MT
F
AF710121
1988

PLYMOUTH COUNTY MASSACHUSETTS PROBATE INDEX

1686-1881

TRANSCRIBED

By

RALPH V. WOOD, JR., C.G.

PICTON PRESS

CAMDEN, MAINE

1988

Library of Congress Cataloging-in-Publication Data

Wood, Ralph V.
Plymouth County Massachusetts probate index, 1686-1881.

1. Plymouth County (Mass.)--Genealogy.
2. Probate records--Massachusetts--Plymouth County--Indexes. I. Title.
F72.P7W66 1988 929'.374482 88-22357

Copyright 1988 Picton Press
All rights reserved
Library of Congress Catalog Card Number: 88-22357
International Standard Book Number 0-929539-04-4

Available from
PICTON PRESS
P.O. Box 1111
Camden, Maine 04843

Manufactured in the United States of America

This publication is designed as a finding aid for researchers working with the probate records of Plymouth County, Massachusetts. These "old series" probate records, covering the time period 1686 (when the county was formed) until 1881, are organized on a docket system and include both original papers (filed in envelopes) and the probate court books.

A handwritten docket index to these records, in 15 volumes, is available at the Registry of Probate in the town of Plymouth. The volumes have been microfilmed for the LDS and most of the material for this publication was taken from a microfilm copy. When the microfilm was not readable, due to tight book bindings, the handwritten index at Plymouth was consulted.

Several of my colleagues suggested that including volume/page references along with the docket numbers would increase the utility of this book to the researcher. This was an excellent suggestion. However experimentation showed that including the volume/page entries would increase the book size by a factor of about $3\frac{1}{2}$, raising the book price proportionally.

Most of the case entries fall into one of four categories. I have used "will" to indicate a case where a will is among the papers, whether the proceedings were testate or intestate. "Admn" applies to intestate proceedings where no will was involved. "Grdn" applies to guardianships. In proceedings where a guardian was appointed for a number of children, the index at Plymouth has one docket entry, listing all the children but located under the name of the first child on the list. In this publication I have made a separate entry for each child. "Adop" signifies an adoption, often with a change in both surname and given name. The index entry is for the name after adoption. It is worth noting that 90% of the adoption records include the name both before and after adoption.

The four case categories above include over 99% of all cases. For the few cases which do not fit the four categories, the following abbreviations have been used in this index.

abse absentee (found mostly 1776-1781)
acct account
affi affidavit

agre	agreement
appt	appointment (such as Register of Probate)
atta	attachment on an estate
bond	bond
cita	citation
clai	claim
comp	complaint
cont	contract (such as a marriage contract)
decr	decree (on an estate); judge's decree
divi	division (of an estate)
dowe	dower assignment
inve	inventory
name	change of name
oath	oath, usually an oath of office
part	partition, usually of real estate
peti	petition
powe	power of attorney
quit	quit claim
rece	receipt
rost	roster
seve	severance
trus	trustee
warr	warrant

In this published index a single character sometimes appears immediatedly to the right of the DOCKET column. The meanings of such characters is as follows:

- a An adult guardianship, usually further identified in the manuscript index by such phrases as "insane," "non compos," "spendthrift," "intemperate," etc.
- \+ Some cases were evidently unearthed after the manuscript index was made. Volume/page citations for these cases are in the Appendix at the end of Volume 15, usually with a fraction added to the Docket Number. Here all such fractions are put as "+".
- b Black
- i Indian

Spellings of surnames and given names are given here as they appear in the manuscript index headings.

Ralph V. Wood, Jr., C.G.
Cambridge, Massachusetts
28 June 1988

SURNAME	FIRST NAME	YEAR	PLACE	CASE	DOCKET
ABEL	Robert	1664	Rehoboth	admn	1
ACKLEY	Elizabeth V	1853	Connecticut	grdn	3
	Lucy A	1853	Connecticut	grdn	3
	Mary J	1853	Connecticut	grdn	3
	Susan	1861	Easton	part	2
	Susan T	1853	Connecticut	grdn	3
ADAMS	Asa F	1877	Plymouth	admn	4
	Charles	1868	Kingston	admn	5
	Charles T	1853	Kingston	grdn	34
	Columbus	1853	Kingston	grdn	34
	Deborah	1826	Kingston	will	6
	Delia J	1851	Portage OH	grdn	27
	Ebenezer	1820	Kingston	will	7
	Elizabeth M	1881	Plymouth	admn	8
	Francis	1755	Plymouth	admn	10
	Francis	1755	Plymouth	grdn	11
	Francis	1825	Kingston	admn	9
	Francis B	1851	Portage OH	grdn	27
	Frederick C	1874	Kingston	will	12
	Gamaliel B	1853	Kingston	will	13
	George	1812	Boston	grdn	21
	George	1867	Plymouth	will	15
	George	1870	Kingston	admn	14
	George N	1863	Plymouth	admn	16
	Harriet S	1842	-----	grdn	17
	Harriet S	1873	Kingston	admn	18
	Helen F	1851	Portage OH	grdn	27
	Jedediah	1850	N. Bridgewater	will	19
	Joanna	1739	Mendon	grdn	20
	John	1812	Boston	grdn	21
	Joseph	1750	Marshfield	will	22
	Joseph	1803	Hingham	admn	24
	Joseph	1803	Hingham	grdn	25
	Joseph	1815	Kingston	will	23
	Joshua	1782	Kingston	admn	26
	Louisa Q	1851	Portage OH	grdn	27
	Lucy	1863	Kingston	will	28
	Lucy E	1881	Kingston	will	29
	Lydia	1755	Plymouth	grdn	11
	Lydia	1803	Hingham	grdn	25
	Lydia	1870	Hingham	will	30
	Mary	1812	Boston	grdn	21
	Mary	1851	Kingston	will	32
	Mary	1854	Abington	admn	31
	Mary (House)	1778	Abington	part	39
	Melzar	1826	Kingston	will	33
	Nancy J	1853	Kingston	grdn	34
	Nathan H	1803	Hingham	grdn	25
	Olive T	1853	Kingston	grdn	34
	Peter	1845	N. Bridgewater	will	35
	Rufus	1823	Middleboro	grdn	36
	Samuel	1755	Plymouth	grdn	11
	Samuel	1777	Abington	admn	38
	Samuel	1863	Kingston	will	37
	Samuel W	1853	Kingston	grdn	34
	Sarah	1778	Abington	part	39
	Susan C	1870	Kingston	grdn	40 a
	Susan C	1871	Kingston	admn	41
	Sylvia	1825	Kingston	will	42
	Thankful	1854	Kingston	will	43
	Thomas	1769	Kingston	admn	44
	Thomas	1812	Boston	grdn	21
	Thomas	1818	Boston	warr	45
	William H	1876	Bridgewater	admn	46
AHERN	Annie	1877	Brockton	grdn	48
	William	1877	Brockton	admn	47
	William	1877	Brockton	grdn	48
AKIN	Elizabeth	1793	Rochester	will	49
ALBRO	Frank	1878	Brockton	admn	50
ALDEN	Abbie W	1880	Abington	admn	51
	Abiathar	1741	Duxbury	grdn	191

SURNAME	FIRST NAME	YEAR	PLACE	CASE	DOCKET
ALDEN	Abiathar	1790	Duxbury	admn	52
	Abigail	1740	Duxbury	grdn	54
	Abigail	1771	Bridgewater	grdn	186
	Abigail	1875	Bridgewater	admn	53
	Abner	1848	Duxbury	admn	55
	Adam	1769	Bridgewater	grdn	140
	Alexander	1881	S. Abington	admn	56
	Alpheus	1801	Bridgewater	grdn	159
	Alton G	1878	Middleboro	grdn	62
	Amandar	1860	Bridgewater	will	57
	Amasa	1837	Bridgewater	admn	58
	Amelia F	1860	Bridgewater	grdn	59
	Amherst	1805	Duxbury	will	60
	Amherst A	1845	Duxbury	grdn	170
	Andrew	1836	Middleboro	will	61
	Annie M	1878	Middleboro	grdn	62
	Arthur P	1860	Bridgewater	grdn	59
	Asaba C	1870	E. Bridgewater	grdn	105
	Bartlett	1818	Bridgewater	grdn	175
	Bela H	1860	Bridgewater	grdn	59
	Benjamin	1741	Duxbury	admn	63
	Benjamin	1769	Bridgewater	grdn	140
	Benjamin	1818	Bridgewater	grdn	175
	Benjamin	1835	Duxbury	admn	64
	Benjamin	1870	Duxbury	admn	65
	Benjamin R	1870	E. Bridgewater	grdn	105
	Betsey	1843	Middleboro	admn	66
	Betsey W	1838	Middleboro	grdn	67
	Bezaleel	1741	Duxbury	grdn	191
	Bezaleel	1803	Duxbury	admn	68
	Briggs	1740	Duxbury	grdn	54
	Briggs	1796	Duxbury	will	69
	Caleb	1863	Middleboro	will	70
	Caroline F	1838	Middleboro	grdn	67
	Carrie E	1878	Middleboro	grdn	62
	Cromwell	1878	Bridgewater	admn	71
	Cyrus	1849	Middleboro	grdn	72
	Daniel	1799	Bridgewater	will	73
	Daniel	1801	Bridgewater	grdn	159
	Daniel	1879	Middleboro	admn	74
	Darius G	1855	Middleboro	grdn	75
	David	1719	Duxbury	admn	76
	David	1763	Middleboro	will	77
	David	1814	Middleboro	will	78
	David	1850	Middleboro	will	79
	Deborah H	1879	Wareham	admn	80
	Earl	1864	Middleboro	admn	81
	Ebenezer	1732	Middleboro	grdn	133
	Ebenezer	1748	Middleboro	admn	83
	Ebenezer	1773	Middleboro	admn	82
	Ebenezer	1788	Middleboro	grdn	84
	Edith	1815	Duxbury	will	85
	Edward V	1822	Bridgewater	admn	86
	Eleazer	1773	Bridgewater	will	87
	Eleazer	1803	Bridgewater	will	88
	Eleazer	1851	Bridgewater	will	89
	Elijah	1840	W. Bridgewater	grdn	90
	Elijah	1879	Bridgewater	will	91
	Elizabeth	1772	Duxbury	admn	92
	Elizabeth	1836	Duxbury	admn	93
	Eunice	1830	Bridgewater	will	94
	Ezra	1768	Bridgewater	will	95
	Ezra	1867	Abington	will	97
	Ezra H	1870	Bridgewater	admn	96
	Frank R	1881	S. Abington	grdn	98
	Frederick D	1855	Middleboro	grdn	75
	Gustavus	1859	N. Bridgewater	grdn	99
	Gustavus L	1849	Middleboro	grdn	100
	Hannah	1732	Middleboro	will	101
	Hannah	1739	Duxbury	will	102
	Hannah	1850	Duxbury	admn	103

SURNAME	FIRST NAME	YEAR	PLACE	CASE	DOCKET
ALDEN	Hannah B	1880	Bridgewater	admn	104
	Harriet	1870	E. Bridgewater	grdn	105
	Harry W	1880	Abington	grdn	106
	Henry	1858	Abington	will	108
	Henry Pierce	1857	E. Bridgewater	name	107
	Hettie	1881	S. Abington	grdn	98
	Hosea	1837	Abington	admn	109
	Ichabod	1779	Duxbury	admn	110
	Isaac	1727	Bridgewater	will	111
	Isaac	1771	Bridgewater	grdn	186
	Isaac	1781	Bridgewater	will	112
	Isaac	1835	Bridgewater	will	114
	Isaac	1844	E. Bridgewater	admn	113
	Isaac C	1858	Abington	grdn	116
	Isaac F	1837	Bridgewater	grdn	115
	Isaiah	1831	Scituate	admn	118
	Isaiah	1845	Duxbury	will	117
	Israel	1829	Middleboro	grdn	119 a
	James	1769	Bridgewater	grdn	140
	James	1848	N. Bridgewater	grdn	120
	James S	1875	Bridgewater	will	121
	Jared	1872	Middleboro	will	122
	Jedidah	1826	Middleboro	admn	123
	Job	1825	Middleboro	admn	124
	Job	1850	Middleboro	admn	125
	John	1687	Duxbury	admn	126
	John	1730/1	Middleboro	will	132
	John	1732	Middleboro	grdn	133
	John	1739	Duxbury	admn	127
	John	1759	Bridgewater	will	131
	John	1779	Duxbury	grdn	130
	John	1854	Duxbury	will	128
	John 2nd	1871	Duxbury	will	129
	Jonathan	1696/7	Duxbury	admn	134
	Jonathan	1825	E. Bridgewater	admn	135
	Joseph	1696/7	Bridgewater	will	138
	Joseph	1769	Bridgewater	grdn	140
	Joseph	1787	Middleboro	admn	136
	Joseph	1788	Middleboro	grdn	84
	Joseph	1803	Bridgewater	will	137
	Joseph	1853	E. Bridgewater	admn	139
	Joseph T	1860	Bridgewater	grdn	59
	Joshua	1809	Bridgewater	will	141
	Judah	1741	Duxbury	admn	142
	Judah	1845	Duxbury	will	143
	Judah	1845	Duxbury	grdn	170
	Lewis T	1881	Bridgewater	will	144
	Lucinda	1855	Middleboro	admn	145
	Lucy	1825	Middleboro	grdn	146
	Luther E	1844	Abington	grdn	147
	Lyman	1865	Abington	will	148
	Martha C	1878	Duxbury	will	149
	Mary	1812	Bridgewater	will	152
	Mary	1849	Duxbury	will	150
	Mary A	1881	Duxbury	admn	151
	Mary H	1875	Bridgewater	admn	153
	Mercy	1812	Duxbury	will	154
	Minerva	1837	Bridgewater	grdn	115
	Myra	1868	Duxbury	admn	155
	Nabbie	1769	Bridgewater	grdn	140
	Nathan	1843	E. Bridgewater	will	156
	Noah	1732	Middleboro	grdn	133
	Oliver	1825	Bridgewater	will	157
	Oliver	1827	Bridgewater	grdn	158 a
	Otis	1801	Bridgewater	grdn	159
	Priscilla	1860	N. Bridgewater	admn	160
	Rebecca	1844	W. Bridgewater	grdn	161 a
	Rebecca P	1779	Duxbury	grdn	130
	Rhoda R	1870	E. Bridgewater	grdn	105
	Richard H L	1860	Bridgewater	grdn	59
	Rocinda	1770	Middleboro	grdn	181

SURNAME	FIRST NAME	YEAR	PLACE	CASE	DOCKET
ALDEN	Ruel P	1849	Middleboro	grdn	72
	Rufus	1825	Middleboro	will	162
	Rufus	1835	Middleboro	grdn	163
	Ruth	1788	Middleboro	grdn	84
	Ruth	1871	Duxbury	will	164
	Sabra	1842	Duxbury	admn	165
	Sally H	1845	Bridgewater	will	166
	Sally S	1857	Middleboro	will	167
	Samuel	1781	Duxbury	will	168
	Samuel	1799	Duxbury	admn	169
	Samuel	1814	Bridgewater	admn	174
	Samuel	1816	Abington	admn	171
	Samuel	1818	Bridgewater	grdn	175
	Samuel	1870	E. Bridgewater	grdn	105
	Samuel B	1845	Duxbury	grdn	170
	Samuel F	1874	N. Bridgewater	admn	172
	Samuel G	1870	E. Bridgewater	will	173
	Sarah	1801	Bridgewater	grdn	159
	Seth	1783	Bridgewater	grdn	178
	Seth	1784	Bridgewater	will	177
	Seth	1808	Bridgewater	grdn	179
	Seth Jr	1776	Bridgewater	will	176
	Silas	1764	Middleboro	admn	180
	Silence	1770	Middleboro	grdn	181
	Solomon	1814	Bridgewater	will	182
	Solomon	1852	Bridgewater	will	183
	Solomon	1866	Bridgewater	admn	184
	Southworth	1828	-----	grdn	185
	Susanna	1771	Bridgewater	grdn	186
	Thomas	1850	Bridgewater	admn	187
	Thomas R	1835	E. Bridgewater	admn	188
	Vienna	1868	Middleboro	will	189
	William C	1849	Middleboro	grdn	100
	William H	1858	Abington	grdn	116
	William S	1871	Bridgewater	admn	190
	Wrestling	1741	Duxbury	grdn	191
ALDRICH	Harriet A	1863	Middleboro	grdn	195
	Henry S	1868	E. Bridgewater	grdn	192
	Ira F	1868	E. Bridgewater	grdn	192
	James	1829	Bridgewater	admn	193
	Joseph	1863	Middleboro	admn	194
	Mary A	1863	Middleboro	grdn	195
	Nathan	1821	Middleboro	grdn	196 a
	Stillman	1868	Hanson	admn	197
ALEXANDER	John K	1866	Plymouth	admn	198
ALGER	Abbie B	1860	W. Bridgewater	grdn	199
	Abiel	1786	Bridgewater	grdn	200
	Abiezer	1830	W. Bridgewater	admn	201
	Abiezer	1863	W. Bridgewater	admn	202
	Abigail	1832	W. Bridgewater	grdn	230
	Anna C	1863	W. Bridgewater	admn	203
	Anne C	1878	W. Bridgewater	grdn	204
	Austin W	1863	Bridgewater	grdn	235
	Betsey	1858	Bridgewater	admn	205
	Caroline B	1869	W. Bridgewater	will	206
	Chester W	1879	W. Bridgewater	grdn	225
	Clydia M	1879	W. Bridgewater	grdn	225
	Daniel	1786	Bridgewater	admn	207
	Ebenezer	1791	Bridgewater	grdn	208
	Ebenezer	1844	W. Bridgewater	will	209
	Ebenezer	1876	Brockton	will	210
	Edmund	1832	W. Bridgewater	grdn	230
	Elvira	1842	W. Bridgewater	grdn	211 a
	Everett M	1879	W. Bridgewater	grdn	225
	Harry E	1879	W. Bridgewater	grdn	225
	Helen D	1878	W. Bridgewater	grdn	204
	Henry W	1878	W. Bridgewater	will	212
	Hephsibah	1841	W. Bridgewater	will	213
	Isaac	1832	W. Bridgewater	grdn	230
	Israel	1730	Bridgewater	admn	214
	Israel Jr	1755	Bridgewater	will	215

SURNAME	FIRST NAME	YEAR	PLACE	CASE	DOCKET
ALGER	Israel S	1840	W. Bridgewater	grdn	216
	James	1810	Bridgewater	will	217
	James	1822	Bridgewater	will	218
	James	1833	Bridgewater	grdn	219 a
	James	1878	W. Bridgewater	will	220
	John	1730	Bridgewater	admn	221
	Joseph	1791	Bridgewater	admn	222
	Joseph	1852	W. Bridgewater	will	223
	Leonard	1838	W. Bridgewater	will	224
	Louisa E	1879	W. Bridgewater	grdn	225
	Mary	1858	Bridgewater	admn	226
	Nathan	1832	W. Bridgewater	will	227
	Nathan	1859	W. Bridgewater	admn	228
	Nathan J	1860	W. Bridgewater	grdn	199
	Otis	1869	W. Bridgewater	will	229
	Polly	1832	W. Bridgewater	grdn	230
	Roland F	1840	W. Bridgewater	grdn	216
	Ruth	1832	W. Bridgewater	grdn	230
	Salome	1834	E. Bridgewater	grdn	231 a
	Sanford	1878	W. Bridgewater	will	232
	Sanford	1879	W. Bridgewater	grdn	225
	Sarah S	1880	W. Bridgewater	will	233
	Simeon	1832	W. Bridgewater	grdn	230
	Stillman	1840	W. Bridgewater	admn	234
	Stillman	1863	Bridgewater	grdn	235
	Susan	1863	W. Bridgewater	will	236
	Susan E	1860	W. Bridgewater	grdn	199
	William	1880	W. Bridgewater	admn	237
ALLEN	Adeline H	1856	E. Bridgewater	grdn	249
	Alexander	1836	Duxbury	admn	238
	Alpheus	1805	Bridgewater	grdn	239
	Ambrose	1796	Bridgewater	grdn	262
	Anthony S	1852	Plymouth	will	240
	Barzillai	1826	E. Bridgewater	admn	241
	Benjamin	1737	Bridgewater	admn	243
	Benjamin	1737	Bridgewater	grdn	244
	Benjamin	1768	Plymouth	admn	242
	Bethia	1733	Bridgewater	grdn	300
	Betsey	1833	Rochester	grdn	248
	Betsey	1853	Marion	admn	245
	Betsey	1858	Plymouth	admn	246
	Betsey B	1879	Plymouth	admn	247
	Betty	1733/4	Bridgewater	grdn	344
	Clara A	1860	N. Bridgewater	grdn	270
	Clara D	1856	E. Bridgewater	grdn	249
	Clothier	1876	Lakeville	will	250
	Daniel	1817	Pembroke	will	251
	David	1757	Middleboro	admn	252
	David	1845	E. Bridgewater	will	253
	Dinah (Nye)	1833	Rochester	grdn	248
	Ebenezer	1730	Bridgewater	will	254
	Ebenezer	1733	Bridgewater	admn	255
	Eleazer	1789	Rochester	admn	256
	Eliashib	1814	Rochester	admn	257
	Elisha	1727	Bridgewater	admn	258
	Elisha	1731	Bridgewater	grdn	309
	Elizabeth	1716	Scituate	admn	259
	Ephraim	1734	Bridgewater	admn	260
	Ephraim	1737	Bridgewater	grdn	244
	Ephraim	1848	Rochester	will	261
	Esther	1733/4	Bridgewater	grdn	344
	Ethan	1796	Bridgewater	grdn	262
	Ezra	1779	Plymouth	will	263
	Ezra	1795	Bridgewater	will	264
	Ezra T	1879	Marion	admn	265
	Florence R	1878	Plymouth	adop	266
	Francis	1749	Plymouth	admn	267
	George G	1865	Marion	grdn	268
	George M	1878	Scituate	will	269
	Hannah	1737	Bridgewater	grdn	244
	Henry P	1860	N. Bridgewater	grdn	270

SURNAME	FIRST NAME	YEAR	PLACE	CASE	DOCKET
ALLEN	Isaac	1732	Bridgewater	grdn	273
	Isaac	1791	Bridgewater	admn	271
	Isaac	1822	Bridgewater	will	272
	Jacob	1751	Bridgewater	admn	274
	James	1732	Bridgewater	grdn	273
	James	1789	Bridgewater	will	275
	James O	1881	Brockton	admn	276
	Jane	1749	Plymouth	grdn	277
	Jane S	1872	Rochester	will	278
	Joann	1845	E. Bridgewater	grdn	279 a
	John	1773	Pembroke	will	280
	John	1789	Rochester	will	281
	John	1824	Rochester	admn	282
	John	1833	Duxbury	will	286
	John	1842	Middleboro	will	284
	John	1867	Plymouth	admn	285
	John Jr	1824	Rochester	admn	283
	Joseph	1828	E. Bridgewater	will	288
	Joseph	1860	Marion	admn	290
	Joseph	1872	Plymouth	will	287
	Joseph C	1858	E. Bridgewater	admn	289
	Joshua	1833	Rochester	grdn	248
	Joshua	1835	Rochester	admn	291
	Josiah	1733	Bridgewater	admn	292
	Josiah	1745	Bridgewater	grdn	293
	Josiah	1745	Bridgewater	admn	295
	Josiah	1785	Bridgewater	will	294
	Justus	1821	Rochester	admn	296
	Louisa A	1867	Plymouth	will	297
	Lucy	1827	E. Bridgewater	grdn	328
	Lydia	1733	Bridgewater	grdn	300
	Lydia	1831	Plymouth	will	298
	Marcia	1859	Plymouth	admn	299
	Martha	1733	Bridgewater	grdn	300
	Mary	1731	Bridgewater	grdn	309
	Mary	1733/4	Bridgewater	grdn	344
	Mary	1736	Bridgewater	admn	310
	Mary	1759	Bridgewater	will	304
	Mary	1785	Plymouth	will	301
	Mary	1818	Salem	grdn	305
	Mary M	1852	Bridgewater	will	303
	Mary S	1874	Plymouth	admn	302
	Mathew	1784	Bridgewater	admn	306
	Mathew	1787	Bridgewater	will	307
	Mathew	1803	Bridgewater	admn	308
	Mehitable	1731	Bridgewater	grdn	309
	Mehitable	1736	Bridgewater	admn	310
	Mehitable	1737	Bridgewater	grdn	244
	Micah	1745	Bridgewater	will	311
	Morrill	1876	Pembroke	admn	312
	Nathan	1733/4	Bridgewater	grdn	344
	Nehemiah	1733	Bridgewater	admn	313
	Noble B	1853	Marion	admn	314
	Oliver	1802	Rochester	admn	315
	Oliver	1843	Bridgewater	will	316
	Oliver	1856	Bridgewater	will	317
	Pamelia D	1874	Plymouth	admn	318
	Phebe	1819	Bridgewater	will	319
	Priscilla	1830	Pembroke	will	321
	Priscilla P	1838	Kingston	will	320
	Samuel	1705	Bridgewater	will	322
	Samuel	1735	Bridgewater	admn	323
	Samuel	1750	Bridgewater	will	325
	Samuel	1827	E. Bridgewater	grdn	328
	Samuel B	1874	E. Bridgewater	will	326
	Samuel Jr	1735	Bridgewater	admn	324
	Samuel P	1874	E. Bridgewater	will	327
	Sarah	1733/4	Bridgewater	grdn	344
	Sarah	1812	Bridgewater	will	329
	Seth	1784	Bridgewater	admn	330
	Seth	1835	Halifax	will	331

SURNAME	FIRST NAME	YEAR	PLACE	CASE	DOCKET
ALLEN	Silence	1731	Bridgewater	grdn	309
	Simeon	1805	Bridgewater	will	332
	Stephen	1872	Marion	admn	333
	Susanna	1731	Bridgewater	grdn	309
	Susanna	1739	Bridgewater	will	334
	Susannah	1844	Bridgewater	admn	335
	Sylvia	1830	Rochester	admn	336
	Theophilus P	1860	Marion	admn	337
	Thomas	1853	N. Bridgewater	grdn	338
	Timothy	1827	Plymouth	admn	339
	Walter D	1860	N. Bridgewater	grdn	270
	Weston	1810	Rochester	will	340
	Weston	1879	Marion	admn	341
	William	1733/4	Bridgewater	grdn	344
	William	1827	E. Bridgewater	grdn	328
	William	1829	Plymouth	grdn	342 a
	William B	1876	E. Bridgewater	grdn	343
	Willie E	1865	N. Bridgewater	grdn	345
	Willie E	1870	N. Bridgewater	admn	346
	Zebina	1856	E. Bridgewater	will	347
	Zebina M	1856	E. Bridgewater	grdn	249
	Zephaniah	1832	Bridgewater	grdn	348 a
	Zephaniah	1842	Bridgewater	admn	349
ALMY	Annie M	1877	Mattapoisett	grdn	350
	John E	1877	Mattapoisett	grdn	350
AMES	Abbie S	1870	N. Bridgewater	grdn	351
	Abiel	1803	Bridgewater	will	352
	Abiel	1838	W. Bridgewater	will	353
	Abigail	1840	N. Bridgewater	grdn	393
	Abigail	1851	N. Bridgewater	will	354
	Abigail P	1877	W. Bridgewater	will	355
	Albert	1859	Marshfield	will	356
	Alexander	1850	Bridgewater	will	357
	Alice	1859	W. Bridgewater	will	358
	Ambrose	1781	Bridgewater	grdn	375
	Annie F	1877	Hingham	will	359
	Annie L	1863	Marshfield	grdn	400
	Arabella	1854	N. Bridgewater	grdn	391
	Azel	1842	Marshfield	admn	360
	Benjamin	1773	Bridgewater	will	361
	Benjamin	1850	N. Bridgewater	grdn	362 a
	Benjamin	1850	N. Bridgewater	will	363
	Calvin	1874	Marshfield	grdn	364
	Calvin	1880	Marshfield	admn	365
	Charles	1781	Bridgewater	grdn	375
	Charles	1867	W. Bridgewater	admn	366
	Charles F	1874	Mattapoisett	grdn	367
	Cornelia J	1870	N. Bridgewater	grdn	351
	Daniel F	1849	N. Bridgewater	admn	368
	Daniel H	1872	Mattapoisett	admn	369
	David	1726	Bridgewater	admn	370
	David	1794	Bridgewater	will	371
	David	1856	N. Bridgewater	will	372
	Dorcas	1816	Bridgewater	will	373
	Ebenezer	1779	Bridgewater	admn	374
	Ebenezer	1781	Bridgewater	grdn	375
	Edward	1869	Marshfield	will	376
	Edwin	1832	Bridgewater	admn	377
	Edwin W	1870	N. Bridgewater	grdn	351
	Elbridge G	1879	Brockton	will	378
	Elijah	1866	Marshfield	will	379
	Eliza A	1833	Bridgewater	grdn	435
	Elizabeth	1843	Marshfield	grdn	381
	Elizabeth	1865	Mattapoisett	admn	380
	Ellis F	1881	Brockton	admn	382
	Emma A	1874	Mattapoisett	grdn	367
	Eugene A	1871	Bridgewater	admn	383
	Fanny H	1855	Rochester	grdn	442
	Fisk	1790	Bridgewater	grdn	399
	Fisk	1852	N. Bridgewater	will	384
	Frank T	1881	Marshfield	grdn	385

SURNAME	FIRST NAME	YEAR	PLACE	CASE	DOCKET
AMES	Franklin	1804	Bridgewater	grdn	413
	Hannah	1802	Bridgewater	will	388
	Hannah	1855	Plympton	admn	386
	Hannah	1855	N. Bridgewater	will	387
	Hannah L	1861	W. Bridgewater	grdn	390
	Hannah W	1854	Bridgewater	will	389
	Henry C	1854	N. Bridgewater	grdn	391
	Hiram	1854	Rochester	admn	392
	Horace	1840	N. Bridgewater	grdn	393
	Howard M	1874	W. Bridgewater	grdn	394
	Isaac	1851	Marshfield	admn	395
	James	1788	Bridgewater	admn	398
	James	1790	Bridgewater	grdn	399
	James	1803	Bridgewater	admn	397
	James	1863	W. Bridgewater	will	396
	Jane F	1863	Marshfield	grdn	400
	Job	1827	N. Bridgewater	will	401
	Joel	1840	N. Bridgewater	admn	402
	John	1726	Bridgewater	admn	403
	John	1756	Bridgewater	will	404
	Jonathan	1775	Bridgewater	will	405
	Jonathan E	1838	Duxbury	will	406
	Joseph	1790	Bridgewater	will	407
	Joseph	1813	Bridgewater	will	408
	Joseph	1813	Bridgewater	admn	409
	Joshua	1773	Bridgewater	grdn	410
	Joshua	1802	Bridgewater	admn	411
	Josiah	1839	N. Bridgewater	will	412
	Jotham	1757	Bridgewater	grdn	440
	Leonard	1804	Bridgewater	grdn	413
	Lewis	1859	Kingston	admn	414
	Lewis	1861	W. Bridgewater	admn	415
	Lois	1843	Marshfield	grdn	381
	Lopha	1867	N. Bridgewater	will	416
	Luceanna	1869	Marshfield	will	417
	Lucy	1849	N. Bridgewater	grdn	418
	Luther	1840	N. Bridgewater	grdn	393
	Marcia	1833	Bridgewater	admn	419
	Marcus	1843	Marshfield	grdn	381
	Marcus	1870	Marshfield	admn	420
	Martha J	1872	Dunn WI	grdn	421
	Mary	1757	Bridgewater	will	422
	Mary E	1870	N. Bridgewater	grdn	351
	Nathan	1756	Bridgewater	will	424
	Nathan	1757	Bridgewater	grdn	425
	Nathan	1776	Bridgewater	will	423
	Nathaniel	1736	Bridgewater	admn	426
	Nathaniel	1805	Bridgewater	will	427
	Nathaniel	1866	N. Bridgewater	grdn	428 a
	Nathaniel	1866	N. Bridgewater	admn	429
	Nathaniel T	1863	Marshfield	grdn	400
	Olive	1840	N. Bridgewater	grdn	393
	Phebe	1794	Bridgewater	will	430
	Phebe	1814	Bridgewater	grdn	431
	Robert	1825	Marshfield	admn	432
	Ruth R	1870	N. Bridgewater	grdn	351
	Sally	1866	N. Bridgewater	grdn	433 a
	Sally	1873	N. Bridgewater	admn	434
	Sarah	1757	Bridgewater	grdn	425
	Sarah O	1855	Rochester	grdn	442
	Serepta J	1833	Bridgewater	grdn	435
	Seth	1828	Rochester	admn	436
	Silence	1781	Bridgewater	grdn	375
	Simeon	1757	Bridgewater	grdn	440
	Simeon	1812	Bridgewater	will	437
	Solomon	1745	Bridgewater	admn	438
	Solomon	1757	Bridgewater	grdn	440
	Solomon	1814	Bridgewater	will	439
	Stephen S	1855	Rochester	grdn	442
	Stephen S	1859	Mattapoisett	admn	441
	Thankful	1861	Marshfield	admn	443

SURNAME	FIRST NAME	YEAR	PLACE	CASE	DOCKET
AMES	Theron	1870	N. Bridgewater	will	444
	Thomas	1737	Bridgewater	will	445
	Thomas	1774	Bridgewater	will	446
	Thomas	1812	Bridgewater	will	447
	Thomas	1828	N. Bridgewater	grdn	448
	Thomas	1873	W. Bridgewater	will	450
	Thomas C	1847	Rochester	will	451
	Thomas L	1874	Mattapoisett	grdn	367
	Thomas T	1854	N. Bridgewater	admn	449
	Tilden	1867	Marshfield	will	452
	Timothy	1814	Bridgewater	admn	453
	Waldo	1851	Bridgewater	admn	454
	Wallace	1880	Marshfield	admn	455
	Walter	1781	Bridgewater	grdn	375
	Willard	1880	W. Bridgewater	grdn	456 a
	William	1712	Bridgewater	admn	459
	William	1781	Bridgewater	grdn	375
	William	1850	W. Bridgewater	admn	458
	William L	1862	Kingston	grdn	457
AMESBURY	William	1759	Rehoboth	grdn	460
AMOS	Edward	1761	-----	grdn	461
ANDERSON	Charles E	1880	Brockton	grdn	462
	Henry	1845	Hingham	admn	463
	Susan	1861	Hingham	grdn	464
ANDREWS	Adelaide L	1865	Hingham	grdn	476
	Benjamin	1832	Hingham	admn	465
	Benjamin	1833	Hingham	grdn	466
	Betsey	1852	Hingham	will	467
	Catherine C	1821	Hingham	grdn	471
	Charlotte J	1821	Hingham	grdn	471
	Christopher AA	1881	Scituate	will	468
	David	1847	Hingham	will	469
	David	1863	Hingham	will	470
	Elizabeth	1821	Hingham	grdn	471
	Elizabeth	1833	Hingham	grdn	466
	Ellen F	1833	Hingham	grdn	466
	George	1823	E. Bridgewater	grdn	472
	Hannah	1764	Norton	grdn	475
	Hannah	1821	Hingham	grdn	471
	Hannah	1856	Hingham	admn	473
	Hannah C	1835	Hingham	admn	474
	Harriet F	1865	Hingham	grdn	476
	Henry	1844	Middleboro	admn	477
	Jerusha	1857	Plymouth	grdn	478 a
	John	1745	Plymouth	admn	479
	Joseph	1805	Hingham	grdn	480 a
	Joseph	1806	Hingham	will	481
	Katy	1837	Hingham	will	482
	Loring	1811	Hingham	admn	483
	Lovice	1866	Middleboro	will	484
	Lydia	1833	Hingham	grdn	466
	Lydia	1872	Hingham	will	485
	Manassah	1881	Bridgewater	will	486
	Mary	1764	Norton	grdn	475
	Mary E	1865	Hingham	grdn	476
	Robert M	1873	Carver	admn	487
	Sally	1852	Hingham	will	488
	Samuel	1807	Hingham	admn	489
	Thomas	1821	Hingham	admn	490
	Thomas	1865	Hingham	admn	491
	William H B	1865	Hingham	grdn	476
	Zephaniah	1857	Bridgewater	admn	492
ANGELL	Thomas C	1835	Plymouth	admn	493
ANGIER	Charles	1786	Bridgewater	grdn	496
	John	1786	Bridgewater	grdn	496
	John	1787	Bridgewater	will	494
	Mary	1786	Bridgewater	grdn	496
	Oakes	1786	Bridgewater	will	495
	Oakes	1786	Bridgewater	grdn	496
	Samuel	1805	Bridgewater	admn	497
	Sarah	1786	Bridgewater	grdn	496

SURNAME	FIRST NAME	YEAR	PLACE	CASE	DOCKET
ANGIER	Susanna	1786	Bridgewater	grdn	497
ANNIS	Sally	1853	Hingham	admn	498
ANTHONY	Charles	1794	Middleboro	admn	499
	Henery	1760	Scituate	admn	500
APPLING	Eliza C	1845	Carver	grdn	502
	George H	1842	Carver	admn	501
	George H	1845	Carver	grdn	502
	Mary A	1845	Carver	grdn	502
ARNOLD	Benjamin	1759	Duxbury	grdn	512
	Edward	1748	Duxbury	will	503
	Elizabeth	1852	Middleboro	name	507
	Elizabeth	1873	Middleboro	will	504
	Ezra	1780	Duxbury	will	505
	Galen	1863	Duxbury	will	506
	George H J	1852	Middleboro	name	507
	Henry	1852	Middleboro	name	508
	Henry	1881	Middleboro	will	509
	Henry F	1878	Brockton	grdn	510
	James	1755	Duxbury	admn	511
	James	1759	Duxbury	grdn	512
	John	1720	Rochester	divi	513
	Samuel	1693	Marshfield	will	516
	Samuel	1709	Rochester	will	515
	Samuel	1728	Rochester	will	514
	Sarah	1724	Rochester	will	517
	Seth	1721	Duxbury	will	518
	Walter F	1881	Hanson	admn	519
	William	1836	Duxbury	will	520
ASBURY	Thomas B	1837	Columbus OH	grdn	521
ASHER	Canada	1822	Plymouth	admn	522
ASHLEY	Abigail	1843	Middleboro	grdn	531
	Abraham	1759	Rochester	admn	523
	Barnabas	1826	Rochester	grdn	524 a
	Barnabas	1833	Rochester	admn	525
	Calvin	1831	Middleboro	grdn	546
	Charles	1835	Rochester	admn	526
	Charles E	1871	Lakeville	grdn	527
	Chester	1880	Lakeville	grdn	528
	Cynthia	1877	Marshfield	admn	529
	David	1880	Lakeville	admn	530
	Earl S	1843	Middleboro	grdn	531
	Elisha	1762	Rochester	grdn	532
	Enoch	1762	Rochester	grdn	532
	Eunice	1762	Rochester	grdn	532
	Frederick G	1871	Lakeville	grdn	527
	Henry	1850	Rochester	admn	533
	Isaac	1762	Rochester	grdn	532
	James	1846	Rochester	admn	534
	John & wife	1816	Rochester	will	535
	John S	1826	Rochester	admn	536
	Joseph	1831	Middleboro	grdn	546
	Josephus P	1843	Middleboro	grdn	531
	Lavinah H	1861	Lakeville	will	537
	Levi L	1843	Middleboro	grdn	531
	Luther	1831	Middleboro	admn	538
	Luther	1831	Middleboro	grdn	546
	Mary	1767	Middleboro	grdn	539 a
	Noah	1843	Middleboro	admn	540
	Paul	1850	Rochester	admn	541
	Percival	1822	Rochester	admn	542
	Ruth	1867	Lakeville	admn	543
	Sarah	1843	Middleboro	grdn	531
	Thomas	1762	Rochester	admn	544
	William	1762	Rochester	grdn	532
	William	1831	Middleboro	grdn	546
	William	1836	Middleboro	admn	545
ASHPORT	Cuff	1827	Bridgewater	admn	547
	Lydia	1843	Bridgewater	admn	548
ASHTON	Betsey A	1867	Wareham	grdn	549
	Hannah F	1867	Wareham	grdn	549
	Olive A	1867	Wareham	grdn	549

SURNAME	FIRST NAME	YEAR	PLACE	CASE	DOCKET
ASHTON	William W	1867	Wareham	grdn	549
ASKIN	Christopher	1776	Abington	will	550
	Elizabeth	1776	Abington	admn	551
	George	1776	Abington	grdn	553
	Jeremiah	1767	Abington	admn	552
	Jeremiah	1776	Abington	grdn	553
	Mary	1776	Abington	grdn	553
	Reed	1776	-----	grdn	554
	Submit	1776	Abington	grdn	553
ASTLE	Abel	1871	N. Bridgewater	admn	555
ATHERTON	Adeline	1872	N. Bridgewater	will	556
	Edith	1867	N. Bridgewater	grdn	557
	Henry H	1867	N. Bridgewater	admn	558
	Hiram	1850	N. Bridgewater	admn	559
	Isaac	1817	Bridgewater	admn	560
	Lemuel B	1860	N. Bridgewater	admn	561
ATKINSON	Charles B	1869	Rochester	grdn	562
	Edward E	1869	Rochester	grdn	562
	Elvira T	1869	Rochester	grdn	562
ATSATT	Edward L	1867	Mattapoisett	grdn	563
	Edward S	1866	Mattapoisett	admn	564
	John	1860	Mattapoisett	admn	565
	William	1874	Mattapoisett	will	566
ATWELL	Russell	1844	Marshfield	admn	567
	Sumner	1871	Duxbury	admn	568
ATWOOD	Abbie A	1864	Middleboro	grdn	569
	Abigail	1767	Plympton	grdn	617
	Abigail	1786	Plympton	grdn	571
	Abigail S	1864	Carver	will	570
	Alexander A	1878	Marion	grdn	572 a
	Amasa	1811	Middleboro	grdn	573 a
	Amasa	1843	Middleboro	will	574
	Asaph Jr	1864	Middleboro	admn	575
	Barnabas	1785	Plympton	will	576
	Charles A	1862	Carver	grdn	577
	Clara	1786	Plympton	grdn	571
	Edward	1757	Halifax	admn	578
	Eli	1833	Middleboro	admn	579
	Eliab	1829	Plympton	grdn	613
	Elijah D	1856	Plymouth	admn	580
	Elizabeth D	1829	Plympton	grdn	613
	Elmira	1845	Middleboro	grdn	581
	Emily W	1829	Plympton	grdn	613
	Experience	1761	Plymouth	admn	582
	Francis	1853	Middleboro	admn	584
	Francis A	1864	Middleboro	grdn	585
	Francis E	1875	Middleboro	name	583
	George H	1829	Plympton	grdn	613
	George W	1854	Carver	grdn	607
	Hannah	1786	Plympton	grdn	571
	Hannah C	1868	Middleboro	admn	586
	Harriet J	1868	Carver	grdn	587
	Isaac	1762	Plymouth	admn	588
	Janet	1786	Plympton	grdn	571
	Jesse	1827	Duxbury	admn	589
	Joanne	1738	Plympton	grdn	590 a
	John	1754	Plymouth	will	591
	John	1773	Plymouth	admn	593
	John	1793	Plymouth	grdn	592
	John	1839	Carver	admn	595
	John B	1864	Plymouth	admn	594
	Jonathan	1854	Carver	will	596
	Joseph	1824	Carver	admn	597
	Joseph	1878	Carver	admn	598
	Julia A	1878	Middleboro	will	599
	Lemuel R	1829	Plympton	grdn	613
	Levi	1868	Middleboro	will	600
	Lucius	1854	Carver	grdn	607
	Luther	1829	Carver	grdn	602 a
	Luther	1868	Abington	will	601
	Luther Jr	1851	Carver	admn	603

SURNAME	FIRST NAME	YEAR	PLACE	CASE	DOCKET
ATWOOD	Lydia	1830	Carver	will	605
	Lydia	1857	Abington	admn	604
	Lydia V	1829	Plympton	grdn	613
	Margaret	1756	Plymouth	grdn	606
	Melissa	1862	Carver	grdn	577
	Miranda	1854	Carver	grdn	607
	Nancy	1873	Carver	will	608
	Nathaniel	1767	Plympton	admn	609
	Nathaniel	1804	Carver	admn	610
	Nathaniel	1838	Carver	admn	611
	Pelham	1832	Middleboro	admn	612
	Persis H	1829	Plympton	grdn	613
	Polly	1815	Plymouth	grdn	623
	Polly D	1864	Middleboro	grdn	585
	Priscilla	1756	Plymouth	grdn	606
	Rebekah	1863	Middleboro	admn	614
	Samuel	1767	Plympton	grdn	617
	Samuel	1834	Carver	admn	615
	Samuel	1840	Middleboro	admn	616
	Sophronia	1833	Duxbury	grdn	618
	Stephen	1767	Plympton	grdn	617
	Stephen	1777	Plympton	admn	619
	Susannah S	1878	Middleboro	will	620
	Thomas	1815	Plymouth	grdn	623
	Thomas	1834	Plymouth	will	622
	Thomas	1880	Marshfield	admn	621
	Tilson	1875	Brockton	admn	624
	William	1814	Carver	admn	625
	William	1851	Middleboro	will	626
	William	1863	Middleboro	will	627
	William F	1864	Middleboro	grdn	585
	Wilson L	1874	Middleboro	grdn	628
AUGUR	John	1756	Bridgewater	admn	629
AUSTIN	David	1765	Westerly RI	will	630
AVERY	Bertha B	1875	Plymouth	grdn	632
	Charles N	1858	Middleboro	grdn	631
	David E	1875	Plymouth	grdn	632
	Elmer E	1875	Plymouth	grdn	632
	Herbert W	1875	Plymouth	grdn	632
	Joseph	1822	Plymouth	admn	633
	Luther	1833	Rochester	admn	634
	Martha E	1873	Plymouth	admn	635
	Mary G	1857	Plymouth	grdn	636
BABCOCK	Frederick A	1854	St Andrews Can	admn	637
	Orville	1863	Plymouth	will	638
BACHELDER	Algernon	1866	Marion	grdn	639
	Antoinette	1866	Marion	grdn	639
	Carrie	1866	Marion	grdn	639
	John	1866	Marion	grdn	639
	John	1876	Plymouth	admn	640
	Minnie	1866	Marion	grdn	639
	Sally	1865	Hingham	will	641
BACKFORD	James	1755	Bridgewater	admn	642
BACKUS	Hannah	1865	Middleboro	will	643
	Isaac	1806	Middleboro	will	644
	Ruth	1858	Middleboro	will	645
	Simon	1833	Middleboro	will	646
BACON	Benjamin	1871	Mattapoisett	will	647
	David	1831	Rochester	admn	648
	George	1826	Plymouth	will	649
	George H	1874	Marion	will	650
	Mary	1832	Rochester	grdn	651 a
	Mary	1871	Mattapoisett	admn	652
	Sarah	1749	Plymouth	admn	653
BADGER	Sarah	1855	Carver	grdn	654 a
BAGNALL	Benjamin	1839	Plymouth	admn	655
	Bethiah	1847	Plymouth	admn	656
	Elizabeth S	1855	Plymouth	grdn	657
	Elizabeth S	1870	Plymouth	admn	658
	Lucy	1856	Plymouth	admn	659
	Minerva	1878	Plymouth	admn	660

SURNAME	FIRST NAME	YEAR	PLACE	CASE	DOCKET
BAGNALL	Richard	1809	Plymouth	admn	662
	Richard	1868	Plymouth	will	661
	Samuel W	1848	Plymouth	will	663
BAILEY	Abby G	1846	Hingham	grdn	664
	Abigail	1768	Scituate	grdn	719
	Abigail	1798	Hanover	grdn	706
	Abigail	1830	Hanover	will	665
	Abner	1768	Scituate	grdn	719
	Abner	1803	Scituate	will	666
	Alice F	1868	Hanover	grdn	688
	Amasa	1788	Scituate	will	667
	Amasa	1794	Scituate	grdn	668
	Ann Maria	1870	Scituate	admn	669
	Anna	1821	Hingham	will	670
	Benjamin	1770	Scituate	will	671
	Benjamin	1808	Nantucket	grdn	718
	Benjamin	1822	Scituate	will	672
	Benjamin	1872	Hanover	admn	673
	Betsey	1816	Scituate	admn	674
	Billings	1809	Scituate	grdn	686
	Caleb	1786	Scituate	admn	675
	Caleb	1794	Scituate	grdn	668
	Caleb	1873	Hingham	grdn	676 a
	Caleb	1877	Hingham	admn	677
	Calvin S	1835	Hanover	grdn	694
	Charles	1783	Hanover	admn	678
	Charles	1820	Hanover	admn	679
	Chloe	1844	Hanover	admn	680
	Cordiann F	1880	Marshfield	admn	681
	Cotton	1828	Scituate	will	682
	David	1837	Scituate	admn	683
	Deborah	1809	Scituate	grdn	686
	Ebenezer	1772	Scituate	will	685
	Ebenezer	1809	Scituate	grdn	686
	Ebenezer	1865	Scituate	will	684
	Elbridge	1835	Hanover	grdn	694
	Elizabeth	1790	Scituate	admn	687
	Eva L	1868	Hanover	grdn	688
	Ezekiel	1792	Hanover	grdn	689
	George	1832	Hanover	will	692
	George	1856	Hanover	admn	690
	George	1856	Hanover	will	691
	George C	1835	Hanover	grdn	694
	George Jr	1835	Hanover	admn	693
	Guido Jr	1690	Bridgewater	admn	695
	Hannah	1809	Scituate	grdn	686
	Hannah	1840	Scituate	admn	696
	Hayward	1845	Hingham	admn	697
	Henry	1832	Hanover	grdn	698 a
	Horatio N	1835	Hanover	grdn	694
	Horatio N	1860	Abington	admn	699
	Israel	1750	Bridgewater	will	701
	Israel	1774	Bridgewater	admn	700
	Israel	1790	Scituate	grdn	702
	Israel	1798	Hanover	grdn	706
	Jacob	1783	Hanover	will	703
	Jael	1792	Scituate	will	704
	James	1798	Hanover	grdn	706
	James	1880	Abington	admn	705
	Joanna	1845	Scituate	will	707
	Job	1768	Scituate	will	708
	Job	1792	Scituate	will	709
	Job	1860	Scituate	will	710
	John	1718	Scituate	will	711
	John	1752	Hanover	will	712
	John	1778	Hanover	will	713
	Joseph	1747	Scituate	will	714
	Joseph	1782	Scituate	will	715
	Joseph	1790	Scituate	grdn	702
	Joseph	1809	Scituate	admn	716
	Joshua	1808	Nantucket	grdn	718

SURNAME	FIRST NAME	YEAR	PLACE	CASE	DOCKET
BAILEY	Joshua	1828	Scituate	grdn	717
	Judith	1768	Scituate	grdn	719
	Lucy	1798	Hanover	grdn	706
	Luther	1819	Hanover	grdn	720 a
	Luther	1820	Hanover	admn	721
	Lydia	1867	Scituate	will	722
	Lydia J	1846	Hingham	grdn	664
	Melzar C	1843	Hanover	admn	723
	Melzar C	1856	Hanover	grdn	724
	Mephibosheth	1794	Bridgewater	grdn	725
	Mercy	1768	Scituate	grdn	719
	Mercy	1827	Scituate	admn	726
	Millard F	1863	Abington	grdn	727
	Nahum	1876	Kingston	will	728
	Noah C	1875	Scituate	admn	729
	Olive	1880	Hanover	will	730
	Olive W	1835	Hanover	grdn	694
	Paul	1831	Scituate	will	731
	Paul	1860	Scituate	admn	732
	Quincy E	1857	Hanover	grdn	750
	Rebecca	1792	Hanover	grdn	689
	Rebecca	1798	Hanover	grdn	706
	Rebecca	1809	Scituate	grdn	686
	Reuben C	1835	Hanover	grdn	694
	Rowland	1829	Scituate	admn	733
	Sally	1875	Middleboro	admn	734
	Sarah	1833	Scituate	will	735
	Sarah M	1830	Scituate	grdn	736
	Sarah M	1880	Hanover	admn	737
	Seth	1746	Scituate	will	739
	Seth	1797	Hanover	admn	738
	Seth K	1862	Scituate	admn	740
	Stephen	1806	Hanover	will	741
	Sukey	1854	Hingham	will	742
	Susan N	1878	Hingham	admn	743
	Sylvia	1789	Hanover	grdn	744
	Thomas	1698	Scituate	will	746 i
	Thomas	1868	Kingston	will	745
	Thomas T	1841	Scituate	will	747
	W Roland	1876	Kingston	admn	751
	Waterman	1872	Scituate	will	748
	Whitman	1809	Scituate	grdn	686
	William	1745	Scituate	will	749
	William E	1857	Hanover	grdn	750
BAKER	Abigail	1713	Marshfield	grdn	804
	Abigail	1786	Marshfield	grdn	814
	Abigail	1854	Duxbury	will	752
	Abigail	1871	Abington	admn	753
	Abner L	1849	Hingham	admn	754
	Abner L	1849	Hingham	grdn	758
	Almira	1813	Duxbury	grdn	771
	Alvin	1875	Duxbury	will	755
	Ann Eliza	1870	Marshfield	grdn	756
	Anna F	1849	Hingham	grdn	758
	Anna W	1851	Duxbury	admn	757
	Arthur	1874	Abington	grdn	759
	Barker	1862	Pembroke	admn	760
	Barker C	1813	Duxbury	grdn	771
	Benjamin	1769	Pembroke	admn	761
	Benjamin	1877	Marshfield	will	762
	Bethiah	1713	Marshfield	grdn	804
	Bradford	1834	Marshfield	admn	763
	Calvin	1837	Marshfield	grdn	764
	Charles	1817	Marshfield	will	765
	Charles	1847	Marshfield	will	766
	Daniel	1789	Pembroke	admn	767
	Daniel	1852	Bridgewater	admn	768
	Daniel	1871	Duxbury	admn	769
	Edward	1713	Marshfield	grdn	804
	Edward	1870	Plympton	grdn	812
	Edward D	1813	Duxbury	grdn	771

SURNAME	FIRST NAME	YEAR	PLACE	CASE	DOCKET
BAKER	Edward D	1824	Duxbury	admn	770
	Elijah	1827	Duxbury	admn	772
	Elijah	1835	Duxbury	admn	773
	Elisha	1721	Marshfield	grdn	796
	Emma C	1873	Duxbury	admn	774
	Francis A	1871	Pembroke	grdn	809
	Francis H	1845	Duxbury	grdn	775
	George	1813	Duxbury	grdn	771
	George	1838	Marshfield	admn	776
	George	1845	E. Bridgewater	grdn	777
	Griswold E	1880	Brockton	grdn	778
	Hannah	1861	Marshfield	grdn	779
	Hannah C	1853	Duxbury	will	780
	Henrietta F	1864	Pembroke	grdn	788
	Henry	1777	Marshfield	grdn	782
	Henry	1826	Marshfield	admn	781
	Hervey	1833	Pembroke	grdn	831 a
	Hervey	1881	Duxbury	will	783
	Hiram	1862	Marshfield	admn	784
	James	1798	Marshfield	admn	785
	James	1875	Marshfield	admn	786
	Jane	1826	N. Bridgewater	will	787
	Jennie F	1864	Pembroke	grdn	788
	John	1813	Pembroke	will	789
	John	1852	Marshfield	bond	790
	John	1854	Plymouth	admn	791
	John	1867	Hingham	will	792
	Joseph	1861	Marshfield	admn	793
	Joseph C	1865	Middleboro	will	794
	Joshua	1721	Marshfield	grdn	796
	Joshua	1753	Pembroke	admn	795
	Josiah	1701	Marshfield	grdn	797
	Josiah	1721	Marshfield	grdn	796
	Josiah	1874	Lakeville	admn	798
	Julianna	1878	Marshfield	admn	799
	Kenelm	1713	Marshfield	will	803
	Kenelm	1713	Marshfield	grdn	804
	Kenelm	1771	Marshfield	will	802
	Kenelm	1777	Marshfield	admn	801
	Kenelm	1826	Pembroke	admn	800
	Keziah	1713	Marshfield	grdn	804
	Levi	1869	Kingston	admn	805
	Levi	1870	Plympton	grdn	812
	Lucy	1837	Marshfield	admn	806
	Lydia	1834	Kingston	will	807
	Marcus	1871	Lakeville	grdn	808 a
	Marcus S	1871	Pembroke	grdn	809
	Marion R	1849	Hingham	grdn	758
	Martha J	1871	Duxbury	admn	810
	Mary A	1868	Kingston	admn	811
	Mary A	1870	Plympton	grdn	812
	Mary C	1865	Middleboro	grdn	813
	Miriam	1786	Marshfield	grdn	814
	Nathaniel	1721	Marshfield	grdn	796
	Nathaniel	1760	Pembroke	admn	815
	Olive	1777	Marshfield	grdn	782
	Orlando L	1868	Middleboro	grdn	837
	Otis	1813	Duxbury	grdn	771
	Otis	1855	Marshfield	bond	816
	Otis	1868	Marshfield	will	817
	Paul	1875	Rockland	admn	818
	Samuel	1700	Marshfield	admn	819
	Samuel	1713	Marshfield	grdn	804
	Samuel	1721	Marshfield	admn	820
	Samuel	1793	Duxbury	will	824
	Samuel	1825	Middleboro	grdn	827
	Samuel	1851	Middleboro	admn	825
	Samuel	1872	Marshfield	will	823
	Samuel C	1862	Marshfield	grdn	822
	Samuel Jr	1825	Middleboro	admn	826
	Samuel Jr	1852	Marshfield	admn	821

SURNAME	FIRST NAME	YEAR	PLACE	CASE	DOCKET
BAKER	Sarah	1721	Marshfield	grdn	796
	Sarah	1827	Duxbury	admn	828
	Sarah L	1872	Hingham	admn	829
	Simeon	1880	Lakeville	admn	830
	Sumner B	1837	Marshfield	grdn	764
	Susannah	1833	Pembroke	grdn	831 a
	Tabatha	1777	Marshfield	grdn	782
	Thomas	1712	Childley Eng	admn	832
	Thomas	1798	Marshfield	grdn	833
	Thomas	1827	Marshfield	admn	834
	Thomas	1827	Duxbury	will	835
	Thomas	1845	E. Bridgewater	admn	836
	Velilla	1868	Middleboro	grdn	837
	Weston	1813	Duxbury	grdn	771
	William	1713	Marshfield	grdn	804
	William	1807	Marshfield	admn	838
	William	1858	Pembroke	admn	839
	William W	1875	Plymouth	will	840
	Winthrop S	1879	Brockton	admn	841
BALDWIN	Alva B	1864	Abington	grdn	842
	Bethiah	1791	Hanover	grdn	843
	Frances	1866	Hanover	will	844
	Francis	1791	Hanover	grdn	843
	Hannah	1791	Hanover	admn	845
	Lucy	1791	Hanover	grdn	843
	Samuel	1782	Hanover	grdn	846 a
	Samuel	1785	Hanover	admn	847
	William	1791	Hanover	grdn	843
BALLARD	James	1879	Abington	will	848
	Lizzie F	1867	Plymouth	grdn	849
	Samuel D	1868	Plymouth	admn	850
BANCROFT	Edmund A	1877	California	admn	851
	Polly	1868	Hingham	admn	852
BANGS	Nabby	1847	Hingham	will	853
	Ruth	1806	Hingham	will	854
BANKS	Clark J	1835	Plymouth	admn	855
BARBER	Elva J	1867	Marshfield	grdn	856
	George O	1867	Marshfield	grdn	856
	James C	1862	Marshfield	admn	857
	Julia A	1866	Marshfield	admn	858
	Marcus N	1867	Marshfield	grdn	856
BARDEN	Benjamin	1757	Middleboro	grdn	859
	Benjamin	1762	Middleboro	grdn	860 a
	Benjamin	1772	Middleboro	admn	861
	Bethiah	1822	Middleboro	will	862
	Consider	1779	Middleboro	admn	863
	Deborah	1721	Middleboro	will	865
	Deborah	1725	Middleboro	grdn	864
	Edward	1860	Middleboro	will	866
	Gershom	1809	Plymouth	admn	867
	Ichabod	1725	Middleboro	grdn	864
	Ichabod	1771	Middleboro	admn	868
	Ichabod	1821	Middleboro	grdn	869 a
	John	1724	Middleboro	admn	870
	John	1815	Middleboro	will	871
	John	1863	Middleboro	will	872
	Joseph	1749	Middleboro	admn	873
	Joseph	1783	Middleboro	will	874
	Mercy	1792	Middleboro	will	875
	Stephen	1814	Rochester	admn	876
	Thomas F	1880	Middleboro	admn	877
	William	1693	Middleboro	will	878
BARKER	Abner	1730	Marshfield	grdn	879
	Alice	1720	Abington	grdn	912
	Alice M	1860	Hanover	grdn	880
	Barnabas	1763	Scituate	will	881
	Barnabas	1795	Marshfield	admn	882
	Barnabas	1834	Pembroke	admn	883
	Barsheba	1756	Scituate	grdn	889
	Benjamin	1837	Pembroke	will	884
	Benjamin	1864	Hanson	will	885

SURNAME	FIRST NAME	YEAR	PLACE	CASE	DOCKET
BARKER	Blaney P	1856	S. Scituate	admn	886
	Bowen	1874	Hanson	will	887
	Charles	1844	Pembroke	admn	888
	Content	1756	Scituate	grdn	889
	Daniel	1720	Abington	grdn	912
	Daniel	1849	Hanson	admn	890
	Deborah	1819	Pembroke	will	891
	Deborah	1832	Hingham	will	892
	Deborah B	1871	S. Scituate	admn	893
	Ebenezer	1756	Pembroke	will	894
	Ebenezer	1781	Pembroke	admn	895
	Elisha	1710	Duxbury	admn	896
	Elisha	1787	Hanover	admn	897
	Eliza	1866	Pembroke	will	898
	Elizabeth	1772	Pembroke	grdn	899 a
	Elizabeth	1775	Pembroke	will	900
	Francis	1721	Pembroke	admn	901
	Francis Jr	1694	Duxbury	admn	902
	George	1720	Abington	grdn	912
	Hannah	1730	Marshfield	grdn	879
	Hannah	1793	Pembroke	grdn	903
	Hannah	1837	Pembroke	will	904
	Isaac	1693	Duxbury	divi	908
	Isaac	1742	Pembroke	grdn	906 a
	Isaac	1788	Middleboro	admn	909
	Isaac	1826	Pembroke	admn	905
	Isaac B	1845	Hanson	admn	910
	Isaac Jr	1725	Pembroke	admn	907
	James	1718	Abington	will	911
	James	1720	Abington	grdn	912
	John	1729	Scituate	will	913
	John	1828	Hingham	will	914
	John	1873	Pembroke	will	915
	Jonathan	1691	Middleboro	admn	916
	Joseph	1815	Middleboro	admn	917
	Joseph	1854	Middleboro	admn	918
	Joshua	1756	Scituate	grdn	889
	Joshua	1805	Pembroke	will	919
	Josiah	1718	Pembroke	will	920
	Josiah	1774	Pembroke	will	921
	Josiah	1789	Pembroke	admn	922
	Josiah	1873	Hanson	will	923
	Lucy	1756	Scituate	grdn	889
	Lydia	1720	Abington	grdn	912
	Lydia	1874	Halifax	admn	924
	Lydia H	1875	Hanson	grdn	925
	Marcy	1756	Scituate	grdn	889
	Mary	1752	Scituate	admn	926
	Mary	1754	Lebanon	grdn	927
	Patience	1802	Scituate	will	928
	Prince	1784	Pembroke	will	929
	Robert	1691/2	Duxbury	will	933
	Robert	1718	Newport	grdn	934
	Robert	1729	Pembroke	will	930
	Robert	1759	Scituate	will	935
	Robert	1836	Pembroke	admn	931
	Robert	1879	Pembroke	admn	932
	Ruth B	1854	Pembroke	grdn	936 a
	Samuel	1782	Scituate	will	938
	Samuel	1840	Hanson	will	937
	Samuel P	1866	Scituate	admn	939
	Samuel W	1755	Scituate	will	940
	Sarah	1730	Scituate	will	941
	Sarah	1786	Pembroke	will	942
	Sarah	1794	Pembroke	admn	943
	Seth	1866	Hanover	admn	944
	Sophia	1872	Wareham	will	945
	Stephen	1720	Abington	grdn	912
	Stephen	1738	Scituate	admn	946
	Susan E	1845	Pembroke	grdn	947
	Thomas	1734	Pembroke	admn	948

SURNAME	FIRST NAME	YEAR	PLACE	CASE	DOCKET
BARKER	Thomas	1780	Pembroke	will	949
	Warren W	1877	Marshfield	will	950
	Zipporah	1756	Scituate	grdn	889
BARLOW	Aaron	1714/5	Rochester	will	951
	Aaron	1744	Rochester	admn	952
	Amity	1783	Rochester	admn	953
	Ebenezer	1754	Rochester	will	954
	Francis	1858	Mattapoisett	admn	955
	George	1775	Rochester	will	956
	George	1847	Rochester	admn	957
	Mary	1714/5	Rochester	grdn	958
	Moses	1742	Rochester	will	959
	Nathan	1714	Rochester	grdn	960
	Nathan	1744	Rochester	admn	961
	Shubael	1770	Rochester	will	962
	Susanna	1786	Rochester	grdn	963
BARNES	Abbie L	1848	Hingham	grdn	994
	Abigail	1824	Hingham	grdn	990
	Adeline L	1849	Hingham	grdn	964 a
	Alice	1773	Plymouth	grdn	965 a
	Allen B	1871	Plymouth	grdn	966
	Anna	1760	Plympton	will	967
	Anna	1856	Hingham	admn	968
	Benjamin	1760	Plymouth	admn	973
	Benjamin	1803	Hingham	admn	969
	Benjamin	1827	Hingham	grdn	979
	Benjamin	1832	Hingham	grdn	970 a
	Benjamin	1834	Hingham	admn	971
	Benjamin	1838	Plymouth	admn	974
	Benjamin	1865	Plymouth	will	975
	Benjamin 2nd	1859	Hingham	will	972
	Betsey	1863	Hingham	admn	976
	Betsey C	1863	Plymouth	admn	977
	Bradford	1851	Plymouth	admn	978
	Caleb B	1827	Hingham	grdn	979
	Canterbury	1833	Hingham	will	980
	Christiana	1844	Hingham	admn	981
	Cromwell	1804	Hingham	grdn	983
	Cromwell	1824	Hingham	admn	982
	Curtis	1834	Hingham	grdn	984 a
	Curtis	1852	Hingham	will	985
	David	1811	Scituate	will	986
	Deborah G	1849	Hingham	grdn	987 a
	Dorcas	1793	Plymouth	admn	988
	Elce	1751	Plymouth	grdn	1021
	Eliza V	1832	Hingham	admn	989
	Elizabeth E	1824	Hingham	grdn	990
	Ellis	1861	Plymouth	will	991
	Ensign	1830	Hingham	will	993
	Ensign	1832	Hingham	will	992
	Ensign	1848	Hingham	grdn	994
	Ezekiel	1819	Hingham	will	995
	Fanny	1845	Plymouth	grdn	1037
	George	1827	Hingham	admn	996
	Hannah	1751	Plymouth	grdn	1021
	Hannah	1837	Hingham	will	997
	Harrison O	1865	Plymouth	grdn	998
	Helen A	1848	Hingham	grdn	994
	Henry	1879	Hingham	admn	999
	Isaac	1842	Plymouth	admn	1001
	Isaac	1848	Plymouth	admn	1002
	Isaac	1874	Hingham	will	1000
	James	1863	Plymouth	will	1003
	Jane	1861	Plymouth	admn	1004
	Jane	1866	Plymouth	admn	1005
	John	1672	Plymouth	admn	1006
	John	1744	Plymouth	admn	1007
	John	1745	Plymouth	admn	1008
	John	1751	Plymouth	grdn	1021
	John	1804	Hingham	grdn	983
	John	1817	Hingham	admn	1009

SURNAME	FIRST NAME	YEAR	PLACE	CASE	DOCKET
BARNES	John	1822	Hingham	admn	1010
	Jonathan	1714	Plymouth	will	1011
	Jonathan	1736	Plymouth	admn	1012
	Jonathan	1748	Plymouth	will	1014
	Jonathan	1754	Plymouth	grdn	1015
	Jonathan	1758	Plymouth	admn	1013
	Joseph	1795	Plymouth	admn	1016
	Joseph	1843	Scituate	admn	1018
	Joseph Jr	1837	Plymouth	admn	1017
	Laura A	1848	Hingham	grdn	994
	Lemuel	1750	Plymouth	admn	1020
	Lemuel	1751	Plymouth	grdn	1021
	Lemuel	1808	Plymouth	admn	1019
	Levi	1853	Plymouth	will	1022
	Lincoln	1823	Hingham	admn	1023
	Luther J	1855	Hingham	admn	1024
	Lydia	1751	Plymouth	grdn	1021
	Lydia	1854	Hingham	will	1025
	Malachi	1853	Hingham	admn	1026
	Martha	1817	Hingham	grdn	1027 a
	Martha	1840	Hingham	admn	1028
	Martha W	1860	Plymouth	will	1030
	Martha et al	1835	Hingham	part	1029
	Martin	1845	Hingham	admn	1031
	Mary	1744	Plymouth	admn	1032
	Mary	1824	Plymouth	admn	1033
	Mary	1836	Plymouth	admn	1034
	Mary A	1879	Plymouth	admn	1035
	Mary W	1836	Plymouth	grdn	1038
	Mercy	1786	Plymouth	admn	1036
	Nancy C	1845	Plymouth	grdn	1037
	Nancy P	1836	Plymouth	grdn	1038
	Nathan	1838	Hingham	will	1039
	Nathaniel	1754	Plymouth	grdn	1015
	Nathaniel	1781	Plymouth	admn	1040
	Nathaniel	1804	Plymouth	admn	1041
	Nathaniel C	1873	Plymouth	admn	1042
	Olive	1824	Hingham	grdn	990
	Phebe	1753	Plymouth	will	1043
	Polly	1838	Hingham	will	1044
	Rachel L	1824	Hingham	grdn	990
	Southworth	1860	Plymouth	admn	1045
	Susan	1849	Hingham	will	1046
	Thomas	1852	Hingham	will	1047
	William	1751	Plymouth	grdn	1021
	William	1751	Plymouth	will	1048
	William	1760	Plymouth	admn	1049
	William	1826	Plymouth	admn	1050
	William	1832	Plymouth	admn	1051
	William B	1870	Plymouth	will	1052
	William E	1870	Plymouth	admn	1053
	William W	1871	Plymouth	grdn	966
	Zacheus	1754	Plymouth	grdn	1015
	Zacheus	1833	Plymouth	admn	1054
BARNEY	George E	1879	Lakeville	grdn	1055
	Jennie H	1879	Lakeville	grdn	1055
	Mary A	1879	Lakeville	grdn	1055
BARRELL	Abigail	1810	Bridgewater	grdn	1062
	Betsey	1850	E. Bridgewater	will	1056
	Carrie Eliz.	1870	Abington	adop	1057
	Elisha	1829	Hanover	will	1058
	George W	1871	E. Bridgewater	will	1059
	Hannah	1810	Bridgewater	grdn	1062
	James	1810	Bridgewater	will	1061
	James	1850	S. Scituate	will	1060
	James C	1810	Bridgewater	grdn	1062
	Jane	1868	S. Scituate	will	1063
	Joseph	1864	S. Scituate	will	1064
	Lydia	1714	Scituate	will	1065
	Noah	1838	Scituate	will	1066
	Noah Jr	1831	Scituate	grdn	1067 a

SURNAME	FIRST NAME	YEAR	PLACE	CASE	DOCKET
BARRELL	Rebecca	1840	Scituate	admn	1068
	Ruth	1863	S. Scituate	will	1069
	William	1689	Scituate	admn	1070
	William	1752	Scituate	admn	1071
	William	1806	Scituate	will	1072
BARRETT	Samuel	1877	Middleboro	will	1073
BARROWS	Abbie D	1872	Pembroke	grdn	1074
	Abisha	1810	Wareham	admn	1075
	Abner	1767	Plympton	admn	1076
	Albert	1848	Wareham	admn	1077
	Alpheus	1834	Rochester	admn	1078
	Amanda N	1867	Middleboro	admn	1079
	Andrew	1809	Carver	will	1080
	Andrew	1850	Carver	grdn	1097
	Andrew F	1881	Carver	admn	1081
	Andrew J	1868	Mattapoisett	grdn	1082 a
	Asa	1840	Middleboro	admn	1083
	Asa	1879	Plymouth	admn	1084
	Bennett	1723	Plympton	grdn	1113
	Carver	1826	Carver	admn	1085
	Charles	1865	Middleboro	will	1086
	Charles C	1845	Middleboro	admn	1087
	Charles H	1838	Middleboro	grdn	1088
	Elisha	1767	Rochester	will	1089
	Elizabeth	1723	Plympton	grdn	1113
	Ephraim	1723	Plympton	grdn	1113
	Fanny E	1878	Wareham	admn	1090
	Frederick S	1867	Wareham	grdn	1091
	Freeman	1813	Middleboro	admn	1092
	George	1759	Plympton	bond	1094
	George	1794	Plympton	will	1095
	George	1854	Rochester	admn	1093
	George D	1863	Plympton	will	1096
	Gustavus H	1850	Carver	grdn	1097
	Hannah S	1855	Carver	grdn	1124
	Harriet A	1855	Carver	grdn	1124
	Hiram	1868	Wareham	admn	1098
	Isaac	1723	Plympton	grdn	1113
	Isaac	1741	Plymouth	admn	1101
	Isaac	1793	Carver	grdn	1099
	Isaac	1807	Plymouth	will	1102
	Isaac	1808	Middleboro	admn	1100
	Isaac N	1879	Plymouth	admn	1103
	Jacob	1853	Middleboro	will	1104
	James	1750	Plympton	admn	1105
	James	1806	Carver	admn	1106
	John	1692	-----	will	1107
	John	1720	Plympton	admn	1112
	John	1723	Plympton	grdn	1113
	John	1743	Rochester	admn	1110
	John	1752	Rochester	grdn	1111
	John	1812	Carver	grdn	1108
	John	1837	Carver	admn	1109
	Joseph	1870	Carver	will	1114
	Josiah	1836	Middleboro	will	1115
	Judith	1855	Wareham	admn	1116
	Lewin	1880	Middleboro	admn	1117
	Lothrop	1857	Carver	admn	1118
	Lothrop	1873	Carver	admn	1119
	Lothrop W	1855	Carver	grdn	1124
	Lucinda A F	1873	Carver	grdn	1120
	Lucy H	1849	Wareham	grdn	1121
	Lydia H	1849	Wareham	grdn	1121
	Mary	1806	Carver	grdn	1123
	Mary A	1870	Middleboro	will	1122
	Mary H	1850	Carver	grdn	1097
	Mercy F	1855	Carver	grdn	1124
	Moses	1769	Plympton	admn	1125
	Nancy	1806	Carver	grdn	1123
	Nathaniel	1803	Middleboro	will	1126
	Nathaniel S	1866	Carver	admn	1127

SURNAME	FIRST NAME	YEAR	PLACE	CASE	DOCKET
BARROWS	Nelson	1803	Middleboro	grdn	1137
	Peleg	1803	Carver	will	1128
	Peleg	1835	Carver	admn	1129
	Rebecca	1873	Wareham	will	1130
	Robert	1707	Plymouth	will	1131
	Robert	1766	Middleboro	admn	1133
	Robert	1768	Plymouth	admn	1132
	Ruth	1723	Plympton	grdn	1113
	Ruth	1848	Middleboro	will	1134
	Sarah S	1877	Middleboro	will	1135
	Seth	1752	Rochester	grdn	1111
	Sophia	1880	Middleboro	admn	1136
	Stillman	1803	Middleboro	grdn	1137
	Sylvanus	1855	Middleboro	admn	1138
	William	1849	Carver	admn	1139
	William	1867	Wareham	will	1140
	Wilson	1854	Carver	admn	1141
	Zenas H	1849	Wareham	grdn	1121
BARRY	John	1870	Hingham	admn	1142
	Patrick	1876	Hingham	will	1143
	Timothy	1856	Plymouth	will	1144
BARRYSVILLE	Jacob	1858	Abington	admn	1145
BARSTOW	Abigail	1728	Hanover	grdn	1194
	Aliston P	1880	Duxbury	grdn	1146
	Andrew	1857	Bridgewater	will	1147
	Benjamin	1751	Pembroke	admn	1148
	Benjamin	1792	Pembroke	will	1149
	Benjamin	1826	Rochester	grdn	1150 a
	Benjamin	1872	Duxbury	admn	1151
	Benjamin F	1867	Chinese Camp CA	admn	1152
	Betsey	1855	Hanover	admn	1153
	Betsey E	1874	Hanover	will	1154
	Burden	1796	Pembroke	admn	1155
	Caleb	1758	Pembroke	grdn	1156
	Charles	1829	Pembroke	admn	1157
	Charles L	1869	Duxbury	will	1158
	Clara A	1880	Duxbury	grdn	1146
	Content	1758	Pembroke	grdn	1156
	Daniel	1842	Hanover	will	1159
	Daniel	1861	Hanover	admn	1160
	Deborah	1731	Hanover	grdn	1196
	Diana	1855	Kingston	admn	1161
	Edward	1833	Hanover	admn	1162
	Edward	1833	Hanover	grdn	1163
	Edwin W	1877	Bridgewater	will	1164
	Eleanor	1847	Scituate	will	1165
	Elijah	1842	Scituate	admn	1166
	Elizabeth	1731	Hanover	grdn	1196
	Elizabeth	1833	Hanover	grdn	1163
	Ezekiel	1815	Hanover	admn	1167
	Frederick O	1833	Hanover	grdn	1163
	George	1826	Hanson	admn	1168
	George	1836	Duxbury	admn	1169
	George B	1836	Duxbury	grdn	1170
	Gideon	1822	Rochester	grdn	1171 a
	Gideon	1826	Rochester	admn	1172
	Gideon	1849	Rochester	will	1173
	Hannah	1868	Hanover	will	1174
	Hatherly	1772	Hanover	grdn	1175
	Henry Jr	1872	Mattapoisett	admn	1176
	Jacob	1796	Pembroke	admn	1177
	Jacob	1807	Scituate	admn	1178
	James	1728	Hanover	grdn	1194
	James	1732	Hanover	will	1179
	James	1809	Duxbury	will	1180
	James	1881	Mattapoisett	admn	1181
	Joanna H	1881	Mattapoisett	grdn	1182
	Job	1731	Hanover	grdn	1196
	Job	1753	Pembroke	admn	1183
	John B	1854	Hanover	will	1185
	John E	1833	Hanover	grdn	1163

SURNAME	FIRST NAME	YEAR	PLACE	CASE	DOCKET
BARSTOW	John S	1869	Mattapoisett	will	1184
	Joseph	1712	Scituate	will	1186
	Joseph	1728	Hanover	will	1187
	Joseph	1731	Hanover	grdn	1196
	Joseph	1836	Duxbury	admn	1188
	Joseph B	1833	Hanover	grdn	1163
	Joseph Jr	1813	Duxbury	admn	1189
	Joshua	1728	Hanover	grdn	1194
	Lydia	1731	Hanover	grdn	1196
	Lydia	1823	Duxbury	warr	1190
	Lydia	1878	Duxbury	admn	1191
	Margaret	1802	Hanover	warr	1192
	Marietta H	1870	Hanover	admn	1193
	Mary	1728	Hanover	grdn	1194
	Mary H	1879	Mattapoisett	grdn	1195 a
	Michael	1731	Hanover	grdn	1196
	Molly	1850	S. Scituate	will	1197
	Priscilla	1731	Hanover	grdn	1196
	Robert	1833	Hanover	grdn	1163
	Rogers L	1860	Mattapoisett	admn	1198
	Ruth	1799	Pembroke	will	1199
	Samuel	1730	Hanover	admn	1200
	Samuel	1801	Hanover	will	1201
	Samuel	1826	Hanover	will	1202
	Samuel	1867	Hanover	will	1203
	Samuel S	1858	Hingham	will	1204
	Sarah	1728	Scituate	grdn	1219
	Sarah	1758	Pembroke	grdn	1156
	Sarah	1858	Duxbury	admn	1205
	Sarah	1863	Bridgewater	will	1206
	Sarah F	1876	Kingston	grdn	1207
	Solomon	1828	Pembroke	admn	1208
	Tamar	1839	Hanson	will	1209
	Thomas	1797	Scituate	will	1210
	Thomas	1835	Scituate	admn	1211
	Thomas	1857	S. Scituate	name	1212
	Thomas H C	1869	Hanover	will	1213
	William	1719	Scituate	will	1217
	William	1724	Scituate	admn	1218
	William	1728	Scituate	grdn	1219
	William	1852	Duxbury	bond	1214
	William	1863	Pembroke	admn	1216
	William	1871	Duxbury	admn	1215
	Zacheus M	1857	Mattapoisett	will	1220
BARTLETT	Abby	1867	Plymouth	admn	1221
	Abner	1813	Plymouth	admn	1222
	Addie L	1869	Plymouth	grdn	1335
	Alexander	1785	Plymouth	grdn	1374
	Alfred	1814	Plymouth	grdn	1270
	Alonzo S	1867	Plymouth	admn	1223
	Amasa	1835	Plymouth	will	1225
	Amasa	1867	Plymouth	admn	1224
	Amasa	1881	Plymouth	will	1226
	Amasa M	1854	Plymouth	grdn	1309
	Andrew	1809	Plymouth	admn	1227
	Andrew P	1866	Plymouth	grdn	1228
	Ann E	1853	Plymouth	grdn	1229
	Anna C	1814	Plymouth	grdn	1270
	Anna M	1864	Plymouth	admn	1230
	Annie W	1878	Hingham	name	1231
	Ansel	1826	Plymouth	admn	1232
	Ansel	1864	Plymouth	admn	1233
	Asa	1839	Wareham	admn	1234
	Asa M	1839	Wareham	grdn	1235
	Benjamin	1691	Duxbury	will	1236
	Benjamin	1704	Plymouth	grdn	1322
	Benjamin	1718	Plymouth	admn	1239
	Benjamin	1724	Duxbury	will	1238
	Benjamin	1726	Plymouth	grdn	1324
	Benjamin	1727	Duxbury	admn	1237
	Benjamin	1760	Plymouth	admn	1240

SURNAME	FIRST NAME	YEAR	PLACE	CASE	DOCKET
BARTLETT	Benjamin Jr	1755	Plymouth	admn	1241
	Bradford	1827	Rochester	will	1242
	Bradford D	1839	Wareham	grdn	1235
	Caleb	1798	Plymouth	admn	1243
	Catherine	1817	Plymouth	grdn	1386
	Cephas	1814	Plymouth	grdn	1270
	Charles	1773	Plymouth	grdn	1244
	Charles	1792	Plymouth	admn	1245
	Charles	1794	Kingston	grdn	1340
	Charles	1847	Plymouth	grdn	1246 a
	Charles	1849	Westbrook ME	will	1248
	Charles	1857	Kingston	will	1247
	Charles G	1854	Plymouth	grdn	1309
	Coleman	1869	Plymouth	will	1249
	Cornelius	1785	Plymouth	grdn	1374
	Cornelius A	1880	Kingston	will	1250
	Cynthia	1844	Plymouth	will	1251
	Cyrus	1833	Plymouth	part	1332
	Daniel	1871	Hingham	will	1252
	Daniel W	1843	Hingham	grdn	1254
	Daniel W	1856	Hingham	admn	1253
	David	1867	W. Bridgewater	will	1255
	Deborah	1852	Kingston	admn	1256
	Dolly	1816	Plymouth	grdn	1257
	Dorothy	1815	Plymouth	admn	1258
	Ebenezer	1697	Duxbury	admn	1259
	Ebenezer	1720	Plymouth	grdn	1365
	Edward	1836	Plymouth	grdn	1260
	Elizabeth	1714	Duxbury	grdn	1262
	Elizabeth	1717	Duxbury	grdn	1354
	Elizabeth	1720	Plymouth	grdn	1365
	Elizabeth	1793	Plymouth	admn	1261
	Elizabeth B	1824	Kingston	grdn	1271
	Elkanah	1844	Plymouth	admn	1263
	Ellis	1833	Plymouth	part	1332
	Elmer H	1879	Plymouth	grdn	1264
	Elnathan	1714	Plymouth	admn	1265
	Elnathan	1727	Plymouth	grdn	1284
	Elnathan	1741	Plymouth	will	1266
	Elnora	1859	Wareham	grdn	1287
	Ephraim 2nd	1833	Plymouth	admn	1268
	Ephraim Jr	1800	Plymouth	admn	1267
	Eva	1879	San Francisco	grdn	1344
	Eva F	1855	Kingston	grdn	1288
	Flavel	1850	Plymouth	admn	1269
	Francis	1814	Plymouth	grdn	1270
	Francis D	1824	Kingston	grdn	1271
	Frank	1846	Plymouth	grdn	1272
	Frederick	1859	Kingston	admn	1273
	Frederick	1867	Plymouth	admn	1274
	Frederick D	1875	Plymouth	grdn	1275
	Freeman	1848	Plymouth	admn	1276
	Freeman P	1833	Plymouth	part	1332
	George	1804	Plymouth	admn	1278
	George	1824	Kingston	grdn	1271
	George	1854	Kingston	admn	1277
	George	1869	Plymouth	admn	1279
	Hannah	1727	Plymouth	grdn	1284
	Hannah	1812	Plymouth	grdn	1281
	Hannah	1844	Plymouth	grdn	1282
	Hannah	1851	Plymouth	admn	1280
	Hannah S	1855	Plymouth	admn	1283
	Harriet	1836	Plymouth	grdn	1260
	Harriet	1859	Wareham	grdn	1287
	Harriet	1862	Kingston	admn	1285
	Harriet B	1839	Wareham	grdn	1235
	Harriet W	1848	Plymouth	admn	1286
	Helen F	1839	Wareham	grdn	1235
	Henrietta J	1855	Kingston	grdn	1288
	Henry	1854	Kingston	admn	1289
	Henry 2nd	1827	Plymouth	admn	1290

SURNAME	FIRST NAME	YEAR	PLACE	CASE	DOCKET
BARTLETT	Herbert W	1869	Plymouth	grdn	1291
	Hosea	1847	Plymouth	admn	1292
	Ichabod	1714	Duxbury	grdn	1262
	Ichabod	1716	Duxbury	admn	1293
	Idella W	1860	Kingston	grdn	1294
	Idella W	1871	Kingston	admn	1295
	Isaac	1816	Kingston	admn	1296
	James	1720	Plymouth	grdn	1365
	James	1724	Plymouth	admn	1297
	James	1808	Plymouth	admn	1298
	James	1842	Middleboro	admn	1300
	James	1845	Plymouth	admn	1299
	John	1773	Plymouth	will	1302
	John	1814	Plymouth	will	1303
	John	1840	Plymouth	grdn	1304
	John	1870	Plymouth	grdn	1305 a
	John E	1833	Plymouth	admn	1307
	John F	1854	Plymouth	grdn	1309
	John Frank	1877	New York	admn	1308
	John Jr	1790	Plymouth	admn	1306
	John Jr	1814	Kingston	admn	1301
	Jonathan	1782	Plymouth	grdn	1310
	Jonathan	1783	Plymouth	admn	1311
	Jonathan	1793	Plymouth	admn	1312
	Joseph	1703	Plymouth	admn	1321
	Joseph	1704	Plymouth	grdn	1322
	Joseph	1711	Plymouth	admn	1315
	Joseph	1717	Duxbury	grdn	1354
	Joseph	1720	Plymouth	grdn	1365
	Joseph	1726	Plymouth	grdn	1324
	Joseph	1756	Plymouth	will	1316
	Joseph	1783	Kingston	admn	1313
	Joseph	1783	Plymouth	will	1318
	Joseph	1788	Kingston	admn	1314
	Joseph	1835	Plymouth	admn	1319
	Joseph	1835	Plymouth	will	1320
	Joseph Jr	1760	Plymouth	admn	1317
	Joseph T	1822	Plymouth	grdn	1323
	Joshua	1807	Plymouth	admn	1325
	Josiah	1717	Duxbury	grdn	1354
	Judah	1853	Plymouth	admn	1326
	Judith	1875	Wareham	will	1327
	Laura A	1824	Kingston	grdn	1271
	Lemuel	1720	Plymouth	grdn	1365
	Lemuel	1792	Plymouth	admn	1328
	Lemuel	1825	Plymouth	admn	1329
	Leroy C	1865	Marshfield	grdn	1401
	Lewis	1853	Plymouth	admn	1330
	Lewis	1879	Plymouth	will	1331
	Lewis L	1833	Plymouth	part	1332
	Lizzie W	1869	Plymouth	grdn	1335
	Lloyd G	1855	Kingston	grdn	1288
	Lois	1798	Plymouth	grdn	1333
	Lucia A	1869	Plymouth	grdn	1335
	Lucia W	1838	Plymouth	grdn	1334
	Lucretia W	1838	Plymouth	grdn	1357
	Lucy	1856	Plymouth	admn	1336
	Lucy D	1853	Plymouth	will	1337
	Lydia	1704	Plymouth	grdn	1322
	Lydia	1714	Duxbury	grdn	1262
	Lydia	1826	Plymouth	admn	1338
	Lydia A	1843	Hingham	grdn	1254
	Lysander	1794	Kingston	grdn	1340
	Lysander	1858	Kingston	will	1339
	M----	1726	Plymouth	grdn	1324
	Marcia	1814	Plymouth	grdn	1270
	Margaret	1805	Plymouth	admn	1341
	Martha W	1814	Plymouth	grdn	1270
	Martha W	1854	Plymouth	grdn	1309
	Mary	1811	Plymouth	will	1342
	Mary	1824	Kingston	grdn	1271

SURNAME	FIRST NAME	YEAR	PLACE	CASE	DOCKET
BARTLETT	Mary	1846	Plymouth	grdn	1272
	Mary	1849	Plymouth	admn	1343
	May M	1879	San Francisco	grdn	1344
	Melatiah	1825	Plymouth	admn	1345
	Mercy	1878	Plymouth	admn	1346
	Nancy C	1877	Plymouth	admn	1347
	Nathaniel	1717	Duxbury	grdn	1354
	Nathaniel	1732	Duxbury	admn	1353
	Nathaniel	1776	Plymouth	admn	1348
	Nathaniel	1785	Plymouth	grdn	1374
	Nathaniel	1802	Plymouth	admn	1349
	Nathaniel	1872	Plymouth	admn	1351
	Nathaniel 2nd	1862	Plymouth	admn	1350
	Nathaniel L	1872	Plymouth	admn	1352
	Olive H	1879	Plymouth	admn	1355
	Oren	1832	Plymouth	grdn	1356
	Paran	1838	Plymouth	grdn	1357
	Patty	1874	W. Bridgewater	admn	1358
	Peleg	1819	Kingston	admn	1359
	Peleg B S	1859	Wareham	grdn	1287
	Phebe	1879	Plymouth	admn	1360
	Polly	1816	Plymouth	grdn	1257
	Priscilla	1822	Plymouth	grdn	1323
	Rebecca	1848	Plymouth	grdn	1361 a
	Rebecca A	1870	Plymouth	admn	1362
	Remember	1872	Wareham	will	1363
	Robert	1718	Plymouth	admn	1364
	Robert	1720	Plymouth	grdn	1365
	Rufus	1847	Plymouth	admn	1366
	Rufus	1863	Wareham	will	1367
	Samuel	1704	Plymouth	grdn	1322
	Samuel	1713	Duxbury	admn	1368
	Samuel	1751	Plymouth	admn	1371
	Samuel	1769	Plymouth	admn	1372
	Samuel	1780	Plymouth	will	1373
	Samuel	1785	Plymouth	grdn	1374
	Samuel	1843	Plymouth	grdn	1370
	Samuel	1865	Plymouth	admn	1369
	Sarah	1704	Plymouth	grdn	1322
	Sarah	1714	Duxbury	grdn	1262
	Sarah	1717	Duxbury	grdn	1354
	Sarah	1726	Plymouth	grdn	1324
	Sarah	1794	Kingston	grdn	1340
	Sarah	1798	Plymouth	grdn	1333
	Sarah C	1873	Kingston	will	1375
	Sarah G	1879	Plymouth	admn	1376
	Sarah J	1839	Wareham	grdn	1235
	Sarah T	1849	Plymouth	admn	1377
	Sarah W	1875	Plymouth	will	1378
	Seth	1717	Duxbury	grdn	1354
	Seth E	1852	Duxbury	admn	1379
	Seth S	1879	Plymouth	grdn	1380
	Solomon	1822	Plymouth	admn	1381
	Stephen	1785	Plymouth	grdn	1374
	Stephen	1835	Plymouth	admn	1382
	Stephen	1877	Plymouth	admn	1383
	Susan	1847	Plymouth	will	1384
	Sylvanus	1811	Plymouth	admn	1385
	Sylvanus	1817	Plymouth	grdn	1386
	Thankful	1782	Plymouth	will	1387
	Thankful	1845	Plymouth	will	1388
	Thomas	1764	Plymouth	will	1389
	Thomas	1824	Plymouth	grdn	1390
	Thomas M	1824	Plymouth	admn	1391
	Truman	1785	Plymouth	grdn	1374
	Truman	1861	Plymouth	will	1392
	Uriah	1818	Kingston	will	1393
	Victor A	1864	Plymouth	admn	1394
	Walter S	1877	Kingston	admn	1395
	William	1717	Duxbury	admn	1396
	William	1816	Plymouth	admn	1397

SURNAME	FIRST NAME	YEAR	PLACE	CASE	DOCKET
BARTLETT	William	1872	Plymouth	will	1399
	William 3rd	1838	Plymouth	admn	1398
	William D	1817	Plymouth	grdn	1386
	William P	1865	Marshfield	grdn	1401
	William S	1872	Plymouth	will	1400
	Zacheus	1800	Plymouth	admn	1402
	Zacheus	1836	Plymouth	will	1403
	Zacheus	1866	Plymouth	admn	1404
BARTON	Jedediah S	1847	Duxbury	will	1405
	Thomas	1880	E. Bridgewater	admn	1406
BASS	Bathsheba	1750	Bridgewater	grdn	1414
	Benjamin	1756	Hanover	admn	1407
	Benjamin	1821	Hanover	admn	1408
	Benjamin	1824	Hanover	admn	1409
	Benjamin	1825	Hanover	admn	1410
	Elisha	1867	Hanover	will	1411
	Eunice	1750	Bridgewater	grdn	1414
	Jonathan	1750	Bridgewater	will	1412
	Sarah	1750	Bridgewater	grdn	1414
	Sarah F	1864	Abington	adpt	1413
	Ziba	1804	Bridgewater	admn	1415
BASSETT	Abner S	1829	Rochester	grdn	1416
	Adoniram Jr	1870	Bridgewater	grdn	1449
	Caleb	1841	Middleboro	will	1417
	Caleb	1860	Middleboro	will	1418
	Cyrus	1850	Bridgewater	admn	1419
	Daniel	1849	Hingham	will	1420
	Desire P	1848	Rochester	grdn	1421
	Dorothy	1746	Bridgewater	grdn	1439
	Elizabeth	1744	Bridgewater	admn	1422
	Eunice M	1859	Marion	grdn	1423
	George	1867	Bridgewater	admn	1424
	George W	1848	Rochester	grdn	1421
	Hannah M	1875	Bridgewater	admn	1425
	Hannah W	1867	Bridgewater	will	1426
	Isabel	1874	Lakeville	grdn	1427
	Jesse	1832	Plymouth	admn	1428
	John	1860	Hingham	admn	1429
	Joseph	1736	Bridgewater	will	1435
	Joseph	1741	Bridgewater	admn	1438
	Joseph	1746	Bridgewater	grdn	1439
	Joseph	1803	Bridgewater	will	1436
	Joseph	1808	Rochester	will	1432
	Joseph	1813	Hingham	admn	1430
	Joseph	1817	Bridgewater	will	1437
	Joseph	1824	Hingham	admn	1431
	Joseph	1854	Bridgewater	will	1433
	Joseph	1858	Bridgewater	will	1434
	Lydia	1834	Rochester	admn	1440
	Martin	1836	Hingham	admn	1441
	Mary	1789	Rochester	grdn	1442
	Mary	1875	Bridgewater	will	1443
	Nathan	1864	Bridgewater	will	1444
	Paschal	1850	Bridgewater	admn	1445
	Perez	1828	Rochester	admn	1446
	Perez Jr	1828	Rochester	admn	1447
	Phebe	1876	Bridgewater	will	1448
	Samuel W	1870	Bridgewater	grdn	1449
	Sarah	1746	Bridgewater	grdn	1439
	Susannah	1771	Wareham	grdn	1450 a
	Tabitha	1826	Hingham	will	1451
	Thomas	1833	Rochester	will	1452
	Thomas Jr	1832	Rochester	admn	1453
	Urania	1854	Bridgewater	bond	1454
	Urania	1868	N. Bridgewater	admn	1455
	Washington	1873	Wareham	will	1456
	William	1755	Rochester	will	1457
	William	1791	Rochester	admn	1458
	William	1798	Rochester	will	1459
	William	1844	Bridgewater	will	1460
BATES	Abbie F	1877	S. Abington	grdn	1461

SURNAME	FIRST NAME	YEAR	PLACE	CASE	DOCKET
BATES	Abby C	1849	N. Bridgewater	grdn	1468
	Abigail	1869	Wareham	admn	1462
	Abiram	1852	Carver	grdn	1509
	Agnes M	1868	Hanover	grdn	1463
	Alexander	1788	Scituate	admn	1464
	Alice M	1871	Mattapoisett	grdn	1465
	Amos	1833	Hanover	will	1466
	Amos Jr	1766	Rochester	will	1467
	Angelina L	1849	N. Bridgewater	grdn	1468
	Anna	1817	Bridgewater	grdn	1469
	Barnabas	1734	Plymouth	grdn	1473
	Barnabas	1795	Wareham	will	1470
	Barnabas	1835	Wareham	will	1472
	Barnabas 2nd	1811	Wareham	admn	1471
	Benjamin	1800	Abington	admn	1476
	Benjamin	1817	Abington	admn	1477
	Benjamin	1840	Hanover	grdn	1475 a
	Benjamin	1869	Plymouth	admn	1474
	Benjamin W	1836	Scituate	admn	1478
	Benjamin W	1850	Bridgewater	admn	1479
	Bethia	1860	Bridgewater	admn	1480
	Betsey	1809	Pembroke	grdn	1602
	Betsey	1825	Hanover	will	1481
	Betsey R	1833	Hanover	grdn	1593
	Betty	1789	Hanover	admn	1482
	Beulah	1861	Scituate	admn	1483
	Caleb	1820	Kingston	admn	1486
	Caleb	1820	Kingston	grdn	1487
	Caleb	1858	Hingham	will	1485
	Caleb	1878	Scituate	will	1484
	Calvin	1843	N. Bridgewater	admn	1488
	Calvin	1855	Hanover	admn	1489
	Carrie G	1870	Plymouth	grdn	1493
	Celia A M	1833	Hanover	grdn	1593
	Charles	1817	Bridgewater	grdn	1469
	Charles	1877	Scituate	will	1490
	Charles C	1870	Plymouth	grdn	1493
	Charles E	1865	Scituate	admn	1491
	Charles F	1869	Plymouth	grdn	1492
	Christopher	1817	Bridgewater	admn	1494
	Christopher	1851	E. Bridgewater	admn	1495
	Clara W	1868	Hanover	grdn	1519
	Clement	1840	Hanover	admn	1496
	Comfort	1756	Pembroke	admn	1497
	Comfort	1802	Pembroke	grdn	1498
	Comfort	1809	Pembroke	admn	1499
	Comfort	1876	Plymouth	will	1500
	Cornelius	1850	Scituate	will	1501
	Daniel	1776	Abington	admn	1502
	Daniel	1826	Abington	admn	1503
	Daniel	1839	Abington	admn	1504
	Daniel W	1863	E. Bridgewater	grdn	1505
	Daniel W	1877	S. Abington	grdn	1506 a
	David	1802	Plymouth	admn	1507
	David	1849	Carver	admn	1508
	David M	1852	Carver	grdn	1509
	Deborah	1879	S. Abington	will	1510
	Delia	1873	Pembroke	will	1511
	Diantha B	1851	Bridgewater	grdn	1588
	Dorothy	1839	Abington	admn	1512
	Dorothy D	1875	Kingston	will	1513
	Edward	1864	Pembroke	admn	1514
	Edward T	1867	Mattapoisett	grdn	1569
	Elbridge G	1868	Hanson	admn	1515
	Eleazer	1750	Abington	will	1516
	Eleazer	1803	Abington	admn	1517
	Elijah	1797	Rochester	admn	1518
	Elizabeth B	1820	Kingston	grdn	1487
	Ellen F	1868	Hanover	grdn	1519
	Elliot L	1868	Hanover	grdn	1463
	Enos	1814	Hanover	admn	1520

SURNAME	FIRST NAME	YEAR	PLACE	CASE	DOCKET
BATES	Enos	1822	Hanover	grdn	1521
	Esther	1826	Abington	admn	1522
	Fanny	1833	Hanover	grdn	1593
	Francis	1866	Plymouth	admn	1523
	Francis C	1866	Plymouth	grdn	1524
	Francis H	1836	Wareham	grdn	1525
	Gamaliel	1823	Hanover	will	1526
	George	1859	Hanover	admn	1527
	George E	1864	Carver	admn	1528
	George H	1837	Scituate	grdn	1529
	George H	1851	Scituate	grdn	1530
	George H	1851	E. Bridgewater	admn	1531
	Hannah	1856	S. Scituate	will	1532
	Hannah J	1876	Hingham	will	1533
	Harriet	1874	Pembroke	admn	1534
	Hira	1828	Plymouth	grdn	1590
	Hira	1870	Plymouth	admn	1535
	Jacob	1853	E. Bridgewater	admn	1536
	Jacob	1877	S. Abington	admn	1537
	James	1849	Abington	will	1538
	James	1876	Plymouth	admn	1539
	James C	1865	Plymouth	grdn	1540
	James H	1864	Carver	grdn	1541
	Jane	1855	N. Bridgewater	admn	1542
	Jared W	1864	Mattapoisett	admn	1543
	Jemima	1875	Marion	will	1544
	Jennie	1760	Abington	grdn	1545
	Jeremiah	1813	Hanover	admn	1546
	Job	1734	Plymouth	grdn	1473
	John	1734	Plymouth	grdn	1473
	John	1761	Abington	admn	1547
	John	1798	Wareham	will	1548
	John	1809	Pembroke	grdn	1602
	John	1856	Scituate	admn	1549
	John	1862	Mattapoisett	admn	1550
	John P	1823	Hanover	grdn	1585
	John R	1826	Hingham	admn	1551
	Jonathan	1807	Rochester	admn	1552
	Jonathan	1877	Plymouth	admn	1553
	Joseph	1778	Middleboro	will	1554
	Joseph	1858	Carver	admn	1555
	Joseph 3rd	1817	Plymouth	admn	1556
	Joseph N	1869	Plymouth	grdn	1557
	Joseph S	1873	Hanover	admn	1558
	Joshua	1804	Pembroke	grdn	1559
	Joshua	1839	Bridgewater	admn	1560
	Lemuel	1750	Abington	grdn	1561
	Lemuel	1794	Abington	admn	1562
	Lizzie P	1874	E. Bridgewater	grdn	1563
	Lois	1839	Scituate	grdn	1564 a
	Lucia E	1820	Kingston	grdn	1487
	Lusanna W	1878	Scituate	will	1565
	Lydia	1822	Hanover	grdn	1521
	Lydia	1860	Rochester	admn	1566
	Lydia C	1872	Hanover	will	1567
	Marcia E	1867	Mattapoisett	admn	1568
	Marcia S	1867	Mattapoisett	grdn	1569
	Margaret	1856	Pembroke	admn	1570
	Marion F	1867	Mattapoisett	grdn	1569
	Marshall L	1880	Hull	admn	1571
	Martin L	1823	Windsor	bond	1572
	Mary	1836	Hanover	will	1573
	Mary C	1877	S. Abington	admn	1574
	Mary E	1851	Bridgewater	grdn	1588
	Mary G	1864	Carver	grdn	1541
	Mary P	1848	Scituate	will	1575
	Mercy	1809	Pembroke	grdn	1602
	Mille	1756	Pembroke	grdn	1576
	Molly	1760	Abington	grdn	1545
	Moses	1859	E. Bridgewater	will	1577
	Moses	1873	E. Bridgewater	admn	1578

SURNAME	FIRST NAME	YEAR	PLACE	CASE	DOCKET
BATES	Moses Jr	1852	-----	oath	1579
	Nahum	1817	Bridgewater	grdn	1469
	Nahum	1821	Bridgewater	admn	1580
	Nahum	1869	Abington	admn	1581
	Nathan	1804	Abington	grdn	1582
	Noble E	1864	Marion	admn	1583
	Ozin	1828	Plymouth	grdn	1590
	Peggy	1760	Abington	grdn	1545
	Peter	1759	Abington	admn	1584
	Phebe	1823	Hanover	grdn	1585
	Polly	1809	Pembroke	grdn	1602
	Rachel	1750	Abington	admn	1586
	Rachel	1852	Scituate	will	1587
	Rebecca W	1833	Hanover	grdn	1593
	Rodney L	1851	Bridgewater	grdn	1588
	Rowland B	1872	Rochester	will	1589
	Ruby	1828	Plymouth	grdn	1590
	Rufus	1878	Hanover	admn	1591
	Ruth	1866	Hanover	admn	1592
	Ruth J	1833	Hanover	grdn	1593
	Samuel	1731	Plymouth	admn	1595
	Samuel	1836	Plymouth	admn	1594
	Samuel Sr	1713	Plymouth	will	1596
	Sarah J	1857	E. Bridgewater	will	1597
	Seth	1821	Hanover	admn	1599
	Seth	1831	Abington	admn	1598
	Seth W	1848	Hanover	admn	1600
	Simeon	1834	Scituate	will	1601
	Spencer	1809	Pembroke	grdn	1602
	Stephen	1864	Hanson	admn	1603
	Susanna	1849	Abington	will	1604
	Sybel R	1833	Hanover	grdn	1593
	Sylvia	1852	Carver	grdn	1509
	Thomas	1804	Wareham	will	1606
	Thomas	1823	Wareham	will	1607
	Thomas	1867	Kingston	will	1605
	Thomas C	1849	Rochester	admn	1608
	Thomas M	1858	Hanover	admn	1609
	Thomas S	1860	Abington	grdn	1610
	Walter	1870	Hanover	admn	1611
	Ward	1859	Hanover	will	1612
	Watson	1880	Abington	admn	1613
	William	1871	Wareham	will	1614
	William H	1864	E. Bridgewater	admn	1615
	William H	1871	Mattapoisett	grdn	1465
	William H	1877	S. Abington	grdn	1461
	William M	1836	Wareham	grdn	1525
	Zephaniah A	1844	Bridgewater	admn	1616
BATTELL	Marcia E	1861	Middleboro	grdn	1617
BATTLES	Benjamin	1835	Scituate	grdn	1618 a
	Benjamin	1836	Scituate	admn	1619
	Caleb	1857	Plymouth	will	1620
	Caleb	1878	Plymouth	will	1621
	Charles L	1873	Monticello IA	grdn	1622
	Ellis	1857	Plymouth	grdn	1623 a
	John	1746	Plympton	admn	1624
	John	1855	Plymouth	will	1625
	John	1878	Brockton	admn	1626
	Samuel	1813	Plymouth	admn	1627
	Samuel	1817	Bridgewater	will	1628
	Sarah H	1873	Monticello IA	grdn	1622
BAULCH	Benjamin	1757	Scituate	admn	1629
BAXTER	Anna	1821	Bridgewater	will	1630
	Josiah D	1859	Plymouth	bond	1631
	Josiah D	1875	Plymouth	admn	1632
	Mary	1868	Plymouth	admn	1633
	Thompson	1813	Bridgewater	will	1634
BEACH	Ambrose N	1881	S. Scituate	will	1635
	Clementina	1855	Hingham	will	1636
	Martha A	1874	S. Scituate	name	1637
BEAL	Abraham	1749	Abington	will	1638

SURNAME	FIRST NAME	YEAR	PLACE	CASE	DOCKET
BEAL	Ada M	1877	Pembroke	grdn	1639
	Adeline M	1862	Abington	admn	1640
	Albert A	1862	Abington	grdn	1641
	Alden	1877	Hanover	will	1642
	Alonzo	1874	Hanover	admn	1643
	Ann	1806	Middleboro	will	1644
	Anna N	1878	S. Abington	will	1645
	Asahel	1875	Rockland	will	1646
	Benjamin	1750	Bridgewater	grdn	1651
	Benjamin	1752	Abington	grdn	1650
	Benjamin	1805	Abington	will	1649
	Benjamin	1814	Hingham	will	1647
	Benjamin	1815	Abington	grdn	1743
	Benjamin	1833	Hingham	will	1648
	Betsey	1823	Hanson	grdn	1652 a
	Betsey S	1869	Hingham	will	1653
	Blaney	1822	Hanson	admn	1654
	Caroline J	1851	Hingham	grdn	1655
	Celia	1849	Hanson	admn	1656
	Charles	1830	Hingham	admn	1657
	Charles	1875	Plymouth	admn	1658
	Charles C	1871	Mattapoisett	admn	1659
	Clifford G	1874	Pembroke	grdn	1660
	Cora M	1866	Abington	grdn	1675
	Daniel	1880	Hingham	will	1661
	Daniel L	1866	Hingham	admn	1662
	David	1769	Hingham	part	1667
	David	1823	Pembroke	will	1666
	David	1849	Hanson	admn	1664
	David	1855	Abington	admn	1665
	David	1864	Kingston	will	1663
	Edwin	1873	Halifax	admn	1668
	Elijah	1805	Hingham	grdn	1705
	Elijah	1866	Hingham	will	1671
	Elijah	1872	Hingham	admn	1672
	Elijah 2nd	1861	Hingham	grdn	1669 a
	Elijah 2nd	1861	Hingham	will	1670
	Elizabeth	1827	Hingham	will	1673
	Elsie	1833	Hanson	will	1674
	Eugene F	1871	Abington	grdn	1708
	Evangeline M	1866	Abington	grdn	1675
	Flora W	1865	E. Bridgewater	grdn	1676
	Frances	1831	Abington	admn	1677
	George A	1843	Abington	grdn	1678
	George E	1866	Abington	admn	1679
	Grace May	1879	Pembroke	name	1680
	Gracie	1880	Rockland	adpt	1681
	Gridley	1881	Abington	admn	1682
	Hannah	1805	Bridgewater	admn	1685
	Hannah	1844	Hingham	will	1683
	Hannah	1862	Abington	will	1684
	Harriet	1869	N. Bridgewater	admn	1686
	Hattie M	1866	Abington	grdn	1675
	Henry	1805	Hingham	grdn	1710
	Henry B	1871	Abington	grdn	1708
	Herman	1874	Pembroke	grdn	1660
	Isaac	1828	Scituate	admn	1687
	Israel	1813	Hingham	will	1688
	Jacob	1819	Hingham	admn	1689
	Jacob Jr	1805	Hingham	admn	1690
	James	1880	Hingham	will	1691
	James F	1837	Abington	grdn	1692
	Jane L	1866	Abington	grdn	1675
	Jane T	1880	Scituate	admn	1693
	Jedediah	1806	Pembroke	admn	1694
	Jeremiah	1752	Abington	admn	1696
	Jeremiah	1832	N. Bridgewater	will	1695
	Jeremiah Jr	1752	Abington	admn	1697
	John	1814	Hingham	will	1699
	John	1863	Hingham	admn	1698
	John Jr	1806	Hingham	will	1700

SURNAME	FIRST NAME	YEAR	PLACE	CASE	DOCKET
BEAL	Jonathan	1750	Bridgewater	grdn	1651
	Jonathan	1813	Bridgewater	will	1701
	Joseph	1822	Hingham	will	1702
	Joseph S	1853	----	oath	1703
	Laban	1805	Hingham	warr	1704
	Laban	1805	Hingham	grdn	1705
	Levi	1752	Abington	grdn	1650
	Levi	1852	Hingham	admn	1706
	Levi Jr	1837	Hingham	admn	1707
	Lottie A	1871	Abington	grdn	1708
	Louisa R	1805	Hingham	grdn	1710
	Louisa R	1873	Hingham	will	1709
	Lucy S	1875	Brockton	grdn	1711 a
	Lydia	1839	Hingham	will	1712
	Lydia	1858	Abington	admn	1713
	Martha C	1871	Mattapoisett	admn	1714
	Martin	1820	Bridgewater	admn	1715
	Martin	1876	Brockton	admn	1716
	Mary W	1879	Hingham	grdn	1717
	Matthew W	1851	Bridgewater	admn	1718
	Maud M	1877	Pembroke	grdn	1639
	Micah P	1836	Abington	admn	1719
	Nathan	1863	Hingham	admn	1720
	Nathan	1872	Abington	admn	1721
	Nathan Jr	1837	Abington	grdn	1722
	Nathaniel	1820	Abington	admn	1723
	Noah	1794	Abington	admn	1724
	Noah	1840	Abington	admn	1725
	Noah	1871	Abington	admn	1726
	Olive	1830	Hingham	will	1727
	Peggy	1805	Hingham	grdn	1705
	Peter W	1862	Abington	admn	1728
	Polly	1881	Abington	admn	1729
	Priscilla	1752	Abington	grdn	1650
	Rachel	1805	Hingham	grdn	1705
	Rebecca	1823	Hingham	will	1730
	Rebecca N	1844	Hingham	grdn	1731
	Rhoda	1858	Hingham	admn	1732
	Samuel	1750	Bridgewater	will	1733
	Samuel	1856	Hingham	will	1734
	Sarah	1838	Hingham	admn	1735
	Sarah B	1843	Abington	grdn	1736
	Sarah D	1873	Hanson	admn	1737
	Sarah F	1881	Scituate	admn	1738
	Solomon	1750	Pembroke	admn	1739
	Susanna	1840	Hingham	will	1740
	Thomas	1815	Abington	grdn	1743
	Thomas	1862	Abington	will	1742
	Thomas P	1852	Kingston	will	1741
	Welcome	1821	Hingham	will	1744
	William	1832	Hingham	admn	1745
	William H	1866	Hingham	admn	1746
	Zadock	1874	Hanover	will	1747
	Zelotes	1842	Abington	admn	1748
	Zelotes	1851	Abington	will	1749
BEARCE	Abiah	1764	Halifax	grdn	1771
	Andrew	1803	Halifax	admn	1750
	Austin	1764	Halifax	will	1751
	Austin	1764	Halifax	grdn	1771
	Calvin	1877	Plymouth	admn	1752
	Dolly	1851	Hanson	will	1753
	Ebenezer	1877	Scituate	admn	1754
	Eunice	1783	Pembroke	grdn	1755
	Gideon	1761	Halifax	admn	1756
	Gideon	1772	Halifax	grdn	1765
	Hannah	1835	Hanson	will	1757
	Isaiah	1805	Pembroke	admn	1758
	Jacob	1763	Pembroke	admn	1759
	Jacob	1857	Hanson	admn	1760
	James	1728	Plympton	admn	1761
	James	1763	Halifax	admn	1762

SURNAME	FIRST NAME	YEAR	PLACE	CASE	DOCKET
BEARCE	Job	1828	E. Bridgewater	will	1763
	John	1761	Halifax	admn	1764
	Jonathan	1772	Halifax	grdn	1765
	Josiah D	1849	Abington	admn	1766
	Levi	1761	Halifax	grdn	1767
	Lucy	1764	Halifax	grdn	1771
	Mial	1753	Halifax	admn	1768
	Mial	1762	Halifax	grdn	1769
	Obadiah	1762	Halifax	grdn	1769
	Sally	1868	Plymouth	admn	1770
	Sarah	1764	Halifax	grdn	1771
	Seth	1777	Pembroke	admn	1772
	Shubael	1774	Pembroke	will	1773
	Thomas	1758	Pembroke	admn	1774
	Thomas	1857	Pembroke	will	1775
BEARD	John	1851	Rochester	admn	1776
BEARY	Thomas J	1879	S. Abington	grdn	1777
BECKMAN	Esther M	1858	Plymouth	grdn	1780
BEEBY	Eliphalet	1788	Bridgewater	admn	1778
	William	1870	Bridgewater	admn	1779
BEGGEN	Patrick	1858	Hanson	grdn	1781
BELCHER	Mayhew	1778	Bridgewater	will	1782
	Sally	1876	E. Bridgewater	will	1783
BELKNAP	Sarah	1820	Hingham	will	1784
	Willie F	1860	Duxbury	name	1785
	Zela	1866	Duxbury	admn	1786
BELL	John	1736	Plympton	admn	1787
	William	1875	Middleboro	will	1788
BEMIS	Ezekiel	1869	Pembroke	admn	1789
BENNER	Joseph	1850	Abington	admn	1790
BENNETT	Allen	1829	Middleboro	grdn	1791
	Anna	1749	Middleboro	grdn	1792
	Arthur	1737	Middleboro	grdn	1793
	Charles	1840	E. Bridgewater	grdn	1854
	Charlotte	1811	Middleboro	grdn	1794
	Cornelius	1766	Middleboro	admn	1795
	Ebenezer	1750	Middleboro	will	1798
	Ebenezer	1779	Middleboro	admn	1799
	Ebenezer L	1794	Rochester	grdn	1796
	Ebenezer L	1806	Rochester	admn	1797
	Eleazer	1840	E. Bridgewater	grdn	1854
	Elizabeth	1761	Seabrook	grdn	1810
	Ezra	1796	Middleboro	admn	1800
	Frank D	1851	N. Bridgewater	grdn	1801
	Frederick	1811	Middleboro	grdn	1794
	Galen T	1839	Rochester	will	1802
	George	1862	Abington	will	1803
	Hannah	1838	Middleboro	will	1804
	Hannah B	1866	Middleboro	will	1805
	Isaac	1755	Middleboro	admn	1806
	Jacob	1761	Seabrook	grdn	1810
	Jacob	1800	Middleboro	will	1807
	Jacob	1833	Middleboro	admn	1808
	Jacob	1866	Middleboro	will	1809
	Jael	1749	Middleboro	grdn	1792
	James	1867	N. Bridgewater	admn	1812
	James	1872	N. Bridgewater	will	1811
	Jedediah	1756	Middleboro	grdn	1836
	Jeremiah H	1793	Middleboro	grdn	1813
	Jeremiah H	1815	Middleboro	admn	1814
	John	1718	Middleboro	admn	1815
	John	1761	Middleboro	will	1816
	John	1811	Middleboro	admn	1817
	John	1816	Rochester	will	1818
	John	1854	Rochester	will	1821
	John	1875	Rochester	will	1822
	John A	1844	Rochester	grdn	1820
	John G	1840	Rochester	grdn	1819
	Joseph	1736	Middleboro	admn	1826
	Joseph	1741	Middleboro	admn	1827
	Joseph	1756	Middleboro	grdn	1836

SURNAME	FIRST NAME	YEAR	PLACE	CASE	DOCKET
BENNETT	Joseph	1761	Seabrook	grdn	1810
	Joseph	1856	Rochester	admn	1823
	Joseph O	1851	N. Bridgewater	admn	1824
	Joseph W	1840	E. Bridgewater	admn	1825
	Mary	1754	Pembroke	grdn	1828
	Mary	1756	Middleboro	grdn	1836
	Mary	1789	Pembroke	admn	1829
	Mary	1864	E. Bridgewater	admn	1831
	Mary O	1851	N. Bridgewater	grdn	1830
	Mercy	1826	Middleboro	admn	1832
	Michael	1851	Rochester	admn	1833
	Michael 2nd	1851	Rochester	grdn	1834
	Nathan	1751	Middleboro	admn	1835
	Nathan	1756	Middleboro	grdn	1836
	Nehemiah	1769	Middleboro	admn	1837
	Nehemiah	1810	Middleboro	admn	1838
	Nehemiah	1815	Middleboro	grdn	1839
	Nehemiah	1869	Middleboro	admn	1840
	Patience	1796	Middleboro	grdn	1843
	Patience	1810	Middleboro	grdn	1841
	Patience	1857	Rochester	will	1842
	Peter	1749	Middleboro	grdn	1792
	Peter	1749	Middleboro	will	1844
	Phillip	1810	Middleboro	will	1845
	Phillip	1811	Middleboro	grdn	1794
	Polly	1857	Bridgewater	will	1846
	Priscilla	1749	Middleboro	admn	1847
	Priscilla	1749	Middleboro	grdn	1855
	Ruth	1792	Middleboro	will	1848
	Sally	1767	Middleboro	grdn	1856
	Samuel	1757	Middleboro	will	1850
	Samuel	1779	Middleboro	admn	1849
	Shepard	1829	Middleboro	grdn	1851
	Silvanus	1767	Middleboro	grdn	1856
	Silvanus	1809	Middleboro	will	1852
	Stephen	1825	Middleboro	grdn	1853
	Susan	1840	E. Bridgewater	grdn	1854
	Susannah	1749	Middleboro	grdn	1855
	Theodata	1767	Middleboro	grdn	1856
	Thomas	1846	Middleboro	admn	1857
	Timothy	1736	Middleboro	grdn	1858
	William	1810	Middleboro	will	1859
	William W	1842	E. Bridgewater	admn	1860
	Winfred S	1867	N. Bridgewater	grdn	1861
	Zephaniah	1796	Middleboro	grdn	1843
BENSON	Alice	1758	Scituate	will	1862
	Alice F	1856	Bridgewater	grdn	1863
	Andrew	1817	Middleboro	admn	1864
	Andrew	1817	Middleboro	grdn	1918
	Ansel	1855	Middleboro	will	1865
	Aquilla	1737	Rochester	admn	1866
	Asa	1836	Middleboro	will	1867
	Asa	1875	Middleboro	will	1868
	Aubrey	1856	Bridgewater	grdn	1863
	Benjamin	1749	Bridgewater	will	1870
	Benjamin	1764	Bridgewater	grdn	1869
	Benjamin Jr	1818	Wareham	admn	1871
	Betsey	1847	Bridgewater	admn	1872
	Caleb	1788	Middleboro	will	1873
	Caleb	1864	Halifax	will	1874
	Calvin	1817	Middleboro	grdn	1918
	Chester A	1877	Bridgewater	grdn	1875
	Chloe	1879	Bridgewater	will	1876
	Cyrus	1805	Bridgewater	grdn	1879
	Cyrus	1858	Bridgewater	will	1877
	Cyrus Jr	1854	Bridgewater	admn	1878
	David	1823	Bridgewater	will	1880
	Ebenezer	1767	Wareham	will	1881
	Elnathan	1859	Wareham	grdn	1882
	Hannah W	1876	Bridgewater	admn	1883
	Isaac	1848	Middleboro	will	1884

SURNAME	FIRST NAME	YEAR	PLACE	CASE	DOCKET
BENSON	Jabez	1803	Wareham	will	1885
	John	1770	Bridgewater	will	1891
	John	1802	Middleboro	will	1889
	John	1805	Bridgewater	admn	1892
	John	1828	Wareham	grdn	1886
	John	1834	Wareham	admn	1887
	John	1848	Middleboro	will	1890
	John W	1835	Wareham	grdn	1888
	Jonah	1842	Bridgewater	will	1893
	Jonah Jr	1865	Bridgewater	admn	1894
	Jonathan	1789	Bridgewater	will	1895
	Jonathan	1802	Bridgewater	admn	1896
	Jonathan	1805	Bridgewater	grdn	1879
	Joseph	1737	Rochester	admn	1902
	Joseph	1745	Scituate	grdn	1897
	Joseph	1753	Scituate	will	1899
	Joseph	1759	Scituate	grdn	1898
	Joseph	1776	Middleboro	will	1903
	Joseph	1807	Scituate	admn	1900
	Joseph Jr	1745	Scituate	admn	1901
	Joshua	1781	Middleboro	will	1904
	Joshua	1828	Rochester	admn	1905
	Kezia	1749	Bridgewater	will	1906
	Lemira	1856	Bridgewater	grdn	1863
	Levi	1815	Wareham	admn	1907
	Linus	1836	Middleboro	grdn	1908
	Linus	1859	Middleboro	will	1909
	Lucia	1826	Scituate	will	1910
	Lydia	1862	Bridgewater	will	1911
	Lydia W	1879	Bridgewater	admn	1912
	Martha	1801	Bridgewater	will	1913
	Nabby	1805	Bridgewater	grdn	1879
	Nahum	1826	Bridgewater	admn	1914
	Patience	1817	Middleboro	grdn	1918
	Polly	1858	Middleboro	will	1916
	Polly P	1828	Rochester	grdn	1915
	Priscilla	1738	Rochester	grdn	1917
	Priscilla	1817	Middleboro	grdn	1918
	Rebecca	1846	Middleboro	admn	1919
	Roxalana	1817	Middleboro	grdn	1918
	Samuel	1778	Middleboro	will	1920
	Samuel	1828	Wareham	grdn	1921
	Samuel	1828	Wareham	admn	1922
	Sarah	1817	Middleboro	grdn	1918
	Sarah	1829	Rochester	will	1923
	Seth	1877	Plymouth	admn	1924
	Seth S	1860	Wareham	admn	1925
	Sheldon	1859	Wareham	admn	1926
	Susanna	1814	Wareham	admn	1927
	Susanna	1820	Scituate	will	1928
	Susanna	1836	Rochester	admn	1929
	Sylvia	1828	Rochester	grdn	1930
	Temperance P	1828	Rochester	grdn	1930
	Walter	1859	Wareham	grdn	1882
	William	1711	Rochester	admn	1931
	Winfield S	1877	Bridgewater	grdn	1875
	Winfield S	1880	Brockton	grdn	1932
	Zeno	1856	Bridgewater	grdn	1863
BENT	Elizabeth	1686	-----	grdn	1938
	Everett	1846	Middleboro	will	1933
	Experience	1754	Middleboro	admn	1934
	George W	1872	Wareham	will	1935
	Isaac	1876	Wareham	admn	1936
	John	1853	Carver	admn	1937
	Joseph	1686	-----	grdn	1938
	Nancy	1837	Middleboro	admn	1939
	Sarah	1832	Middleboro	admn	1940
	William E	1851	Bridgewater	admn	1941
	Winslow	1827	Middleboro	admn	1942
	Zenas	1823	Middleboro	admn	1943
BERRY	Abbie	1877	Bridgewater	grdn	1944

SURNAME	FIRST NAME	YEAR	PLACE	CASE	DOCKET
BERRY	Hannah	1758	Abington	admn	1945
	Hattie	1877	Bridgewater	grdn	1944
	John	1877	Bridgewater	grdn	1944
	Nahum	1877	Bridgewater	grdn	1944
BESSE	Abia	1876	Wareham	admn	1946
	Adelaide S	1853	Wareham	grdn	1947
	Alden	1801	Wareham	will	1948
	Ansel	1806	Wareham	admn	1949
	Ansel	1840	Wareham	admn	1950
	Barzilla	1813	Plymouth	admn	1951
	Benjamin F	1878	Wareham	admn	1952
	David	1738	Rochester	will	1954
	David	1811	Wareham	grdn	1953
	David	1870	Wareham	admn	1955
	Elisha G	1849	Wareham	admn	1956
	George H	1839	Wareham	admn	1957
	Harriet	1870	Wareham	grdn	1964
	Harry R	1875	Wareham	grdn	1958
	Isaac Y	1849	Wareham	admn	1959
	Jabez	1804	Wareham	will	1960
	Jedidah	1823	Wareham	admn	1961
	Jedidah	1864	Wareham	admn	1962
	Joanna	1843	Duxbury	grdn	1966
	Joshua	1870	Wareham	grdn	1964
	Lothrop A	1873	Wareham	will	1963
	Lucius	1843	Duxbury	grdn	1966
	Lydia	1870	Wareham	grdn	1964
	Marshall	1842	Duxbury	admn	1965
	Marshall	1843	Duxbury	grdn	1966
	Martha	1843	Duxbury	grdn	1966
	Mary	1865	Pembroke	grdn	1969
	Nathaniel	1865	E. Bridgewater	admn	1967
	Nathaniel	1865	Pembroke	grdn	1969
	Nathaniel B	1871	Wareham	grdn	1968
	Olive	1825	Wareham	admn	1970
	Orlando	1870	Wareham	grdn	1964
	Pamelia	1843	Duxbury	grdn	1966
	Rodolphus	1878	Wareham	admn	1971
	Samuel	1865	Wareham	admn	1973
	Samuel B	1860	Wareham	admn	1972
	Sarah	1843	Duxbury	grdn	1966
	Silas Jr	1815	Wareham	admn	1974
	Silvanus	1865	Wareham	will	1975
	William D	1875	Wareham	grdn	1958
BETTRIDGE	Agnes	1874	N. Bridgewater	will	1976
	Agnes E	1874	N. Bridgewater	grdn	1977
BICKFORD	Curtis R	1880	S. Abington	grdn	1978
	Myra L	1880	S. Abington	grdn	1978
BICKNELL	Annie	1826	Abington	grdn	1983
	Betsey	1826	Abington	grdn	1983
	Charlotte	1826	Abington	grdn	1983
	Diantha	1826	Abington	grdn	1983
	Elizabeth	1721	Middleboro	grdn	1979
	Frank A	1879	Brockton	grdn	1980
	Hannah	1721	Middleboro	grdn	1979
	Hannah	1870	Hingham	will	1982
	Hannah S	1870	Kingston	admn	1981
	Harriet	1826	Abington	grdn	1983
	Henry	1826	Abington	grdn	1983
	Henry D	1829	Abington	will	1984
	Henry S	1871	Kingston	grdn	1985
	Jacob	1821	Abington	admn	1986
	Jacob	1850	Abington	admn	1987
	James A	1881	Brockton	admn	1988
	Japhet	1721	Middleboro	grdn	1979
	John	1779	Abington	will	1989
	John	1790	Abington	will	1990
	Joseph	1782	Abington	will	1991
	Leavitt L	1880	New York	admn	1992
	Luke	1814	Abington	will	1993
	Mary	1721	Middleboro	grdn	1979

SURNAME	FIRST NAME	YEAR	PLACE	CASE	DOCKET
BICKNELL	Polly	1826	Abington	grdn	1983
	Quincy	1856	Hingham	will	1994
	Randall	1826	Abington	admn	1995
	Thomas	1718	Middleboro	admn	1996
	Thomas	1723	Middleboro	admn	1997
	Thomas	1871	Kingston	will	1998
BIGELOW	James F	1872	Abington	admn	1999
BILLINGTON	Christian	1703	Middleboro	peti	2001
	Francis	1703	Middleboro	peti	2001
	Francis	1799	Middleboro	admn	2000
	Isaac	1712	Middleboro	admn	2002
	Seth	1718	Middleboro	admn	2003
BINNEY	Amos	1811	Hull	grdn	2011
	Ann	1811	Hull	grdn	2011
	Anna	1824	Hull	grdn	2005
	Anna	1863	Hingham	admn	2004
	Barnabas	1811	Hull	grdn	2011
	Barnabas	1824	Hull	grdn	2005
	Elkanah	1853	Hingham	will	2006
	Elmer	1868	Hanover	grdn	2009
	Henry	1868	Hanover	grdn	2009
	Jane	1811	Hull	grdn	2011
	Jane	1819	Hull	will	2007
	Laura	1868	Hanover	grdn	2009
	Lelia	1868	Hanover	grdn	2009
	Margaret	1834	Hull	grdn	2015
	Martin	1811	Hull	grdn	2011
	Molly	1824	Hull	admn	2008
	Nancy	1834	Hull	grdn	2015
	Nancy	1868	Hanover	grdn	2009
	Rachel	1811	Hull	grdn	2011
	Rebecca	1811	Hull	grdn	2011
	Rebecca	1819	Hull	admn	2010
	Sarah Ann	1877	Hingham	admn	2012
	Spencer	1811	Hull	grdn	2011
	Spencer	1811	Hull	admn	2013
	Spencer	1832	Hull	admn	2014
	Spencer	1834	Hull	grdn	2015
BIRD	Sarah	1879	E. Bridgewater	admn	2016
	William	1872	E. Bridgewater	will	2017
BISBEE	Aaron	1753	Pembroke	admn	2018
	Aaron	1799	Duxbury	will	2019
	Adoniram	1817	Bridgewater	grdn	2061
	Aelius	1861	Plympton	grdn	2020
	Alden C	1864	Middleboro	admn	2021
	Alice	1880	Plympton	grdn	2057
	Benjamin	1743	Plympton	grdn	2048
	Benjamin	1749	Pembroke	grdn	2041
	Benjamin	1756	Bridgewater	admn	2022
	Celia	1861	Plympton	grdn	2020
	Charles	1828	Middleboro	grdn	2023
	Daniel	1852	Kingston	will	2024
	Eleanor	1748	Plympton	grdn	2025
	Elijah	1743	Plympton	admn	2026
	Elijah	1805	Plympton	admn	2027
	Elijah	1831	Plympton	will	2028
	Elijah	1869	Plympton	will	2029
	Elisha	1690	Marshfield	will	2030
	Elisha	1737	Pembroke	admn	2031
	Elisha	1756	Pembroke	admn	2032
	Eva	1861	Plympton	grdn	2020
	Felecia	1861	Plympton	grdn	2020
	Franklin	1869	Duxbury	admn	2033
	Frederick	1861	Plympton	grdn	2020
	George H	1865	Duxbury	will	2034
	Gideon	1761	Pembroke	admn	2035
	Hopestill	1695	Marshfield	admn	2036
	Hopestill	1818	Rochester	will	2037
	Hopestill	1852	Middleboro	will	2038
	Ichabod W	1864	Middleboro	grdn	2039
	Ira	1817	Bridgewater	grdn	2061

SURNAME	FIRST NAME	YEAR	PLACE	CASE	DOCKET
BISBEE	Isaac	1819	Pembroke	admn	2040
	Jairus	1749	Pembroke	grdn	2041
	Jairus	1753	Pembroke	peti	2042
	John	1774	Pembroke	admn	2043
	John	1817	Bridgewater	will	2044
	John T	1880	Plympton	will	2045
	Joseph	1743	Plympton	grdn	2048
	Joseph	1827	Middleboro	will	2046
	Joseph	1828	Middleboro	grdn	2023
	Joseph H	1876	Middleboro	admn	2047
	Josiah	1832	Rochester	admn	2049
	Levi	1849	Rochester	admn	2050
	Lovina	1877	E. Bridgewater	will	2051
	Lydia L	1842	Portland ME	grdn	2052
	Mary	1734	Hingham	will	2056
	Mary	1880	Plympton	grdn	2057
	Mary J	1874	Rochester	admn	2053
	Mary W	1877	Middleboro	grdn	2054
	Mary W	1879	Middleboro	admn	2055
	Olive	1832	Pembroke	admn	2058
	Ruben	1743	Plympton	grdn	2048
	Sarah	1842	Kingston	grdn	2059
	Sarah N	1859	Abington	admn	2060
	Sidney	1817	Bridgewater	grdn	2061
	Susannah	1753	Pembroke	peti	2042
	Sylvanus	1812	Plympton	admn	2062
	Wadsworth	1857	Pembroke	will	2063
	William	1816	Kingston	grdn	2064
	William	1831	Plympton	will	2065
	William M	1859	Plympton	admn	2066
	Zebulon	1842	Kingston	admn	2067
BISHOP	Dexter	1873	Lakeville	will	2068
	Henry	1848	Middleboro	admn	2069
	Hudson	1758	Pembroke	will	2070
	James	1715	Pembroke	admn	2071
	John	1756	Pembroke	will	2072
	John	1790	Rochester	admn	2073
	John	1817	Middleboro	will	2074
	John	1830	Plymouth	admn	2075
	Joshua	1756	Pembroke	grdn	2080
	Joshua	1840	Middleboro	will	2076
	Josiah	1749	Pembroke	admn	2077
	Mary	1740	Pembroke	will	2078
	Mary	1756	Pembroke	grdn	2080
	Nathaniel	1839	Pembroke	admn	2079
	Sarah	1756	Pembroke	grdn	2080
	Zenas	1876	Middleboro	will	2081
BISWICK	Everton	1754	Bridgewater	grdn	2082
BLACK	Anna	1849	Middleboro	grdn	2084
	Joseph W	1849	Middleboro	will	2083
	Joseph W	1849	Middleboro	grdn	2084
BLACKMAN	Elizabeth	1872	Hingham	admn	2085
BLACKMER	Arthur L	1871	Rochester	grdn	2086
	Branch	1795	Plymouth	grdn	2094
	Branch	1818	Plymouth	will	2087
	Charles M	1869	Rochester	admn	2088
	Ezra	1881	Plymouth	will	2089
	George E	1822	Plymouth	grdn	2090
	George E	1830	Plymouth	admn	2091
	James	1820	Rochester	admn	2092
	James	1829	Rochester	grdn	2093
	Jerusha	1795	Plymouth	grdn	2094
	John	1750	Wareham	will	2095
	John	1794	Plymouth	will	2096
	John	1847	Plymouth	will	2097
	John 2nd	1829	Rochester	admn	2098
	Lydia D S	1871	Plymouth	part	2099
	Mary	1717	Rochester	grdn	2105
	Nancy	1870	N. Bridgewater	admn	2101
	Nancy S	1847	Rochester	grdn	2100
	Peter	1717	Rochester	will	2102

SURNAME	FIRST NAME	YEAR	PLACE	CASE	DOCKET
BLACKMER	Peter	1717	-----	grdn	2103
	Richard	1808	Plymouth	admn	2104
	Samuel	1717	Rochester	grdn	2105
	Stephen	1717	Rochester	grdn	2105
	William	1698	Plymouth	will	2106
	William	1717	Rochester	grdn	2105
	William	1791	Wareham	will	2107
BLACKWELL	Betsey	1836	Rochester	will	2108
	Caleb	1763	Rochester	will	2109
	Caleb	1816	Rochester	admn	2110
	John	1811	Rochester	grdn	2111
	Seth	1812	Rochester	admn	2112
BLAIR	Priscilla	1864	Middleboro	will	2113
BLAISDELL	Oscar A	1877	Marion	grdn	2114
BLAKE	Jeremiah	1839	N. Bridgewater	grdn	2115
	John A	1866	Plymouth	admn	2116
	Joseph	1813	Hingham	will	2117
	Lucy	1818	Hingham	will	2118
	Phineas	1849	Bridgewater	will	2119
	Samuel	1862	Abington	will	2120
	Samuel	1872	Abington	will	2121
	Thomas C	1876	Bridgewater	admn	2122
BLANCHARD	Alvin	1880	Plymouth	admn	2123
	Anna	1812	Abington	grdn	2131
	Betsey	1823	Abington	admn	2124
	Clarissa	1812	Abington	grdn	2131
	Daniel	1837	Abington	admn	2125
	Daniel	1879	Rockland	will	2126
	Dean	1812	Abington	grdn	2130
	Dean	1812	Abington	grdn	2131
	Dean	1844	Abington	admn	2127
	Dean	1868	Abington	grdn	2128
	Dean	1868	Abington	admn	2129
	Eli	1846	E. Bridgewater	will	2132
	Elizabeth	1861	Abington	admn	2133
	Eunice B	1869	Hingham	grdn	2134
	Horatio	1830	Plympton	grdn	2142
	Irene E	1866	Abington	grdn	2135
	Irving W	1872	Abington	grdn	2140
	Jesse	1804	Abington	admn	2136
	Jesse	1807	Abington	grdn	2137
	Jonathan	1831	Plympton	admn	2138
	Lester	1874	Abington	grdn	2139
	Lizzie B	1872	Abington	grdn	2140
	Lucia	1830	Plympton	grdn	2142
	Lucy W	1865	Abington	will	2141
	Mahala	1848	Abington	admn	2143
	Merril	1812	Abington	grdn	2131
	Merrill	1868	Abington	grdn	2144
	Quincy	1807	Abington	grdn	2137
	Saba	1830	Plympton	grdn	2142
	Sarah	1812	Abington	grdn	2131
	Susan A	1848	N. Bridgewater	grdn	2145
	Theron	1807	Abington	grdn	2137
	Thomas	1803	Abington	will	2146
	Vinson	1873	Abington	admn	2147
	William	1833	Stoughton	grdn	2148
	William W	1865	E. Bridgewater	admn	2149
BLANKINSHIP	Alfred	1853	Marion	grdn	2151
	Alfred	1866	Mattapoisett	grdn	2150
	Barnabas	1799	Rochester	admn	2152
	Betsey	1812	Rochester	admn	2153
	Celia A	1876	Marion	will	2154
	Charles	1810	Rochester	will	2155
	Charles	1833	Rochester	grdn	2174
	Charles	1834	Rochester	admn	2156
	Edwin	1861	Marion	grdn	2168
	Elizabeth M	1869	Marion	admn	2157
	Esther	1861	Marion	grdn	2168
	George	1837	Rochester	admn	2159
	George	1885	Marion	admn	2160

SURNAME	FIRST NAME	YEAR	PLACE	CASE	DOCKET
BLANKINSHIP	George Jr	1831	Rochester	admn	2158
	Hannah	1833	Rochester	grdn	2174
	James	1817	Rochester	admn	2161
	Jared	1832	Rochester	admn	2162
	Jared	1833	Rochester	grdn	2174
	Jared	1858	Marion	admn	2163
	Jarvis	1865	Marion	will	2164
	Job	1800	Rochester	admn	2165
	Job	1868	Marion	will	2166
	Joseph	1879	Marion	will	2167
	Melora	1833	Rochester	grdn	2174
	Owen	1861	Marion	grdn	2168
	Perez	1802	Rochester	admn	2169
	Seth	1851	Rochester	will	2170
	Stephen	1838	Rochester	grdn	2171
	Thankful	1867	Marion	admn	2172
	Walter F	1869	Marion	admn	2173
	Warren	1833	Rochester	grdn	2174
	William	1812	Rochester	admn	2175
BLOMSTRAND	Albert G	1875	E. Bridgewater	grdn	2176
	George W	1875	E. Bridgewater	grdn	2176
	Peter	1875	E. Bridgewater	admn	2177
BLOSSOM	Benjamin	1762	Plympton	grdn	2180
	Charles W	1863	Hingham	admn	2178
	Edward D	1873	Hingham	admn	2179
	John	1762	Plympton	grdn	2180
	Mary	1762	Plympton	grdn	2180
	Sarah	1762	Plympton	grdn	2180
	Thomas D	1871	Hingham	grdn	2181
	Thomas D	1873	Hingham	admn	2182
	Zacheus	1760	Plympton	admn	2183
BOAG	Elizabeth	1871	Plymouth	admn	2184
BOARDMAN	Joseph	1789	Plympton	admn	2185
BOILEAU	Jesse	1813	Duxbury	admn	2186
BOLLES	Almira	1827	Rochester	grdn	2187
	Amaziah	1807	Rochester	admn	2188
	Benjamin	1817	Rochester	admn	2189
	Charlton H	1870	Middleboro	will	2190
	Desire	1864	Mattapoisett	will	2191
	Ebenezer	1827	Rochester	admn	2192
	Ebenezer	1849	Rochester	will	2193
	Elizabeth	1841	Rochester	will	2194
	Ezra	1862	Mattapoisett	admn	2195
	Hosea	1753	Rochester	admn	2196
	Isaac	1821	Rochester	will	2197
	Isaac	1850	Rochester	admn	2198
	John H	1873	Marion	admn	2199
	Jonathan	1773	Rochester	will	2200
	Lydia	1818	Rochester	admn	2201
	Lydia	1845	Rochester	will	2202
	Mary	1827	Rochester	grdn	2187
	Mary	1831	Rochester	grdn	2212
	Obed	1841	Rochester	will	2203
	Ruth	1830	Rochester	admn	2204
	Samuel J	1863	N. Bridgewater	grdn	2205
	Savery	1826	Rochester	admn	2207
	Savery	1827	Rochester	grdn	2187
	Savery A	1860	Wareham	admn	2206
	Stephen W	1879	Mattapoisett	admn	2208
	William	1828	Rochester	admn	2211
	William A	1831	Rochester	grdn	2212
	William N	1863	Middleboro	admn	2210
	William T	1876	Mattapoisett	admn	2209
BOLT	Charles	1768	Plymouth	admn	2213
	Prince	1818	Plymouth	grdn	2214
BOLTON	Abigail	1722	Bridgewater	grdn	2221
	Bethiah	1848	Middleboro	will	2215
	John	1722	Bridgewater	admn	2216
	John	1755	Bridgewater	will	2217
	John	1831	W. Bridgewater	admn	2218
	Joseph	1722	Bridgewater	grdn	2221

SURNAME	FIRST NAME	YEAR	PLACE	CASE	DOCKET
BOLTON	Joseph	1819	Bridgewater	grdn	2219 a
	Mary	1730	Bridgewater	admn	2220
	Nathaniel	1722	Bridgewater	grdn	2221
	Phillip	1764	Bridgewater	grdn	2222
	Phillip	1819	Bridgewater	grdn	2223 a
	Phillip	1823	Bridgewater	admn	2224
	Sarah	1744	Bridgewater	admn	2225
BONNEY	Abiah	1726	Pembroke	grdn	2240
	Alice or Elsie	1864	Duxbury	grdn	2226
	Anna	1847	Abington	grdn	2288
	Ansel F	1865	Duxbury	admn	2227
	Beriah	1768	Plympton	will	2228
	Betsey	1806	Pembroke	grdn	2263
	Cephas	1874	Marshfield	will	2229
	Charles	1817	Pembroke	grdn	2281
	Charles	1835	Rochester	will	2230
	Charles T	1835	Rochester	grdn	2231
	Crowell	1863	Hanson	will	2232
	Cynthia	1794	Hanover	grdn	2272
	Daniel	1799	Plympton	admn	2233
	David	1759	Pembroke	admn	2234
	Ebenezer	1712	Duxbury	admn	2236
	Ebenezer	1763	Pembroke	will	2238
	Ebenezer	1802	Plympton	admn	2237
	Ebenezer	1813	Pembroke	will	2239
	Ebenezer	1843	Hanson	admn	2235
	Elijah	1726	Pembroke	grdn	2240
	Elisha	1776	Pembroke	admn	2241
	Ezekiel	1772	Pembroke	admn	2242
	Ezekiel	1880	Hanson	admn	2243
	George	1869	Rochester	will	2244
	George	1879	Lakeville	grdn	2252
	Gladden	1881	S. Abington	admn	2245
	Hannah	1803	Plympton	will	2246
	Hannah	1803	Pembroke	grdn	2247
	Harriet	1847	Abington	grdn	2288
	Harvey	1841	Plympton	will	2248
	James	1723	Pembroke	admn	2249
	James	1728	Pembroke	admn	2250
	James	1820	Pembroke	will	2251
	Jennie	1879	Lakeville	grdn	2252
	Jeremiah	1817	Pembroke	grdn	2281
	Job	1726	Pembroke	grdn	2240
	John	1746	Pembroke	will	2255
	John	1765	Pembroke	will	2254
	John	1852	Plympton	admn	2253
	Joseph	1720	Pembroke	admn	2256
	Joseph Jr	1808	Pembroke	admn	2257
	Josiah	1872	Hanover	will	2258
	Josiah W	1870	Hanover	admn	2259
	Keturah	1820	Pembroke	will	2251
	Lemuel	1803	Pembroke	admn	2260
	Lemuel	1806	Pembroke	admn	2261
	Lucius L	1866	Marshfield	admn	2262
	Lucy	1806	Pembroke	grdn	2263
	Luther	1804	Pembroke	grdn	2264
	Luther	1807	Pembroke	admn	2265
	Lydia	1868	N. Bridgewater	admn	2266
	Mary	1879	Lakeville	grdn	2252
	Mary C	1853	Plympton	grdn	2267
	Mehitable	1747	-----	admn	2268
	Nathaniel	1776	Plympton	admn	2269
	Noah	1859	Hanson	admn	2270
	Oliver	1773	Pembroke	grdn	2276
	Oliver	1790	Hanover	admn	2271
	Oliver	1794	Hanover	grdn	2272
	Orpha	1806	Pembroke	grdn	2263
	Pelham W	1870	Pembroke	admn	2273
	Polly	1817	Pembroke	grdn	2281
	Samuel	1806	Rochester	admn	2274
	Samuel	1821	Hanson	admn	2275

SURNAME	FIRST NAME	YEAR	PLACE	CASE	DOCKET
BONNEY	Silvester	1773	Pembroke	grdn	2276
	Stephen	1852	Plympton	admn	2277
	Theodore L	1863	Hanson	admn	2278
	Thomas	1693	Duxbury	will	2279
	Thomas	1735	Duxbury	will	2280
	Wealthy	1817	Pembroke	grdn	2281
	William	1687	Duxbury	waiv	2282
	William	1747	Plympton	admn	2284
	William	1773	Plympton	will	2283
	William	1793	Pembroke	admn	2285
	William	1847	Abington	admn	2287
	William	1847	Abington	grdn	2288
	William A	1874	Middleboro	admn	2286
BONUM	Ebenezer	1735	Plympton	admn	2288 +
	George	1748	Plympton	will	2288 +
BOODRY	Benjamin L	1864	Mattapoisett	admn	2289
	Benjamin L	1864	Mattapoisett	grdn	2290
	Nathan	1872	Mattapoisett	admn	2291
	William D	1845	Rochester	grdn	2292
	William D	1845	Rochester	admn	2293
BOOTH	Abiel P	1851	Middleboro	will	2294
	Abigail	1752	Pembroke	will	2295
	Abraham	1742	Pembroke	will	2296
	Elizabeth	1719	Scituate	grdn	2307
	Guilford	1822	Middleboro	grdn	2297
	Guilford	1828	Middleboro	admn	2298
	John	1718	Scituate	admn	2299
	John	1750	Middleboro	will	2300
	John	1802	Middleboro	admn	2301
	John	1865	Lakeville	admn	2302
	Lydia	1719	Scituate	grdn	2307
	Mary	1754	Scituate	will	2303
	William	1825	Middleboro	grdn	2304
	Zebedee	1801	Middleboro	admn	2305
	Zebedee	1813	Middleboro	admn	2306
	Zerviah	1719	Scituate	grdn	2307
BORDEN	Adolphus K	1875	Brockton	will	2308
	Edward A	1876	Brockton	grdn	2309
	Lucy Ann L	1876	Brockton	admn	2310
BOSWORTH	Abby	1865	Pembroke	grdn	2311
	Asaph	1841	Halifax	admn	2312
	Asaph	1871	Pembroke	admn	2313
	Bela	1853	Plympton	will	2314
	Benjamin	1802	Halifax	grdn	2338
	Caroline	1846	Plympton	grdn	2335
	Chloe	1768	Bridgewater	grdn	2315
	Darius	1802	Halifax	grdn	2338
	David	1747	Halifax	will	2316
	David	1808	Halifax	grdn	2317
	Deborah	1846	Plympton	grdn	2335
	Deborah W	1872	Halifax	will	2318
	Earl	1832	E. Bridgewater	admn	2319
	Edwin	1864	Pembroke	admn	2320
	Elizabeth	1777	Halifax	grdn	2340
	Ichabod	1745	Halifax	grdn	2342
	Jabez	1751	Kingston	admn	2321
	James	1831	Halifax	will	2322
	James	1843	Plympton	admn	2323
	John	1769	Halifax	admn	2324
	John	1802	Halifax	admn	2325
	John	1807	Halifax	admn	2326
	John	1827	E. Bridgewater	admn	2327
	Jonathan	1741	Halifax	admn	2329
	Jonathan	1745	Halifax	grdn	2342
	Jonathan	1767	Bridgewater	admn	2328
	Jonathan	1768	Bridgewater	grdn	2315
	Jonathan	1802	Halifax	grdn	2338
	Joseph	1769	Halifax	admn	2330
	Lewis	1802	Halifax	grdn	2338
	Lydia	1867	Halifax	admn	2331
	Nehemiah	1802	Rochester	admn	2332

SURNAME	FIRST NAME	YEAR	PLACE	CASE	DOCKET
BOSWORTH	Nehemiah	1853	Plympton	admn	2333
	Noah	1745	Halifax	grdn	2342
	Noah	1837	Halifax	will	2334
	Priscilla	1846	Plympton	grdn	2335
	Ruth	1832	Halifax	grdn	2336
	Sally	1881	Halifax	admn	2337
	Sarah	1768	Bridgewater	grdn	2315
	Sarah	1802	Halifax	grdn	2338
	Seth	1830	Halifax	will	2339
	Susanna	1802	Halifax	grdn	2338
	Waterman	1777	Halifax	grdn	2340
	Zadoc	1745	Halifax	grdn	2342
	Zadoc	1776	Halifax	will	2341
BOUCHER	John	1875	Brockton	grdn	2343
BOULDRY	Augustus	1869	E. Bridgewater	grdn	2347
	Charlton	1869	E. Bridgewater	grdn	2347
	Frederick	1869	E. Bridgewater	grdn	2347
	Georgianna eta	1865	E. Bridgewater	grdn	2344
	James	1855	Bridgewater	admn	2345
	James	1869	E. Bridgewater	grdn	2347
	Nathaniel	1869	E. Bridgewater	grdn	2347
	Owen	1869	E. Bridgewater	grdn	2347
	Rodney W	1865	E. Bridgewater	grdn	2346
	Roland	1869	E. Bridgewater	grdn	2347
	Thaddeus	1869	E. Bridgewater	grdn	2347
	Thomas	1869	E. Bridgewater	grdn	2347
	Thomas H	1854	Bridgewater	will	2348
BOURASSO	Arabella	1843	Troy NY	grdn	2349
	Francis	1843	Troy NY	grdn	2349
	Mary	1843	Troy NY	grdn	2349
BOURNE	Abel	1822	Hanson	will	2350
	Abel	1871	Hanson	will	2351
	Abner	1806	Middleboro	will	2352
	Alexander	1849	Wareham	admn	2353
	Benjamin	1829	Wareham	will	2354
	Betsey	1878	Marshfield	will	2355
	Calvin F	1868	Hanson	admn	2356
	Charles	1879	Hanson	admn	2357
	Chloe D	1870	Hanson	grdn	2358
	Daniel	1864	Hanson	will	2359
	Earl	1839	Middleboro	will	2360
	Ebenezer	1709	Marshfield	grdn	2372
	Ebenezer	1763	Wareham	admn	2363
	Ebenezer	1802	Wareham	admn	2364
	Ebenezer	1810	Wareham	grdn	2367
	Ebenezer	1868	Wareham	will	2366
	Ebenezer	1877	Wareham	grdn	2368
	Ebenezer 2nd	1854	Wareham	admn	2365
	Ebenezer B	1879	Hanson	grdn	2362
	Ebenezer L	1821	Rochester	admn	2361
	Elizabeth	1709	Marshfield	grdn	2372
	Ellen	1877	Wareham	grdn	2368
	Ellen T	1876	St.Johns NB	name	2369
	Ellsworth T	1869	Hanson	grdn	2370
	Everline	1839	Middleboro	grdn	2399
	George	1709	Marshfield	grdn	2372
	George	1864	Abington	grdn	2379
	George Henry	1868	Marshfield	name	2371
	Hannah	1848	Middleboro	admn	2374
	Hannah D	1833	Hingham	admn	2373
	Harriet J	1869	Hanson	grdn	2370
	Helen M	1849	Wareham	grdn	2375
	Hezekiah	1745	Wareham	grdn	2376
	Horace	1877	Wareham	grdn	2368
	James	1810	Pembroke	will	2377
	James	1864	Abington	grdn	2379
	James A	1869	Pembroke	admn	2378
	Jane F	1841	Middleboro	grdn	2381
	Jane T	1880	S. Abington	admn	2380
	Jedediah	1709	Marshfield	grdn	2372
	Jedediah	1765	Marshfield	will	2382

SURNAME	FIRST NAME	YEAR	PLACE	CASE	DOCKET
BOURNE	John	1686	Marshfield	admn	2383
	John	1750	Marshfield	admn	2384
	John	1789	Marshfield	will	2385
	John	1824	Hanson	admn	2388
	John	1859	Marshfield	admn	2386
	John	1877	Marshfield	admn	2387
	Josiah	1709	Marshfield	grdn	2372
	Josiah	1770	Pembroke	will	2389 +
	Josiah	1803	Pembroke	admn	2389
	Josiah	1810	Wareham	grdn	2367
	Josiah	1864	Abington	grdn	2379
	Josiah	1879	Hanson	grdn	2390
	Keziah	1832	Middleboro	will	2391
	Lemuel	1831	Middleboro	will	2392
	Lemuel	1838	Middleboro	will	2393
	Leonard B	1808	Rochester	admn	2394
	Loritta	1864	Abington	grdn	2379
	Loruhama	1761	Rochester	will	2395
	Lucy	1860	Middleboro	will	2396
	Mary	1839	Middleboro	grdn	2399
	Mary	1864	Abington	grdn	2379
	Mary Emma	1871	Marshfield	name	2398
	Nancy E	1864	Wareham	grdn	2400
	Nary B	1863	Abington	will	2397
	Newcomb	1843	Halifax	admn	2401
	Olive S	1855	Marshfield	admn	2402
	Owen	1877	Wareham	grdn	2368
	Proctor	1858	Marshfield	will	2403
	Richard	1682	Sandwich	admn	2404
	Rouse	1768	Marshfield	admn	2405
	Ruth	1861	Rochester	will	2406
	Ruth	1861	Marshfield	admn	2407
	Samuel S	1877	Wareham	will	2408
	Sarah	1854	Marshfield	admn	2409
	Shearjashub	1742	Scituate	grdn	2410
	Silvanus	1861	Wareham	will	2411
	Sylvanus	1864	Wareham	grdn	2400
	Thomas	1704	Marshfield	will	2412
	Thomas	1762	Marshfield	admn	2413
	Thomas	1831	Marshfield	admn	2415
	Thomas	1859	E. Bridgewater	will	2414
	Timothy	1860	Wareham	will	2416
	William	1846	Middleboro	will	2419
	William	1878	Hanson	will	2418
	William H	1852	Hanson	admn	2417
	William L	1867	Mattapoisett	admn	2420
	Wilson	1864	Abington	grdn	2379
	Zebia	1855	Middleboro	will	2421
BOUTELLE	Ann	1874	Plymouth	admn	2422
	Caleb	1819	Plymouth	will	2423
	Mary Ann	1878	Norfolk VA	grdn	2424
BOUVE	John	1855	Scituate	admn	2425
BOVEY	John	1817	Boston	grdn	2426
BOWEN	Elizabeth	1737	Stoughton	grdn	2427
	James A	1864	Duxbury	will	2428
BOWERS	Charles	1833	Scituate	grdn	2429
	George	1833	Scituate	grdn	2429
	Henry	1833	Scituate	grdn	2429
	Mary	1833	Scituate	grdn	2429
	William	1833	Scituate	grdn	2429
	William C	1839	Scituate	admn	2430
BOWKER	Allen	1824	Scituate	will	2431
	Almira	1826	Scituate	grdn	2452
	Andrew J	1869	S. Scituate	admn	2432
	Anna	1816	Scituate	will	2433
	Anna	1816	Scituate	admn	2434
	Anna R	1875	S. Scituate	grdn	2475
	Benjamin	1754	Scituate	admn	2435
	Benjamin	1798	Pembroke	will	2436
	Benjamin	1849	Hanson	will	2437
	Catherina	1800	Scituate	grdn	2441

SURNAME	FIRST NAME	YEAR	PLACE	CASE	DOCKET
BOWKER	Catherine	1834	Scituate	grdn	2438
	Charles	1827	Scituate	admn	2439
	Charles	1834	Scituate	grdn	2438
	Charlotte	1817	Scituate	grdn	2440
	David	1800	Scituate	grdn	2441
	David	1832	Scituate	grdn	2442
	David	1842	Scituate	admn	2443
	Dimmick	1862	S. Scituate	admn	2444
	Dorcassina	1817	Scituate	grdn	2440
	Edmund	1827	Scituate	will	2445
	Edwin	1834	Scituate	grdn	2438
	Elijah	1812	Scituate	admn	2446
	Esther	1845	Scituate	admn	2447
	Eunice	1761	Scituate	grdn	2450
	Eunice	1826	Scituate	grdn	2452
	Everlina	1874	S. Scituate	admn	2448
	George	1834	Scituate	grdn	2438
	George E	1878	Hingham	grdn	2449
	Gustavus	1828	S. Scituate	grdn	2455
	Hannah	1761	Scituate	grdn	2450
	Harriet	1826	Scituate	grdn	2452
	Harriet	1855	Hanson	will	2451
	Harriet T	1853	Hanson	grdn	2465
	Helen	1834	Scituate	grdn	2438
	Henry	1828	S. Scituate	grdn	2455
	Henry W	1831	Scituate	grdn	2454
	Henry W	1847	Scituate	admn	2453
	Howard	1858	S. Scituate	will	2456
	Isaac	1856	S. Scituate	will	2457
	Ishmael	1773	Pembroke	grdn	2458
	James	1724	Scituate	admn	2459
	James	1763	Scituate	will	2460
	James	1834	Scituate	grdn	2438
	John	1807	Scituate	will	2461
	Joshua	1761	Scituate	grdn	2450
	Laurinda	1834	Scituate	grdn	2438
	Lazarus	1798	Scituate	will	2462
	Lazarus	1832	Scituate	will	2463
	Lucretia	1826	Scituate	grdn	2471
	Lyman	1834	Scituate	grdn	2438
	Margaret	1761	Scituate	grdn	2450
	Martha	1826	Scituate	grdn	2452
	Mary	1826	Scituate	grdn	2452
	Mary A	1874	Hanson	admn	2464
	Mary J	1853	Hanson	grdn	2465
	Molly	1773	Pembroke	grdn	2458
	Parsons	1800	Scituate	grdn	2441
	Parsons	1820	Hingham	will	2466
	Parsons	1831	Scituate	grdn	2454
	Perez G	1881	Hingham	will	2467
	Rebecca	1817	Scituate	grdn	2440
	Richard	1873	Hanson	will	2468
	Rosilla	1874	Hanson	admn	2469
	Ruth	1817	Scituate	grdn	2440
	Sally	1826	Scituate	grdn	2471
	Sally	1860	S. Scituate	will	2470
	Sarah	1832	Scituate	will	2472
	Stephen	1827	Scituate	grdn	2473
	Susannah	1826	Scituate	grdn	2471
	Turner	1853	Hanson	admn	2474
	Wilfred C	1875	S. Scituate	grdn	2475
BOWLAND	Thomas	1783	Rochester	will	2476
BOWLIN	John	1861	Marion	grdn	2479
	John L	1861	Marion	admn	2477
	Josiah	1868	Mattapoisett	will	2478
	Susan B	1861	Marion	grdn	2479
BOWMAN	John W	1859	Scituate	admn	2480
	Luther A	1875	Mattapoisett	admn	2481
BOYCE	Jane	1752	Pembroke	admn	2482
	Jean	1752	Duxbury	admn	2483
	Joseph	1778	Pembroke	admn	2484

SURNAME	FIRST NAME	YEAR	PLACE	CASE	DOCKET
BOYCE	William	1795	Plymouth	admn	2485
BOYLE	Johanna	1859	N. Bridgewater	admn	2486
	William H	1873	N. Bridgewater	grdn	2488
BOYLES	Thomas	1730	Plymouth	admn	2487
BOYLSTON	Benjamin	1864	Duxbury	grdn	2489
	Joseph	1873	Pembroke	will	2490
	Mary	1864	Duxbury	grdn	2489
	Mehitable	1864	Duxbury	grdn	2489
BRACKETT	Arthur	1872	N. Bridgewater	grdn	2491
	Sarah E	1872	N. Bridgewater	grdn	2491
BRADBURY	Charles W	1863	Abington	grdn	2492
BRADFORD	-----	1730	Kingston	grdn	2506
	Abigail	1742	Plympton	grdn	2606
	Abigail	1788	Plympton	grdn	2617
	Abigail	1838	Duxbury	grdn	2493
	Abraham	1828	Plympton	admn	2494
	Albion	1858	Kingston	grdn	2495
	Alice	1700	Plymouth	grdn	2628
	Allen	1876	Plymouth	admn	2496
	Allen N	1877	Plymouth	grdn	2497
	Anna R	1857	Duxbury	grdn	2498
	Bartlett	1821	Plymouth	admn	2500
	Bartlett	1822	Plymouth	grdn	2567
	Bartlett	1849	Plymouth	admn	2499
	Bathsheba	1861	Plymouth	admn	2501
	Benjamin	1784	Kingston	admn	2502
	Charles	1730	Kingston	grdn	2506
	Charles	1783	Duxbury	grdn	2542
	Charles	1837	Plympton	admn	2504
	Charles	1849	Plymouth	admn	2503
	Charles S	1867	Kingston	grdn	2505
	Clara J	1857	Kingston	grdn	2507
	Consider	1825	Kingston	admn	2508
	Cornelius F	1853	Illinois	grdn	2509
	Daniel	1861	Kingston	admn	2510
	David	1730	Kingston	admn	2511
	David	1811	Plymouth	grdn	2513
	David	1840	Kingston	will	2512
	David	1860	Plymouth	admn	2514
	Ebenezer N	1870	Plymouth	admn	2515
	Edward W	1875	Plymouth	admn	2516
	Eleanor	1840	Plymouth	grdn	2517
	Elihu	1778	Duxbury	grdn	2536
	Eliphalet	1735	Kingston	grdn	2545 +
	Elisha	1750	Kingston	admn	2518
	Elizabeth	1778	Plymouth	admn	2521
	Elizabeth	1807	Plympton	admn	2520
	Elizabeth	1863	Duxbury	admn	2519
	Ellis	1848	Kingston	admn	2522
	Emily	1873	Kingston	admn	2523
	Ephraim	1746	Kingston	will	2524
	Ephraim	1870	Duxbury	will	2525
	Eunice	1876	Plymouth	admn	2526
	Evelina	1822	Plymouth	grdn	2567
	Ezekiel	1747	Kingston	grdn	2612
	Gamaliel	1778	Duxbury	will	2527
	Gamaliel	1807	Duxbury	will	2528
	George	1778	Duxbury	grdn	2536
	George A	1834	Kingston	grdn	2561
	George A	1837	Kingston	grdn	2529
	George F	1815	Plymouth	grdn	2541
	George F	1876	Plymouth	grdn	2530
	George R	1853	Illinois	grdn	2509
	Gershom	1837	Duxbury	grdn	2532
	Gershom	1844	Duxbury	admn	2531
	Gideon	1793	Plympton	will	2533
	Gideon	1805	Plympton	will	2534
	Grace	1778	Duxbury	grdn	2536
	Grace	1853	Plympton	admn	2535
	Hannah	1824	Plymouth	will	2537
	Hannah	1832	Plympton	grdn	2538

SURNAME	FIRST NAME	YEAR	PLACE	CASE	DOCKET
BRADFORD	Hannah	1837	Duxbury	grdn	2532
	Harriet	1837	Duxbury	grdn	2532
	Harriet P	1872	Duxbury	admn	2539
	Hezekiah	1837	Plympton	will	2540
	Hitty A	1815	Plymouth	grdn	2541
	Ira	1783	Duxbury	grdn	2542
	Isaiah	1778	Duxbury	grdn	2536
	Isaiah	1858	Duxbury	admn	2543
	Israel	1855	Plympton	admn	2544
	Jael	1730	Kingston	will	2545
	James	1735	Kingston	grdn	2545 +
	James	1822	Plymouth	grdn	2567
	James	1836	Plymouth	admn	2547
	James	1840	Plymouth	grdn	2517
	James	1850	Plymouth	grdn	2548
	James H	1863	Duxbury	admn	2546
	Jane	1794	Plympton	will	2550
	Jane	1816	Kingston	will	2549
	Jason	1871	Kingston	will	2551
	Jerusha	1730	Kingston	grdn	2506
	Joah	1783	Duxbury	grdn	2542
	John	1736	Kingston	will	2553
	John	1770	Plympton	admn	2555
	John	1807	Plympton	will	2556
	John	1831	Plympton	admn	2557
	John C	1857	Middleboro	admn	2554
	John Jr	1724	Plymouth	will	2552
	Johnson	1850	Plymouth	grdn	2548
	Jonathan	1733	Kingston	grdn	2582
	Joseph	1715	Plymouth	will	2559 +
	Joseph	1791	Plympton	admn	2559
	Joseph	1853	Plymouth	admn	2558
	Josiah	1730	Kingston	grdn	2508
	Josiah	1730	Kingston	grdn	2506
	Josiah	1818	Plymouth	grdn	2560
	Julia	1834	Kingston	grdn	2561
	Lemuel	1733	Kingston	grdn	2582
	Lemuel	1751	Plymouth	grdn	2563
	Lemuel	1855	Plymouth	admn	2562
	Leonicy B	1875	Brockton	will	2564
	Lewis	1851	Plympton	admn	2565
	Louis	1822	Plymouth	grdn	2567
	Lucy	1783	Duxbury	grdn	2542
	Lucy	1822	Plymouth	grdn	2567
	Lucy	1875	Duxbury	admn	2566
	Lusannah	1878	Kingston	admn	2568
	Luther	1861	Plympton	will	2569
	Lydia	1733	Kingston	grdn	2582
	Lydia	1776	Plympton	grdn	2610
	Lydia	1837	Duxbury	grdn	2532
	Lydia	1869	Kingston	admn	2570
	Lydia	1877	Kingston	admn	2571
	Lydia D	1877	Plymouth	grdn	2497
	Lydia T	1861	Plymouth	name	2572
	Lyman	1840	Duxbury	admn	2573
	Maria	1832	Plympton	grdn	2538
	Maria W	1865	Duxbury	admn	2574
	Martha D	1841	Duxbury	grdn	2575
	Mary	1790	Kingston	grdn	2576
	Mary	1803	Duxbury	will	2579
	Mary	1814	Plympton	grdn	2577
	Mary	1839	Plympton	grdn	2632
	Mary	1863	Plympton	admn	2578
	Matilda	1854	Duxbury	grdn	2580
	Mercy	1730	Kingston	grdn	2507
	Mercy	1776	Plympton	grdn	2610
	Mercy	1806	Plympton	grdn	2591
	Minerva	1839	Plympton	grdn	2632
	Nathan	1733	Kingston	grdn	2582
	Nathan	1787	Kingston	will	2581
	Nathaniel	1733	Kingston	grdn	2582

SURNAME	FIRST NAME	YEAR	PLACE	CASE	DOCKET
BRADFORD	Nathaniel	1751	Plymouth	grdn	2563
	Nathaniel	1751	Plymouth	admn	2583
	Nathaniel	1840	Plymouth	grdn	2517
	Nathaniel N	1861	Plympton	adpt	2584
	Noah	1746	Plymouth	will	2585
	Olive	1776	Plympton	grdn	2610
	Olive	1859	Duxbury	admn	2586
	Otis	1837	Duxbury	grdn	2532
	Pamelia D	1881	Middleboro	will	2587
	Patience	1832	Plympton	grdn	2538
	Peabody	1782	Duxbury	admn	2588
	Peleg	1869	Kingston	admn	2589
	Perez	1802	Duxbury	will	2590
	Phebe	1742	Plympton	grdn	2606
	Polly	1806	Plympton	grdn	2591
	Prince	1836	Duxbury	admn	2592
	Priscilla	1850	Kingston	admn	2593
	Rebecca D	1866	Duxbury	admn	2594
	Robert	1782	Kingston	will	2595
	Robert	1818	Kingston	admn	2596
	Ruth	1813	Plymouth	admn	2597
	Saba	1806	Plympton	grdn	2591
	Sally C H	1864	Kingston	will	2598
	Samuel	1714	Duxbury	will	2599
	Samuel	1740	Plympton	will	2605
	Samuel	1742	Plympton	grdn	2606
	Samuel	1779	Duxbury	admn	2600
	Samuel	1788	Plympton	grdn	2617
	Samuel	1816	Duxbury	admn	2601
	Samuel	1857	Duxbury	admn	2602
	Samuel	1861	Plympton	admn	2604
	Samuel Jr	1856	Duxbury	will	2603
	Sarah	1700	Plymouth	grdn	2628
	Sarah	1730	Kingston	grdn	2506
	Sarah	1776	Plympton	grdn	2610
	Sarah	1822	Plymouth	admn	2607
	Sarah	1834	Kingston	admn	2608
	Sarah B	1861	Duxbury	admn	2609
	Silvanus	1811	Kingston	admn	2611
	Simeon	1747	Kingston	grdn	2612
	Sophia M	1867	New Bedford	grdn	2613
	Stephen	1857	Duxbury	admn	2614
	Stephen	1867	Kingston	admn	2615
	Stetson	1826	Kingston	will	2616
	Susan	1837	Duxbury	grdn	2532
	Susannah	1788	Plympton	grdn	2617
	Sylvia	1783	Duxbury	grdn	2542
	Thomas	1832	Plympton	grdn	2538
	Thomas	1857	Kingston	admn	2618
	Thomas B	1855	Kingston	admn	2619
	Thomas B	1857	Kingston	grdn	2507
	Waite	1747	Kingston	grdn	2612
	Waldo	1875	Brockton	will	2620
	William	1687	Plymouth	admn	2625
	William	1700	Plymouth	grdn	2628
	William	1703	Plymouth	will	2626
	William	1730	Kingston	admn	2621
	William	1742	Plympton	grdn	2606
	William	1776	Plympton	grdn	2610
	William	1802	Plympton	admn	2629
	William	1806	Plympton	grdn	2591
	William	1813	Plymouth	admn	2627
	William	1832	Plympton	grdn	2538
	William	1838	Plympton	admn	2630
	William	1839	Plympton	grdn	2632
	William	1875	Duxbury	admn	2623
	William H	1870	Plymouth	admn	2624
	William Jr	1728	Kingston	admn	2622
	William L	1843	Plympton	admn	2631
	Winslow	1788	Plympton	grdn	2617
	Winslow	1814	Plympton	admn	2633

SURNAME	FIRST NAME	YEAR	PLACE	CASE	DOCKET
BRADFORD	Winslow	1871	Wareham	admn	2634
	Zadoc	1745	Kingston	admn	2635
	Zadock	1735	Kingston	grdn	2545 +
	Zadock	1860	Duxbury	admn	2636
	Zeuma	1858	Kingston	grdn	2495
BRADLEY	William A	1881	Middleboro	will	2637
BRADY	Thomas C	1861	N. Bridgewater	admn	2638
BRALEY	Abner	1869	Rochester	will	2639
	Albert G	1880	Acushnet	adpt	2640
	Anna	1876	Rochester	admn	2641
	Elijah	1816	Rochester	will	2642
	Ezekiel	1841	Rochester	admn	2643
	George	1793	Rochester	will	2644
	George	1846	Rochester	admn	2645
	James	1863	Rochester	will	2646
	John	1875	Rochester	admn	2647
	Roger	1777	Rochester	grdn	2648
	Roger	1778	Rochester	will	2649
	Russell	1815	Rochester	will	2650
	Russell	1862	Rochester	admn	2651
	Samuel T	1871	Rochester	admn	2652
	Seth	1787	Rochester	grdn	2653
	Stephen	1787	Rochester	grdn	2653
BRAMHALL	Benjamin	1779	Plymouth	grdn	2654
	Betty	1772	Abington	grdn	2655
	Caleb	1772	Abington	grdn	2655
	Charles	1840	Plymouth	admn	2656
	Edmund	1764	Plymouth	grdn	2657
	Ellis B	1865	Plymouth	will	2658
	George	1796	Plymouth	admn	2659
	George	1856	Plymouth	admn	2661
	George	1872	Plymouth	admn	2662
	George Jr	1826	Plymouth	grdn	2660
	Gideon	1772	Abington	grdn	2655
	Hannah	1772	Abington	grdn	2655
	Joseph	1806	Plymouth	admn	2663
	Joshua	1763	Plymouth	will	2664
	Joshua	1772	Abington	grdn	2655
	Keziah	1772	Abington	grdn	2655
	Lydia	1804	Plymouth	grdn	2665
	Molly	1772	Abington	grdn	2655
	Nancy E	1846	Plymouth	admn	2666
	Remember	1824	Plymouth	admn	2667
	Samuel	1772	Abington	admn	2668
	Sarah	1754	Plymouth	admn	2669
	Sarah	1810	Plymouth	grdn	2670
	Sylvanus	1772	Abington	grdn	2655
	Sylvanus	1779	Plymouth	will	2671
	Sylvanus	1827	Plymouth	admn	2672
BRANCH	Experience	1697	Marshfield	admn	2673
	Experience	1745	Plymouth	grdn	2674
	John	1711	Marshfield	will	2676
	John	1745	Plymouth	grdn	2674
	John	1748	Plymouth	admn	2675
	Lydia	1752	Plymouth	admn	2677
	Remember	1711	Marshfield	admn	2678
	Thankful	1745	Plymouth	grdn	2674
	Thomas	1712	Marshfield	grdn	2679
	Thomas	1731	Plymouth	admn	2680
BRANNAGAN	Ellen	1867	N. Bridgewater	grdn	2681
	Eugene	1867	N. Bridgewater	grdn	2681
	John	1867	N. Bridgewater	grdn	2681
	Joseph	1867	N. Bridgewater	grdn	2681
	Margaret	1867	N. Bridgewater	grdn	2681
	Mary	1867	N. Bridgewater	grdn	2681
	Thomas	1867	N. Bridgewater	grdn	2681
	William	1867	N. Bridgewater	grdn	2681
BRANNING	John	1867	Hanson	admn	2682
BRAYTON	Bessie	1879	Brockton	grdn	2683
	Francis	1879	Brockton	grdn	2683
	Harry	1879	Brockton	grdn	2683

SURNAME	FIRST NAME	YEAR	PLACE	CASE	DOCKET
BRAYTON	Howard	1879	Brockton	grdn	2683
	Julius F	1879	Brockton	admn	2684
	William	1879	Brockton	grdn	2683
BREACH	Henry F	1871	Kingston	grdn	2685
	William	1869	Carver	will	2686
BRECK	Joseph	1815	Pembroke	grdn	2690
	Moses	1807	Plymouth	admn	2687
	Richard A	1874	Bridgewater	admn	2688
	Samuel	1809	Pembroke	admn	2689
	Samuel	1815	Pembroke	grdn	2690
BREEN	John	1865	Hingham	admn	2691
BRENEN	Elizabeth	1863	Scituate	will	2692
BRENTON	William	1675	-----	admn	2693
BRESSENHAM	Henry W	1870	E. Bridgewater	grdn	2694
BRETT	Addie A U	1870	Bridgewater	name	2694 +
	Algernon	1851	E. Bridgewater	peti	2704
	Algernon S	1850	E. Bridgewater	admn	2695
	Antoinette T	1869	Bridgewater	name	2696
	Arvilla	1851	E. Bridgewater	peti	2704
	Avis	1852	N. Bridgewater	will	2697
	Calvin	1801	Bridgewater	admn	2698
	Daniel	1779	Bridgewater	grdn	2700
	Daniel	1851	N. Bridgewater	admn	2699
	Edward	1844	N. Bridgewater	grdn	2712
	Elihu	1711	Bridgewater	admn	2702
	Elihu	1745	Bridgewater	will	2701
	Francis	1844	N. Bridgewater	grdn	2712
	Francis	1872	N. Bridgewater	admn	2703
	Huldah	1851	E. Bridgewater	peti	2704
	Isaac	1828	N. Bridgewater	will	2705
	Isaac	1866	N. Bridgewater	admn	2708
	Isaac M	1867	N. Bridgewater	grdn	2707
	Isaac M P	1863	N. Bridgewater	name	2706
	John	1763	Bridgewater	grdn	2709
	Joseph	1846	N. Bridgewater	admn	2710
	Lavina	1844	N. Bridgewater	grdn	2712
	Lavina S	1866	N. Bridgewater	grdn	2711
	Mary	1780	Bridgewater	admn	2713
	Nathaniel	1741	Bridgewater	will	2714
	Nathaniel	1779	Bridgewater	admn	2715
	Royal T	1870	Duxbury	admn	2716
	Samuel	1844	N. Bridgewater	grdn	2712
	Samuel	1844	N. Bridgewater	will	2717
	Samuel Jr	1844	N. Bridgewater	admn	2718
	Sanford	1838	N. Bridgewater	will	2719
	Sarah	1865	N. Bridgewater	will	2720
	Seth	1741	Bridgewater	grdn	2721
	Simeon	1792	Bridgewater	will	2722
	Simeon Jr	1786	Bridgewater	admn	2723
	Susan W	1866	Duxbury	admn	2724
	Uriah	1779	Bridgewater	grdn	2700
	William	1724	Bridgewater	will	2725
	William	1851	E. Bridgewater	peti	2704
	Zibeon	1874	N. Bridgewater	admn	2726
BREWER	James	1806	Plymouth	admn	2727
	John	1814	Plymouth	admn	2728
BREWSTER	Aaron	1842	Kingston	admn	2729
	Abigail	1780	Kingston	will	2730
	America	1848	Plymouth	will	2731
	Anne	1858	Kingston	will	2732
	Arunah	1808	Duxbury	grdn	2770
	Asa	1875	Duxbury	will	2733
	Aseneth	1808	Duxbury	grdn	2770
	Caroline	1840	Duxbury	grdn	2766
	Clement D	1862	Kingston	will	2734
	Daniel W	1877	Duxbury	will	2735
	Deborah	1860	Duxbury	admn	2736
	Deborah	1867	Kingston	admn	2738
	Deborah S	1875	Duxbury	admn	2737
	Elisha	1801	Kingston	will	2739
	Elisha	1820	Kingston	grdn	2740

SURNAME	FIRST NAME	YEAR	PLACE	CASE	DOCKET
BREWSTER	Elizabeth	1828	Kingston	grdn	2750
	Ellis	1818	Plymouth	admn	2741
	Emma et als	1878	Kingston	part	2742
	George W	1877	Hanson	grdn	2743
	Harriet	1840	Duxbury	grdn	2766
	Henry G	1877	Hanson	grdn	2744
	Hosea	1794	Kingston	admn	2745
	Hosea	1810	Kingston	grdn	2746
	Hosea	1832	Kingston	will	2747
	Irene	1857	Duxbury	will	2748
	James B	1877	Hanson	admn	2749
	James D	1828	Kingston	grdn	2750
	Jane	1840	Duxbury	grdn	2766
	Job E	1834	Duxbury	admn	2751
	John	1770	Kingston	will	2752
	Joseph	1767	Duxbury	will	2753
	Joseph	1791	Duxbury	will	2754
	Joseph	1807	Duxbury	admn	2755
	Joseph	1846	Duxbury	admn	2756
	Joshua	1831	Duxbury	grdn	2757
	Joshua	1832	Duxbury	admn	2758
	Joshua	1851	Duxbury	admn	2759
	Joshua	1853	Duxbury	will	2760
	Joshua	1875	Duxbury	grdn	2762
	Joshua T	1863	Duxbury	admn	2761
	Judith	1820	Kingston	grdn	2740
	Judith	1842	Kingston	grdn	2763
	Lemuel	1774	Kingston	admn	2764
	Louis	1808	Duxbury	grdn	2770
	Lydia	1840	Duxbury	grdn	2766
	Lydia	1851	Duxbury	admn	2765
	Martin Jr	1828	Kingston	admn	2767
	Mary	1871	Kingston	peti	2768
	Melzar	1808	Duxbury	grdn	2770
	Melzar	1870	Duxbury	admn	2769
	Nathan C	1861	Duxbury	will	2771
	Nathaniel	1755	Duxbury	will	2772
	Olive	1808	Duxbury	grdn	2770
	Pelham	1850	Kingston	admn	2774
	Pelham	1877	Plymouth	will	2773
	Persis	1848	Kingston	admn	2775
	Phillippa	1869	Duxbury	grdn	2776
	Phillippa	1869	Duxbury	will	2777
	Rachel S	1877	Hanson	grdn	2778
	Rachel S	1877	Hanson	admn	2779
	Rebecca	1801	Kingston	admn	2780
	Ruth	1866	Duxbury	will	2781
	Sarah	1851	Kingston	will	2782
	Sarah	1851	Plymouth	will	2783
	Sophia	1820	Kingston	grdn	2740
	Spencer	1844	Kingston	will	2784
	Stephen	1840	Duxbury	will	2785
	Thomas	1815	Kingston	admn	2786
	Warren W	1851	Duxbury	grdn	2787
	William	1822	Hanson	grdn	2788 a
	William	1825	Hanson	admn	2789
	Wrestling	1696	Duxbury	admn	2790
	Wrestling	1767	Kingston	will	2791
	Wrestling	1816	Kingston	admn	2792
	Zilpha	1875	Duxbury	grdn	2762
BRIDGEWATER	West Precinct	1784	Bridgewater	bond	2793
BRIDGHAM	Joseph	1754	Plympton	will	2794
BRIEN	Catherine	1873	Kingston	grdn	2795
BRIGDEN	Zachariah	1829	Kingston	admn	2796
BRIGGS	Abigail B	1875	Rochester	will	2797
	Achsah	1865	Marion	grdn	2802
	Adoniram	1867	Abington	admn	2798
	Alden	1849	Pembroke	will	2799
	Alden	1861	Pembroke	admn	2800
	Almira	1841	Scituate	grdn	2900
	Almira	1873	Rochester	admn	2801

SURNAME	FIRST NAME	YEAR	PLACE	CASE	DOCKET
BRIGGS	Alpheus	1865	Marion	grdn	2802
	Ann	1835	Rochester	grdn	2925
	Anna	1851	Plymouth	grdn	2896
	Ansel	1834	Wareham	admn	2803
	Arnold	1777	Rochester	grdn	2926
	Arnold	1825	Rochester	admn	2804
	Arthur S	1875	Marion	grdn	2805
	Barnabas	1793	Halifax	admn	2806
	Bartlett	1825	Scituate	admn	2807
	Benjamin	1757	Scituate	will	2810
	Benjamin	1802	Halifax	admn	2809
	Benjamin	1806	Wareham	admn	2811
	Benjamin	1826	Wareham	admn	2812
	Benjamin S	1873	Marion	admn	2808
	Betsey	1848	Wareham	admn	2814
	Betsey	1859	E. Bridgewater	will	2815
	Betsey	1868	Wareham	will	2813
	Caroline	1868	Marion	grdn	2944
	Catherine	1855	Lakeville	admn	2816
	Catherine W	1855	Rochester	will	2817
	Charles	1840	Scituate	grdn	2825
	Charles C	1843	Scituate	admn	2819
	Charles H	1872	Plymouth	grdn	2820
	Charles Jr	1828	Scituate	grdn	2818
	Charlotte	1841	Scituate	grdn	2900
	Cornelius	1694	Scituate	will	2824
	Cornelius	1764	Rochester	will	2822
	Cornelius	1769	Scituate	admn	2823
	Cornelius	1845	Rochester	will	2821
	Cynthia	1840	Scituate	grdn	2825
	Daniel	1822	Pembroke	admn	2826
	Daniel	1849	Middleboro	admn	2827
	David	1872	Scituate	will	2828
	Deborah	1785	Pembroke	grdn	2937
	Deborah	1841	Scituate	grdn	2943
	Deborah C	1796	Scituate	grdn	2829
	Deborah C	1800	Scituate	admn	2830
	Deborah C	1876	S. Scituate	will	2831
	Drusilla	1776	Rochester	grdn	2832
	Ebenezer	1795	Middleboro	will	2833
	Ebenezer	1808	Middleboro	will	2834
	Ebenezer	1824	Middleboro	will	2835
	Ebenezer	1840	Scituate	grdn	2825
	Ebenezer	1851	Middleboro	will	2836
	Elihu	1778	Rochester	admn	2837
	Elijah	1808	Rochester	will	2838
	Elisha	1836	Pembroke	admn	2839
	Elisha	1857	Pembroke	will	2840
	Elizabeth	1728	Rochester	grdn	2841
	Elizabeth	1865	Marion	grdn	2802
	Emeline	1841	Scituate	grdn	2900
	Ephraim	1800	Halifax	admn	2842
	Esther	1851	Middleboro	will	2843
	Ezra	1804	Hanover	will	2845
	Ezra	1806	Hanover	grdn	2846
	Ezra	1845	Middleboro	grdn	2847
	Ezra Jr	1804	Hanover	grdn	2844
	Frances	1687	Scituate	admn	2848
	Fred	1868	Marion	grdn	2944
	George	1845	Middleboro	grdn	2847
	George	1865	Scituate	will	2849
	George H	1881	S. Scituate	admn	2850
	Hannah	1725	Scituate	grdn	2851
	Hannah	1806	Hanover	grdn	2846
	Harriet	1834	Scituate	grdn	2949
	Harvey	1872	Plymouth	admn	2852
	Henrietta C	1854	Rochester	admn	2853
	Henry	1838	Scituate	admn	2854
	Hervey	1837	Wareham	admn	2855
	Huldah	1863	S. Scituate	will	2856
	Ida P	1875	Plymouth	grdn	2857

SURNAME	FIRST NAME	YEAR	PLACE	CASE	DOCKET
BRIGGS	Isaac	1802	Plymouth	will	2858
	Israel	1856	Wareham	grdn	2859
	Israel	1856	Wareham	will	2860
	James	1703	Scituate	admn	2861
	James	1754	Scituate	will	2863
	James	1756	Scituate	grdn	2862
	James	1804	Scituate	will	2865
	James	1833	Scituate	will	2866
	James 3rd	1792	Scituate	admn	2864
	James F	1869	Lakeville	admn	2869
	James S	1879	Scituate	will	2867
	James W	1850	Bristol RI	grdn	2868
	Jedediah	1751	Wareham	admn	2870
	Jedediah	1823	Wareham	admn	2871
	Jerome	1861	Pembroke	grdn	2872
	Jesse	1844	Wareham	admn	2873
	John	1710	Scituate	admn	2874
	John	1723	Boston	warr	2879
	John	1727	Rochester	will	2880
	John	1728	Rochester	grdn	2841
	John	1771	Rochester	admn	2881
	John	1790	Scituate	admn	2875
	John	1800	Scituate	admn	2876
	John	1807	Scituate	will	2877
	John	1840	Scituate	admn	2878
	John	1841	Scituate	grdn	2943
	John	1865	Marion	admn	2882
	John E	1872	N. Bridgewater	admn	2883
	Jonathan	1802	Middleboro	admn	2884
	Joseph	1770	Scituate	will	2885
	Joseph	1806	Hanover	grdn	2846
	Joseph	1820	Woodstock VT	admn	2888
	Joseph	1846	Scituate	admn	2887
	Joseph Jr	1747	Scituate	will	2886
	Joshua	1797	Wareham	admn	2889
	Judson	1846	Middleboro	admn	2890
	Lemuel	1849	Middleboro	will	2891
	Leonard	1845	Middleboro	will	2892
	Livonia	1868	Marion	grdn	2944
	Lucy	1833	Scituate	will	2893
	Lucy	1841	Scituate	grdn	2900
	Lucy	1841	Scituate	grdn	2943
	Lucy	1845	Middleboro	grdn	2847
	Luther	1864	Pembroke	will	2894
	Luther	1864	Scituate	will	2895
	Lydia	1806	Hanover	grdn	2846
	Marianna	1851	Plymouth	grdn	2896
	Mary	1725	Scituate	grdn	2851
	Mary	1776	Rochester	grdn	2832
	Mary	1835	Rochester	grdn	2925
	Mary	1841	Scituate	grdn	2900
	Mary	1850	Rochester	grdn	2951
	Mary	1862	E. Bridgewater	admn	2897
	Mary	1880	Hanover	admn	2898
	Mary T	1841	Scituate	grdn	2899
	Matilda	1845	Middleboro	grdn	2847
	Mirabah	1864	Rochester	will	2901
	Moses	1835	Rochester	grdn	2925
	Nathan	1798	Wareham	will	2905
	Nathan	1817	Rochester	admn	2902
	Nathan	1832	Rochester	admn	2903
	Nathan	1835	Rochester	grdn	2925
	Nathan	1870	Marion	admn	2904
	Nathaniel	1776	Rochester	grdn	2832
	Nathaniel	1776	Rochester	admn	2906
	Nathaniel	1778	Pembroke	will	2907
	Nathaniel	1818	Hanover	will	2908
	Oliver E	1873	Marion	admn	2909
	Otis	1880	Scituate	will	2910
	Pamelia	1880	Wareham	will	2911
	Paul	1863	Marion	admn	2912

SURNAME	FIRST NAME	YEAR	PLACE	CASE	DOCKET
BRIGGS	Peleg A	1870	Marion	grdn	2814
	Peleg T	1870	Marion	will	2913
	Perez	1834	Wareham	will	2915
	Perez F	1838	Wareham	admn	2916
	Phebe N	1860	Wareham	admn	2917
	Priscilla	1866	Marion	will	2918
	Rachel	1870	S. Scituate	admn	2919
	Rebecca	1777	Rochester	grdn	2926
	Rebecca	1832	Rochester	admn	2920
	Rebecca	1837	Scituate	will	2921
	Rebecca	1841	Halifax	will	2922
	Reuben	1830	Rochester	will	2923
	Rhoda	1834	Scituate	grdn	2949
	Richard	1799	Halifax	will	2924
	Roland	1835	Rochester	grdn	2925
	Ruth	1777	Rochester	grdn	2926
	Sally	1806	Hanover	grdn	2846
	Samuel	1750	Rochester	will	2927
	Samuel	1826	Wareham	will	2929
	Samuel	1843	Plympton	will	2928
	Samuel	1845	Middleboro	grdn	2847
	Samuel	1845	Middleboro	admn	2930
	Samuel	1850	Rochester	grdn	2951
	Samuel	1869	Plymouth	will	2931
	Sarah	1840	Scituate	grdn	2825
	Sarah	1841	Scituate	grdn	2943
	Sarah	1848	Scituate	will	2932
	Sarah M	1868	Scituate	name	2933
	Seth	1785	Pembroke	grdn	2937
	Seth	1801	Pembroke	will	2936
	Seth	1852	Hanson	admn	2935
	Seth Jr	1781	Marshfield	admn	2934
	Shadrach	1869	Scituate	admn	2938
	Silas	1833	Rochester	will	2939
	Susan	1863	Rochester	will	2940
	Thomas	1806	Hanover	grdn	2846
	Thomas	1841	Scituate	grdn	2943
	Thomas	1868	Marion	grdn	2944
	Thomas C	1861	Bridgewater	admn	2942
	Thomas Wales	1816	S. Scituate	grdn	2941
	Timothy H	1877	Marion	will	2945
	William	1799	Wareham	admn	2946
	William	1816	Scituate	admn	2948
	William	1834	Scituate	grdn	2949
	William	1848	E. Bridgewater	will	2947
	William	1849	Rochester	admn	2950
	William	1850	E. Bridgewater	admn	2947 +
	William	1850	Rochester	grdn	2951
	Zalmon	1873	Hanson	will	2952
	Zenas	1870	Marion	admn	2953
BRIGHAM	Antipas	1832	Plymouth	admn	2954
	Antipas	1834	Plymouth	grdn	2955
	Henry H	1879	S. Abington	admn	2956
	Mercy	1834	Plymouth	grdn	2955
BRIGHTMAN	Charles	1858	Rochester	will	2957
	Davenport	1821	Rochester	will	2958
	Edith C	1876	Middleboro	will	2959
	Ruby	1822	Rochester	will	2960
BRINNAN	James	1867	Scituate	grdn	2961
BRISLEN	Fanny	1833	Hingham	admn	2962
	John	1825	Hingham	admn	2963
BRITTON	Abby	1864	Middleboro	grdn	2964
	Hermon S	1864	Middleboro	grdn	2964
	Zephaniah L P	1862	Halifax	admn	2965
BROADHURST	Chloe	1876	Bridgewater	will	2966
	Thomas	1872	Bridgewater	will	2967
BRONSDON	Deborah K	1876	Hingham	admn	2968
BRONSON	George	1819	Hingham	grdn	2969
	George	1830	Hingham	admn	2970
	Shubael G	1819	Hingham	admn	2971
BROOKER	Benjamin D	1822	Hingham	admn	2972

SURNAME	FIRST NAME	YEAR	PLACE	CASE	DOCKET
BROOKS	Cecilia	1838	Hingham	will	2973
	Curtis	1817	Hanover	admn	2974
	Deborah	1847	Scituate	admn	2975
	Elijah	1854	S. Scituate	will	2976
	Elizabeth	1753	Scituate	grdn	2977
	Ella	1865	Hanover	grdn	2978
	Gilbert	1768	Scituate	will	2979
	Hannah	1818	Hanover	grdn	2980
	John	1754	Weymouth	grdn	2981
	John	1818	Hanover	grdn	2980
	Joseph	1822	Hanover	will	2982
	Nancy C	1857	Hanover	grdn	2983
	Nathaniel	1763	Scituate	will	2984
	Nathaniel	1873	S. Scituate	admn	2985
	Noah	1791	Scituate	admn	2986
	Rufus	1819	Scituate	grdn	2988
	Ruth	1818	Hanover	grdn	2980
	Samuel	1858	Hanover	will	2987
	Sarah	1819	Scituate	grdn	2988
	Simeon	1774	Scituate	admn	2989
	Simeon	1793	Scituate	grdn	2990
	Simeon	1818	Scituate	grdn	2991
	Thomas	1752	Scituate	admn	2992
	Walter	1865	Hanover	grdn	2978
	William	1794	Scituate	admn	2993
	William	1821	Scituate	admn	2994
BROWN	Abel	1866	Scituate	will	2995
	Abigail	1863	S. Scituate	admn	2996
	Abijah	1827	Scituate	will	2997
	Adelaide	1853	Marion	grdn	2998
	Alden	1842	E. Bridgewater	grdn	3027
	Alfred	1817	Bridgewater	grdn	3062
	Amos	1823	Duxbury	admn	2999
	Ann	1847	Plymouth	admn	3000
	Anna	1863	Abington	grdn	3061
	Ansel W	1864	Pembroke	admn	3001
	Arthur H	1866	E. Bridgewater	grdn	3095
	Austin	1814	Abington	grdn	3083
	Barnabas A	1846	Plymouth	admn	3002
	Bela	1814	Abington	grdn	3083
	Benjamin	1773	Scituate	admn	3003
	Benjamin	1848	Scituate	will	3004
	Betsey	1819	Bridgewater	will	3005
	Betsey	1843	Scituate	will	3006
	Betsey	1872	Abington	admn	3007
	Betty	1774	Scituate	grdn	3008
	Caleb	1860	New Ipswich NH	grdn	3009
	Catherine B	1861	Abington	grdn	3011
	Catherine H	1861	Abington	will	3010
	Charles	1846	Kingston	will	3013
	Charles	1852	E. Bridgewater	will	3012
	Charles	1863	S. Scituate	grdn	3029
	Charles	1864	Abington	grdn	3014
	Charles	1864	Abington	grdn	3038
	Charles	1868	Scituate	grdn	3015
	Charles	1874	Scituate	admn	3016
	Charles L	1874	Plymouth	grdn	3060
	Charles T	1865	Plymouth	grdn	3017
	Charlotte	1824	Hingham	grdn	3018
	Cyrus L	1864	Abington	admn	3019
	Damon	1863	S. Scituate	grdn	3029
	Daniel	1815	Abington	grdn	3020
	David	1753	Bridgewater	will	3021
	David	1864	E. Bridgewater	admn	3022
	David	1865	Hingham	admn	3024
	David 2nd	1855	Hingham	will	3025
	David Jr	1878	Kingston	admn	3023
	Ebenezer	1874	S. Scituate	admn	3026
	Edward	1842	E. Bridgewater	grdn	3027
	Elisha	1876	Marshfield	will	3028
	Elizabeth	1863	S. Scituate	grdn	3029

SURNAME	FIRST NAME	YEAR	PLACE	CASE	DOCKET
BROWN	Ella	1860	New Ipswich NH	grdn	3009
	Ellis	1863	S. Scituate	grdn	3029
	Elwyn M	1860	S. Scituate	grdn	3030
	Emery	1842	E. Bridgewater	admn	3031
	Enoch	1795	Abington	grdn	3032
	Enos	1843	Scituate	admn	3033
	Eunice	1879	E. Bridgewater	grdn	3034
	Frank	1864	Abington	grdn	3038
	George	1850	Kingston	grdn	3035
	George	1853	Marion	grdn	2998
	George	1863	S. Scituate	grdn	3029
	Harriet	1864	Abington	grdn	3038
	Harriet C	1870	Scituate	grdn	3037
	Harriet M	1832	E. Bridgewater	grdn	3036
	Henry	1851	Scituate	grdn	3039
	Horace	1863	S. Scituate	grdn	3029
	Isaac	1835	E. Bridgewater	admn	3040
	Isaac	1863	E. Bridgewater	admn	3041
	James	1831	E. Bridgewater	admn	3042
	James L	1865	Scituate	admn	3043
	Jared	1853	Marion	grdn	2998
	John	1821	Duxbury	admn	3047
	John	1864	Scituate	admn	3045
	John Jr	1817	Bridgewater	admn	3044
	John R	1860	Abington	will	3046
	Joseph	1791	Abington	grdn	3050
	Joseph	1826	E. Bridgewater	admn	3049
	Joseph P	1877	Plymouth	will	3048
	Josiah	1770	(see # 2389+)		3051
	Laura	1863	S. Scituate	grdn	3029
	Lemuel	1846	Plymouth	admn	3052
	Lizzie	1860	New Ipswich NH	grdn	3009
	Lizzie Adams	1880	Abington	adop	3053
	Lorenzo	1842	E. Bridgewater	grdn	3027
	Lucy J	1861	S. Scituate	admn	3054
	Lydia	1817	Bridgewater	grdn	3062
	Lydia A	1832	Plymouth	admn	3055
	Mary	1810	Plymouth	admn	3058
	Mary	1850	Plymouth	will	3059
	Mary	1863	Abington	grdn	3061
	Mary	1877	E. Bridgewater	admn	3056
	Mary E	1874	Plymouth	grdn	3060
	Mary F	1846	Hingham	grdn	3057
	Mehitable	1817	Bridgewater	grdn	3062
	Millard E	1879	E. Bridgewater	will	3063
	Molly	1877	E. Bridgewater	will	3064
	Moses	1862	Pembroke	admn	3065
	Nabby	1858	Plymouth	will	3066
	Nancy	1865	Scituate	admn	3067
	Nellie	1863	Abington	grdn	3061
	Nellie J	1877	Scituate	grdn	3068
	Rachel	1873	Scituate	will	3069
	Rhoda	1833	Duxbury	admn	3070
	Robert	1810	Plymouth	admn	3071
	Robert	1873	Plymouth	will	3072
	SAmuel	1835	Halifax	admn	3075
	Sally	1857	S. Scituate	will	3073
	Samuel	1768	Abington	admn	3079
	Samuel	1783	Scituate	will	3074
	Samuel	1787	Abington	will	3080
	Samuel	1814	Abington	grdn	3083
	Samuel	1844	Abington	will	3081
	Samuel	1848	Hingham	will	3077
	Samuel	1868	Pembroke	will	3076
	Samuel Jr	1845	Hingham	admn	3078
	Samuel N	1870	Abington	will	3082
	Sarah	1860	New Ipswich NH	grdn	3009
	Sarah T	1870	Duxbury	peti	3084
	Smith	1827	Pembroke	admn	3085
	Susannah	1850	Abington	will	3086
	Thomas	1824	Hingham	admn	3087

SURNAME	FIRST NAME	YEAR	PLACE	CASE	DOCKET
BROWN	Walston	1857	Abington	will	3088
	William	1805	Plymouth	grdn	3089
	William	1846	Plymouth	admn	3090
	William	1865	Plymouth	admn	3092
	William	1868	Plymouth	will	3091
	William H	1854	Abington	grdn	3093
	William H	1866	E. Bridgewater	admn	3094
	William H	1866	E. Bridgewater	grdn	3095
	Woodbridge	1784	Abington	will	3096
	Woodbridge	1811	Abington	admn	3097
BROWNELL	Abbie M	1866	Middleboro	grdn	3098
	Cook	1851	Mattapoisett	admn	3099
	Mabel F	1866	Middleboro	grdn	3098
	Stafford	1848	Rochester	admn	3100
BRUCE	James R	1875	Scituate	will	3101
	Susan L	1877	Scituate	grdn	3102
	William G	1874	Marion	admn	3103
BRYAN	Francis	1739	Middleboro	will	3104
	Patrick	1834	Hingham	admn	3105
BRYANT	Abel T	1862	Halifax	admn	3106
	Abigail	1768	Pembroke	grdn	3107
	Abigail	1871	N. Bridgewater	admn	3108
	Abijah	1874	Bridgewater	admn	3109
	Adeline	1828	Plympton	grdn	3110
	Alvin	1845	Plympton	admn	3111
	Amos	1789	Middleboro	admn	3112
	Annah	1776	Scituate	grdn	3169
	Barza	1871	Pembroke	will	3113
	Bathsheba	1731	Scituate	grdn	3174
	Benjamin	1702	Scituate	will	3114
	Benjamin	1724	Plympton	admn	3115
	Betsey	1878	Plympton	admn	3116
	Caleb	1778	Middleboro	admn	3117
	Cephas	1858	Hingham	admn	3118
	Charles M	1871	Bridgewater	grdn	3119
	Cyrus W	1868	Fairhaven	grdn	3120
	Daniel	1777	Halifax	grdn	3123
	Daniel	1816	Bridgewater	grdn	3121
	Daniel	1818	Bridgewater	grdn	3122
	David	1731	Scituate	admn	3124
	Deborah	1731	Scituate	grdn	3174
	Deborah L	1839	Scituate	admn	3125
	Dion	1871	Bridgewater	admn	3126
	Edward	1772	Scituate	grdn	3127
	Edward	1875	Brockton	grdn	3216
	Elijah	1807	Scituate	admn	3128
	Eliza	1828	Plympton	grdn	3110
	Elizabeth	1839	Scituate	grdn	3204
	Elizabeth	1846	Scituate	admn	3129
	Ellen	1868	Halifax	grdn	3163
	Emma F	1862	Kingston	name	3130
	Ephraim	1784	Plympton	admn	3131
	Ephraim	1791	Middleboro	admn	3132
	Eunice	1840	Scituate	admn	3133
	Ezekiel	1774	Plympton	admn	3134
	Ford	1779	Plympton	grdn	3196
	Francis	1868	Halifax	grdn	3163
	George	1769	Kingston	admn	3136
	George	1773	Kingston	grdn	3138
	George	1779	Plympton	admn	3135
	George	1791	Kingston	admn	3137
	George	1875	Brockton	grdn	3216
	Gridley	1867	Scituate	will	3139
	Hannah	1725	Kingston	grdn	3177
	Hannah	1736	Scituate	will	3140
	Hannah	1823	Middleboro	will	3141
	Henrietta	1878	Plymouth	grdn	3207
	Hervey	1870	Pembroke	will	3142
	Hiram	1881	Duxbury	grdn	3143
	Hopestill	1732	Plympton	grdn	3201
	Horace	1879	Brockton	admn	3144

SURNAME	FIRST NAME	YEAR	PLACE	CASE	DOCKET
BRYANT	Israel	1779	Plympton	grdn	3196
	Jabez	1697	Scituate	admn	3145
	Jacob	1731	Scituate	grdn	3174
	Jacob M	1881	Pembroke	will	3146
	James	1777	Plympton	will	3147
	James	1819	Wareham	grdn	3158
	Jerusha	1725	Kingston	grdn	3177
	Jesse	1725	Kingston	grdn	3177
	Jesse	1759	Middleboro	admn	3148
	Job	1808	Bridgewater	will	3149
	John	1707	Scituate	will	3151
	John	1716	Scituate	admn	3152
	John	1732	Scituate	grdn	3150
	John	1736	Plympton	will	3153
	John	1819	Wareham	grdn	3158
	Jonathan	1730	Plymouth	admn	3154
	Joseph	1738	Scituate	admn	3155
	Joseph	1796	Marshfield	will	3156
	Joseph	1796	Marshfield	grdn	3157
	Joseph	1819	Wareham	grdn	3158
	Joshua	1799	Plympton	admn	3160
	Joshua	1817	Scituate	admn	3159
	Judith L	1879	Plympton	will	3161
	Lawrence	1819	Wareham	grdn	3158
	Lawrence	1863	Wareham	admn	3162
	Leavitt	1868	Halifax	grdn	3163
	Lemuel	1768	Braintree	grdn	3164
	Lemuel	1826	Plympton	admn	3165
	Lemuel	1828	Plympton	grdn	3110
	Lewis	1837	Kingston	admn	3166
	Lillian	1874	E. Bridgewater	grdn	3167
	Lucretia H	1878	Bridgewater	will	3168
	Lucy	1868	Fairhaven	grdn	3120
	Lydia	1776	Scituate	grdn	3169
	Mabel	1874	E. Bridgewater	grdn	3167
	Maria W	1877	Scituate	will	3170
	Martha	1772	Scituate	grdn	3127
	Martin	1871	Pembroke	will	3171
	Mary	1725	Kingston	grdn	3177
	Mary	1731	Scituate	grdn	3174
	Mary	1761	Hanover	will	3172
	Mary	1776	Scituate	grdn	3169
	Mary	1790	Plympton	admn	3173
	Mary	1828	Plympton	grdn	3110
	Mary C	1871	Bridgewater	grdn	3119
	Mercy N	1861	Halifax	admn	3175
	Micah	1725	Kingston	grdn	3177
	Micah	1776	Middleboro	admn	3176
	Myron L	1875	Bridgewater	grdn	3178
	Nathan	1809	Bridgewater	grdn	3179
	Nathaniel	1794	Plympton	will	3180
	Noah	1820	Scituate	admn	3181
	Paul	1857	Halifax	admn	3182
	Peleg	1772	Scituate	will	3183
	Peleg	1821	Kingston	admn	3185
	Peleg	1875	Kingston	will	3186
	Peleg Jr	1774	Scituate	admn	3184
	Perez	1777	Halifax	grdn	3123
	Phebe	1725	Kingston	grdn	3177
	Philander	1844	Middleboro	will	3187
	Phillip	1816	Bridgewater	will	3188
	Richard	1773	Kingston	grdn	3138
	Ruth	1777	Halifax	grdn	3123
	Saba	1877	Duxbury	will	3189
	Salome	1864	Plympton	admn	3190
	Samuel	1690/1	Scituate	admn	3191
	Samuel	1750	Plympton	will	3192
	Samuel	1774	Plympton	will	3193
	Samuel	1865	Kingston	will	3194
	Sarah	1796	Marshfield	grdn	3157
	Sarah	1874	E. Bridgewater	grdn	3167

SURNAME	FIRST NAME	YEAR	PLACE	CASE	DOCKET
BRYANT	Sarah E	1880	Middleboro	name	3195
	Sears	1779	Plympton	grdn	3196
	Seth	1732	Plympton	grdn	3201
	Seth	1772	Marshfield	will	3199
	Seth	1774	Halifax	admn	3198
	Seth	1779	Marshfield	abse	3197
	Seth	1822	Middleboro	will	3200
	Silvanus	1770	Plympton	admn	3202
	Snow	1835	Scituate	admn	3203
	Snow	1839	Scituate	grdn	3204
	Sophia	1880	Pembroke	admn	3205
	Stephen	1748	Halifax	admn	3206
	Susan	1878	Plymouth	grdn	3207
	Theron	1860	W. Bridgewater	will	3208
	Thomas	1748	Scituate	will	3210
	Thomas	1757	Halifax	admn	3211
	Thomas H B	1867	Halifax	will	3209
	Timothy	1848	Hingham	will	3212
	Vashty	1773	Marshfield	grdn	3213
	William	1773	Middleboro	admn	3214
	William	1864	Rochester	will	3215
	William	1875	Brockton	grdn	3216
BUCK	Abigail	1700	Scituate	grdn	3228
	Eunice P	1879	Mattapoisett	will	3217
	Isaac	1695	Scituate	admn	3218
	Isaac Jr	1710	Scituate	admn	3219
	John	1697	Scituate	will	3220
	John	1700	Scituate	grdn	3228
	Jonathan	1703	Scituate	admn	3221
	Joseph	1775	Scituate	admn	3222
	Lydia	1791	Scituate	admn	3223
	Martha E	1880	Brockton	admn	3224
	Mary	1767	Scituate	admn	3225
	Thomas	1700	Scituate	grdn	3228
	Thomas	1703	Scituate	admn	3226
	Thomas	1737	Scituate	admn	3227
BUCKER	Molly	1782	Bridgewater	grdn	3229
BUCKLEY	Deborah	1858	Bridgewater	admn	3230
	Denis	1879	Brockton	grdn	3231
	John	1879	Brockton	grdn	3231
	Mary C	1874	Halifax	admn	3232
	Nellie	1879	Brockton	grdn	3231
	William	1871	N. Bridgewater	admn	3233
BUELL	Edward W	1867	Mattapoisett	grdn	3234
BUGBEE	James H	1834	Plymouth	admn	3235
BUKER	Richard Jr	1756	Pembroke	admn	3236
BULLARD	Mary A	1880	W. Bridgewater	admn	3238
	Mary L	1871	N. Bridgewater	grdn	3237
BUMP	Annah	1772	Wareham	grdn	3284
	Hannah S	1869	Middleboro	will	3257
	James	1821	Middleboro	grdn	3260
	Jeremiah	1771	Wareham	will	3267
	Jeremiah	1806	Wareham	will	3266
	Jeremiah	1828	Wareham	will	3268
	John	1762	Wareham	will	3272
	John	1822	Wareham	admn	3271
	Joshua	1772	Wareham	admn	3283
	Joshua	1772	Wareham	grdn	3284
	Noble P	1872	Bridgewater	admn	3297
	Warren	1838	Bridgewater	will	3306
BUMPUS	Achsah	1845	Wareham	admn	3239
	Andrew J	1858	Wareham	grdn	3240
	Anna	1745	Wareham	grdn	3305
	Anna	1855	Wareham	grdn	3304
	Asa	1837	Wareham	will	3241
	Benjamin	1743	Wareham	admn	3242
	Benjamin	1816	Rochester	will	3246
	Benjamin	1828	Carver	admn	3245
	Benjamin	1859	Wareham	admn	3243
	Benjamin	1865	Wareham	will	3244
	Betsey	1868	Middleboro	will	3247

SURNAME	FIRST NAME	YEAR	PLACE	CASE	DOCKET
BUMPUS	Braddock	1853	Wareham	admn	3248
	Chloe	1855	Middleboro	will	3249
	Edward	1745	Wareham	admn	3250
	Eliphalet	1860	Wareham	will	3251
	Elisha B	1867	N. Bridgewater	will	3252
	Elizabeth	1861	Wareham	admn	3253
	Ellinor	1748	Wareham	grdn	3264
	Ernest F	1882	Wareham	name	3254
	Estill P	1852	Wareham	will	3255
	Eunice	1824	Rochester	will	3256
	Harvey	1875	Wareham	will	3258
	Isaac	1779	Middleboro	grdn	3292
	Jacob	1720	Rochester	admn	3259
	James	1727	Rochester	admn	3262
	James	1748	Wareham	grdn	3264
	James	1750	Middleboro	will	3261
	James	1756	Middleboro	grdn	3265
	James F	1847	Wareham	admn	3263
	Jedediah	1748	Wareham	grdn	3264
	Jedediah	1756	Middleboro	grdn	3265
	Jeremiah G	1855	Wareham	admn	3269
	Jeremiah Jr	1859	Wareham	admn	3270
	John	1764	Wareham	will	3274
	John	1775	Rochester	will	3273
	John	1813	Carver	grdn	3275
	John	1875	Carver	admn	3276
	Jonathan	1847	Wareham	will	3277
	Joseph	1705	Middleboro	admn	3278
	Josepn	1739	Middleboro	admn	3279
	Joseph	1750	Middleboro	admn	3280
	Joseph	1756	Middleboro	grdn	3265
	Joseph	1817	Middleboro	admn	3281
	Joshua	1841	Middleboro	admn	3282
	Lemuel	1840	Plympton	grdn	3285
	Lemuel J	1861	Wareham	admn	3286
	Lewin	1857	Wareham	admn	3287
	Lois	1748	Wareham	grdn	3264
	Lucy	1779	Middleboro	grdn	3292
	Lydia	1711	Middleboro	admn	3288
	Martha	1727	Rochester	grdn	3289
	Mary	1739	Middleboro	grdn	3291
	Mary	1756	Middleboro	grdn	3265
	Mary	1779	Middleboro	grdn	3292
	Mary	1878	Carver	admn	3290
	Mercy	1745	Wareham	grdn	3305
	Mercy	1855	Wareham	admn	3293
	Nathan	1813	Wareham	admn	3294
	Nathaniel	1778	Middleboro	will	3295
	Noah	1799	Wareham	grdn	3296
	Rebecca	1712	Middleboro	admn	3298
	Rhoda	1745	Wareham	grdn	3305
	Rowland	1853	Wareham	will	3299
	Ruth	1749	Wareham	grdn	3309
	Samuel	1727	Rochester	grdn	3303
	Samuel	1842	Rochester	admn	3301
	Samuel	1870	Rochester	admn	3302
	Samuel B	1875	Wareham	will	3300
	Susan	1855	Wareham	grdn	3304
	Susannah	1745	Wareham	grdn	3305
	Walter	1855	Wareham	grdn	3304
	Wiberry	1739	Middleboro	grdn	3291
	Wibra	1712	Middleboro	admn	3307
	Zackary	1727	Rochester	grdn	3303
	Zenas	1779	Middleboro	grdn	3292
	Zenas	1862	Wareham	admn	3308
	Zilpha	1749	Wareham	grdn	3309
BUNDY	John	1681	Taunton	will	3310
BUNKER	Isaac L	1858	N. Bridgewater	will	3311
	Valentine	1863	Plymouth	admn	3312
BURBANK	Adeline S	1873	Mattapoisett	admn	3313
	Andrew R	1839	Hingham	admn	3314

SURNAME	FIRST NAME	YEAR	PLACE	CASE	DOCKET
BURBANK	David	1814	Plymouth	admn	3315
	David	1855	Plymouth	admn	3316
	Ezra	1800	Plymouth	admn	3317
	Ezra	1879	Mattapoisett	admn	3318
	John	1822	Plymouth	admn	3319
	Lucy	1825	Plymouth	grdn	3320
	Mary	1842	Plymouth	admn	3321
	Nehemiah	1814	Plymouth	admn	3322
	Nehemiah	1825	Plymouth	grdn	3320
	Olive	1878	Plymouth	admn	3323
	Priscilla	1825	Plymouth	will	3324
	Priscilla L	1826	Plymouth	bond	3325
	Rebecca	1866	Plymouth	admn	3326
	Samuel	1816	Plymouth	admn	3327
	Samuel	1877	Hingham	will	3328
	Sarah	1859	Plymouth	admn	3329
	Tirzah	1847	Wareham	will	3330
	William S	1873	Plymouth	admn	3331
BURBECK	Edward	1855	E. Bridgewater	admn	3332
BURDITT	Alfred	1855	Duxbury	admn	3333
	Andrew	1870	Duxbury	will	3334
	Hannah	1871	Duxbury	admn	3335
BURGE	Benjamin	1751	Dartmouth	grdn	3339
	Ebenezer	1750	Wareham	will	3336
	Phebe	1764	Rochester	grdn	3337
	Samuel	1772	Wareham	will	3338
	Seth	1751	Dartmouth	grdn	3339
	Silas	1751	Dartmouth	grdn	3339
	Thomas	1751	Dartmouth	grdn	3339
	Thomas	1770	Rochester	admn	3340
BURGESS	Abigail	1836	Rochester	will	3341
	Abner S	1864	Plymouth	will	3342
	Abraham	1853	Rochester	will	3343
	Alice E	1875	Rockland	grdn	3355
	Barzilla	1823	Wareham	admn	3344
	Barzillai	1832	Wareham	grdn	3346
	Benjamin	1832	Wareham	grdn	3346
	Benjamin	1860	Duxbury	admn	3347
	Benjamin F	1864	Wareham	admn	3345
	Betsey O	1856	Plymouth	admn	3348
	Caroline	1867	Plymouth	admn	3349
	Catherine	1832	Wareham	grdn	3346
	Catherine	1854	Plymouth	grdn	3352
	Catherine S	1838	Wareham	will	3350
	Catherine S	1866	Wareham	grdn	3351
	Chandler	1851	Plymouth	admn	3353
	Chandler Jr	1849	Plymouth	admn	3354
	Clara E	1875	Rockland	grdn	3355
	Cornelius S	1860	Middleboro	will	3356
	Deborah K	1876	Kingston	admn	3357
	Ebenezer	1832	Wareham	grdn	3346
	Eliza A	1880	Kingston	will	3358
	Elizabeth C	1868	Plymouth	admn	3359
	Emery	1872	Abington	will	3360
	Emma	1854	Plymouth	grdn	3352
	Emma C	1855	Plymouth	admn	3361
	Henry	1872	Wareham	will	3362
	Ichabod	1820	Rochester	grdn	3363
	Ichabod	1835	Rochester	admn	3364
	Jacob S	1865	Duxbury	admn	3365
	James	1812	Wareham	will	3366
	Jemima	1859	Plymouth	admn	3367
	John	1792	Rochester	will	3368
	John	1814	Wareham	grdn	3372
	John	1847	Rochester	admn	3369
	John	1850	Plymouth	admn	3370
	John G	1836	Wareham	admn	3373
	John Jr	1850	Plymouth	will	3371
	John S	1803	Wareham	will	3374
	Joseph H	1863	Wareham	grdn	3376
	Joseph S	1836	Wareham	admn	3375

SURNAME	FIRST NAME	YEAR	PLACE	CASE	DOCKET
BURGESS	Joseph W B	1863	Plymouth	grdn	3377
	Josiah	1845	Abington	admn	3378
	Lancelot	1822	Kingston	admn	3379
	Lemuel	1828	Wareham	admn	3380
	Lewis	1857	Plymouth	admn	3381
	Lillie E	1872	Duxbury	grdn	3382
	Lucy	1843	Plymouth	admn	3383
	Martha D	1839	Wareham	grdn	3384
	Melissa	1864	Middleboro	admn	3385
	Mercy K	1850	N. Bridgewater	grdn	3386
	Nathan	1855	Plymouth	will	3387
	Nathan	1863	Plymouth	admn	3388
	Nathaniel	1798	Plymouth	admn	3389
	Prince	1833	Wareham	will	3390
	Prince Jr	1839	Wareham	will	3391
	Rebecca E	1868	Plymouth	will	3392
	Resolved H	1868	Wareham	admn	3393
	Samuel	1784	Middleboro	admn	3394
	Sarah H	1858	Duxbury	admn	3395
	Stephen	1866	Wareham	grdn	3351
	Stephen C	1866	Wareham	will	3396
	Susan H	1858	Plymouth	grdn	3397
	Sylvanus W	1879	Plymouth	admn	3398
	Thomas	1796	Plymouth	grdn	3399
	Thomas	1828	Plymouth	admn	3400
	Thomas A	1874	Middleboro	admn	3401
	Vinal	1866	Plymouth	admn	3402
	Whiton H	1865	Middleboro	grdn	3403
	William	1836	Plymouth	will	3405
	William	1875	Plymouth	admn	3404
	Winslow	1861	Plymouth	admn	3406
BURKE	Hugh	1874	N. Bridgewater	admn	3407
	John	1869	Abington	admn	3408
	John K	1878	Abington	will	3409
	Margaret	1874	Scituate	admn	3410
	Margaret	1877	Abington	admn	3411
BURLEIGH	Henry	1850	E. Bridgewater	admn	3412
BURLEY	John	1862	Abington	will	3413
BURNHAM	Anna W	1873	N. Bridgewater	name	3414
	Francis A	1873	Hanson	admn	3415
	Mary	1874	Hanson	will	3416
BURNS	John	1879	Plymouth	admn	3417
	Phillip	1875	Abington	admn	3418
	Russell B	1868	Middleboro	will	3419
BURPEE	Varnum	1855	Rochester	admn	3420
BURR	Arthur A	1879	Hingham	admn	3421
	David	1797	Bridgewater	grdn	3425
	David	1814	Hingham	will	3424
	David	1852	Hingham	admn	3423
	David	1879	Hingham	admn	3422
	Elijah	1859	Hingham	will	3426
	Elisha	1854	Hingham	grdn	3427
	Elisha	1863	Hingham	will	3428
	Emma	1848	Hingham	grdn	3429
	Emma	1854	Hingham	will	3430
	Emma	1881	Hingham	admn	3431
	Fearing	1866	Hingham	admn	3432
	Hannah R	1861	Hingham	will	3433
	Joanna	1865	Hingham	admn	3434
	John	1857	Hingham	will	3435
	John W	1857	Hingham	grdn	3436
	Jonathan	1769	Bridgewater	grdn	3442
	Jonathan	1797	Bridgewater	will	3437
	Jonathan	1805	Hingham	admn	3438
	Levi	1839	Hingham	will	3439
	Lincoln	1868	Hingham	will	3440
	Lucy L	1863	Hingham	admn	3441
	Martha	1769	Bridgewater	grdn	3442
	Mary	1859	Hingham	will	3444
	Mary	1865	Hanover	will	3443
	Mary	1871	Hingham	admn	3445

SURNAME	FIRST NAME	YEAR	PLACE	CASE	DOCKET
BURR	Matthew	1847	Hingham	admn	3446
	Olive	1812	Hingham	grdn	3447
	Priscilla W	1822	Hingham	grdn	3449
	Priscilla W	1846	Hingham	admn	3450
	Priscilla etal	----	Plymouth	peti	3448
	Robert	1853	Hingham	will	3451
	Ruth	1797	Bridgewater	grdn	3425
	Seth	1840	W. Bridgewater	grdn	3452
	Susan	1851	Middleboro	admn	3453
	Theophilus	1835	Hingham	admn	3454
	Thomas	1812	Hingham	grdn	3447
	Thomas	1812	Hingham	admn	3455
	Warren	1825	Hingham	will	3456
	Waters	1819	Hingham	will	3457
BURRELL	Abraham	1763	Abington	admn	3458
	Addie	1864	Middleboro	grdn	3459
	Alice	1864	Middleboro	grdn	3459
	Benjamin	1807	Hingham	grdn	3460
	Daniel	1820	Hingham	admn	3461
	Daniel	1879	S. Abington	admn	3462
	Henry	1874	Rockland	admn	3463
	Henry H	1870	Abington	admn	3464
	Humphries	1757	Abington	admn	3465
	Isaac	1878	S. Scituate	will	3466
	John	1754	Abington	will	3469
	John	1828	N. Bridgewater	admn	3467
	John	1836	N. Bridgewater	admn	3468
	John H	1865	Abington	name	3470
	Lydia	1816	Hingham	admn	3471
	Malachi	1858	Hingham	will	3472
	Malachi	1864	Middleboro	admn	3473
	Mary	1772	Abington	will	3474
	Mary	1809	Hingham	will	3475
	Nicholas	1871	N. Bridgewater	admn	3476
	Oliver	1851	Hingham	grdn	3478
	Stephen	1868	Hingham	will	3477
	Waterman	1851	Hingham	grdn	3478
BURROWS	James H	1858	Scituate	grdn	3479 +
	Jeremiah	1714	Marshfield	admn	3479
	Sarah L	1858	Scituate	grdn	3479 +
	Thomas J	1846	Scituate	admn	3480
	William T	1858	Scituate	grdn	3479 +
BURT	Ruth	1881	Middleboro	admn	3481
	Silence	1818	Rochester	will	3482
	William E	1851	Bridgewater	admn	3483
BURTCH	William D	1879	Bridgewater	admn	3484
BUSH	Frederick	1855	E. Bridgewater	will	3485
BUTLER	Joanna	1748	Marshfield	will	3486
	John	1880	Marshfield	grdn	3488
	Judah	1699	Falmouth	atta	3487
	Mary	1880	Marshfield	grdn	3488
	Patrick	1869	Wareham	will	3490
	Patrick	1872	Scituate	admn	3489
	Valeria C	1872	N. Bridgewater	admn	3491
BUTTERFIELD	Jonathan	1769	Bridgewater	will	3492
	Rachel	1779	Bridgewater	will	3493
BUTTERLY	Christopher	1875	Scituate	will	3494
BUTTERWORTH	Alford	1839	Bridgewater	grdn	3496
	John	1862	Middleboro	admn	3495
	Ruth	1839	Bridgewater	grdn	3496
	Sarah	1839	Bridgewater	grdn	3496
BUTTIMER	John	1881	Hingham	will	3497
BUTTOMER	John	1881	W. Bridgewater	will	3498
BUTTS	Patrick M	1871	Mattapoisett	admn	3499
BYRAM	Anna	1771	Bridgewater	grdn	3500
	Benjamin	1748	Bridgewater	grdn	3501
	George H	1879	E. Bridgewater	will	3502
	Joseph	1744	Bridgewater	admn	3503
	Josiah	1806	Bridgewater	will	3504
	Josiah	1851	E. Bridgewater	admn	3505
	Martha	1748	Bridgewater	grdn	3501

SURNAME	FIRST NAME	YEAR	PLACE	CASE	DOCKET
BYRAM	Mary	1748	Bridgewater	grdn	3501
	Matilda	1807	Bridgewater	admn	3507
	Nary	1806	Bridgewater	grdn	3506
	Nicholas	1688	Bridgewater	will	3508
	Nicholas	1727	Bridgewater	will	3509
	Seth	1782	Bridgewater	admn	3510
	Susannah	1700	Bridgewater	will	3511
CAHOON	Betsey M	1855	Wareham	name	3511 +
	Ebenezer Y	1852	Wareham	will	3512
	Freeman H	1867	Plymouth	will	3513
	Jesse	1872	Wareham	will	3514
	Mark	1852	Plymouth	will	3515
	Samuel	1879	Plymouth	admn	3516
	Stephen	1818	Plymouth	will	3517
CAIN	Daniel	1821	Hingham	admn	3518
	Daniel	1835	Hingham	admn	3519
	Priscilla	1868	Hingham	admn	3520
CALDERWOOD	John	1795	Plymouth	admn	3521
CALDWELL	Alice	1869	W. Bridgewater	grdn	3522
	Bertha	1869	W. Bridgewater	grdn	3522
	Charles	1869	W. Bridgewater	grdn	3522
	Edward E	1873	W. Bridgewater	admn	3523
	Ella H	1865	W. Bridgewater	grdn	3526
	Hannah H	1869	E. Bridgewater	will	3524
	Lizzie M	1865	Middleboro	grdn	3527
	Sarah E	1865	W. Bridgewater	grdn	3526
	Sarah S	1865	W. Bridgewater	admn	3525
	Warren H	1865	Middleboro	grdn	3527
CALKINS	Clara	1873	N. Bridgewater	grdn	3529
	Clarence	1873	N. Bridgewater	admn	3528
	Clarence	1873	N. Bridgewater	grdn	3529
	Oscar	1873	N. Bridgewater	grdn	3529
CALLAHAN	Anthony	1881	Hanover	will	3530
	John	1879	Brockton	will	3531
CAMPEN	Ellen H	1880	Wareham	admn	3532
CANDEDO	Sarah A	1869	Mattapoisett	admn	3533
CANEDY	Abigail A W	1837	Middleboro	grdn	3534
	Alexander	1855	Lakeville	admn	3535
	Benjamin B	1856	Lakeville	admn	3536
	Betsey	1841	Middleboro	grdn	3541
	Elkanah	1841	Middleboro	grdn	3541
	Mary	1841	Middleboro	grdn	3541
	Micah	1780	Middleboro	admn	3537
	Sally V	1865	Lakeville	admn	3538
	Salmond	1841	Middleboro	grdn	3541
	William	1804	Middleboro	will	3540
	William	1837	Middleboro	will	3539
	William	1841	Middleboro	grdn	3541
	Zebulon L	1840	Middleboro	admn	3542
CANNAWAY	Tina	1874	Abington	name	3543
CANNON	Caleb L	1844	Rochester	admn	3544
	Calvin C	1841	Rochester	admn	3545
	Ebenezer	1842	Rochester	admn	3546
	Elisha 2nd	1869	Mattapoisett	admn	3547
	Frederick J	1857	Mattapoisett	grdn	3548
	Frederick J	1868	Mattapoisett	admn	3549
	Hallet M	1868	Mattapoisett	admn	3550
	Harriet	1871	Mattapoisett	grdn	3553
	Mary Blankins.	1871	Mattapoisett	grdn	3553
	Melinda	1841	Rochester	grdn	3551
	Minerva B	1871	Mattapoisett	admn	3552
	Minnie	1871	Mattapoisett	grdn	3553
CANTFELT	Andrew	1875	E. Bridgewater	grdn	3554
	Ellen	1875	E. Bridgewater	grdn	3554
	Mary	1875	E. Bridgewater	grdn	3554
	William	1875	E. Bridgewater	admn	3555
CAPEN	Abby G	1871	W. Bridgewater	will	3556
	Edward	1820	Boston	grdn	3557
	Esther	1847	N. Bridgewater	will	3558
	Mary T	1866	Middleboro	admn	3559
	Samuel	1844	N. Bridgewater	will	3560

SURNAME	FIRST NAME	YEAR	PLACE	CASE	DOCKET
CAPLICE	Michael	1878	Rockland	grdn	3561
CARBEY	John	1743	Rochester	grdn	3562
	Mary	1743	Rochester	grdn	3562
CARLAND	Daniel	1864	Plymouth	grdn	2563
	Ellen	1864	Plymouth	grdn	3563
	John	1862	Plymouth	admn	2564
CARNES	John	1875	Hingham	admn	3565
	Margaret	1877	Hingham	grdn	3566
	Patrick	1877	Hingham	grdn	3566
CARR	Andrew	1873	Plymouth	admn	3567
	Henry	1870	N. Bridgewater	admn	3568
	Moses	1877	Hanson	admn	3569
	Redden Jr	1833	W. Bridgewater	grdn	3570
	Simeon	1879	Brockton	will	3571
	Sylvia	1878	Wareham	will	3572
CARRIER	Henry L	1847	Bridgewater	will	3573
CARROLL	Elizabeth	1871	Wareham	grdn	3574
	Maria	1871	Wareham	grdn	3574
	Mary	1860	Marshfield	grdn	3575
CARTER	Henry	1879	Plymouth	will	3576
	Lydia G H	1852	Middleboro	grdn	3577
CARVER	Abigail	1766	Marshfield	admn	3578
	Abigail	1773	Plymouth	will	3579
	Alanson	1820	Marshfield	admn	3580
	Barstow	1872	Marshfield	will	3581
	Bathsheba	1860	Bridgewater	will	3582
	Bethiah	1762	Bridgewater	grdn	3592
	Betsey	1816	Plymouth	grdn	3583
	Caleb	1786	Marshfield	admn	3584
	David	1853	Marshfield	will	3585
	David	1870	Marshfield	grdn	3586
	David	1870	Marshfield	will	3587
	Deborah	1868	Middleboro	admn	3588
	Eleazer	1743	Bridgewater	will	3590
	Eleazer	1762	Bridgewater	grdn	3592
	Eleazer	1866	E. Bridgewater	will	3589
	Eleazer Jr	1755	Bridgewater	admn	3591
	Ellen	1853	Bridgewater	grdn	3626
	Ellen	1859	Bridgewater	admn	3593
	Emeline	1840	Plymouth	grdn	3594
	Hannah	1728	Plympton	grdn	3603
	Ichabod	1840	Plymouth	admn	3595
	Israel	1868	Marshfield	will	3597
	James	1761	Plymouth	admn	3598
	James	1761	Plymouth	grdn	3599
	James	1787	Plymouth	admn	3600
	John	1715	Marshfield	admn	3606
	John	1728	Plympton	grdn	3603
	John	1747	Plympton	admn	3602
	John	1754	Plymouth	admn	3605
	John	1803	Bridgewater	will	3607
	John	1816	Plymouth	grdn	3583
	John	1834	Middleboro	will	3604
	John	1870	Bridgewater	admn	3608
	John Jr	1724	Plympton	admn	3601
	Joseph	1764	Bridgewater	grdn	3609
	Joseph	1778	Bridgewater	will	3610
	Joshua	1771	Marshfield	admn	3611
	Joshua	1827	Marshfield	will	3612
	Josiah	1731	Plymouth	grdn	3614
	Josiah	1750	Plymouth	admn	3615
	Josiah	1799	Middleboro	will	3613
	Josiah	1825	Plymouth	admn	3616
	Lucinda	1867	Bridgewater	will	3617
	Mary	1762	Bridgewater	grdn	3592
	Mary J	1875	Marshfield	will	3618
	Mercy	1841	Middleboro	will	3619
	Nathaniel	1762	Bridgewater	grdn	3592
	Nathaniel	1815	Carver	admn	3621
	Nathaniel	1842	Plymouth	admn	3622
	Nathaniel	1853	Bridgewater	grdn	3626

SURNAME	FIRST NAME	YEAR	PLACE	CASE	DOCKET
CARVER	Rachel F	1874	Marshfield	admn	3623
	Rebecca	1874	Marshfield	admn	3624
	Richard	1853	Bridgewater	grdn	3626
	Richard et al	1878	Bridgewater	peti	3625
	Sarah	1728	Plympton	grdn	3603
	Sarah	1879	Bridgewater	admn	3627
	William	1760	Marshfield	will	3628
	William	1764	Marshfield	admn	3629
CARVER MASS	Indians (of)	1827	Carver	acct	3596
CARY	Abigail	1777	Bridgewater	admn	3630
	Bethiah H	1874	N. Bridgewater	will	3631
	Bethuel Jr	1852	Abington	admn	3632
	Caleb	1767	Bridgewater	grdn	3633
	Caleb	1816	Bridgewater	will	3634
	Charles	1847	N. Bridgewater	grdn	3644
	Charles	1854	E Machias ME	grdn	3655
	Charles	1871	N. Bridgewater	will	3635
	Eleazer	1769	Bridgewater	grdn	3665
	Eleazer	1806	Bridgewater	will	3636
	Eleazer	1815	Bridgewater	admn	3637
	Eliphalet	1820	Bridgewater	admn	3638
	Ephraim	1792	Bridgewater	will	3639
	Eunice	1769	Bridgewater	grdn	3665
	Experience	1828	Bridgewater	admn	3640
	Frabcis	1833	N. Bridgewater	admn	3642
	Francis	1728	Bridgewater	will	3641
	Francis	1870	E. Bridgewater	will	3643
	George	1847	N. Bridgewater	grdn	3644
	Hannah	1855	N. Bridgewater	admn	3645
	Helen	1858	N. Bridgewater	name	3646
	James	1706	Bridgewater	will	3647
	James	1850	N. Bridgewater	admn	3648
	John	1709	Bridgewater	grdn	3661
	John	1770	Bridgewater	will	3649
	Jonathan	1695	Bridgewater	admn	3650
	Jonathan	1709	Bridgewater	grdn	3661
	Jonathan	1745	Bridgewater	admn	3651
	Jonathan	1766	Bridgewater	admn	3652
	Jonathan	1769	Bridgewater	grdn	3665
	Jonathan	1813	Bridgewater	will	3653
	Jonathan	1852	N. Bridgewater	will	3654
	Josiah	1760	Bridgewater	grdn	3668
	Lewis	1854	E Machias ME	grdn	3655
	Lois	1769	Bridgewater	grdn	3665
	Louisa	1858	N. Bridgewater	name	3646
	Lydia	1760	Bridgewater	grdn	3668
	Martin	1847	N. Bridgewater	admn	3656
	Mary	1760	Bridgewater	grdn	3668
	Mary	1815	Bridgewater	will	3658
	Mary Alice	1858	N. Bridgewater	name	3657
	Mehitable	1760	Bridgewater	grdn	3659
	Recompence	1709	Bridgewater	grdn	3661
	Recompence	1759	Bridgewater	will	3660
	Recompence	1760	Bridgewater	grdn	3668
	Sally	1838	Bridgewater	will	3662
	Simeon	1760	Bridgewater	grdn	3668
	Simeon	1802	Bridgewater	will	3663
	William	1769	Bridgewater	grdn	3665
	William	1879	Brockton	will	3664
	Zachariah	1788	Bridgewater	will	3666
	Zebulon	1759	Bridgewater	admn	3667
	Zebulon	1760	Bridgewater	grdn	3668
CASAR	(Indian man)	1747	Carolina	admn	3669
CASEY	Edmund	1875	E. Bridgewater	admn	3670
	Hannah	1879	Middleboro	admn	3671
	Henry	1869	E. Bridgewater	name	3672
CASHMAN	James	1879	Hanover	will	3673
	Timothy	1858	S. Scituate	admn	3674
CASHWELL	William	1841	Plymouth	grdn	3675
CASSIN	Catherine	1880	E. Bridgewater	admn	3676
CASTRO	Jose M	1808	-----	grdn	3677

SURNAME	FIRST NAME	YEAR	PLACE	CASE	DOCKET
CASWELL	Abiathar	1829	Taunton	grdn	3698
	Abraham	1880	Lakeville	admn	3678
	Albert Elmer	1866	Plympton	name	3679
	Almeda J	1879	Middleboro	admn	3680
	Azubah	1864	Middleboro	will	3681
	Cyrus P	1853	Middleboro	admn	3682
	Daniel	1761	Middleboro	admn	3683
	David	1838	Middleboro	admn	3684
	David B	1873	Lakeville	grdn	3685
	Edward T	1873	Lakeville	grdn	3685
	Elbridge G	1871	Mattapoisett	will	3686
	Eliab	1875	Lakeville	admn	3687
	Everett	1865	Middleboro	admn	3688
	Jacob	1756	Middleboro	admn	3689
	Job	1838	Hanover	admn	3690
	John	1778	Rochester	admn	3691
	John	1834	Rochester	admn	3692
	Jonathan	1824	Middleboro	admn	3693
	Loring F	1876	Mattapoisett	admn	3694
	Nancy	1872	Middleboro	admn	3695
	Nathaniel	1867	Lakeville	admn	3696
	Nathaniel Jr	1859	Lakeville	admn	3697
	Sally	1829	Taunton	grdn	3698
	Thomas	1726	Middleboro	will	3699
	Zephaniah	1851	Bridgewater	admn	3700
CATHELL	James	1858	Rochester	admn	3701
	Jane	1876	Rochester	admn	3702
CAVENDER	John	1773	Middleboro	admn	3703
CAZNEAN	Edward	1868	Hingham	admn	3704
CHADDOCK	Joseph	1813	Hanover	admn	3705
CHAMBERLAIN	Amos	1838	Hanover	grdn	3719
	Arza	1846	E. Bridgewater	admn	3706
	Benjamin	1724	Pembroke	admn	3707
	Benjamin	1803	Bridgewater	will	3708
	Calvin	1863	E. Bridgewater	will	3709
	Chloe	1829	E. Bridgewater	will	3710
	Deliverance	1826	E. Bridgewater	admn	3711
	Elizabeth	1844	Abington	admn	3712
	Eunice	1721	Pembroke	bond	3721
	Flora W	1857	N. Abington	name	3713
	Hannah	1828	E. Bridgewater	admn	3714
	Isaac	1807	Bridgewater	admn	3715
	Job	1788	Bridgewater	admn	3716
	John	1834	Abington	will	3717
	John	1838	Hanover	grdn	3719
	John	1870	Abington	admn	3718
	Joseph	1721	Pembroke	bond	3721
	Joseph	1880	E. Bridgewater	will	3720
	Josiah	1829	Hanover	will	3722
	Lewis	1826	E. Bridgewater	admn	3723
	Luther	1843	E. Bridgewater	admn	3724
	Mary	1838	Hanover	grdn	3719
	Mary R	1876	Hanover	admn	3725
	Myron	1838	Hanover	grdn	3719
	Nathan	1870	E. Bridgewater	admn	3726
	Nathaniel	1716	Pembroke	admn	3727
	Nathaniel	1814	Bridgewater	will	3728
	Nathaniel	1838	Hanover	grdn	3719
	Nathaniel F	1854	Hanover	admn	3729
	Patience	1721	Pembroke	bond	3721
	Phillip	1761	Plympton	admn	3730
	Silvina	1829	E. Bridgewater	admn	3731
	Thomas	1837	E. Bridgewater	will	3732
	William H	1862	Abington	grdn	3733
CHAMPNEY	Abigail	1847	Abington	grdn	3736
	John S	1847	Abington	admn	3735
	John S Jr	1827	E. Bridgewater	grdn	3734
	Sarah	1847	Abington	grdn	3736
CHANDLER	Aaron	1801	Duxbury	admn	3737
	Abbott	1869	Duxbury	grdn	3738
	Albert W	1877	Kingston	admn	3739

SURNAME	FIRST NAME	YEAR	PLACE	CASE	DOCKET
CHANDLER	Alden	1788	Plympton	grdn	3784
	Arthur	1869	Duxbury	grdn	3738
	Asa	1825	Duxbury	admn	3740
	Asa	1843	Duxbury	admn	3741
	Bartlett	1825	Pembroke	admn	3742
	Benjamin	1692	Duxbury	admn	3743
	Benjamin	1728	Pembroke	grdn	3737
	Benjamin	1745	Duxbury	grdn	3744
	Benjamin	1771	Duxbury	admn	3745
	Benjamin	1800	Duxbury	grdn	3746
	Charles	1814	Duxbury	admn	3748
	Charles	1820	Duxbury	grdn	3819
	Charles J	1863	Duxbury	admn	3749
	Christian	1820	Duxbury	will	3750
	David	1877	Kingston	admn	3751
	Diana	1862	Duxbury	will	3752
	Edith	1872	Kingston	admn	3753
	Edmund	1721	Duxbury	admn	3754
	Eli	1877	Duxbury	will	3755
	Elijah	1764	Duxbury	grdn	3756
	Eliza	1869	Duxbury	grdn	3738
	Eliza	1881	Kingston	admn	3757
	Elizabeth	1732	Duxbury	will	3758
	Elmer	1869	Duxbury	grdn	3738
	Ephraim	1794	Kingston	admn	3759
	Ephraim	1796	Kingston	grdn	3760
	George	1801	Duxbury	grdn	3761
	George 2nd	1874	Duxbury	admn	3762
	Hannah	1877	Kingston	admn	3763
	Henry	1859	Duxbury	will	3764
	Hiram	1880	Duxbury	admn	3765
	Howard	1877	Duxbury	admn	3766
	Ira	1848	Duxbury	admn	3767
	Ira	1868	Kingston	admn	3768
	Isaac	1796	Kingston	grdn	3760
	Isaac	1838	Duxbury	admn	3769
	James	1850	Pembroke	will	3770
	James	1866	Duxbury	admn	3772
	James H	1861	Kingston	admn	3771
	Jesse	1865	Duxbury	will	3773
	John	1728	Pembroke	grdn	3747
	John	1780	Duxbury	will	3776
	John	1796	Kingston	grdn	3760
	John	1825	Duxbury	grdn	3801
	John	1859	Marshfield	will	3778
	John B	1846	Plymouth	will	3777
	John Sr	1759	Duxbury	will	3774
	John Sr	1764	Duxbury	will	3775
	Jonathan	1775	Bridgewater	will	3779
	Joseph	1721	Duxbury	will	3780
	Joseph	1759	Duxbury	admn	3781
	Joseph	1788	Plympton	grdn	3784
	Joseph	1794	Kingston	admn	3783
	Joseph	1795	Kingston	grdn	3820
	Joseph 2nd	1873	Duxbury	admn	3782
	Joshua	1782	Duxbury	will	3785
	Levi	1869	Duxbury	will	3786
	Louisa	1869	Duxbury	grdn	3738
	Lucretia	1856	Kingston	admn	3787
	Lucy T	1859	Duxbury	will	3788
	Lydia	1788	Plympton	grdn	3784
	Lydia	1825	Duxbury	grdn	3801
	Margaret	1758	Pembroke	will	3789
	Martin S	1874	Duxbury	will	3790
	Mary	1808	Kingston	admn	3791
	Mary	1820	Duxbury	grdn	3819
	Mary	1851	Duxbury	admn	3792
	Mary A	1878	Duxbury	admn	3793
	Mercy	1778	Plymouth	grdn	3794
	Nancy	1801	Duxbury	grdn	3803
	Nathan	1795	Duxbury	will	3795

SURNAME	FIRST NAME	YEAR	PLACE	CASE	DOCKET
CHANDLER	Nathan	1796	Kingston	grdn	3760
	Nathan	1857	Kingston	will	3797
	Nathan	1864	Duxbury	admn	3796
	Noah	1854	Duxbury	admn	3798
	Peleg	1825	Duxbury	admn	3800
	Peleg	1825	Duxbury	grdn	3801
	Peleg	1841	Duxbury	will	3799
	Pelham	1801	Duxbury	grdn	3803
	Pelham	1879	Duxbury	will	3802
	Perez	1800	Duxbury	will	3805
	Perez	1832	Duxbury	admn	3806
	Perez	1870	Abington	admn	3804
	Phillip	1764	Duxbury	will	3807
	Phillip	1795	Duxbury	admn	3808
	Phillip	1801	Duxbury	admn	3809
	Phillip	1820	Duxbury	grdn	3819
	Phillip	1836	Duxbury	admn	3810
	Polly	1825	Duxbury	grdn	3801
	Prudence	1874	Duxbury	will	3811
	Rachel	1788	Plympton	grdn	3784
	Rebecca	1859	Kingston	will	3812
	Rispa	1796	Kingston	grdn	3760
	Sally	1861	Kingston	admn	3813
	Samuel	1742	Duxbury	will	3815
	Samuel	1822	Duxbury	will	3814
	Samuel	1866	Duxbury	admn	3816
	Sceva	1880	S. Scituate	admn	3817
	Simeon	1728	Pembroke	grdn	3747
	Simeon Sr	1856	Pembroke	will	3818
	Sophia	1820	Duxbury	grdn	3819
	Spencer	1795	Kingston	grdn	3820
	Sylvia	1831	Duxbury	will	3821
	Wadsworth	1820	Duxbury	grdn	3819
	Wadsworth	1842	Duxbury	will	3822
	Wendell O	1865	Duxbury	grdn	3823
	Willard M	1860	Kingston	adop	3824
	William	1870	Duxbury	admn	3825
	Zebedee	1778	Plympton	admn	3826
	Zebedee	1844	Plympton	admn	3827
CHAPEN	Elizabeth M	1861	Hingham	will	3828
CHAPLAIN	William G	1874	N. Bridgewater	will	3829
CHAPMAN	Abraham B	1793	Pembroke	admn	3830
	Catherine	1868	Plymouth	grdn	3836
	Edward E	1877	Hanover	grdn	3831
	Joseph	1793	Pembroke	grdn	3832
	Lillie M	1877	Hanover	grdn	3831
	Luther	1880	Hanson	admn	3833
	Mary	1793	Pembroke	grdn	3832
	Richard	1778	Pembroke	admn	3834
	Ruth	1793	Pembroke	quit	3835
	Sarah E	1868	Plymouth	grdn	3836
CHARD	Caleb	1709	Bridgewater	admn	3837
	Caleb	1749	Abington	grdn	3838
	Samuel	1710	Middleboro	admn	3839
CHASE	Anna	1795	Middleboro	grdn	3843
	Benjamin	1795	Middleboro	grdn	3843
	Benjamin	1833	Middleboro	will	3842
	Benjamin	1853	Carver	admn	3841
	Benjamin F	1877	Marion	admn	3840
	Charles	1853	Middleboro	grdn	3844
	Charles	1858	Lakeville	grdn	3863
	Clarissa	1877	Rochester	will	3845
	Consider	1801	Carver	will	3847
	Consider	1846	Abington	will	3846
	Diana	1795	Middleboro	grdn	3843
	Elias S	1874	Rochester	will	3848
	Ezra	1864	Middleboro	will	3849
	Henry	1860	Plymouth	admn	3850
	Isaac	1824	Carver	grdn	3852
	Isaac	1833	Carver	admn	3851
	Job	1795	Middleboro	will	3853

SURNAME	FIRST NAME	YEAR	PLACE	CASE	DOCKET
CHASE	John	1824	Carver	grdn	3852
	John	1857	Plymouth	admn	3854
	John	1867	Carver	will	3855
	Lemuel	1853	Middleboro	grdn	3844
	Levi	1821	Carver	will	3856
	Lewis	1857	Lakeville	admn	3857
	Louisa P	1838	Carver	grdn	3858
	Lucinda	1842	Middleboro	grdn	3859
	Mary	1833	Middleboro	grdn	3860
	Mary R	1836	Middleboro	grdn	3861
	Peter	1781	Scituate	admn	3862
	Phebe	1858	Lakeville	grdn	3863
	Plummer	1837	Carver	admn	3864
	Polly	1795	Middleboro	grdn	3843
	Polly	1841	Middleboro	will	3865
	Rhoda A	1855	Rochester	grdn	3866
	Richmond	1852	Middleboro	admn	3867
	Sarah B	1863	Lakeville	will	3868
	Silvanus	1824	Carver	grdn	3852
	Thomas	1777	Middleboro	admn	3869
	Welcome	1795	Middleboro	grdn	3843
CHENEY	Samuel C	1861	Plympton	admn	3870
CHESMAN	John W	1866	Hingham	grdn	3871
	Noah	1825	N. Bridgewater	admn	3872
	Noah	1825	N. Bridgewater	grdn	3873
	Samuel	1846	N. Bridgewater	will	3874
CHESNUT	Mary	1857	Bridgewater	admn	3875
CHILDS	Anna A	1878	Hingham	admn	3876
	Benjamin	1709	Marshfield	admn	3877
	James	1880	Hingham	will	3878
	Joseph	1718	Marshfield	will	3879
	Richard	1691	Marshfield	admn	3880
	Richard	1720	Marshfield	grdn	3881
	Sarah D	1864	N. Bridgewater	admn	3882
CHIPMAN	Content	1778	Halifax	grdn	3888
	Hasadiah K	1880	Bridgewater	will	3883
	Jacob	1741	Halifax	will	3884
	Jacob	1748	Halifax	grdn	3885
	Jacob	1778	Halifax	admn	3886
	Jacob	1778	Halifax	grdn	3888
	Joseph	1778	Halifax	grdn	3888
	Lloyd	1863	Wareham	grdn	3887
	Lucy	1778	Halifax	grdn	3888
	Lydia	1778	Halifax	grdn	3888
	Mercy	1771	Kingston	grdn	3889
	Sarah	1771	Kingston	grdn	3889
	Seth	1766	Kingston	admn	3890
	Silas	1830	Hingham	admn	3891
CHITTENDEN	Desire	1773	Scituate	grdn	3901
	Elizabeth	1733	Scituate	admn	3892
	Gideon	1789	Scituate	grdn	3893
	Henry	1713	Scituate	will	3894
	Isaac	1744	Scituate	will	3895
	Isaac	1773	Scituate	grdn	3901
	Israel	1722	Scituate	admn	3896
	Israel	1768	Scituate	will	3897
	Israel	1788	Scituate	admn	3898
	Israel	1799	Scituate	grdn	3899
	Joseph	1708	Scituate	admn	3900
	Luther	1773	Scituate	grdn	3901
	Mary	1793	Scituate	will	3902
	Nathaniel	1759	Scituate	admn	3903
	Nathaniel	1796	Scituate	admn	3904
	Stephen	1723	Scituate	admn	3905
	Susannah	1732	Scituate	will	3906
	Thomas	1747	Scituate	will	3907
CHRISTIAN	Caleb	1873	Bridgewater	will	3908
	George	1841	Bridgewater	admn	3909
CHRISTIE	Carrie	1878	Wareham	grdn	3910
	Everett	1878	Wareham	grdn	3910
	Hattie	1878	Wareham	grdn	3910

SURNAME	FIRST NAME	YEAR	PLACE	CASE	DOCKET
CHRISTIE	John	1838	Wareham	admn	3911
	Lois	1869	Middleboro	admn	3912
	Warren M	1876	Wareham	admn	3913
CHUBBUCK	Anthony	1863	Scituate	will	3914
	Daniel	1866	Scituate	grdn	3923
	Eleazer	1878	Hingham	admn	3915
	Eleazer Jr	1879	Hingham	admn	3916
	Elizabeth	1802	Pembroke	admn	3917
	Elizabeth	1878	Hingham	admn	3918
	Esther L	1880	Hingham	grdn	3919
	Francis G	1841	Scituate	admn	3920
	Henry	1836	Hingham	will	3921
	James	1801	Abington	admn	3922
	James	1866	Scituate	grdn	3923
	Jeremiah	1801	Scituate	admn	3924
	Lot	1820	Plymouth	admn	3925
	Lydia	1858	Scituate	admn	3926
	Nathaniel	1739	Wareham	will	3927
	Weldon	1860	Middleboro	admn	3928
	Willis	1819	Wareham	admn	3929
	Willis B	1853	Wareham	admn	3930
CHUMMUCK	Andrew	1851	Plymouth	admn	3931
	Jesse	1824	Plymouth	admn	3932
CHURCH	Abigail	1784	Rochester	grdn	3948
	Albert	1816	Rochester	grdn	3979
	Anna	1872	S. Scituate	grdn	3933
	Benjamin	1816	Rochester	grdn	3971
	Benjamin	1875	Duxbury	admn	3934
	Bethiah	1832	Rochester	will	3935
	Betsey	1840	Marshfield	will	3936
	Betsey	1848	Marshfield	grdn	3945
	Charles	1729	Freetown	warr	3937
	Charles	1773	Scituate	admn	3938
	Charles	1779	Scituate	grdn	3969
	Charles	1842	Rochester	grdn	3960
	Charles	1857	Pembroke	admn	3939
	Christopher	1779	Scituate	grdn	3969
	Constant	1815	Pembroke	admn	3940
	Cornelius	1872	S. Scituate	admn	3942
	Cornelius B	1851	S. Scituate	admn	3941
	David	1839	Marshfield	will	3944
	David	1848	Marshfield	grdn	3945
	David F	1826	Pembroke	admn	3943
	Earl	1843	Rochester	will	3946
	Ebenezer	1784	Rochester	grdn	3948
	Ebenezer	1816	Rochester	admn	3947
	Edwin	1848	Marshfield	grdn	3945
	Elizabeth	1756	Scituate	grdn	3949
	Florence	1872	S. Scituate	grdn	3933
	George	1816	Rochester	grdn	3971
	George	1869	Duxbury	grdn	3980
	Hannah	1777	Hanover	grdn	3950
	Hannah	1779	Scituate	grdn	3969
	Hulday	1802	Kingston	will	3951
	Jael	1822	Scituate	admn	3952
	John	1784	Rochester	grdn	3948
	John	1878	Marshfield	will	3953
	Jonathan	1816	Rochester	will	3954
	Jonathan	1841	Rochester	will	3955
	Joseph	1707	Plymouth	admn	3956
	Joseph	1816	Rochester	grdn	3971
	Lemuel	1772	Rochester	admn	3958
	Lemuel	1776	Rochester	admn	3959
	Lemuel	1829	Scituate	will	3957
	Lemuel	1842	Rochester	grdn	3960
	Lewis	1831	Pembroke	grdn	3962
	Lewis C	1866	Hanover	will	3961
	Lucy H	1831	Fairhaven	grdn	3963
	Lydia	1842	Rochester	grdn	3960
	Martha	1869	Duxbury	grdn	3980
	Martha G	1871	Rochester	admn	3964

SURNAME	FIRST NAME	YEAR	PLACE	CASE	DOCKET
CHURCH	Martin	1831	Pembroke	grdn	3962
	Martin	1868	Duxbury	admn	3965
	Mary	1779	Scituate	grdn	3966
	Mary	1779	Scituate	grdn	3969
	Mary	1816	Rochester	grdn	3979
	Mary	1866	Pembroke	admn	3967
	Mary H	1866	Abington	admn	3968
	Mehitable	1779	Scituate	grdn	3969
	Meribah	1858	Rochester	will	3970
	Millie	1869	Duxbury	grdn	3980
	Nabby	1816	Rochester	grdn	3971
	Nathaniel	1689	Scituate	admn	3972
	Nathaniel	1753	Scituate	admn	3973
	Nathaniel	1778	Scituate	admn	3974
	Richard	1703	Scituate	grdn	3975
	Richard	1703	Scituate	admn	3976
	Richard	1816	Rochester	grdn	3979
	Richard	1856	Bridgewater	will	3978
	Richard Jr	1776	Rochester	will	3977
	Ruth	1869	Duxbury	grdn	3980
	Sally	1816	Rochester	grdn	3971
	Samuel	1779	Scituate	grdn	3969
	Samuel T	1867	Duxbury	will	3981
	Sarah	1712	Plymouth	grdn	3982
	Sarah	1842	Rochester	will	3983
	Sarah K	1871	Pembroke	admn	3984
	Susan	1842	Rochester	grdn	3960
	Sylvia	1756	Scituate	grdn	3949
	Thomas	1792	Scituate	admn	3985
	Timothy	1777	Hanover	grdn	3950
	Timothy	1777	Hanover	admn	3986
	Timothy	1828	Hanover	will	3987
	Walter	1816	Rochester	grdn	3971
	William	1816	Rochester	grdn	3971
	William	1821	Scituate	will	3988
	William Jr	1864	Hanover	admn	3989
CHURCHILL	Alfred	1865	Plympton	admn	3990
	Almira	1838	Plymouth	grdn	3991
	Ansill	1752	Plymouth	grdn	4113
	Barnabas	1720	Plymouth	admn	3992
	Barnabas	1760	Plymouth	admn	3993
	Barnabas	1821	Plymouth	will	3994
	Bathsheba	1793	Plymouth	grdn	3995
	Benjamin	1772	Middleboro	admn	3996
	Benjamin	1806	NewBrunswick	grdn	3999
	Bethiah	1784	Plymouth	grdn	3997 a
	Bethiah	1818	Plymouth	grdn	4031
	Betsey	1859	Plymouth	admn	3998
	Betty	1806	NewBrunswick	grdn	3999
	Branch	1814	Plymouth	admn	4000
	Branch	1854	NewPlymothOH	will	4001
	Charles	1752	Plymouth	grdn	4113
	Charles	1784	Plymouth	grdn	4002
	Charles	1851	Abington	will	4005
	Charles	1864	W. Bridgewater	will	4004
	Charles A J	1870	Bridgewater	grdn	4003
	Charlotte	1842	Plymouth	grdn	4044
	Chloe J	1877	Lakeville	will	4006
	Cornelius B	1840	Plymouth	grdn	4007
	Cyrus	1856	Duxbury	admn	4008
	Daniel	1850	Plympton	will	4009
	Daniel	1855	Plymouth	will	4010
	Desire	1761	Plymouth	admn	4011
	Ebenezer	1731	Plymouth	grdn	4014
	Ebenezer	1751	Plympton	admn	4012
	Ebenezer	1781	Plymouth	admn	4013
	Edwin C	1858	Plymouth	grdn	4015
	Eleazer	1715/6	Plymouth	will	4018 +
	Eleazer	1754	Plymouth	admn	4016
	Eleazer	1819	Bridgewater	admn	4018
	Eleazer Jr	1781	Plymouth	admn	4017

SURNAME	FIRST NAME	YEAR	PLACE	CASE	DOCKET
CHURCHILL	Elizabeth	1813	Plymouth	grdn	4112
	Elizabeth	1850	Plymouth	admn	4019
	Elkanah	1764	Plymouth	will	4020
	Ellis	1752	Plymouth	grdn	4113
	Emma	1861	Plympton	adop	4021
	Ephraim	1748	Plymouth	admn	4022
	Ephraim	1752	Plymouth	grdn	4113
	Ephraim	1762	Plymouth	admn	4023
	Ephraim	1797	Plymouth	grdn	4024
	Ephraim	1818	Bridgewater	admn	4026
	Ephraim F	1865	Plymouth	admn	4025
	Ezra	1832	Plymouth	admn	4027
	Ezra	1842	Plymouth	grdn	4035
	Ezra	1850	N. Bridgewater	admn	4028
	Ezra H	1865	Hanson	grdn	4073
	George	1797	Plymouth	admn	4030
	George	1818	Plymouth	grdn	4031
	George	1871	Plymouth	will	4029
	Hannah	1752	Plymouth	grdn	4101
	Hannah	1811	Plymouth	admn	4032
	Hannah	1818	Plymouth	grdn	4031
	Harvey	1831	Plympton	admn	4033
	Heman	1841	Plymouth	will	4034
	Howard	1842	Plymouth	grdn	4035
	Ichabod	1760	Plymouth	grdn	4060
	Ichabod	1784	Plympton	grdn	4036 a
	Isaac	1751	Plympton	grdn	4088
	Isaac	1761	Plymouth	admn	4040
	Isaac	1761	Plymouth	grdn	4041
	Isaac	1778	Plympton	will	4038
	Isaac	1842	Abington	will	4037
	Isaac Jr	1822	Plympton	grdn	4039
	Isaiah	1805	Plympton	admn	4042
	Jabez	1842	Plymouth	grdn	4044
	Jabez Jr	1842	Plymouth	admn	4043
	Jacob	1803	Plympton	admn	4045
	James	1755	Plympton	will	4046
	James	1803	Plympton	admn	4047
	Jane	1848	Plymouth	will	4049
	Jane B	1861	Plympton	admn	4048
	Jenny	1784	Plymouth	grdn	4050
	Jerusha	1806	NewBrunswick	grdn	3999
	Jesse	1871	Hingham	admn	4051
	Job	1826	Plymouth	admn	4052
	John	1723	Plymouth	admn	4054
	John	1731	Plymouth	grdn	4014
	John	1745	Plymouth	admn	4056
	John	1751	Plympton	grdn	4088
	John	1752	Plymouth	grdn	4113
	John	1780	Plymouth	admn	4057
	John	1796	Plymouth	grdn	4065
	John	1814	Plymouth	admn	4058
	John D	1877	Plymouth	bond	4059 +
	John Jr	1730	Plymouth	admn	4055
	John S	1839	Duxbury	grdn	4053
	Joseph	1710/0	Plymouth	will	4059
	Joseph	1760	Plymouth	grdn	4060
	Joseph	1794	Plympton	grdn	4102
	Joshua	1751	Plympton	grdn	4088
	Leah	1751	Plympton	grdn	4088
	Leah	1781	Plympton	admn	4061
	Levi	1794	Plympton	grdn	4102
	Levi	1845	E. Bridgewater	admn	4062
	Lillis	1818	Plymouth	grdn	4031
	Lizzie F	1873	Plymouth	grdn	4063
	Lucy	1760	Plymouth	grdn	4060
	Lucy	1760	Plymouth	grdn	4064
	Lucy	1796	Plymouth	grdn	4065
	Lydia	1736	Plympton	will	4067
	Lydia L	1875	Plymouth	admn	4066
	Martha	1873	Plymouth	will	4068

SURNAME	FIRST NAME	YEAR	PLACE	CASE	DOCKET
CHURCHILL	Martha H	1880	Plymouth	admn	4069
	Mary	1770	Plympton	will	4070
	Mary	1806	NewBrunswick	grdn	3999
	Mary A	1878	Plympton	grdn	4071
	Mary B	1877	Carver	admn	4072
	Mary E	1865	Hanson	grdn	4073
	Mercy	1876	Kingston	admn	4074
	Nancy	1818	Plymouth	grdn	4031
	Nancy	1838	Duxbury	admn	4075
	Nancy	1857	Plymouth	will	4076
	Nathaniel	1767	Plymouth	grdn	4077
	Nathaniel	1794	Plympton	grdn	4102
	Nathaniel	1803	Plympton	will	4081
	Nathaniel	1838	Plymouth	grdn	3991
	Nathaniel	1838	Plymouth	admn	4078
	Nathaniel Jr	1785	Plympton	admn	4080
	Nathaniel Jr	1834	Plymouth	admn	4079
	Olive	1881	Pembroke	will	4082
	Oliver	1852	Plympton	will	4083
	Oliver	1878	Plympton	will	4084
	Orin W	1861	Plympton	adop	4021
	Patience	1784	Plymouth	grdn	4050
	Peleg	1810	Duxbury	admn	4086
	Peleg	1860	Kingston	will	4085
	Perez	1797	Middleboro	will	4087
	Priscilla	1752	Plymouth	grdn	4113
	Rebecca	1751	Plympton	grdn	4088
	Rebecca	1760	Plymouth	grdn	4089
	Reuben	1797	Plymouth	admn	4090
	Rose S	1873	Plymouth	grdn	4063
	Ruth	1751	Plympton	grdn	4088
	Sally	1818	Plymouth	grdn	4031
	Samuel	1751	Plympton	will	4093
	Samuel	1818	Plymouth	admn	4091
	Samuel	1843	Halifax	will	4092
	Sarah	1842	Plymouth	grdn	4035
	Seth	1761	Plymouth	grdn	4041
	Seth	1798	Plymouth	admn	4094
	Seth	1856	Plympton	admn	4095
	Silence	1839	N. Bridgewater	admn	4096
	Stephen	1750	Plymouth	will	4099
	Stephen	1751	Plymouth	admn	4100
	Stephen	1752	Plymouth	grdn	4101
	Stephen	1794	Plympton	grdn	4102
	Stephen	1806	NewBrunswick	grdn	3999
	Stephen	1824	Plymouth	will	4098
	Stephen	1835	Duxbury	admn	4097
	Susan A	1879	Plymouth	admn	4103
	Susanna	1760	Plymouth	grdn	4089
	Sylvanus	1866	Plympton	grdn	4105
	Sylvanus	1866	Plympton	admn	4106
	Sylvanus B	1839	Plympton	grdn	4104
	Sylvester	1842	Plymouth	grdn	4044
	Thaddeus	1810	Plymouth	admn	4107
	William	1760	Plymouth	grdn	4089
	William	1760	Plympton	will	4109
	William	1813	Plymouth	grdn	4112
	William	1824	Plympton	admn	4110
	William	1842	Plymouth	grdn	4044
	William Jr	1841	Plymouth	admn	4111
	William Sr	1723	Plympton	will	4108
	Zacheus	1752	Plymouth	grdn	4113
	Zadock	1752	Plymouth	grdn	4101
	Zadock	1858	Plympton	admn	4114
	Zebedee	1768	Middleboro	admn	4115
CILE	Arthur	1719	Scituate	admn	4116
CLAGHORN	James	1723	Rochester	admn	4117
	Lemuel	1743	Wareham	admn	4118
CLAPP	Abigail	1789	Scituate	grdn	4119 a
	Abigail	1811	Scituate	will	4120
	Abijah Jr	1792	Scituate	admn	4121

SURNAME	FIRST NAME	YEAR	PLACE	CASE	DOCKET
CLAPP	Albert	1838	Scituate	admn	4122
	Albert	1850	S. Scituate	admn	4123
	Alexander	1830	Scituate	will	4124
	Alfred	1836	Scituate	admn	4125
	Alfred	1836	Scituate	grdn	4191
	Allen	1827	Scituate	will	4126
	Allen	1870	S. Scituate	will	4127
	Anna	1827	Scituate	grdn	4187
	Anna	1879	S. Scituate	admn	4128
	Arethusa	1804	Scituate	grdn	4145
	Augustus	1827	Scituate	will	4130
	Augustus	1840	Scituate	grdn	4129
	Benjamin	1775	Rochester	will	4131
	Benjamin	1793	Scituate	admn	4132
	Benjamin	1794	Scituate	grdn	4235
	Benjamin	1815	Scituate	admn	4133
	Betsey	1855	Scituate	admn	4134
	Chandler	1833	Scituate	will	4135
	Charles	1780	Scituate	grdn	4156
	Charles	1793	Scituate	admn	4136
	Charles	1866	Scituate	admn	4137
	Charlotte	1827	Scituate	grdn	4187
	Charlotte	1843	Scituate	will	4138
	Charlotte	1865	S. Scituate	admn	4139
	Chloe	1823	Scituate	will	4140
	Cora	1874	S. Scituate	grdn	4141
	Daniel	1804	Scituate	grdn	4145
	David	1773	Scituate	will	4143
	David Jr	1752	Scituate	admn	4142
	Deborah	1804	Scituate	grdn	4145
	Deborah B	1878	S. Scituate	admn	4144
	Desire	1795	Scituate	will	4146
	Dwelly	1752	Scituate	grdn	4147
	Dwelly	1820	Scituate	admn	4148
	Ebenezer	1792	Rochester	will	4150
	Ebenezer Jr	1769	Rochester	admn	4149
	Edward S	1805	Scituate	grdn	4151
	Elijah	1761	Middleboro	grdn	4154
	Elijah	1776	Middleboro	will	4153
	Elijah	1859	S. Scituate	will	4152
	Elizabeth	1819	Marshfield	will	4155
	Elizabeth	1828	Scituate	grdn	4200
	Enos	1780	Scituate	grdn	4156
	Eunice	1800	Rochester	grdn	4199
	Experience	1831	Marshfield	will	4157
	Ezra	1761	Middleboro	will	4158
	Frank A	1843	Scituate	grdn	4159
	Galen	1776	Scituate	will	4160
	George	1875	S. Scituate	will	4161
	Georgiana	1840	Scituate	grdn	4129
	Gorham	1828	Scituate	grdn	4200
	Hannah	1780	Scituate	grdn	4156
	Hannah	1828	Scituate	grdn	4200
	Hannah	1840	Scituate	admn	4162
	Helen	1827	Scituate	grdn	4187
	Hiram	1851	Scituate	admn	4163
	Increase	1716	Rochester	will	4164
	Increase	1778	Scituate	admn	4165
	James	1803	Scituate	admn	4166
	James	1804	Scituate	grdn	4145
	Job	1781	Scituate	will	4167
	Job	1826	Scituate	admn	4168
	John	1730	Scituate	will	4172
	John	1754	Rochester	will	4169
	John	1767	Scituate	will	4173
	John	1791	Rochester	admn	4170
	John	1810	Scituate	will	4174
	John	1841	Rochester	will	4171
	John Sr	1855	S. Scituate	will	4175
	Joseph	1747	Scituate	grdn	4177
	Joseph	1747	Scituate	will	4178

SURNAME	FIRST NAME	YEAR	PLACE	CASE	DOCKET
CLAPP	Joseph	1752	Scituate	grdn	4179
	Joseph	1770	Scituate	will	4180
	Joseph	1819	Scituate	grdn	4182
	Joseph S	1804	Scituate	will	4181
	Joseph S	1876	S. Scituate	admn	4176
	Jotham	1804	Scituate	grdn	4145
	Julia	1827	Scituate	grdn	4187
	Kenelm	1826	Abington	will	4183
	Leonard	1852	Scituate	will	4184
	Lucretia	1827	Scituate	grdn	4187
	Lucy	1780	Scituate	grdn	4156
	Lucy	1827	Scituate	grdn	4187
	Lucy	1860	S. Scituate	admn	4186
	Lucy W	1854	S. Scituate	admn	4185
	Luther L	1881	Scituate	admn	4188
	Manassah	1757	Middleboro	admn	4189
	Manassah	1778	Middleboro	will	4190
	Mandana	1836	Scituate	grdn	4191
	Martha	1827	Scituate	grdn	4194
	Martha D	1879	Duxbury	will	4192
	Martha H	1861	S. Scituate	will	4193
	Martha J	1851	Rochester	grdn	4198
	Mary	1800	Rochester	grdn	4199
	Mary	1827	Scituate	grdn	4194
	Mary	1830	Scituate	will	4195
	Mary	1851	Rochester	grdn	4198
	Mary B	1871	S. Scituate	will	4197
	Mary F	1875	Scituate	grdn	4196
	Meltiah	1828	Scituate	grdn	4200
	Mercy	1781	Scituate	grdn	4201 a
	Michael	1760	Scituate	will	4202
	Michael	1766	Scituate	grdn	4203
	Michael	1800	Hanover	admn	4204
	Michael T	1875	Hingham	admn	4205
	Nathaniel	1783	Scituate	will	4206
	Nathaniel	1829	Rochester	will	4208
	Nathaniel	1851	Rochester	admn	4209
	Nathaniel	1854	S. Scituate	will	4207
	Noah	1776	Scituate	admn	4210
	Otis	1828	Scituate	grdn	4200
	Owen	1853	S. Scituate	grdn	4211
	Patience	1780	Scituate	grdn	4156
	Paul	1853	S. Scituate	admn	4212
	Perkins	1812	Scituate	admn	4213
	Perkins	1819	Scituate	grdn	4182
	Polly	1800	Rochester	grdn	4199
	Polly	1827	Scituate	grdn	4187
	Priscilla	1836	Scituate	will	4214
	Rachel	1819	Scituate	grdn	4182
	Rachel	1842	Scituate	will	4215
	Roger	1797	Scituate	admn	4216
	Rufus	1834	Scituate	will	4217
	Sally	1862	Scituate	will	4219
	Sally S	1835	Hanover	grdn	4218
	Samuel	1733	Scituate	will	4220
	Samuel	1767	Scituate	will	4221
	Samuel	1796	Scituate	grdn	4222 a
	Samuel	1800	Rochester	grdn	4199
	Samuel S	1853	Rochester	will	4223
	Sarah	1763	-----	grdn	4224
	Sarah	1770	Scituate	grdn	4225 a
	Sarah	1775	Scituate	admn	4226
	Sarah	1780	Scituate	grdn	4156
	Serena	1804	Scituate	grdn	4145
	Silas	1826	Scituate	will	4227
	Silas	1827	Scituate	grdn	4194
	Stephen	1756	Scituate	will	4228
	Stephen	1825	Scituate	admn	4229
	Stephen	1828	Scituate	grdn	4200
	Stephen	1873	S. Scituate	will	4230
	Sylvanus	1811	Scituate	admn	4231

SURNAME	FIRST NAME	YEAR	PLACE	CASE	DOCKET
CLAPP	Temperance	1828	Scituate	grdn	4200
	Thomas	1770	Scituate	grdn	4233 a
	Thomas	1774	Scituate	will	4234
	Thomas	1780	Scituate	grdn	4156
	Thomas	1794	Scituate	grdn	4235
	Thomas	1819	Scituate	grdn	4182
	Thomas	1850	Scituate	admn	4232
	William	1761	Middleboro	grdn	4154
	William	1805	Scituate	will	4236
	William	1827	Scituate	grdn	4187
	Zilpha	1803	Scituate	admn	4237
CLARK	Abigail	1712	Plymouth	grdn	4334
	Abigail	1804	Plymouth	grdn	4417
	Abigail M	1835	Plymouth	grdn	4238
	Abishai T	1854	Middleboro	admn	4239
	Abner	1830	Middleboro	admn	4240
	Abner Jr	1840	Middleboro	admn	4241
	Alexander	1869	Rochester	grdn	4291
	Amasa	1843	Plymouth	will	4242
	Amos	1852	Middleboro	grdn	4265
	Amos D	1849	Middleboro	admn	4243
	Amos O	1881	Marshfield	admn	4244
	Annie	1881	Rochester	admn	4245
	Annie M	1864	W. Bridgewater	grdn	4362
	Ansel	1831	Rochester	will	4246
	Artemas E	1865	Rochester	admn	4247
	Augusta	1876	Middleboro	will	4248
	Barnabas	1845	Rochester	admn	4249
	Benjamin	1832	Bridgewater	admn	4250
	Benjamin	1878	Plymouth	admn	4253
	Benjamin H	1858	Marshfield	admn	4251
	Benjamin W	1863	Marshfield	admn	4252
	Betsey	1810	Plymouth	grdn	4255
	Betsey M	1881	Plymouth	admn	4254
	Charity W	1879	Middleboro	will	4256
	Charles H	1875	Rochester	admn	4257
	Charlotte	1871	Hingham	grdn	4258
	Chloe	1818	Bridgewater	grdn	4385
	Consider	1797	Plymouth	grdn	4268
	Consider	1831	Plymouth	admn	4259
	Cornelius	1783	Rochester	will	5260
	Cynthia	1881	Plympton	admn	4261
	Daniel	1853	Plymouth	will	4262
	Darius	1819	Rochester	admn	4263
	David	1798	Middleboro	grdn	4289
	David	1852	Middleboro	grdn	4265
	David	1861	Plymouth	grdn	4284
	David G	1851	Middleboro	admn	4264
	Deborah	1797	Plymouth	grdn	4268
	Deborah	1815	Plymouth	grdn	4267
	Deborah	1841	Rochester	Grdn	4361
	Deborah F	1835	Plymouth	grdn	4266
	Delia	1880	Brockton	grdn	4318
	Dorothy	1728	Plympton	admn	4269
	Ebenezer	1760	Halifax	grdn	4270
	Ebenezer	1765	Rochester	will	4271
	Ebenezer	1831	Middleboro	grdn	4272
	Ebenezer	1849	Middleboro	admn	4273
	Edward D	1876	Plymouth	admn	4274
	Elias	1833	Duxbury	admn	4275
	Elijah M	1878	Mattapoisett	will	4276
	Elisha	1798	Middleboro	grdn	4289
	Elisha	1835	Middleboro	will	4277
	Eliza	1816	Pittsfield	grdn	4354
	Elizabeth	1753	Plymouth	grdn	4357
	Elizabeth	1772	Plymouth	will	4278
	Elizabeth	1792	Plymouth	admn	4279
	Elizabeth	1844	Rochester	admn	4280
	Elizabeth	1863	Middleboro	admn	4282
	Elizabeth E	1850	Middleboro	will	4281
	Elizabeth F	1870	E. Bridgewater	adop	4283

SURNAME	FIRST NAME	YEAR	PLACE	CASE	DOCKET
CLARK	Ella	1861	Plymouth	grdn	4284
	Elmer H	1866	Middleboro	grdn	4285
	Emily K	1864	Middleboro	admn	4286
	Emma	1867	Middleboro	grdn	4363
	Ezekiel	1795	Rochester	will	4287
	Ezra	1793	Middleboro	will	4288
	Ezra	1798	Middleboro	grdn	4289
	Ezra	1880	Plymouth	admn	4290
	Frederick G	1869	Rochester	grdn	4291
	Freeman C	1827	Plymouth	admn	4292
	George	1852	Middleboro	grdn	4265
	George E	1863	Hanover	grdn	4294
	George H	1865	Rochester	admn	4293
	Gideon	1861	Plymouth	grdn	4284
	Granville	1871	Hingham	grdn	4258
	Hannah	1867	Middleboro	grdn	4363
	Hannah G	1854	Middleboro	will	4295
	Henrietta F	1878	Plymouth	grdn	4356
	Henry	1696	Duxbury	admn	4296
	Henry A	1881	Marshfield	grdn	4297
	Hope	1827	Middleboro	admn	4298
	Ira	1871	Rochester	will	4299
	Isaac	1881	Middleboro	will	4300
	Israel	1788	Plymouth	will	4302
	Israel	1808	Plymouth	admn	4303
	Israel	1810	Plymouth	grdn	4255
	Israel 2nd	1877	Plymouth	admn	4301
	Ivory H	1879	Plymouth	admn	4304
	James	1716	Pembroke	admn	4308
	James	1731	Plymouth	will	4311
	James	1747	Plymouth	grdn	4312
	James	1750	Plymouth	will	4313
	James	1794	Pembroke	admn	4309
	James	1815	Plymouth	will	4314
	James	1819	Rochester	will	4305
	James	1821	Plymouth	will	4315
	James	1822	Rochester	admn	4306
	James	1871	Hingham	grdn	4258
	James	1880	Brockton	grdn	4318
	James E	1831	Plymouth	grdn	4316
	James E	1836	Rochester	grdn	4307
	James Jr	1726	Plymouth	admn	4310
	James M	1865	Scituate	admn	4317
	Jane	1777	Middleboro	admn	4319
	Jennie	1867	Middleboro	grdn	4363
	Joanna G	1848	Rochester	grdn	4320
	Job P	1852	Middleboro	will	4321
	John	1712	Plymouth	admn	4333
	John	1712	Plymouth	grdn	4334
	John	1727	Rochester	will	4322
	John	1770	Hanover	admn	4330
	John	1794	Rochester	admn	4324
	John	1810	Plymouth	grdn	4255
	John	1837	Rochester	will	4325
	John	1862	Plymouth	will	4331
	John	1863	Marion	admn	4327
	John 3rd	1784	Rochester	admn	4323
	John 3rd	1807	Plymouth	admn	4332
	John C	1851	E. Bridgewater	will	4329
	John H	1867	Rochester	admn	4326
	John W	1880	Brockton	grdn	4384
	John W	1881	Brockton	admn	4328
	Jonathan	1791	Rochester	admn	4335
	Jonathan	1827	Abington	admn	4336
	Joseph	1712	Plymouth	grdn	4334
	Joseph	1765	Rochester	will	4337
	Joseph	1773	Rochester	will	4338
	Joseph	1843	Middleboro	will	4340
	Joseph	1870	Rochester	will	4339
	Joseph W	1858	Hanover	admn	4341
	Josiah	1792	Plymouth	warr	4342

SURNAME	FIRST NAME	YEAR	PLACE	CASE	DOCKET
CLARK	Josiah	1818	Plymouth	admn	4343
	Josiah	1839	Plymouth	will	4344
	Julia	1880	Brockton	admn	4346
	Julia A	1871	N. Bridgewater	will	4345
	Kezia	1874	Rochester	admn	4347
	Lemuel	1798	Halifax	admn	4348
	Lemuel	1818	Rochester	admn	4349
	Lois G	1876	Middleboro	admn	4350
	Lothrop	1842	Plymouth	will	4352
	Lothrop Jr	1806	Plymouth	admn	4351
	Louisa	1858	Middleboro	will	4353
	Louisa	1867	Middleboro	grdn	4363
	Lucretia	1816/0	Pittsfield	grdn	4354
	Lucy	1848	Middleboro	will	4355
	Lucy B	1863	Hanover	grdn	4294
	Lucy T	1878	Plymouth	grdn	4356
	Lydia	1798	Middleboro	grdn	4289
	Martha	1712	Plymouth	grdn	4334
	Martha	1816	Pittsfield	grdn	4354
	Mary	1712	Plymouth	grdn	4334
	Mary	1753	Plymouth	grdn	4357
	Mary	1785	Plymouth	clai	4358
	Mary	1816	Pittsfield	grdn	4354
	Mary	1855	Plymouth	admn	4359
	Mary	1867	Middleboro	grdn	4363
	Mary A	1841	Rochester	grdn	4361
	Mary A	1864	W. Bridgewater	grdn	4362
	Mary J	1880	Hingham	will	4360
	Matilda	1816	Pittsfield	grdn	4354
	Mercy	1793	Middleboro	will	4364
	Michael	1880	Brockton	grdn	4318
	Nathan	1866	Rochester	will	4365
	Nathaniel	1709	Plymouth	admn	4366
	Nathaniel	1718	Plymouth	will	4367
	Nathaniel	1863	Mattapoisett	admn	4370
	Nathaniel	1874	Plymouth	will	4369
	Nathaniel 3rd	1820	Plymouth	admn	4368
	Nellie O	1881	Marshfield	grdn	4297
	Noah	1830	Plymouth	will	4371
	Noah	1841	Middleboro	will	4372
	Noah	1879	Middleboro	will	4373
	Parnal	1818	Bridgewater	grdn	4385
	Patience C	1868	Middleboro	will	4374
	Paul O	1849	Middleboro	grdn	4375
	Peleg	1869	Rochester	admn	4376
	Phillip W	1873	Halifax	admn	4377
	Polly	1804	Plymouth	grdn	4417
	Presbury	1858	Rochester	will	4378
	Richard	1830	Middleboro	will	4379
	Richard	1863	Middleboro	admn	4380
	Robert	1817	Middleboro	will	4381
	Robert	1873	Middleboro	admn	4382
	Roger	1800	Middleboro	grdn	4383 a
	Rosanna	1880	Brockton	grdn	4384
	Sally	1818	Bridgewater	grdn	4385
	Samuel	1763	Plymouth	admn	4386
	Samuel	1874	Plymouth	admn	4387
	Samuel S	1850	Middleboro	will	4388
	Sarah	1804	Plymouth	grdn	4417
	Sarah	1863	Hanover	admn	4389
	Sarah	1875	Mattapoisett	admn	4390
	Seth	1805	Plymouth	admn	4391
	Stella	1876	Halifax	admn	4392
	Stephen	1863	Plympton	admn	4393
	Stephen	1881	Carver	admn	4394
	Stephen Jr	1865	Duxbury	admn	4395
	Susan S	1875	Middleboro	will	4396
	Susannah	1744	-----	grdn	4397
	Susannah B	1866	Mattapoisett	grdn	4398
	Sylvanus W	1838	Plymouth	admn	4399
	Thomas	1727	Plymouth	admn	4400

SURNAME	FIRST NAME	YEAR	PLACE	CASE	DOCKET
CLARK	Thomas	1728	Plymouth	admn	4401
	Thomas	1744	Plymouth	admn	4402
	Thomas	1747	Rochester	will	4406
	Thomas	1753	Plymouth	admn	4403
	Thomas	1795	Plymouth	admn	4404
	Thomas	1800	Plymouth	will	4405
	Thomas	1810	Plymouth	grdn	4255
	Thomas	1837	Rochester	will	4407
	Thomas A	1866	Middleboro	admn	4408
	Thurston	1696	Duxbury	admn	4296
	Timothy H	1858	Rochester	admn	4409
	Warren	1848	Rochester	admn	4410
	Willard	1819	Rochester	will	4411
	Willard E	1865	Rochester	admn	4412
	William	1687	Duxbury	will	4418
	William	1755	Rochester	will	4419
	William	1782	Plymouth	admn	4416
	William	1792	Rochester	admn	4420
	William	1804	Plymouth	grdn	4417
	William	1816	Pittsfield	grdn	4354
	William	1817	Plymouth	will	4414
	William	1845	Rochester	admn	4421
	William	1877	Plymouth	will	4413
	William	1879	Marion	will	4423
	William A	1860	New Bedford	grdn	4422
	William Jr	1800	Plymouth	admn	4415
	Zilpha M	1873	Middleboro	will	4424
	Zoath	1826	Plymouth	admn	4425
CLEARY	Charles	1867	Pembroke	admn	4426
	James Jr	1859	Pembroke	admn	4427
CLEMONS	John	1792	Pembroke	admn	4428
CLIFFORD	Lucy T	1875	Plymouth	admn	4429
	Mary J	1876	Kingston	adop	4430
CLIFT	Adeline	1841	Marshfield	admn	4431
	Adna	1761	Marshfield	grdn	4432
	Belus	1875	S. Abington	admn	4433
	Bethiah	1838	E. Bridgewater	admn	4434
	Church	1761	Marshfield	grdn	4449
	Church	1769	Marshfield	will	4435
	Deborah	1761	Marshfield	grdn	4432
	Deborah	1873	E. Bridgewater	will	4437
	Deborah T	1873	Marshfield	admn	4436
	Eunice	1834	Marshfield	will	4438
	Israel	1784	Marshfield	grdn	4439
	Joseph	1849	Marshfield	will	4440
	Mary	1724	Marshfield	grdn	4442
	Mary	1875	Marshfield	admn	4441
	Nathaniel	1761	Marshfield	grdn	4432
	Nathaniel	1762	Marshfield	admn	4443
	Nathaniel	1773	Bridgewater	admn	4447
	Nathaniel	1784	Marshfield	grdn	4444
	Nathaniel	1818	Bridgewater	admn	4448
	Nathaniel	1833	Marshfield	admn	4446
	Nathaniel Jr	1833	Marshfield	admn	4445
	Rhoda	1761	Marshfield	grdn	4449
	Samuel	1724	Marshfield	grdn	4442
	William	1723	Marshfield	admn	4450
	William	1749	Marshfield	admn	4451
	William	1778	Marshfield	admn	4452
	William 2nd	1834	Marshfield	grdn	4453
	Wills	1832	Marshfield	admn	4454
	Winslow	1773	Bridgewater	grdn	4455
CLIFTON	Anna	1766	Rochester	grdn	4462
	Benjamin	1731	Rochester	will	4456
	Benjamin	1808	Rochester	admn	4457
	Benjamin S	1870	Marion	admn	4458
	Cynthia D	1853	Marion	will	4459
	Dennis	1817	Rochester	grdn	4460
	Ellen M	1853	Marion	grdn	4461
	Lydia	1766	Rochester	grdn	4462
	Mary	1766	Rochester	grdn	4462

SURNAME	FIRST NAME	YEAR	PLACE	CASE	DOCKET
CLIFTON	Meribah	1766	Rochester	grdn	4462
	Savery	1814	Rochester	admn	4463
	Stephen	1803	Rochester	admn	4464
	Thankful	1817	Rochester	admn	4465
	Timothy	1766	Rochester	grdn	4462
	Timothy	1766	Rochester	admn	4466
	Timothy	1840	Rochester	admn	4467
	Timothy	1876	Marion	will	4468
CLOUD	H H	1877	Abington	admn	4469
COADE	Hannah G	1864	Middleboro	will	4470
COBB	Alanson M	1880	Middleboro	admn	4471
	Albert	1858	Middleboro	admn	4472
	Almira	1863	Middleboro	will	4473
	Andrew	1800	Middleboro	will	4474
	Anna	1815	Abington	grdn	4475
	Ansell	1815	Bridgewater	admn	4476
	Artemas	1858	Wareham	grdn	4478
	Artemas C	1842	Middleboro	will	4477
	Asaph	1827	Rochester	grdn	4581
	Asenath	1777	Middleboro	grdn	4599
	Austin	1815	Abington	grdn	4475
	Baxter	1877	Abington	admn	4479
	Benjamin	1811	Carver	will	4480
	Benjamin	1869	Kingston	admn	4481
	Bertha H	1854	Pembroke	adop	4482
	Betsey	1850	Hanson	admn	4484
	Betsey	1863	Hanson	admn	4485
	Betsey C	1849	Middleboro	grdn	4483
	Catherine S	1879	Plymouth	peti	4486
	Charles	1879	Plymouth	will	4487
	Clarence O	1860	Kingston	adop	4488
	Consider	1815	Abington	grdn	4475
	Cornelius	1761	Plymouth	grdn	4592
	Cornelius	1830	Plymouth	will	4489
	Cornelius	1834	Hanson	admn	4491
	Cornelius	1835	Hanson	grdn	4492
	Cornelius	1852	Hanson	admn	4490
	David	1745	Abington	grdn	4506
	David	1761	Plymouth	grdn	4592
	David	1872	N. Bridgewater	will	4493
	David W	1869	N. Bridgewater	grdn	4494
	Deliverance	1845	Middleboro	will	4495
	Deliverance	1865	Middleboro	admn	4496
	Dorothy C	1858	Middleboro	will	4497
	Ebenezer	1752	Plymouth	admn	4498
	Ebenezer	1801	Kingston	will	4500
	Ebenezer	1864	Carver	will	4501
	Ebenezer Jr	1783	Kingston	admn	4499
	Edward	1745	Abington	grdn	4506
	Edward	1797	Abington	admn	4505
	Edward	1815	Abington	grdn	4475
	Edward	1843	Abington	will	4504
	Edward 2nd	1841	Abington	admn	4502
	Edward W	1841	Abington	grdn	4503
	Elizabeth	1743	Middleboro	grdn	4598
	Elizabeth	1821	Plymouth	grdn	4507
	Elizabeth	1845	Abington	grdn	4573
	Elizabeth	1853	Kingston	will	4508
	Elvira C	1866	Hanson	admn	4509
	Ephraim	1775	Plymouth	will	4510
	Florence L	1866	Hanover	grdn	4511
	Frank W	1859	Carver	grdn	4560
	Frederick	1824	Carver	admn	4512
	Frederick	1825	Carver	grdn	4513
	George	1803	Plympton	will	4515
	George A	1847	Baltimore MD	grdn	4516
	George W	1854	Marion	admn	4514
	Gershom	1770	Middleboro	admn	4517
	Gideon	1778	Middleboro	admn	4518
	Hannah	1777	Middleboro	grdn	4599
	Hannah	1862	Marion	admn	4520

SURNAME	FIRST NAME	YEAR	PLACE	CASE	DOCKET
COBB	Hannah B	1870	Carver	admn	4519
	Harvey R	1852	Rochester	admn	4521
	Hattie T	1863	N. Bridgewater	adop	4522
	Helen	1835	Hanson	grdn	4492
	Helen F	1847	Baltimore MD	grdn	4516
	Helen M	1843	Carver	grdn	4524
	Helen P	1863	N. Bridgewater	adop	4523
	Heman	1857	Plymouth	will	4525
	Heman	1871	Middleboro	admn	4526
	Isaac E	1821	Plymouth	admn	4527
	Isaiah	1854	Rochester	will	4528
	Jacob	1854	Abington	admn	4529
	James	1743	Middleboro	admn	4531
	James	1767	Kingston	admn	4530
	James	1773	Middleboro	admn	4532
	James	1834	Middleboro	admn	4533
	Jeremiah	1801	Middleboro	admn	4534
	Job	1761	Plymouth	admn	4535
	Job	1761	Plymouth	grdn	4592
	Job Jr	1825	Plymouth	admn	4536
	John	1715	Plymouth	will	4537
	John	1750	Plymouth	admn	4538
	John	1750	Middleboro	will	4547
	John	1752	Plymouth	grdn	4539
	John	1752	Middleboro	grdn	4549
	John	1763	Plymouth	admn	4540
	John	1814	Abington	admn	4544
	John	1822	Middleboro	will	4550
	John	1824	Wareham	admn	4542
	John	1824	Kingston	will	4543
	John B	1834	Middleboro	admn	4551
	John B	1869	N. Bridgewater	grdn	4494
	John F	1875	Abington	will	4545
	John Jr	1750	Middleboro	will	4548
	John K	1879	Plymouth	will	4541
	John Sr	1728	Middleboro	will	4546
	Jonathan	1756	Middleboro	admn	4552
	Joseph	1804	Carver	admn	4553
	Joseph	1807	Kingston	admn	4554
	Joseph	1866	Pembroke	will	4556
	Joseph W	1866	Hull	admn	4555
	Josephus G	1861	Middleboro	admn	4557
	Josiah	1854	Kingston	will	4558
	Julia A	1877	Marion	admn	4559
	Laura A	1859	Carver	grdn	4560
	Lazarus	1770	Plymouth	admn	4561
	Leander	1872	Marion	will	4562
	Lemuel	1743	Plymouth	admn	4563
	Lemuel	1761	Plymouth	grdn	4572
	Lemuel	1841	Plymouth	admn	4564
	Lemuel	1868	Plympton	admn	4565
	Lewis	1842	Middleboro	admn	4566
	Lewis A	1879	Halifax	grdn	4567
	Lucia	1835	Hanson	grdn	4492
	Lucia	1852	Hanson	admn	4568
	Lucy	1825	Carver	grdn	4513
	Lucy	1858	Wareham	grdn	4478
	Lucy	1864	Carver	admn	4569
	Luther	1815	Abington	grdn	4475
	Luther	1828	Abington	grdn	4570
	Lydia	1761	Plymouth	grdn	4572
	Lydia	1845	Abington	grdn	4573
	Lydia	1849	Abington	will	4571
	Marcia R	1867	Kingston	adop	4574
	Margaret	1796	Plymouth	admn	4575
	Marston	1858	Carver	admn	4577
	Marston F	1855	Carver	admn	4576
	Martha	1752	Middleboro	grdn	4549
	Martin	1870	Kingston	will	4578
	Mary	1745	Abington	grdn	4506
	Mary	1827	Rochester	grdn	4581

SURNAME	FIRST NAME	YEAR	PLACE	CASE	DOCKET
COBB	Mary	1855	Kingston	will	4579
	Mary	1858	Wareham	grdn	4478
	Mary F	1874	Plymouth	admn	4580
	Meletiah	1773	Middleboro	grdn	4582
	Mercy	1859	Carver	admn	4585
	Mercy B	1842	Carver	admn	4583
	Mercy B	1842	Carver	grdn	4584
	Michal	1878	Hingham	will	4586
	Nathan	1800	Plympton	will	4587
	Nathaniel	1793	Carver	admn	4589
	Nathaniel Jr	1768	Plymouth	admn	4588
	Nehemiah	1761	Plymouth	grdn	4592
	Nehemiah	1805	Plymouth	admn	4591
	Nehemiah	1841	Carver	will	4590
	Nellie W	1878	Carver	grdn	4593
	Oliver	1849	Rochester	will	4594
	Otis	1838	Middleboro	grdn	4595
	Otis	1840	Carver	admn	4596
	Patience	1761	Plymouth	grdn	4592
	Philander 2nd	1870	Kingston	grdn	4597
	Priscilla	1743	Middleboro	grdn	4598
	Priscilla	1777	Middleboro	grdn	4599
	Richard	1745	Abington	admn	4600
	Richard H	1880	Abington	admn	4601
	Rowland	1760	Plympton	admn	4602
	Samuel	1823	Rochester	admn	4603
	Samuel S	1837	Middleboro	will	4604
	Sarah	1805	Plymouth	will	4605
	Sarah	1820	Middleboro	admn	4607
	Sarah	1859	Kingston	will	4606
	Seth	1740	Plymouth	admn	4608
	Seth	1821	Kingston	admn	4610
	Seth	1855	Marion	grdn	4609
	Stevens	1805	Kingston	will	4611
	Susan	1845	Abington	grdn	4573
	Susan G W	1877	Marion	grdn	4612
	Susannah	1813	Middleboro	will	4613
	Susannah	1815	Abington	grdn	4475
	Susannah	1858	Kingston	admn	4614
	Syene	1854	Middleboro	admn	4615
	Thomas	1841	Carver	admn	4616
	Timothy	1806	Carver	will	4617
	William	1764	Kingston	admn	4618
	William	1804	Carver	admn	4619
	William	1827	Rochester	grdn	4581
	William	1844	Plymouth	admn	4621
	William H	1852	Rochester	grdn	4620
	Wilson	1859	Carver	admn	4622
	Wilson	1873	Middleboro	admn	4623
	Zebedee	1859	Middleboro	admn	4624
	Zilpha	1777	Middleboro	grdn	4599
COBBETT	Charles T	1865	Marshfield	grdn	4625
	Ella M	1865	Marshfield	grdn	4625
	Ellsworth	1881	Rockland	grdn	4625 +
	Lewis	1881	Rockland	admn	4626
COCKS	John	1761	Middleboro	will	4627
	Mary	1798	Pembroke	will	4628
	William	1712	Scituate	will	4629
	William	1784	Pembroke	will	4630
CODDEMON	Solomon Jr	1745	Middleboro	grdn	4631
CODDING	Isaac	1832	Plainfield	Peti	4632
	Sally	1832	Plainfield	Peti	4632
	Samuel	1832	Plainfield	Peti	4632
CODMENT	John	1740	Middleboro	will	4633 i
	Solomon	1759	Bridgewater	will	4634 i
COE	James H	1863	Athens NY	grdn	4635
	William W	1863	Athens NY	grdn	4635
COFFIN	Joseph	1726	Nantucket	part	4636
	Thomas M	1876	Plymouth	will	4637
COGGESHALL	Gideon	1849	Middleboro	admn	4638
	Hannah P	1868	Duxbury	will	4639

SURNAME	FIRST NAME	YEAR	PLACE	CASE	DOCKET
COGGESHALL	Jeremiah	1812	Middleboro	admn	4640
COLBATH	Charles E	1877	Hingham	will	4641
COLBURN	Charles H	1880	Hingham	admn	4642
	Willis W	1880	Hingham	grdn	4643
COLBY	Elizabeth	1860	Carver	admn	4644
	Oriana	1861	Carver	grdn	4645
COLE	Albert L	1866	Lakeville	admn	4646
	Alden	1855	Lakeville	will	4647
	Ambrose	1738	Scituate	will	4648
	Ambrose	1777	Scituate	will	4649
	Amos	1729	Scituate	grdn	4650
	Andrew	1841	Middleboro	will	4651
	Andrew	1862	Middleboro	admn	4652
	Avery	1840	Abington	admn	4653
	Bartlett B	1841	Carver	grdn	4654
	Bartlett B	1869	Carver	admn	4655
	Benjamin	1727	Plympton	grdn	4658
	Benjamin	1748	Plympton	admn	4657
	Benjamin	1764	Plymouth	admn	4656
	Bethana	1859	Middleboro	will	4659
	Braddock	1799	Scituate	grdn	4718
	Bradford	1841	Carver	admn	4660
	Charles	1828	Middleboro	grdn	4681
	Charles	1840	Scituate	will	4661
	Chloe	1857	Lakeville	admn	4662
	Consider	1776	Pembroke	will	4663
	David	1760	Scituate	will	4664
	David	1806	Scituate	admn	4665
	Ebenezer	1790	Plympton	grdn	4667
	Ebenezer	1793	Carver	admn	4666
	Edward	1802	Plympton	admn	4668
	Edward	1858	Middleboro	will	4669
	Edward W	1877	Middleboro	admn	4670
	Elizabeth	1727	Plympton	grdn	4658
	Elizabeth	1729	Scituate	grdn	4650
	Elizabeth	1801	Middleboro	grdn	4671
	Ensign	1761	Scituate	admn	4672
	Ephraim	1731	Plymouth	will	4673
	Ephraim	1776	Bridgewater	will	4674
	Ephraim	1828	N. Bridgewater	will	4675
	Ephraim	1837	N. Bridgewater	will	4676
	Esther	1850	S. Scituate	will	4677
	Frank L	1876	Kingston	grdn	4678
	Frank T	1866	Lakeville	grdn	4679
	George	1783	Scituate	admn	4680
	George W	1828	Middleboro	grdn	4681
	Gridley	1799	Scituate	grdn	4718
	Gridley	1815	Scituate	admn	4682
	Hannah L	1869	Carver	grdn	4683
	Hezediah	1825	E. Bridgewater	will	4684
	Hezekiah	1797	Carver	will	4685
	Hezekiah	1843	Carver	admn	4686
	Isaac	1790	Plympton	grdn	4667
	Isaiah	1811	Middleboro	admn	4687
	James	1702	Plymouth	deed	4688
	James	1870	Kingston	admn	4689
	James	1871	Middleboro	will	4690
	Jane	1863	Plymouth	admn	4691
	Jemima	1798	Carver	admn	4692
	Job	1712	Duxbury	admn	4693
	John	1724	Plympton	will	4694
	John	1778	Plympton	will	4695
	John	1790	Plympton	grdn	4667
	John	1792	Carver	admn	4696
	John Q A	1845	Abington	grdn	4697
	Jonathan	1772	Scituate	will	4698
	Jonathan	1787	Scituate	will	4699
	Joseph	1786	Plympton	will	4700
	Joseph O	1880	Scituate	admn	4701
	Joshua	1852	Carver	will	4702
	Joshua	1860	Carver	admn	4703

SURNAME	FIRST NAME	YEAR	PLACE	CASE	DOCKET
COLE	Laura	1843	Carver	grdn	4709
	Lemuel	1858	Middleboro	admn	4704
	Levi	1864	Abington	admn	4705
	Lillie J	1875	Bridgewater	grdn	4706
	Lucy F	1850	Carver	admn	4707
	Mabel H	1875	Bridgewater	grdn	4706
	Marcia	1843	Carver	grdn	4709
	Margaret	1831	Hanson	will	4708
	Margaret	1843	Carver	grdn	4709
	Mary	1779	Middleboro	admn	4711
	Mary	1843	Carver	grdn	4709
	Mary D	1846	Hanson	grdn	4710
	Mary H	1864	Middleboro	grdn	4712
	Mehitable	1791	Scituate	will	4713
	Nathaniel	1747	Pembroke	will	4714
	Nathaniel	1779	Pembroke	grdn	4715
	Ornan	1833	N. Bridgewater	will	4716
	Phebe	1852	Plympton	admn	4717
	Rachel	1799	Scituate	grdn	4718
	Rebecca	1733	Plymouth	grdn	4729
	Rebecca	1742	Plymouth	will	4719
	Ruth	1862	Lakeville	will	4720
	Samuel	1724	Plympton	admn	4723
	Samuel	1727	Plympton	grdn	4722
	Samuel	1731	Plymouth	admn	4724
	Samuel	1733	Plymouth	grdn	4725
	Samuel	1757	Duxbury	will	4721
	Samuel	1812	Plymouth	admn	4726
	Samuel	1843	Plymouth	admn	4727
	Sarah	1733	Plymouth	grdn	4729
	Sarah	1811	Carver	will	4728
	Susan E	1852	Middleboro	will	4730
	Susannah	1727	Plympton	admn	4732
	Susannah	1865	N. Bridgewater	will	4731
	Sylvester	1856	Hanover	will	4733
	Thomas	1759	Middleboro	will	4734
	Thomas	1763	Middleboro	admn	4735
	Thomas E	1875	Kingston	admn	4736
	West	1777	Pembroke	admn	4737
	William	1738	Scituate	will	4738
	William	1790	Plympton	grdn	4667
	William	1799	Scituate	admn	4739
	William H	1864	Lakeville	admn	4740
	Zibeon	1821	N. Bridgewater	admn	4741
COLEMAN	Aurelia	1854	Lakeville	will	4742
	David	1814	Scituate	admn	4743
	David	1839	Scituate	admn	4744
	David E	1839	Scituate	grdn	4745
	Jane A	1876	Scituate	will	4746
	Joseph	1694	Scituate	admn	4747
	Joseph	1826	Scituate	admn	4748
	Joseph	1877	Scituate	will	4749
	Thomas	1737	Scituate	will	4750
COLLAMORE	Abigail	1746	Scituate	grdn	4755
	Abigail	1754	Scituate	will	4751
	Anthony	1694	Scituate	admn	4753
	Anthony	1746	Scituate	admn	4754
	Anthony	1746	Scituate	grdn	4755
	Anthony	1847	Pembroke	admn	4752
	Arabella	1848	Pembroke	grdn	4773
	Benjamin	1803	Scituate	admn	4756
	Betty	1818	Scituate	will	4757
	Caroline	1848	Pembroke	grdn	4773
	Charles	1802	Pembroke	admn	4758
	Ellen	1848	Pembroke	grdn	4773
	Enoch	1824	Scituate	will	4759
	Enoch	1839	Scituate	will	4760
	Flora	1880	Pembroke	grdn	4769 +
	George	1824	Pembroke	grdn	4762
	George	1848	Pembroke	grdn	4773
	Gilman	1823	Pembroke	will	4761

SURNAME	FIRST NAME	YEAR	PLACE	CASE	DOCKET
COLLAMORE	Gilman	1824	Pembroke	grdn	4762
	Henry	1848	Pembroke	grdn	4773
	Horace	1867	Pembroke	will	4763
	Isaac	1759	Scituate	will	4764
	John	1755	Scituate	will	4765
	John	1824	Pembroke	grdn	4762
	John	1859	S. Scituate	will	4766
	Margaret	1793	Scituate	admn	4767
	Martha	1702	Scituate	admn	4768
	Mary	1756	Scituate	will	4769
	Nancy M Tower	1880	Pembroke	grdn	4769 +
	Peter	1748	Scituate	will	4770
	Polly L	1869	S. Scituate	admn	4771
	Rachel	1878	Rockland	will	4772
	Samuel	1746	Scituate	grdn	4755
	Sarah	1848	Pembroke	grdn	4773
	Susannah	1746	Scituate	grdn	4755
	Thomas	1812	Pembroke	admn	4774
	William	1811	Pembroke	admn	4775
COLLER	G Alfred	1864	N. Bridgewater	grdn	4776
	S Edwin	1864	N. Bridgewater	grdn	4776
COLLEY	John	1748	Bridgewater	admn	4777
COLLIER	Christopher	1850	Scituate	bond	4778
	Hannah	1828	Scituate	admn	4779
	Isaac	1814	Scituate	admn	4780
	James	1850	Scituate	will	4781
	Jonathan	1817	Scituate	grdn	4782 a
	Mary L	1847	Scituate	grdn	4783
	Peleg H	1848	Scituate	admn	4784
	William	1878	S. Scituate	admn	4785
COLLINGWOOD	Charles S	1870	Plymouth	grdn	4786
	George et al	1856	Plymouth	peti	4787
	Joseph W	1863	Plymouth	admn	4788
	Nellie F	1870	Plymouth	grdn	4786
	Robert S	1856	Plymouth	grdn	4789
COLLINS	Sally	1864	Plymouth	will	4790
	Silvanus	1819	Plymouth	admn	4791
COLSON	Samuel Jr	1873	Abington	will	4792
	Winfield	1878	Abington	admn	4793
COLTRAIN	John	1761	Wareham	grdn	4794
COLWELL	Cordelia C	1867	W. Bridgewater	peti	4795
	Ebenezer	1842	Middleboro	admn	4796
	Ebenezer	1846	N. Bridgewater	admn	4797
	Elizabeth	1873	Middleboro	admn	4798
	John	1858	W. Bridgewater	will	4799
	John W	1866	W. Bridgewater	admn	4800
COMSTOCK	William W	1878	Middleboro	will	4801
CONANT	Albert	1836	Bridgewater	grdn	4802
	Andrew	1858	Bridgewater	will	4803
	Andrew	1879	Bridgewater	will	4804
	Benjamin	1825	Paxton MA	grdn	4805
	David	1793	Bridgewater	will	4807
	David Jr	1761	Bridgewater	admn	4806
	Deborah	1778	Bridgewater	grdn	4808
	Ellen L	1879	Bridgewater	admn	4809
	Ezra	1825	Paxton	grdn	4805
	Ezra	1840	Bridgewater	admn	4810
	Galen	1863	Bridgewater	will	4811
	George	1829	Marshfield	admn	4812
	Gershom	1792	Bridgewater	will	4813
	John	1816	Bridgewater	will	4814
	John	1832	Bridgewater	admn	4815
	John A	1868	E. Bridgewater	will	4817
	John A 2nd	1842	E. Bridgewater	admn	4816
	Joseph	1726	Middleboro	grdn	4818
	Josiah	1721	Middleboro	admn	4819
	Josiah	1726	Middleboro	grdn	4818
	Marshall	1873	Bridgewater	will	4820
	Mary	1825	Paxton	grdn	4805
	Nathan	1778	Bridgewater	will	4821
	Nathaniel	1745	Bridgewater	will	4823

SURNAME	FIRST NAME	YEAR	PLACE	CASE	DOCKET
CONANT	Nathaniel	1812	Bridgewater	will	4824
	Nathaniel Sr	1732	Bridgewater	will	4822
	Phineas	1798	Bridgewater	will	4825
	Prudence	1726	Middleboro	grdn	4818
	Sarah	1879	E. Bridgewater	admn	4826
	Silence	1862	Bridgewater	will	4827
	Susanna	1863	Bridgewater	will	4828
	Susannah	1726	Middleboro	grdn	4818
	Sylvanus	1778	Bridgewater	grdn	4808
	Sylvanus	1778	Middleboro	will	4829
	Thomas	1787	Bridgewater	will	4830
	Thomas	1870	Scituate	will	4831
	William	1754	Bridgewater	will	4832
	William	1827	Wareham	admn	4833
	Zenas	1829	Bridgewater	will	4834
CONDON	Samuel P	1858	E. Bridgewater	will	4835
	William	1881	Hingham	will	4836
CONNELLY	John	1862	Abington	admn	4837
	Winnie	1864	Scituate	will	4838
CONNOR	Daniel	1727	Plympton	admn	4839
CONROY	Ann	1880	Scituate	admn	4840
CONRY	Annie	1871	Abington	name	4841
	Barna	1865	Abington	will	4842
	Luke	1873	Abington	admn	4843
	Thomas	1880	Hull	admn	4844
CONVERSE	Albert D	1872	E. Bridgewater	admn	4845
CONWAY	Catherine	1870	Bridgewater	will	4846
	Daniel	1876	Brockton	will	4847
COOGAN	Alice	1857	Bridgewater	grdn	4850
	Ann	1857	Bridgewater	grdn	4850
	Edward	1876	Bridgewater	will	4848
	Mary	1857	Bridgewater	grdn	4850
	Mary A	1856	Bridgewater	admn	4849
	Patrick O'Mara	1857	Bridgewater	grdn	4850
	William Joseph	1857	Bridgewater	grdn	4850
COOK	Abigail	1752	Kingston	grdn	4897
	Amos	1762	Kingston	grdn	4851
	Asa	1869	Kingston	admn	4852
	Barnabas	1757	Marshfield	admn	4853
	Bartlett	1762	Kingston	grdn	4851
	Benjamin	1800	Kingston	admn	4855
	Benjamin	1829	Kingston	grdn	4856
	Benjamin	1880	Kingston	admn	4854
	Caleb	1724	Plymouth	admn	4858
	Caleb	1757	Kingston	admn	4859
	Caleb	1762	Kingston	will	4860
	Caleb Sr	1722	Plymouth	will	4857
	Caroline	1877	Hingham	will	4861
	Charles	1732	Kingston	grdn	4906
	Charles	1795	Plympton	grdn	4929
	Charles	1831	Scituate	admn	4862
	Christina	1853	Kingston	admn	4863
	Clarence	1857	Abington	grdn	4867
	Deborah	1857	Abington	grdn	4867
	Ebed	1860	Scituate	grdn	4865
	Edward B	1874	Lakeville	admn	4864
	Edwin	1860	Scituate	grdn	4865
	Eli	1845	Kingston	will	4866
	Eliza	1857	Abington	grdn	4867
	Elizabeth	1864	Kingston	admn	4868
	Elkanah	1839	Kingston	admn	4869
	Eunice	1851	Kingston	will	4870
	Fanny	1839	Scituate	grdn	4872
	Fanny D	1865	Kingston	admn	4871
	Francis	1732	Kingston	grdn	4906
	Francis	1746	Plympton	will	4874
	Francis Jr	1724	Plympton	admn	4873
	Frederick	1863	Abington	admn	4875
	George	1857	Abington	grdn	4867
	Hannah	1760	Kingston	admn	4876
	Hannah	1862	Kingston	will	4877

SURNAME	FIRST NAME	YEAR	PLACE	CASE	DOCKET
COOK	Hannah B	1872	Pembroke	grdn	4878
	Hannah B	1872	Pembroke	admn	4879
	Harriet	1839	Scituate	grdn	4872
	Harriet	1857	Abington	grdn	4867
	Henry	1860	Scituate	grdn	4865
	Ira	1864	Kingston	admn	4880
	Isaac	1798	Kingston	grdn	4881
	Isaac	1866	Hanson	will	4882
	Jacob	1747	Kingston	will	4883
	James	1860	Scituate	grdn	4865
	Jane	1736	Kingston	will	4884
	Jane	1879	Kingston	admn	4885
	Joanna	1837	Kingston	will	4886
	John	1741	Kingston	will	4887
	John	1744	Kingston	admn	4888
	John	1795	Plympton	grdn	4929
	John	1819	Pembroke	grdn	4889
	Josiah	1752	Kingston	grdn	4897
	Josiah	1827	Kingston	admn	4890
	Josiah	1837	Kingston	admn	4891
	Josiah	1857	Abington	grdn	4867
	Josiah	1861	Kingston	admn	4892
	Judith	1845	Scituate	will	4893
	Kingman	1861	Bridgewater	admn	4894
	Kucy	1819	Pembroke	grdn	4889
	Lucy	1859	Hanson	will	4895
	Lucy	1877	Kingston	admn	4896
	Lydia	1752	Kingston	grdn	4897
	Lydia	1753	Kingston	grdn	4902
	Lydia	1837	Kingston	admn	4891
	Margaret	1753	Kingston	grdn	4902
	Maria A	1850	Middleboro	grdn	4898
	Martin	1847	Kingston	will	4899
	Martin	1880	Kingston	admn	4900
	Mary	1829	Kingston	grdn	4856
	Molly	1753	Kingston	grdn	4902
	Molly	1857	Kingston	admn	4901
	Nathan F	1875	S. Abington	adop	4903
	Nathaniel	1732	Kingston	grdn	4906
	Nathaniel	1760	Kingston	admn	4905
	Nathaniel	1864	Abington	admn	4904
	Patience	1838	Kingston	admn	4907
	Peleg	1770	Kingston	admn	4908
	Peleg	1829	Kingston	grdn	4856
	Phebe	1816	Kingston	grdn	4909
	Randall	1871	Abington	will	4910
	Robert	1732	Kingston	grdn	4906
	Robert	1732	Kingston	will	4911
	Robert	1743	Kingston	admn	4912
	Robert	1776	Scituate	grdn	4916
	Robert	1828	Kingston	admn	4914
	Robert	1832	Scituate	admn	4917
	Robert	1844	Kingston	will	4915
	Robert	1855	Abington	admn	4918
	Robert Jr	1744	Kingston	grdn	4913
	Ruth	1725	Plympton	grdn	4919
	Sarah	1732	Kingston	grdn	4906
	Sarah	1828	Kingston	will	4920
	Sarah E	1858	Hingham	admn	4921
	Simeon	1732	Kingston	grdn	4906
	Simeon	1744	Plymouth	grdn	4922
	Susanna	1861	Bridgewater	grdn	4923
	Susannah	1725	Plympton	grdn	4919
	Sylvanus	1753	Kingston	grdn	4902
	Sylvanus	1815	Kingston	admn	4924
	William A	1852	Scituate	grdn	4925
	Zenas	1794	Plympton	admn	4926
	Zenas	1795	Plympton	grdn	4929
	Zenas	1819	Plympton	admn	4927
	Zenas	1835	Kingston	will	4928
	Zilpha	1829	Kingston	grdn	4856

SURNAME	FIRST NAME	YEAR	PLACE	CASE	DOCKET
COOMBS	Abigail C	1864	Rochester	will	4930
	Asa	1788	Middleboro	grdn	4936
	Asa	1858	Rochester	will	4931
	Benjamin	1790	Rochester	will	4932
	Benjamin	1792	Rochester	grdn	4933
	Caleb	1813	Rochester	will	4934
	Elnathan	1788	Middleboro	admn	4935
	Elnathan	1788	Middleboro	grdn	4936
	Hannah	1788	Middleboro	grdn	4936
	Hannah	1827	Rochester	admn	4937
	Ithamar	1768	Rochester	will	4938
	John B	1879	S. Abington	grdn	4939 a
COOMER	Joanna	1743	Plympton	grdn	4940
	Lois	1743	Plympton	grdn	4940
	Ruth	1743	Plympton	grdn	4940
	William	1741	Plympton	admn	4941
	William	1803	Duxbury	grdn	4942
COOPER	Arabella	1878	Duxbury	admn	4943
	Deborah	1861	Plympton	will	4944
	Experience	1813	Kingston	will	4945
	John	1755	Plymouth	admn	4946
	John	1761	Plymouth	grdn	4948
	John	1779	Plymouth	admn	4947
	Joseph	1761	Plymouth	grdn	4948
	Joseph	1763	Plymouth	admn	4949
	Joseph	1851	Plymouth	will	4951
	Joseph Jr	1830	Plymouth	admn	4950
	Nathaniel	1761	Plymouth	grdn	4948
	Nathaniel	1822	Kingston	admn	4952
	Polly	1859	Plympton	admn	4953
	Richard	1724	Plymouth	admn	4954
	Richard	1852	Plympton	admn	4955
	Sally	1827	Kingston	grdn	4956
	Thomas	1761	Plymouth	grdn	4948
	Thomas	1808	Kingston	will	4957
	William H	1866	N. Bridgewater	admn	4958
COPELAND	Abby G	1855	W. Bridgewater	will	4959
	Albert	1860	W. Bridgewater	will	4960
	Alice W	1867	W. Bridgewater	will	4961
	Amelia P	1871	Bridgewater	grdn	4984
	Anne	1874	Marion	will	4962
	Asa	1871	Bridgewater	grdn	4964
	Asa E	1871	Bridgewater	admn	4963
	Azel	1871	Bridgewater	grdn	4964
	Azel H	1865	W. Bridgewater	admn	4965
	Betsey W	1876	Brockton	admn	4966
	Caleb	1828	W. Bridgewater	admn	4967
	Caleb	1878	Brockton	will	4968
	Chester	1871	Bridgewater	grdn	4964
	Cyrus	1841	Bridgewater	admn	4969
	Cyrus	1879	Bridgewater	will	4970
	Daniel	1827	Bridgewater	will	4971
	Deborah O	1837	W. Bridgewater	grdn	4972
	Ebenezer	1810	Scituate	will	4973
	Elizabeth	1810	Scituate	grdn	4997
	Ephraim	1879	Brockton	admn	4974
	Ezra S	1873	W. Bridgewater	grdn	4975
	Ezra S	1874	W. Bridgewater	will	4976
	Hannah	1837	Scituate	will	4977
	Hannah	1877	Brockton	admn	4978
	Hulda	1810	Scituate	grdn	4997
	Jonathan	1821	Bridgewater	will	4979
	Jonathan	1837	W. Bridgewater	admn	4980
	Jonathan	1870	W. Bridgewater	will	4981
	Joseph	1793	Scituate	will	4983
	Joseph	1811	Bridgewater	will	4982
	Lestina M	1871	Bridgewater	grdn	4984
	Lucinda	1870	S. Scituate	will	4985
	Lucius	1865	W. Bridgewater	grdn	4986
	Lydia	1842	Scituate	will	4987
	Marcus	1880	Brockton	grdn	4988

SURNAME	FIRST NAME	YEAR	PLACE	CASE	DOCKET
COPELAND	Martha	1856	W. Bridgewater	admn	4989
	Mary	1871	Bridgewater	grdn	4964
	Mary H	1862	N. Bridgewater	will	4990
	Mary W	1877	W. Bridgewater	admn	4991
	Nathan	1880	W. Bridgewater	will	4992
	Rachel	1853	W. Bridgewater	grdn	4993
	Rachel A	1878	Bridgewater	will	4994
	Richard	1871	Bridgewater	grdn	4964
	Salmon	1848	W. Bridgewater	admn	4995
	Sarah	1810	Scituate	grdn	4997
	Sarah	1857	Halifax	will	4996
	Seth	1859	W. Bridgewater	will	4998
	Susan	1837	W. Bridgewater	grdn	4972
	Ward	1856	N. Bridgewater	admn	4999
	William	1838	Scituate	admn	5000
	William	1857	S. Scituate	will	5001
	William	1861	W. Bridgewater	grdn	5002
	William	1861	W. Bridgewater	admn	5003
	William H	1868	E. Bridgewater	admn	5004
CORBETT	Mary	1845	Hingham	grdn	5005
	Sarah	1845	Hingham	grdn	5006
	Thomas Jr	1843	Hingham	admn	5007
CORCORAN	Andrew	1878	Brockton	grdn	5009
	Johanna	1878	Brockton	admn	5008
	Katie	1878	Brockton	grdn	5009
	Nellie	1878	Brockton	grdn	5009
	Patrick	1878	Brockton	grdn	5009
COREY	Mary	1865	Rochester	admn	5010
CORLEW	Anna	1845	Scituate	will	5011
	Bill	1831	Scituate	admn	5012
	Daniel	1819	Scituate	grdn	5013
	Daniel	1823	Scituate	admn	5014
	Jane	1867	S. Scituate	will	5015
	John	1792	Scituate	admn	5016
	Joseph	1864	S. Scituate	admn	5017
	Noah	1792	Scituate	admn	5018
	Noah	1833	Scituate	admn	5019
CORNELL	Daniel	1779	Rochester	admn	5020
CORNISH	Bailey	1822	Plymouth	grdn	5021
	Benjamin	1781	Plymouth	admn	5022
	Benjamin	1864	Plymouth	will	5023
	Betsey	1852	Plymouth	admn	5024
	David	1826	Plymouth	admn	5025
	Deborah	1848	Halifax	admn	5026
	Elizabeth D F	1854	Plymouth	admn	5027
	Ellis	1878	Halifax	admn	5028
	Emma K	1873	Plymouth	grdn	5049
	Eunice T	1841	Middleboro	grdn	5029
	Freeman	1822	Plymouth	admn	5030
	Freeman	1873	Plymouth	grdn	5049
	Giles	1850	Plymouth	admn	5031
	Giles W	1851	Plymouth	grdn	5032
	Hannah F	1857	Middleboro	grdn	5033
	Isaiah	1864	Plymouth	will	5034
	John	1818	Plymouth	will	5035
	John	1842	Plymouth	admn	5036
	Lucy	1847	Plymouth	grdn	5037
	Lydia	1862	Plympton	will	5038
	Nathaniel	1851	Plymouth	will	5039
	Sabiah F	1870	Halifax	admn	5040
	Samuel	1730	-----	will	5041
	Samuel	1818	Plymouth	admn	5042
	Samuel	1846	Plymouth	admn	5043
	Spooner	1856	Plymouth	admn	5044
	Stephen	1866	Bridgewater	will	5045
	Thomas	1757	Bridgewater	will	5046
	Thomas	1838	Plymouth	will	5047
	Thomas	1873	Plymouth	grdn	5049
	Thomas Jr	1872	Plymouth	admn	5048
	William	1832	Middleboro	grdn	5050
	William	1841	Middleboro	will	5051

SURNAME	FIRST NAME	YEAR	PLACE	CASE	DOCKET
CORNISH	William D	1857	Middleboro	grdn	5033
CORNWALL	Louisa P	1865	N. Bridgewater	will	5052
CORTHELL	Calvin	1839	Hanover	will	5053
	Fred Loring	1880	Hingham	name	5054
	Hattie A	1872	Abington	grdn	5055
	John	1784	Scituate	will	5056
	John	1793	Scituate	admn	5057
	John	1854	Abington	will	5058
	Levi	1827	Hingham	admn	5059
	Loring	1877	Hingham	admn	5060
	Mary K	1877	Hingham	admn	5062
	Mary L	1868	Hingham	admn	5061
	Patience L	1862	Hanover	will	5063
	Theophilus	1858	Scituate	will	5064
	William P	1877	S. Abington	admn	5065
COSTELLO	Bridget	1875	Bridgewater	will	5066
	John	1873	Bridgewater	grdn	5067
	Michael	1873	Bridgewater	will	5068
	Thomas	1873	Abington	admn	5069
COTTLE	Charles E	1861	Scituate	admn	5070
	Harrison W	1877	Middleboro	admn	5071
COTTON	John	1700	Plymouth	will	5072
	John	1790	Plymouth	will	5073
	John	1803	Plymouth	admn	5074
	John	1808	Plymouth	grdn	5080
	Josiah	1756	Plymouth	will	5075
	Josiah	1819	Plymouth	will	5076
	Josiah	1829	Plymouth	admn	5077
	Lydia	1843	Plymouth	admn	5078
	Martha	1797	Plymouth	cita	5079
	Mary A	1808	Plymouth	grdn	5080
	Priscilla	1859	Plymouth	will	5082
	Priscilla 2nd	1841	Plymouth	admn	5081
	Rosseter	1837	Plymouth	will	5083
	Theophilus	1782	Plymouth	will	5084
	Thomas E S	1848	Plymouth	grdn	5086
	Thomas J	1819	Plymouth	admn	5085
COUGHLAN	Mary M	1878	Abington	admn	5088
	Patrick	1876	Hingham	admn	5089
COUGHLIN	Bartholomew	1871	E. Bridgewater	admn	5087
	Timothy	1862	E. Bridgewater	grdn	5090
COURT	Probate	1798	Plymouth	acct	5091
	Probate	1839	Plymouth	acct	5092
COURTNEY	Harriet N	1869	Plymouth	admn	5093
COVINGTON	Edwin	1835	Plymouth	grdn	5094
	Elam	1835	Plymouth	grdn	5094
	Harriet	1835	Plymouth	grdn	5094
	Harriet	1847	Plymouth	admn	5095
	Helen	1835	Plymouth	grdn	5094
	Jacob	1835	Plymouth	grdn	5094
	Jacob	1835	Plymouth	admn	5096
	Leonard	1835	Plymouth	grdn	5094
	Martha	1835	Plymouth	grdn	5094
	Martha	1865	Plymouth	admn	5098
	Martha A	1848	Plymouth	admn	5097
	Mary	1807	Plymouth	grdn	5099
	Mary	1835	Plymouth	grdn	5094
	Thomas	1825	Plymouth	admn	5100
COWDEN	Mary C	1874	Duxbury	will	5101
COWELL	William G	1879	Mattapoisett	grdn	5102
COWEN	Eliza W	1872	Rochester	name	5103
	Gathelus	1720	Scituate	grdn	5107
	Isaac B	1864	Mattapoisett	grdn	5104
	Israel	1715	Scituate	admn	5106
	Israel	1720	Scituate	grdn	5107
	Israel	1859	Rochester	admn	5105
	Jesse H	1863	Mattapoisett	admn	5108
	Job	1720	Scituate	grdn	5107
	Joseph	1720	Scituate	grdn	5107
	Josiah	1720	Scituate	grdn	5107
	Rachel	1720	Scituate	grdn	5107

SURNAME	FIRST NAME	YEAR	PLACE	CASE	DOCKET
COWEN	Robert	1863	Plymouth	grdn	5109
	Robert	1863	Plymouth	admn	5110
COWING	Abbie	1847	Rochester	grdn	5135
	Abner P	1843	Rochester	grdn	5111
	Anna	1783	Rochester	grdn	5112
	Baulch	1748	Scituate	grdn	5113
	Caleb	1777	Rochester	dowe	5114
	Hannah	1748	Scituate	will	5115
	Hannah	1828	Bridgewater	will	5116
	Henry	1855	Rochester	admn	5117
	Israel	1733	Scituate	admn	5119
	Israel	1779	Scituate	admn	5120
	Israel	1855	Rochester	will	5118
	Jane	1794	Bridgewater	will	5121
	Jeremiah H	1851	Rochester	admn	5122
	Jonathan	1842	Rochester	will	5123
	Jonathan 2nd	1847	Rochester	admn	5124
	Joseph	1781	Bridgewater	admn	5125
	Joseph	1828	Bridgewater	admn	5126
	Josiah	1760	Scituate	admn	5127
	Lot	1814	Rochester	will	5128
	Lydia	1868	Mattapoisett	admn	5129
	Mary A	1879	Duxbury	will	5130
	Phebe J	1851	Rochester	grdn	5131
	Priscilla	1847	Rochester	grdn	5135
	Robert	1719	Scituate	admn	5132
	Robert	1818	Plymouth	grdn	5133
	Samuel	1836	Rochester	admn	5134
	Sarah	1847	Rochester	grdn	5135
	Sophronia	1847	Rochester	grdn	5135
	Thomas	1726	Scituate	will	5136
	William H	1857	Rochester	name	5139
	William W	1848	Rochester	admn	5137
	William W	1849	Rochester	grdn	5138
COX	Cora	1877	Bridgewater	grdn	5147
	Daniel	1779	Middleboro	grdn	5155
	Ebenezer	1774	Middleboro	admn	5140
	Elias	1845	Plymouth	admn	5141
	Elias	1878	Plymouth	will	5142
	Elisha	1812	Middleboro	grdn	5154
	Elisha	1813	Middleboro	admn	5143
	Elisha	1873	Middleboro	admn	5144
	Elizabeth	1812	Middleboro	grdn	5154
	Ephraim	1835	Hanson	admn	5145
	Ephraim	1873	Hanson	will	5146
	Francis	1877	Bridgewater	grdn	5147
	George	1812	Middleboro	grdn	5154
	George	1875	Middleboro	admn	5149
	George A	1875	Middleboro	grdn	5148
	James	1826	Pembroke	admn	5150
	John	1770	Middleboro	admn	5151
	John	1779	Middleboro	grdn	5155
	Patience	1779	Middleboro	grdn	5155
	Patience	1854	Plymouth	admn	5152
	Priscilla	1779	Middleboro	grdn	5155
	Priscilla	1812	Middleboro	grdn	5154
	Priscilla	1847	Middleboro	admn	5153
	Ruth	1812	Middleboro	grdn	5154
	Ruth	1873	Middleboro	admn	5156
	Seth	1806	Pembroke	will	5157
	Seth	1835	Hanson	will	5158
	Timothy	1779	Middleboro	grdn	5155
	William A	1864	Middleboro	grdn	5159
	William A	1872	Middleboro	admn	5160
COY	Caroline K	1842	Bridgewater	admn	5161
	George W	1838	Bridgewater	admn	5162
COYNE	John	1869	Wareham	grdn	5164
	Julia	1869	Wareham	admn	5163
	Thomas P	1869	Wareham	grdn	5164
CRAFTS	John	1849	N. Bridgewater	will	5165
	Mary	1843	N. Bridgewater	admn	5166

SURNAME	FIRST NAME	YEAR	PLACE	CASE	DOCKET
CRAFTS	Mary S	1874	N. Bridgewater	admn	5167
	Thomas	1819	Middleboro	will	5168
CRAMPTON	Demetrius	1874	Marion	grdn	5169
CRANDON	Benjamin	1842	Plymouth	admn	5170
	James	1756	Plymouth	admn	5171
	John	1759	Plymouth	grdn	5173
	John	1766	Plymouth	grdn	5172
	Phillip	1847	Rochester	will	5174
	Phillip	1876	Middleboro	will	5175
CRANE	Amelia	1827	Bridgewater	grdn	5178
	Daniel	1827	Bridgewater	admn	5177
	Daniel	1827	Bridgewater	grdn	5178
	Daniel	1841	W. Bridgewater	admn	5176
	Frederick	1842	W. Bridgewater	grdn	5179
	Jonathan	1814	Bridgewater	will	5180
	Jonathan	1827	Bridgewater	grdn	5178
	Julia	1875	Hingham	will	5181
	Lydia	1826	Bridgewater	will	5182
	Morton E	1857	Bridgewater	admn	5183
	Sally	1875	Lakeville	admn	5184
	Samuel	1809	Bridgewater	admn	5185
CRAPO	Abner B	1853	Rochester	admn	5186
	Alice	1880	Rochester	will	5187
	Earl	1840	Rochester	admn	5188
	Harriet	1879	Bridgewater	will	5189
	Hezekiah	1795	Rochester	admn	5190
	John	1832	Rochester	will	5191
	Jonathan S	1832	Rochester	grdn	5192
	Lot	1805	Rochester	will	5193
	Nicholas	1793	Rochester	will	5194
	Nicholas	1816	Rochester	admn	5195
	Peter	1756	Rochester	will	5196
	Phillip	1865	Bridgewater	will	5197
	Phillip	1874	Rochester	will	5198
	Sally H	1856	Rochester	will	5199
CREHAN	Honora	1863	Hingham	admn	5200
	Patrick	1872	Hingham	admn	5201
CRESWELL	James	1876	Hingham	will	5202
CRIGHTON	Nathan	1876	Bridgewater	will	5203
CRIMBLE	Murney H	1748	Plymouth	admn	5204
CRIMMINS	Agnes	1881	Brockton	grdn	5206
	Dennis	1877	Brockton	will	5205
	Elizabeth	1881	Brockton	grdn	5206
	Frederick	1881	Brockton	grdn	5206
	John	1881	Brockton	grdn	5206
	Mary E	1881	Brockton	grdn	5206
	Patrick	1881	Brockton	grdn	5206
CRITTENDEN	Frederick H	1860	Wareham	admn	5207
	John S	1870	Wareham	admn	5208
CROADE	Deborah	1745	-----	peti	5209
	Ruth	1789	Halifax	will	5210
	Thomas	1773	Halifax	will	5211
CROCKER	Calvin	1854	Bridgewater	admn	5212
	Caroline H	1880	Brockton	will	5213
	Daniel	1801	Carver	admn	5214
	Daniel	1871	N. Bridgewater	admn	5215
	Eleazer	1784	Plympton	admn	5216
	Eleazer	1810	Carver	admn	5217
	Elizabeth	1873	Wareham	grdn	5229
	Emeline	1855	Bridgewater	grdn	5234
	Ensign	1869	Hanover	admn	5218
	Florintine	1855	Bridgewater	grdn	5234
	Frederick C	1873	Abington	admn	5219
	George	1873	Wareham	grdn	5229
	Hannah	1822	Carver	admn	5220
	Hannah N	1811	Carver	grdn	5221
	Harvey	1844	Barnstable	grdn	5222
	Helen	1855	Bridgewater	grdn	523[illegible]
	Heman	1801	Carver	admn	5223
	Heman	1857	Carver	will	5224
	John W	1850	Wareham	admn	5225

SURNAME	FIRST NAME	YEAR	PLACE	CASE	DOCKET
CROCKER	Nathaniel	1864	Wareham	admn	5226
	Perez	1854	N. Bridgewater	will	5227
	Rebecca	1858	Carver	admn	5228
	Samuel	1873	Wareham	grdn	5229
	Stephen	1865	Halifax	admn	5230
	Susanna	1743	Plympton	grdn	5231
	Theophilus	1734	Middleboro	admn	5232
	Timothy	1822	Wareham	admn	5233
	Volucy	1855	Bridgewater	grdn	5234
	Walton	1873	Wareham	grdn	5229
	Walton N	1872	Wareham	will	5235
	William H	1878	Halifax	admn	5236
CROMBIE	Calvin	1815	Plymouth	admn	5237
	Deborah	1806	Plymouth	grdn	5239
	Kimball	1791	Plymouth	admn	5238
	Kimball	1806	Plymouth	grdn	5239
	Nancy	1806	Plymouth	grdn	5239
	William	1806	Plymouth	grdn	5239
	William	1815	Plymouth	will	5241
	William Jr	1804	Plymouth	admn	5240
CROOKER	Abigail	1733	Pembroke	grdn	5242
	Abner	1776	Scituate	admn	5243
	Bethiah	1773	Pembroke	grdn	5244
	Charles	1835	-----	grdn	5264
	Charles H	1873	Halifax	grdn	5245
	Daniel	1693	Marshfield	admn	5246
	Daniel	1724	Pembroke	admn	5247
	Daniel	1733	Pembroke	grdn	5242
	Daniel	1773	Pembroke	will	5248
	Daniel	1818	Pembroke	will	5249
	David	1801	Pembroke	will	5249 +
	David	1812	Pembroke	admn	5249 +
	Deborah	1773	Pembroke	grdn	5244
	Elijah	1805	Pembroke	admn	5250
	Elizabeth	1733	Pembroke	grdn	5242
	Elizabeth	1805	Pembroke	grdn	5251
	Francis	1701	Marshfield	will	5252
	Hannah	1790	Pembroke	grdn	5253
	Harriet	1835	-----	grdn	5264
	Henry S	1836	Plympton	will	5254
	Isaac	1779	Pembroke	will	5255
	James	1818	Pembroke	grdn	5256
	Jeremiah	1758	Marshfield	will	5257
	Joanna	1771	Marshfield	will	5258
	John	1834	Plympton	will	5259
	John H	1836	Plymouth	grdn	5260
	Jonathan	1757	Pembroke	admn	5261
	Judith	1790	Pembroke	grdn	5253
	Lemuel	1795	Carver	will	5262
	Marcia	1805	Pembroke	grdn	5251
	Martilla	1790	Pembroke	grdn	5253
	Mary	1733	Pembroke	grdn	5242
	Melzar	1849	Pembroke	admn	5263
	Molly	1790	Pembroke	grdn	5253
	Priscilla	1835	-----	grdn	5264
	Sally	1790	Pembroke	grdn	5253
	Tilden	1773	Pembroke	grdn	5244
	Tilden	1818	Hanover	admn	5265
	Ursula B	1880	Bridgewater	will	5266
	Zenas	1827	Bridgewater	admn	5267
CROSBY	Alfred K	1848	Rochester	grdn	5268
	Harriet W	1854	Rochester	admn	5269
	John W	1874	Brockton	will	5270
	Joseph A	1868	Mattapoisett	grdn	5271
	Mary E	1857	N. Bridgewater	grdn	5272
	Mary H	1873	Mattapoisett	will	5273
	Nathan	1865	Mattapoisett	will	5274
	Nathaniel A	1868	Mattapoisett	will	5275
	Waterman	1849	Rochester	admn	5276
	William K	1854	Rochester	grdn	5277
CROSS	Catherine	1875	Mattapoisett	admn	5278

SURNAME	FIRST NAME	YEAR	PLACE	CASE	DOCKET
CROSS	Henry	1843	N. Bridgewater	grdn	5282
	Lucy	1843	N. Bridgewater	grdn	5282
	Margaret	1843	N. Bridgewater	grdn	5282
	Nathaniel	1840	E. Bridgewater	admn	5279
	Nathaniel	1843	N. Bridgewater	grdn	5282
	Nathaniel	1861	N. Bridgewater	admn	5280
	Nathaniel H	1843	N. Bridgewater	admn	5281
	Susan	1843	N. Bridgewater	grdn	5282
	William	1843	N. Bridgewater	grdn	5282
CROSSAN	John	1872	Bridgewater	admn	5283
CROSSLEY	Eliza S	1866	Marshfield	grdn	5284
	Henry T	1875	Abington	admn	5285
	John N	1876	Brockton	admn	5286
CROSSMAN	Barnabas	1744	Middleboro	admn	5287
	Barnabas	1746	Middleboro	grdn	5289
	Elisha	1746	Middleboro	grdn	5289
	Elisha	1780	Middleboro	admn	5288
	Elkanah	1746	Middleboro	grdn	5289
	Hannah	1746	Middleboro	grdn	5289
	Rufus	1838	W. Bridgewater	grdn	5290
	Theophilus	1746	Middleboro	grdn	5289
CROSSWELL	Andrew	1796	Plymouth	admn	5291
	Benjamin	1820	Bridgewater	will	5292
CROWELL	Angeline E	1859	Middleboro	will	5293
	Emma A	1854	Duxbury	admn	5294
	Francis D	1872	Marion	admn	5295
	Hannah B	1866	Wareham	will	5296
	Obed	1835	Wareham	admn	5297
CROWLEY	Thomas	1873	E. Bridgewater	grdn	5298
CRUDEN	Cornelius	1880	Brockton	will	5299
CUDWORTH	Abigail	1774	Scituate	grdn	5300
	Ann	1828	Marshfield	grdn	5303
	Benjamin	1730	Scituate	grdn	5304
	Benjamin	1828	Marshfield	admn	5302
	Benjamin	1828	Marshfield	grdn	5303
	Benjamin	1858	Lakeville	admn	5301
	David	1800	Scituate	cita	5305
	Elijah	1878	S. Scituate	admn	5306
	Elisha G	1863	Lakeville	admn	5307
	Elizabeth	1723	Scituate	grdn	5312
	Hannah	1730	Scituate	grdn	5304
	Isabella	1828	Marshfield	grdn	5303
	Isabella G	1830	Marshfield	admn	5308
	Israel	1723	Scituate	grdn	5312
	Israel	1727	Scituate	will	5311
	Israel	1741	Scituate	admn	5310
	Israel	1762	Scituate	will	5309
	James	1697	Scituate	admn	5313
	James	1781	Scituate	admn	5314
	James	1828	Marshfield	grdn	5303
	James	1853	Scituate	admn	5315
	Joanna	1730	Scituate	grdn	5304
	John	1755	Scituate	admn	5316
	John	1776	Scituate	will	5317
	John Jr	1829	Scituate	admn	5319
	John Sr	1829	Scituate	admn	5318
	Jonathan	1718	Scituate	admn	5320
	Jonathan	1730	Scituate	grdn	5304
	Jonathan	1763	Scituate	admn	5321
	Martha	1742	Scituate	grdn	5322
	Mary	1699	Scituate	will	5323
	Mary	1792	Scituate	will	5324
	Mary	1828	Marshfield	grdn	5303
	Melzar	1814	Scituate	admn	5325
	Nancy	1828	Marshfield	grdn	5303
	Nancy	1865	Marshfield	will	5326
	Nathaniel	1724	Scituate	admn	5327
	Noah	1803	Scituate	admn	5328
	Rachel	1730	Scituate	grdn	5304
	Ruth	1742	Scituate	grdn	5322
	Sarah	1768	Scituate	will	5329

SURNAME	FIRST NAME	YEAR	PLACE	CASE	DOCKET
CUDWORTH	William	----	Scituate	will	5330
	William	1828	Marshfield	grdn	5303
CUFF	Hannah	1815	Plymouth	will	5331
CULLIHAM	Owen	1736	Plymouth	admn	5332
CUMMINGS	George	1866	Lakeville	admn	5333
	Jason	1845	Middleboro	grdn	5334
	Mary	1872	Plymouth	grdn	5335
	Mary E	1872	Hull	grdn	5336
	Seth	1844	Middleboro	admn	5337
CUNDALL	Enoch	1809	Rochester	admn	5338
CUNDELL	Joseph	1820	Rochester	admn	5339
CUNNET	Isaac Jr	1748	Plymouth	admn	5340 i
CUNNINGHAM	Guilford E	1880	Plymouth	will	5341
	Jesse	1847	Plymouth	will	5342
	Phebe B	1872	Kingston	admn	5343
CURRAN	Christopher	1870	N. Bridgewater	will	5344
	Christopher	1870	N. Bridgewater	grdn	5345
	John	1868	Wareham	will	5346
	Mary Ann	1870	N. Bridgewater	grdn	5345
CURRIER	Susan E	1864	Plymouth	admn	5347
CURTIS	Abel	1793	Hanover	grdn	5349
	Abel Jr	1784	Hanover	grdn	5348
	Abner	1777	Plymouth	grdn	5351
	Abner	1799	Hanover	will	5350
	Abner	1812	Hanover	grdn	5482
	Adison	1876	Mattapoisett	1876	5400
	Alice M	1866	Middleboro	grdn	5352
	Amos	1748	Scituate	admn	5353
	Amos	1763	Hanover	grdn	5415
	Amos T	1863	Scituate	will	5354
	Ann F	1849	Hanover	grdn	5389
	Anna	1823	Hanover	will	5356
	Anna	1834	Hanover	will	5355
	Asa	1803	Scituate	grdn	5390
	Asa	1858	Scituate	will	5357
	Asa F	1881	Scituate	admn	5358
	Barnabas	1821	N. Bridgewater	will	5359
	Bela	1854	N. Bridgewater	admn	5360
	Benjamin	1727	Pembroke	admn	5361
	Benjamin	1743	Hanover	admn	5364
	Benjamin	1756	Halifax	admn	5366
	Benjamin	1757	Hanover	will	5365
	Benjamin	1763	Halifax	grdn	5367
	Benjamin	1770	Scituate	will	5362
	Benjamin	1778	Scituate	admn	5363
	Beriah	1757	Scituate	grdn	5368
	Betty	1811	Hanover	admn	5369
	Bezaleel	1792	Hanover	will	5370
	Cassandra	1875	Hanover	admn	5371
	Charles	1763	Hanover	grdn	5415
	Charles	1782	Scituate	admn	5372
	Charles E	1859	S. Scituate	admn	5373
	Christopher	1756	Scituate	grdn	5374
	David	1756	Bridgewater	admn	5375
	David	1867	Middleboro	grdn	5376
	Deborah	1763	Hanover	grdn	5415
	Deborah	1834	Hanover	will	5377
	Deborah	1836	Scituate	will	5378
	Ebenezer	1753	Hanover	admn	5379
	Ebenezer	1807	Hanover	will	5380
	Edward	1845	Hanover	will	5381
	Edwin	1865	Marshfield	admn	5382
	Eli	1777	Plymouth	grdn	5351
	Eli	1818	Scituate	will	5383
	Eli	1830	Scituate	admn	5384
	Eli Jr	1852	Scituate	admn	5385
	Elijah	1794	Scituate	will	5386
	Elijah	1829	Scituate	admn	5387
	Elisha	1726	Scituate	grdn	5414
	Elizabeth	1733	Pembroke	grdn	5440
	Elizabeth	1754	Scituate	will	5388

SURNAME	FIRST NAME	YEAR	PLACE	CASE	DOCKET
CURTIS	Elizabeth	1756	Scituate	grdn	5374
	Ellen M	1849	Hanover	grdn	5389
	Emily	1803	Scituate	grdn	5390
	Emma	1881	Brockton	will	5391
	Enoch	1756	Scituate	grdn	5374
	Enos	1812	Hanover	grdn	5482
	Experience	1842	Hanover	will	5392
	Fanny	1801	Scituate	grdn	5393
	Francis	1739	Plymouth	admn	5394
	Frederick	1795	Scituate	grdn	5395
	Gershom	1763	Hanover	grdn	5415
	Hannah	1812	Hanover	grdn	5482
	Hannah	1847	Rochester	will	5396
	Harriet	1878	Hingham	admn	5397
	Harriet F	1856	Scituate	grdn	5398
	Hette	1873	S. Scituate	will	5399
	Horace	1876	Mattapoisett	grdn	5400
	Hulda	1770	Hanover	grdn	5480
	Isaac	1867	N. Bridgewater	will	5401
	Isaac F	1867	N. Bridgewater	will	5402
	Jacob	1752	Plymouth	admn	5403
	Jacob	1873	Pembroke	admn	5404
	Jael	1784	Hanover	will	5405
	James	1767	Plymouth	will	5406
	James	1795	Scituate	grdn	5395
	James	1859	S. Scituate	admn	5407
	James	1867	Duxbury	will	5410
	James B	1863	Pembroke	will	5408
	James T	1861	Duxbury	admn	5409
	Japhet	1759	Middleboro	admn	5411
	Jesse	1726	Scituate	grdn	5414
	Jesse	1759	Hanover	admn	5412
	Jesse	1763	Hanover	grdn	5415
	Jesse	1812	Hanover	will	5413
	Job	1756	Scituate	grdn	5374
	Job	1804	Hanover	will	5416
	Job	1833	Scituate	will	5417
	Job	1880	Rockland	admn	5418
	John	1730	Scituate	will	5422
	John	1750	Hanover	will	5419
	John	1759	Scituate	admn	5423
	John	1799	Hanover	will	5420
	John	1813	Scituate	admn	5424
	John	1837	Scituate	grdn	5425
	John	1841	Scituate	will	5426
	John	1852	Hanover	admn	5421
	John	1865	Abington	admn	5427
	John B	1864	Pembroke	admn	5428
	Jonathan	1733	Pembroke	grdn	5440
	Jonathan	1763	Halifax	grdn	5367
	Joseph	1726	Scituate	admn	5431
	Joseph	1754	Hanover	will	5429
	Joseph	1759	Hanover	will	5430
	Joseph	1760	Hanover	grdn	5514
	Joseph	1834	Scituate	admn	5432
	Joseph	1835	Scituate	grdn	5473
	Joseph	1845	Scituate	will	5433
	Joseph W	1878	Hingham	grdn	5434
	Joseph W	1879	Hingham	admn	5435
	Joshua	1733	Pembroke	grdn	5440
	Joshua	1754	Hanover	grdn	5441
	Joshua	1763	Halifax	grdn	5367
	Joshua	1775	Halifax	admn	5439
	Joshua	1792	Abington	admn	5436
	Joshua	1823	Abington	admn	5437
	Joshua	1869	Abington	will	5438
	Judith	1868	N. Bridgewater	will	5442
	Keturah	1881	Hanover	admn	5443
	Lauraette	1876	Mattapoisett	grdn	5400
	Lemuel	1741	Hanover	grdn	5541
	Lemuel	1807	Hanover	will	5444

SURNAME	FIRST NAME	YEAR	PLACE	CASE	DOCKET
CURTIS	Lemuel	1842	Hanover	will	5445
	Levi	1853	Hanover	will	5446
	Loring	1812	Hanover	grdn	5482
	Lucinda	1854	Hanover	admn	5447
	Lucius	1802	Hanover	grdn	5507
	Lucy	1831	Scituate	will	5448
	Luther	1801	Hanover	grdn	5450
	Luther	1843	Hanover	admn	5451
	Luther N	1841	Scituate	admn	5449
	Lydia	1836	Hanover	will	5452
	Mabel A	1878	S. Scituate	adop	5453
	Margaret	1741	Hanover	grdn	5541
	Maria	1801	Scituate	grdn	5393
	Marietta	1874	Rockland	admn	5454
	Martha	1792	Hanover	admn	5455
	Martha	1828	Scituate	admn	5456
	Martin	1838	Scituate	admn	5457
	Martin	1841	Pembroke	admn	5458
	Martin	1848	Hanover	admn	5459
	Mary	1802	Hanover	grdn	5507
	Mary	1830	Hanover	will	5460
	Mary E	1875	Hanover	grdn	5532
	Mary R	1864	Hanover	will	5461
	Mehitable	1741	Hanover	grdn	5541
	Mehitable	1744	Scituate	admn	5462
	Melzar	1801	Hanover	will	5463
	Melzar	1836	Hanover	will	5464
	Mercy	1828	Marshfield	will	5465
	Miriam	1755	Scituate	will	5466
	Nancy	1858	N. Bridgewater	will	5467
	Nathaniel	1802	Hanover	grdn	5507
	Nathaniel	1849	Hanover	admn	5468
	Nehemiah	1770	Middleboro	grdn	5469
	Nehemiah	1795	Scituate	grdn	5395
	Nehemiah	1849	Scituate	admn	5470
	Orphan	1763	Hanover	grdn	5415
	Peleg	1726	Scituate	grdn	5414
	Peleg	1797	Scituate	will	5471
	Peleg	1835	Scituate	will	5472
	Peleg	1835	Scituate	grdn	5473
	Persis	1825	Hanover	will	5474
	Peter	1812	Hanover	grdn	5482
	Peter	1880	Rockland	admn	5475
	Polly	1862	Scituate	admn	5476
	Prince	1815	Hanover	will	5477
	Rachel B	1785	Scituate	grdn	5478
	Rachel C	1863	Hanover	will	5479
	Rebecca	1733	Pembroke	grdn	5440
	Rebecca	1770	Hanover	grdn	5480
	Rebecca	1794	Hanover	grdn	5481
	Rebecca	1812	Hanover	grdn	5482
	Reuben	1741	Hanover	grdn	5541
	Reuben	1758	Hanover	admn	5484
	Reuben	1806	Scituate	admn	5483
	Reuben	1850	Hanover	will	5486
	Reuben 2nd	1818	Hanover	admn	5485
	Richard	1693	Scituate	will	5487
	Richard	1760	Scituate	grdn	5488
	Richard	1766	Hanover	will	5489
	Robert	1858	Hanover	will	5490
	Robert	1880	E. Bridgewater	will	5491 +
	Robert S	1873	Hanover	admn	5491
	Rufus	1878	Scituate	admn	5492
	Ruth	1846	Scituate	will	5493
	Ruth	1876	S. Scituate	will	5494
	Ruth T	1865	Hanover	admn	5495
	Saba	1794	Hanover	grdn	5481
	Salina	1803	Scituate	grdn	5390
	Samuel	1742	Scituate	admn	5497
	Samuel	1746	Scituate	will	5505
	Samuel	1756	Scituate	grdn	5374

SURNAME	FIRST NAME	YEAR	PLACE	CASE	DOCKET
CURTIS	Samuel	1756	Scituate	admn	5498
	Samuel	1760	Scituate	grdn	5499
	Samuel	1794	Hanover	will	5504
	Samuel	1802	Hanover	grdn	5507
	Samuel	1803	Scituate	admn	5500
	Samuel	1826	Hanover	will	5503
	Samuel	1827	Scituate	will	5501
	Samuel	1835	Scituate	will	5502
	Samuel	1879	Marshfield	admn	5496
	Samuel Jr	1783	Hanover	will	5506
	Sarah	1740	Scituate	grdn	5508
	Sarah	1763	Hanover	grdn	5415
	Sarah	1802	Hanover	will	5510
	Sarah	1812	Hanover	grdn	5482
	Sarah	1861	Hanover	admn	5511
	Sarah	1878	Scituate	will	5509
	Selina B	1856	Scituate	grdn	5398
	Seth	1760	Hanover	grdn	5514
	Seth	1770	Hanover	grdn	5480
	Seth	1812	Hanover	grdn	5482
	Seth	1812	Scituate	will	5513
	Seth	1860	S. Scituate	admn	5512
	Shadrach B	1871	Scituate	will	5515
	Simeon	1757	Scituate	grdn	5368
	Simeon	1800	Hanover	will	5516
	Simeon	1837	E. Bridgewater	will	5517
	Snow	1758	Hanover	grdn	5518
	Snow	1824	Hanover	will	5519
	Sophia	1866	S. Scituate	will	5520
	Stephen	1758	Scituate	admn	5521
	Stephen	1832	Scituate	admn	5522
	Thankful	1726	Scituate	grdn	5414
	Thankful	1754	Hanover	grdn	5441
	Thomas	1712	Scituate	grdn	5523
	Thomas	1757	Scituate	admn	5524
	Thomas	1800	Scituate	will	5525
	Thomas	1800	Scituate	admn	5526
	Thomas W	1865	Abington	admn	5527
	William	1737	Hanover	admn	5534
	William	1741	Hanover	grdn	5541
	William	1748	Scituate	will	5528
	William	1749	Hanover	admn	5533
	William	1759	Hanover	admn	5535
	William	1768	Hanover	grdn	5536
	William	1793	Hanover	will	5537
	William	1793	Hanover	warr	5538
	William	1800	Hanover	admn	5540
	William	1811	Duxbury	admn	5529
	William	1821	Pembroke	will	5530
	William 2nd	1871	Hanover	will	5531
	William G	1794	Hanover	grdn	5481
	William G	1795	Hanover	admn	5539
	William S	1875	Hanover	grdn	5532
	Zacheus	1773	Plymouth	admn	5542
CUSHING	Abigail	1824	Scituate	will	5543
	Abigail	1830	Hingham	grdn	5777
	Abigail	1841	Hingham	grdn	5544
	Abigail B	1846	Hingham	admn	5545
	Adam	1774	Abington	admn	5546
	Adeline	1810	Hingham	grdn	5745
	Alfred	1866	Hingham	grdn	5547
	Alice	1767	Scituate	grdn	5673
	Alice	1848	Scituate	will	5548
	Allen	1862	Hingham	admn	5549
	Almira	1877	Hingham	admn	5550
	Andrew	1816	Hingham	grdn	5664
	Andrew	1830	Hingham	grdn	5777
	Anna	1837	Hanover	grdn	5584
	Anna	1859	Hanson	admn	5551
	Annie S	1880	Mattapoisett	grdn	5552
	Bela	1810	Scituate	admn	5553

SURNAME	FIRST NAME	YEAR	PLACE	CASE	DOCKET
CUSHING	Bela	1839	Hingham	will	5554
	Benjamin	1791	Pembroke	grdn	5769
	Benjamin	1792	Hanover	grdn	5557
	Benjamin	1810	Hull	will	5555
	Benjamin	1810	Hingham	grdn	5731
	Benjamin	1812	Hingham	will	5556
	Betsey	1811	Hingham	grdn	5579
	Betsey	1878	S. Scituate	will	5558
	Betty	1819	Hingham	will	5559
	Brackley	1831	Abington	admn	5560
	Brackley	1839	Abington	admn	5561
	Caleb	1767	Scituate	grdn	5673
	Caleb	1826	Hingham	will	5562
	Caleb	1829	Wareham	will	5563
	Catherine A	1874	Hingham	admn	5564
	Charles	1791	Pembroke	grdn	5769
	Charles	1829	Hingham	grdn	5569
	Charles	1837	Hanover	grdn	5584
	Charles	1843	Hanson	will	5565
	Charles	1875	Hingham	grdn	5620
	Charles S	1870	Hingham	grdn	5568
	Charles S	1871	Abington	grdn	5566
	Charles W	1828	Hingham	will	5567
	Chrisey	1804	Hingham	grdn	5570
	Christiana	1822	Hingham	will	5571
	Christopher	1820	Scituate	will	5572
	Daniel	1811	Hingham	grdn	5573
	Daniel	1826	Hingham	admn	5574
	Deborah	1816	Hingham	grdn	5664
	Deborah	1842	Hingham	will	5575
	Deborah	1845	Hingham	will	5576
	Deborah	1854	Hingham	grdn	5667
	Delia	1870	Pembroke	will	5577
	Ebed	1808	Hingham	will	5578
	Ebed	1811	Hingham	grdn	5579
	Ebenezer	1816	Hingham	admn	5580
	Edward	1827	Scituate	grdn	5583
	Edward	1837	Hanover	grdn	5584
	Edward	1842	Hanson	will	5581
	Edward	1847	Hingham	will	5582
	Elijah	1762	Pembroke	will	5585
	Elijah	1801	Kingston	admn	5587
	Elijah	1807	Pembroke	will	5586
	Elisha	1795	Rochester	will	5589
	Elisha	1829	Hingham	admn	5588
	Elizabeth	1803	Hingham	grdn	5590
	Elizabeth	1804	Hingham	admn	5591
	Elizabeth	1831	Hingham	admn	5592
	Elizabeth	1875	Hingham	will	5593
	Elnathan	1833	Scituate	admn	5594
	Elnathan H	1851	Rochester	admn	5595
	Emma	1845	Hingham	admn	5596
	Ensign	1864	Hingham	will	5597
	Ezekiel	1706/7	Scituate	grdn	5635
	Ezekiel D	1828	Hanover	admn	5598
	Ezra	1820	Abington	admn	5599
	Fanny	1804	Hingham	grdn	5570
	Fatima	1847	Hingham	grdn	5600
	Fatima	1847	Hingham	will	5601
	Francis	1822	Hingham	grdn	5602
	Francis	1832	Hingham	admn	5603
	Francis	1837	Hanover	grdn	5584
	Francis	1845	Hingham	admn	5604
	Frank	1854	Hingham	grdn	5667
	Frank E	1875	Hingham	grdn	5620
	Freddie B	1875	Hingham	grdn	5605
	George	1814	Scituate	will	5606
	George	1857	S. Scituate	will	5607
	Greenwood	1872	Abington	will	5608
	Hannah	1810	Hingham	grdn	5731
	Hannah	1827	Scituate	grdn	5609

SURNAME	FIRST NAME	YEAR	PLACE	CASE	DOCKET
CUSHING	Hannah	1834	Scituate	will	5610
	Hannah	1854	Scituate	admn	5611
	Harriet	1830	Hingham	grdn	5777
	Henrietta	1843	Hingham	grdn	5686
	Henry	1809	Hingham	admn	5614
	Henry	1810	Hingham	grdn	5745
	Henry	1862	Abington	admn	5612
	Henry	1864	Abington	grdn	5613
	Henry	1864	Hingham	will	5615
	Horatio	1792	Hanover	grdn	5557
	Horatio	1836	Hanover	admn	5616
	Hosea	1811	Hingham	grdn	5617 a
	Hosea	1837	Hingham	admn	5619
	Hosea Jr	1815	Hingham	admn	5618
	Ida	1875	Hingham	grdn	5620
	Ignatius	1706/7	Scituate	grdn	5635
	Ignatius	1767	Halifax	admn	5621
	Isaac	1815	Hingham	admn	5622
	Isaiah	1816	Hingham	will	5623
	Jacob	1814	Hingham	admn	5624
	Jacob	1868	Hingham	admn	5626
	Jacob G	1864	Hingham	admn	5625
	Jairus	1768	Duxbury	admn	5627
	James	1772	Scituate	grdn	5628
	James	1812	Scituate	will	5629
	James	1829	Hingham	grdn	5569
	Jane	1829	Hull	grdn	5633
	Jane	1830	Hull	admn	5632
	Jane	1878	Hingham	admn	5630
	Jane L	1857	Hull	admn	5631
	Jennie F	1868	Abington	grdn	5770
	Jeremiah	1706	Scituate	will	5634
	Jeremiah	1706/7	Scituate	grdn	5635
	Jerome	1824	Hingnam	will	5636
	Jerusha	1862	Hingham	will	5637
	Joanna	1816	Hingham	grdn	5664
	Joanna W	1870	Hingham	grdn	5568
	John	1736	Scituate	will	5643
	John	1778	Scituate	will	5644
	John	1798	Scituate	admn	5645
	John	1804	Hingham	grdn	5570
	John	1819	Pembroke	grdn	5638
	John	1837	Hanover	grdn	5584
	John	1837	Hanson	admn	5639
	John	1842	Abington	admn	5640
	John	1871	Hanover	admn	5641
	John Sr	1708	Scituate	will	5642
	John W	1836	Plymouth	grdn	5646
	Jonathan	1800	-----	grdn	5690
	Jonathan	1847	Hingham	will	5647
	Jonathan	1877	Bridgewater	will	5648
	Joseph	1767	Scituate	admn	5649
	Joseph	1792	Hanover	will	5650
	Joseph	1810	Hingham	will	5652
	Joseph	1829	Hingham	grdn	5569
	Joseph	1837	Hanover	grdn	5584
	Joseph	1839	Hanover	admn	5651
	Joseph	1846	Hingham	will	5653
	Joshua	1822	Duxbury	admn	5654
	Joshua	1860	Mattapoisett	will	5656
	Joshua	1876	Duxbury	will	5655
	Josiah	1794	Pembroke	will	5659
	Josiah	1819	Pembroke	will	5660
	Josiah	1881	S. Scituate	will	5657
	Josiah C	1880	Middleboro	will	5658
	Judith	1829	Hull	grdn	5633
	Judith S	1857	Hull	admn	5661
	Laban	1877	Hingham	admn	5662
	Lemuel	1780	Hanover	admn	5663
	Leonard	1816	Hingham	grdn	5664
	Loring	1856	Hingham	will	5665

SURNAME	FIRST NAME	YEAR	PLACE	CASE	DOCKET
CUSHING	Loring	1862	Hingham	admn	5666
	Lucas	1854	Hingham	grdn	5667
	Lucy	1837	Hanover	grdn	5584
	Lucy T	1814	Hingham	will	5668
	Lydia	1767	Scituate	grdn	5673
	Lydia	1791	Middleboro	will	5669
	Lydia	1837	Scituate	admn	5672
	Lydia	1843	Hingham	grdn	5686
	Lydia	1868	Kingston	adop	5670
	Lydia	1880	Hingham	admn	5671
	Lysander F	1862	Abington	will	5674
	Margaret	1857	Hingham	will	5675
	Mary	1804	Hingham	grdn	5687
	Mary	1811	Hingham	grdn	5579
	Mary	1816	Hingham	grdn	5664
	Mary	1829	Hull	grdn	5633
	Mary	1832	Hingham	admn	5682
	Mary	1837	Hanover	grdn	5584
	Mary	1843	Hingham	grdn	5686
	Mary	1857	Hull	admn	5680
	Mary	1857	Hull	will	5681
	Mary	1868	Hanover	grdn	5677
	Mary	1874	S. Scituate	will	5679
	Mary	1874	Hingham	will	5685
	Mary B	1810	Hingham	grdn	5745
	Mary B	1824	Hingham	grdn	5683
	Mary B	1843	Hingham	will	5684
	Mary S	1820	Scituate	grdn	5678
	Mary T	1847	Boston	grdn	5676
	Matthew	1803	Hingham	admn	5688
	Matthew	1820	Middleboro	admn	5689
	Morgianna	1854	Hingham	grdn	5667
	Nancy	1800	-----	grdn	5690
	Nathan	1812	Scituate	will	5691
	Nathan G	1834	Plymouth	admn	5692
	Nathan G	1836	Plymouth	grdn	5646
	Nathaniel	1789	Middleboro	will	5697
	Nathaniel	1791	Pembroke	will	5698
	Nathaniel	1795	Scituate	admn	5693
	Nathaniel	1824	Rochester	will	5701
	Nathaniel	1827	Scituate	admn	5694
	Nathaniel	1827	Hanson	grdn	5699 a
	Nathaniel	1827	Hanson	admn	5700
	Nathaniel	1841	Rochester	will	5702
	Nathaniel	1863	Scituate	admn	5695
	Nathaniel	1872	S. Scituate	admn	5696
	Ned	1863	Hingham	will	5703
	Nehemiah	1775	Pembroke	will	5706
	Nehemiah	1829	Hingham	admn	5704
	Nehemiah	1844	Boston	grdn	5707
	Nehemiah Jr	1763	Pembroke	admn	5705
	Noah	1797	Halifax	admn	5708
	Olive	1848	Hull	will	5709
	Olive	1863	Scituate	grdn	5710 a
	Oliver	1816	Hingham	grdn	5664
	Oliver	1857	Hingham	will	5711
	Oliver W	1857	Hingham	admn	5712
	Perry L	1877	SantaBarbara CA	admn	5713
	Peter	1804	Hingham	grdn	5570
	Peter	1837	Hingham	grdn	5714 a
	Pickels	1842	Scituate	will	5715
	Polly	1852	Hingham	will	5716
	Pyam	1841	Hull	will	5717
	Pyam	1866	Hingham	will	5718
	Pyam	1868	Hingham	will	5719
	Rachel	1857	Hanson	will	5720
	Rachel	1868	S. Scituate	will	5721
	Rebecca	1830	Hingham	grdn	5777
	Robert	1825	Hingham	will	5722
	Robert	1869	Hingham	admn	5723
	Robert	1870	Hingham	admn	5725

SURNAME	FIRST NAME	YEAR	PLACE	CASE	DOCKET
CUSHING	Robert F	1869	Hingham	grdn	5724
	Rowland	1840	Hingham	admn	5726
	Ruth	1830	Hull	will	5727
	Ruth	1839	Scituate	will	5728
	Ruth	1852	S. Scituate	will	5729
	Ruth	1879	S. Scituate	admn	5730
	Ruthy	1810	Hingham	grdn	5731
	Sabina L	1877	Bridgewater	admn	5732
	Sally	1850	Hingham	will	5733
	Samuel	1770	Scituate	admn	5734
	Samuel W	1873	Kingston	will	5735
	Sarah	1742	Scituate	admn	5739
	Sarah	1828	Hull	will	5736
	Sarah	1829	Hull	grdn	5633
	Sarah	1833	Abington	admn	5740
	Sarah	1845	Hingham	will	5742
	Sarah	1854	Hingham	grdn	5667
	Sarah	1857	Hull	grdn	5737 a
	Sarah	1858	Hull	admn	5738
	Sarah	1860	Hingham	admn	5743
	Sarah	1872	Hingham	will	5745 +
	Sarah C	1879	Hanover	admn	5741
	Sarah J	1810	Hingham	grdn	5745
	Sarah J	1861	Hingham	admn	5744
	Seth	1761	Plympton	will	5746
	Seth	1810	Plympton	will	5747
	Seth	1816	Hingham	grdn	5664
	Seth	1830	Hingham	grdn	5777
	Seth	1847	Hingham	will	5749
	Seth	1854	Hingham	grdn	5667
	Seth B	1854	Hingham	will	5750
	Seth Jr	1829	Hingham	admn	5748
	Silence	1829	Hingham	admn	5751
	Silent	1804	Hingham	grdn	5570
	Sophia	1866	Hingham	will	5752
	Stephen	1803	Hingham	will	5753
	Stephen	1804	Hingham	grdn	5687
	Stephen	1818	Hingham	admn	5754
	Susan	1874	Hingham	admn	5755
	Susannah	1833	Abington	admn	5756
	Sylvanus	1819	Abington	admn	5757
	Sylvanus	1870	Abington	admn	5758
	Theodore	1855	Hingham	will	5759
	Theophilus	1788	Pembroke	admn	5760
	Theophilus	1820	Hingham	will	5761
	Theophilus	1866	Hingham	will	5762
	Thomas	1783	Halifax	admn	5767
	Thomas	1791	Pembroke	grdn	5769
	Thomas	1824	Scituate	will	5766
	Thomas	1833	Hingham	admn	5763
	Thomas	1837	Hanson	admn	5768
	Thomas	1865	Hingham	will	5765
	Thomas 2nd	1858	Hingham	will	5764
	Thomas R	1868	Abington	grdn	5770
	Volney	1830	Hingham	grdn	5777
	Washington	1849	Hingham	will	5771
	Wendell	1816	Hingham	grdn	5664
	Wendell H	1858	Hingham	grdn	5772
	William	1810	Scituate	will	5773
	William	1825	Pembroke	will	5774
	William	1830	Hingham	grdn	5777
	William	1837	Hanover	grdn	5584
	William	1844	Boston	grdn	5707
	William	1848	Hingham	will	5776
	William 2nd	1835	Hingham	admn	5775
	Zattu	1768	Rochester	admn	5778
	Zeba	1854	Scituate	will	5779
CUSHMAN	Abigail	1728	Plympton	grdn	5881
	Abigail	1746	Plympton	grdn	5849
	Abigail	1832	Rochester	admn	5780
	Abner	1766	Halifax	admn	5781

SURNAME	FIRST NAME	YEAR	PLACE	CASE	DOCKET
CUSHMAN	Abner	1807	Middleboro	grdn	5783
	Abner W	1812	Middleboro	admn	5782
	Adoniram	1788	Middleboro	grdn	5867
	Albert	1872	Bridgewater	grdn	5784
	Alethea	1875	Marshfield	will	5785
	Allerton	1730	Plympton	will	5786
	Allerton	1730	Plympton	grdn	5873
	Andrew	1769	Middleboro	grdn	5879
	Andrew	1777	Middleboro	admn	5787
	Anna	1858	Duxbury	will	5788
	Bartholomew	1779	Plympton	grdn	5797
	Bartholomew	1795	Kingston	grdn	5901
	Benjamin	1813	Plympton	will	5790
	Benjamin	1833	Plympton	grdn	5791 a
	Benjamin	1842	Plympton	admn	5792
	Benjamin	1869	Duxbury	will	5789
	Betsey	1870	Duxbury	admn	5794
	Betsey C	1864	Duxbury	admn	5793
	Caleb	1777	Plympton	admn	5795
	Cephas	1808	Rochester	admn	5796
	Chipman	1779	Plympton	grdn	5797
	Consider	1767	Marshfield	grdn	5798
	Cornelia R	1871	Kingston	grdn	5799
	David	1857	Duxbury	will	5800
	Deborah	1767	Marshfield	grdn	5798
	Dennis W	1860	Middleboro	admn	5801
	Earl	1778	Middleboro	grdn	5894
	Earl	1847	Middleboro	will	5802
	Ebenezer	1793	Plympton	admn	5803
	Ebenezer	1827	Kingston	will	5804
	Edwin	1871	Kingston	will	5805
	Eleazer	1758	Plympton	will	5806
	Elias	1832	Middleboro	will	5807
	Elias	1878	Middleboro	will	5809
	Elias A	1855	Middleboro	will	5808
	Eliphalet	1805	Plymouth	admn	5810
	Elisha	1790	Kingston	admn	5811
	Elisha	1795	Kingston	grdn	5901
	Elizabeth	1717	Plymouth	grdn	5819
	Elizabeth	1832	Middleboro	grdn	5874
	Elizabeth	1871	Middleboro	admn	5812
	Elkanah	1714	Plymouth	admn	5818
	Elkanah	1717	Plymouth	grdn	5819
	Elkanah	1727	Plympton	will	5813
	Elkanah	1742	Plymouth	admn	5816
	Elkanah	1743	Plymouth	grdn	5817
	Elkanah	1857	Kingston	admn	5815
	Elkanah Jr	1787	Plympton	admn	5814
	Experience	1736	Middleboro	grdn	5836
	Ezekiel	1832	Rochester	will	5820
	Ezra	1771	Marshfield	admn	5823
	Ezra	1797	Plympton	admn	5822
	Ezra	1855	Duxbury	will	5821
	Fear	1728	Plympton	grdn	5881
	Flora E	1868	Kingston	grdn	5824
	Gardner	1816	Rochester	will	5825
	George	1788	Middleboro	grdn	5867
	George	1840	Kingston	grdn	5907
	George	1875	Duxbury	will	5826
	George	1875	Middleboro	will	5827
	Gilson	1841	Rochester	grdn	5828 a
	Hannah	1717	Plymouth	grdn	5819
	Hannah	1840	Kingston	grdn	5907
	Hannah	1875	Duxbury	admn	5830
	Hannah S	1853	Duxbury	will	5829
	Harvey	1828	Kingston	admn	5831
	Henry W	1866	Kingston	admn	5832
	Hercules	1832	Middleboro	will	5833
	Holmes	1778	Middleboro	grdn	5894
	Hulda	1746	Plympton	grdn	5849
	Ichabod	1732	Middleboro	admn	5835

SURNAME	FIRST NAME	YEAR	PLACE	CASE	DOCKET
CUSHMAN	Ichabod	1736	Middleboro	grdn	5836
	Ichabod	1778	Middleboro	admn	5834
	Isaac	1732	Plympton	will	5843
	Isaac	1736	Middleboro	grdn	5836
	Isaac	1760	Kingston	grdn	5837
	Isaac	1769	Middleboro	grdn	5879
	Isaac	1777	Middleboro	admn	5838
	Isaac	1807	Middleboro	grdn	5783
	Isaac	1820	Middleboro	admn	5839
	Isaac	1822	Carver	admn	5844
	Isaac	1832	Middleboro	will	5841
	Isaac Jr	1727	Plympton	admn	5842
	Isaac M	1828	Middleboro	admn	5840
	Isaac N	1880	Bridgewater	admn	5845
	Jabez	1786	Middleboro	admn	5846
	James	1717	Plymouth	grdn	5819
	James	1730	Plympton	grdn	5873
	James	1742	Plymouth	admn	5847
	James	1769	Kingston	grdn	5854
	James	1833	Kingston	will	5848
	Jane	1788	Middleboro	grdn	5867
	Jerusha	1746	Plympton	grdn	5849
	Joanna	1814	Middleboro	will	5850
	Joanna	1816	Plympton	will	5851
	Job	1739	Plymouth	admn	5852
	John	1769	Kingston	grdn	5854
	John	1778	Middleboro	grdn	5894
	John W	1866	Duxbury	will	5853
	Jonathan	1776	Kingston	will	5855
	Joseph	1730	Plympton	grdn	5873
	Joseph	1807	Middleboro	grdn	5783
	Joseph	1818	Middleboro	grdn	5859
	Joseph	1822	Middleboro	admn	5858
	Joseph	1864	Duxbury	admn	5857
	Joseph P	1858	Marshfield	admn	5860
	Joseph S	1796	Duxbury	admn	5856
	Joshua	1765	Marshfield	will	5861
	Joshua	1808	Rochester	grdn	5862 a
	Josiah	1750	Plympton	will	5863
	Josiah	1784	Plympton	will	5864
	Jotham	1817	Halifax	admn	5865
	Levi	1800	Wareham	admn	5866
	Lewis	1788	Middleboro	grdn	5867
	Lydia	1749	Plymouth	will	5868
	Lydia	1779	Plympton	grdn	5797
	Marcia A	1879	Marshfield	admn	5869
	Margaret	1860	Kingston	admn	5870
	Mary	1730	Plympton	grdn	5873
	Mary	1736	Middleboro	grdn	5836
	Mary	1832	Middleboro	grdn	5874
	Mary	1858	Kingston	will	5871
	Mary L	1878	Kingston	admn	5872
	Mercy	1740	Plympton	will	5875
	Miel	1767	Marshfield	grdn	5798
	Molly	1779	Plympton	grdn	5797
	Nathaniel	1728	Plympton	grdn	5881
	Nellie E	1868	Kingston	grdn	5824
	Nellie E	1877	Kingston	admn	5876
	Noah	1818	Middleboro	will	5877
	Oramelle B	1875	Brockton	grdn	5878 a
	Patience	1736	Middleboro	grdn	5836
	Patience	1769	Middleboro	grdn	5879
	Perez	1769	Middleboro	grdn	5879
	Priscilla	1728	Plympton	grdn	5881
	Priscilla	1769	Middleboro	grdn	5879
	Priscilla	1769	Middleboro	will	5880
	Rebecca	1736	Middleboro	grdn	5836
	Robert	1757	Kingston	will	5883
	Robert	1767	Marshfield	grdn	5798
	Robert	1778	Middleboro	grdn	5894
	Robert	1802	Plympton	admn	5884

SURNAME	FIRST NAME	YEAR	PLACE	CASE	DOCKET
CUSHMAN	Robert	1837	Marshfield	will	5885
	Robert Jr	1751	Kingston	will	5882
	Ruth	1776	Marshfield	grdn	5886
	Ruth	1776	Marshfield	admn	5887
	Salome	1818	Middleboro	grdn	5859
	Samuel	1786	Middleboro	admn	5888
	Samuel	1788	Middleboro	grdn	5867
	Sarah	1746	Plympton	admn	5889
	Sarah E	1832	Middleboro	grdn	5890
	Spencer	1864	Kingston	will	5891
	Stephen	1870	Carver	will	5892
	Susanna	1856	Carver	will	5893
	Susannah	1769	Middleboro	grdn	5879
	Sylvanus	1778	Middleboro	grdn	5894
	Sylvia D	1866	Kingston	admn	5895
	Thomas	1691	Plymouth	will	5896
	Thomas	1746	Plympton	grdn	5849
	Thomas	1768	Kingston	will	5900
	Thomas	1778	Plympton	admn	5898
	Thomas	1795	Kingston	grdn	5901
	Thomas	1854	Kingston	will	5899
	Thomas M	1858	Middleboro	will	5897
	Venus	1869	Middleboro	will	5902
	William	1769	Middleboro	admn	5903
	William	1785	Middleboro	grdn	5904 a
	William	1832	Middleboro	grdn	5874
	William	1840	Kingston	grdn	5907
	William	1868	Kingston	admn	5906
	William P	1872	Marshfield	will	5905
	Zebedee	1779	Plympton	grdn	5797
	Zebulon	1832	Middleboro	admn	5908
CUTBERT	Samuel	1699	Middleboro	admn	5909
CUTLER	Charles	1845	N. Bridgewater	grdn	5910
	Everett H	1845	N. Bridgewater	grdn	5910
DACEY	Timothy	1873	Hingham	will	5911
DAILEY	Lewis	1823	N. Bridgewater	admn	5912
	Rebecca	1850	N. Bridgewater	will	5913
DALEY	Thomas	1865	Hingham	admn	5914
DAMON	Abiel	1733	Scituate	grdn	5973
	Abigail	1799	Scituate	will	5915
	Abigail	1863	S. Scituate	admn	5916
	Abigail	1873	Pembroke	admn	5917
	Albert	1875	Scituate	grdn	5918
	Alexander	1828	Scituate	grdn	5919
	Alice	1859	S. Scituate	will	5920
	Amos	1733	Scituate	grdn	5973
	Amos	1859	Marshfield	will	5921
	Ann	1812	Scituate	grdn	6020
	Anna L	1782	Scituate	will	5922
	Arthur	1866	S. Scituate	grdn	5933
	Arvilla	1877	Scituate	will	5923
	Bathsheba	1733	Scituate	grdn	5973
	Bathsheba	1833	Scituate	admn	5924
	Benjamin Jr	1793	Marshfield	admn	5925
	Caleb	1857	Scituate	will	5926
	Calvin	1801	Scituate	admn	5927
	Calvin	1865	Marshfield	will	5928
	Calvin S	1878	Plymouth	will	5929
	Carrie A	1869	Scituate	grdn	5930
	Charles	1866	S. Scituate	grdn	5933
	Charles H	1866	S. Scituate	admn	5931
	Charles L	1872	S. Scituate	grdn	5932
	Cora	1875	Scituate	grdn	5918
	Daniel	1695/6	Scituate	will	5934
	Daniel	1733	Scituate	admn	5935
	Daniel	1733	Scituate	grdn	5973
	Daniel	1788	Scituate	will	5936
	Daniel	1859	S. Scituate	will	5937
	Daniel E	1859	Plymouth	oath	5938
	David	1734	Scituate	grdn	5988
	David	1760	Scituate	admn	5939

SURNAME	FIRST NAME	YEAR	PLACE	CASE	DOCKET
DAMON	David	1863	S. Scituate	grdn	5975 a
	David	1867	Abington	admn	5940
	Deborah	1817	Pembroke	grdn	5951
	Doan	1826	Scituate	admn	5941
	Ebenezer	1780	Marshfield	will	5942
	Edward	1826	Scituate	admn	5943
	Edwin W	1866	Scituate	admn	5944
	Eells	1805	Hanover	admn	5945
	Eells	1831	Hanover	will	5946
	Eleanor	1876	Hanover	will	5947
	Elijah	1810	Pembroke	admn	5949
	Elijah	1811	Pembroke	admn	5950
	Elijah	1817	Pembroke	grdn	5951
	Elijah	1872	Hanson	admn	5948
	Ernest	1872	Abington	grdn	5956
	Eugene	1872	Abington	grdn	5956
	Eunice	1834	Scituate	admn	5952
	Eunice B	1870	S. Scituate	will	5953
	Experience	1732	Scituate	admn	5955
	Experience Jr	1725	Scituate	admn	5954
	Frank	1866	S. Scituate	grdn	5933
	Frank	1872	Abington	grdn	5956
	Franklin	1872	Scituate	will	5957
	Freeman	1822	Scituate	admn	5958
	Galen	1826	Scituate	grdn	5959 a
	Galen	1829	Scituate	admn	5960
	Galen	1864	S. Scituate	admn	5961
	George B	1850	Marshfield	admn	5962
	George W	1875	Scituate	admn	5963
	Harriet T	1867	Scituate	admn	5964
	Harris	1846	Scituate	will	5965
	Hattie	1866	S. Scituate	grdn	5933
	Henry	1860	Scituate	will	5966
	Howard	1825	Scituate	admn	5967
	Howard W	1874	Abington	will	5968
	Ichabod	1731	Scituate	will	5969
	Ichabod	1760	Scituate	admn	5970
	Ichabod	1776	Scituate	will	5971
	Isaac	1733	Scituate	grdn	5973
	Isaac B	1878	Scituate	will	5972
	Isabel M	1877	Scituate	name	5974
	Jacob	1863	S. Scituate	grdn	5975 a
	James	1845	Scituate	admn	5976
	James D	1855	Scituate	admn	5977
	Jefferson	1863	S. Scituate	grdn	5975 a
	Jemina	1733	Scituate	grdn	5973
	Joanna	1734	Scituate	grdn	5988
	John	1735	Scituate	admn	5981
	John	1815	Scituate	will	5983
	John	1836	Scituate	admn	5984
	John	1837	Scituate	bond	5987 +
	John	1869	Scituate	admn	5987
	John C	1831	Scituate	grdn	5985
	John C	1845	Scituate	admn	5986
	John H	1879	Plymouth	grdn	5980
	John Jr	1794	Scituate	admn	5982
	John M	1851	Pembroke	grdn	5978 a
	John M	1855	Hanson	will	5979
	Jonathan	1734	Scituate	grdn	5988
	Joseph	1733	Scituate	grdn	5973
	Joseph	1807	Abington	will	5989
	Joseph	1870	Hanover	will	5990
	Joseph	1879	Scituate	will	5991
	Joshua	1848	Scituate	will	5992
	Joshua S	1864	Scituate	admn	5993
	Josiah	1787	Scituate	admn	5994
	Josiah	1831	Scituate	admn	5995
	Josiah	1852	Scituate	will	5996
	Judith	1878	Scituate	will	5997
	Julia	1870	S. Scituate	grdn	5998
	Lazarus B	1822	Scituate	admn	5999

SURNAME	FIRST NAME	YEAR	PLACE	CASE	DOCKET
DAMON	Lewis	1867	Bridgewater	will	6000
	Lincoln	1878	Marshfield	admn	6001
	Lucy A	1867	Bridgewater	grdn	6002
	Lucy P	1872	S. Scituate	will	6003
	Luther	1762	Scituate	grdn	6005
	Luther	1875	S. Scituate	will	6004
	Lydia	1851	Hanover	will	6007
	Lydia T J	1834	Scituate	grdn	6006
	Marcus M	1867	Scituate	admn	6008
	Martha	1734	Scituate	grdn	5988
	Martha	1870	S. Scituate	grdn	5998
	Mary	1734	Scituate	grdn	5988
	Mary	1817	Pembroke	grdn	5951
	Mehitable	1768	Scituate	will	6009
	Melzar	1822	Scituate	will	6010
	Nabby	1862	S. Scituate	admn	6011
	Nancy T	1817	Pembroke	grdn	5951
	Nathaniel	1817	Pembroke	grdn	5951
	Nathaniel	1828	Marshfield	admn	6012
	Nathaniel	1862	Pembroke	will	6014
	Nathaniel	1878	Marshfield	admn	6013
	Nellie	1866	S. Scituate	grdn	5933
	Nelson	1870	S. Scituate	grdn	5998
	Obadiah	1847	Scituate	admn	6015
	Philanda L	1784	Scituate	bond	6017
	Philenda L	1862	S. Scituate	will	6016
	Rachel	1734	Scituate	grdn	5988
	Reuben	1838	Scituate	will	6018
	Robert	1733	Scituate	grdn	5973
	Ruth	1762	Scituate	grdn	6005
	Ruth T	1856	Hingham	admn	6019
	Samuel	1812	Scituate	grdn	6020
	Seth	1726	Scituate	grdn	6024
	Simeon	1811	Scituate	admn	6021
	Stephen	1771	Scituate	grdn	6022
	Sylvanus	1836	Scituate	admn	6023
	Thankful	1726	Scituate	grdn	6024
	Willie	1875	Scituate	grdn	5918
	Zachariah	1730	Scituate	admn	6028
	Zachariah	1764	Scituate	will	6025
	Zachariah	1771	Scituate	admn	6026
	Zachariah	1773	Scituate	will	6027
	Zadock	1815	Scituate	admn	6029
DANA	Francis	1876	Wareham	will	6030
	Henry B	1878	Scituate	will	6031
DANFORTH	Allen	1872	Plymouth	will	6032
	Lydia P	1859	Plymouth	admn	6033
	Polly	1877	Plymouth	will	6034
DANIELS	Edward	1857	Plymouth	grdn	6040
	George	1858	Wareham	admn	6035
	Hannah O	1865	Pembroke	grdn	6036
	Sally	1863	Scituate	will	6037
	William	1826	Hingham	admn	6039
	William	1865	Pembroke	admn	6038
	William H	1857	Plymouth	grdn	6040
DARLING	Alanson	1822	Middleboro	grdn	6051
	Aurilla	1822	Middleboro	grdn	6051
	Benjamin	1709	Plympton	admn	6041
	Benjamin	1808	Middleboro	will	6042
	Benjamin	1822	Middleboro	grdn	6051
	Bennet	1856	Middleboro	admn	6043
	Betsey	1794	Duxbury	grdn	6061
	Betsey	1822	Middleboro	grdn	6051
	Daniel	1814	Middleboro	admn	6044
	Daniel	1822	Middleboro	grdn	6051
	David	1785	Pembroke	will	6045
	David	1876	Hanover	will	6046
	Deborah	1794	Duxbury	grdn	6061
	Eva	1873	Plymouth	grdn	6067
	Fanny E	1869	Plymouth	admn	6047
	George	1748	Middleboro	admn	6048

SURNAME	FIRST NAME	YEAR	PLACE	CASE	DOCKET	
DARLING	Grace	1879	Bridgewater	grdn	6049	
	Hannah	1822	Middleboro	grdn	6051	
	Hannah	1828	Middleboro	admn	6050	
	John	1747	Middleboro	admn	6052	
	John	1794	Duxbury	admn	6053	
	Joseph	1793	Duxbury	will	6054	
	Martha	1812	Middleboro	admn	6055	
	Melissa	1822	Middleboro	grdn	6051	
	Mina	1873	Plymouth	grdn	6067	
	Nathan	1811	Middleboro	grdn	6056	a
	Nathan	1812	Middleboro	grdn	6057	a
	Nathan	1812	Middleboro	admn	6058	
	Polly	1814	Plymouth	will	6059	
	Polly	1843	Middleboro	admn	6060	
	Rebecca	1794	Duxbury	grdn	6061	
	Rhoda	1794	Duxbury	grdn	6061	
	Samuel	1751	Pembroke	grdn	6062	
	Samuel	1805	Duxbury	grdn	6063	
	Samuel	1807	Duxbury	admn	6064	
	Thomas	1716	Middleboro	will	6065	
	Thomas	1748	Middleboro	admn	6066	
	William	1873	Plymouth	grdn	6067	
DARRY	Harriet L	1847	Hanson	grdn	6068	
	William	1846	Hanson	admn	6069	
DARWIN	Eliza	1857	Rochester	grdn	6071	
	Rebecca A	1857	Rochester	admn	6070	
	Sarah	1857	Rochester	grdn	6071	
DAVENPORT	Richard	1786	Bridgewater	will	6072	
	William R	1865	Mattapoisett	admn	6073	
DAVID	Sampson	1794	Middleboro	admn	6074	
	Stephen	1754	Titicut	deed	6075	i
DAVIDSON	Martha	1872	Bangor ME	admn	6076	
DAVIE	Betsey	1849	Plymouth	will	6077	
	Deborah	1771	Plymouth	grdn	6078	
	Hannah	1880	Plymouth	admn	6079	
	Ichabod	1848	Plymouth	will	6080	
	Isaac	1865	Plymouth	will	6081	
	Jedidah	1849	Plymouth	will	6082	
	Jerusha	1809	Plymouth	grdn	6088	
	John	1841	Plymouth	will	6083	
	Marcia T	1852	Plymouth	grdn	6084	
	Nancy	1867	Plymouth	will	6085	
	Robert	1809	Plymouth	warr	6087	
	Robert	1809	Plymouth	grdn	6088	
	Robert	1829	Plymouth	admn	6086	
	Sarah D	1868	Kingston	admn	6089	
	Sarah J	1875	Plymouth	will	6090	
	Solomon	1842	Kingston	admn	6091	
	Solomon	1843	Kingston	grdn	6092	
	Sylvester	1834	Plymouth	admn	6093	
	Thomas	1771	Plymouth	grdn	6078	
	Thomas	1771	Plymouth	admn	6094	
DAVIS	Abby	1858	Rochester	grdn	6143	
	Abby W	1867	Plymouth	grdn	6095	
	Alice	1857	Rochester	will	6096	
	Anna	1843	Rochester	will	6097	
	Annie	1858	Rochester	grdn	6143	
	Arthur	1869	Abington	grdn	6145	
	Charles G	1826	Plymouth	grdn	6111	
	Charles S	1878	Plymouth	grdn	6098	
	Cyrus W	1869	Hanover	grdn	6099	
	David J	1869	Hanover	admn	6100	
	Deborah	1830	Hingham	grdn	6103	
	Deborah	1877	Hingham	will	6101	
	Deborah L	1848	Hingham	will	6102	
	Dorcas	1721	Rochester	grdn	6104	
	Edward	1806	Kingston	admn	6105	
	Elizabeth H	1879	Bridgewater	adpt	6106	
	Elizabeth T	1831	Hingham	grdn	6107	
	Enoch	1853	Lakeville	admn	6108	
	Enoch	1878	Middleboro	admn	6109	

SURNAME	FIRST NAME	YEAR	PLACE	CASE	DOCKET
DAVIS	Frederick	1780	Pembroke	grdn	6110
	George	1869	Abington	grdn	6145
	Hannah	1826	Plymouth	grdn	6111
	Harriet	1830	Hingham	grdn	6103
	Harriet	1847	Plymouth	will	6112
	Henry	1808	Kingston	admn	6113
	Isaac	1786	Plymouth	grdn	6144
	Joanna	1871	Plymouth	admn	6114
	John	1825	Barnstable	will	6115
	John	1829	Rochester	admn	6116
	John	1831	Hingham	grdn	6107
	John	1831	Hingham	admn	6117
	John	1875	Plymouth	grdn	6118
	John C	1877	Duxbury	will	6119
	Lemuel	1847	Hingham	grdn	6120
	Lemuel	1849	Hingham	will	6121
	Marilla	1869	Abington	admn	6122
	Martha	1841	Kingston	admn	6123
	Mary	1880	Middleboro	will	6124
	Nathan	1827	Rochester	will	6125
	Nathan S	1851	Middleboro	admn	6126
	Nathaniel M	1848	Plymouth	will	6128
	Nathaniel T	1829	Hingham	admn	6127
	Nicholas	1733	Kingston	admn	6129
	Nicholas	1755	Rochester	will	6131
	Nicholas	1822	Rochester	will	6132
	Nicholas Jr	1799	Kingston	will	6130
	Peace	1721	Rochester	grdn	6104
	Rebecca	1777	Pembroke	admn	6133
	Rebecca	1826	Plymouth	grdn	6111
	Samuel	1793	Kingston	admn	6134
	Samuel	1829	Plymouth	admn	6135
	Samuel W	1856	Rochester	admn	6136
	Sarah	1826	Plymouth	grdn	6111
	Sarah	1830	Hingham	grdn	6103
	Susan	1830	Hingham	grdn	6103
	Thomas	1785	Plymouth	admn	6137
	Thomas	1808	Boston	warr	6138
	Timothy	1721	Rochester	admn	6141
	Timothy	1802	Kingston	admn	6139
	Timothy	1843	Rochester	will	6142
	Timothy	1858	Rochester	grdn	6143
	Timothy	1864	Kingston	will	6140
	Wendell	1786	Plymouth	grdn	6144
	Willard	1869	Abington	grdn	6145
	William	1826	Plymouth	admn	6147
	William	1853	Plymouth	will	6148
	William	1870	Abington	grdn	6151
	William	1872	Middleboro	will	6149
	William Frank	1873	Middleboro	adop	6150
	William Jr	1824	Plymouth	admn	6146
	William R	1875	Hingham	will	6153
	William S	1861	Hanover	admn	6152
	William T	1826	Plymouth	grdn	6111
	Zebulon R	1853	Hingham	will	6154
DAWES	Abraham	1868	Duxbury	admn	6155
	Albert	1857	Duxbury	grdn	6156
	Allen	1857	Duxbury	admn	6157
	Ambrose	1724	Duxbury	admn	6158
	Amy B	1855	Hanover	admn	6159
	Cleora	1866	Abington	will	6160
	David H	1855	Abington	admn	6161
	Ebenezer	1791	Scituate	admn	6162
	Eliza	1857	Duxbury	grdn	6156
	Jacob	1853	Abington	will	6163
	Jonathan	1751	Bridgewater	grdn	6164
	Nathan	1757	Abington	grdn	6167
	Nathan	1837	E. Bridgewater	admn	6165
	Nathan	1868	Abington	admn	6166
	Robert	1755	Bridgewater	will	6168
	Robert	1757	Abington	grdn	6167

SURNAME	FIRST NAME	YEAR	PLACE	CASE	DOCKET
DAWES	Ruel	1811	Hingham	admn	6169
	Samuel	1750	Bridgewater	admn	6170
	Samuel	1784	Duxbury	grdn	6171
	Sylvester H	1879	Rockland	will	6172
	William	1867	Hanover	will	6173
DAY	David	1871	Middleboro	grdn	6174
	George	1871	Middleboro	grdn	6174
	Herbert	1871	Middleboro	grdn	6174
	John	1871	Middleboro	grdn	6174
	Norman	1871	Middleboro	grdn	6174
DAYTON	Lucy	1831	Hingham	will	6175
	Nathaniel L	1832	Hingham	grdn	6176
DEALTRY	Charles W	1864	Middleboro	grdn	6176 +
DEAN	Abba	1871	Lakeville	grdn	6184
	Achsah	1823	Middleboro	will	6177
	Carrie L	1877	Brockton	grdn	6194
	Charles J	1864	N. Bridgewater	admn	6178
	Ebenezer	1855	Plympton	will	6180
	Ebenezer T	1843	Plympton	admn	6179
	Edmund W	1879	Middleboro	admn	6181
	Eliab	1871	Middleboro	admn	6182
	Eva	1871	Lakeville	grdn	6184
	Fanny	1819	Bridgewater	will	6183
	Frank	1871	Lakeville	grdn	6184
	Freeman	1832	Rochester	will	6185
	George Delbert	1874	Marion	name	6187
	George W	1855	Plympton	admn	6186
	Hannah	1739	Raynham	grdn	6188
	Hannah	1825	Plympton	will	6189
	Horatio B	1847	Plympton	admn	6190
	Juliet T	1857	Plymouth	grdn	6191
	Leonard	1854	Middleboro	admn	6192
	Mary	1843	Middleboro	admn	6193
	Nellie	1877	Brockton	grdn	6194
	Randall	1854	Middleboro	admn	6195
	Ruth	1857	Plympton	will	6197
	Ruth E	1872	Middleboro	admn	6196
	Sally	1866	Middleboro	admn	6198
	Samuel	1834	Scituate	will	6199
	Samuel D	1845	E. Bridgewater	admn	6200
	Sarah	1836	Plympton	admn	6201
	Silas W	1880	Middleboro	admn	6202
	Simon	1788	Bridgewater	admn	6203
	William H	1878	N. Bridgewater	admn	6204
	Winslow	1867	Plympton	will	6205
DEARBORN	Harrison	1854	Bridgewater	admn	6206
	Olive F	1856	Bridgewater	grdn	6207
	Sarah M	1864	E. Bridgewater	admn	6208
DEBLOIS	Ruth	1837	E. Bridgewater	admn	6209
DECORT	Jacob	1746	Plymouth	admn	6210
DECOST	Anthony	1764	Plymouth	admn	6211
DECROW	John	1760	Marshfield	admn	6212
	John	1761	Marshfield	warr	6213
	Martha	1761	Marshfield	warr	6213
	Martha	1761	Marshfield	grdn	6214 a
	Robert	1761	Marshfield	admn	6215
	Seth	1872	Marshfield	will	6216
	Susanna	1761	Marshfield	warr	6213
	Volentine	1697	Marshfield	admn	6217
DEERING	John	1855	Hingham	name	6218
DELANO	Abel	1799	Pembroke	admn	6219
	Abigail	1838	Pembroke	grdn	6220
	Amasa	1754	Rochester	grdn	6221
	Amasa	1760	Scituate	admn	6222
	Anna	1869	Marion	grdn	6335
	Asa	1851	Duxbury	admn	6223
	Avery	1805	Plymouth	admn	6224
	Barker	1837	Pembroke	admn	6225
	Benjamin	1748	Duxbury	grdn	6340
	Benjamin	1808	Duxbury	admn	6226
	Benjamin	1816	Scituate	will	6227

SURNAME	FIRST NAME	YEAR	PLACE	CASE	DOCKET
DELANO	Benjamin	1817	Scituate	grdn	6303
	Benjamin	1868	Kingston	admn	6230
	Benjamin	1869	Marion	grdn	6335
	Benjamin	1870	Marion	admn	6231
	Benjamin F	1851	Rochester	admn	6228
	Benjamin H	1866	Abington	admn	6229
	Benoni	1738	Duxbury	admn	6232
	Beriah	1748	Duxbury	admn	6233
	Caleb	1827	Rochester	grdn	6270
	Celia	1878	E. Bridgewater	will	6234
	Charles	1806	Duxbury	admn	6236
	Charles	1826	Rochester	admn	6235
	Charles	1856	Marion	grdn	6327
	Charles C	1856	Duxbury	grdn	6237
	Charles W	1876	Marion	grdn	6239
	Clark	1876	Marion	will	6238
	Cornelius	1801	Duxbury	admn	6240
	Cornelius	1801	Duxbury	grdn	6241
	Cynthia	1861	E. Bridgewater	will	6242
	Daniel C	1867	Pembroke	will	6243
	David	1755	Middleboro	will	6244
	David	1761	Duxbury	admn	6245
	David	1825	Duxbury	admn	6246
	Edith	1867	Abington	grdn	6251
	Edward	1817	Scituate	grdn	6303
	Elijah	1872	Abington	will	6248
	Elijah 2nd	1867	Duxbury	will	6247
	Elisha	1820	Duxbury	admn	6249
	Elisha	1879	Duxbury	will	6250
	Elizabeth	1748	Duxbury	grdn	6340
	Eva	1867	Abington	grdn	6251
	Ezra	1867	Abington	grdn	6251
	Faith	1749	Duxbury	grdn	6252
	Genella	1867	Abington	grdn	6251
	George	1801	Duxbury	grdn	6241
	George	1853	Kingston	admn	6254
	George E	1847	Duxbury	grdn	6253
	Hannah	1855	Duxbury	admn	6255
	Harper	1825	Rochester	will	6257
	Harper Jr	1819	Rochester	admn	6256
	Harvey	1860	Duxbury	admn	6258
	Hosea Jr	1847	Duxbury	admn	6259
	Ichabod	1728	Plymouth	admn	6260
	Ichabod	1748	Duxbury	grdn	6340
	Ichabod	1786	Duxbury	will	6261
	Ichabod	1831	Duxbury	admn	6262
	Isaac	1856	Marion	admn	6263
	Isaac	1856	Marion	grdn	6327
	Israel	1704	Duxbury	admn	6264
	Jabez	1768	Rochester	admn	6267
	Jabez	1770	Rochester	grdn	6268
	Jabez	1817	Rochester	admn	6266
	Jabez	1827	Rochester	grdn	6270
	Jabez	1854	Marion	admn	6265
	James	1875	Marion	admn	6269
	Jane	1827	Rochester	grdn	6270
	Jane	1838	Pembroke	grdn	6220
	Jeptha	1844	Duxbury	will	6271
	Jesse	1758	Duxbury	admn	6272
	Jesse	1875	Duxbury	admn	6273
	John	1749	Duxbury	grdn	6252
	John	1771	Pembroke	admn	6276
	John	1776	Pembroke	will	6277
	John	1825	Duxbury	admn	6274
	John P	1861	Duxbury	admn	6275
	Jonathan	1745	Rochester	will	6280
	Jonathan	1763	Duxbury	grdn	6278
	Jonathan	1765	Duxbury	will	6279
	Joseph	1770	Duxbury	will	6281
	Joshua	1750	Kingston	will	6283
	Joshua	1759	Kingston	grdn	6282

SURNAME	FIRST NAME	YEAR	PLACE	CASE	DOCKET
DELANO	Joshua	1816	Kingston	admn	6285
	Joshua	1845	Duxbury	admn	6286
	Joshua Jr	1801	Kingston	will	6284
	Laura	1838	Pembroke	grdn	6220
	Leander T	1871	Kingston	grdn	6287
	Lemuel	1748	Duxbury	grdn	6340
	Lemuel	1763	Middleboro	grdn	6288
	Lewis S	1871	Kingston	admn	6289
	Lucy	1817	Scituate	grdn	6303
	Lucy	1877	Rockland	will	6290
	Luther	1852	Plymouth	admn	6291
	Lydia	1735	Duxbury	grdn	6310
	Lydia	1819	Duxbury	admn	6294
	Lydia	1837	Rochester	will	6292
	Lydia	1856	Plymouth	admn	6293
	Lydia S	1865	Duxbury	will	6295
	Malachi	1745	Duxbury	admn	6296
	Mary	1735	Duxbury	grdn	6310
	Mary	1747	Duxbury	grdn	6298 a
	Mary	1817	Scituate	grdn	6303
	Mary	1824	Kingston	will	6297
	Mary	1829	Duxbury	admn	6299
	Mary	1846	Duxbury	will	6301
	Mary E	1872	S. Scituate	will	6302
	Mary S	1838	Duxbury	admn	6300
	Nathan	1770	Rochester	grdn	6268
	Nathan	1851	Plympton	admn	6306
	Nathan	1857	Duxbury	admn	6304
	Nathan	1862	Duxbury	admn	6305
	Nathaniel	1735	Duxbury	grdn	6310
	Nathaniel	1751	Duxbury	admn	6307
	Nathaniel	1812	Duxbury	admn	6308
	Nathaniel	1855	Duxbury	will	6309
	Otis B	1836	Duxbury	admn	6311
	Phillip	1708	Duxbury	will	6312
	Phillip	1761	Duxbury	will	6313
	Polly	1827	Rochester	grdn	6270
	Prudence	1817	Scituate	grdn	6303
	Reuben	1797	Duxbury	admn	6314
	Rufus	1867	Abington	grdn	6251
	Ruth	1852	Marion	admn	6315
	Ruth	1872	Duxbury	admn	6316
	Sally	1817	Scituate	grdn	6303
	Sally	1858	Kingston	admn	6317
	Sally	1869	Marion	grdn	6335
	Samuel	1728	Duxbury	admn	6318
	Samuel	1732	Duxbury	admn	6319
	Samuel	1739	Duxbury	will	6320
	Samuel	1814	Duxbury	will	6321
	Samuel	1861	Duxbury	will	6322
	Samuel	1873	Duxbury	admn	6323
	Sarah	1853	Marion	admn	6325
	Sarah	1856	Marion	grdn	6327
	Sarah	1861	S. Scituate	will	6324
	Sarah	1875	Marion	admn	6326
	Seth	1805	Duxbury	admn	6328
	Seth	1867	Abington	grdn	6251
	Silva	1748	Duxbury	grdn	6340
	Silvanus	1818	Duxbury	will	6329
	Sophia	1869	Marion	grdn	6335
	Stephen	1821	Rochester	will	6330
	Stephen	1827	Rochester	grdn	6270
	Stephen	1858	New Bedford	will	6331
	Susanna	1844	Duxbury	admn	6332
	Thomas	1723	Duxbury	will	6333
	Ward	1869	Marion	grdn	6335
	Ward P	1867	Marion	admn	6334
	William	1748	Duxbury	grdn	6340
	William	1798	Kingston	admn	6336
	William	1815	Scituate	admn	6337
	William	1817	Scituate	grdn	6303

SURNAME	FIRST NAME	YEAR	PLACE	CASE	DOCKET
DELANO	William	1824	Hanson	will	6338
	William	1856	Marion	grdn	6327
	William A	1854	Marion	admn	6339
	Zenas	1827	Duxbury	admn	6341
	Zerviah	1735	Duxbury	grdn	6310
DELILE	Peter	1744	(transient)	admn	6342
DELIS	Simon	1748	Scituate	will	6343
DENHAM	George	1880	Plymouth	admn	6344
	Sarah E	1874	Mattapoisett	adop	6345
DENNIHER	John	1873	Bridgewater	will	6346
DENNIS	Annie D	1866	Mattapoisett	grdn	6347
	Carrie B	1866	Mattapoisett	grdn	6347
	John S	1865	Mattapoisett	admn	6348
DENTON	Catherine	1865	Rochester	grdn	6349
DESPARD	John	1723	Plympton	will	6350
DEUEL	Hattie B	1875	Rockland	grdn	6351
	Lottie H	1875	Rockland	grdn	6351
	Thorne	1875	Abington	admn	6352
DEXTER	Abby	1841	Rochester	grdn	6431
	Albert	1872	Mattapoisett	grdn	6353 a
	Alden	1842	Rochester	grdn	6357
	Alden	1850	Rochester	admn	6356
	Alden	1869	Mattapoisett	admn	6354
	Alden D	1841	Rochester	admn	6355
	Allen	1848	Rochester	admn	6358
	Benjamin	1737	Rochester	admn	6360
	Benjamin	1755	Rochester	grdn	6364
	Benjamin	1792	Rochester	grdn	6434
	Benjamin	1842	Rochester	grdn	6357
	Benjamin	1846	Rochester	admn	6363
	Benjamin Jr	1791	Rochester	admn	6361
	Benjamin P	1828	Rochester	admn	6362
	Bethiah	1805	Rochester	grdn	6365
	Bethuel	1856	Marion	will	6366
	Caleb	1832	Rochester	grdn	6368
	Caleb	1833	Rochester	admn	6369
	Caleb	1851	Rochester	admn	6370
	Caleb Jr	1827	Rochester	admn	6367
	Catherine S	1879	Mattapoisett	will	6371
	Constant	1757	Rochester	will	6372
	David	1768	Rochester	grdn	6400
	David	1864	Middleboro	admn	6373
	Deborah	1712	Rochester	grdn	6416
	Denjamin	1734	Rochester	will	6359
	Ebenezer	1738	Rochester	grdn	6420
	Ebenezer 2nd	1854	Rochester	will	6374
	Edward	1798	Rochester	will	6375
	Elijah	1829	Rochester	will	6376
	Elisha L	1876	Mattapoisett	admn	6377
	Eliza B	1835	Rochester	grdn	6378
	Ellen	1880	Mattapoisett	admn	6379
	Elnathan	1759	Rochester	admn	6380
	Elnathan	1788	Rochester	admn	6381
	Enoch	1738	Rochester	grdn	6420
	Ephraim	1775	Rochester	will	6382
	Ephraim 2nd	1863	Mattapoisett	will	6383
	Eunice	1842	Rochester	grdn	6357
	Francis E	1856	Rochester	grdn	6384
	George	1842	Rochester	grdn	6357
	Gideon	1830	Rochester	admn	6385
	Hannah	1792	Rochester	grdn	6434
	Harper D	1821	Rochester	admn	6386
	Harvey	1854	Rochester	admn	6387
	Henry N	1856	Rochester	will	6388
	Isaac	1738	Rochester	grdn	6420
	Isaiah	1784	Rochester	admn	6389
	Jabez	1773	Rochester	will	6390
	James	1776	Rochester	will	6391
	Jane	1755	Rochester	grdn	6364
	Jane	1874	Marion	admn	6392
	Jedidah	1755	Rochester	grdn	6364

SURNAME	FIRST NAME	YEAR	PLACE	CASE	DOCKET
DEXTER	Joanna	1734	Rochester	grdn	6393
	John	1738	Rochester	grdn	6420
	John	1744	Rochester	will	6394
	John	1813	Rochester	admn	6395
	John	1814	Rochester	grdn	6417
	John 2nd	1880	Mattapoisett	will	6397
	John G	1834	Rochester	will	6396
	John G	1835	Rochester	grdn	6378
	Jonathan	1768	Rochester	grdn	6400
	Jonathan	1841	Rochester	admn	6399
	Jonathan	1860	Marion	will	6398
	Joseph	1738	Rochester	grdn	6420
	Joseph	1842	Rochester	grdn	6357
	Joseph	1875	Mattapoisett	will	6402
	Joseph B	1854	Rochester	admn	6401
	Joshua	1793	Rochester	admn	6403
	Josiah	1768	Rochester	admn	6404
	Josiah	1792	Rochester	grdn	6434
	Keziah L	1835	Rochester	grdn	6405
	Lemuel LeBaron	1876	Mattapoisett	grdn	6406
	Leonard	1867	Mattapoisett	admn	6407
	Luke	1856	Rochester	admn	6408
	Lydia	1793	Rochester	grdn	6410
	Lydia T	1861	Middleboro	will	6409
	Martha	1835	Rochester	admn	6411
	Martha M	1849	Rochester	grdn	6412
	Mary	1712	Rochester	grdn	6416
	Mary	1761	Rochester	will	6415
	Mary	1773	Rochester	will	6390
	Mary	1814	Rochester	grdn	6417
	Mary A	1869	Rochester	grdn	6414
	Mary A	1872	Mattapoisett	admn	6413
	Nancy	1793	Rochester	grdn	6410
	Nellie	1880	Mattapoisett	admn	6379
	Noah	1745	Rochester	admn	6418
	Noah	1816	Rochester	admn	6419
	Obadiah D	1835	Rochester	grdn	6405
	Peleg	1738	Rochester	grdn	6420
	Phillip	1792	Rochester	grdn	6434
	Phillip	1833	Rochester	admn	6421
	Prince	1813	Rochester	admn	6422
	Prince	1834	Rochester	grdn	6423
	Rebecca	1793	Rochester	grdn	6410
	Reuben	1846	Rochester	will	6424
	Rufus	1866	Marion	admn	6426
	Rufus A	1853	Rochester	grdn	6425 a
	Ruth	1849	Rochester	admn	6427
	Ruth	1866	Marion	grdn	6428 a
	Sabina L	1854	Hingham	will	6429
	Sally	1814	Rochester	grdn	6417
	Samuel B	1861	Mattapoisett	will	6430
	Samuel S	1841	Rochester	grdn	6431
	Seth	1734	Rochester	grdn	6393
	Seth	1792	Rochester	grdn	6434
	Seth	1793	Rochester	will	6432
	Seth	1832	Rochester	admn	6433
	Sophia M	1880	Mattapoisett	admn	6435
	Stephen	1849	Rochester	grdn	6412
	Stephen	1865	Mattapoisett	admn	6436
	Stillman	1847	Rochester	admn	6438
	Sumner	1868	Mattapoisett	admn	6439
	Thankful	1768	Rochester	grdn	6400
	Thomas	1752	Rochester	will	6440
	Thomas	1842	Rochester	grdn	6357
	Thomas	1871	Mattapoisett	will	6441
	Warren	1880	Mattapoisett	will	6442
	William B	1866	Mattapoisett	admn	6445
	William P	1850	Rochester	admn	6443
	William R	1856	Rochester	grdn	6384
	William R	1856	Rochester	grdn	6444
	Zoath	1875	Marion	will	6446

SURNAME	FIRST NAME	YEAR	PLACE	CASE	DOCKET	
DICKERMAN	Horace W	1865	Plymouth	grdn	6448	
	Ira	1834	N. Bridgewater	grdn	6447	
	Isaac W	1865	Plymouth	grdn	6448	
	Julia	1831	N. Bridgewater	grdn	6449	
	Lydia	1831	N. Bridgewater	grdn	6449	
	Lyman	1818	Bridgewater	grdn	6451	
	Manassah	1818	Bridgewater	will	6450	
	Manassah	1818	Bridgewater	grdn	6451	
	Nahum	1831	N. Bridgewater	grdn	6449	
	Oliver	1818	Bridgewater	grdn	6451	
	Rowana	1818	Bridgewater	grdn	6451	
	Samuel	1819	Plymouth	admn	6452	
	Samuel	1831	N. Bridgewater	admn	6453	
DICKSEY	John	1674	Swansey	bond	6454	
DIKE	Bela C	1837	N. Bridgewater	grdn	6455	
	Lois F	1876	Brockton	will	6456	
	Mary	1819	Plymouth	admn	6457	
	Oliver	1865	N. Bridgewater	will	6458	
	Samuel	1813	Plymouth	admn	6459	
	Samuel	1842	N. Bridgewater	will	6460	
	Samuel	1864	N. Bridgewater	will	6461	
	Simeon	1843	Plymouth	will	6462	
DILL	Daniel	1806	Hull	admn	6463	
	Henry	1836	Hull	grdn	6468	
	Mary	1857	Hull	admn	6464	
	Moses	1855	Scituate	grdn	6465	a
	Seth	1817	Scituate	admn	6466	
	Solomon	1849	Hull	admn	6467	
	Susan	1836	Hull	grdn	6468	
DILLARD	Benjamin	1857	Plymouth	admn	6469	
	Betsey	1870	Plymouth	will	6470	
DILLAWAY	Thomas	1784	Boston	grdn	6471	
DILLINGHAM	Abigail	1864	Wareham	admn	6472	
	Drusilla B	1864	Scituate	admn	6473	
	John	1761	Middleboro	grdn	6476	
	John	1769	Pembroke	will	6474	
	Paul	1761	Middleboro	admn	6475	
	Paul	1761	Middleboro	grdn	6476	
	Prudence	1761	Middleboro	grdn	6476	
	Ruth	1761	Middleboro	grdn	6476	
DIMAN	Alice	1879	Plymouth	grdn	6490	
	Annie B	1879	Plymouth	grdn	6490	
	Benjamin	1857	Plymouth	grdn	6477	a
	Charles B	1879	McClintockv' PA	grdn	6478	
	Daniel	1798	Plymouth	will	6479	
	Daniel	1848	Plymouth	grdn	6480	a
	Daniel	1856	Plymouth	admn	6481	
	David	1835	Hull	admn	6482	
	David	1842	Plymouth	admn	6483	
	David Jr	1850	Plymouth	admn	6484	
	Edward F	1879	McClintockv' PA	grdn	6478	
	Elizabeth	1807	Plymouth	will	6485	
	Jonathan	1797	Plymouth	will	6486	
	Josiah	1829	Plymouth	admn	6487	
	Judith G	1872	Holbrook	peti	6488	
	Samuel N	1830	Plymouth	grdn	6489	
	William B	1879	Plymouth	grdn	6490	
DIMMICK	Braddock	1845	Falmouth	will	6491	
DINGLEY	Abner	1807	Duxbury	admn	6492	
	Elizabeth	1718	Marshfield	will	6493	
	Esther	1807	Duxbury	grdn	6494	
	Hannah	1807	Duxbury	grdn	6494	
	Isaac	1860	Marshfield	admn	6495	
	Isaac P	1881	Marshfield	will	6496	
	Jabez	1809	Marshfield	will	6497	
	Jacob	1691	Marshfield	admn	6498	
	Jacob	1773	Duxbury	will	6499	
	John	1689/0	Marshfield	admn	6500	
	John	1764	Marshfield	will	6501	+
	John	1779	Marshfield	will	6501	
	John	1806	Marshfield	admn	6502	

SURNAME	FIRST NAME	YEAR	PLACE	CASE	DOCKET	
DINGLEY	John T	1806	Marshfield	grdn	6503	
	Joseph	1807	Duxbury	grdn	6494	
	Mary	1733	Marshfield	grdn	6504	a
	Rebecca	1818	Marshfield	will	6505	
	Ruth S	1846	Pembroke	will	6506	
	Thomas	1806	Marshfield	will	6507	
	Thomas	1831	Marshfield	admn	6508	
DINNAN	James B	1879	Brockton	will	6509	
DITMER	Valentine	1866	Kingston	admn	6510	
DIXON	Alfred E	1878	Plymouth	grdn	6511	
	Charles	1878	Plymouth	grdn	6513	
	David	1864	Plymouth	admn	6512	
	Edward L	1878	Plymouth	grdn	6513	
	Mary J	1872	Plymouth	admn	6514	+
	Ruby F	1880	Plymouth	will	6515	
	Samuel	1819	Plymouth	admn	6516	
	Thomas J	1878	Scituate	admn	6517	
DOANE	Arthur H	1880	Middleboro	grdn	6518	
	George H	1880	Middleboro	admn	6519	
	John	1805	Scituate	admn	6520	
	Lucy	1839	Scituate	admn	6521	
	Mercy A	1854	Marshfield	grdn	6522	
	Reuben H	1854	Marshfield	grdn	6522	
DOBSON	Bertha M	1878	S. Abington	adop	6523	
DODD	Harriet L	1875	W. Bridgewater	will	6524	
DODGE	Ezekiel	1770	Abington	admn	6525	
	Ezekiel	1776	Abington	grdn	6526	
	Mehitable	1776	Abington	grdn	6526	
DODSON	Mary	1695/6	Scituate	will	6527	
DOGGETT	Abigail	1784	Nova Scotia	powe	6528	
	Amos	1737	Marshfield	admn	6529	
	Elkanah	1787	Middleboro	admn	6530	
	Experience	1825	Middleboro	will	6531	
	John	1718	Marshfield	will	6532	
	John	1751	Scituate	admn	6533	
	Perez	1849	Middleboro	will	6534	
	Perez F	1875	Wareham	admn	6535	
	Samuel	1725	Marshfield	will	6536	
	Seth	1734	Plymouth	admn	6537	
	Seth	1816	Middleboro	will	6538	
	Simeon	1823	Middleboro	will	6539	
	Thomas	1692/3	Marshfield	will	6540	
	Thomas	1736	Marshfield	will	6541	
	Thomas	1788	Middleboro	will	6542	
	Thomas	1831	Middleboro	will	6543	
	Thomas	1865	Lakeville	will	6544	
DOHER	Edward	1862	S. Scituate	will	6545	
DOLAN	Patrick	1875	Hingham	admn	6546	
	Patsy	1875	Hingham	admn	6546	
DONALDSON	Christian	1860	Scituate	admn	6547	
DONNELL	Charles	1808	Hanover	grdn	6548	a
	Charles	1832	Hanover	admn	6549	
	Jane	1810	Hanover	grdn	6552	
	John	1810	Hanover	grdn	6552	
	Joseph	1785	Hanover	admn	6550	
	Samuel	1807	Hanover	admn	6551	
	Samuel	1810	Hanover	grdn	6552	
	Thomas	1810	Hanover	grdn	6552	
	Thomas B	1865	Hanover	admn	6553	
DONOHOE	Ann	1879	Brockton	admn	6554	
	Daniel T	1867	N. Bridgewater	adop	6555	
	Mary Ann	1870	N. Bridgewater	grdn	6558	
	Patrick et al	1882	Brockton	peti	6556	
	Phillip	1870	N. Bridgewater	grdn	6558	
	Sarah Ann	1880	Brockton	grdn	6557	
	Thomas	1870	N. Bridgewater	grdn	6558	
DONOVAN	Jeremiah	1860	Abington	grdn	6559	
	John	1867	Bridgewater	will	6560	
	John	1880	S. Abington	admn	6561	
	John Eddy	1880	S. Abington	grdn	6562	
	Martin	1862	New Haven CT	will	6563	

SURNAME	FIRST NAME	YEAR	PLACE	CASE	DOCKET
DONOVAN	Susanna	1873	Bridgewater	admn	6564
DORNIN	John B	1874	Rochester	will	6565
DOROTHY	Eunice	1838	Scituate	admn	6566
	John	1790	Scituate	admn	6567
DORREN	Aaron	1839	N. Bridgewater	grdn	6568 a
DOTEN	Abigail	1805	Plymouth	admn	6569
	Daniel	1853	Middleboro	will	6570
	Deborah	1808	Plymouth	grdn	6571
	Ebenezer	1786	Plympton	admn	6572
	Edward	1765	Plympton	admn	6573
	Edward	1787	Plympton	grdn	6574
	Edward	1805	Plymouth	admn	6575
	Edward	1819	Plymouth	grdn	6576 a
	Elisha	1754	Plymouth	will	6577
	Elisha	1828	Plymouth	admn	6578
	Elmer C	1879	Plymouth	grdn	6579
	Esther H	1862	Plymouth	will	6580
	Hannah	1749	Plympton	grdn	6584
	Hannah	1754	Plymouth	will	6581
	Hannah	1799	Plymouth	admn	6582
	Hannah	1805	Kingston	admn	6583
	Ichabod	1730	Plymouth	grdn	6599
	Isaac	1770	Plymouth	will	6585
	Jabez	1730	Plymouth	grdn	6586
	Jacob	1747	Plympton	admn	6587
	Jacob	1749	Plympton	grdn	6584
	Jacob	1785	Kingston	admn	6588
	James	1786	Plymouth	will	6589
	James	1817	Plymouth	will	6591
	James	1859	Plymouth	will	6592
	James Jr	1797	Plymouth	admn	6590
	Jemima	1749	Plympton	grdn	6584
	John	1747	Plympton	will	6593
	John	1749	Plympton	will	6594
	John	1797	Plymouth	grdn	6595
	Joseph	1851	Plymouth	admn	6596
	Josiah	1771	Plymouth	admn	6597
	Mary	1730	Plymouth	grdn	6599
	Mary	1861	Plymouth	will	6598
	Mary (Polly)	1808	Plymouth	grdn	6571
	Nathaniel	1750	Plympton	grdn	6600
	Nathaniel	1801	Plymouth	admn	6601
	Neviah	1730	Plymouth	grdn	6586
	Neviah	1738	Plymouth	will	6602
	Peter B	1852	Plymouth	grdn	6603 a
	Prince	1870	Plymouth	admn	6604
	Priscilla A	1853	Plymouth	grdn	6605
	Rebecca	1730	Plymouth	grdn	6599
	Samuel	1861	Plymouth	admn	6609
	Samuel 2nd	1850	Plymouth	admn	6607
	Samuel H	1856	Plymouth	oath	6608
	Samuel Jr	1763	Plymouth	admn	6606
	Sarah	1749	Plympton	grdn	6584
	Stephen	1802	Plymouth	admn	6610
	Stephen	1831	Plymouth	will	6611
	Stephen	1861	Plymouth	will	6612
	Susan	1853	Plymouth	admn	6613
	Susanna	1804	Plymouth	grdn	6614
	William	1813	Plymouth	will	6615
	William W	1855	Plymouth	admn	6616
	Zephaniah	1749	Plympton	grdn	6584
DOTY	Albert	1874	Wareham	will	6617
	Barnabas	1759	Rochester	admn	6618
	Benjamin	1695	Plymouth	grdn	6630
	Bethiah	1826	Wareham	grdn	6628
	Calvin	1826	Wareham	grdn	6628
	Cyrus	1826	Wareham	grdn	6628
	Desire	1701	Plymouth	grdn	6626
	Edward	1689	Plymouth	admn	6619
	Edward Jr	1776	Rochester	admn	6620
	Elisha	1701	Plymouth	grdn	6626

SURNAME	FIRST NAME	YEAR	PLACE	CASE	DOCKET
DOTY	Isaac	1724	Plymouth	admn	6621
	Isaac	1740	Wareham	admn	6622
	John	1701	Plymouth	will	6623
	Joseph	1734	Rochester	peti	6624
	Joseph	1850	Rochester	admn	6625
	Josiah	1701	Plymouth	grdn	6626
	Martha	1701	Plymouth	grdn	6626
	Mercy	1695	Plymouth	grdn	6630
	Nathaniel	1820	Wareham	admn	6627
	Nathaniel	1826	Wareham	grdn	6628
	Parnam	1826	Wareham	grdn	6628
	Samuel	1695	Plymouth	grdn	6630
	Samuel	1701	Plymouth	grdn	6626
	Samuel	1740	Plymouth	admn	6629
	Thomas	1721	Cape Cod	admn	6631
	Thomas	1721	-----	grdn	6632
DOUGLASS	Baker L	1843	Middleboro	admn	6633
	Eliza	1838	E. Bridgewater	grdn	6634
	Emma E	1880	Rochester	admn	6635
	George	1843	Rochester	admn	6636
	George	1859	E. Bridgewater	admn	6637
	Hannah	1838	E. Bridgewater	grdn	6634
	John	1776	Middleboro	will	6638
	John Jr	1819	Plymouth	admn	6639
	Joshua	1879	Plymouth	admn	6640
	Mary	1853	Plymouth	will	6641
	William	1851	Plymouth	admn	6642
DOW	Alexander	1747	Plymouth	admn	6643
	Alexander	1755	Plymouth	grdn	6644
DOWNEY	Benjamin	1869	Abington	grdn	6647
	Dennis	1869	Abington	admn	6645
	Dennis	1869	Abington	grdn	6647
	James	1872	Abington	grdn	6646
	John	1869	Abington	grdn	6647
	Margaret	1872	Abington	grdn	6646
	Mary	1869	Abington	grdn	6647
	William	1869	Abington	grdn	6647
DOYLE	Thomas	1856	Pembroke	admn	6648
DRAKE	Aaron B	1868	N. Bridgewater	will	6649
	Abby	1862	N. Bridgewater	grdn	6657
	Alvin	1868	Rochester	will	6650
	Amelia	1849	Middleboro	admn	6651
	Beza L	1845	Scituate	admn	6652
	Ebenezer F	1861	Pembroke	admn	6653
	Edith	1869	Hanson	grdn	6664
	Elizabeth	1865	S. Scituate	admn	6654
	Enoch	1866	Middleboro	admn	6655
	Enos	1868	Middleboro	will	6656
	Frank	1862	N. Bridgewater	grdn	6657
	Jane B	1871	N. Bridgewater	will	6658
	Joseph	1769	Middleboro	admn	6659
	Lewis A	1873	N. Bridgewater	grdn	6660
	Margaret	1876	Brockton	grdn	6661 a
	Mary E	1868	Rochester	grdn	6662
	Peter	1759	Bridgewater	admn	6663
	Samuel	1869	Hanson	grdn	6664
	Stafford	1876	Brockton	grdn	6665 a
	Stafford	1876	Brockton	will	6666
	Thomas	1869	Hanson	grdn	6664
	Timothy	1869	Hanson	grdn	6664
	Timothy	1879	E. Bridgewater	will	6667
	Urana W	1859	Pembroke	admn	6668
	Ursula	1861	Pembroke	admn	6669
	William	1862	N. Bridgewater	grdn	6657
	William Jr	1851	Middleboro	admn	6671
	William Sr	1849	Middleboro	will	6670
DRAYTON	Daniel W	1860	Hanson & Maine	grdn	6672
	Florinda	1860	Hanson & Maine	grdn	6672
	George	1860	Hanson & Maine	grdn	6672
DREW	Abijah	1819	Hingham	admn	6673
	Adeline	1879	Plymouth	admn	6674

SURNAME	FIRST NAME	YEAR	PLACE	CASE	DOCKET
DREW	Atwood	1823	Plymouth	will	6675
	Atwood	1827	Plymouth	grdn	6691
	Atwood L	1878	Plymouth	admn	6676
	Austin	1855	Plymouth	grdn	6685
	Benjamin	1821	Plymouth	admn	6677
	Betsey L	1792	Plymouth	grdn	6678
	Caleb	1795	Plymouth	grdn	6679
	Charles	1842	Duxbury	grdn	6681
	Charles	1855	Plymouth	grdn	6685
	Charles Jr	1836	Duxbury	admn	6680
	Clara	1842	Duxbury	grdn	6681
	Clark	1797	Duxbury	admn	6682
	Clement	1798	Kingston	admn	6683
	Cornelius	1815	Kingston	will	6684
	David	1855	Plymouth	grdn	6685
	Ebenezer	1831	Kingston	will	6686
	Ebenezer	1853	Plymouth	admn	6687
	Eliza	1827	Plymouth	grdn	6691
	Florence	1855	Plymouth	grdn	6685
	George	1827	Plymouth	grdn	6691
	George	1844	Plymouth	admn	6689
	George	1866	Halifax	admn	6688
	George H	1830	Plymouth	grdn	6690 a
	Hannah	1832	Kingston	will	6692
	Harrison	1855	Plymouth	grdn	6685
	Henry J	1873	Plymouth	grdn	6721
	Isaac	1844	Plymouth	admn	6693
	James	1738	Plymouth	grdn	6712
	James	1788	Plymouth	admn	6695
	James	1800	Kingston	grdn	6697
	James	1807	Kingston	admn	6696
	James	1826	Middleboro	will	6694
	Joanna	1733	Plymouth	grdn	6718
	Job	1833	Halifax	will	6698
	Job W	1869	Kingston	will	6699
	John	1721	Plymouth	admn	6700
	John	1745	Halifax	will	6701
	John	1877	Kingston	will	6702
	Joseph	1808	Duxbury	admn	6703
	Joshua	1748	Plymouth	admn	6704
	Joshua	1799	Duxbury	grdn	6705
	Joshua	1863	Duxbury	will	6706
	Josiah	1741	Plymouth	admn	6707
	Josiah	1827	Plymouth	grdn	6691
	Josiah	1854	Plymouth	admn	6708
	Katie Louisa	1874	Duxbury	adop	6709
	Lemuel	1738	Plymouth	admn	6710
	Lemuel	1738	Plymouth	grdn	6712
	Lemuel	1755	Plymouth	admn	6711
	Levi	1749	Plymouth	grdn	6713
	Lewis	1823	Duxbury	admn	6714
	Lucinda	1862	Plymouth	admn	6715
	Lucy	1799	Duxbury	grdn	6746
	Lucy	1870	Duxbury	will	6716
	Lydia	1733	Plymouth	grdn	6718
	Lydia	1827	Plymouth	grdn	6691
	Lydia	1861	Plymouth	will	6717
	Malachi	1853	Plymouth	admn	6719
	Mary	1868	Kingston	admn	6720
	Mary C	1873	Plymouth	grdn	6721
	Mercy	1807	Plymouth	will	6722
	Nathaniel D	1879	Kingston	admn	6723
	Nehemiah	1813	Kingston	admn	6724
	Nicholas	1734	Plymouth	admn	6725
	Nicholas H	1848	Plymouth	will	6727
	Nicholas Jr	1777	Plymouth	admn	6726
	Rebecca	1733	Plymouth	grdn	6718
	Saba	1800	Kingston	grdn	6697
	Sally	1829	Plymouth	admn	6728
	Sally	1855	Plymouth	grdn	6685
	Samuel	1824	Plymouth	admn	6729

SURNAME	FIRST NAME	YEAR	PLACE	CASE	DOCKET
DREW	Sarah	1738	Plymouth	grdn	6712
	Sarah	1852	Middleboro	will	6730
	Seth	1740	Plymouth	admn	6731
	Seth	1824	Kingston	will	6732
	Seth	1854	Kingston	will	6733
	Sophia	1859	Plymouth	admn	6734
	Spencer	1813	Duxbury	grdn	6735 a
	Stephen	1835	Kingston	will	6736
	Susan H	1872	Plymouth	admn	6737
	Sylvanus	1829	Duxbury	will	6738
	Sylvia	1837	Kingston	will	6739
	Thankful D	1841	Kingston	will	6740
	Thomas	1770	Halifax	admn	6741
	Thomas	1861	Halifax	will	6742
	Viana	1842	Duxbury	grdn	6681
	Wallace	1842	Duxbury	grdn	6681
	Wealthy	1799	Duxbury	grdn	6746
	William	1738	Plymouth	grdn	6712
	William	1795	Kingston	will	6743
	William	1827	Plymouth	grdn	6691
	William	1840	Plymouth	admn	6744
	William T	1861	Plymouth	will	6745
	Zilpha	1799	Duxbury	grdn	6746
DRINKWATER	Thomas	1715	Taunton	admn	6747
DUGGAN	Michael	1852	Abington	will	6748
DUNBAR	Abel	1781	Bridgewater	grdn	6819
	Albert	1879	W. Bridgewater	grdn	6761
	Alice	1879	W. Bridgewater	grdn	6761
	Alice Ann	1880	Plymouth	will	6749
	Asa	1856	W. Bridgewater	admn	6750
	Asaph	1868	Abington	will	6751
	Atlanta	1858	E. Bridgewater	grdn	6783
	Atwood L	1875	Scituate	grdn	6752 a
	Azuba	1817	Bridgewater	will	6754
	Barnabas	1817	Bridgewater	will	6755
	Benjamin	1782	Halifax	grdn	6757
	Benjamin	1810	Hingham	grdn	6756 a
	Betsey	1866	N. Bridgewater	admn	6759
	Betsey M	1847	N. Bridgewater	admn	6758
	Bradford	1844	N. Bridgewater	will	6760
	Caroline	1856	Hingham	grdn	6799
	Channing	1879	W. Bridgewater	grdn	6761
	Charles	1848	N. Bridgewater	admn	6763
	Charles A	1874	N. Bridgewater	admn	6765
	Charles F	1810	Bridgewater	grdn	6762
	Charles H	1849	N. Bridgewater	grdn	6764
	Clara	1868	N. Bridgewater	grdn	6822
	Daniel	1777	Halifax	abse	6766
	Daniel	1870	W. Bridgewater	will	6767
	David	1725	Bridgewater	grdn	6794
	David	1781	Bridgewater	warr	6768
	David	1826	Hingham	admn	6769
	Davis R	1846	N. Bridgewater	will	6770
	Dinah	1869	Bridgewater	will	6771
	Ebenezer	1826	N. Bridgewater	will	6772
	Edwin	1843	N. Bridgewater	admn	6773
	Elias	1824	Bridgewater	admn	6774
	Elisha	1773	Bridgewater	will	6775
	Eliza	1856	Scituate	grdn	6776 a
	Enoch	1862	Hingham	will	6777
	Etta C	1879	S. Abington	grdn	6778
	Francis B	1834	N. Bridgewater	will	6779
	George B	1875	Brockton	admn	6781
	George L	1866	E. Bridgewater	admn	6780
	Grace	1879	W. Bridgewater	grdn	6761
	Harriet	1875	Hingham	admn	6782
	Horace	1858	E. Bridgewater	grdn	6783
	Hosea	1782	Halifax	grdn	6757
	Hosea	1789	Halifax	admn	6785
	Hosea	1794	Halifax	grdn	6825
	Hosea	1873	Hingham	admn	6784

SURNAME	FIRST NAME	YEAR	PLACE	CASE	DOCKET
DUNBAR	Jacob	1827	N. Bridgeer	admn	6786
	Jacob	1859	Hingham	will	6787
	James	1690	Bridgewater	admn	6788
	Jennet	1830	Halifax	will	6789
	Jesse	1816	Bridgewater	admn	6790
	Jesse	1836	Scituate	will	6792
	Jesse Jr	1830	Scituate	admn	6791
	John	1725	Bridgewater	grdn	6794
	John	1794	Halifax	grdn	6825
	John D	1810	Plymouth	admn	6793
	Joseph	1782	Halifax	will	6795
	Josiah	1862	N. Bridgewater	will	6796
	Julia	1868	N. Bridgewater	grdn	6822
	Louisa	1868	N. Bridgewater	grdn	6822
	Lydia	1843	Bridgewater	will	6797
	Martin V B	1879	W. Bridgewater	admn	6798
	Mary	1856	Hingham	grdn	6799
	Mercy	1781	Bridgewater	grdn	6819
	Nancy	1794	Halifax	grdn	6825
	Olive	1783	Bridgewater	grdn	6800
	Peter	1720	Bridgewater	admn	6801
	Phebe	1786	Bridgewater	admn	6802
	Sally P	1821	Hingham	grdn	6803
	Sally P	1846	Hingham	will	6804
	Salmon	1863	E. Bridgewater	will	6805
	Samuel	1786	Bridgewater	will	6806
	Samuel	1856	Hingham	grdn	6799
	Samuel	1866	N. Bridgewater	will	6808
	Samuel Jr	1853	Hingham	admn	6807
	Sarah	1839	Scituate	admn	6809
	Sarah	1863	W. Bridgewater	will	6810
	Sarah	1864	Hingham	will	6811
	Sarah H	1881	Brockton	will	6812
	Sibyl	1877	Brockton	admn	6813
	Simeon	1792	Abington	admn	6814
	Simeon	1810	Bridgewater	will	6815
	Simeon	1874	W. Bridgewater	admn	6816
	Stillman	1879	Brockton	will	6817
	Susan W	1874	W. Bridgewater	grdn	6818
	Sylvester	1781	Bridgewater	grdn	6819
	Thankful	1828	Abington	will	6820
	Thaxter	1783	Bridgewater	admn	6821
	Walter	1868	N. Bridgewater	grdn	6822
	Walton	1781	Bridgewater	grdn	6819
	Willard	1868	N. Bridgewater	grdn	6822
	William	1794	Halifax	grdn	6825
	William	1847	W. Bridgewater	will	6823
	William	1876	Bridgewater	admn	6824
DUNCAN	Abel G	1874	Hanover	will	6826
DUNHAM	Abigail	1827	Carver	grdn	6865
	Andrew	1861	Mattapoisett	will	6827
	Angelo L	1875	Carver0	admn	6828
	Anna Elizabeth	1877	Plymouth	name	6829
	Annis	1729	Middleboro	will	6830
	Annis	1770	Middleboro	grdn	6861
	Benjamin	1827	Carver	grdn	6865
	Benjamin	1853	Abington	admn	6831
	Benjamin W	1862	Carver	admn	6832
	Cornelius	1765	Plympton	admn	6833
	Cornelius	1876	Brockton	admn	6834
	Ebenezer	1737	Plympton	grdn	6858
	Ebenezer	1766	Plympton	admn	6835
	Ebenezer	1773	Plymouth	admn	6836
	Ebenezer	1821	Carver	will	6837
	Elijah	1827	Plymouth	admn	6838
	Elijah	1871	Middleboro	admn	6839
	Elizabeth	1854	Plymouth	admn	6840
	Ephraim	1756	Middleboro	will	6841
	Ephraim	1770	Middleboro	grdn	6861
	Eunice	1874	Plymouth	admn	6842
	George	1801	Plymouth	admn	6843

SURNAME	FIRST NAME	YEAR	PLACE	CASE	DOCKET
DUNHAM	George	1810	Plymouth	admn	6844
	George	1820	Bridgewater	admn	6846
	George	1859	Abington	admn	6847
	George F	1868	Plymouth	admn	6845
	Hannah J	1872	Plymouth	admn	6848
	Harvey	1833	Plymouth	admn	6849
	Harvey	1870	Plymouth	admn	6850
	Henry	1806	Abington	admn	6851
	Ichabod Jr	1826	Plymouth	will	6852
	Ira	1821	Kingston	admn	6853
	Israel	1726	Plympton	admn	6854
	Israel	1828	Carver	will	6855
	Jacob	1829	Plymouth	grdn	6856 a
	James	1737	Plympton	grdn	6858
	James	1758	Plympton	admn	6857
	Jane P	1842	Rochester	admn	6859
	John	1692	Plymouth	will	6860
	Jonathan	1770	Middleboro	grdn	6861
	Joseph	1703	Plymouth	will	6863
	Joseph	1782	Middleboro	admn	6862
	Joseph	1827	Carver	grdn	6865
	Joseph	1842	Plymouth	admn	6864
	Josiah	1748	Plymouth	grdn	6866
	Josiah	1757	Plymouth	admn	6867
	Lucas	1874	Plymouth	will	6868
	Lydia	1827	Carver	grdn	6865
	Mary T	1880	Carver	will	6869
	Nancy T	1880	Plymouth	admn	6870
	Nathan	1875	Plymouth	will	6871
	Nathaniel	1763	Plymouth	admn	6872
	Nathaniel	1783	Plymouth	admn	6873
	Patience	1850	Plymouth	will	6874
	Robert	1824	Plymouth	admn	6875
	Robert	1833	Plymouth	admn	6876
	Samuel	1687/8	Plymouth	admn	6877
	Samuel	1718	Plymouth	admn	6878
	Samuel	1761	Plymouth	admn	6879
	Samuel T	1841	Rochester	admn	6880
	Sarah C B	1859	Carver	admn	6881
	Silas	1825	Pembroke	admn	6882
	Solomon	1792	Middleboro	admn	6883
	Susanna	1737	Plympton	grdn	6858
	Thomas S	1870	Carver	admn	6884
	Warren	1838	Middleboro	will	6885
	William	1745	Plymouth	will	6887
	William	1761	Plymouth	will	6888
	William	1816	Halifax	admn	6886
	William	1833	Plymouth	admn	6889
	William G	1833	Plymouth	grdn	6890 a
	William G	1864	Plymouth	admn	6891
DUNN	Alexander	1880	Hingham	admn	6892
	Ann	1878	Scituate	will	6893
	Cornelius	1870	Hingham	will	6894
	Joseph	1872	Abington	will	6895
	Joseph	1880	Rockland	admn	6896
	Margaret	1869	W. Bridgewater	will	6897
	Mary E	1880	Hingham	grdn	6898
	Matthew	1880	Hingham	grdn	6898
	Thomas	1880	Hingham	will	6899
	William	1841	Plympton	admn	6900
DUNPHE	Imogene D	1880	E. Bridgewater	will	6901
	Jotham	1870	Bridgewater	admn	6902
DUNSTER	Hannah	1853	Pembroke	admn	6903
DUNTON	Stimpson	1879	Plymouth	admn	6904
DURANT	Esmerelda F	1880	Abington	peti	6905
DURFEY	Benjamin	1765	Middleboro	will	6906
	Edward	1832	Middleboro	grdn	6909 a
	Edward B	1854	Rochester	grdn	6907 a
	Edward B	1868	Mattapoisett	admn	6908
	Elizabeth	1767	Middleboro	admn	6910
	Elizabeth	1808	Plymouth	will	6911

SURNAME	FIRST NAME	YEAR	PLACE	CASE	DOCKET
	Mary	1733	Plymouth	grdn	6912
	Peleg	1730	Plymouth	admn	6913
DURGIN	Benjamin F	1867	Halifax	admn	6914
DWELLEY	Abner	1732	Hanover	will	6915
	Abner	1743	Scituate	grdn	6928
DWELLEY	Amey	1748	Scituate	will	6916
	Amy M	1880	Hanson	will	6917
	Anna D	1874	Hanover	grdn	6918
	Betsey	1842	Hanover	grdn	6936
	Deborah	1743	Scituate	grdn	6928
	Deborah	1748	Scituate	admn	6919
	Elizabeth	1717	Scituate	will	6920
	Elizabeth	1743	Scituate	grdn	6928
	Elizabeth	1879	Pembroke	admn	6921
	Frances	1865	Pembroke	admn	6922
	Frank C	1874	Hanover	grdn	6918
	George	1862	Pembroke	admn	6923
	Hosea	1866	Hanover	will	6924
	Ichabod	1709	Plymouth	admn	6925
	James H	1854	Pembroke	admn	6926
	Jedediah	1738	Scituate	admn	6927
	Jedediah	1743	Scituate	grdn	6928
	John	1718	Scituate	will	6929
	John	1743	Scituate	admn	6930
	John	1750	Scituate	grdn	6942
	John	1857	Hanover	will	6931
	Joseph	1745	Scituate	admn	6932
	Joseph	1750	Scituate	grdn	6942
	Joseph	1868	Hanover	admn	6933
	Joshua	1743	Scituate	grdn	6928
	Joshua	1787	Hanover	admn	6934
	Joshua	1842	Hanover	grdn	6936
	Joshua Jr	1842	Hanover	will	6935
	Judith	1757	Scituate	admn	6937
	Laurentia	1842	Hanover	grdn	6936
	Lemuel	1740	Scituate	admn	6941
	Lemuel	1750	Scituate	grdn	6942
	Lemuel	1846	Hanover	admn	6939
	Lemuel	1878	Hanover	will	6940
	Lemuel Jr	1841	Hanover	grdn	6938 a
	Lot	1752	-----	grdn	6943
	Lot	1780	Pembroke	admn	6944
	Lucy	1743	Scituate	grdn	6928
	Lucy	1790	Hanover	grdn	6949
	Melzar	1829	Hanover	will	6945
	Melzar	1842	Hanover	grdn	6936
	Melzar	1842	Hanover	admn	6946
	Nathan	1835	Pembroke	will	6947
	Nathan H	1862	Hanover	admn	6948
	Priscilla	1790	Hanover	grdn	6949
	Richard	1692	Scituate	admn	6950
	Richard	1709	Scituate	admn	6951
	Ruth	1750	Scituate	grdn	6942
	Sally	1879	Hanover	admn	6952
	Samuel	1690	Scituate	admn	6953
	Sarah	1750	Scituate	grdn	6942
	Simeon	1724	Scituate	will	6954
	William	1732	Hanover	grdn	6955
DWYER	Ellen	1867	Abington	admn	6956
DYER	Alice	1865	Abington	grdn	6977
	Anna	1864	Abington	admn	6957
	Bela	1830	Abington	will	6958
	Bela	1875	S. Abington	will	6959
	Bethiah	1837	Plymouth	will	6960
	Celia	1863	Bridgewater	admn	6961
	Charles	1750	Plymouth	admn	6962
	Charles	1787	Plymouth	admn	6963
	Christopher	1786	Abington	will	6965
	Christopher	1800	Bridgewater	will	6964
	Christopher	1853	Abington	admn	6967
	Christopher	1868	Abington	will	6968

SURNAME	FIRST NAME	YEAR	PLACE	CASE	DOCKET
DYER	Christopher Jr	1787	Abington	admn	6966
	Cynthia	1838	Hanover	grdn	6973
	Cyrus	1865	Abington	grdn	6977
	Cyrus A	1865	Abington	admn	6969
	Daniel	1866	Bridgewater	will	6970
	Dorothy	1846	Hanover	grdn	6979
	Ebenezer A	1864	Abington	grdn	6972
	Edward L	1864	Abington	admn	6971
	Edward O	1864	Abington	grdn	6972
	Eliza	1838	Hanover	grdn	6973
	Ezekiel	1825	Bridgewater	comp	6974 a
	Ezekiel D	1865	Abington	admn	6975
	Frank	1865	Abington	grdn	6977
	Frank W	1880	Hanover	grdn	6976
	Hannah	1793	Plymouth	will	6978
	Hervey	1846	Hanover	grdn	6979
	Jacob	1807	Abington	admn	6980
	James	1829	Abington	admn	6981
	James B	1877	Abington	admn	6982
	Jason	1838	Bridgewater	admn	6983
	John	1714	Plymouth	bond	6984
	John	1740	Plymouth	grdn	6985 a
	John	1741	Plymouth	will	6986
	John	1773	Plymouth	admn	6987
	John	1777	Boston	grdn	6988
	Lucia	1846	Hanover	grdn	6979
	Lucy	1838	Hanover	grdn	6973
	Mary C	1859	Abington	grdn	6989
	Nathaniel N	1876	S. Abington	will	6990
	Polly	1850	Bridgewater	admn	6991
	Rufus	1789	Bridgewater	grdn	6992
	Ruth	1846	Hanover	grdn	6979
	Samuel	1867	S. Scituate	will	6993
	Samuel N	1879	S. Abington	will	6994
	Sarah	1805	Bridgewater	will	6995
	Sarah	1842	Bridgewater	admn	6996
	Willia	1859	Abington	grdn	6989
	Willia S	1881	S. Abington	admn	6997
	William	1740	Plymouth	admn	6998
	William	1740	Plymouth	grdn	6999
EAMES	Abner	1767	Marshfield	admn	7000
	Abner	1830	Marshfield	admn	7001
	Anthony	1729	Marshfield	will	7003
	Anthony	1739	Marshfield	will	7002
	Benjamin	1789	Marshfield	will	7004
	Bethiah	1713	Bridgewater	grdn	7019
	Betsey	1830	N. Bridgewater	grdn	7020
	Daniel	1830	N. Bridgewater	grdn	7020
	Diantha	1830	N. Bridgewater	grdn	7020
	Ephraim	1830	N. Bridgewater	grdn	7020
	Hannah	1713	Bridgewater	grdn	7019
	Isaac	1868	N. Bridgewater	admn	7005
	James	1859	Marshfield	admn	7006
	Jedediah	1738	Marshfield	admn	7007
	Jedediah	1744	Marshfield	grdn	7008
	Jonathan	1724	Marshfield	will	7009
	Josiah	1738	Marshfield	admn	7010
	Josiah 2nd	1831	Ilsboro ME	seve	7011
	Justus	1706	Marshfield	will	7012
	Lemuel	1773	Marshfield	will	7013
	Luther	1830	N. Bridgewater	grdn	7020
	Mark	1693	Marshfield	will	7014
	Mark	1723	Marshfield	admn	7015
	Martha	1713	Bridgewater	grdn	7019
	Mary	1713	Bridgewater	grdn	7019
	Nathaniel	1773	Abington	will	7016
	Penelope	1744	Marshfield	grdn	7008
	Ruth	1784	Marshfield	admn	7017
	Sarah	1703	Marshfield	powe	7018
	Sarah	1713	Bridgewater	grdn	7019
	Sarah	1830	N. Bridgewater	grdn	7020

SURNAME	FIRST NAME	YEAR	PLACE	CASE	DOCKET
EAMES	Silvanus	1761	Marshfield	admn	7021
	Spencer	1830	N. Bridgewater	grdn	7020
	William	1713	Bridgewater	grdn	7019
EARL	Abbie	1847	Middleboro	grdn	7023
	Charles	1847	Middleboro	grdn	7023
	Mary	1847	Middleboro	grdn	7023
	Peter J	1824	Rochester	admn	7022
	Sarah	1847	Middleboro	grdn	7023
EASDELL	Rebecca	1762	Plymouth	admn	7024
EASTERBROOK	Charles	1836	Hingham	grdn	7027
	Charles G	1865	Abington	grdn	7025 a
	Isaac	1835	Hingham	admn	7026
	Isaac	1836	Hingham	grdn	7027
	Joseph	1836	Hingham	grdn	7027
	Joseph	1879	Hingham	admn	7028
	Susan	1836	Hingham	grdn	7027
EASTLAND	John	1726	Plymouth	admn	7029
EATON	Abby	1849	Middleboro	grdn	7030
	Alden	1849	Middleboro	admn	7031
	Alfred	1840	Middleboro	will	7032
	Apollos	1849	Middleboro	admn	7033
	Arabella	1832	W. Bridgewater	admn	7034
	Barzillai	1869	Middleboro	will	7035
	Benjamin	1745	Kingston	will	7036
	Benjamin	1746	Kingston	grdn	7062
	Benjamin	1751	Kingston	admn	7037
	Benjamin	1755	Middleboro	grdn	7038
	Consider	1769	Kingston	grdn	7039
	Cyrus	1834	Middleboro	grdn	7040
	David	1759	Kingston	admn	7041
	Elijah	1755	Middleboro	grdn	7038
	Elijah	1831	Middleboro	will	7042
	Elisha	1738	Plympton	admn	7043
	Enos	1856	Middleboro	admn	7044
	Eunice	1769	Kingston	grdn	7039
	Francis	1749	Middleboro	admn	7045
	Freedom	1827	Halifax	admn	7046
	Harriet A	1849	Middleboro	grdn	7047
	Henry	1849	Middleboro	grdn	7030
	Israel	1833	Middleboro	will	7048
	Jabez	1805	Plympton	admn	7049
	James	1746	Kingston	grdn	7062
	Job	1769	Kingston	grdn	7039
	Job	1812	Kingston	admn	7050
	John	1750	Kingston	grdn	7052 a
	John	1755	Middleboro	grdn	7038
	John	1755	Halifax	grdn	7051 a
	John C H	1880	Brockton	will	7053
	Joshua	1769	Kingston	grdn	7039
	Marcy	1719	Plymouth	grdn	7054
	Mary	1755	Middleboro	grdn	7038
	Noah	1746	Kingston	grdn	7062
	Noah	1795	Plympton	grdn	7055 a
	Olive	1812	Middleboro	grdn	7056
	Oliver	1799	Middleboro	admn	7057
	Philena	1857	Middleboro	will	7058
	Ruel	1849	Middleboro	grdn	7030
	Samuel	1724	Middleboro	admn	7059
	Samuel	1820	Middleboro	will	7060
	Seth	1746	Kingston	grdn	7062
	Seth	1849	Middleboro	will	7061
	Shepherd T P	1856	Boston	grdn	7063
	Sidney	1857	Middleboro	admn	7064
	Solomon	1834	Middleboro	will	7065
	Solomon K	1872	Mattapoisett	will	7066
	Susanna	1755	Middleboro	grdn	7038
	William	1690	-----	will	7067
	Williams	1879	Middleboro	admn	7068
	Ziba	1858	Middleboro	will	7069
ECHE	Elizabeth	1731	Titicut	will	7070 i
ECHES	John	1720	Titicut	will	7071

SURNAME	FIRST NAME	YEAR	PLACE	CASE	DOCKET
EDDY	Addie G	1870	Abington	grdn	7079
	Benjamin	1742	Halifax	admn	7072
	Benjamin J	1862	E. Bridgewater	admn	7073
	Clara	1870	Petoluma CA	grdn	7074
	Ebenezer	1830	Middleboro	admn	7075
	Ezra	1859	Plympton	admn	7076
	Francis	1870	Petoluma CA	grdn	7074
	George A	1870	Petoluma CA	grdn	7074
	Henry	1859	N. Bridgewater	grdn	7078
	Henry	1872	N. Bridgewater	admn	7077
	Ida M	1870	Abington	grdn	7079
	John	1816	Plymouth	admn	7080
	Jonathan	1744	Halifax	admn	7081
	Joshua	1864	Middleboro	admn	7082
	Louisa D	1865	Middleboro	grdn	7083
	Mariah F	1865	Middleboro	grdn	7083
	Moses	1785	Middleboro	will	7084
	Nathaniel	1869	Middleboro	will	7085
	Obadiah	172-	Middleboro	will	7086
	Samuel	1746	Middleboro	admn	7087
	Samuel	1757	Middleboro	grdn	7088
	Sarah	1779	Middleboro	grdn	7089
	Sarah	1859	N. Bridgewater	grdn	7078
	Sarah W	1869	Plymouth	admn	7090
	Seth	1839	Middleboro	admn	7091
	Willard	1859	N. Bridgewater	grdn	7078
	William H	1838	Middleboro	admn	7092
	Zachariah	1779	Middleboro	admn	7093
	Zachariah	1860	Middleboro	will	7094
EDES	William	1866	Plymouth	admn	7095
EDMONDS	Elizabeth	1777	Plymouth	admn	7096
EDSON	Abiezer	1749	Bridgewater	grdn	7097
	Alanson	1871	W. Bridgewater	will	7098
	Anna	1811	Marshfield	will	7099
	Barnabas	1859	N. Bridgewater	admn	7100
	Benjamin	1758	Bridgewater	will	7101
	Betsey G	1873	N. Bridgewater	will	7102
	Caleb	1764	Bridgewater	grdn	7159
	Calvin	1764	Bridgewater	grdn	7159
	Calvin	1791	Bridgewater	grdn	7103
	Charles	1797	Bridgewater	grdn	7151
	Charles	1800	Bridgewater	grdn	7104 a
	Charlotte	1797	Bridgewater	grdn	7151
	Charlotte	1863	Middleboro	grdn	7105
	Cyrus	1794	Bridgewater	grdn	7157
	Daniel	1764	Bridgewater	grdn	7159
	David	1795	Bridgewater	will	7106
	David	1832	N. Bridgewater	will	7107
	David	1876	Brockton	admn	7108
	David	1881	Brockton	admn	7109
	Ebenezer	1829	N. Bridgewater	will	7110
	Elijah	1762	Bridgewater	will	7111
	Eunice	1785	Bridgewater	grdn	7112
	Ezra	1794	Bridgewater	admn	7113
	Ezra	1828	Bridgewater	admn	7114
	Galen	1852	N. Bridgewater	admn	7115
	George	1865	E. Bridgewater	will	7116
	Hannah	1794	Bridgewater	grdn	7157
	Henry	1840	W. Bridgewater	admn	7117
	Henry	1864	N. Bridgewater	admn	7118
	Horace O	1875	Abington	grdn	7119
	Hosea	1764	Bridgewater	grdn	7159
	Huldah	1785	Bridgewater	grdn	7112
	Ichabod	1811	Bridgewater	admn	7120
	James	1808	Bridgewater	will	7121
	James	1818	Middleboro	admn	7122
	Jennett	1880	E. Bridgewater	will	7123
	Jesse	1784	Bridgewater	admn	7124
	Jesse	1792	Bridgewater	grdn	7125
	Joanna	1785	Bridgewater	grdn	7112
	Joel	1830	E. Bridgewater	admn	7126

SURNAME	FIRST NAME	YEAR	PLACE	CASE	DOCKET
EDSON	John	1865	Bridgewater	will	7127
	Jonah	1874	E. Bridgewater	will	7128
	Joseph	1711	Bridgewater	admn	7129
	Joseph Jr	1791	Bridgewater	admn	7130
	Josiah	1734	Bridgewater	will	7131
	Josiah	1762	Bridgewater	will	7132
	Josiah	1782	Bridgewater	grdn	7135
	Josiah	1820	Bridgewater	will	7136
	Josiah Jr	1779	Bridgewater	admn	7133
	Josiah(absent)	1779	Bridgewater	admn	7134
	Levi	1777	Bridgewater	admn	7137
	Lucy	1797	Bridgewater	grdn	7151
	Lydia	1785	Bridgewater	grdn	7112
	Lydia	1830	E. Bridgewater	grdn	7144 a
	Marshal	1768	Bridgewater	admn	7138
	Martha	1805	Bridgewater	admn	7139
	Mary	1873	N. Bridgewater	will	7140
	Mary A	1879	Brockton	will	7141
	Mary R	1881	W. Bridgewater	admn	7142
	Mehitable	1830	E. Bridgewater	grdn	7144 a
	Mehitable	1879	Brockton	admn	7143
	Nathan	1751	Bridgewater	admn	7145
	Nathaniel	1741	Bridgewater	grdn	7156
	Nathaniel	1785	Bridgewater	grdn	7112
	Nathaniel	1785	Bridgewater	admn	7146
	Olive	1764	Bridgewater	grdn	7159
	Peter	1750	Bridgewater	will	7148
	Policarpus	1796	Bridgewater	admn	7149
	Rebecca	1784	Bridgewater	grdn	7150
	Ruth	1764	Bridgewater	grdn	7159
	Sally	1792	Bridgewater	grdn	7125
	Sally	1797	Bridgewater	grdn	7151
	Samuel	1692	Bridgewater	will	7152
	Samuel	1719	Bridgewater	will	7153
	Samuel	1741	Bridgewater	grdn	7156
	Samuel	1772	Bridgewater	will	7154
	Samuel	1785	Bridgewater	admn	7155
	Sarah	1794	Bridgewater	grdn	7157
	Susanna	1712	Bridgewater	grdn	7160
	Susanna	1742	Bridgewater	will	7158
	Susanna	1764	Bridgewater	grdn	7159
	Sylvester	1764	Bridgewater	grdn	7159
	Timothy	1712	Bridgewater	grdn	7160
	William	1800	Bridgewater	will	7161
	William	1849	N. Bridgewater	will	7162
	liver	1809	Middleboro	admn	7147
EDWARDS	Charles	1835	Rochester	admn	7163
	Corrella C	1870	Wareham	will	7164
	George G	1872	Middleboro	grdn	7167
	George W	1849	Rochester	grdn	7165
	George W	1879	Rochester	grdn	7166 a
	Hannah H	1836	Rochester	grdn	7168
	John F	1879	Plymouth	admn	7169
	Joseph	1833	Rochester	will	7170
	Mary	1797	Plymouth	grdn	7171
	Mary H	1878	Brockton	peti	7172
	Nye	1819	Rochester	admn	7173
	Robert	1843	Scituate	admn	7174
	Sarah A	1849	Rochester	grdn	7165
	Shubael G	1872	Middleboro	will	7175
	Susan A	1821	Rochester	grdn	7176
EELLS	Abigail	1757	Scituate	grdn	7183
	Bradbury	1757	Hanover	grdn	7185
	George W	1837	Hanover	grdn	7180
	George W	1857	Hanover	admn	7177
	Hannah	1754	Scituate	will	7178
	Hannah	1757	Hanover	grdn	7185
	Hannah	1784	Hanover	admn	7179
	James G	1837	Hanover	grdn	7180
	John	1757	Scituate	grdn	7183
	John	1760	Scituate	admn	7181

SURNAME	FIRST NAME	YEAR	PLACE	CASE	DOCKET
EELLS	Joseph	1757	Scituate	grdn	7183
	Joseph	1837	Hanover	will	7182
	Linthal	1757	Scituate	grdn	7183
	Lusanna	1757	Scituate	grdn	7183
	Marcy B	1865	Hanover	will	7184
	Mary	1757	Hanover	grdn	7185
	Nathaniel	1750	Scituate	will	7186
	Nathaniel	1806	Scituate	admn	7187
	Nathaniel	1830	Scituate	admn	7188
	Robert	1844	Hanover	will	7190
	Robert	1872	Hanover	will	7191
	Robert L	1800	Hanover	will	7189
	Sally	1854	Hanover	admn	7192
	Samuel	1871	Hanover	admn	7193
	Sarah	1718	Scituate	admn	7194
EGGERTON	Dennis	1734	Bridgewater	admn	7195
ELDRIDGE	Amasa E	1876	Middleboro	grdn	7196
	Anna F	1869	Wareham	grdn	7197
	Benjamin F	1876	Middleboro	admn	7198
	Darius	1880	Wareham	peti	7199
	George	1876	Middleboro	grdn	7196
	Harrison L	1861	Duxbury	grdn	7200
	Joseph A	1877	Wareham	admn	7201
	Julia A	1881	Kingston	admn	7202
	Laura E	1869	Wareham	grdn	7197
	Mary C	1859	Hingham	grdn	7203
	Rebecca T	1868	Duxbury	grdn	7204 a
	Samuel	1762	Falmouth	grdn	7205
	Sylvester	1853	Duxbury	admn	7206
ELLERSON	Joseph D	1863	Bridgewater	grdn	7207
ELLIOT	Clara	1869	Rochester	grdn	7208
	Eliza	1869	Rochester	grdn	7208
	Frank	1869	Rochester	grdn	7208
	Harriet	1869	Rochester	grdn	7208
	James	1869	Rochester	grdn	7208
	John	1869	Rochester	grdn	7208
	Margaret	1869	Rochester	grdn	7208
	Samuel	1868	Rochester	admn	7209
	Samuel	1869	Rochester	grdn	7208
	William	1869	Rochester	grdn	7208
ELLIS	Abner	1732	Roch'str/M'boro	will	7210
	Albert	1840	Rochester	admn	7211
	Anson B	1854	Plymouth	admn	7212
	Ansonia	1854	Plymouth	grdn	7232
	Arthur	1876	Plymouth	grdn	7252
	Benjamin	1853	Carver	will	7213
	Betsey	1796	Plymouth	grdn	7214
	Carrie	1875	Mattapoisett	grdn	7217
	Charles	1870	E. Bridgewater	grdn	7306
	Charles	1875	Mattapoisett	grdn	7217
	Charles C	1839	Wareham	admn	7215
	Charles L	1851	Plympton	grdn	7216
	Clarence S	1873	Hanson	grdn	7218
	Clark	1782	-----	grdn	7220
	Clark	1877	Plymouth	name	7219
	Cora	1870	E. Bridgewater	grdn	7306
	Cornelius	1807	Middleboro	admn	7221
	David	1859	Plymouth	admn	7222
	Deborah	1796	Plymouth	grdn	7214
	Ebenezer	1821	Bridgewater	will	7223
	Ebenezer	1845	Rochester	admn	7224
	Ebenezer	1856	Middleboro	admn	7225
	Edward	1828	Duxbury	grdn	7309
	Edward	1870	E. Bridgewater	grdn	7306
	Edward	1878	Bridgewater	will	7226
	Elihu	1854	Plympton	admn	7227
	Elnathan	1849	Wareham	admn	7228
	Etta	1870	E. Bridgewater	grdn	7306
	Francis B	1843	Hanover	admn	7229
	Freeman	1728	Rochester	will	7230
	Hannah	1835	Carver	grdn	7231

SURNAME	FIRST NAME	YEAR	PLACE	CASE	DOCKET
ELLIS	Hannah	1854	Plymouth	grdn	7232
	Harriet	1854	Plymouth	grdn	7232
	Harrison	1864	Wareham	admn	7233
	Helen L	1841	Rochester	grdn	7235
	Helen M	1870	E. Bridgewater	will	7234
	Helena F	1879	Carver	grdn	7236
	James	1832	Carver	admn	7237
	James	1876	Bridgewater	admn	7238
	James C	1875	Plympton	admn	7239
	James W	1875	Plymouth	admn	7240
	Jesse	1732	Middleboro	admn	7241
	Joel	1731	Rochester	admn	7242
	Joel	1803	Plympton	will	7244
	Joel	1808	Rochester	will	7243
	Joel	1814	Plympton	admn	7245
	John P	1877	Plympton	will	7246
	Joseph	1880	Hanover	will	7248
	Joseph M	1868	Carver	admn	7247
	Joshua J	1835	Scituate	grdn	7249
	Josiah T	1850	Plympton	admn	7250
	Judith	1862	Mattapoisett	will	7251
	Laura	1875	Mattapoisett	grdn	7217
	Lena	1876	Plymouth	grdn	7252
	Lizzie L	1865	Duxbury	adop	7253
	Lucy	1835	Scituate	will	7254
	Lydia	1854	Plymouth	grdn	7232
	Malachi	1818	Rochester	admn	7255
	Mariah	1733	Middleboro	grdn	7302
	Marick	1827	Plympton	admn	7256
	Marie	1879	Carver	grdn	7236
	Mary	1744	Rochester	admn	7257
	Mary	1849	Carver	admn	7258
	Mary	1868	Plymouth	admn	7259
	Mary	1880	Hanover	will	7260
	Mathias	1782	Middleboro	admn	7261
	Mathias	1790	Middleboro	admn	7262
	Mathias	1813	Wareham	admn	7263
	Mathias	1879	Carver	admn	7263 +
	Mercy	1825	Plymouth	grdn	7264
	Molly	1766	Plympton	grdn	7296
	Mordecai	1810	Hanover	will	7265
	Mordecai	1829	Hanover	will	7266
	Nancy	1876	Plymouth	grdn	7252
	Nathan	1731	Middleboro	admn	7267
	Nathaniel	1817	Hanover	admn	7268
	Nathaniel	1859	Plymouth	will	7269
	Nathaniel	1876	Plymouth	grdn	7252
	Otis	1860	Hanover	admn	7270
	Phebe	1854	Plymouth	grdn	7232
	Rebecca	1759	Hanover	grdn	7272
	Rebecca	1854	Plymouth	admn	7271
	Ruth	1782	-----	grdn	7220
	Sally	1855	Plymouth	admn	7273
	Samuel	1745	Plymouth	will	7274
	Samuel	1770	Plympton	admn	7277
	Samuel	1777	Plymouth	admn	7275
	Samuel	1782	Middleboro	grdn	7279
	Samuel	1817	Plympton	will	7278
	Samuel	1838	Wareham	will	7280
	Samuel	1842	Plymouth	admn	7276
	Sarah	1759	Hanover	grdn	7272
	Sarah	1816	Bridgewater	admn	7281
	Sarah F	1877	Carver	admn	7281 +
	Seth	1749	Wareham	admn	7282
	Southworth	1841	Middleboro	will	7284
	Southworth	1866	Middleboro	will	7283
	Spooner	1868	Hanover	will	7285
	Stephen	1766	Plympton	grdn	7296
	Stephen	1796	Plymouth	grdn	7214
	Stephen	1824	Plympton	will	7286
	Stephen	1874	Marion	will	7287

SURNAME	FIRST NAME	YEAR	PLACE	CASE	DOCKET
ELLIS	Susannah	1835	Plympton	admn	7288
	Thomas	1800	Plymouth	will	7291
	Thomas	1813	Rochester	will	7289
	Thomas	1830	Plympton	admn	7290
	Thomas	1848	Plymouth	will	7292
	Thomas S	1875	Middleboro	will	7293
	Timothy	1811	Rochester	admn	7294
	Wallace	1876	Plymouth	grdn	7252
	Willard	1766	Plympton	grdn	7296
	Willard	1852	Plympton	will	7295
	William	1716	Middleboro	will	7301
	William	1733	Middleboro	grdn	7302
	William	1768	Plymouth	admn	7297
	William	1778	Rochester	will	7303
	William	1795	Plymouth	will	7298
	William	1837	Plymouth	admn	7299
	William	1859	Mattapoisett	will	7304
	William	1870	E. Bridgewater	grdn	7306
	William G	1879	Hanover	admn	7305
	William W	1857	Middleboro	grdn	7300
ELLISON	William	1828	Duxbury	grdn	7309
	William	1858	Duxbury	will	7307
	William P	1855	Duxbury	name	7308
ELMER	Lizzie N	1877	Wareham	grdn	7338
ELMES	Ann	1816	Scituate	grdn	7312
	Charles	1814	Scituate	admn	7311
	Charles	1816	Scituate	grdn	7312
	Charles	1878	Scituate	will	7310
	Charlotte	1846	Hanson	will	7313
	Chloe	1836	Middleboro	admn	7314
	Daniel	1842	Scituate	admn	7315
	Daniel R	1880	Hanover	will	7316
	Elizabeth	1844	Scituate	grdn	7328
	Ignatius	1763	Middleboro	admn	7317
	Isaac	1844	Scituate	grdn	7328
	James H	1864	Scituate	admn	7318
	John	1783	Scituate	admn	7319
	John Jr	1775	Scituate	admn	7320
	Jonathan	1742	Scituate	will	7321
	Joseph Jr	1823	Scituate	will	7322
	Joseph N	1858	Scituate	admn	7323
	Joshua	1816	Scituate	grdn	7312
	Judith	1840	Scituate	admn	7324
	Lucy	1866	Scituate	will	7325
	Mary	1816	Scituate	grdn	7312
	Mary	1844	Scituate	will	7326
	Mary	1858	Scituate	grdn	7327 a
	Nancy	1844	Scituate	grdn	7328
	Nathaniel	1824	Scituate	admn	7329
	Nathaniel	1875	S. Scituate	will	7330
	Robert	1786	Scituate	will	7331
	Robert	1836	Scituate	will	7332
	Rodulphus	1748	Middleboro	will	7333
	Sally B	1878	Lakeville	admn	7334
	Theodore S	1840	Middleboro	grdn	7335
	Thomas T	1876	Scituate	admn	7336
	William	1881	Scituate	will	7337
EMBREE	Thomas J	1837	Louisanna	grdn	7339
EMERSON	Jeremiah	1879	Scituate	grdn	7340 a
EMERY	Moses	1861	Lakeville	will	7341
ENGLISH	John	1867	Abington	admn	7342
ENOS	Elmer E	1873	Plymouth	adop	7343
ENWRIGHT	John	1876	Bridgewater	will	7344
ERLAND	Henry	1853	Plymouth	will	7345
	Henry T	1864	Carver	admn	7346
	Sally C	1873	Plymouth	admn	7347
ERSKINE	Elizabeth	1784	Bridgewater	warr	7348
	Jane	1867	Abington	admn	7349
ESCHEMBACH	George C D	1882	Brockton	adop	7350
ESKRIDGE	Thomas	1781	Middleboro	admn	7351
ESPELL	Susan	1863	Middleboro	will	7352

SURNAME	FIRST NAME	YEAR	PLACE	CASE	DOCKET
ESTES	Annette	1877	Rockland	grdn	7356
	Barsheba	1791	Wareham	admn	7353
	Barsheba	1791	Wareham	grdn	7354
	Betsey	1853	Hanson	grdn	7362
	Betsey J	1867	Abington	will	7355
	Edith	1877	Rockland	grdn	7356
	Edward	1802	Hanover	grdn	7368
	Edward	1867	Abington	will	7357
	Elijah	1877	Rockland	will	7358
	Elmer F	1869	Abington	grdn	7359
	Emma J	1868	Hanover	grdn	7360
	Eugene B	1867	E. Bridgewater	grdn	7361
	Floran P	1853	Hanson	grdn	7362
	Fred C	1869	Abington	grdn	7359
	Irene A	1866	Duxbury	adop	7363
	Job	1845	Hanson	admn	7364
	Joseph 2nd	1837	Pembroke	admn	7365
	Joseph C	1867	N. Bridgewater	will	7366
	Mathew	1791	Wareham	grdn	7354
	Matthew	1774	Hanover	will	7367
	Mercy	1802	Hanover	grdn	7368
	Richard	1797	Hanover	admn	7369
	Richard	1878	Hanover	admn	7370
	Robert	1804	Hanover	admn	7371
	Robert Jr	1843	Abington	admn	7372
	Saba	1877	Rockland	grdn	7356
	Stephen	1791	Wareham	grdn	7354
	William	1791	Wareham	grdn	7354
	William	1794	Hanover	will	7373
	William	1802	Hanover	grdn	7368
	William	1864	Hanson	admn	7374
	Zacheus	1846	Hanson	will	7375
EVANS	Jane M	1881	Middleboro	admn	7376
	John	1802	Edentown NC	grdn	7377
EVERETT	Abby A H	1879	Wareham	admn	7378
	Hannah B	1880	Wareham	will	7379
	John L	1868	Wareham	will	7380
	Lucy	1867	Wareham	will	7381
	Noble	1820	Wareham	will	7382
	Noble	1840	Wareham	admn	7383
EVERSON	Abigail	1780	Kingston	will	7384
	Abigail	1802	Pembroke	grdn	7385
	Barnabas	1802	Pembroke	grdn	7385
	Barnabas	1821	Hanson	admn	7386
	Caroline	1865	Hanson	grdn	7387
	Charles	1872	Kingston	admn	7388
	Charlotte	1802	Pembroke	grdn	7385
	Clarissa	1802	Pembroke	grdn	7385
	Dulcinea	1802	Pembroke	grdn	7385
	Ephraim	1757	Kingston	will	7389
	Ephraim	1787	Kingston	admn	7390
	Ephraim	1820	Plymouth	admn	7391
	Fred W	1868	Hanover	grdn	7404
	Frederick O	1867	Hanson	admn	7392
	Hannah	1857	Kingston	will	7393
	James Jr	1787	Kingston	admn	7394
	John	1766	Kingston	admn	7395
	John	1780	Kingston	admn	7396
	Josiah	1843	Kingston	will	7397
	Judith	1865	Kingston	admn	7398
	Levi	1800	Pembroke	admn	7399
	Levi	1845	Hanson	admn	7400
	Levi	1860	Hanson	will	7401
	Lois	1880	Kingston	will	7402
	Lucy A	1873	Kingston	admn	7403
	Lunette L F	1868	Hanover	grdn	7404
	Lydia	1780	Kingston	grdn	7405
	Lydia	1813	Kingston	will	7406
	Mary T	1865	Hanson	admn	7407
	Mercy	1878	Hanson	grdn	7408 a
	Mercy	1880	Hanson	admn	7409

SURNAME	FIRST NAME	YEAR	PLACE	CASE	DOCKET
EVERSON	Patty	1802	Pembroke	grdn	7385
	Richard	1802	Pembroke	grdn	7385
	Richard	1851	Kingston	admn	7410
	Richard	1868	Hanson	will	7411
	Robert	1776	Kingston	admn	7412
	Samuel	1747	Middleboro	admn	7413
	Samuel	1802	Pembroke	grdn	7385
	Samuel	1833	Kingston	will	7415
	Seth	1763	Kingston	admn	7415
	Seth	1832	Kingston	admn	7416
	Sidney	1848	Kingston	will	7417
	Silvanus	1757	Kingston	grdn	7418
	Spencer	1862	Kingston	will	7419
	Susan	1873	Kingston	grdn	7420 a
	Susan	1874	Kingston	will	7421
	Sylvanus	1802	Pembroke	grdn	7385
EWELL	Allen	1804	Marshfield	grdn	7423
	Allen	1870	Marshfield	will	7422
	Charles	1865	Marshfield	grdn	7424
	Eliza	1880	Marshfield	will	7425
	Eunice	1880	Hingham	grdn	7426
	Eva	1880	Hingham	grdn	7426
	Fred	1880	Hingham	grdn	7426
	George L	1874	Duxbury	grdn	7427
	Gershom	1716/8	Scituate	will	7431
	Gershom	1726	Scituate	will	7432
	Gershom	1728	Scituate	grdn	7433
	Gershom	1758	Scituate	grdn	7445
	Gershom	1821	Scituate	admn	7430
	Gershom	1835	Marshfield	admn	7428
	Gershom	1867	Marshfield	admn	7429
	Hannah	1728	Scituate	grdn	7433
	Harriet C	1820	Marshfield	grdn	7434
	Henry	1697	Scituate	will	7435
	Herbert	1865	Marshfield	grdn	7424
	Ichabod	1718	Scituate	will	7436
	Isaac	1859	Marshfield	admn	7437
	Jedediah	1814	Marshfield	will	7438
	Job	1804	Marshfield	admn	7439
	Job	1865	Marshfield	grdn	7424
	Job L	1865	Marshfield	admn	7440
	John	1758	Scituate	will	7441
	Joseph	1837	Marshfield	admn	7442
	Malichy	1758	Scituate	grdn	7445
	Mary	1710	Boston	powe	7443
	Mehitable	1742	Scituate	admn	7444
	Peleg	1758	Scituate	grdn	7445
	Rachel	1835	Marshfield	grdn	7446
	Rachel	1843	Marshfield	grdn	7447 a
	Relief	1728	Scituate	grdn	7433
	Rizpah	1852	Hingham	admn	7448
	Sarah	1709	Scituate	will	7449
	Seth	1728	Scituate	grdn	7433
	Seth	1804	Marshfield	will	7450
	Solomon	1858	E. Bridgewater	admn	7451
	Turner	1804	Marshfield	grdn	7423
	Turner Jr	1863	Marshfield	will	7452
	Walter F	1880	++ngham	admn	7453
	Zenas T	1875	Marshfield	will	7454
EWER	Seth	1870	Middleboro	will	7455
FABORNE	Robert	1838	Plymouth	admn	7456
FAIRBANKS	Ann H	1861	Abington	admn	7457
	Charles H	1874	Abington	grdn	7458
	George L	1875	Bridgewater	admn	7459
	Ida S	1862	Abington	grdn	7460
	Laura E	1874	Abington	grdn	7458
	Lewis E	1861	Abington	admn	7461
FALLOWELL	William	1727	Plymouth	admn	7462
FARMER	George W	1860	Halifax	admn	7463
	Jedediah	1875	Hingham	will	7464
	Margaret	1812	Plymouth	admn	7465

SURNAME	FIRST NAME	YEAR	PLACE	CASE	DOCKET
FARMER	Phebe	1839	Plymouth	admn	7466
	Thomas	1827	Plymouth	admn	7467
FARNHAM	George	1880	Brockton	admn	7468
FARNSWORTH	James D	1855	Bridgewater	will	7469
FARRAN	Polly	1849	Scituate	will	7470
FARRAR	Arthur M	1861	N. Bridgewater	admn	7471
	Deborah	1871	S. Scituate	will	7472
	Henry T	1878	S. Scituate	grdn	7473
	Lucy	1867	S. Scituate	will	7474
	Sally	1875	S. Scituate	admn	7475
	William C	1863	S. Scituate	admn	7476
FARRELL	Alice G	1881	Brockton	grdn	7477
	John	1876	Hingham	admn	7478
	Mary	1876	Hingham	admn	7479
	William	1880	Brockton	will	7480
FARRINGTON	Harriet A	1836	Marshfield	grdn	7481
FARRIS	Jeremiah	1878	Plymouth	will	7482
	Mary C	1879	Plymouth	will	7483
FARROW	Abial	1847	Scituate	will	7484
	Abial Jr	1847	Scituate	admn	7485
	Benjamin	1768	Scituate	will	7486
	Nathaniel	1842	Scituate	admn	7487
	Rufus	1866	S. Scituate	will	7488
	Thomas	1806	Scituate	will	7489
FARWELL	Benjamin	1815	Fitchburg	grdn	7490
	Mary	1815	Fitchburg	grdn	7490
FAUGHT	Charles E	1868	Plymouth	grdn	7492
	Lizzie M	1868	Plymouth	adop	7491
	Lizzie M	1868	Plymouth	grdn	7492
FAULKNER	Anna D	1878	Plymouth	grdn	7493
FAUNCE	Albert	1876	Brockton	admn	7494
	Aubrey D W	1874	Abington	grdn	7495
	Barnaba	1782	Halifax	grdn	7554
	Barnabus	1853	Plymouth	admn	7496
	Benjamin	1752	Kingston	grdn	7497
	Benjamin	1777	Kingston	admn	7498
	Benjamin	1802	Kingston	grdn	7499 a
	Benjamin	1842	Kingston	admn	7500
	Caleb	1818	Plymouth	grdn	7517
	Caroline	1818	Carver	grdn	7537
	Charles A	1875	Brockton	will	7502
	Charles C	1878	Kingston	admn	7503
	Charles L	1843	Plymouth	admn	7501
	Daniel	1803	Carver	admn	7504
	Dorcas	1818	Plymouth	grdn	7517
	Eleanor	1817	Kingston	will	7505
	Eleazer	1746	Plymouth	admn	7506
	Eleazer	1837	Kingston	admn	7507
	Elijah	1823	Kingston	admn	7508
	Elizabeth	1859	Plymouth	will	7509
	Emeline	1818	Carver	grdn	7537
	Ezra	1818	Carver	admn	7510
	George	1802	Duxbury	grdn	7511
	George	1818	Carver	grdn	7537
	George H	1874	N. Bridgewater	admn	7512
	Hannah	1796	Middleboro	grdn	7526
	Hannah	1827	Kingston	will	7513
	Jabez	1736	Plymouth	grdn	7514
	James	1782	Halifax	admn	7515
	James V	1871	Carver	admn	7516
	Jane	1818	Plymouth	grdn	7517
	John	1751	Kingston	will	7523
	John	1769	Kingston	will	7524
	John	1787	Duxbury	admn	7519
	John	1787	Kingston	grdn	7525
	John	1796	Middleboro	grdn	7526
	John	1815	Kingston	admn	7522
	John	1829	Kingston	will	7521
	John	1834	Plymouth	admn	7518
	John	1874	Kingston	admn	7520
	Joseph	1724	Plymouth	will	7527

SURNAME	FIRST NAME	YEAR	PLACE	CASE	DOCKET
FAUNCE	Joseph	1761	Middleboro	admn	7528
	Joseph	1795	Middleboro	admn	7529
	Joseph	1823	Middleboro	will	7530
	Kilborn	1871	Kingston	admn	7531
	Lucy	1782	Halifax	grdn	7554
	Lydia	1742	Kingston	admn	7532
	Lydia	1749	Plymouth	admn	7533
	Lydia	1749	Plymouth	grdn	7543
	Martha E	1839	Plymouth	grdn	7545
	Martin	1879	Kingston	admn	7534
	Mary	1818	Carver	grdn	7537
	Mary	1872	Carver	admn	7535
	Mary A	1872	Carver	admn	7536
	Molly	1787	Kingston	grdn	7525
	N Arthur	1874	Abington	admn	7538
	Nathaniel	1818	Plymouth	grdn	7517
	Nathaniel	1839	Plymouth	grdn	7545
	Nathaniel	1866	Kingston	admn	7540
	Nathaniel B	1839	Plymouth	admn	7539
	Olive	1877	Plymouth	admn	7541
	Peleg	1749	Plymouth	grdn	7543
	Peleg	1878	Plymouth	admn	7542
	Rebecca	1862	Plymouth	will	7544
	Rebecca J	1839	Plymouth	grdn	7545
	Sarah	1736	Plymouth	admn	7546
	Sarah	1849	Kingston	will	7547
	Sarah	1874	Kingston	admn	7548
	Stephen	1787	Kingston	grdn	7525
	Thaddeus	1809	Plymouth	admn	7549
	Thomas	1745	Plymouth	will	7550
	Thomas	1747	Plymouth	admn	7551
	Thomas	1761	Plympton	grdn	7552
	Tilden	1787	Kingston	grdn	7525
	Tilden	1855	Kingston	admn	7553
	William	1782	Halifax	grdn	7554
	Zenas	1854	Duxbury	admn	7555
FAXON	Alathea	1853	Abington	grdn	7561
	Alfred	1853	Abington	grdn	7561
	Eliashib	1761	Pembroke	admn	7556
	Elijah	1763	Pembroke	will	7557
	Elisha	1777	Halifax	admn	7558
	Elisha	1842	Abington	admn	7559
	George L	1851	E. Bridgewater	grdn	7560
	Maria	1853	Abington	grdn	7561
	Micah	1858	N. Bridgewater	will	7562
	Rectina	1873	N. Bridgewater	will	7563
	Susanna	1777	Halifax	grdn	7564
	William	1853	Abington	grdn	7561
FEARING	Abel	1852	Hingham	will	7565
	Abigail	1761	Wareham	grdn	7566
	Albert	1875	Hingham	will	7567
	Anna	1879	Hingham	will	7568
	Annes	1837	Hingham	will	7569
	Aurelia	1875	Hingham	grdn	7570
	Benjamin	1774	Wareham	will	7571
	Benjamin	1824	Wareham	grdn	7577
	Benjamin	1830	Wareham	will	7572
	Benjamin	1866	Wareham	admn	7573
	Betsey	1848	Hingham	will	7574
	Betsey	1864	Hingham	will	7575
	Caroline	1824	Wareham	grdn	7577
	Caroline	1834	Wareham	admn	7576
	Charles	1880	Hingham	admn	7578
	Chloe	1864	Hingham	will	7579
	Cushing	1833	Boston	peti	7613
	David	1760	Wareham	admn	7580
	David	1820	Wareham	admn	7581
	David	1824	Wareham	grdn	7577
	David	1876	Hingham	admn	7582
	Deborah	1818	Hingham	admn	7583
	Edwin	1861	Hingham	admn	7584

SURNAME	FIRST NAME	YEAR	PLACE	CASE	DOCKET
FEARING	Elijah	1812	Hingham	will	7585
	Elizabeth	1834	Wareham	grdn	7586
	Ezekiel	1865	Hingham	will	7587
	George B	1824	Bridgewater	grdn	7588
	Hawkes	1826	Hingham	will	7589
	Hawkes	1863	Hingham	admn	7590
	Henry	1868	Hingham	admn	7591
	Hepsibah	1861	Wareham	admn	7592
	Israel	1754	Wareham	will	7596
	Israel	1757	Wareham	grdn	7597
	Israel	1761	Wareham	grdn	7566
	Israel	1826	Wareham	will	7594
	Israel G	1856	Bridgewater	will	7593
	Israel Jr	1753	Wareham	admn	7595
	Jerome	1837	Hingham	will	7598
	Joanna G	1878	Wareham	will	7599
	John	1788	Wareham	will	7602
	John	1836	Hingham	will	7600
	John	1853	Wareham	will	7604
	John	1872	Hingham	will	7601
	John Jr	1823	Wareham	admn	7603
	Judith	1869	Hingham	will	7606
	Judith W	1866	Hingham	admn	7605
	Leah	1844	Hingham	admn	7607
	Lydia	1847	Hingham	will	7608
	Maria B	1841	Hingham	grdn	7609
	Marilla	1824	Wareham	grdn	7577
	Martha S	1879	Hingham	will	7610
	Martin	1868	Hingham	will	7611
	Mary	1832	Hingham	grdn	7612 a
	Matilda D	1833	Boston	peti	7613
	Mercy	1871	Hingham	will	7614
	Morris	1875	Hingham	admn	7615
	Moses	1827	Wareham	admn	7616
	Noah	1824	Bridgewater	will	7617
	Samuel	1837	Hingham	grdn	7618 a
	Samuel	1841	Hingham	admn	7619
	Sarah	1757	Wareham	grdn	7597
	Shubael	1812	Hingham	grdn	7620 a
	Tamar	1832	Hingham	will	7621
	Thomas	1820	Hingham	will	7622
	Thomas	1824	Bridgewater	grdn	7588
	Thomas	1827	Hingham	admn	7623
	Thomas	1832	Hingham	grdn	7624
	William	1832	Hingham	grdn	7624
	William S	1862	Wareham	will	7625
FEARO	John	1846	Kingston	will	7626
FEE	John	1880	Hingham	will	7627
	Michael	1863	Hingham	admn	7628
FEELEY	Daniel	1870	N. Bridgewater	admn	7629
FELIX	Israel	1793	Middleboro	admn	7630 i
FELLOWS	Lewis	1881	Brockton	will	7631
FELT	Desire H	1873	Greenwood ME	admn	7632
FELTON	Mary	1838	Hingham	admn	7633
	Mary W	1867	Abington	will	7634
FERGUSON	George H	1868	Bridgewater	grdn	7635
	Mary	1865	Bridgewater	admn	7636
FERNOLD	Benjamin W	1864	Abington	admn	7637
FERRY	Robert	1845	Hull	admn	7638
FESSENDEN	John	1852	Carver	admn	7639
FIELD	Abigail	1750	Bridgewater	will	7640
	Abigail	1755	Bridgewater	grdn	7660
	Amasa	1864	W. Bridgewater	admn	7641
	Barzillai	1839	N. Bridgewater	will	7642
	Bethuel	1849	N. Bridgewater	will	7643
	Chloe	1878	W. Bridgewater	grdn	7644
	Daniel	1746	Bridgewater	will	7645
	Daniel	1757	Bridgewater	will	7646
	Daniel	1834	N. Bridgewater	peti	7648
	Daniel	1836	N. Bridgewater	will	7647
	Eliza J	1863	E. Bridgewater	admn	7649

SURNAME	FIRST NAME	YEAR	PLACE	CASE	DOCKET
FIELD	Elizabeth	1881	S. Abington	admn	7650
	Fobes	1826	N. Bridgewater	will	7651
	George	1834	N. Bridgewater	peti	7648
	Hannah	1699	Bridgewater	grdn	7659
	Henry G	1879	E. Bridgewater	grdn	7652
	Jabez	1731	Bridgewater	grdn	7667
	Jabez	1805	Bridgewater	will	7653
	Jabez	1809	Bridgewater	grdn	7664
	Jabez	1868	N. Bridgewater	admn	7654
	Job	1748	Bridgewater	will	7655
	John	1697/8	Bridgewater	admn	7656
	John	1699	Bridgewater	grdn	7659
	John	1755	Bridgewater	grdn	7660
	John	1866	N. Bridgewater	will	7658
	John Jr	1729	Bridgewater	admn	7657
	Joseph	1754	Bridgewater	will	7661
	Lucy Ann	1866	E. Bridgewater	adop	7662
	Marshall	1842	N. Bridgewater	admn	7663
	Mercy	1731	Bridgewater	grdn	7667
	Ozias	1809	Bridgewater	grdn	7664
	Richard	1725	Bridgewater	admn	7665
	Richard	1731	Bridgewater	grdn	7667
	Richard	1734	Bridgewater	admn	7666
	Ruth	1699	Bridgewater	grdn	7659
	Ruth	1731	Bridgewater	grdn	7667
	Sally	1878	Brockton	admn	7668
	Serena	1809	Bridgewater	grdn	7664
	Silas E	1881	Halifax	admn	7669
	Susanna	1731	Bridgewater	grdn	7667
	Waldo	1826	N. Bridgewater	admn	7670
	William	1808	Bridgewater	admn	7671
	William G	1879	E. Bridgewater	admn	7672
	Zabia	1731	Bridgewater	grdn	7667
	Zilpha	1809	Bridgewater	grdn	7664
FILLMORE	Lydia	1839	Hanover	admn	7673
	Spiller	1820	Hanover	will	7674
FINNEGAN	John	1873	N. Bridgewater	grdn	7675
	Patrick	1867	N. Bridgewater	admn	7676
FINNEY	Abigail	1756	-----	grdn	7677
	Amanda	1851	Plymouth	grdn	7678
	Angeline	1826	Plymouth	grdn	7718
	Anna D	1868	Plymouth	grdn	7682
	Betsey	1837	Plymouth	grdn	7683
	Betsey	1868	Plymouth	admn	7679
	Betsey	1868	Plymouth	will	7680
	Caleb	1846	Plymouth	admn	7681
	Charles L	1868	Plymouth	grdn	7682
	Clark	1837	Plymouth	grdn	7683
	Cornelia	1850	Plymouth	grdn	7685
	Ebenezer	1745	(Middleboro	admn	7684
	Edna	1850	Plymouth	grdn	7685
	Eliza	1811	Plymouth	grdn	7722
	Elizabeth	1738	Middleboro	grdn	7686
	Elizabeth	1795	Plymouth	will	7687
	Elizabeth A	1843	Plymouth	grdn	7688
	Elkanah	1837	Plymouth	admn	7689
	Elkanah C	1873	Plymouth	will	7690
	Emily Y	1832	Middleboro	grdn	7735
	Ephraim	1862	Plymouth	will	7691
	Eveline	1873	Abington	grdn	7694
	Ezra	1811	Plymouth	grdn	7722
	Ezra	1860	Plymouth	grdn	7692 a
	Ezra	1861	Plymouth	will	7693
	George	1873	Abington	grdn	7694
	Harriet C	1844	Plymouth	will	7695
	Harrison	1826	Plymouth	grdn	7718
	Harrison	1878	Plymouth	admn	7696
	Henry	1867	Plymouth	admn	7697
	Ichabod	1750	Barnstable	grdn	7698
	James	1841	Middleboro	admn	7699
	Jane	1745	Middleboro	admn	7700

SURNAME	FIRST NAME	YEAR	PLACE	CASE	DOCKET
FINNEY	Jane	1756	-----	grdn	7677
	John	1785	Middleboro	admn	7702
	John	1787	Kingston	will	7701
	Jonathan	1738	Middleboro	will	7703
	Jonathan	1739	Middleboro	admn	7704
	Jonathan	1822	Middleboro	admn	7705
	Joseph	1726	Plympton	will	7707
	Joseph	1726	Plympton	grdn	7708
	Joseph	1876	Plymouth	admn	7706
	Joshua	1726	Plymouth	grdn	7709
	Joshua	1739	Middleboro	grdn	7738
	Joshua	1745	Plymouth	admn	7710
	Joshua	1829	Middleboro	admn	7711
	Josiah	1726	Plymouth	will	7713
	Josiah	1814	Plymouth	admn	7714
	Josiah	1841	Plymouth	admn	7715
	Josiah T	1827	Carver	grdn	7712
	Lewis	1822	Plymouth	admn	7717
	Lewis	1826	Plymouth	grdn	7718
	Lewis	1849	Plymouth	admn	7716
	Lewis	1850	Plymouth	grdn	7685
	Lucinda	1872	Lakeville	will	7719
	Lucy	1868	Plymouth	admn	7720
	Lucy	1873	Abington	grdn	7694
	Lydia	1811	Plymouth	grdn	7722
	Lydia	1855	Lakeville	will	7721
	Mary	1857	Plymouth	admn	7723
	Mercy	1726	Plympton	grdn	7708
	Nancy D	1845	Plymouth	grdn	7724
	Nelson	1745	Middleboro	grdn	7725
	Nelson	1781	Middleboro	admn	7726
	Palatiah	1726	Plympton	grdn	7708
	Patience	1726	Plympton	grdn	7708
	Pelham	1826	Plymouth	grdn	7718
	Pelham	1868	Plymouth	admn	7727
	Pella F	1873	Plymouth	admn	7728
	Phebe	1851	Plymouth	grdn	7729 a
	Phebe	1852	Plymouth	admn	7730
	Robert	1690	Plymouth	will	7731
	Robert	1712	Plymouth	admn	7732
	Robert	1864	Plymouth	will	7733
	Solomon B	1832	Middleboro	grdn	7735
	Solomon B	1879	Middleboro	will	7734
	Susan	1872	Plymouth	will	7736
	Thomas	1796	Plymouth	grdn	7737
	Timothy	1739	Middleboro	grdn	7738
FISH	Abigail	1739	Kingston	grdn	7773
	Absalom	1811	Kingston	grdn	7739
	Adam	1815	Duxbury	admn	7740
	Amy W	1864	Duxbury	grdn	7741
	Andrew W	1863	Hanson	admn	7742
	Caleb	1825	Pembroke	admn	7743
	Charles	1793	Scituate	admn	7744
	Charles	1817	Kingston	will	7745
	Charles	1825	Kingston	admn	7746
	Christina	1825	Pembroke	grdn	7747
	Daniel C	1856	Hanson	admn	7748
	Deborah	1815	Duxbury	grdn	7749
	Deborah	1852	Hanson	will	7750
	Eben	1862	Duxbury	admn	7751
	Elizabeth H	1835	Kingston	grdn	7752
	Elnathan	1738	Kingston	admn	7753
	Harriet	1872	Marshfield	admn	7754
	Isaac L	1873	Bridgewater	will	7755
	Jacob	1811	Pembroke	admn	7756
	Joanna	1880	S. Abington	will	7757
	Job	1868	Pembroke	will	7758
	John	1739	Kingston	grdn	7773
	John	1857	Pembroke	will	7759
	Jonathan	1792	Scituate	admn	7760
	Lucinda	1825	Pembroke	grdn	7747

SURNAME	FIRST NAME	YEAR	PLACE	CASE	DOCKET
FISH	Lydia	1739	Kingston	grdn	7773
	Lydia	1837	Marshfield	will	7761
	Mary	1813	Kingston	admn	7762
	Mary C	1825	Pembroke	grdn	7747
	Melzar W	1864	Duxbury	grdn	7741
	Nathaniel	1809	Kingston	admn	7763
	Nathaniel	1811	Kingston	grdn	7739
	Reuben	1875	Mattapoisett	admn	7764
	Samuel	1817	Duxbury	admn	7765
	Sarah	1739	Kingston	grdn	7773
	Susan W	1876	Brockton	admn	7766
	Thomas	1736	Duxbury	admn	7767
	Thomas	1828	Pembroke	will	7768
	Ursula	1850	Pembroke	will	7769
	Zacheus	1739	Kingston	grdn	7773
	Zacheus	1777	Pembroke	will	7770
	Zacheus	1807	Pembroke	admn	7771
	Zacheus	1836	Marshfield	admn	7772
FISHER	Cynthia	1869	N. Bridgewater	admn	7774
	John	1864	Plymouth	admn	7775
	Mary	1702	Scituate	will	7776
	Timothy W	1881	W. Bridgewater	grdn	7777 a
FISHLEY	Harriet A	1844	Marshfield	grdn	7778
	William H	1844	Marshfield	grdn	7778
FISKE	Robert T P	1866	Hingham	admn	7779
FITTZ	Hervey	1878	Middleboro	will	7780
FITZGERALD	Ellen	1864	N. Bridgewater	grdn	7781
	Louisa	1864	N. Bridgewater	grdn	7781
	Margaret	1763	Hanover	will	7782
	Mary	1864	N. Bridgewater	grdn	7781
	Richard	1746	Hanover	will	7783
FITZPATRICK	Anthony	1857	Kingston	admn	7784
	Bridget	1872	Middleboro	will	7785
	Darbey	1751	Marshfield	admn	7786
	Edmund	1757	Marshfield	grdn	7787
	Elinor	1757	Marshfield	grdn	7787
	James	1857	N. Bridgewater	grdn	7788
	Joanna	1764	-----	decr	7789
	John	1757	Marshfield	grdn	7787
	Lidia	1757	Marshfield	grdn	7787
	Mary Ann	1857	N. Bridgewater	grdn	7788
FLAGG	George N	1869	W. Bridgewater	admn	7790
FLANAGAN	Anna	1875	Abington	grdn	7792
	Charles	1875	Abington	grdn	7792
	George	1875	Abington	grdn	7792
	John	1873	Abington	admn	7791
	Peter	1875	Abington	grdn	7792
	Thomas	1875	Abington	grdn	7792
	William	1875	Abington	grdn	7792
FLANIGAN	Frederick	1863	N. Bridgewater	grdn	7793
	Lawrence	1863	N. Bridgewater	grdn	7793
	Mary	1863	N. Bridgewater	grdn	7793
	Thomas J	1863	N. Bridgewater	grdn	7793
	William	1863	N. Bridgewater	admn	7794
FLANNERY	Thomas	1873	Wareham	admn	7795
FLEMMING	John B	1876	Kingston	grdn	7796
	Morris	1875	Duxbury	admn	7797
FLETCHER	Arthur B	1876	Hingham	grdn	7799
	Charles H	1876	Hingham	admn	7798
	Grace C	1876	Hingham	grdn	7799
	John	1723	Harwich	grdn	7800
FLING	Eliza	1877	Hingham	admn	7801
FLOURE	Lydia	1736	Plympton	grdn	7802
FLOYD	Francis	1746	Plymouth	admn	7803
FLYNN	Mary E	1880	Plymouth	grdn	7804
FOBES	Alanson	1852	E. Bridgewater	admn	7805
	Albert	1813	Bridgewater	grdn	7835
	Alpheus	1839	Bridgewater	will	7806
	Amelia W	1879	Bridgewater	will	7807
	Andrew J	1863	Bridgewater	admn	7808
	Aretas	1873	Bridgewater	admn	7809

SURNAME	FIRST NAME	YEAR	PLACE	CASE	DOCKET
FOBES	Avery	1845	Bridgewater	will	7810
	Avery	1879	W. Bridgewater	admn	7811
	Caleb	1833	Bridgewater	admn	7812
	Caroline	1806	Bridgewater	grdn	7845
	Charles	1862	Plymouth	grdn	7814
	Charles F	1880	Carver	admn	7813
	Dwelley	1813	Bridgewater	grdn	7835
	Edmund	1862	Plymouth	grdn	7814
	Edward	1736	Bridgewater	will	7815
	Eliab	1779	Bridgewater	admn	7816
	Eliab	1781	Bridgewater	grdn	7822
	Eliab	1806	Bridgewater	grdn	7845
	Elijah	1781	Bridgewater	grdn	7822
	Ellen Amelia	1836	Hanover	adop	7817
	Emma	1862	Plymouth	grdn	7814
	Ephraim	1755	Bridgewater	will	7818
	Ezra	1823	Bridgewater	will	7819
	Franklin	1874	N. Bridgewater	will	7820
	Freelove	1811	Bridgewater	will	7821
	Hannah	1781	Bridgewater	grdn	7822
	Isaac	1855	Bridgewater	will	7823
	Jason	1809	Bridgewater	admn	7824
	Jason	1833	Bridgewater	grdn	7836
	John	1725	Bridgewater	admn	7825
	John	1728	Bridgewater	grdn	7844
	John	1783	Bridgewater	will	7826
	Joseph P	1784	Greenwich NH	grdn	7827
	Joshua	1767	Bridgewater	admn	7828
	Joshua	1787	Bridgewater	will	7829
	Joshua	1827	Bridgewater	admn	7830
	Josiah	1728	Bridgewater	grdn	7844
	Josiah	1794	Bridgewater	will	7831
	Laban	1806	Bridgewater	grdn	7845
	Lois	1872	Bridgewater	will	7832
	Lucy	1806	Bridgewater	grdn	7845
	Lurana	1859	Bridgewater	admn	7833
	Martha	1795	Bridgewater	will	7834
	Mary	1813	Bridgewater	grdn	7835
	Mary	1833	Bridgewater	grdn	7836
	Mary	1862	Plymouth	grdn	7814
	Molly	1842	Bridgewater	admn	7837
	Nathan	1814	Plympton	admn	7838
	Olive M	1874	Bridgewater	will	7839
	Polly	1806	Bridgewater	grdn	7845
	Rhoda	1813	Bridgewater	grdn	7835
	Robert	1836	Bridgewater	admn	7840
	Ruel	1857	Bridgewater	will	7841
	Salmon	1832	Bridgewater	admn	7842
	Sarah	1728	Bridgewater	grdn	7844
	Sarah	1833	Bridgewater	grdn	7836
	Sarah R	1867	Bridgewater	admn	7843
	Silence	1728	Bridgewater	grdn	7844
	Solomon	1806	Bridgewater	grdn	7845
	Stella	1806	Bridgewater	grdn	7845
	Susan	1781	Bridgewater	grdn	7822
	Thomas	1781	Bridgewater	grdn	7822
	Timothy	1803	Bridgewater	will	7846
	Timothy	1855	Bridgewater	will	7847
	William	1764	Bridgewater	will	7848
	William	1797	Bridgewater	will	7849
	William	1812	Bridgewater	admn	7850
	Zephaniah	1846	Bridgewater	admn	7851
FOGG	Betsey	1876	S. Scituate	will	7852
	Ebenezer T	1861	S. Scituate	will	7853
	Jonathan	1879	Brockton	admn	7854
FOLEY	Alice	1878	Rockland	grdn	7855
	Ann	1870	N. Bridgewater	grdn	7858
	Ann	1878	Rockland	grdn	7855
	Ellen	1870	N. Bridgewater	will	7856
	Ellen	1878	Rockland	grdn	7855
	Hannah	1880	E. Bridgewater	admn	7857

SURNAME	FIRST NAME	YEAR	PLACE	CASE	DOCKET
FOLEY	Hugh	1870	N. Bridgewater	grdn	7858
	James	1870	N. Bridgewater	grdn	7858
	Margaret	1878	Rockland	grdn	7855
	Mary	1878	Rockland	grdn	7855
	Thomas	1870	N. Bridgewater	grdn	7858
	William	1878	Rockland	grdn	7855
FOLSOM	Eunice M	1864	W. Bridgewater	grdn	7859
	Frederick	1864	W. Bridgewater	grdn	7859
	Henry M	1864	W. Bridgewater	admn	7860
	Seneca	1877	W. Bridgewater	will	7861
FORD	Adam	1805	Pembroke	admn	7862
	Adam	1806	Pembroke	admn	7863
	Albert J	1841	Pembroke	grdn	7864
	Almira R	1871	Marshfield	will	7865
	Amos	1789	Duxbury	admn	7866
	Andrew	1725	Abington	will	7867
	Andrew	1750	Abington	will	7868
	Anna	1873	Bridgewater	will	7870
	Anna D	1872	Duxbury	will	7869
	Arunah T	1869	E. Bridgewater	admn	7871
	Asa	1833	N. Bridgewater	admn	7872
	Aseneth	1861	Duxbury	will	7873
	Barnabas	1773	Pembroke	will	7875
	Barnabas	1785	Pembroke	admn	7874
	Briggs	1873	Pembroke	admn	7876
	Briggs	1874	Pembroke	grdn	7957
	Chandler	1799	Marshfield	grdn	7882
	Chandler	1850	Marshfield	will	7877
	Charles H	1865	Pembroke	grdn	7880
	Charles Jr	1859	S. Scituate	admn	7879
	Charles R	1881	Brockton	admn	7878
	Consider	1799	Marshfield	grdn	7882
	Consider	1840	Marshfield	admn	7881
	Cora	1863	Abington	grdn	7906
	Daniel	1872	Scituate	will	7885
	Daniel A	1839	Abington	grdn	7883 a
	Daniel A	1868	Abington	will	7884
	David	1850	N. Bridgewater	admn	7886
	David F	1841	N. Bridgewater	grdn	7909
	Deborah L	1812	Marshfield	grdn	7887
	Edward T	1881	Brockton	grdn	7888
	Elijah	1792	Marshfield	will	7889
	Elijah	1844	Marshfield	grdn	7890 a
	Elijah	1845	Marshfield	will	7891
	Elijah T	1856	Duxbury	will	7892
	Elijah T	1858	Duxbury	name	7893
	Elisha	1758	Marshfield	will	7895
	Elisha	1803	Marshfield	will	7894
	Elisha	1811	Marshfield	admn	7896
	Eliza	1864	Duxbury	will	7897
	Elizabeth	1812	Marshfield	grdn	7887
	Elizabeth	1841	Duxbury	admn	7898
	Emily	1874	Pembroke	grdn	7957
	Ephraim	1834	Marshfield	admn	7899
	Erasmus H	1843	Hingham	grdn	7900
	Erasmus H	1852	Hingham	will	7901
	Ezra J	1877	Brockton	will	7902
	Francis	1799	Marshfield	grdn	7882
	Francis	1863	Abington	grdn	7906
	Francis A	1837	Hingham	admn	7903
	Francis G	1843	Hingham	will	7904
	Frank B	1865	Pembroke	grdn	7880
	George H	1863	Pembroke	admn	7905
	Georgianna	1863	Abington	grdn	7906
	Hannah	1785	Pembroke	admn	7907
	Harriet E	1865	Duxbury	grdn	7908
	Henry A	1841	N. Bridgewater	grdn	7909
	Hezekiah	1722	Abington	will	7910
	Hezekiah	1723	Abington	grdn	7911
	Hiram L	1850	Marshfield	grdn	7912
	Isaac et al	1773	Marshfield	peti	7913

SURNAME	FIRST NAME	YEAR	PLACE	CASE	DOCKET
FORD	James	1735	Marshfield	will	7914
	James	1796	Abington	grdn	7915
	James	1812	Marshfield	grdn	7887
	James	1855	Abington	admn	7916
	James	1866	Pembroke	admn	7918
	James	1879	Pembroke	admn	7919
	James T	1852	Duxbury	will	7917
	Jane	1812	Marshfield	grdn	7887
	Jennie	1881	Brockton	grdn	7888
	John	1693	Marshfield	admn	7925
	John	1738	Hanover	admn	7920
	John	1776	Pembroke	will	7921
	John	1792	Abington	admn	7923
	John	1880	Rockland	will	7924
	John	1880	Marshfield	grdn	7926 a
	John	1881	Marshfield	admn	7927
	John Jr	1793	Pembroke	will	7922
	Joseph	1749	Pembroke	admn	7928
	Joseph	1848	Abington	admn	7929
	Joshua H	1877	Duxbury	admn	7930
	Lemuel	1812	Marshfield	will	7931
	Lilless	1782	Duxbury	grdn	7975
	Lot	1821	Pembroke	will	7932
	Lucy B	1862	Marshfield	grdn	7933 a
	Lucy B	1863	Marshfield	admn	7934
	Lydia	1874	Pembroke	admn	7936
	Lydia T	1867	Duxbury	admn	7935
	Lydia T	1878	Abington	admn	7937
	Martin	1872	Pembroke	will	7938
	Mary	1861	Abington	admn	7941
	Mary C	1856	Pembroke	will	7940
	Mary N S	1840	Marshfield	grdn	7942
	Mary N S	1848	Pembroke	admn	7939
	Mercy	1853	E. Bridgewater	will	7943
	Michael	1729	Marshfield	will	7944
	Michael	1764	Marshfield	will	7955
	Michael	1807	Scituate	admn	7946
	Michael	1878	S. Scituate	will	7947
	Nathan	1860	Duxbury	admn	7948
	Nathan W	1861	Duxbury	grdn	7949
	Nathaniel	1749	Marshfield	grdn	7950
	Nathaniel	1812	Marshfield	grdn	7887
	Nathaniel	1859	Pembroke	grdn	7951 a
	Nathaniel	1862	Pembroke	will	7952
	Noah	1817	Abington	admn	7953
	Noah	1878	Brockton	will	7955
	Noah P	1865	Abington	admn	7954
	Obadiah	1782	Pembroke	admn	7956
	Pamelia	1874	Pembroke	grdn	7957
	Peleg	1769	Marshfield	will	7958
	Peleg	1799	Marshfield	grdn	7882
	Peleg	1799	Marshfield	admn	7959
	Peleg	1812	Marshfield	grdn	7887
	Peleg	1814	Scituate	will	7960
	Peleg	1876	Duxbury	will	7962
	Peleg B	1878	Rockland	admn	7961
	Phebe	1863	Pembroke	will	7963
	Priscilla	1812	Marshfield	grdn	7887
	Priscilla B	1857	Pembroke	will	7964
	Rebecca	1799	Marshfield	grdn	7882
	Rebecca	1875	Marshfield	admn	7965
	Rhoda	1869	S. Scituate	will	7966
	Rosella	1812	Marshfield	grdn	7887
	Ruth	1723	Abington	grdn	7911
	Ruth	1799	Marshfield	grdn	7882
	Samuel	1781	Marshfield	will	7967
	Samuel	1809	Marshfield	will	7968
	Samuel	1838	N. Bridgewater	admn	7971
	Samuel	1849	Marshfield	admn	7969
	Samuel	1875	Marshfield	will	7970
	Sarah	1750	Marshfield	will	7973

SURNAME	FIRST NAME	YEAR	PLACE	CASE	DOCKET
FORD	Sarah	1782	Duxbury	admn	7974
	Sarah	1782	Duxbury	grdn	7975
	Sarah	1871	S. Scituate	will	7972
	Seth	1807	Marshfield	admn	7976
	Solomon	1877	Abington	admn	7977
	Sophronia	1877	Scituate	admn	7978
	Susanner B	1879	Hingham	will	7979
	Thomas	1765	Marshfield	grdn	7980 a
	Thomas	1788	Marshfield	will	7981
	Thomas	1829	Marshfield	admn	7982
	Thomas P	1840	Marshfield	grdn	7942
	Waterman	1826	Marshfield	will	7983
	William	1721	Marshfield	will	7984
	William	1761	Marshfield	admn	7985
	William	1787	Marshfield	admn	7986
	William	1845	Pembroke	will	7989
	William	1861	Marshfield	admn	7987
	William Jr	1830	Pembroke	grdn	7988 a
FORREST	Asa	1806	Halifax	admn	7990
FORSBERG	Clement W	1881	Brockton	admn	7991
FOSS	Edward	1874	N. Bridgewater	grdn	7992
	Eli	1874	N. Bridgewater	grdn	7992
	Eunice	1874	N. Bridgewater	grdn	7992
	Nelson J	1873	N. Bridgewater	will	7993
	S Nellie	1875	Brockton	admn	7994
	Walter	1874	N. Bridgewater	grdn	7992
FOSTER	Abigail	1848	Scituate	admn	7995
	Alexander B	1869	Kingston	will	7997
	Alexander G	1825	Kingston	grdn	7996
	Anna M	1854	New York	grdn	7998
	Asenath P	1881	Kingston	grdn	7999 a
	Augusta C	1879	S. Scituate	will	8000
	Benjamin	1757	Pembroke	admn	8001
	Betsey	1876	S. Scituate	will	8002
	Betsey S	1880	Kingston	admn	8003
	Catherine	1881	Lakeville	will	8004
	Charles	1805	Kingston	will	8005
	Charles Jr	1813	Kingston	grdn	8006
	Charles Jr	1821	Kingston	admn	8007
	Daniel	1807	Pembroke	will	8008
	David	1739	Scituate	admn	8009
	David	1806	Pembroke	admn	8010
	David H	1880	Pembroke	will	8011
	Deborah	1732	Marshfield	will	8012
	Eleanor	1837	Rochester	grdn	8013
	Elisha	1771	Scituate	admn	8014
	Elisha	1827	Scituate	will	8015
	Elisha	1852	S. Scituate	admn	8016
	Elizabeth	1802	Pembroke	will	8017
	Emily A	1876	Marshfield	grdn	8018
	Emma F	1870	Hingham	peti	8019
	Freeman	1863	S. Scituate	will	8020
	Grace	1836	Scituate	admn	8021
	Hatherly	1751	Scituate	will	8022
	Hector	1862	Abington	admn	8023
	Hester A	1837	Rochester	grdn	8013
	Horatio	1862	Hanson	will	8024
	Isaiah D	1813	Rochester	admn	8025
	James	1878	Kingston	will	8028
	James C	1854	Brooklyn	will	8027
	James Jr	1811	Rochester	admn	8026
	Joanna	1872	Kingston	will	8029
	John	1738	Scituate	admn	8032
	John	1741	Plymouth	will	8030
	John	1760	Kingston	admn	8031
	John	1816	Scituate	will	8033
	John B	1836	Pembroke	admn	8034
	Joseph	1735	Plymouth	grdn	8075
	Joseph	1826	Kingston	admn	8035
	Joseph H	1827	Hingham	grdn	8036
	Josiah	1757	Pembroke	admn	8037

SURNAME	FIRST NAME	YEAR	PLACE	CASE	DOCKET
FOSTER	Josiah	1780	Pembroke	will	8038
	Josiah D	1812	Rochester	admn	8039
	Lydia	1795	Kingston	will	8040
	Lydia	1846	Kingston	admn	8041
	Marion	1873	Hingham	grdn	8071
	Mary	1735	Plymouth	grdn	8075
	Mary	1772	Scituate	grdn	8055
	Mary	1781	Plymouth	will	8042
	Mary	1816	Scituate	grdn	8043 a
	Mary	1819	Scituate	admn	8044
	Mary	1879	Lakeville	will	8046
	Mary A M	1832	N. Bridgewater	grdn	8047
	Mary J	1866	Hanson	grdn	8045
	Melzar A	1838	Kingston	admn	8048
	Mercy	1796	Plymouth	will	8049
	Micah	1829	Pembroke	admn	8050
	Nathaniel	1793	Middleboro	will	8051
	Nathaniel	1848	Kingston	will	8052
	Olive P	1832	N. Bridgewater	grdn	8047
	Robert	1791	Kingston	admn	8053
	Robert	1811	Kingston	admn	8054
	Ruth	1772	Scituate	grdn	8055
	Samuel	1778	Kingston	admn	8056
	Samuel	1859	S. Scituate	will	8057
	Sarah	1731	Marshfield	will	8058
	Sarah	1830	Scituate	grdn	8059 a
	Sarah	1832	Scituate	will	8060
	Sarah	1865	S. Scituate	admn	8061
	Seth	1827	Scituate	will	8062
	Seth	1848	Hanson	will	8063
	Susanna	1837	Rochester	grdn	8013
	Temperance F	1863	S. Scituate	grdn	8064 a
	Thomas	1758	Marshfield	admn	8065
	Thomas	1778	Plymouth	admn	8066
	Thomas	1796	Plymouth	admn	8067
	Timothy	1854	S. Scituate	will	8068
	Walter	1867	S. Scituate	will	8069
	Walter	1873	Hingham	grdn	8071
	Walter 2nd	1872	S. Scituate	admn	8070
	William	1735	Plymouth	grdn	8075
	William	1736	Plymouth	admn	8074
	William	1873	Hingham	grdn	8071
	William	1877	Hingham	admn	8073
	William A	1861	Kingston	admn	8072
	William G	1876	Marshfield	grdn	8018
FOWLER	John Sumner	1871	Hingham	grdn	8076
FOYE	Esther A	1881	Brockton	admn	8077
FRAHER	Bridget	1874	W. Bridgewater	grdn	8080
	Julia	1874	W. Bridgewater	admn	8078
	Michael	1874	W. Bridgewater	admn	8079
	Michael	1874	W. Bridgewater	grdn	8080
FRANCIS	Anthony	1840	Plymouth	admn	8081
	James	1841	Plymouth	grdn	8082
	John	1841	Plymouth	grdn	8082
	Ruphe	1841	Plymouth	grdn	8082
	Susan	1863	Middleboro	admn	8083
	Sylvester	1841	Plymouth	grdn	8082
FRANK	Antonio	1875	Plymouth	will	8084
FRANKLIN	John	1765	Scituate	admn	8085
FRAWLEY	Henry T	1878	Brockton	grdn	8086
	Patrick	1875	Bridgewater	will	8087
FRAZIER	Henry	1862	Plymouth	admn	8088
	Rebecca	1841	Duxbury	will	8089
	Samuel A	1823	Duxbury	bond	8090
	Samuel A	1838	Duxbury	will	8091
	Thomas	1782	Duxbury	admn	8092
FREDRICKSON	Charles	1845	Hull	admn	8093
FREELOVE	John	1755	Bridgewater	will	8094
	John	1756	Bridgewater	grdn	8095
	Thankful	1756	Bridgewater	grdn	8095
FREEMAN	Abijah	1831	Duxbury	will	8096

SURNAME	FIRST NAME	YEAR	PLACE	CASE	DOCKET
FREEMAN	Andrew	1837	W. Bridgewater	grdn	8097 a
	Andrew	1845	N. Bridgewater	admn	8098
	Asher	1820	Scituate	admn	8099
	Bathsheba	1836	E. Bridgewater	admn	8100
	Benjamin	1769	Middleboro	grdn	8101
	Benjamin	1836	Plymouth	grdn	8131
	Bethiah	1835	E. Bridgewater	grdn	8102
	Daniel	1825	Duxbury	admn	8103
	David H	1880	Duxbury	will	8104
	Deborah	1837	Duxbury	grdn	8105
	Edmund	1766	Rochester	grdn	8106
	Elisha	1846	Middleboro	admn	8107
	Elizabeth	1833	Plymouth	grdn	8108
	Frederick	1833	Plymouth	grdn	8108
	George	1836	Plymouth	grdn	8131
	Hannah	1837	Duxbury	grdn	8105
	Hezekiah	1839	Wareham	admn	8109
	Howard	1841	Scituate	admn	8110
	Isaac	1766	Rochester	will	8111
	James O	1880	Duxbury	admn	8112
	John	1847	Carver	admn	8113
	Jonathan	1748	Halifax	will	8114
	Joseph	1790	Duxbury	will	8115
	Josephus	1835	E. Bridgewater	grdn	8102
	Josiah	1769	Middleboro	will	8116
	Lemuel	1864	S. Scituate	will	8117
	Margaret	1833	Plymouth	grdn	8108
	Martin	1837	Rochester	admn	8118
	Nancy	1837	Duxbury	grdn	8105
	Nancy	1847	Duxbury	will	8119
	Nathaniel	1836	Plymouth	grdn	8131
	Nathaniel	1839	Rochester	admn	8120
	Olivia	1840	Rochester	grdn	8124
	Otis	1833	Plymouth	grdn	8108
	Polly C	1852	Carver	admn	8121
	Rachel L	1854	Wareham	will	8122
	Sarah	1833	Plymouth	grdn	8108
	Seth	1840	Rochester	grdn	8124
	Seth	1861	Mattapoisett	will	8123
	Seth	1879	Mattapoisett	grdn	8125 a
	Sprague	1810	Duxbury	admn	3126
	Sprague	1879	Duxbury	admn	8127
	Susan M	1858	N. Bridgewater	grdn	8128
	Timothy	1855	Wareham	will	8129
	Wallace S	1881	Duxbury	grdn	8130
	Weston	1836	Plymouth	grdn	8131
	William	1858	Duxbury	grdn	8132
	William A	1837	Duxbury	admn	8133
FRENCH	Albert N	1838	Kingston	admn	8134
	Amasa	1803	Bridgewater	admn	8135
	Betsey	1820	Bridgewater	grdn	8160
	Brosard	1870	Hingham	will	8136
	Charles E	1865	Hingham	admn	8137
	Daniel	1809	Bridgewater	grdn	8138
	Daniel	1876	E. Bridgewater	admn	8139
	Dependance	1770	Bridgewater	admn	8140
	Edmund	1858	Hingham	admn	8141
	Frederick	1860	N. Bridgewater	grdn	8146
	George H	1867	Hingham	admn	8142
	Henrietta A	1872	Scituate	admn	8143
	Henry	1860	N. Bridgewater	grdn	8146
	Henry C	1865	Hingham	admn	8144
	Henry V	1859	N. Bridgewater	admn	8145
	Isaac	1796	Bridgewater	grdn	8151
	Isaac K	1839	N. Bridgewater	admn	8147
	John	1710	Marshfield	admn	8148
	Joseph	1876	Rockland	admn	8149
	Lemuel	1796	Bridgewater	grdn	8151
	Lemuel	1850	N. Bridgewater	admn	8150
	Levi	1796	Bridgewater	admn	8152
	Levi	1820	Bridgewater	admn	8153

SURNAME	FIRST NAME	YEAR	PLACE	CASE	DOCKET
FRENCH	Levi	1820	Bridgewater	grdn	8160
	Levi	1875	Hingham	will	8154
	Levi	1876	Brockton	will	8155
	Mary	1741	Abington	grdn	8156
	Mary	1850	N. Bridgewater	grdn	8176
	Mary	1874	N. Bridgewater	will	8157
	Mary F	1876	Rockland	grdn	8158
	Merritt	1820	Bridgewater	grdn	8160
	Merritt	1872	N. Bridgewater	admn	8159
	Molly	1770	Bridgewater	grdn	8161
	Moses C	1840	TuftonboroNH	admn	8162
	Nathaniel	1818	Hingham	admn	8163
	Nathaniel	1854	E. Bridgewater	will	8164
	Persis	1821	Hingham	admn	8165
	Richard	1688	Marshfield	admn	8166
	Robert T	1858	Abington	admn	8167
	Sally	1864	Hingham	admn	8168
	Samuel	1735	Abington	will	8169
	Silvanus Jr	1855	N. Bridgewater	admn	8170
	Sylvanus	1796	Bridgewater	grdn	8151
	Sylvanus	1856	N. Bridgewater	admn	8171
	Theodore	1819	Hingham	grdn	8172
	Theodore	1820	Hingham	admn	8173
	Timothy	1877	Kingston	will	8174
	William	1850	N. Bridgewater	grdn	8176
	William Jr	1849	N. Bridgewater	admn	8175
FROST	Benjamin	1861	Abington	will	8177
	Matilda	1872	Hanover	admn	8178
	Susan E	1854	Abington	adop	8179
FROWLEY	James	1864	Bridgewater	admn	8180
	James	1864	Bridgewater	grdn	8181
FRYE	Anthony	1802	Middleboro	admn	8182
FULGHAM	Charles	1764	Plymouth	grdn	8183
	Joseph	1764	Plymouth	will	8184
	Lurania	1779	Plymouth	admn	8185
FULLER	Abiel	1720	Plympton	admn	8186
	Abigail	1766	Halifax	grdn	8187
	Abigail	1859	Halifax	admn	8188
	Ada	1863	Halifax	grdn	8189
	Alexander	1877	Kingston	will	8191
	Alexander Jr	1869	Kingston	admn	8190
	Allen	1810	Middleboro	grdn	8291
	Amos	1875	Plympton	admn	8192
	Andrew A	1865	Carver	admn	8193
	Annie	1877	Middleboro	grdn	8256
	Barzillai	1850	Hanover	admn	8194
	Benjamin	1836	Halifax	admn	8195
	Benjamin	1839	Kingston	will	8196
	Caroline	1869	Kingston	admn	8198
	Caroline	1877	Kingston	grdn	8217
	Caroline H P	1857	N. Bridgewater	adop	8197
	Charles	1862	Plympton	will	8200
	Charles	1863	Kingston	admn	8199
	Charles	1877	Middleboro	grdn	8256
	Charles A	1872	Plympton	admn	8201
	Charles F	1863	Halifax	grdn	8189
	Charles W	1873	Plympton	grdn	8202
	Charlotte	1877	Middleboro	grdn	8256
	Chipman	1771	Halifax	grdn	8278
	Chipman	1796	Halifax	admn	8203
	Consider	1810	Middleboro	grdn	8291
	Consider	1829	Kingston	will	8204
	Consider	1875	Middleboro	will	8205
	Cyrus	1816	Halifax	admn	8206
	Cyrus	1874	Halifax	peti	8207
	Darius A	1849	Duxbury	admn	8208
	Ebenezer	1712	Middleboro	grdn	8268
	Ebenezer	1772	Kingston	will	8209
	Ebenezer	1786	Halifax	will	8211
	Ebenezer	1844	Halifax	will	8212
	Ebenezer Jr	1770	Halifax	admn	8210

SURNAME	FIRST NAME	YEAR	PLACE	CASE	DOCKET
FULLER	Eliza	1878	Plympton	admn	8214
	Eliza C	1847	Plympton	grdn	8213
	Eliza P	1844	Middleboro	grdn	8215
	Elkanah	1726	Plympton	grdn	8216
	Emily J	1877	Kingston	grdn	8217
	Ephraim	1813	Halifax	admn	8218
	Ephraim	1844	Halifax	admn	8219
	Ephraim	1847	Plympton	admn	8220
	Ephraim	1872	Kingston	will	8221
	Eunice	1771	Halifax	grdn	8278
	Ezra	1771	Kingston	will	8222
	Ezra	1857	Carver	admn	8223
	Freeman	1840	Middleboro	grdn	8251
	Gamaliel	1866	Wareham	admn	8224
	George	1838	Kingston	admn	8225
	Hannah	1814	Halifax	admn	8226
	Hannah	1830	Kingston	grdn	8286
	Hannah	1869	Halifax	admn	8227
	Harvey	1867	Plympton	admn	8228
	Isaac	1695	Middleboro	grdn	8229
	Isaac	1727	Middleboro	admn	8230
	Issachar	1867	Hingham	will	8230 +
	Jabez	1712	Middleboro	admn	8231
	Jabez	1729	Middleboro	admn	8232
	Jabez	1757	Kingston	admn	8233
	Jabez	1813	Kingston	admn	8234
	James	1760	Kingston	admn	8235
	James	1859	Kingston	admn	8236
	James D	1864	Halifax	admn	8237
	James T	1864	Halifax	grdn	8238
	John	1709	Middleboro	admn	8248
	John	1766	Halifax	admn	8244
	John	1778	Kingston	will	8239
	John	1809	Middleboro	admn	8249
	John	1827	Kingston	grdn	8240 a
	John	1828	Kingston	admn	8241
	John	1840	Middleboro	grdn	8251
	John	1857	Halifax	will	8245
	John	1878	Kingston	admn	8243
	John A	1877	Kingston	admn	8242
	John B	1835	Middleboro	admn	8250
	John E	1878	Hingham	will	8246
	John S	1879	Brockton	will	8247
	Jonathan	1802	Middleboro	admn	8252
	Josiah	1820	Kingston	will	8253
	Josiah	1845	Duxbury	admn	8255
	Josiah	1868	Kingston	will	8254
	Julia	1877	Middleboro	grdn	8256
	Laura	1868	Kingston	grdn	8257
	Lois	1712	Middleboro	grdn	8268
	Lois S	1880	Halifax	will	8258
	Lucy	1839	Middleboro	will	8259
	Lucy	1849	Kingston	admn	8260
	Lydia	1748	Plympton	grdn	8263
	Lydia	1771	Halifax	grdn	8278
	Lydia	1803	Middleboro	admn	8261
	Lydia	1812	Halifax	will	8262
	Marcus	1877	Middleboro	admn	8264
	Mary	1712	Middleboro	grdn	8268
	Mary	1857	Middleboro	grdn	8265 a
	Mary E	1844	Middleboro	grdn	8215
	Mary H	1879	Middleboro	will	8266
	Mercy	1712	Middleboro	grdn	8268
	Mercy	1875	Middleboro	admn	8267
	Miranda	1847	Halifax	will	8269
	Nancy	1804	Halifax	grdn	8274
	Nathan	1761	Halifax	will	8271
	Nathan	1804	Halifax	grdn	8274
	Nathan	1832	Kingston	admn	8270
	Nathan	1875	Halifax	will	8272
	Nathan H	1854	Halifax	grdn	8273

SURNAME	FIRST NAME	YEAR	PLACE	CASE	DOCKET
FULLER	Nathaniel	1750	Plympton	will	8275
	Noel B	1857	Carver	grdn	8276
	Philemon	1839	Plympton	admn	8277
	Priscilla	1771	Halifax	grdn	8278
	Priscilla	1804	Halifax	grdn	8274
	Rolinda	1854	Halifax	grdn	8273
	Sally	1813	Kingston	grdn	8292
	Sally	1881	Brockton	admn	8279
	Samuel	1695	Middleboro	admn	8280
	Samuel	1714/5	Middleboro	admn	8281
	Samuel	1728	Plympton	admn	8283
	Samuel	1758	Plympton	admn	8284
	Samuel	1830	Kingston	grdn	8286
	Samuel	1843	Middleboro	admn	8182
	Samuel	1843	Halifax	will	8285
	Sarah	1836	W. Bridgewater	admn	8287
	Sarah	1868	Kingston	grdn	8257
	Sarah T	1846	Halifax	grdn	8288
	Seth	1870	Middleboro	will	8290
	Seth Jr	1756	Plympton	admn	8289
	Silvia	1810	Middleboro	grdn	8291
	Sophia	1813	Kingston	grdn	8292
	Susannah	1783	Pembroke	will	8293
	Sylvanus	1851	Halifax	will	8294
	Sylvanus R	1876	Plymouth	admn	8295
	Theodore S	1865	Plymouth	admn	8296
	Thomas	1811	Halifax	admn	8297
	Thomas	1846	Halifax	admn	8298
	Waldo A	1830	Kingston	grdn	8299
	Waldo A	1872	Kingston	admn	8300
	Warren	1866	Plympton	admn	8301
	Wheelock	1812	Halifax	grdn	8302 a
	William	1748	Plympton	grdn	8263
	William	1791	Middleboro	grdn	8303
	William	1868	Kingston	grdn	8257
	William H	1844	Halifax	grdn	8304
	Zebedee C	1875	Plympton	admn	8305
	Zephaniah	1816	Kingston	admn	8307
	Zephaniah Jr	1807	Kingston	admn	8306
FULLERTON	Annie L	1878	S. Abington	grdn	8308
	Edward	1870	Abington	admn	8309
	Edward S	1871	Abington	grdn	8310
	Henry W	1870	Abington	admn	8311
	Jairus	1859	Abington	admn	8312
	Mary	1848	N. Bridgewater	admn	8313
	Oliver	1849	N. Bridgewater	admn	8314
	Silence D	1876	S. Abington	will	8315
FUNNELL	Mr (absent)	1779	Boston	acct	8316
FURNSIDE	James	1877	Duxbury	admn	8317
	John H	1877	Duxbury	grdn	8318
	William H	1877	Duxbury	grdn	8318
FYFE	John	1874	Hingham	admn	8319
	Sarah	1860	Hingham	will	8320
GALE	Rebecca	1843	Plymouth	will	8321
GALLIGAN	Andrew	1853	Wareham	admn	8322
	Bernard	1861	N. Bridgewater	will	8323
GALLIGHER	John	1878	Bridgewater	admn	8324
GALLON	Sophia	1870	Mattapoisett	admn	8325
GALLT	John	1813	Wareham	will	8326
	John	1861	Wareham	admn	8327
GAMMONS	Ebenezer N	1880	Middleboro	admn	8328
	Edward L	1873	Middleboro	admn	8329
	Emma C	1871	Bridgewater	admn	8330
	Jairus	1846	Middleboro	admn	8331
	John	1822	Middleboro	admn	8332
	John W	1879	Middleboro	grdn	8333 a
	Keziah	1847	Middleboro	admn	8334
	Lena M	1880	Middleboro	grdn	8335
	Lizzie S	1880	Middleboro	grdn	8335
	Louisa	1833	Middleboro	grdn	8336
	Roland E	1879	Middleboro	will	8337

SURNAME	FIRST NAME	YEAR	PLACE	CASE	DOCKET
	Thomas	1859	Middleboro	name	8338
GANNETT	Angelina	1877	S. Abington	admn	8339
	Benjamin	1690/1	Scituate	admn	8340
	Edward	1828	Scituate	grdn	8341
	Elizabeth	1828	Scituate	grdn	8341
	Elkanah	1832	Scituate	will	8342
	Freeman	1877	Scituate	admn	8343
	Hannah	1701	Scituate	will	8344
	John	1780	Scituate	will	8345
	Joseph	1789	Bridgewater	will	8346
	Joseph	1829	E. Bridgewater	admn	8347
	Joseph	1840	E. Bridgewater	admn	8348
	Joseph	1860	Scituate	admn	8349
	Joy K	1860	Scituate	grdn	8350
	Judith	1860	Scituate	admn	8351
	Lucy T	1873	Scituate	grdn	8352 a
	Matthew	1694	Scituate	will	8354
	Matthew	1702	Scituate	admn	8355
	Matthew	1736	Scituate	will	8356
	Matthew	1764	Bridgewater	will	8353
	Matthew	1786	Scituate	will	8357
	Mercy	1849	Scituate	admn	8358
	Robert R	1877	S. Abington	admn	8359
	Samuel	1847	Scituate	will	8360
	Seth	1775	Scituate	admn	8361
	Simeon	1836	E. Bridgewater	will	8362
	Submit	1803	Scituate	will	8363
	Thomas	1811	Plympton	admn	8364
	Thomas	1848	Scituate	admn	8365
	Thomas	1877	S. Abington	admn	8366
GARDNER	Albert	1847	Hingham	grdn	8416
	Alexander	1822	Hingham	admn	8367
	Alfred	1845	Hanover	grdn	8379
	Andrew	1847	Hingham	grdn	8416
	Anthony	1839	Hingham	admn	8368
	Beatrice	1833	E. Bridgewater	admn	8369
	Caleb	1821	Abington	admn	8370
	Calvin	1847	Hingham	admn	8371
	Charles	1839	Hingham	will	8373
	Charles	1874	Hingham	admn	8374
	Charles T	1829	Pembroke	admn	8372
	Cynthia	1879	Rockland	will	8375
	David	1833	Hingham	grdn	8376 a
	Deborah	1860	Hanover	admn	8377
	Deren P	1823	Hingham	grdn	8378
	Ebenezer	1845	Hanover	grdn	8379
	Edgar	1881	Hingham	grdn	8380
	Elijah L	1879	Hingham	will	8381
	Emeline W	1879	Marshfield	will	8382
	Enoch W	1864	Hingham	admn	8383
	Ephraim N	1859	Scituate	admn	8384
	Esther	1845	Hingham	will	8385
	Francis A	1869	Hingham	admn	8387
	Francis L	1865	Plymouth	grdn	8386
	Frank	1874	Waubeck WI	grdn	8388
	Franklin	1870	Hingham	admn	8389
	George	1861	Hanover	grdn	8408
	George D	1864	Hingham	admn	8391
	George L	1854	Hingham	grdn	8392
	George P	1853	Hingham	admn	8390
	Giles	1834	Hingham	admn	8393
	Granville	1865	Plymouth	admn	8394
	Harriet B	1876	Hanover	will	8395
	Helen M	1851	Hingham	grdn	8396
	Henry F	1871	Hingham	grdn	8398
	Henry W	1861	Hanover	will	8397
	Hepsibath	1874	Hingham	admn	8399
	Hiram	1873	Hingham	will	8400
	Hiram	1877	Hanover	will	8401
	Hosea	1840	Hingham	admn	8402
	Hosea J	1857	Hingham	admn	8403

SURNAME	FIRST NAME	YEAR	PLACE	CASE	DOCKET
GARDNER	Isaac	1879	Hingham	admn	8405
	Isaac C	1858	E. Bridgewater	will	8404
	James	1739	Marshfield	will	8406
	James	1814	Hingham	grdn	8423
	James	1860	Hingham	will	8407
	James	1861	Hanover	grdn	8408
	Jeremiah	1822	Hingham	admn	8409
	Jeremiah	1826	Hingham	admn	8410
	Jesse	1851	Hingham	admn	8411
	Joanna	1879	Rockland	will	8412
	Justus W	1866	Hanover	grdn	8413
	Katy	1881	Hingham	grdn	8380
	Leavitt	1814	Hingham	grdn	8423
	Lewis Albert	1873	Marshfield	will	8414
	Lucy	1847	Hingham	grdn	8416
	Lucy	1873	Hingham	will	8415
	Luther T	1880	Duxbury	admn	8417
	Lydia	1814	Hingham	grdn	8423
	Lydia	1854	Hingham	grdn	8392
	Marcus H	1858	Hingham	grdn	8418
	Marcy	1829	Hingham	will	8419
	Mariah J	1823	Hingham	grdn	8378
	Mary	1814	Hingham	grdn	8423
	Mary	1874	Hingham	will	8422
	Mary E	1871	Hingham	will	8421
	Mary L	1859	E. Bridgewater	grdn	8420
	Melzar	1824	Hingham	admn	8424
	Merlin	1870	Duxbury	will	8425
	Minot T	1860	Hanover	admn	8426
	Nancy	1870	Hingham	admn	8427
	Nellie J	1872	Bridgewater	adop	8428
	Nelson W	1857	Plymouth	grdn	8429
	Noah	1828	Abington	admn	8430
	Orra	1876	Hingham	admn	8431
	Perez	1818	Hingham	grdn	8432
	Reuben	1846	Hingham	admn	8433
	Robert	1815	Hingham	admn	8434
	Robert D	1847	Hingham	admn	8435
	Ruth	1842	Pembroke	will	8436
	Samuel	1689	Plymouth	admn	8437
	Samuel	1859	-----	peti	8438
	Sarah	1861	Hanover	grdn	8408
	Saunders	1879	Rockland	admn	8439
	Seth	1845	Hanover	grdn	8379
	Seth Jr	1830	Scituate	admn	8440
	Solomon	1814	Hingham	grdn	8423
	Solomon	1814	Hingham	admn	8441
	Solomon	1861	Hingham	admn	8442
	Stephen	1815	Hingham	admn	8443
	Susan	1845	Hingham	admn	8444
	Thankful	1838	Hanover	will	8445
	Thomas	1707	Plymouth	grdn	8446
	Thomas	1711	Plymouth	admn	8447
	Thomas J	1868	Hanover	will	8448
GARLAND	Lydia	1877	Middleboro	admn	8449
GARNET	Zenas	1799	Pembroke	grdn	8453
GARRETT	Joseph	1714	Scituate	will	8450
	Richard	1742	Scituate	will	8451
	Ruth	1717	Scituate	will	8452
GARY	Abbie	1879	Rockland	grdn	8454
	Ada	1879	Rockland	grdn	8454
	Amy	1879	Rockland	grdn	8454
	Joseph D	1836	Duxbury	grdn	8455
	Thomas	1879	Rockland	admn	8456
	Zephaniah	1847	Duxbury	admn	8457
GATES	Betsey	1851	Hanover	will	8458
	Joshua	1870	Hanover	will	8459
	Marcia E	1873	Bridgewater	admn	8460
GAY	Abigail	1804	Hingham	will	8461
	Austin S	1869	Boston	adop	8462
	Ebenezer	1842	Hingham	will	8463

SURNAME	FIRST NAME	YEAR	PLACE	CASE	DOCKET
GAY	Mary A	1867	Hingham	will	8464
GAYNER	Lillian A	1877	Brockton	adop	8465
GEGAN	William	1868	N. Bridgewater	admn	8466
GELATT	Deborah	1866	Mattapoisett	admn	8467
	Holder	1858	Mattapoisett	will	8468
GIBBS	Abraham	1844	Wareham	will	8469
	Alvin	1872	Wareham	will	8471
	Alvina	1855	Middleboro	grdn	8470
	Andrew	1796	Wareham	admn	8472
	Andrew 2nd	1859	Wareham	admn	8473
	Ansel E	1855	Middleboro	grdn	8474 a
	Azel W	1852	Wareham	grdn	8475
	Benjamin	1799	Wareham	admn	8476
	Benjamin	1816	Wareham	grdn	8477
	Benjamin	1835	Plymouth	admn	8478
	Calvin	1869	Wareham	admn	8479
	Constant	1817	Wareham	admn	8480
	Elisha	1827	Middleboro	grdn	8481 a
	Ellen	1881	Middleboro	will	8482
	Elnathan	1825	Wareham	admn	8483
	Esther	1736	Plymouth	will	8484
	Fannie F	1863	Wareham	adop	8485
	George	1794	Wareham	grdn	8486
	George	1801	Wareham	admn	8487
	George	1859	Wareham	will	8488
	George	1859	Wareham	grdn	8497
	George W	1860	Wareham	admn	8489
	Henry	1871	Plymouth	will	8490
	John	1717	Plymouth	admn	8491
	John	1801	Wareham	will	8492
	John	1826	Rochester	admn	8493
	Joseph	1847	Wareham	will	8494
	Joshua	1793	Wareham	admn	8495
	Joshua	1839	Wareham	will	8496
	Mary	1859	Wareham	grdn	8497
	Moses	1829	Middleboro	will	8498
	Moses	1858	Wareham	admn	8499
	Pelham E	1856	Middleboro	will	8500
	Reuben	1877	Middleboro	admn	8501
	Rufus	1822	Plymouth	admn	8502
	Stephen	1871	Wareham	will	8503
	Sylvanus	1784	Rochester	admn	8504
	William	1832	Wareham	admn	8505
	William B	1875	Carver	admn	8506
GIFFORD	David	1881	Mattapoisett	admn	8507
	George W	1816	Rochester	admn	8508
	Hannah	1857	Rochester	will	8509
	Harriet J	1874	Brockton	will	8510
	Henry A	1874	N. Bridgewater	admn	8511
	John	1750	Rochester	will	8512
	Nathan N	1875	Rochester	will	8513
	Samuel	1750	Rochester	admn	8514
	Susan A	1873	Mattapoisett	admn	8515
	Sylvanus	1875	Mattapoisett	admn	8516
GILBERT	Benjamin	1763	Halifax	admn	8517
	Benjamin	1800	Halifax	admn	8518
	Benjamin D	1876	Mattapoisett	admn	8520
	Benjamin D Jr	1865	Mattapoisett	admn	8519
	Caroline E	1879	Plymouth	will	8521
	Gustavus	1865	Plymouth	will	8522
	Joseph D	1875	Abington	grdn	8523
	Martha	1870	Mattapoisett	admn	8524
	Mary	1875	Plymouth	admn	8525
	Nathaniel	1765	Halifax	grdn	8530
	Nathaniel	1837	Bridgewater	admn	8526
	Oscar G	1863	Abington	admn	8527
	Samuel	1852	Hingham	will	8528
	William	1765	Halifax	grdn	8530
	William	1800	Halifax	grdn	8529
GILES	John	1873	Abington	admn	8531
	Susan H	1866	Abington	will	8532

SURNAME	FIRST NAME	YEAR	PLACE	CASE	DOCKET
GILKEY	Hariot J	1824	Hingham	grdn	8533
	Jacob	1809	Hingham	admn	8534
	Jacob	1851	Hingham	will	8535
	James	1754	Scituate	admn	8536
	John	1754	Scituate	grdn	8537
GILL	Abby	1863	Hingham	admn	8538
	Abner	1878	Brockton	grdn	8542
	Bessie	1878	Brockton	grdn	8542
	Caleb	1855	Hingham	will	8539
	Caleb	1869	Hingham	will	8540
	Capen	1878	Brockton	grdn	8542
	Charles	1859	Hingham	admn	8541
	Clara	1878	Brockton	grdn	8542
	Elisha	1878	Brockton	admn	8543
	Irene	1878	Brockton	grdn	8542
	John	1849	Hingham	admn	8544
	John E	1865	N. Bridgewater	grdn	8545
	Laura	1878	Brockton	grdn	8542
	Mary	1818	Hingham	will	8546
	Nathaniel	1839	Hingham	grdn	8547 a
	Nathaniel	1840	Hingham	will	8548
	Thomas	1812	Hingham	will	8549
GILLIS	Alexander	1877	Wareham	admn	8550
GILMORE	Samuel	1868	Middleboro	will	8551
GISBY	John	1824	Middleboro	will	8552
	Mary	1848	Middleboro	admn	8553
	William	1870	Middleboro	admn	8554
GLASCO	Jean	1752	Pembroke	admn	8555
GLASS	Abram	1864	Duxbury	grdn	8556
	Caroline A	1869	Plymouth	admn	8557
	Charles Soule	1864	Duxbury	grdn	8556
	Consider	1859	Scituate	will	8558
	Daniel R	1839	Duxbury	admn	8559
	Elizabeth	1718	Scituate	will	8560
	James	1691	Duxbury	will	8561
	James	1760	Duxbury	will	8562
	James Jr	1826	Duxbury	grdn	8563 a
	John	1726	Duxbury	admn	8564
	John	1819	Duxbury	grdn	8565 a
	John	1828	Duxbury	admn	8566
	Lucy	1849	Duxbury	admn	8567
	Marcia	1864	Duxbury	grdn	8556
	Nancy	1868	Duxbury	admn	8568
	Roger	1692/3	Duxbury	will	8569
	Sarah	1873	Scituate	will	8570
	Seth	1864	Duxbury	admn	8571
GLASURE	James L	1864	Abington	admn	8572
GLEASON	Gertrude M	1876	Abington	grdn	8574
	James H	1876	Abington	admn	8573
	Marion H	1876	Abington	grdn	8574
	Mary	1872	N. Bridgewater	admn	8575
GLOVER	Elijah	1812	Pembroke	grdn	8576
	George	1812	Pembroke	grdn	8576
	George S	1856	Hingham	grdn	8577 a
	George S	1867	Hingham	will	8578
	James	1820	Pembroke	admn	8579
	John J	1812	Pembroke	grdn	8576
	Joseph W	1868	S. Scituate	grdn	8580
	Martin C	1868	S. Scituate	will	8581
	Robert	1787	Pembroke	will	8582
	Thomas	1761	Pembroke	admn	8583
GLOYD	David	1836	Abington	admn	8584
	James	1748	Abington	admn	8585
GLYNN	Julia G	1840	Kingston	grdn	8586
GODDARD	Benjamin	1828	Plymouth	admn	8587
	Catherine	1849	Plymouth	grdn	8588
	Charles	1849	Plymouth	grdn	8588
	Daniel	1844	Plymouth	will	8589
	Daniel	1849	Plymouth	admn	8590
	Grace H	1851	Plymouth	will	8591
	John	1795	Plymouth	admn	8592

SURNAME	FIRST NAME	YEAR	PLACE	CASE	DOCKET
GODFREY	John	1803	Plymouth	admn	8593
	Lydia	1872	Plymouth	admn	8594
	William	1799	Plymouth	admn	8595
	William	1843	Plymouth	admn	8596
	Rufus	1878	Middleboro	admn	8597
GODIN	Louis B	1873	Abington	grdn	8598
GOLDSBORO	John F	1863	Plympton	grdn	8599
GOMES	Antonio	1874	Scituate	grdn	8600
	Francisco	1874	Scituate	grdn	8600
	Joaquiña	1874	Scituate	grdn	8600
	John J	1874	Scituate	admn	8601
GOOCH	John	1772	Marshfield	will	8602
	Mary	1779	Marshfield	will	8603
	Samuel D	1860	Hingham	admn	8604
GOODING	Deborah	1871	Plymouth	admn	8605
	John	1870	Plymouth	will	8606
	John T	1880	Plymouth	admn	8607
GOODNOW	Joshua	1847	Goshen OH	admn	8608
GOODRICH	Hosea G	1879	Bridgewater	will	8609
	Martha	1873	Scituate	admn	8610
GOODSPEED	Ezra	1868	Bridgewater	admn	8611
	Ezra C	1868	Bridgewater	grdn	8612
	Jabez	1862	Mattapoisett	will	8613
	Sarah D	1877	Plymouth	admn	8614
GOODWIN	Abigail T	1865	Plymouth	admn	8615
	Amaziah	1808	Pembroke	grdn	8616 a
	Charles	1871	Plymouth	admn	8617
	Charles	1878	Middleboro	admn	8618
	Charles H	1881	Middleboro	admn	8619
	Eliza H	1847	Plymouth	grdn	8620
	Frank	1775	Plymouth	grdn	8638
	George	1775	Plymouth	grdn	8638
	Hannah J	1855	Plymouth	will	8621
	Hannaj J	1794	Portland	grdn	8622
	Hersey B	1822	Plymouth	grdn	8623
	Lazarus	1795	Plymouth	admn	8624
	Lucy	1819	Plymouth	admn	8625
	Lucy	1825	Middleboro	admn	8626
	Lydia	1801	Plymouth	admn	8627
	Mercy	1775	Plymouth	grdn	8638
	Nathaniel	1771	Plymouth	admn	8628
	Nathaniel	1819	Plymouth	will	8629
	Nathaniel	1857	Plymouth	will	8630
	Rowland	1766	Pembroke	will	8631
	Ruth	1825	Plymouth	admn	8632
	Samuel B	1862	Abington	will	8633
	Sarah	1794	Portland	grdn	8622
	Sylvia F	1879	Middleboro	admn	8634
	Thomas	1775	Plymouth	grdn	8638
	Timothy	1817	Plymouth	admn	8635
	William	1775	Plymouth	grdn	8638
	William	1825	Plymouth	will	8637
	William Jr	1822	Plymouth	will	8636
GORDAK	Clarentine	1835	Scituate	grdn	8639
	William W	1853	Boston	grdn	8640
GORDON	Jane B	1877	Plymouth	admn	8641
	Timothy	1877	Plymouth	admn	8642
GORHAM	Fannie W	1867	Marshfield	grdn	8643 a
	Jabez	1830	Middleboro	admn	8644
	Jabez	1862	Mattapoisett	admn	8645
	John	1759	Scituate	admn	8646
	Mercy A	1835	Marshfield	grdn	8647
GORMAN	John	1869	Abington	will	8648
GOULD	Anna	1800	Plymouth	admn	8649
	Brister	1823	Abington	admn	8650
	Edward	1860	(see # 6672)	grdn	8652
	Edward L	1865	Wayne ME	grdn	8651
	Elisha	1817	Hull	will	8652
	Eliza P	1879	Hingham	admn	8653
	Elizabeth	1820	Boston	grdn	8661
	Emery	1872	Abington	grdn	8656

SURNAME	FIRST NAME	YEAR	PLACE	CASE	DOCKET
GOULD	Ephraim	1766	Plymouth	admn	8654
	Frederick	1872	Abington	grdn	8656
	Frederick J	1876	Brockton	grdn	8655
	George	1860	(see # 6672)	grdn	8652
	George	1872	Abington	grdn	8656
	Granville	1862	Bridgewater	grdn	8657
	Hannah	1779	Pembroke	grdn	8678
	Hattie	1862	Bridgewater	grdn	8657
	Jabez	1875	Brockton	admn	8658
	Jane	1820	Boston	grdn	8661
	Jane	1837	Hingham	will	8659
	John	1779	Pembroke	grdn	8678
	John	1820	Boston	grdn	8661
	John	1859	Hull	will	8660
	Josiah L	1849	Hingham	admn	8662
	Lydia	1844	Hingham	will	8663
	Martha	1820	Boston	grdn	8661
	Mary	1820	Boston	grdn	8661
	Mary	1845	Hingham	grdn	8665 a
	Mary	1859	Hull	will	8666
	Mary Jr	1810	Pembroke	will	8664
	Myron	1864	E. Bridgewater	admn	8667
	Peltiah	1861	Bridgewater	admn	8668
	Robert	1837	Hull	bond	8669
	Robert	1864	Hingham	admn	8670
	Robert et al	1879	Cambridge	peti	8671
	Samuel	1791	Pembroke	admn	8672
	Sarah	1862	Bridgewater	grdn	8657
	Thomas	1820	Boston	grdn	8661
	Tilson	1777	Pembroke	admn	8673
	Tilson	1778	Hanover	grdn	8674
	William	1759	Scituate	admn	8675
	William	1778	Pembroke	admn	8676
	William	1779	Pembroke	grdn	8678
	William	1806	Pembroke	grdn	8677 a
GRACE	Anastacia	1880	Rockland	grdn	8679
	James	1874	Rockland	admn	8680
	Sarah E	1880	Rockland	grdn	8679
	William	1879	Rockland	admn	8681
	William	1880	Rockland	grdn	8679
GRADY	Dennis	1879	Brockton	admn	8682
	James	1858	Bridgewater	admn	8683
GRAHAM	James	1871	Bridgewater	admn	8684
	Thomas	1872	Abington	admn	8685
	Thomas F	1876	Abington	grdn	8686
GRANDERSON	Charles	1878	S. Scituate	will	8687
	Simeon	1835	Scituate	grdn	8688 a
GRAVES	Ruth B	1869	Bridgewater	admn	8689
GRAY	Anna	1718	-----	grdn	8700
	Edith	1879	Marion	grdn	8691
	Edward	1877	Kingston	admn	8690
	Estella	1879	Marion	grdn	8691
	Helen M	1857	Kingston	name	8692
	John	1732	Kingston	will	8693
	John	1811	Kingston	admn	8694
	John	1848	Kingston	admn	8695
	John	1859	Kingston	admn	8696
	Judith	1869	Kingston	admn	8697
	Lena	1879	Marion	grdn	8691
	Lewis	1860	Kingston	admn	8698
	Lillie Burges	1879	Marion	grdn	8691
	Molly	1843	Plympton	will	8699
	Rebecca	1718	-----	grdn	8700
	Rufus	1872	Marion	admn	8701
	Samuel	1738	Kingston	admn	8702
	Samuel	1753	Kingston	grdn	8703
	Sarah	1853	Kingston	admn	8705
	Sarah B	1867	Kingston	admn	8706
	Sarah D	1846	Hingham	admn	8704
	Wait	1753	Kingston	grdn	8703
	Wait	1763	Kingston	admn	8707

SURNAME	FIRST NAME	YEAR	PLACE	CASE	DOCKET
GRAY	Waity	1771	Kingston	grdn	8708
GREATON	Charles A	1843	Plymouth	admn	8709
GREEN	Abby	1872	Wareham	will	8710
	Barnabas	1827	Rochester	admn	8711
	Barnabas	1863	Wareham	grdn	8712 a
	Catherine	1858	Wareham	admn	8713
	Jeremiah	1806	(transient)	grdn	8714 b
	John	1855	Wareham	admn	8715
	Joseph	1813	Hanover	will	8717
	Joseph(absent)	1779	Boston	acct	8716
	Paul	1783	Rochester	will	8718
	Robert	1821	Bridgewater	grdn	8719 a
	Robert	1827	W. Bridgewater	admn	8720
	Samuel	1756	Abington	admn	8721
	Samuel	1795	Middleboro	grdn	8722
	Sarah	1795	Middleboro	grdn	8722
	Thomas B	1873	S. Scituate	admn	8723
	Thomas C	1877	Plymouth	admn	8724
	William C	1847	Plymouth	admn	8725
GREENFIELD	Harriet E	1865	Plympton	grdn	8726
	Mary D	1865	Middleboro	admn	8727
GREENLEAF	John	1828	Hull	will	8728
GREW	Benjamin R	1874	Lakeville	admn	8729
GRIFFIN	George W	1879	Plymouth	will	8730
	Olive W	1858	Plymouth	admn	8731
	William	1864	N. Bridgewater	will	8732
GRIFFITH	Ephraim	1834	Carver	will	8733
	Ephraim	1838	Carver	grdn	8734 a
	Jedidah	1854	Carver	will	8735
	Stephen	1839	Middleboro	grdn	8736 a
	Stephen A	1863	Carver	will	8737
GRIHM	William	1864	Abington	grdn	8738
GROSS	Betty	1793	Pembroke	grdn	8739
	Cornelia	1812	Scituate	grdn	8744
	Deborah	1841	Scituate	will	8740
	Deborah F	1880	S. Scituate	will	8741
	Edmond Jr	1768	Scituate	admn	8742
	Edmund	1794	Scituate	admn	8743
	Edmund	1812	Scituate	grdn	8744
	Elisha	1829	Scituate	admn	8745
	Elizabeth	1812	Scituate	grdn	8744
	Isaac	1774	Hanover	admn	8746
	Jane	1812	Scituate	grdn	8744
	Jonathan Y	1875	Duxbury	admn	8747
	Lewis	1869	S. Scituate	will	8748
	Mary	1812	Scituate	grdn	8744
	Polly	1793	Pembroke	grdn	8739
	Ruth	1793	Pembroke	grdn	8739
	Ruth	1820	Hanover	will	8749
	Thomas	1798	Hanover	will	8750
	Thomas	1811	Scituate	admn	8751
	Thomas	1812	Scituate	grdn	8744
GROVER	Hiram	1881	W. Bridgewater	will	8752
GUARD	Mary J	1874	Abington	grdn	8753
GUILD	Elisha F	1845	Hingham	admn	8754
	Elisha F	1846	Hingham	grdn	8755
GULLIFER	John	1837	Duxbury	admn	8756
	Peleg	1806	Duxbury	admn	8757
	Peleg	1827	Duxbury	admn	8758
	Thomas	1764	Duxbury	grdn	8760
	Thomas	1765	Duxbury	will	8759
GULLIFORD	John	1733	Marshfield	grdn	8761
GUNDAWAY	Betty	1840	Hanover	admn	8762
	Richard	1820	Pembroke	grdn	8763 a
GUNN	Justin L	1879	Bridgewater	admn	8764
GURNEY	Abbie A	1870	Hanover	grdn	8765
	Almon	1873	E. Bridgewater	will	8766
	Anna	1803	Bridgewater	grdn	8797
	Asa	1843	Abington	will	8767
	Azel	1859	N. Bridgewater	will	8768
	Benjamin	1739	Middleboro	will	8769

SURNAME	FIRST NAME	YEAR	PLACE	CASE	DOCKET
GURNEY	Benjamin	1828	Rochester	will	8770
	Charlotte H	1868	Middleboro	admn	8771
	Cyrus	1868	E. Bridgewater	will	8772
	Daniel	1848	Middleboro	admn	8773
	Daniel	1871	Abington	admn	8774
	David	1815	Middleboro	will	8777
	David	1842	Middleboro	grdn	8778
	David	1850	E. Bridgewater	admn	8776
	David	1862	Abington	will	8775
	Deborah	1880	S. Abington	admn	8779
	Edmund	1870	Abington	admn	8780
	Elbridge	1827	E. Bridgewater	grdn	8781
	Elbridge T	1866	Rochester	admn	8782
	Eli E	1866	Abington	grdn	8783
	Emily	1844	E. Bridgewater	grdn	8790
	Ephraim	1851	Abington	admn	8784
	George	1851	Wareham	admn	8785
	George	1851	E. Bridgewater	grdn	8811
	George H	1874	N. Bridgewater	will	8786
	Gilbert T	1877	Marion	grdn	8787
	Harriet E	1878	Rockland	grdn	8788
	Henry	1842	Middleboro	grdn	8778
	Henry	1844	E. Bridgewater	grdn	8790
	Henry	1863	Bridgewater	admn	8789
	Ira	1856	Abington	admn	8791
	Jane	1842	Middleboro	grdn	8778
	Jane	1842	Middleboro	will	8792
	Jeremiah	1848	Abington	will	8793
	John	1797	Bridgewater	admn	8796
	John	1803	Bridgewater	grdn	8797
	John	1829	Abington	will	8795
	John	1867	Abington	admn	8794
	Jonathan	1842	Middleboro	grdn	8778
	Joseph P	1851	Abington	will	8798
	Lebbeus	1862	Abington	admn	8799
	Lemuel	1803	Bridgewater	grdn	8797
	Lemuel	1835	Wareham	admn	8800
	Lucius	1869	N. Bridgewater	will	8801
	Marcus A	1879	Middleboro	admn	8802
	Maria A	1876	S. Abington	admn	8803
	Martha	1803	Bridgewater	grdn	8797
	Mary	1765	Bridgewater	grdn	8819
	Mary	1860	E. Bridgewater	will	8804
	Mary C	1880	Rockland	admn	8805
	Mehitable	1849	N. Bridgewater	will	8806
	Melvin Jr	1845	Abington	will	8807
	Noah	1846	Abington	admn	8808
	Ozen	1858	N. Bridgewater	will	8809
	Perkins	1792	Bridgewater	will	8810
	Polly Ann	1851	E. Bridgewater	grdn	8811
	Rhoda	1803	Bridgewater	grdn	8797
	Richard	1855	Marion	will	8812
	Richard S	1876	Marion	admn	8813
	Ruth	1861	Abington	admn	8814
	Samuel	1717	Abington	will	8815
	Samuel	1803	Bridgewater	grdn	8797
	Samuel	1822	Abington	admn	8816
	Samuel	1862	Rochester	will	8817
	Samuel N	1877	Rochester	will	8818
	Sarah	1765	Bridgewater	grdn	8819
	Seth	1842	E. Bridgewater	will	8820
	Seth	1844	E. Bridgewater	admn	8821
	Stephen	1822	Rochester	warr	8822
	Stephen	1822	Rochester	grdn	8826
	Sybyl	1803	Bridgewater	grdn	8797
	Thomas	1878	Rockland	grdn	8788
	Thomas	1880	Rockland	admn	8824
	Thomas J	1878	Brockton	admn	8823
	Tirzah	1822	Rochester	grdn	8826
	Wesley	1878	Rockland	admn	8825
	Wilson	1822	Rochester	grdn	8826

SURNAME	FIRST NAME	YEAR	PLACE	CASE	DOCKET
GURNEY	Zachariah	1765	Bridgewater	will	8827
	Zachariah	1813	Bridgewater	will	8828
	Zachariah	1846	N. Bridgewater	will	8829
GUSTAVASON	John	1856	Rochester	admn	8830
GWYNNETH	John	1835	Bridgewater	admn	8831
HACKETT	Asael	1829	Middleboro	admn	8832
	Augusta	1855	Indiana	grdn	8845
	Benjamin	1802	Middleboro	admn	8833
	Elizabeth A	1866	Middleboro	admn	8834
	Elkanah	1872	Carver	admn	8835
	George	1732	Middleboro	admn	8837
	George Jr	1819	Middleboro	admn	8836
	Horatio A	1866	Middleboro	admn	8838
	John	1712	Middleboro	admn	8839
	John	1768	Middleboro	will	8840
	John	1786	Middleboro	admn	8841
	Lovisa	1811	Middleboro	grdn	8842
	Molly	1811	Middleboro	grdn	8842
	Peleg	1807	Middleboro	admn	8843
	Peleg	1811	Middleboro	grdn	8842
	Samuel	1785	Middleboro	admn	8844
	Samuel	1811	Middleboro	grdn	8842
	Samuel	1855	Indiana	grdn	8845
	Sarah	1811	Middleboro	grdn	8842
	Sylvanus	1855	Indiana	grdn	8845
	Zilpha	1857	Middleboro	will	8846
HADAWAY	Charles S	1877	Plymouth	grdn	8847
	Thomas	1879	Plymouth	admn	8848
HADLEY	Amos	1874	Marion	will	8849
	Amos J	1875	Marion	grdn	8850
	Byron F	1875	Marion	grdn	8850
	Eliza C	1866	Marion	admn	8851
HAFFORD	Reuben	1879	Lakeville	will	8852
	Sylvia	1873	Lakeville	will	8853
	William F	1876	Lakeville	will	8854
HAGAR	William	1881	Plymouth	admn	8855
HALDEN	Selma	1877	Brockton	adop	8856
HALE	Artemas Jr	1854	Bridgewater	admn	8857
	Caroline A	1856	Bridgewater	grdn	8858
	Chester	1869	E. Bridgewater	grdn	8860
	Deborah L	1877	Bridgewater	admn	8859
	Edith	1869	E. Bridgewater	grdn	8860
	Ellen	1856	Bridgewater	grdn	8858
	Lucy	1876	Bridgewater	will	8861
	Mabel	1869	E. Bridgewater	grdn	8860
	Zacheus	1869	Abington	admn	8862
HALEY	Agnes	1876	Plympton	grdn	8865
	Almira	1866	Marshfield	grdn	8864
	Edward J	1864	Plympton	grdn	8863
	Elizabeth	1876	Plympton	grdn	8865
	Henrietta	1866	Marshfield	grdn	8864
	Henry T	1864	Plympton	grdn	8863
	Imogene	1876	Plympton	grdn	8865
	Mary	1866	Marshfield	grdn	8864
HALL	Abigail D	1880	S. Abington	will	8866
	Abner	1866	Mattapoisett	admn	8867
	Adam	1808	Marshfield	will	8868
	Adrastus	1802	Raynham	grdn	8869
	Albert	1873	Middleboro	grdn	8870
	Allen	1800	Rochester	admn	8871
	Almira	1818	Middleboro	grdn	8873
	Almira	1834	Scituate	grdn	8872
	Amariah	1742	Taunton	grdn	8874
	Anna	1867	Mattapoisett	admn	8875
	Arethusa	1877	Mattapoisett	admn	8876
	Asa	1816	Bridgewater	grdn	8877 a
	Asahel	1761	Kingston	grdn	8878
	Asenath	1837	Kingston	admn	8879
	Augusta	1814	Duxbury	grdn	8880
	Beza	1802	Raynham	grdn	8869
	Catherine	1826	Scituate	grdn	8881

SURNAME	FIRST NAME	YEAR	PLACE	CASE	DOCKET
HALL	Charles	1837	Kingston	grdn	8882
	Christiana	1859	Kingston	grdn	8883
	Clarissa	1802	Raynham	grdn	8869
	Clarissa	1869	N. Bridgewater	grdn	8886
	Cyrus	1873	Middleboro	grdn	8870
	Daniel	1847	Duxbury	admn	8884
	Daniel	1869	N. Bridgewater	admn	8885
	Daniel E	1869	N. Bridgewater	grdn	8886
	David	1810	Duxbury	admn	8887
	David	1869	N. Bridgewater	admn	8888
	David	1877	Bridgewater	grdn	8889 a
	David	1877	Bridgewater	admn	8890
	Davis	1811	Pembroke	grdn	8891
	Ebenezer	1874	Bridgewater	will	8892
	Eber	1806	Plymouth	grdn	8893
	Elisha	1818	Kingston	admn	8894
	Elisha	1837	Kingston	grdn	8882
	Elizabeth	1728	Kingston	will	8895
	Emeline	1818	Middleboro	grdn	8873
	Frederick O	1863	Stoughton	adop	8896
	George	1876	Rochester	admn	8899
	George H	1856	Marshfield	bond	8898
	George W	1837	Kingston	grdn	8897
	Gracey L	1843	Pembroke	grdn	8900
	Henry A	1879	Bridgewater	will	8901
	Horace	1876	Pembroke	will	8902
	Huldah	1876	Rochester	will	8903
	Huldah B	1879	Marshfield	admn	8904
	James	1757	Pembroke	admn	8905
	James	1797	Plymouth	grdn	8909
	James	1818	Middleboro	grdn	8873
	James	1818	Middleboro	admn	8907
	James	1824	Middleboro	admn	8908
	James	1836	Hingham	admn	8906
	James	1873	Plymouth	will	8910
	Jeremiah	1807	Pembroke	will	8911
	Job	1778	Kingston	admn	8912
	Job	1779	Kingston	grdn	8929
	Job	1810	Pembroke	admn	8913
	John	1763	Middleboro	admn	8914
	John	1859	Kingston	will	8915
	John	1878	Bridgewater	admn	8916
	John O	1879	Marshfield	admn	8917
	Joseph	1836	Rochester	admn	8918
	Joseph	1841	Halifax	will	8919
	Joshua	1797	Duxbury	admn	8920
	Joshua	1869	N. Bridgewater	grdn	8924
	Judah	1747	Kingston	admn	8921
	Judah	1826	Kingston	admn	8922
	Kezia	1809	Marshfield	will	8923
	Laura	1869	N. Bridgewater	grdn	8924
	Lot	1841	Duxbury	will	8925
	Lucretia	1811	Pembroke	grdn	8891
	Lucy	1803	Middleboro	admn	8926
	Luke	1815	Marshfield	admn	8927
	Lydia	1811	Pembroke	grdn	8891
	Lydia	1825	Hanson	admn	8928
	Maria	1814	Duxbury	grdn	8880
	Mary	1742	Taunton	grdn	8874
	Mary	1779	Kingston	grdn	8929
	Mary	1811	Pembroke	grdn	8891
	Mary	1869	N. Bridgewater	grdn	8924
	Mason	1821	Middleboro	will	8930
	Mercy	1825	Scituate	will	8931
	Patience	1742	Taunton	grdn	8874
	Phebe	1779	Kingston	grdn	8929
	Phebe	1796	Kingston	grdn	8932 a
	Rebecca	1814	Duxbury	grdn	8880
	Rebecca	1814	Duxbury	admn	8933
	Rebecca W	1880	S. Abington	admn	8934
	Reuben	1789	Bridgewater	admn	8935

SURNAME	FIRST NAME	YEAR	PLACE	CASE	DOCKET
HALL	Rhoda	1816	Middleboro	grdn	8943
	Robert	1875	Scituate	will	8937
	Robert B	1868	Plymouth	will	8936
	Rufus	1873	Middleboro	grdn	8870
	Ruth	1838	Kingston	will	8938
	Sally	1802	Raynham	grdn	8869
	Sally	1856	W. Bridgewater	will	8939
	Samuel	1803	Marshfield	admn	8940
	Samuel	1820	Scituate	admn	8941
	Sarah	1753	Marshfield	grdn	8953
	Sarah	1779	Kingston	grdn	8929
	Seth	1816	Middleboro	admn	8942
	Seth	1816	Middleboro	grdn	8943
	Silas	1878	S. Abington	will	8944
	Silvanus	1815	Bridgewater	will	8945
	Simeon	1778	Kingston	admn	8946
	Simeon	1779	Kingston	grdn	8929
	Simeon	1784	Kingston	admn	8947
	Stillman	1822	Carver	will	8948
	Susanna	1859	Hingham	will	8949
	Thomas	1748	Kingston	admn	8950
	Thomas	1751	Pembroke	admn	8951
	Thomas	1761	Kingston	grdn	8878
	Timothy	1753	Marshfield	will	8952
	Timothy	1753	Marshfield	grdn	8953
	Washington	1834	Kingston	admn	8954
	William	1763	Marshfield	admn	8955
	William	1864	Duxbury	admn	8956
	Winslow	1828	Middleboro	grdn	8957
HALLY	Ellen	1873	Hingham	admn	8958
HAMBLIN	Amanda	1857	Wareham	grdn	8960
	Charles	1857	Wareham	grdn	8960
	Charles	1873	Wareham	admn	8959
	Eliza	1857	Wareham	grdn	8960
	Elkanah	1881	Wareham	admn	8961
	Emeline	1878	Wareham	admn	8962
	George S	1867	Wareham	admn	8963
	Hope	1872	Rochester	will	8964
	Isaac	1762	Bridgewater	admn	8965
	John	1773	Bridgewater	grdn	8966
	Joseph	1773	Bridgewater	grdn	8966
	Nathan C	1857	Wareham	admn	8967
	Nathaniel	1856	Wareham	will	8968
	Reuben	1799	Rochester	admn	8969
	Sarah	1773	Bridgewater	grdn	8966
HAMMATT	Abraham	1774	Plymouth	admn	8970
	Abraham	1797	Plymouth	admn	8971
	Hannah	1857	Marion	will	8972
	John	1808	Rochester	will	8973
	Joseph	1853	Marion	will	8974
	Robert W	1879	California	admn	8975
HAMMOND	Abigail	1803	Rochester	will	8976
	Agnes	1874	Marion	grdn	9001
	Alexander B	1869	California	admn	8977
	Alice	1839	Scituate	admn	8978
	Allen	1827	Herculan NY	grdn	9040
	Almira	1828	Carver	grdn	8979
	Annetta	1874	Marion	grdn	9001
	Antipas	1773	Rochester	will	8980
	Arthur H	1833	Wareham	grdn	8981
	Barzilla	1779	Rochester	admn	8982
	Benjamin	1758	Rochester	will	8985
	Benjamin	1786	Plympton	grdn	8991
	Benjamin	1789	Scituate	admn	8983
	Benjamin	1819	Hingham	grdn	8984
	Benjamin	1826	Carver	admn	8987
	Benjamin	1826	Carver	grdn	8988
	Benjamin 3rd	1836	Rochester	admn	8986
	Betsey	1867	Mattapoisett	admn	8989
	Betsey B	1880	Marion	admn	8990
	Betty	1786	Plympton	grdn	8991

SURNAME	FIRST NAME	YEAR	PLACE	CASE	DOCKET
HAMMOND	Bruce F	1854	Rochester	admn	8992
	Bulah	1839	Rochester	admn	8993
	Caleb	1840	Rochester	grdn	8994
	Charles B	1837	Rochester	admn	8995
	Charles B	1857	Marion	will	8996
	Charlotte E	1864	Carver	grdn	8997
	Christopher	1842	Rochester	admn	8998
	Clement	1850	Rochester	admn	8999
	Clement	1874	Marion	admn	9000
	Clement	1874	Marion	grdn	9001
	David	1837	Pembroke	admn	9002
	Deborah	1767	Rochester	grdn	9005
	Deborah	1823	Rochester	will	9004
	Deborah	1865	Marion	admn	9003
	Edmund D	1830	Rochester	admn	9006
	Edward	1802	Rochester	admn	9007
	Edwin	1852	Rochester	grdn	9039
	Elihu	1872	Mattapoisett	will	9008
	Elijah	1831	Rochester	admn	9009
	Eliza W	1870	Marion	admn	9010
	Elizabeth	1854	Rochester	will	9012
	Elizabeth	1877	Mattapoisett	admn	9011
	Elizabeth B	1841	Rochester	grdn	9013
	Elnathan	1831	Rochester	will	9014
	Eloisa M	1872	Mattapoisett	grdn	9015
	Emma	1874	Marion	grdn	9001
	Enoch	1800	Rochester	will	9016
	Ethan	1810	Rochester	grdn	9018
	Ethan A	1810	Rochester	admn	9017
	Eunice A	1878	Marion	grdn	9019
	Experience	1823	Scituate	grdn	9020
	Experience	1825	Scituate	admn	9021
	Frederick	1874	Scituate	will	9022
	George	1782	Plympton	admn	9023
	George	1786	Plympton	grdn	8991
	George	1826	Carver	grdn	8988
	George	1828	Carver	grdn	8979
	George	1870	Marion	admn	9024
	Gideon 2nd	1848	Rochester	will	9025
	Hannah	1786	Plympton	grdn	8991
	Hannah	1826	Carver	grdn	8988
	Hannah	1870	Carver	will	9026
	Harper	1810	Rochester	grdn	9018
	Henry	1852	Rochester	admn	9027
	Hunnewill	1807	Rochester	will	9028
	Ida	1874	Marion	grdn	9001
	Isaac	1850	Bridgewater	grdn	9029
	Israel	1839	Rochester	admn	9030
	James	1780	Rochester	will	9031
	James	1826	Rochester	will	9032
	James	1840	Rochester	grdn	8994
	James	1852	Rochester	admn	9033
	Jesse	1838	Rochester	grdn	9035
	Jesse	1845	Rochester	admn	9034
	Jirah	1773	Rochester	admn	9036
	John	1787	Rochester	will	9037
	John	1827	Herculaneum NY	grdn	9040
	John	1852	Rochester	grdn	9039
	John W	1843	Rochester	admn	9038
	Joseph	1777	Scituate	admn	9041
	Joseph	1819	Hingham	admn	9042
	Joseph	1827	Herculan NY	grdn	9040
	Joseph	1835	Hingham	admn	9043
	Joseph F	1857	Rochester	admn	9044
	Josephus	1779	Rochester	will	9045
	Josiah	1826	Carver	grdn	8988
	Josiah N	1874	Marion	admn	9046
	Leonard	1864	Mattapoisett	will	9047
	Lettice	1795	Rochester	grdn	9048
	Loring	1865	Hingham	will	9049
	Lucy	1786	Plympton	grdn	8991

SURNAME	FIRST NAME	YEAR	PLACE	CASE	DOCKET
HAMMOND	Mary	1788	Plympton	admn	9050
	Mary	1852	Rochester	grdn	9039
	Mary	1874	Marion	grdn	9001
	Mary D	1864	Mattapoisett	will	9051
	Melissa	1828	Carver	grdn	8979
	Moses	1800	Rochester	will	9052
	Nathan	1803	Rochester	will	9053
	Nathaniel	1827	Rochester	will	9055
	Nathaniel 2nd	1822	Rochester	grdn	9054 a
	Nathaniel Jr	1829	Rochester	grdn	9056
	Nehemiah	1828	Carver	grdn	8979
	Noah	1834	Rochester	admn	9057
	Orin	1853	Rochester	admn	9058
	Phillip T	1834	Rochester	admn	9059
	Polly	1804	Rochester	grdn	9060
	Polly	1879	Scituate	admn	9061
	Priscilla	1786	Plympton	grdn	8991
	Rachel	1821	Middleboro	will	9062
	Rebecca	1794	Wareham	grdn	9063
	Reuben B	1829	Rochester	admn	9064
	Reuben B	1856	Marion	admn	9065
	Roger	1758	Rochester	will	9066
	Roger W	1850	Bridgewater	admn	9067
	Samuel	1728	Rochester	will	9068
	Seth	1737	Rochester	admn	9069
	Seth	1841	Rochester	admn	9070
	Stafford	1809	Rochester	will	9071
	Stephen	1840	Rochester	will	9072
	Susan	1838	Rochester	grdn	9035
	Sylvanus	1776	Rochester	admn	9073
	Sylvia P	1857	Mattapoisett	admn	9074
	Thankful	1767	Rochester	grdn	9005
	Thomas	1786	Plympton	grdn	8991
	Thomas	1827	Carver	will	9075
	Thomas	1864	Carver	admn	9076
	Thomas C	1851	Rochester	admn	9077
	Thomas P	1879	Mattapoisett	admn	9078
	Timothy	1792	Rochester	admn	9079
	Timothy	1852	Rochester	admn	9081
	Timothy Jr	1838	Rochester	admn	9080
	William	1813	Rochester	admn	9082
	William	1828	Carver	grdn	8979
	William	1838	Carver	will	9083
HANAN	Sarah C H	1852	Wareham	adop	9084
	Sarah E H	1852	Wareham	grdn	9085
HANCOCK	Moses W	1877	Brockton	will	9086
HANDY	Ansel	1849	Rochester	admn	9087
	Augustus H	1870	Marion	admn	9088
	Benjamin	1848	Rochester	admn	9089
	Caleb	1856	Marion	will	9090
	Daniel	1864	Middleboro	will	9091
	Ebenezer	1874	Marion	admn	9092
	Edward Jr	1822	Rochester	admn	9093
	Elisha	1833	Rochester	grdn	9110
	Elizabeth N	1844	Rochester	grdn	9094
	Freeman	1837	Rochester	will	9095
	Hanable	1754	Rochester	admn	9096
	Hannah W	1875	Marion	admn	9097
	Isaac	1858	Marion	admn	9098
	Isabella	1856	Hanover	admn	9099
	Isabella	1856	Hanover	grdn	9100
	Jabez	1844	Rochester	admn	9101
	Jonathan	1857	Marion	admn	9102
	Joseph	1833	Rochester	will	9103
	Levi	1850	Rochester	admn	9104
	Lucien N	1833	Rochester	grdn	9105
	Margaret	1838	Rochester	grdn	9106
	Obed	1838	Rochester	grdn	9106
	Orville	1870	Marion	grdn	9107
	Priscilla	1870	Marion	grdn	9107
	Silas Jr	1830	Rochester	admn	9108

SURNAME	FIRST NAME	YEAR	PLACE	CASE	DOCKET
HANDY	Silvia	1838	Rochester	admn	9109
	Theophilus	1870	Marion	grdn	9107
	William	1833	Rochester	grdn	9110
	William	1856	Hanover	grdn	9100
	Zacheus	1787	Rochester	will	9111
HANEY	Dennis	1870	Hanson	grdn	9112
HANKS	John	1742	Duxbury	admn	9113
	John	1804	Duxbury	will	9114
HANLEY	Bridget	1852	Wareham	grdn	9116
	Catherine	1852	Wareham	grdn	9116
	Ellen	1852	Wareham	grdn	9116
	John	1850	Wareham	admn	9115
	John	1852	Wareham	grdn	9116
	Margaret	1852	Wareham	grdn	9116
	Mary	1852	Wareham	grdn	9116
HANMER	Joseph	1699	Scituate	admn	9117
HANMOR	Isaac	1702	Scituate	admn	9118
HANOVER	(town)	1879	Hanover	peti	9119
HAPGOOD	Charles W	1879	Hingham	will	9120
HARADON	Eleanor	1874	Middleboro	admn	9121
	Isaac	1862	Middleboro	will	9122
HARDEN	Abraham	1778	Pembroke	grdn	9123
	Amos	1782	Bridgewater	will	9125
	Benjamin F	1863	E. Bridgewater	grdn	9127
	Benjamin F	1864	E. Bridgewater	admn	9128
	Cushing	1857	Abington	admn	9129
	Daniel	1765	Bridgewater	grdn	9159
	Deborah	1834	Bridgewater	will	9131
	Harriet	1859	Hingham	will	9133
	Harriet	1860	Abington	grdn	9132 a
	Hartey	1852	Hingham	admn	9134
	Harvey	1851	Hanson	will	9135
	Jabez	1879	Bridgewater	will	9137
	Jacob	1805	Abington	admn	9138
	Jacob	1839	Abington	admn	9139
	Jacob	1851	Abington	admn	9140
	James	1839	Abington	grdn	9141
	John	1719	Bridgewater	will	9143
	John	1751	Bridgewater	will	9144
	John	1784	Abington	will	9142
	John	1835	Bridgewater	admn	9146
	John	1839	Bridgewater	admn	9147
	Lucy	1839	Abington	grdn	9141
	Lydia	1765	Bridgewater	grdn	9159
	Mary	1765	Bridgewater	grdn	9159
	Mary	1835	Bridgewater	will	9148
	Nathan	1765	Bridgewater	grdn	9159
	Nathaniel	1771	Pembroke	admn	9153
	Prescott	1839	Abington	grdn	9141
	Prescott A	1853	Abington	admn	9154
	Reuben	1771	Pembroke	grdn	9155
	Samuel	1759	Bridgewater	admn	9158
	Samuel	1765	Bridgewater	grdn	9159
	Samuel	1793	Bridgewater	admn	9157
	Seth	1784	Abington	grdn	9160
	Seth	1822	Abington	admn	9161
	Seth	1856	E. Bridgewater	admn	9162
	Syntha	1778	Pembroke	grdn	9123
	Thomas	1860	Abington	admn	9165
	Ward	1832	Bridgewater	admn	9166
HARDING	Agnes B	1878	E. Bridgewater	adop	9124
	Amos	1875	Hanson	will	9126
	Ander	1854	Abington	grdn	9152
	David	1874	Hingham	admn	9130
	Edward	1854	Abington	grdn	9152
	Howes	1809	Hingham	admn	9136
	John	1822	Bridgewater	admn	9145
	Mary	1862	E. Bridgewater	admn	9149
	Mehitable	1869	Abington	grdn	9150
	Melvin	1863	E. Bridgewater	will	9151
	Morton	1854	Abington	grdn	9152

SURNAME	FIRST NAME	YEAR	PLACE	CASE	DOCKET
HARDING	Samuel	1823	Bridgewater	admn	9156
	Thomas	1821	Hingham	admn	9163
	Thomas	1850	Hingham	admn	9164
HARDWICK	George	1868	Abington	admn	9167
	William F	1868	Abington	grdn	9168
HARLOW	Abner	1864	Mattapoisett	admn	9169
	Alathea	1858	Marshfield	admn	9170
	Alvin	1842	Carver	grdn	9171
	Amaziah	1755	Plymouth	admn	9174
	Amaziah	1762	Plymouth	grdn	9175
	Amaziah	1804	Plymouth	admn	9172
	Amaziah	1806	Plymouth	admn	9173
	Annie	1875	Middleboro	grdn	9176
	Ansel	1832	Plymouth	admn	9177
	Barnabas	1796	Plympton	will	9178
	Benjamin	1779	Middleboro	will	9179
	Benjamin	1816	Plymouth	admn	9181
	Benjamin	1821	Plymouth	grdn	9182
	Benjamin 2nd	1846	Carver	admn	9180
	Betsey	1821	Plymouth	grdn	9182
	Betsey	1833	Middleboro	admn	9185
	Betsey	1878	Lakeville	will	9186
	Betsey H	1872	Plymouth	admn	9184
	Betsey Jr	1866	Plymouth	admn	9183
	Bradford	1853	Middleboro	will	9187
	Briggs	1875	Duxbury	admn	9188
	Calvin F	1868	E. Bridgewater	admn	9189
	Carrie	1868	Plymouth	grdn	9218
	Charles	1868	Plymouth	grdn	9218
	Cordelia	1842	Carver	grdn	9171
	David	1872	Plymouth	admn	9190
	Deborah T	1855	Duxbury	admn	9191
	Eleazer	1738	Duxbury	grdn	9193
	Eleazer	1748	Plymouth	admn	9192
	Eleazer	1812	Duxbury	admn	9194
	Eleazer	1857	Marshfield	admn	9195
	Eliphas	1728	Plymouth	grdn	9257
	Eliza W	1865	Mattapoisett	grdn	9196
	Elizabeth	1865	Hingham	grdn	9243
	Ella	1852	N. Bridgewater	grdn	9271
	Ellis	1857	Middleboro	admn	9198
	Ellis I	1829	Plymouth	admn	9197
	Ephraim	1797	Middleboro	admn	9199
	Ephraim	1797	Plymouth	grdn	9200
	Ephraim	1809	Plymouth	grdn	9229
	Ephraim	1841	Carver	admn	9201
	Ephraim	1842	Carver	grdn	9171
	Ephraim	1860	Plymouth	will	9203
	Ephraim T	1867	Carver	admn	9202
	Ezra	1808	Middleboro	admn	9204
	Ezra	1839	Plymouth	admn	9206
	Ezra	1841	Plymouth	admn	9207
	Ezra	1873	Middleboro	will	9205
	Frank	1873	Middleboro	grdn	9208
	Franklin	1868	Plymouth	grdn	9218
	George	1767	Plymouth	grdn	9290
	George	1795	Plymouth	admn	9209
	George	1865	Plymouth	will	9210
	Gideon	1811	Duxbury	admn	9211
	Gideon	1853	Duxbury	will	9212
	Grace	1875	Middleboro	grdn	9176
	Hannah	1848	Plymouth	admn	9213
	Hannah	1868	Middleboro	will	9215
	Hannah A	1863	Middleboro	will	9214
	Harriet	1852	N. Bridgewater	grdn	9271
	Henry	1834	Plymouth	admn	9216
	Huldah H	1840	Plymouth	grdn	9217
	Ida	1868	Plymouth	grdn	9218
	Isaac	1712	Plymouth	grdn	9267
	Isaac	1724	Plymouth	admn	9219
	Isaac	1827	Middleboro	will	9221

SURNAME	FIRST NAME	YEAR	PLACE	CASE	DOCKET
HARLOW	Isaac	1875	Middleboro	admn	9222
	Isaac 2nd	1806	Bridgewater	will	9220
	Ivory	1875	Middleboro	grdn	9176
	Jabez	1773	Plymouth	admn	9223
	Jabez	1809	Plymouth	grdn	9229
	Jabez	1872	Plympton	admn	9224
	James	1757	Plympton	will	9225
	James	1797	Plymouth	grdn	9226
	James	1832	Plymouth	grdn	9227 a
	James	1847	Plymouth	admn	9228
	Jedidah	1746	Plymouth	grdn	9280
	Jerusha	1767	Plymouth	grdn	9290
	Jerusha	1809	Plymouth	grdn	9229
	Jerusha T	1870	Carver	grdn	9314
	Jesse	1809	Plymouth	will	9230
	Jesse	1811	Plymouth	admn	9231
	Jesse	1844	Plymouth	admn	9232
	Joanna	1860	Middleboro	admn	9233
	John	1814	Middleboro	will	9234
	John	1839	Plymouth	admn	9236
	John	1840	Plymouth	grdn	9238
	John 2nd	1851	Plymouth	admn	9237
	John A	1852	Duxbury	grdn	9235
	Jonathan	1786	Plymouth	will	9239
	Jonathan	1824	Duxbury	admn	9240
	Jonathan	1833	Middleboro	will	9241
	Jonathan	1865	Hingham	grdn	9243
	Jonathan E	1880	Hingham	admn	9242
	Joseph	1845	Plymouth	will	9244
	Joseph	1868	Plymouth	admn	9245
	Josiah	1767	Plymouth	grdn	9290
	Josiah	1799	Middleboro	will	9246
	Josiah	1861	Middleboro	will	9247
	Judah	1868	Duxbury	admn	9248
	Justus	1860	Plymouth	admn	9249
	Justus W	1863	Plymouth	will	9250
	Kimball	1861	Duxbury	grdn	9251 a
	Kimball	1862	Duxbury	will	9252
	Kimball F	1866	Duxbury	grdn	9253
	Lemuel	1728	Plymouth	grdn	9257
	Lemuel	1759	Middleboro	admn	9258
	Lemuel	1759	Middleboro	grdn	9259
	Lemuel	1799	Plymouth	admn	9256
	Lemuel	1852	Duxbury	will	9254
	Lemuel	1864	S. Scituate	will	9255
	Levi Jr	1816	Plympton	admn	9260
	Lewis	1807	Plymouth	admn	9261
	Lewis	1859	Bridgewater	will	9262
	Lillian May	1871	Minnesota	grdn	9263
	Lois	1762	Plymouth	grdn	9175
	Lot	1832	Plymouth	admn	9264
	Lucy	1865	Hingham	grdn	9243
	Lucy	1868	Plymouth	grdn	9218
	Lurabella	1875	Middleboro	grdn	9176
	Lydia	1712	Plymouth	grdn	9267
	Lydia	1720	Plymouth	admn	9266
	Lydia	1863	Duxbury	admn	9265
	Marcus	1855	Middleboro	grdn	9274
	Mary	1692	Plymouth	cont	9268
	Mary	1720	Plymouth	admn	9269
	Mary	1840	Plymouth	grdn	9238
	Mary	1852	N. Bridgewater	grdn	9271
	Mary L	1875	Plymouth	admn	9270
	Mercy	1767	Plymouth	grdn	9290
	Mercy	1835	Plymouth	grdn	9272 a
	Nancy	1840	Plymouth	will	9273
	Nancy	1855	Middleboro	grdn	9274
	Nathaniel	1721/2	Plympton	admn	9276
	Nathaniel	1746	Plymouth	grdn	9280
	Nathaniel	1795	Plympton	will	9277
	Nathaniel	1827	Plympton	admn	9278

SURNAME	FIRST NAME	YEAR	PLACE	CASE	DOCKET
HARLOW	Nathaniel	1831	Plympton	admn	9279
	Nathaniel B	1852	N. Bridgewater	admn	9275
	Patience	1831	Plympton	admn	9281
	Pelham	1822	Plympton	admn	9282
	Rebecca	1712	Plymouth	grdn	9267
	Rebecca	1853	Plymouth	will	9283
	Rebecca	1863	Mattapoisett	admn	9284
	Reuben	1837	Plymouth	admn	9285
	Robert	1712	Plymouth	grdn	9267
	Ruth	1863	Plymouth	admn	9286
	Samuel	1728	Plymouth	will	9288
	Samuel	1767	Plymouth	will	9289
	Samuel	1767	Plymouth	grdn	9290
	Samuel	1840	Plymouth	grdn	9238
	Samuel	1850	Plymouth	will	9287
	Sarah	1824	Plymouth	admn	9291
	Sarah	1828	Plymouth	will	9292
	Seth	1802	Plymouth	will	9293
	Stephen	1853	Middleboro	admn	9294
	Stephen	1874	Halifax	will	9295
	Susannah	1839	Plymouth	admn	9296
	Sylvanus	1800	Plymouth	admn	9297
	Sylvanus	1847	Halifax	will	9299
	Sylvanus	1863	Plymouth	admn	9298
	Sylvia A	1877	Mattapoisett	admn	9300
	Tekoah	1875	Penfield GA	grdn	9301
	Thomas	1746	Plymouth	admn	9302
	Thomas	1759	Middleboro	grdn	9259
	Thomas	1809	Plymouth	grdn	9229
	Thomas	1855	Middleboro	grdn	9274
	Thomas	1874	Plymouth	admn	9304
	Thomas P	1832	Plymouth	grdn	9303
	William	1691	Plymouth	admn	9305
	William	1711	Plymouth	admn	9306
	William	1749	Bridgewater	admn	9310
	William	1752	Plymouth	admn	9307
	William	1793	Middleboro	will	9312
	William	1797	Plymouth	grdn	9200
	William	1810	Plymouth	grdn	9308
	William	1870	Lakeville	will	9313
	William Jr	1781	Middleboro	admn	9311
	William O	1866	Duxbury	grdn	9253
	William R	1834	Plymouth	grdn	9309
	Wilson T	1870	Carver	grdn	9314
	Zenas	1847	Middleboro	will	9315
HARRIMAN	Allen W	1875	Duxbury	grdn	9316
	Henry B	1875	Duxbury	grdn	9316
HARRINGTON	Celestia	1879	Wareham	grdn	9317
	John	1869	Wareham	admn	9318
	Minnie	1879	Wareham	grdn	9317
	William	1854	Marshfield	bond	9319
HARRIS	Abiah	1792	Abington	grdn	9343
	Abigail	1875	Mattapoisett	admn	9320
	Abner	1722	Bridgewater	grdn	9321
	Ann	1722	Bridgewater	grdn	9321
	Arthur	1722	Bridgewater	grdn	9321
	Arthur	1750	Bridgewater	will	9322
	Arthur	1813	Bridgewater	will	9323
	Azor	1873	E. Bridgewater	will	9324
	Benjamin	1706	Bridgewater	grdn	9326
	Benjamin	1750	Bridgewater	grdn	9338
	Benjamin	1828	E. Bridgewater	will	9325
	Bethia	1750	Bridgewater	grdn	9338
	Caleb	1750	Bridgewater	grdn	9338
	Elizabeth	1722	Bridgewater	grdn	9321
	Florence W	1863	Wareham	adop	9327
	Isaac	1706	Bridgewater	admn	9328
	Isaac	1738	Bridgewater	admn	9329
	James	1858	Hingham	will	9330
	Jane	1722	Bridgewater	grdn	9321
	John	1829	E. Bridgewater	admn	9331

SURNAME	FIRST NAME	YEAR	PLACE	CASE	DOCKET
HARRIS	John B	1869	Abington	will	9332
	Leonard	1854	N. Bridgewater	grdn	9333
	Lucy	1750	Bridgewater	admn	9334
	Lucy	1866	S. Scituate	admn	9335
	Marcy	1706	Bridgewater	grdn	9326
	Martha	1706	Bridgewater	grdn	9326
	Martin	1792	Abington	grdn	9343
	Mary	1816	Abington	will	9336
	Mary	1869	S. Scituate	will	9337
	Mehitable	1750	Bridgewater	grdn	9338
	Olive	1792	Abington	grdn	9343
	Polly	1792	Abington	grdn	9343
	Rhoda	1792	Abington	grdn	9343
	Samuel	1854	N. Bridgewater	admn	9339
	Sarah	1877	E. Bridgewater	admn	9340
	Seth	1792	Abington	grdn	9343
	Seth	1797	Abington	admn	9341
	Seth Jr	1792	Abington	will	9342
	Silas	1750	Bridgewater	grdn	9338
	Susan	1876	Hingham	will	9344
	Susanna	1792	Abington	grdn	9343
	William	1750	Bridgewater	grdn	9338
	William	1831	E. Bridgewater	will	9345
	William	1865	Mattapoisett	admn	9346
HARRISON	Alexander M	1879	Plymouth	name	9347
	Alexander M	1881	Plymouth	will	9348
	Jennie	1877	Plymouth	grdn	9349
	William Henry	1854	Boston	name	9350
	William S	1877	Plymouth	grdn	9349
HARRUB	Charles	1851	Scituate	grdn	9357
	George W	1869	Plympton	admn	9351
	Isaac M	1842	Scituate	admn	9352
	Isaac Thomas	1861	Scituate	admn	9353
	John W	1866	Plympton	admn	9354
	Lucy	1860	Bridgewater	will	9355
	Maria	1851	Scituate	grdn	9357
	Maria L	1856	Scituate	will	9356
	Mercy	1851	Scituate	grdn	9357
	Thomas B	1853	Plympton	admn	9358
	Webster	1869	Plympton	grdn	9359
HART	Lydia T	1838	Marshfield	admn	9360
	Mary B	1871	Lakeville	will	9361
	Sarah M	1858	Hingham	admn	9362
	Swanzy	1825	Carver	will	9363
HARTFORD	Patrick	1834	Wareham	admn	9364
HARTWELL	Abihal	1857	N. Bridgewater	admn	9365
	Amy H	1880	W. Bridgewater	will	9366
	Hannah H	1880	Brockton	admn	9367
	Isaac	1763	Bridgewater	grdn	9374
	Isaac	1831	W. Bridgewater	admn	9368
	Isaac H	1875	Brockton	will	9369
	Jonas	1761	Bridgewater	admn	9370
	Jonas	1763	Bridgewater	grdn	9374
	Jonas	1873	W. Bridgewater	admn	9371
	Myron L	1875	Bridgewater	adop	9372
	Samuel	1761	Bridgewater	will	9373
	Samuel	1763	Bridgewater	grdn	9374
HARVEY	Azubah C	1878	Rochester	admn	9375
	Daniel	1800	Bridgewater	admn	9376
	David	1814	Bridgewater	admn	9377
	David	1828	W. Bridgewater	admn	9378
	David	1828	W. Bridgewater	grdn	9382
	David B	1857	Plymouth	admn	9379
	Hannah M	1858	Plymouth	grdn	9380
	Lorenzo	1828	W. Bridgewater	grdn	9382
	Nathan	1815	Bridgewater	will	9381
	Olive	1828	W. Bridgewater	grdn	9382
	Oliver	1828	W. Bridgewater	grdn	9382
	Oliver	1855	Lakeville	admn	9383
	Sylvanus	1871	Plymouth	admn	9384
	Thankful	1858	Plymouth	grdn	9380

SURNAME	FIRST NAME	YEAR	PLACE	CASE	DOCKET
HARVEY	Thaxter	1828	W. Bridgewater	grdn	9382
HASKELL	Abiah	1803	Middleboro	will	9385
	Andrew	1822	Rochester	grdn	9386
	Benjamin	1778	Middleboro	admn	9387
	Betsey	1798	Rochester	grdn	9388
	Charles H	1863	Abington	admn	9389
	Charlotte	1872	Rochester	will	9390
	David	1821	Rochester	will	9392
	David	1822	Rochester	grdn	9386
	David 2nd	1815	Rochester	will	9391
	Delia	1856	Rochester	will	9393
	Ebenezer	1772	Rochester	admn	9394
	Elisha	1829	Middleboro	will	9395
	Elnathan	1783	Rochester	admn	9396
	Elnathan H	1845	Rochester	will	9397
	Elnathan W	1855	Rochester	admn	9398
	Elnathan W	1863	Abington	grdn	9399
	Ephraim	1773	Rochester	will	9400
	George B	1873	Rochester	grdn	9402
	George W	1873	Rochester	admn	9401
	Harriet M	1845	Rochester	grdn	9403
	Hiram	1822	Rochester	grdn	9386
	Israel	1787	Rochester	grdn	9408
	Israel F	1839	Rochester	admn	9404
	James	1793	Rochester	admn	9405
	Jesse	1829	Rochester	admn	9406
	Joanna	1787	Rochester	grdn	9408
	Joanna	1802	Rochester	will	9407
	John	1706	Middleboro	inve	9409
	John	1728	Rochester	admn	9411
	John	1792	Rochester	will	9413
	John	1832	Middleboro	admn	9410
	John	1842	Rochester	admn	9414
	John Jr	1784	Rochester	admn	9412
	Joseph	1787	Rochester	grdn	9415 a
	Joseph	1798	Rochester	grdn	9416 a
	Joseph	1873	Rochester	will	9418
	Joseph H	1863	Abington	grdn	9399
	Joseph Jr	1800	Rochester	admn	9417
	Julia H	1846	Rochester	will	9419
	Lot	1844	Rochester	will	9420
	Lucy T	1854	Rochester	admn	9421
	Lydia	1822	Rochester	grdn	9386
	Mark	1764	Rochester	will	9422
	Mark	1769	Rochester	admn	9423
	Mark	1785	Middleboro	will	9424
	Micah	1807	Rochester	will	9425
	Nathan	1798	Rochester	grdn	9388
	Nathaniel	1827	Rochester	admn	9426
	Nathaniel	1841	Rochester	will	9427
	Noah	1799	Middleboro	admn	9428
	Patty	1787	Rochester	grdn	9408
	Priscilla	1822	Rochester	grdn	9386
	Priscilla	1825	Rochester	will	9429
	Sally	1798	Rochester	grdn	9388
	Samuel	1820	Rochester	admn	9430
	Seth	1769	Rochester	will	9431
	Seth	1793	Middleboro	will	9432
	Seth	1845	Rochester	admn	9433
	Thomas Allen	1816	Middleboro	admn	9434
	Zebulon	1820	Middleboro	will	9435
HASKINS	Amos	1838	Rochester	admn	9436
	Andrew	1856	Lakeville	admn	9437
	Apollos	1865	Lakeville	will	9438
	Enoch	1863	Lakeville	will	9439
	Gideon	1858	Lakeville	will	9440
	Gilbert T	1873	Lakeville	admn	9441
	Hannah	1801	Middleboro	will	9443
	Hannah M	1812	Middleboro	grdn	9442
	Harrison	1851	Rochester	admn	9444
	James	1862	Plymouth	admn	9445

SURNAME	FIRST NAME	YEAR	PLACE	CASE	DOCKET
HASKINS	Jesse	1817	-----	grdn	9446
	Job	1847	Middleboro	grdn	9447 a
	Job	1848	Middleboro	admn	9448
	John C	1868	Lakeville	admn	9449
	Lemuel	1836	Scituate	admn	9450
	Levi	1862	Lakeville	admn	9451
	Mirick	1810	Middleboro	admn	9452
	Nathan	1778	Middleboro	will	9453
	Orrin E	1863	Lakeville	grdn	9454
	Susannah	1876	Lakeville	admn	9455
	Thomas	1817	Rochester	admn	9456
	William	1807	Scituate	will	9457
HASTINGS	Anna M	1854	Plymouth	admn	9458
	Richard L	1854	Bridgewater	will	9459
HATCH	Abby	1855	Marshfield	grdn	9460
	Abigail	1816	Plympton	admn	9461
	Abigail	1818	Beverly	grdn	9572
	Abigail	1832	Pembroke	admn	9462
	Abigail	1862	Marshfield	will	9463
	Abigail	1868	Marshfield	will	9464
	Abijah	1866	Marshfield	admn	9465
	Agathy	1771	-----	warr	9515
	Amos	1810	Marshfield	will	9466
	Anna	1818	Beverly	grdn	9572
	Anna B	1874	Marshfield	grdn	9468
	Anna G	1857	Middleboro	adop	9467
	Anson	1832	Scituate	admn	9469
	Anthony E	1842	Marshfield	will	9470
	Asa	1745	Plymouth	admn	9471
	Asa	1748	Plymouth	grdn	9472
	Asa	1832	Scituate	grdn	9473
	Bathsheba	1807	Hanover	grdn	9577
	Benjamin	1731	Scituate	grdn	9479
	Benjamin	1796	Marshfield	admn	9474
	Benjamin	1817	Rochester	admn	9477
	Benjamin	1830	Hanover	grdn	9480
	Benjamin	1835	Marshfield	admn	9475
	Benjamin	1877	Marshfield	admn	9476
	Benjamin	1878	Scituate	grdn	9478 a
	Bethiah	1846	Marshfield	admn	9481
	Briggs	1769	Scituate	grdn	9615
	Caroline	1823	Marshfield	grdn	9556
	Celia	1870	Marshfield	admn	9482
	Charles	1828	Marshfield	will	9483
	Charles	1836	Marshfield	grdn	9579
	Charles	1870	Marshfield	will	9484
	Daniel	1878	Scituate	admn	9485
	David	1772	Scituate	admn	9486
	David	1823	Marshfield	grdn	9556
	David P	1876	Marshfield	will	9487
	Deborah	1832	Scituate	grdn	9473
	Deborah F	1866	Marshfield	admn	9488
	Ebenezer	1724	Pembroke	will	9490
	Ebenezer	1725	Pembroke	grdn	9491
	Ebenezer	1756	Pembroke	admn	9489
	Eddie	1873	Hingham	grdn	9492
	Edmond	1760	Marshfield	will	9494
	Edmond	1794	Westmoreland NH	warr	9493
	Elizabeth	1823	Marshfield	grdn	9556
	Elizabeth	1855	Marshfield	grdn	9460
	Emmons	1880	Marshfield	will	9495
	Ezekiel	1768	Rochester	will	9406
	Ezekiel	1830	Hanover	grdn	9480
	Ezekiel T	1797	Hanover	admn	9497
	Ezra	1864	Marshfield	will	9498
	Francis	1836	Marshfield	grdn	9579
	Frederick	1769	Scituate	grdn	9615
	Frederick	1843	Marshfield	grdn	9499
	George	1810	Scituate	admn	9500
	George	1831	Scituate	grdn	9600
	Gibbs	1823	Rochester	admn	9501

SURNAME	FIRST NAME	YEAR	PLACE	CASE	DOCKET
HATCH	Grace	1731	Scituate	grdn	9479
	Hannah	1818	Beverly	grdn	9572
	Hannah	1823	Marshfield	grdn	9556
	Henry	1836	Marshfield	grdn	9579
	Hercules	1853	E. Bridgewater	admn	9502
	Hezekiah	1779	Scituate	will	9503
	Ichabod	1845	Marshfield	will	9504
	Ichabod	1876	Marshfield	admn	9505
	Isaac	1724/5	-----	grdn	9547
	Isaac	1759	Pembroke	will	9506
	Isaac	1800	Pembroke	will	9507
	Isaac	1845	Pembroke	will	9508
	Isaac	1850	Pembroke	admn	9509
	Isaac	1877	E. Bridgewater	admn	9510
	Israel	1740	Scituate	will	9514
	Israel	1771	-----	warr	9515
	Israel	1809	Marshfield	will	9511
	Israel	1822	Marshfield	admn	9512
	Israel	1823	Marshfield	grdn	9556
	Israel	1854	Marshfield	admn	9513
	Israel	1855	Marshfield	grdn	9460
	Israel	1864	S. Scituate	grdn	9551
	Jabesh	1724	Rochester	grdn	9516
	Jabez	1758	Marshfield	admn	9517
	Jabez	1842	Marshfield	admn	9518
	Jabez	1855	Marshfield	will	9519
	James	1741	Hanover	will	9520
	James	1769	Scituate	grdn	9615
	James	1836	Marshfield	admn	9521
	Jemima	1786	Scituate	will	9522
	Jennie G	1880	Hanover	adop	9523
	Jeremiah	1712/3	Scituate	will	9524
	Jeremiah	1727	Abington	will	9526
	Jeremiah	1728	-----	grdn	9525
	Jerusha	1771	-----	warr	9515
	Joanna	1840	Marshfield	will	9527
	Job W	1825	Marshfield	will	9528
	Joel	1849	Marshfield	will	9529
	John	1728	N Carolina	grdn	9530
	John	1737	Scituate	will	9533
	John	1804	Bridgewater	will	9531
	John	1809	Hanover	will	9535
	John	1819	Scituate	admn	9534
	John	1868	Hanover	admn	9536
	John	1873	Hanover	will	9537
	John Jr	1730	Scituate	admn	9532
	Jonathan	1775	Scituate	admn	9538
	Jonathan	1840	Marshfield	will	9539
	Joseph	1749	Scituate	will	9540
	Joseph H etal	1881	S. Scituate	peti	9541
	Josiah	1715	Rochester	admn	9542
	Josiah	1724	Rochester	grdn	9516
	Josiah	1724/5	-----	grdn	9547
	Josiah	1758	Pembroke	admn	9546
	Josiah	1763	Pembroke	admn	9545
	Josiah	1831	Pembroke	admn	9544
	Josiah	1848	Pembroke	admn	9543
	Jotham	1832	Marshfield	will	9548
	Julia	1872	Scituate	will	9548
	Lavina	1879	Pembroke	will	9550
	Lavinia A	1850	Pembroke	grdn	9563
	Lizzie	1864	S. Scituate	grdn	9551
	Lizzie	1873	Hingham	grdn	9492
	Lucretia F	1876	Marshfield	admn	9552
	Lucy	1801	Rochester	will	9553
	Lucy	1823	Marshfield	grdn	9556
	Lucy	1827	Scituate	grdn	9554 a
	Lucy	1829	Scituate	will	9555
	Lusanna R	1812	Scituate	grdn	9557
	Luther	1872	Marshfield	will	9558
	Lydia	1765	Scituate	admn	9559

SURNAME	FIRST NAME	YEAR	PLACE	CASE	DOCKET
HATCH	Lydia	1769	Scituate	grdn	9615
	Lydia S	1875	Marshfield	admn	9560
	Marshall	1853	Scituate	will	9561
	Martin	1850	Pembroke	grdn	9563
	Martin H	1849	Scituate	will	9562
	Mary	1716	Scituate	will	9564
	Mary	1731	Scituate	grdn	9479
	Mary	1742	Scituate	admn	9565
	Mary	1767	Scituate	admn	9566 a
	Mary	1818	Beverly	grdn	9572
	Mary	1832	Scituate	grdn	9473
	Mary A	1881	S. Scituate	admn	9567
	Mary A	1881	Marshfield	admn	9671
	Mary F	1876	Wareham	admn	9568
	Mary H C	1877	S. Abington	will	9569
	Mary S	1874	Marshfield	grdn	9570
	Melzar	1807	Hanover	admn	9576
	Melzar	1807	Hanover	grdn	9577
	Melzar	1819	Scituate	grdn	9573 a
	Melzar	1865	Hanover	will	9574
	Melzar Jr	1854	Hanover	admn	9575
	Mercy	1771	-----	warr	9515
	Mercy	1836	Marshfield	grdn	9579
	Mercy P	1874	Marshfield	admn	9578
	Nathaniel	1737	Plymouth	grdn	9580
	Nathaniel	1749	Plymouth	admn	9581
	Nathaniel	1833	Hanson	grdn	9583
	Noah	1808	Marshfield	will	9582
	Olive	1833	Hanson	grdn	9583
	Orpha B	1815	Pembroke	grdn	9584
	Penelope	1776	Pembroke	admn	9585
	Phillips	1769	Scituate	grdn	9615
	Prince	1769	Scituate	grdn	9615
	Rachel	1769	Scituate	grdn	9615
	Reliance	1772	Marshfield	admn	9586
	Richard	1748	Plymouth	grdn	9472
	Rodulphus	1744	Plymouth	admn	9587
	Rosa	1864	S. Scituate	grdn	9551
	Rosella	1855	Marshfield	grdn	9460
	Roxanna	1832	Lynn	grdn	9588
	Ruth	1830	Hanover	grdn	9480
	Sally	1807	Hanover	grdn	9577
	Samuel	1735	Scituate	will	9591
	Samuel	1767	Scituate	will	9592
	Samuel	1776	Pembroke	admn	9589
	Samuel	1783	Pembroke	grdn	9590
	Samuel	1844	Scituate	admn	9593
	Samuel S	1860	Wareham	admn	9595
	Samuel et al	1878	Scituate	peti	9594
	Sarah	1725	Pembroke	grdn	9491
	Sarah	1791	Marshfield	will	9598
	Sarah	1818	Pembroke	grdn	9596 a
	Sarah	1823	Marshfield	grdn	9556
	Sarah	1827	Scituate	will	9597
	Sarah	1831	Scituate	grdn	9600
	Sarah	1833	Hanson	grdn	9583
	Sarah W	1836	Marshfield	grdn	9599
	Seth	1799	Pembroke	will	9601
	Seth	1804	Pembroke	grdn	9602 a
	Thankful	1769	Scituate	grdn	9615
	Thomas	1751	Scituate	will	9607
	Thomas	1792	Hanover	grdn	9603
	Thomas	1807	Hanover	will	9604
	Thomas	1807	Georgia	grdn	9606
	Thomas	1825	Hanover	grdn	9605 a
	Thomas M	1872	Scituate	admn	9608
	Walter	1701	Scituate	will	9609
	Walter	1873	Hingham	grdn	9492
	Warren	1818	Scituate	grdn	9610 a
	Warren	1831	Scituate	grdn	9600
	Warren	1873	Hingham	admn	9611

SURNAME	FIRST NAME	YEAR	PLACE	CASE	DOCKET
HATCH	Willard	1855	Marshfield	grdn	9460
	Willard	1864	S. Scituate	grdn	9551
	William	1702/3	Swansey	agre	9612
	William	1811	Hingham	admn	9613
	William	1832	Scituate	grdn	9473
	William	1876	S. Scituate	admn	9614
	Zachariah	1769	Scituate	grdn	9615
	Zephaniah	1805	Duxbury	admn	9616
HATFIELD	George	1774	Plymouth	admn	9617
	Joseph	1872	Hingham	admn	9618
HATHAWAY	Abby S	1841	Plymouth	grdn	9619
	Abigail	1878	Marion	will	9620
	Abner	1835	Rochester	admn	9621
	Abraham	1814	Rochester	admn	9622
	Alanson	1820	Plymouth	admn	9623
	Albert	1851	Plymouth	grdn	9633
	Albert F	1874	Wareham	admn	9626
	Albert S	1873	Wareham	admn	9624
	Albert S	1873	Wareham	grdn	9625
	Alexander	1856	Wareham	grdn	9627 a
	Alexander	1859	Wareham	will	9628
	Andrew	1809	Rochester	admn	9629
	Ann E	1855	Rochester	grdn	9630
	Anne	1851	Plymouth	grdn	9633
	Benjamin	1851	Plymouth	grdn	9633
	Benjamin	1854	Wareham	will	9631
	Benjamin	1880	Plymouth	admn	9631
	Charles	1851	Wareham	admn	9634
	Charles	1872	Plymouth	will	9635
	Cushman	1874	Bridgewater	admn	9636
	David	1861	Marion	will	9639
	David 2nd	1839	Rochester	will	9637
	David E	1853	Marion	admn	9638
	Dorothy	1796	Rochester	grdn	9640 a
	Dorothy	1839	Rochester	will	9641
	Ebenezer	1830	E. Bridgewater	will	9642
	Ebenezer	1856	E. Bridgewater	admn	9643
	Elmer W	1875	Plymouth	grdn	9644
	Elnathan P	1858	Freetown	bond	9645
	Eugene	1869	Plymouth	admn	9646
	Eunice	1809	Rochester	grdn	9648
	Eunice	1812	Rochester	admn	9647
	Experience	1855	Rochester	will	9649
	Freeman	1839	Middleboro	admn	9650
	George	1851	Plymouth	grdn	9633
	George A	1874	Plymouth	admn	9651
	George B	1878	Plymouth	admn	9652
	George C	1875	Rutland VT	admn	9653
	Hannah	1808	Rochester	will	9654
	Hannah	1839	Bridgewater	will	9655
	Hannah	1874	E. Bridgewater	will	9656
	Ira	1835	Wareham	grdn	9698
	Ira F	1874	Wareham	adop	9657
	Isaac	1793	Middleboro	grdn	9658 a
	Isaac	1875	E. Bridgewater	admn	9661
	Isaac Jr	1826	Wilton ME	admn	9659
	Isaac Jr	1868	Mattapoisett	admn	9660
	Jairus S	1872	Middleboro	admn	9662
	Jerusha F	1854	Duxbury	grdn	9676
	John	1809	Camden	grdn	9663
	John K	1879	Marion	admn	9664
	Joseph	1815	Rochester	admn	9665
	Joseph	1878	Middleboro	admn	9666
	Joshua	1855	Plymouth	will	9667
	Josiah	1778	Halifax	will	9668
	Josiah	1878	E. Bridgewater	admn	9671
	Josiah D D F	1840	Rochester	grdn	9669 a
	Josiah D D F	1879	Rochester	admn	9670
	Judah	1834	Wareham	admn	9672
	Judah	1835	Wareham	grdn	9698
	Leander	1822	Wareham	grdn	9673

SURNAME	FIRST NAME	YEAR	PLACE	CASE	DOCKET
HATHAWAY	Levi	1823	Middleboro	will	9674
	Lucy	1854	Duxbury	grdn	9676
	Lucy C	1878	Plymouth	grdn	9675
	Mabel	1875	E. Bridgewater	grdn	9677
	Mary	1825	Middleboro	will	9678
	Mary	1835	Wareham	grdn	9698
	Mary H	1879	Marion	grdn	9679
	Merick	1795	Middleboro	grdn	9680
	Nathaniel P	1861	Mattapoisett	admn	9681
	Paul	1812	Middleboro	warr	9682
	Paul	1865	Middleboro	admn	9683
	Peleg	1838	Rochester	will	9684
	Priscilla	1855	Rochester	admn	9685
	Rebecca	1851	Plymouth	grdn	9633
	Rufus	1822	Duxbury	admn	9686
	Ruth A	1863	Rochester	will	9687
	Sarah	1835	Wareham	grdn	9698
	Sarah	1851	Rochester	admn	9688
	Sarah E C	1855	Rochester	grdn	9630
	Savory	1811	Wareham	will	9689
	Savory	1855	Rochester	will	9690
	Seabury C	1877	S. Abington	will	9691
	Selathiel	1792	Wareham	will	9692
	Seth	1791	Middleboro	admn	9693
	Silas Jr	1811	Plymouth	admn	9694
	Simon	1799	Rochester	admn	9695
	Simon	1809	Rochester	grdn	9648
	Thomas	1878	Abington	will	9696
	Walter Lloyd	1867	Abington	name	9697
	William	1835	Wareham	grdn	9698
	William	1851	Plymouth	grdn	9633
HATTON	John	1878	Plymouth	will	9699
	Mary A	1880	Plymouth	will	9700
HAVEN	Curtis	1878	Brockton	will	9701
HAVERSTOCK	James	1856	Abington	grdn	9702
	John	1856	Abington	grdn	9702
HAWTHORNE	Samuel	1839	Scituate	admn	9703
	Thomas	1871	Scituate	will	9704
HAY	Charles	1838	Wareham	admn	9705
	Charles H	1844	Wareham	grdn	9706
HAYDEN	Aaron	1852	Bridgewater	grdn	9727
	Abner	1811	Roxbury	grdn	9726
	Abner N	1852	Bridgewater	admn	9707
	Benjamin	1845	Hull	admn	9708
	Caroline H	1816	Boston	grdn	9709
	Deborah	1811	Bridgewater	admn	9710
	Eliza	1869	N. Bridgewater	will	9711
	Frank	1868	N. Bridgewater	grdn	9712
	George	1767	Plymouth	will	9713
	Hannah	1861	Scituate	will	9714
	Hattie	1868	N. Bridgewater	grdn	9712
	Hosea M	1868	Hanover	grdn	9715
	Joseph	1784	Scituate	admn	9716
	Joseph P	1878	Wareham	admn	9717
	Kate W	1859	Bridgewater	admn	9718
	Lettice	1805	Scituate	admn	9719
	Lewis	1872	Bridgewater	will	9720
	Lizzie	1867	Plymouth	grdn	9728
	Lothrop	1867	Plymouth	grdn	9728
	Luther	1873	N. Bridgewater	will	9721
	Marietta	1852	Bridgewater	grdn	9727
	Mary	1860	N. Bridgewater	will	9722
	Mary	1861	Mattapoisett	admn	9723
	Minot H	1868	Hanover	admn	9724
	Rhoda	1871	Scituate	will	9725
	Sally	1811	Roxbury	grdn	9726
	Sarah W	1852	Bridgewater	grdn	9727
	Willie	1867	Plymouth	grdn	9728
HAYES	Bertha Gray	1879	Middleboro	adop	9729
	Daniel	1872	N. Bridgewater	admn	9730
HAYFORD	Benjamin	1761	Middleboro	will	9731

SURNAME	FIRST NAME	YEAR	PLACE	CASE	DOCKET
HAYFORD	Daniel	1765	Pembroke	will	9732
	Ebenezer	1724	Middleboro	grdn	9736
	Ebenezer	1781	Middleboro	admn	9733
	John	1724	Middleboro	admn	9734
	John	1724	Middleboro	grdn	9736
	John	1813	Middleboro	admn	9735
	Samuel	1724	Middleboro	grdn	9736
HAYNES	Albert S	1864	Hingham	admn	9737
	Hettie M	1862	Abington	grdn	9738
	James M	1875	Abington	admn	9739
	Minnie L	1875	Abington	grdn	9740
HAYWARD	Abiel	1761	Bridgewater	grdn	9767
	Abner	1796	Bridgewater	will	9741
	Alden	1870	Middleboro	will	9742
	Almira	1837	N. Bridgewater	grdn	9749
	Almira	1871	Abington	will	9744
	Almira	1877	Brockton	will	9743
	Alvin	1849	Bridgewater	admn	9745
	Alvinna	1849	Bridgewater	grdn	9746
	Amasa	1761	Bridgewater	grdn	9767
	Ambrose	1870	N. Bridgewater	will	9747
	Anna	1781	Bridgewater	grdn	9819
	Azariah	1802	Bridgewater	will	9748
	Barzillai	1818	Bridgewater	grdn	9768
	Bela	1817	Bridgewater	grdn	9777
	Bela	1837	N. Bridgewater	grdn	9749
	Benjamin	1733	Bridgewater	will	9750
	Benjamin	1741	Bridgewater	admn	9751
	Benjamin	1774	Bridgewater	admn	9752
	Benjamin	1774	Bridgewater	grdn	9762
	Benjamin	1807	Bridgewater	admn	9753
	Benjamin F	1859	N. Bridgewater	will	9754
	Benoni	1744	Bridgewater	admn	9755
	Bethia	1751	Bridgewater	grdn	9779
	Bethia	1827	Bridgewater	admn	9756
	Betsey	1824	W. Bridgewater	grdn	9758
	Betsey	1857	Bridgewater	will	9757
	Beza	1830	Plymouth	admn	9759
	Caleb	1847	Bridgewater	grdn	9781
	Caleb	1870	Bridgewater	admn	9760
	Calvin	1854	Bridgewater	will	9761
	Cary	1774	Bridgewater	grdn	9762
	Charity	1778	Bridgewater	grdn	9763
	Cordelia	1870	Plympton	grdn	9764 a
	Cornelius	1813	Bridgewater	will	9765
	Daniel	1750	Bridgewater	grdn	9771
	Daniel L	1871	Bridgewater	will	9766
	David	1761	Bridgewater	grdn	9767
	Davis	1818	Bridgewater	grdn	9768
	Deborah	1852	Bridgewater	will	9769
	Ebenezer	1750	Bridgewater	grdn	9771
	Ebenezer	1786	Bridgewater	will	9770
	Edmund	1781	Bridgewater	admn	9772
	Edmund	1781	Bridgewater	grdn	9819
	Edward	1771	Bridgewater	will	9773
	Edward	1817	Bridgewater	grdn	9777
	Edward	1818	Bridgewater	will	9774
	Edward	1825	W. Bridgewater	admn	9775
	Edward	1856	W. Bridgewater	will	9776
	Eli	1819	Bridgewater	admn	9778
	Eliakim	1751	Bridgewater	grdn	9779
	Elijah	1781	Bridgewater	grdn	9819
	Elijah	1815	Bridgewater	will	9780
	Elijah	1847	Bridgewater	grdn	9781
	Elisha	1710	Bridgewater	will	9782
	Elisha	1748	Bridgewater	will	9783
	Ellen	1869	Plympton	grdn	9784
	Ephraim	1750	Bridgewater	will	9785
	Erastus	1844	Bridgewater	admn	9786
	Eunice	1847	Bridgewater	grdn	9781
	Ezra	1750	Bridgewater	grdn	9771

SURNAME	FIRST NAME	YEAR	PLACE	CASE	DOCKET
HAYWARD	Ezra	1761	Bridgewater	grdn	9787 a
	Ezra	1782	Duxbury	admn	9788
	George P	1831	-----	grdn	9789
	Grace	1802	Bridgewater	will	9790
	Hannah	1741	Bridgewater	grdn	9794
	Hannah	1765	Bridgewater	grdn	9791
	Hannah	1781	Bridgewater	grdn	9819
	Hannah	1785	Bridgewater	will	9792
	Hannah	1788	Bridgewater	grdn	9870
	Hannah	1796	Bridgewater	admn	9793
	Harriet W	1847	Bridgewater	grdn	9795
	Harrison	1833	Bridgewater	grdn	9796
	Hezekiah	1790	Bridgewater	will	9797
	Hezekiah	1811	Bridgewater	admn	9798
	Hope W	1878	Bridgewater	grdn	9854
	Horace	1866	Bridgewater	grdn	9799
	Ira	1850	Kingston	admn	9800
	Jacob	1778	Bridgewater	will	9801
	James	1690/1	Bridgewater	admn	9802
	James	1824	W. Bridgewater	grdn	9758
	Janny	1848	Bridgewater	will	9803
	John	1701	Bridgewater	admn	9804
	John	1705	Bridgewater	admn	9805
	John	1710	Bridgewater	admn	9806
	John	1790	Bridgewater	will	9807
	John	1874	Scituate	admn	9809
	John R	1836	Middleboro	admn	9808
	Jonathan	1737	Bridgewater	admn	9810
	Jonathan	1762	Bridgewater	admn	9811
	Jonathan	1824	W. Bridgewater	will	9812
	Joseph	1718	Bridgewater	will	9813
	Joseph	1758	Bridgewater	will	9814
	Joseph	1826	N. Bridgewater	grdn	9829
	Joseph	1881	Brockton	admn	9815
	Josiah	1764	Bridgewater	will	9816
	Josiah	1765	Bridgewater	grdn	9817
	Josiah	1847	Bridgewater	grdn	9781
	Katherine	1751	Bridgewater	grdn	9779
	Laura	1847	Bridgewater	grdn	9781
	Laura A	1871	Scituate	admn	9818
	Lebbeus	1781	Bridgewater	grdn	9819
	Leonard	1837	E. Bridgewater	grdn	9822
	Lois	1765	Bridgewater	grdn	9817
	Lucius	1850	Kingston	grdn	9820
	Lucy	1837	E. Bridgewater	grdn	9822
	Lucy	1868	Bridgewater	will	9821
	Lucy F	1869	Plympton	grdn	9784
	Luther	1824	W. Bridgewater	grdn	9758
	Luther	1832	W. Bridgewater	will	9824
	Luther	1859	Bridgewater	will	9825
	Luther Jr	1824	W. Bridgewater	admn	9823
	Lydia	1808	Bridgewater	warr	9826
	Lysander	1818	Bridgewater	grdn	9768
	Lysander	1858	Halifax	will	9827
	Manley	1825	N. Bridgewater	admn	9828
	Martha	1826	N. Bridgewater	grdn	9829
	Martin	1869	Plympton	will	9831
	Martin	1879	Phila PA	will	9832
	Martin Jr	1855	Plympton	will	9830
	Mary	1751	Bridgewater	grdn	9779
	Mary	1788	Bridgewater	grdn	9870
	Mary	1834	N. Bridgewater	admn	9833
	Mary Ann	1826	N. Bridgewater	grdn	9829
	Mary E	1875	Brockton	grdn	9834
	Mehitable	1846	W. Bridgewater	will	9835
	Nahum	1866	N. Bridgewater	will	9836
	Nathan	1794	N. Bridgewater	admn	9837
	Nathan	1848	Plymouth	will	9840
	Nathan	1859	N. Bridgewater	admn	9838
	Nathan W	1864	Bridgewater	admn	9839
	Nathaniel	1734	Bridgewater	will	9841

SURNAME	FIRST NAME	YEAR	PLACE	CASE	DOCKET
HAYWARD	Nathaniel	1755	Bridgewater	admn	9842
	Nathaniel	1780	Bridgewater	will	9843
	Nellie M	1866	Bridgewater	grdn	9799
	Olive	1856	Kingston	admn	9844
	Oliver	1831	Bridgewater	admn	9845
	Otho	1858	E. Bridgewater	will	9846
	Otis	1877	Brockton	will	9847
	Peter	1765	Bridgewater	will	9848
	Phebe	1741	Bridgewater	grdn	9849
	Pliny	1863	W. Bridgewater	will	9850
	Rebecca	1741	Bridgewater	grdn	9794
	Rhoda	1861	N. Bridgewater	grdn	9851
	Rhoda	1864	N. Bridgewater	admn	9852
	Robert	1813	Bridgewater	will	9853
	Ruth	1741	Bridgewater	grdn	9794
	Samuel	1837	N. Bridgewater	grdn	9749
	Samuel D	1878	Bridgewater	grdn	9854
	Saphronia	1818	Bridgewater	grdn	9768
	Sarah	1705	Bridgewater	grdn	9861
	Sarah	1741	Bridgewater	grdn	9794
	Sarah	1765	Bridgewater	grdn	9817
	Sarah	1794	Bridgewater	will	9855
	Seth	1741	Bridgewater	grdn	9849
	Seth	1778	Bridgewater	will	9856
	Silas	1852	Bridgewater	will	9857
	Simeon	1751	Bridgewater	grdn	9779
	Solomon	1832	Bridgewater	will	9858
	Solomon	1867	Bridgewater	will	9859
	Susan	1837	E. Bridgewater	grdn	9822
	Susan	1853	Plymouth	admn	9860
	Susanna	1705	Bridgewater	grdn	9861
	Sylvanus	1797	Bridgewater	admn	9862
	Sylvanus	1850	E. Bridgewater	admn	9863
	Thomas	1699	Bridgewater	admn	9864
	Thomas	1741	Bridgewater	will	9865
	Thomas	1754	Bridgewater	admn	9866
	Thomas J	1869	Bridgewater	admn	9867
	Timothy	1750	Bridgewater	grdn	9771
	Timothy	1750	Bridgewater	will	9868
	Timothy	1788	Bridgewater	admn	9869
	Timothy	1788	Bridgewater	grdn	9870
	Waldo	1864	E. Bridgewater	will	9871
	Zeruiah	1844	Bridgewater	will	9872
	Zina	1873	N. Bridgewater	will	9873
HAZARD	Barney	1875	Hingham	admn	9874
HEALEY	Oliver G	1876	S. Abington	will	9875
	Reuben Jr	1880	Brockton	will	9876
	Timothy	1746	Plymouth	admn	9877
HEANCE	George	1876	Plymouth	adop	9878
HEANEY	Dennis	1866	Abington	grdn	9879
	Edward	1866	Abington	grdn	9879
HEARD	Jerusha	1867	N. Bridgewater	admn	9880
HEBARD	Amanda R	1853	N. Bridgewater	grdn	9881
	John C	1876	Rockland	admn	9882
HEDGE	Barnabas	1762	Plymouth	admn	9883
	Barnabas	1840	Plymouth	admn	9884
	Edward G	1869	Plymouth	will	9885
	Eunice D	1850	Plymouth	will	9886
	Helena A	1877	Plymouth	grdn	9887
	Isaac L	1867	Plymouth	will	9888
	Jacob	1713	Plymouth	admn	9889
	Mercy	1792	Plymouth	admn	9890
	Thomas	1865	Plymouth	will	9891
	William	1713	Plymouth	admn	9892 i
HEDLEY	Henry	1793	Rochester	will	9893
	Joseph	1821	Rochester	admn	9894
	Stephen	1816	Rochester	admn	9895
HENBURY	Nicholas	1723	Bridgewater	admn	9896
HENDERSON	Frederick	1790	Scituate	will	9897
	Samuel J	1880	Hingham	admn	9898
HENDLEY	Ellen A	1854	Abington	grdn	9899

SURNAME	FIRST NAME	YEAR	PLACE	CASE	DOCKET
	Susan E	1854	Abington	grdn	9899
HENEBRY	Catharine	1877	Brockton	grdn	9900
HENNESSEY	David	1867	N. Bridgewater	grdn	9903
	Edward	1867	N. Bridgewater	grdn	9903
	John	1867	N. Bridgewater	admn	9902
	John	1867	N. Bridgewater	grdn	9903
	John	1869	Kingston	will	9901
	Lawrence	1867	N. Bridgewater	grdn	9903
	Mary	1867	N. Bridgewater	grdn	9903
	William	1867	N. Bridgewater	grdn	9903
HENNEY	Joseph	1849	Duxbury	admn	9904
HERRICK	John W	1875	E. Bridgewater	grdn	9905
	Thomas W	1865	Duxbury	name	9906
HERSEY	Abel	1804	Hingham	grdn	9933
	Abigail	1816	Hingham	will	9907
	Abner	1849	Hingham	admn	9908
	Adelaide W	1869	Hingham	grdn	9909
	Anna	1754	Milton	grdn	9910
	Anna	1862	Lakeville	grdn	9938
	Avery	1872	Abington	admn	9911
	Bela	1829	Hingham	admn	9912
	Bela F	1879	Hingham	admn	9914
	Bela S	1861	Hingham	admn	9913
	Benjamin	1855	Hingham	admn	9915
	Catharine S	1877	Hingham	will	9916
	Celia	1856	Hingham	will	9917
	Charles	1858	Hingham	admn	9918
	Clarissa	1857	Hingham	will	9919
	Cushing	1870	Hingham	admn	9920
	Daniel	1836	Abington	will	9921
	Daniel	1837	Abington	grdn	9922
	Daniel	1844	Abington	will	9923
	David	1763	Abington	grdn	9927
	David	1827	Abington	admn	9926
	David	1851	Abington	admn	9925
	David	1862	Hanover	will	9924
	Ebed	1837	Hingham	will	9928
	Ebed	1859	Hingham	will	9929
	Edith H L	1874	Hingham	adop	9930
	Edmund	1827	Hingham	will	9931
	Edward L	1853	Hingham	admn	9932
	Elias	1804	Hingham	grdn	9933
	Eliza C	1858	Hingham	admn	9934
	Eliza L	1871	Hingham	will	9935
	Elizabeth	1877	Hingham	will	9936
	Ella M	1866	Hingham	grdn	9937
	Emily A	1862	Lakeville	grdn	9938
	Emma	1861	Hingham	adop	9939
	Emma L	1855	Hingham	grdn	9940
	Ezekiel	1845	Hingham	admn	9941
	George	1871	Hingham	will	9942
	George W	1875	Hingham	will	9943
	Gideon	1759	Abington	will	9944
	Gilbert	1804	Hingham	grdn	9945 a
	Gilbert	1804	Hingham	admn	9946
	Gridley	1827	Hingham	admn	9947
	Hannah	1803	Hingham	will	9948
	Hannah	1872	Abington	admn	9949
	Harriet D	1876	Hingham	admn	9950
	Henry	1877	Hingham	will	9953
	Henry E	1863	Hingham	admn	9951
	Henry M	1876	Hingham	admn	9952
	Hosea	1826	Hingham	admn	9954
	Isaac	1762	Abington	admn	9955
	Isaac	1763	Abington	grdn	9927
	Isaac	1763	Abington	grdn	9956
	Isaac	1865	Hingham	will	9957
	Isaiah	1868	Hingham	will	9958
	Israel	1823	Hingham	will	9959
	Jacob	1854	Pembroke	will	9960
	Jacob	1872	Hingham	admn	9962

SURNAME	FIRST NAME	YEAR	PLACE	CASE	DOCKET
HERSEY	Jacob F	1876	Hingham	grdn	9963
	Jacob Jr	1836	Hingham	admn	9961
	James	1837	Hingham	admn	9964
	James	1860	Abington	admn	9965
	Jeremiah	1814	Hingham	warr	9966
	Jeremiah	1846	Hingham	will	9967
	Jeremiah S	1862	Lakeville	admn	9968
	Job R	1849	Middleboro	admn	9969
	John	1857	W. Bridgewater	admn	9970
	John	1876	W. Bridgewater	admn	9971
	John P	1875	Hingham	will	9972
	Joseph	1807	Abington	will	9973
	Joshua	1807	Hingham	will	9974
	Joshua	1853	Hingham	will	9975
	Joshua	1872	BangorME/Hing'm	admn	9976
	Laban	1842	Hingham	will	9977
	Lucy	1867	Hingham	will	9978
	Lucy A	1854	Hingham	will	9979
	Lydia A	1818	Hingham	grdn	9980
	Lydia A	1878	Hingham	admn	9981
	Maria	1853	Hingham	grdn	9989
	Maria	1880	Hingham	will	9982
	Maria	1881	Hingham	will	9983
	Martin	1858	Hingham	will	9984
	Mary	1838	Abington	will	9985
	Mary	1853	Hingham	grdn	9989
	Mary A	1855	Hingham	grdn	9987
	Mary A	1875	Hingham	will	9988
	Mary J	1863	Hingham	admn	9986
	Molly P	1780	Bridgewater	grdn	9990
	Nancy	1863	Hingham	will	9991
	Naomi	1837	Abington	admn	9992
	Noah	1826	Hingham	will	9993
	Peggy S	1875	Hingham	will	9994
	Persis	1867	Hingham	admn	9995
	Priscilla	1837	Hingham	will	9996
	Rebecca	1803	Hingham	admn	9997
	Relief	1877	E. Bridgewater	will	9998
	Reuben	1846	Hingham	admn	10000
	Reuben Jr	1844	Hingham	will	9999
	Robert	1839	Hingham	admn	10001
	Robert	1878	Hanover	admn	10002
	Rufus	1867	Hingham	admn	10003
	Seth S	1878	Hingham	will	10004
	Stephen	1727	Abington	admn	10005
	Stephen	1828	E. Bridgewater	admn	10006
	Stephen	1851	Hingham	admn	10007
	Sukey	1804	Hingham	grdn	9933
	Susan	1853	Hingham	grdn	9989
	Susanna	1804	Hingham	will	10008
	Susanna	1856	Hingham	admn	10009
	Thomas	1810	Hingham	will	10010
	Thomas J	1868	Hingham	admn	10011
	Willace H	1866	Hingham	grdn	9937
	William	1819	Bridgewater	admn	10012
	William	1846	Hingham	grdn	10015
	William	1857	E. Bridgewater	admn	10014
	William A	1850	Hingham	admn	10016
	William H	1852	W. Bridgewater	admn	10013
	Zadock	1814	Hingham	grdn	10017
HERVEY	Betty	1777	Bridgewater	grdn	10018
	David B	1873	N. Bridgewater	name	10019
	David B	1881	Brockton	admn	10020
	Dorcas	1838	Wareham	admn	10021
	Eliphalet W	1834	Wareham	admn	10022
	Eliphalet W	1837	Wareham	grdn	10023
	James M	1864	Bridgewater	admn	10024
	Jonathan	1777	Bridgewater	grdn	10018
	Joseph	1777	Bridgewater	admn	10026
	Joseph 2nd	1756	Bridgewater	inve	10025
	Joseph Jr	1777	Bridgewater	admn	10027

SURNAME	FIRST NAME	YEAR	PLACE	CASE	DOCKET
HERVEY	Sarah L	1881	Brockton	grdn	10028
	Seth	1777	Bridgewater	admn	10029
	William	1831	Wareham	admn	10030
HEWETT	Abigail	1867	N. Bridgewater	admn	10032
	Abigail Jr	1843	Marshfield	admn	10031
	Ann	1811	Marshfield	admn	10033
	Asa	1857	Marshfield	admn	10034
	Eliza	1875	Brockton	admn	10035
	George	1860	Marshfield	admn	10036
	Hannah	1749	Marshfield	grdn	10046
	James	1750	Bridgewater	admn	10037
	John	1717/8	Marshfield	admn	10038
	John	1749	Marshfield	grdn	10046
	Joseph	1748	Marshfield	John	10039
	Joseph	1749	Marshfield	grdn	10046
	Joseph	1806	Marshfield	admn	10040
	Joseph	1833	Marshfield	admn	10041
	Lucy	1828	Marshfield	grdn	10042 a
	Lydia S	1860	Marshfield	grdn	10043
	Martha	1691	Marshfield	will	10044
	Nancy	1843	Marshfield	admn	10045
	Sarah	1749	Marshfield	grdn	10046
	Solomon	1715	Marshfield	will	10047
	Solomon	1749	Marshfield	grdn	10046
	Tabitha	1749	Marshfield	grdn	10046
	Winter	1718	Marshfield	admn	10048
HEWINS	Anna C	1876	W. Bridgewater	admn	10049
	Edwin W	1849	N. Bridgewater	admn	10050
	Sophia	1875	Pembroke	will	10051
HICHBORN	Benjamin 2nd	1808	Hingham	will	10052
	Cinderilla	1857	Hingham	admn	10053
	Frank	1856	Hingham	grdn	10054
	Lucy	1856	Hingham	grdn	10054
	William	1856	Hingham	grdn	10054
HICKEY	Bridget	1873	Hingham	will	10055
	Bridget	1877	Middleboro	admn	10056
	John	1866	Hingham	will	10057
	Margaret	1875	E. Bridgewater	admn	10058
	William	1877	Middleboro	admn	10059
HICKLING	Elizabeth	1828	Duxbury	admn	10060
HICKS	Elizabeth	1767	Rochester	admn	10061
	John	1813	Pembroke	grdn	10062 a
	John	1844	Pembroke	will	10063
HIGGINS	Arthur	1875	Rockland	grdn	10064
	Bernard	1875	Rockland	grdn	10064
	Bridget	1875	Rockland	grdn	10064
	David G	1881	Brockton	admn	10065
	Eliza G	1880	Abington	admn	10066
	Ellen	1875	Rockland	grdn	10064
	Heman	1842	Hingham	admn	10067
	James	1875	Rockland	grdn	10064
	Joel	1827	Rochester	admn	10068
	Joshua L	1881	Scituate	admn	10069
	Lillie	1875	Rockland	grdn	10064
	Patrick	1874	Abington	admn	10070
	Sullivan	1865	Hingham	admn	10071
	Willard S	1866	N. Bridgewater	will	10072
HILBURN	Alexander	1831	Pembroke	admn	10073
	Charles J	1832	Pembroke	grdn	10074
	Mary J	1832	Pembroke	grdn	10074
HILER	Mary	1881	Kingston	admn	10075
HILL	Barnum	1859	Bridgewater	admn	10076
	Bela	1863	E. Bridgewater	will	10077
	Benjamin	1838	Middleboro	admn	10078
	Beza	1821	Bridgewater	admn	10079
	Charles	1848	Hanson	admn	10080
	Charles	1848	Hanson	grdn	10081
	Daniel	1870	Hingham	will	10082
	Ebenezer	1696	Bridgewater	admn	10083
	Ebenezer	1760	Bridgewater	admn	10084
	Edgar S	1878	Scituate	adop	10085

SURNAME	FIRST NAME	YEAR	PLACE	CASE	DOCKET
HILL	Eleazer	1791	Bridgewater	will	10086
	Elizabeth	1868	Hingham	admn	10087
	Isaac	1848	Hanson	grdn	10081
	Joanna	1848	Hanson	grdn	10081
	John B	1834	E. Bridgewater	grdn	10088
	Josiah	1805	Bridgewater	will	10089
	Leonard	1818	Pembroke	grdn	10090 a
	Leonard	1820	Pembroke	admn	10091
	Lucinda	1825	Hanson	grdn	10092
	Marcia A	1834	E. Bridgewater	grdn	10088
	Phillip E	1877	Bridgewater	will	10093
	Richard	1779	Pembroke	admn	10095
	Richard	1818	Hingham	admn	10096
	Richard Jr	1757	Pembroke	admn	10094
	Samuel	1824	Hanson	admn	10097
	Thomas	1807	Pembroke	will	10098
HILLER	Amasa	1772	Rochester	grdn	10135
	Amasa	1781	Rochester	grdn	10099 a
	Anna	1825	Rochester	grdn	10100
	Barnabas	1875	Marion	will	10101
	Benjamin	1775	Rochester	admn	10102
	Benjamin	1777	Rochester	grdn	10103
	Benjamin	1823	Rochester	admn	10104
	Betsey	1879	Mattapoisett	admn	10105
	Caleb	1805	Rochester	grdn	10118
	David	1825	Rochester	will	10106
	Dorcas	1778	Rochester	will	10107
	Dorcas	1820	Rochester	admn	10108
	Eliza	1867	Mattapoisett	admn	10109
	Hezadiah H	1860	Mattapoisett	admn	10110
	Isaac	1781	Rochester	admn	10112
	Isaac	1803	Rochester	admn	10111
	Jabez	1755	Rochester	will	10113
	Jabez	1772	Rochester	grdn	10135
	Jonathan	1821	Rochester	will	10114
	Joseph	1864	Mattapoisett	admn	10115
	Levi	1768	Rochester	admn	10116
	Levi	1772	Rochester	grdn	10135
	Levi	1805	Rochester	grdn	10118
	Levi	1841	Rochester	admn	10117
	Lois	1772	Rochester	grdn	10135
	Lucy	1865	Marion	will	10119
	Lydia	1876	Mattapoisett	admn	10120
	Mary	1835	Rochester	admn	10121
	Moses	1790	Rochester	grdn	10122 a
	Moses	1818	Rochester	grdn	10123 a
	Nathan	1860	Mattapoisett	will	10124
	Nathaniel	1872	Mattapoisett	admn	10125
	Patience	1860	Mattapoisett	will	10126
	Priscilla	1788	Rochester	will	10127
	Sarah	1812	Rochester	will	10128
	Seth	1796	Rochester	will	10129
	Seth	1831	Rochester	grdn	10130 a
	Seth	1835	Rochester	grdn	10131
	Seth	1835	Rochester	admn	10132
	Seth C	1845	Rochester	admn	10133
	Seth Jr	1805	Rochester	grdn	10118
	Stephen	1844	Rochester	grdn	10134 a
	Thomas	1772	Rochester	grdn	10135
	Timothy	1772	Rochester	grdn	10135
	Timothy	1847	Rochester	will	10137
	Timothy Jr	1816	Rochester	admn	10136
	Zuriah	1868	Mattapoisett	admn	10138
HINCKLEY	Ann	1818	Hingham	grdn	10144
	Ann	1831	Marshfield	admn	10139
	Elizabeth	1818	Hingham	grdn	10144
	Hannah	1818	Hingham	grdn	10144
	Hannah	1871	Hingham	will	10140
	Isaac	1818	Hingham	admn	10141
	Isaac	1818	Hingham	grdn	10144
	Julia E	1870	Middleboro	admn	10142

SURNAME	FIRST NAME	YEAR	PLACE	CASE	DOCKET
HINCKLEY	Thomas	1818	Hingham	grdn	10144
	William	1818	Hingham	grdn	10144
	William H	1840	Hingham	grdn	10143
HIND	John Jr	1741	Bridgewater	admn	10148
HINDE	Keziah	1761	Middleboro	grdn	10150
	Salome	1761	Middleboro	grdn	10150
HINDS	Abia	1756	Bridgewater	grdn	10145
	Ezekiel	1803	Plymouth	grdn	10147
	John	1803	Plymouth	grdn	10149
	Nancy J	1875	Lakeville	admn	10151
HINES	Edward	1876	Hingham	will	10146
HIRSCH	Cyrenious	1873	Plymouth	grdn	10152
	Ella	1873	Plymouth	grdn	10152
	Eunice	1873	Plymouth	grdn	10152
	Maria	1873	Plymouth	grdn	10152
	Mary	1873	Plymouth	will	10153
HITCHCOCK	Anjeannette M	1880	Marshfield	grdn	10154
	Charles	1848	Pembroke	admn	10155
	Daniel	1831	Hanson	admn	10156
	Henry D	1847	Middleboro	admn	10158
	Henry S	1847	Middleboro	grdn	10157
	Lyman A	1879	Marshfield	admn	10159
HOAR	Katharine	1854	Lakeville	will	10160
	Luther	1841	Middleboro	admn	10161
	Lydia B	1841	Middleboro	grdn	10162
	Mercy	1847	Middleboro	will	10163
	Peter	1815	Middleboro	will	10164
	Phebe	1841	Middleboro	grdn	10166
	Samuel	1841	Middleboro	admn	10165
	Tisdale	1841	Middleboro	grdn	10166
	William	1827	Middleboro	admn	10167
	William	1841	Middleboro	admn	10168
HOARD	David S	1872	Lakeville	grdn	10169
	Tisdale W	1866	Lakeville	admn	10170
HOBART	Aaron	1808	Abington	will	10171
	Aaron	1818	Abington	will	10172
	Aaron	1843	-----	oath	10173
	Aaron	1858	E. Bridgewater	will	10174
	Abigail S	1870	Hingham	admn	10175
	Bela	1840	Hingham	will	10176
	Bela	1862	Hingham	admn	10177
	Benjamin	1877	S. Abington	will	10178
	Betsey	1876	Plymouth	admn	10179
	Caleb	1846	Hingham	will	10180
	Caleb	1865	Hingham	will	10181
	Catherine	1856	Irvington NY	admn	10182
	Ebed	1840	Hingham	grdn	10220
	Ebed	1863	Hingham	will	10183
	Edmund	1840	Hingham	grdn	10220
	Edmund	1847	Hingham	will	10184
	Elihu	1842	Abington	admn	10185
	Elijah	1847	Abington	will	10186
	Else	1830	Hingham	will	10187
	Esther	1814	Bridgewater	grdn	10202
	George	1843	E. Bridgewater	admn	10188
	George	1874	Hingham	admn	10189
	Hawkes	1831	Hingham	will	10190
	Isaac	1760	Abington	will	10191
	Isaac	1873	Hanson	admn	10192
	Israel	1731	Scituate	will	10193
	Israel	1876	E. Bridgewater	admn	10194
	Jacob	1777	Abington	grdn	10198
	Jeremiah	1803	Hingham	admn	10195
	Joanna	1835	Massillon OH	peti	10196
	John	1777	Abington	admn	10197
	John	1777	Abington	grdn	10198
	John	1857	Hingham	will	10199
	Jonathan	1819	Bridgewater	will	10200
	Joseph	1814	Bridgewater	grdn	10202
	Joseph	1851	Abington	will	10201
	Leavitt	1869	Hingham	will	10203

SURNAME	FIRST NAME	YEAR	PLACE	CASE	DOCKET
HOBART	Lydia	1862	Hingham	grdn	10218
	Martin	1858	Hingham	admn	10204
	Mary	1778	Abington	will	10207
	Mary	1808	Abington	grdn	10208
	Mary C	1878	Plymouth	admn	10206
	Mary E	1877	Hingham	admn	10205
	Mercy	1848	Hanson	grdn	10209 a
	Molly	1777	Abington	grdn	10198
	Nathaniel	1838	Abington	will	10210
	Nathaniel	1851	N. Bridgewater	will	10211
	Nettie	1862	Hingham	grdn	10218
	Olive B	1873	Hingham	will	10212
	Peter	1793	Hanover	will	10213
	Sabina	1854	Hingham	grdn	10214 a
	Sabina	1855	Hingham	will	10215
	Sally	1848	Abington	will	10216
	Sarah	1862	Hingham	grdn	10218
	Sarah W	1872	Hingham	admn	10217
	Seth	1814	Bridgewater	admn	10219
	Seth	1840	Hingham	grdn	10220
	Susanna	1827	Abington	admn	10221
	Thankful	1808	Abington	grdn	10208
	Thankful	1822	Abington	will	10222
	Thomas	1794	Pembroke	will	10223
	Thomas	1848	Hanson	will	10223
	Thomas A	1853	N. Bridgewater	grdn	10225
	William	1819	Hingham	grdn	10226
	William	1857	Abington	will	10228
	William	1875	Hingham	admn	10227
HODGE	Betsey H	1871	Plymouth	will	10229
	Fannie L	1874	Alto IL	adop	10230
	James T	1816	Plymouth	grdn	10231
	James T	1872	Plymouth	admn	10232
	Mary	1873	Plymouth	grdn	10233
	Michael	1816	Plymouth	admn	10234
HODGES	Francis M	1864	Middleboro	will	10235
	Nathaniel	1837	Duxbury	grdn	10236 a
	Nathaniel	1877	Plymouth	will	10237
	Rebecca	1878	Plymouth	admn	10238
HODGKIN	Betsey	1868	Duxbury	will	10239
HODSDON	Sarah	1875	Scituate	will	10240
HOGAN	Mary	1862	Abington	admn	10241
HOLBROOK	Abigail	1707	Scituate	will	10242
	Albert	1862	Hanover	admn	10243
	Arvin	1874	E. Bridgewater	admn	10244
	Charles E	1851	Abington	grdn	10245
	Daniel	1845	W. Bridgewater	will	10246
	Dexter	1842	Abington	grdn	10259
	Eliphalet	1815	Plymouth	will	10247
	George A	1851	Abington	grdn	10245
	Gideon	1842	Plymouth	will	10248
	Gideon 2nd	1853	Plymouth	admn	10249
	Henry W	1870	Abington	grdn	10250
	Jane	1765	Scituate	admn	10251
	Jeremiah	1815	Plymouth	admn	10252
	Josiah	1840	Abington	admn	10253
	Margaret D	1818	Plymouth	grdn	10254
	Mary	1863	N. Bridgewater	will	10256
	Mary W	1830	Abington	grdn	10255
	Naaman	1796	Plymouth	will	10257
	Nancy	1864	Plymouth	will	10258
	Quincy	1842	Abington	grdn	10259
	Reuben	1842	Abington	admn	10260
	Richard	1873	Abington	will	10261
	Robert	1854	N. Bridgewater	admn	10262
	Ruth	1842	Abington	grdn	10259
	Samuel	1719	Scituate	will	10263
	Samuel	1759	Scituate	will	10264
	Samuel	1763	Scituate	grdn	10265 a
	Samuel	1778	Scituate	admn	10266
	Samuel	1778	Scituate	will	10267

SURNAME	FIRST NAME	YEAR	PLACE	CASE	DOCKET
HOLBROOK	Sarah J	1874	E. Bridgewater	admn	10268
	Silas	1877	E. Bridgewater	admn	10269
	William	1699	Scituate	will	10270
	William	1764	Scituate	grdn	10271
	William	1829	Abington	will	10273
	William	1842	Abington	grdn	10259
	William Jr	1815	Abington	admn	10272
HOLDEN	Adrianna	1866	N. Bridgewater	grdn	10275
	Edward E	1866	N. Bridgewater	admn	10274
	Mary E	1866	N. Bridgewater	grdn	10275
HOLLAND	Cecelia P	1880	Brockton	admn	10276
	William	1786	Plymouth	grdn	10277
HOLLIS	Abel	1863	Hanover	will	10278
	Abigail	1859	Plymouth	admn	10279
	John E	1873	N. Bridgewater	admn	10280
	Samuel W	1875	Hanover	grdn	10281
HOLLM	Christian	1861	Scituate	will	10282
HOLLOWAY	Alice	1876	Brockton	grdn	10284
	Benjamin	1863	Lakeville	grdn	10285
	Benjamin F	1863	Lakeville	admn	10283
	Cassius	1863	Lakeville	grdn	10285
	Elbridge	1863	Lakeville	grdn	10285
	George	1863	Lakeville	grdn	10285
	George	1876	Brockton	grdn	10284
	Harriet	1863	Lakeville	grdn	10285
	Hiram	1876	Brockton	grdn	10284
	Isaac N	1876	Brockton	admn	10286
	Jedidah	1760	Middleboro	grdn	10289
	John	1785	Middleboro	admn	10287
	John	1863	Lakeville	grdn	10285
	Josiah	1816	Middleboro	admn	10288
	Lois	1760	Middleboro	grdn	10289
	Nathan	1758	Middleboro	grdn	10290
	Nathaniel	1757	Middleboro	admn	10291
	Rebecca	1746	Pembroke	admn	10292
	Samuel	1765	Middleboro	admn	10293
	Sarah	1863	Lakeville	grdn	10285
	Thomas	1739	Pembroke	admn	10294
HOLMAN	Abigail	1757	Bridgewater	grdn	10299
	Ann	1757	Bridgewater	admn	10295
	Jane	1757	Bridgewater	grdn	10299
	John	1759	Bridgewater	will	10296
	John Jr	1753	Bridgewater	will	10297
	William	1757	Bridgewater	grdn	10299
	William	1762	Bridgewater	admn	10298
HOLME	James	1850	Wareham	admn	10300
HOLMES	Abba T	1829	Plymouth	grdn	10301
	Abigail	1747	Plymouth	grdn	10551
	Abigail	1763	Plymouth	grdn	10374
	Abigail	1808	Plymouth	will	10302
	Abigail	1818	Bridgewater	grdn	10408
	Abigail	1820	Plymouth	admn	10303
	Abigail	1839	Plymouth	admn	10304
	Abigail	1840	W. Bridgewater	admn	10305
	Abijah	1818	Bridgewater	grdn	10408
	Abijah T	1862	W. Bridgewater	will	10306
	Abner	1765	Plymouth	admn	10309
	Abner	1769	Plymouth	grdn	10308
	Abner	1813	Plymouth	grdn	10307
	Abner	1814	Kingston	will	10310
	Alexander	1856	Plympton	admn	10311
	Alexander	1857	Plympton	admn	10312
	Alexander	1869	Kingston	will	10313
	Allyn Jr	1863	Kingston	admn	10314
	Amasa	1846	Plymouth	will	10316
	Amasa D	1834	Kingston	admn	10315
	Andrew	1806	Plymouth	admn	10317
	Andrew	1862	Marshfield	admn	10319
	Andrew T	1876	Plymouth	admn	10318
	Anna	1757	Kingston	grdn	10489
	Anna	1818	Bridgewater	grdn	10408

SURNAME	FIRST NAME	YEAR	PLACE	CASE	DOCKET
HOLMES	Anna	1865	Plymouth	grdn	10558
	Ansel	1846	Kingston	grdn	10321
	Ansel Jr	1841	Plymouth	admn	10320
	Araunah F	1831	Kingston	admn	10322
	Asaph	1845	Kingston	will	10323
	Barnabas	1799	Rochester	admn	10324
	Barnabas	1803	Rochester	grdn	10325
	Barnabas	1837	Plymouth	admn	10327
	Barnabas	1855	Marion	will	10326
	Barshaba	1763	Halifax	will	10328
	Bartlett	1805	Plymouth	admn	10329
	Bartlett	1861	Plymouth	will	10330
	Barzillai	1848	Plymouth	grdn	10568
	Barzillai	1859	Kingston	admn	10331
	Beeri	1850	Kingston	admn	10332
	Benjamin	1745	Plymouth	admn	10333
	Benjamin	1797	Scituate	admn	10334
	Benjamin	1836	Kingston	will	10335
	Benjamin	1866	Bridgewater	admn	10336
	Betsey	1862	Bridgewater	admn	10341
	Betsey	1864	Plymouth	admn	10338
	Betsey	1870	Mattapoisett	admn	10342
	Betsey	1874	Plymouth	admn	10339
	Betsey	1876	Plymouth	admn	10340
	Betsey D	1832	Plymouth	grdn	10337
	Beulah S	1878	Marshfield	will	10343
	Bradford	1858	Duxbury	will	10344
	Branch B	1875	Plymouth	admn	10345
	Bulah	1824	Duxbury	grdn	10600
	Caleb	1766	Plymouth	grdn	10404
	Caleb B	1878	Plymouth	will	10346
	Calvin	1818	Plymouth	admn	10347
	Chandler	1845	Plymouth	admn	10349
	Chandler Jr	1831	Plymouth	admn	10348
	Charles	1840	Bridgewater	admn	10352
	Charles	1846	Bridgewater	grdn	10353
	Charles C	1877	Hanson	grdn	10402
	Charles F	1873	N. Bridgewater	admn	10351
	Charles H	1851	Kingston	grdn	10350
	Church	1826	Bridgewater	admn	10354
	Clark	1857	Plymouth	admn	10355
	Cornelius	1847	Bridgewater	admn	10356
	Cornelius	1850	Bridgewater	admn	10357
	Cornelius	1869	Kingston	will	10358
	Crymble M	----	Plymouth	----	10359
	Cynthia	1821	Plymouth	grdn	10360
	Cyrus	1849	Hanover	will	10361
	David	1870	Plymouth	admn	10362
	David C	1871	Plymouth	admn	10363
	David S	1881	Plymouth	will	10364
	Davis	1848	Plymouth	grdn	10365
	Deborah	1843	Kingston	will	10366
	Ebenezer	1750	Plymouth	admn	10372
	Ebenezer	1760	Plymouth	admn	10373
	Ebenezer	1763	Plymouth	grdn	10374
	Ebenezer	1835	Middleboro	admn	10367
	Ebenezer	1837	Plymouth	will	10371
	Ebenezer	1869	Marion	will	10368
	Ebenezer	1876	Marion	admn	10369
	Ebenezer	1878	Marion	grdn	10370
	Edgar D	1875	Kingston	admn	10375
	Eleazer	1754	Plymouth	admn	10376
	Eleazer	1798	Plymouth	will	10377
	Eleazer	1804	Plymouth	will	10378
	Eleazer	1811	Plymouth	grdn	10379
	Elisha	1753	Plymouth	will	10380
	Elisha	1779	Plymouth	will	10381
	Elisha	1855	Duxbury	bond	10383
	Elisha	1879	Plymouth	admn	10382
	Elisha T	1860	Kingston	admn	10384
	Eliza	1861	Duxbury	admn	10386

SURNAME	FIRST NAME	YEAR	PLACE	CASE	DOCKET
HOLMES	Eliza J	1817	Plymouth	grdn	10385
	Eliza K	1880	Bridgewater	will	10387
	Elizabeth	1763	Plymouth	admn	10388
	Elizabeth	1818	Bridgewater	grdn	10408
	Elizabeth	1865	Plymouth	grdn	10558
	Elkanah	1754	Plymouth	grdn	10479
	Elkanah	1818	Plymouth	admn	10389
	Elkanah C	1827	Plymouth	grdn	10390
	Ellis	1824	Halifax	will	10391
	Ellis	1824	Duxbury	grdn	10600
	Ellis	1826	Bridgewater	will	10393
	Ellis	1855	Plymouth	admn	10392
	Ellis	1872	E. Bridgewater	will	10394
	Elnathan	1754	Plymouth	grdn	10396
	Elnathan	1823	Plymouth	admn	10395
	Ephraim	1733	Middleboro	grdn	10401
	Ephraim	1780	Kingston	will	10397
	Ephraim	1811	Plymouth	admn	10398
	Ephraim	1877	Plymouth	admn	10399
	Ephraim B	1878	Plymouth	will	10400
	Ernest P	1877	Hanson	grdn	10402
	Esther	1763	Plymouth	grdn	10374
	Esther	1825	Plymouth	grdn	10559
	Experience	1735	Middleboro	grdn	10403
	Ezra	1766	Plymouth	grdn	10404
	Florence M	1875	Plymouth	adop	10405
	Florence W	1881	Plymouth	grdn	10406
	Francis	1812	Plympton	will	10407
	Frederick E	1835	Middleton CT	grdn	10420
	Freeman	1818	Bridgewater	grdn	10408
	Freeman	1846	Bridgewater	grdn	10353
	George	1746	Plymouth	will	10409
	George	1760	Plymouth	admn	10410
	George	1823	Plymouth	admn	10411
	George	1878	Kingston	will	10413
	George E	1854	N. Bridgewater	adop	10415 +
	George W	1872	Bridgewater	admn	10415
	George W	1873	Duxbury	admn	10414
	George W	1875	Plymouth	grdn	10412
	Gershom	1729	Plymouth	grdn	10596
	Gilbert	1763	Plymouth	grdn	10374
	Hannah	1758	Plymouth	admn	10416
	Hannah	1846	Bridgewater	grdn	10353
	Hannah	1860	Halifax	admn	10419
	Hannah	1864	Plymouth	admn	10417
	Hannah	1875	Plymouth	admn	10418
	Hannah P	1835	Middleton CT	grdn	10420
	Heman	1810	Plymouth	admn	10421
	Henry	1834	Bridgewater	admn	10422
	Henry	1845	Middleboro	will	10424
	Henry	1846	Bridgewater	grdn	10423
	Henry B	1871	Marshfield	admn	10426
	Henry W	1868	Marshfield	admn	10425
	Hiram	1825	Plymouth	grdn	10559
	Horace	1855	Kingston	admn	10427
	Horace	1866	Plymouth	admn	10428
	Howland	1854	Bridgewater	will	10429
	Ichabod	1817	Plymouth	will	10431
	Ichabod Jr	1802	Plymouth	admn	10430
	Ichabod S	1876	Plymouth	admn	10432
	Isaac	1724	Rochester	will	10433
	Isaac	1738	Kingston	will	10435
	Isaac	1746	Rochester	will	10434
	Isaac	1756	Kingston	will	10436
	Isabella F	1854	Bridgewater	adop	10437
	Israel	1701	Marshfield	grdn	10439
	Israel	1706	Marshfield	warr	10438
	Jabez	1760	Plymouth	admn	10440
	Jacob	1874	Middleboro	admn	10441
	James	1766	Plymouth	admn	10442
	James	1808	Plymouth	will	10443

SURNAME	FIRST NAME	YEAR	PLACE	CASE	DOCKET
HOLMES	James	1824	Duxbury	grdn	10600
	James H	1844	Kingston	admn	10444
	Jane	1811	Plymouth	grdn	10379
	Jane	1862	Marion	admn	10446
	Jane A	1827	Plymouth	grdn	10445
	Jean	1754	Plymouth	grdn	10479
	Jedediah	1829	Kingston	will	10447
	Jedediah	1862	Kingston	admn	10448
	Jeremiah	1799	Plymouth	grdn	10451
	Jeremiah	1802	Plymouth	admn	10449
	Jeremiah Jr	1798	Plymouth	will	10450
	Joanna	1747	Plymouth	grdn	10452
	John	1697	Plymouth	admn	10466
	John	1701	Marshfield	grdn	10439
	John	1728	Middleboro	admn	10454
	John	1730	Middleboro	will	10455
	John	1733	Middleboro	grdn	10401
	John	1746	Kingston	will	10462
	John	1751	Plymouth	admn	10467
	John	1754	Plymouth	grdn	10468
	John	1774	Halifax	admn	10458
	John	1804	Middleboro	will	10456
	John	1807	Duxbury	admn	10460
	John	1824	Kingston	admn	10463
	John	1836	Plymouth	admn	10464
	John	1841	Pembroke	will	10457
	John	1876	Duxbury	will	10461
	John 2nd	1879	Halifax	admn	10459
	John C	1826	Plymouth	admn	10465
	John et al	1773	Marshfield	peti	10453
	Jonathan	1787	Kingston	will	10469
	Jonathan	1806	Kingston	admn	10470
	Jonathan	1808	Kingston	will	10471
	Joseph	1733	Kingston	will	10472
	Joseph	1737	Plymouth	admn	10477
	Joseph	1748	Plymouth	admn	10478
	Joseph	1754	Plymouth	grdn	10479
	Joseph	1756	Kingston	will	10473
	Joseph	1778	Plymouth	admn	10476
	Joseph	1780	Middleboro	admn	10475
	Joseph	1863	Kingston	will	10474
	Joshua	1733	Plymouth	admn	10518
	Joshua	1754	Plymouth	grdn	10480
	Joshua	1813	Kingston	admn	10481
	Josiah	1725	Pembroke	grdn	10482
	Josiah	1761	Marshfield	admn	10483
	Josiah	1783	Kingston	admn	10484
	Josiah	1860	Kingston	will	10485
	Josiah	1860	Mattapoisett	will	10486
	Josiah	1860	Plymouth	admn	10487
	Lemuel	1757	Kingston	grdn	10489
	Lemuel	1770	Kingston	admn	10488
	Levi	1795	Kingston	will	10490
	Levi	1828	Duxbury	admn	10491
	Lewis	1799	Plymouth	admn	10492
	Lewis	1865	Middleboro	admn	10493
	Lizzie M	1873	N. Bridgewater	grdn	10495
	Lizzie S	1873	Plymouth	adop	10494
	Lois	1754	Plymouth	grdn	10468
	Lois	1815	Kingston	grdn	10513
	Lucretia B	1866	Duxbury	admn	10496
	Lucy	1825	Plymouth	grdn	10559
	Luzania	1757	Kingston	grdn	10489
	Lydia	1827	Carver	admn	10497
	Lydia T	1873	Kingston	admn	10498
	Marcia	1817	-----	rece	10499
	Marcia D	1817	Kingston	grdn	10500
	Marcus	1846	Bridgewater	grdn	10353
	Marcus	1880	Brockton	admn	10501
	Margaret	1754	Plymouth	grdn	10468
	Maria	1850	Plymouth	admn	10502

SURNAME	FIRST NAME	YEAR	PLACE	CASE	DOCKET
HOLMES	Martin W	1864	Halifax	admn	10503
	Mary	1729	Plymouth	grdn	10596
	Mary	1754	Plymouth	grdn	10396
	Mary	1754	Plymouth	grdn	10468
	Mary	1830	Plymouth	admn	10504
	Mary W	1856	Kingston	grdn	10505
	Matilda	1870	Plymouth	admn	10506
	Mehitable	1876	Plymouth	admn	10507
	Melatiah	1757	Kingston	grdn	10489
	Melatiah	1827	Kingston	will	10508
	Melatiah	1861	Kingston	will	10509
	Melvin	1860	Halifax	admn	10510
	Mendall	1856	Kingston	grdn	10505
	Mercy	1841	Plympton	will	10511
	Mercy E	1874	Plymouth	grdn	10563
	Merlie	1873	N. Bridgewater	grdn	10495
	Minnie A	1881	Hanover	grdn	10512
	Mira	1846	Bridgewater	grdn	10353
	Molly	1815	Kingston	grdn	10513
	Myra	1818	Bridgewater	grdn	10408
	Nancy	1799	Plymouth	grdn	10451
	Nancy	1866	Duxbury	will	10514
	Nancy B	1818	Kingston	will	10515
	Nathan E	1871	N. Bridgewater	admn	10516
	Nathaniel	1727	Plymouth	will	10517
	Nathaniel	1733	Plymouth	admn	10518
	Nathaniel	1737	Plymouth	will	10520
	Nathaniel	1746	Plymouth	will	10519
	Nathaniel	1802	Plymouth	will	10521
	Nathaniel	1830	Plymouth	admn	10523
	Nathaniel	1841	Halifax	admn	10526
	Nathaniel	1849	Kingston	admn	10524
	Nathaniel 3rd	1806	Plymouth	admn	10522
	Nathaniel 3rd	1821	Duxbury	admn	10525
	Nehemiah	1754	Plymouth	grdn	10468
	Nellie S	1871	Middleboro	grdn	10527
	Oliver	1808	Halifax	admn	10528
	Oliver	1864	Halifax	admn	10529
	Orren D	1865	Plymouth	admn	10530
	Paraclete	1867	Kingston	admn	10531
	Patience	1763	Plymouth	grdn	10374
	Patience	1787	Kingston	admn	10532
	Peggy	1866	Pembroke	admn	10533
	Pelham	1832	Plympton	will	10534
	Persis H	1874	Plymouth	admn	10535
	Peter	1795	Plymouth	admn	10536
	Peter	1870	Plymouth	admn	10538
	Peter	1880	Plymouth	will	10539
	Peter 2nd	1860	Plymouth	admn	10537
	Peter A	1875	Marion	admn	10540
	Phebe	1772	Plymouth	will	10541
	Phebe	1829	Carver	will	10542
	Philander	1856	N. Bridgewater	admn	10543
	Polly	1811	Plymouth	grdn	10379
	Polly	1814	Plymouth	grdn	10544
	Polly	1830	Carver	will	10545
	Priscilla	1728	Middleboro	grdn	10594
	Priscilla	1747	Plymouth	grdn	10452
	Prudence	1862	Middleboro	admn	10548
	Rachel L	1874	Halifax	admn	10549
	Rebecca	1747	Plymouth	grdn	10551
	Rebecca	1757	Kingston	grdn	10489
	Rebecca	1811	Kingston	admn	10550
	Richard	1697	Plymouth	grdn	10552
	Richard	1718	Plymouth	admn	10553
	Richard	1787	Plymouth	admn	10554
	Richard	1820	Plymouth	will	10555
	Richard	1825	Plymouth	grdn	10559
	Richard	1841	Plymouth	will	10556
	Richard	1846	Bridgewater	grdn	10423
	Richard	1865	Plymouth	grdn	10558

SURNAME	FIRST NAME	YEAR	PLACE	CASE	DOCKET
HOLMES	Richard W	1862	Plymouth	admn	10557
	Robert	1817	Kingston	will	10560
	Robert	1852	Kingston	will	10561
	Robert M	1874	Plymouth	grdn	10563
	Robert W	1878	Kingston	admn	10562
	Rufus	1796	Middleboro	admn	10564
	Ruth	1754	Plymouth	grdn	10468
	Ruth	1792	Kingston	admn	10565
	Ruth	1848	Plymouth	grdn	10568
	Ruth B	1873	Plymouth	admn	10566
	Ruth C	1879	Plymouth	admn	10567
	Sally	1813	Plympton	grdn	10569
	Sally	1814	Plymouth	grdn	10570
	Sally	1859	Kingston	admn	10571
	Sally B	1845	Scituate	grdn	10572
	Samuel	1690	Marshfield	admn	10573
	Samuel	1818	Plymouth	grdn	10574
	Samuel	1830	Kingston	will	10576
	Samuel	1852	Kingston	grdn	10577
	Samuel D	1861	Plymouth	will	10575
	Sarah	1737	Plymouth	grdn	10578
	Sarah	1810	Duxbury	grdn	10582
	Sarah	1820	Marshfield	admn	10583
	Sarah	1835	Kingston	will	10581
	Sarah	1868	Plymouth	will	10579
	Sarah	1879	Plymouth	will	10580
	Seth	1804	Plymouth	will	10584
	Seth	1815	Plymouth	admn	10585
	Seth	1829	Plymouth	admn	10586
	Solomon	1848	Plymouth	grdn	10568
	Solomon M	1847	Plymouth	admn	10587
	Spencer	1846	Kingston	admn	10589
	Spencer Jr	1841	Kingston	will	10588
	Stephen	1855	Plymouth	admn	10591
	Stephen	1865	Kingston	admn	10592
	Stephen Jr	1834	Plymouth	will	10590
	Susan	1873	N. Bridgewater	grdn	10495
	Susan W	1857	Plymouth	admn	10593
	Susanna	1728	Middleboro	grdn	10594
	Susie E	1871	Middleboro	grdn	10527
	Sylvanus	1729	Plymouth	grdn	10596
	Sylvanus	1821	Plymouth	will	10595
	Sylvester	1810	Kingston	admn	10597
	Sylvia	1824	Duxbury	grdn	10600
	Sylvia	1825	Duxbury	admn	10599
	Sylvia	1861	Marion	admn	10598
	Thomas	1728	Middleboro	grdn	10594
	Thomas	1733	Middleboro	will	10601
	Thomas	1754	Plymouth	admn	10605
	Thomas	1779	Plymouth	admn	10603
	Thomas	1798	Plymouth	admn	10604
	Thomas	1799	Plymouth	grdn	10451
	Thomas	1824	Duxbury	grdn	10600
	Thomas C	1853	Kingston	will	10606
	Thomas Jr	1768	Plymouth	admn	10602
	Tilden	1843	Kingston	admn	10607
	Walter M	1880	Brockton	admn	10608
	William	1760	Halifax	admn	10609
	William	1799	Plymouth	grdn	10451
	William	1852	Plymouth	will	10611
	William	1860	Marshfield	will	10613
	William 3rd	1832	Plymouth	admn	10610
	William M	1875	Wareham	admn	10614
	William W	1857	Duxbury	adop	10612
	Winslow	1838	Plymouth	admn	10615
	Zacheus	1769	Plymouth	admn	10616
	Zacheus	1829	Plympton	admn	10617
	Zephaniah	1814	Plymouth	admn	10618
	riscilla	1735	Middleboro	admn	10546
	riscilla	1742	Plympton	grdn	10547
HOLT	Richard	1719	Bridgewater	will	10619

SURNAME	FIRST NAME	YEAR	PLACE	CASE	DOCKET
HOMER	Joseph	1855	Wareham	admn	10620
HOMMEDIEU	Mary C	1820	New York	bond	10621
HOOD	Anna C	1873	Abington	grdn	10622
HOOKER	Helen C	1864	Bridgewater	admn	10623
	Joseph E	1864	Abington	grdn	10624
	Joseph E	1871	Abington	admn	10625
	Sarah H	1864	Bridgewater	admn	10626
HOOPER	Apollos	1851	Bridgewater	admn	10627
	Apollos	1858	W. Bridgewater	admn	10628
	Avery	1833	Bridgewater	grdn	10652
	Calvin	1755	Bridgewater	grdn	10634
	Charles	1833	Bridgewater	grdn	10652
	Charles	1865	Rochester	grdn	10629
	Charles	1867	Rochester	admn	10630
	Charles E	1865	Rochester	grdn	10631
	David	1755	Bridgewater	grdn	10634
	David	1831	Bridgewater	admn	10632
	David	1841	Bridgewater	admn	10633
	Elizabeth	1744	Bridgewater	will	10635
	Elizabeth	1861	Bridgewater	admn	10636
	Fannie K	1879	Bridgewater	admn	10637
	Hannah	1833	Bridgewater	grdn	10652
	Hezekiah	1742	Bridgewater	grdn	10651
	Hezekiah	1813	Bridgewater	will	10638
	James	1719	-----	grdn	10665
	James	1784	Bridgewater	will	10639
	James	1828	Bridgewater	will	10640
	Jerusha	1762	Bridgewater	grdn	10641
	John	1709	Bridgewater	admn	10642
	John	1719	Bridgewater	admn	10643
	John	1741	Bridgewater	will	10650
	John	1742	Bridgewater	admn	10645
	John	1742	Bridgewater	grdn	10646
	John	1742	Bridgewater	grdn	10651
	John	1750	Bridgewater	will	10648
	John	1751	Bridgewater	grdn	10649
	John	1782	Bridgewater	grdn	10644
	John	1807	Bridgewater	will	10647
	Joseph	1742	Bridgewater	grdn	10651
	Julia	1833	Bridgewater	grdn	10652
	Julia M	1860	W. Bridgewater	grdn	10653
	Luther	1755	Bridgewater	grdn	10634
	Luther	1831	Bridgewater	admn	10654
	Lyman	1833	Bridgewater	admn	10655
	Martha D	1858	Rochester	admn	10656
	Mary	1856	Bridgewater	will	10657
	Melansa	1869	Bridgewater	admn	10658
	Nathaniel	1719	-----	grdn	10665
	Philo	1880	Bridgewater	admn	10659
	Rebecca	1744	Bridgewater	grdn	10660
	Russell E	1877	E. Bridgewater	admn	10661
	Sarah	1719	-----	grdn	10665
	Sarah	1751	Bridgewater	grdn	10649
	Sarah	1833	Bridgewater	grdn	10652
	Susan C	1839	Bridgewater	will	10662
	Thomas	1719	-----	grdn	10665
	Thomas	1759	Bridgewater	will	10663
	Thomas	1789	Bridgewater	will	10664
	William	1719	-----	grdn	10665
	William	1755	Bridgewater	admn	10666
	William	1773	Bridgewater	admn	10667
	William	1825	Bridgewater	admn	10668
	William	1860	W. Bridgewater	grdn	10653
	Winslow	1742	Bridgewater	grdn	10651
	Winslow	1750	Bridgewater	admn	10669
	Winslow	1835	Bridgewater	admn	10670
HOPKINS	Samuel P	1852	Plymouth	admn	10671
	Samuel P	1852	Plymouth	grdn	10672
HORN	Rachel	1850	Hingham	admn	10673
HORR	Chloe A	1865	Lakeville	grdn	10674
	Helen M	1865	Lakeville	grdn	10674

SURNAME	FIRST NAME	YEAR	PLACE	CASE	DOCKET
	John E	1865	Lakeville	grdn	10675
	Mary E	1865	Lakeville	grdn	10675
	William	1872	S. Francisco CA	admn	10676
HORRIL	Humphrey	1720	Beverly	grdn	10677
HORTON	Ariel	1865	Buckfield ME	grdn	10678
	Barnabas	1825	Bridgewater	admn	10679
	Jabez	1828	Hingham	admn	10680
	Phebe	1878	Bridgewater	admn	10681
	Robert J B	1865	Buckfield ME	grdn	10678
	Simmons	1848	Scituate	will	10682
HOUSE	Abel	1760	Hanover	admn	10683
	Abigail	1779	Scituate	admn	10684
	Abner	1785	Scituate	admn	10685
	Bathsheba	1779	Hanover	grdn	10705
	Benjamin	1778	Scituate	will	10686
	Betty	1771	Abington	grdn	10687
	Betty	1778	Abington	grdn	10697
	Deborah	1748	Hanover	grdn	10688
	Deborah	1778	Abington	grdn	10697
	Elizabeth T	1866	Hanover	admn	10689
	James	1767	Hanover	admn	10690
	James	1876	S. Scituate	admn	10691
	Job	1771	Abington	grdn	10687
	John	1726	Scituate	grdn	10702
	John	1732	Scituate	admn	10692
	John	1777	Hanover	will	10693
	Joseph	1732	Scituate	will	10694
	Laura C et al	1880	Hanover	peti	10695
	Lydia	1778	Abington	grdn	10697
	Mary	1726	Scituate	grdn	10702
	Mary	1778	Abington	admn	10696
	Mary	1778	Abington	grdn	10697
	Rebecca	1779	Hanover	grdn	10705
	Samuel	1718	Scituate	will	10701
	Samuel	1726	Scituate	grdn	10702
	Samuel	1771	Abington	will	10700
	Samuel	1828	Hanson	will	10699
	Samuel	1860	Hanover	will	10698
	Sarah	1726	Scituate	grdn	10702
	Sarah	1728	Scituate	admn	10703
	Seth	1748	Hanover	grdn	10688
	Seth	1777	Hanover	will	10704
	Seth	1779	Hanover	grdn	10705
	William Lester	1879	Hanover	grdn	10706
HOVEY	Dominicus	1818	Rochester	will	10707
	Ivory	1803	Plymouth	admn	10708
	James	1781	Plymouth	will	10709
	Josiah C	1870	Plymouth	will	10710
	Mary S	1864	N. Bridgewater	admn	10711
	Olive	1805	Plymouth	will	10712
	Ruth H	1865	Hingham	will	10713
HOWARD	Abiel	1777	Bridgewater	admn	10714
	Abigail	1814	Bridgewater	grdn	10723
	Abigail	1848	N. Bridgewater	will	10715
	Adam	1781	Bridgewater	admn	10716
	Adonis	1797	Bridgewater	grdn	10814
	Adonis	1866	E. Bridgewater	admn	10717
	Agnes	1838	E. Bridgewater	grdn	10718
	Alden	1863	Pembroke	admn	10719
	Alice	1855	E. Bridgewater	grdn	10720
	Alpheus	1822	W. Bridgewater	admn	10721
	Amasa	1797	Bridgewater	will	10722
	Ambrose	1782	Bridgewater	grdn	10798
	Apollos	1814	Bridgewater	grdn	10723
	Arabella	1797	Bridgewater	grdn	10814
	Arthur	1862	N. Bridgewater	grdn	10779
	Asa	1828	N. Bridgewater	admn	10724
	Austin	1869	N. Bridgewater	admn	10725
	Azel	1831	W. Bridgewater	grdn	10820
	Barnabas	1813	Bridgewater	will	10726
	Benjamin	1831	W. Bridgewater	grdn	10820

SURNAME	FIRST NAME	YEAR	PLACE	CASE	DOCKET
HOWARD	Benjamin B	1867	W. Bridgewater	will	10727
	Betsey	1814	Randolph	grdn	10728
	Betsey	1860	Wareham	admn	10729
	Caleb	1812	Bridgewater	admn	10730
	Caleb	1831	N. Bridgewater	will	10731
	Caleb	1872	W. Bridgewater	will	10733
	Caleb H	1850	W. Bridgewater	admn	10732
	Calvin	1833	Wareham	admn	10734
	Charles	1810	Scituate	grdn	10841
	Charles	1816	Bridgewater	grdn	10763
	Charles	1838	Wareham	grdn	10832
	Charles	1860	W. Bridgewater	admn	10736
	Charles	1861	Hingham	admn	10735
	Charles	1870	Pembroke	admn	10738
	Charles E	1864	W. Bridgewater	admn	10737
	Charlotte	1849	W. Bridgewater	grdn	10773
	Chelcias	1861	Hanson	admn	10739
	Cordelia	1818	Plymouth	grdn	10794
	Curtis C	1818	Plymouth	grdn	10794
	Curtis C	1879	Plymouth	will	10740
	Cyrus	1873	N. Bridgewater	will	10741
	Damaris	1795	Bridgewater	will	10742
	Daniel	1779	Bridgewater	will	10743
	Daniel	1782	Bridgewater	will	10744
	Daniel	1813	Bridgewater	admn	10745
	Daniel	1814	Bridgewater	grdn	10723
	Daniel	1821	Bridgewater	will	10747
	Daniel 3rd	1814	Bridgewater	admn	10746
	David	1751	Bridgewater	will	10748
	David	1760	Bridgewater	admn	10749
	Dulcena	1877	W. Bridgewater	will	10750
	Edith F	1863	W. Bridgewater	grdn	10751
	Edith M	1877	Brockton	grdn	10752
	Edmund	1859	W. Bridgewater	will	10753
	Edmund	1865	Hingham	will	10754
	Edmund T	1876	Hingham	grdn	10755
	Edward	1809	Bridgewater	will	10756
	Edward	1826	Bridgewater	admn	10757
	Edwin	1820	Bridgewater	admn	10758
	Elam	1832	W. Bridgewater	grdn	10827
	Elbridge G	1874	W. Bridgewater	will	10759
	Eleanor	1818	Plymouth	grdn	10794
	Eleanor W	1863	W. Bridgewater	grdn	10760
	Eliakim	1827	W. Bridgewater	will	10761
	Eliakim	1878	Brockton	will	10762
	Elijah	1816	Bridgewater	grdn	10763
	Eliza	1807	Bridgewater	grdn	10764
	Elizabeth	1828	N. Bridgewater	grdn	10765
	Ella	1849	W. Bridgewater	grdn	10773
	Ellen	1871	N. Bridgewater	will	10766
	Ellen	1875	Brockton	will	10767
	Elma	1855	N. Bridgewater	grdn	10819
	Elmer E	1874	W. Bridgewater	grdn	10780
	Enos	1828	Wareham	admn	10768
	Ephraim	1874	Brockton	admn	10769
	Eunice	1873	Hingham	admn	10771
	Eunice S	1856	N. Bridgewater	admn	10770
	Francis	1831	W. Bridgewater	grdn	10820
	Francis Y	1865	Pembroke	will	10772
	Fred	1855	N. Bridgewater	grdn	10819
	Frederick	1849	W. Bridgewater	grdn	10773
	Freeman	1867	W. Bridgewater	admn	10774
	Galen	1842	W. Bridgewater	will	10775
	Gamaliel	1831	W. Bridgewater	admn	10776
	George	1815	Plymouth	will	10777
	George	1862	N. Bridgewater	grdn	10779
	George Jr	1812	Bridgewater	will	10778
	George W	1874	W. Bridgewater	grdn	10780
	Gideon	1842	N. Bridgewater	admn	10781
	Hannah	1818	Plymouth	grdn	10794
	Hannah	1870	Plymouth	admn	10782

SURNAME	FIRST NAME	YEAR	PLACE	CASE	DOCKET
HOWARD	Hannah	1879	Hingham	admn	10783
	Harriet	1853	W. Bridgewater	grdn	10786
	Harriet	1878	W. Bridgewater	will	10784
	Harrison	1861	N. Bridgewater	will	10785
	Henry F	1853	W. Bridgewater	grdn	10786
	Hepsibah	1849	W. Bridgewater	admn	10787
	Isaac	1878	W. Bridgewater	admn	10788
	Jacob	1822	W. Bridgewater	will	10789
	James	1809	Bridgewater	admn	10790
	James	1818	Plymouth	admn	10793
	James	1818	Plymouth	grdn	10794
	James Jr	1749	Plymouth	will	10792
	James Jr	1809	Bridgewater	will	10791
	Jane	1872	W. Bridgewater	will	10795
	Janet	1861	W. Bridgewater	will	10796
	Jason	1782	Bridgewater	grdn	10798
	Jason	1801	Bridgewater	admn	10797
	Jerusha	1812	Hingham	will	10799
	Jesse Jr	1815	Bridgewater	admn	10800
	John	1713	Bridgewater	admn	10801
	John	1726	Bridgewater	admn	10802
	John	1793	Bridgewater	will	10803
	John	1805	Bridgewater	admn	10804
	John E	1851	W. Bridgewater	will	10805
	John J	1877	Bridgewater	admn	10806
	John T	1874	Plymouth	grdn	10828
	Jonas	1841	W. Bridgewater	grdn	10808
	Jonas Jr	1825	N. Bridgewater	admn	10807
	Jonathan	1809	Bridgewater	will	10810
	Jonathan	1834	W. Bridgewater	admn	10811
	Jonathan 2nd	1805	Bridgewater	will	10809
	Jonathan 2nd	1869	W. Bridgewater	admn	10812
	Joseph	1792	Bridgewater	will	10813
	Joshua	1782	Bridgewater	grdn	10798
	Justin	1862	N. Bridgewater	grdn	10779
	Katie	1797	Bridgewater	grdn	10814
	Leavitt T	1828	W. Bridgewater	grdn	10815
	Lewis	1827	W. Bridgewater	grdn	10816
	Lewis	1865	N. Bridgewater	will	10817
	Lloyd	1838	W. Bridgewater	will	10818
	Louisa	1838	Wareham	grdn	10832
	Louisa	1855	N. Bridgewater	grdn	10819
	Lucy	1831	W. Bridgewater	grdn	10820
	Lysander	1835	N. Bridgewater	admn	10821
	Malcome	1862	N. Bridgewater	grdn	10779
	Marcus	1853	W. Bridgewater	will	10822
	Martha	1837	W. Bridgewater	will	10823
	Martha J	1828	N. Bridgewater	grdn	10765
	Mary	1782	Bridgewater	grdn	10798
	Mary	1823	N. Bridgewater	will	10825
	Mary A	1832	W. Bridgewater	grdn	10827
	Mary C	1874	N. Bridgewater	will	10826
	Mary F	1838	Wareham	grdn	10824 a
	Mary M	1874	Plymouth	grdn	10828
	Nancy H	1874	Hingham	grdn	10829 a
	Nathan	1800	Bridgewater	will	10830
	Nathaniel	1836	Wareham	admn	10831
	Nathaniel	1838	Wareham	grdn	10832
	Ned	1825	Hingham	admn	10833
	Nehemiah	1837	W. Bridgewater	will	10834
	Nicholas P	1866	W. Bridgewater	admn	10835
	Octavia W	1877	Bridgewater	admn	10836
	Oliver	1798	Bridgewater	admn	10837
	Oliver	1838	Wareham	grdn	10832
	Oliver	1845	N. Bridgewater	will	10838
	Parnel	1819	Bridgewater	will	10839
	Peggy	1876	Hingham	will	10840
	Perez	1810	Scituate	grdn	10841
	Perez	1838	Wareham	grdn	10832
	Phebe	1854	W. Bridgewater	will	10842
	Polly	1807	Bridgewater	grdn	10764

SURNAME	FIRST NAME	YEAR	PLACE	CASE	DOCKET
HOWARD	Polly	1870	Hingham	will	10843
	Rhoda	1862	N. Bridgewater	grdn	10779
	Robert	1779	Bridgewater	will	10844
	Robert	1808	Bridgewater	will	10845
	Robert	1846	N. Bridgewater	will	10846
	Roger	1862	N. Bridgewater	grdn	10779
	Rufus E	1838	N. Bridgewater	admn	10847
	Sally	1806	Bridgewater	grdn	10848
	Sally	1807	Bridgewater	grdn	10764
	Salmon	1849	W. Bridgewater	admn	10849
	Salmon W	1849	W. Bridgewater	admn	10850
	Samuel	1859	N. Bridgewater	will	10851
	Sarah	1777	Bridgewater	will	10852
	Sibil	1793	Bridgewater	grdn	10853
	Silas	1821	Bridgewater	admn	10854
	Simeon	1857	Bridgewater	will	10855
	Sophia	1806	Bridgewater	grdn	10848
	Stillman	1810	Scituate	grdn	10841
	Sukey	1816	Bridgewater	grdn	10763
	Susannah	1852	W. Bridgewater	admn	10856
	Thaddeus	1837	W. Bridgewater	admn	10857
	Thomas	1752	Plymouth	grdn	10858
	Thomas	1818	Plymouth	grdn	10859 a
	Thomas	1828	Plymouth	admn	10860
	Thomas	1831	W. Bridgewater	will	10861
	Thomas	1876	W. Bridgewater	will	10862
	Uriel	1870	W. Bridgewater	will	10863
	Waters	1870	Hingham	admn	10864
	Welcome	1870	N. Bridgewater	admn	10865
	William	1872	Wareham	will	10868
	William G	1853	N. Bridgewater	admn	10866
	William P	1855	N. Bridgewater	grdn	10819
	William P	1855	N. Bridgewater	admn	10867
	William W	1878	E. Bridgewater	will	10869
	Zadock	1761	Bridgewater	grdn	10870
	Zephaniah	1854	W. Bridgewater	will	10871
HOWDEE	John	1711/2	Middleboro	will	10872 i
HOWE	Alma	1865	Hanson	grdn	10882
	Azor	1782	Bridgewater	grdn	10873
	Azor	1842	Bridgewater	will	10874
	Betsey	1815	Abington	grdn	10875
	Betsey	1831	Abington	grdn	10876
	Cato	1818	Plymouth	grdn	10877 a
	Edward C	1856	Abington	admn	10879
	Frederic	1865	Hanson	grdn	10882
	Joshua	1802	Abington	admn	10880
	Joshua	1815	Abington	admn	10881
	Mabel	1865	Hanson	grdn	10882
	Melvina	1865	Hanson	grdn	10882
	Nathaniel	1814	Abington	will	10883
	Ruth	1845	Abington	admn	10884
HOWELL	Daniel	1726/7	Bridgewater	grdn	10886
	Hannah	1726/7	Bridgewater	grdn	10886
	Jeremiah	1726	Bridgewater	admn	10885
	Lydia	1726/7	Bridgewater	grdn	10886
	Sarah	1726/7	Bridgewater	grdn	10886
	Susanna	1726/7	Bridgewater	grdn	10886
HOWES	Abel	1841	Rochester	will	10887
	Charles F	1873	Bridgewater	grdn	10888
	Hannah	1793	Plymouth	admn	10889
	Jeremiah	1783	Plymouth	admn	10890
	Mehitable H	1873	Bridgewater	admn	10891
	Oakes R	1850	Rochester	admn	10892
	Paul	1859	N. Bridgewater	will	10893
	Phineas	1871	Bridgewater	will	10894
	Sarah C	1874	Bridgewater	admn	10895
	Thomas	166-	Yarmouth	admn	10896
	Thomas A	1862	Mattapoisett	admn	10897
HOWLAND	Abraham	1747	Pembroke	will	10898
	Albert	1860	Abington	grdn	10954
	Alice	1713	Marshfield	grdn	10956

SURNAME	FIRST NAME	YEAR	PLACE	CASE	DOCKET
HOWLAND	Allen	1853	Pembroke	will	10899
	Allen	1874	Pembroke	admn	10900
	Alvin	1823	Hanson	grdn	10968
	Arthur	1727	Marshfield	will	10901
	Arthur	1749	Marshfield	will	10902
	Arthur	1797	Marshfield	admn	10903
	Arthur	1818	Marshfield	admn	10904
	Caleb	1799	Plymouth	admn	10905
	Caleb	1823	Hanson	grdn	10968
	Calvin L	1879	Hanson	admn	10906
	Celia S	1849	Pembroke	grdn	10907
	Charles	1828	Hanson	grdn	10908
	Charles	1860	Abington	grdn	10954
	Charles	1866	Hanson	will	10909
	Consider	1759	Plymouth	admn	10910
	Deborah C	1848	Plymouth	grdn	10911
	Eden W	1852	Marshfield	admn	10912
	Elizabeth	1727/8	Middleboro	will	10913
	Ethan	1847	Hanson	admn	10914
	Etta	1860	Abington	grdn	10954
	Evelyn H	1866	Hanson	grdn	10915
	Friend	1823	Hanson	grdn	10968
	Friend W	1874	Hanson	will	10916
	Hannah	1865	Pembroke	admn	10917
	Henry	1670	Duxbury	admn	10918
	Henry	1827	Plymouth	admn	10919
	Ichabod	1826	N. Bridgewater	admn	10920
	Ichabod	1846	Plymouth	admn	10921
	Isaac	1724	Middleboro	will	10923
	Isaac	1724	Middleboro	grdn	10930
	Isaac	1787	Middleboro	admn	10924
	Isaac	1832	Plymouth	admn	10925
	Isaac	1863	Plymouth	admn	10926
	Isaac J	1867	Hanson	admn	10927
	Isaac Jr	1723/4	Middleboro	admn	10922
	Jacob	1818	Plymouth	admn	10928
	James	1828	Hanson	grdn	10946
	Jeremiah	1724	Middleboro	grdn	10930
	Jeremiah	1790	Middleboro	admn	10929
	Jerusha	1802	Marshfield	admn	10931
	John	1672	Plymouth	admn	10932
	John	1745	Middleboro	admn	10934
	John	1768	Plymouth	admn	10933
	John	1804	Carver	will	10935
	John	1860	Pembroke	admn	10936
	Jonathan	1828	Hanson	admn	10937
	Jonathan	1850	Abington	admn	10938
	Joseph	1692	Duxbury	admn	10939
	Joseph	1703	Plymouth	will	10940
	Joseph	1724	Middleboro	grdn	10930
	Joseph	1822	Hanson	will	10941
	Joseph B	1881	Hanson	admn	10942
	Joseph L	1877	Lakeville	admn	10943
	Lewis	1846	Hanson	admn	10944
	Luther	1864	Pembroke	will	10945
	Lydia	1828	Hanson	grdn	10946
	Lydia M	1851	Abington	grdn	10948
	Mary V	1871	Hanson	admn	10947
	Nancy S	1851	Abington	grdn	10948
	Nathan	1759	Middleboro	grdn	10949
	Nathan	1857	Plymouth	admn	10950
	Patience	1793	Plymouth	admn	10951
	Perez Jr	1855	E. Bridgewater	will	10952
	Permelia T	1870	Bridgewater	admn	10953
	Prescott	1860	Abington	grdn	10954
	Prince	1713	Marshfield	admn	10955
	Prince	1713	Marshfield	grdn	10956
	Rebecca	1872	Plymouth	admn	10957
	Robert	1713	Marshfield	grdn	10956
	Robert	1821	Pembroke	admn	10958
	Rouse	1774	Pembroke	admn	10959

SURNAME	FIRST NAME	YEAR	PLACE	CASE	DOCKET
HOWLAND	Ruby	1861	Marshfield	will	10960
	Ruth	1829	Pembroke	grdn	10961 a
	Ruth	1838	Pembroke	admn	10962
	Samuel	1753	Pembroke	admn	10963
	Samuel	1796	Plymouth	grdn	10965
	Samuel	1798	Pembroke	admn	10964
	Samuel	1823	Hanson	grdn	10968
	Samuel	1825	Scipio NY	admn	10966
	Samuel H	1873	Duxbury	grdn	10967
	Sapphira	1823	Hanson	grdn	10968
	Sarah P	1818	Marshfield	grdn	10969
	Seth	1729	Middleboro	admn	10970
	Thomas	1737	Pembroke	admn	10971
	Thomas	1739	Plymouth	will	10972
	Thomas S	1780	Plymouth	admn	10973
	Wait W	1851	Marshfield	will	10974
	Warren	1819	Pembroke	admn	10975
	Warren	1828	Hanson	grdn	10946
	Warren	1846	Hanson	will	10976
	Wealthy	1828	Hanson	grdn	10946
	William	1784	Pembroke	will	10977
	William N	1879	Plymouth	admn	10978
	Zerujah	1842	Hanson	will	10979
HOWLEY	Johanna	1868	Abington	admn	10980
HOXIE	Abiathar	1848	Plymouth	admn	10981
	Edward	1849	Plymouth	grdn	10984
	Lydia	1849	Plymouth	grdn	10984
	Sarah	1864	Hanover	will	10982
	Simeon	1851	Hanover	will	10983
	William	1849	Plymouth	grdn	10984
HOY	Patrick	1866	Abington	admn	10985
HOYT	Curtis	1860	Plymouth	admn	10986
	Damon	1851	E. Bridgewater	grdn	10987
	Frederick C	1877	Plymouth	grdn	10988
	Israel	1842	Plymouth	will	10989
	James H	1872	Carver	admn	10990
	Moses	1859	Hingham	admn	10991
	Samuel J	1878	E. Bridgewater	admn	10992
HUBBARD	Harriet	1830	Middleboro	bond	10994
	Nathaniel		(see HOBART)		10993
	Paulina	1830	Middleboro	bond	10994
	William	1858	Lakeville	admn	10995
HUDSON	Ann M	1869	Mattapoisett	grdn	10996 a
	Anne	1712	Duxbury	admn	10997
	Daniel	1751	Bridgewater	will	10998
	Daniel	1775	Bridgewater	will	10999
	Daniel	1839	E. Bridgewater	admn	11000
	Ebenezer	1842	Hingham	admn	11001
	Emmons A	1878	Carver	admn	11002
	Ezra	1814	Hingham	will	11003
	Isaac	1866	Halifax	admn	11004
	John	1684	Duxbury	will	11005
	John	1820	Bridgewater	will	11006
	John O	1866	E. Bridgewater	admn	11007
	Joseph	1867	Mattapoisett	will	11008
	Jotham J	1876	Hingham	admn	11009
	Melzar	1846	E. Bridgewater	will	11010
	Molly	1866	Halifax	admn	11011
	Nathan	1835	E. Bridgewater	will	11012
	Otis	1844	E. Bridgewater	will	11013
	Rebecca	1875	Hingham	will	11014
	Sabra	1852	Hingham	admn	11015
	Sarah A	1866	E. Bridgewater	grdn	11016
	Scarlet	1864	Hingham	will	11017
	Tamar	1875	Hingham	admn	11018
	William	1728	Bridgewater	will	11019
	William	1797	Bridgewater	will	11020
	William	1865	E. Bridgewater	admn	11021
	William	1867	Hingham	will	11022
HUESTON	William	1766	Plymouth	admn	11023
	William	1835	Plymouth	will	11024

SURNAME	FIRST NAME	YEAR	PLACE	CASE	DOCKET
HUGHES	Elizabeth	1727	Plymouth	admn	11025
	Mary A	1877	Rockland	will	11026
	Thomas	1697	Plymouth	will	11027
	William	1824	Hingham	will	11028
HULL	Mary J	1851	Berlin NY	will	11029
HULL (town)	Parsonage Land	1869	Hull	peti	11030
HUMBLE	Charles H etal	1876	Weymouth	peti	11031
	David	1866	Abington	will	11032
	Dorothy	1870	Abington	will	11033
	Major	1870	Abington	admn	11034
	N G	1868	Abington	grdn	11035
HUMPHREY	Clarissa	1871	E. Bridgewater	admn	11036
	Elmira	1835	Hingham	grdn	11040
	George	1857	Duxbury	will	11038
	George 2nd	1839	Duxbury	admn	11037
	Henry A	1854	Bridgewater	grdn	11039
	Isabella	1835	Hingham	grdn	11040
	John	1767	Scituate	grdn	11042
	John	1829	Hingham	admn	11041
	Joshua	1839	Hingham	admn	11043
	Levi	1829	Hingham	will	11044
	Lucy	1864	Hingham	admn	11045
	Mary	1767	Scituate	grdn	11042
	Moses L	1834	Hingham	will	11046
	Ned	1875	Hingham	grdn	11047 a
	Noah	1842	Hingham	will	11048
	Peter	1826	Hingham	admn	11049
	Sophia	1842	Hingham	grdn	11050
	Thomas	1864	N. Bridgewater	grdn	11051
HUNT	Alan	1824	Duxbury	grdn	11070
	Allen M	1843	Duxbury	admn	11052
	Ann	1864	N. Bridgewater	admn	11053
	Asa	1752	Plymouth	admn	11054
	Asa	1791	Middleboro	admn	11055
	Barker	1868	Duxbury	will	11056
	Benoni	1740	Weymouth	grdn	11105
	Betsey	1825	Abington	grdn	11067
	Betsey	1831	Abington	will	11057
	Caleb S	1876	Hingham	will	11058
	Cora	1870	Duxbury	grdn	11066
	David	1860	Abington	will	11059
	Ebenezer	1818	Abington	admn	11060
	Ebenezer K	1831	Abington	will	11061
	Edward	1824	Duxbury	grdn	11070
	Elizabeth	1740	Weymouth	grdn	11105
	Elizabeth C	1878	Abington	admn	11062
	Elizabeth L	1878	Hingham	admn	11063
	Ephraim	1833	Abington	will	11064
	Ephraim	1879	Middleboro	will	11065
	Experience	1827	Abington	divi	11102
	Fred	1870	Duxbury	grdn	11066
	George	1870	Duxbury	grdn	11066
	Hannah	1824	Duxbury	grdn	11070
	Hannah	1825	Abington	grdn	11067
	Harriet	1825	Abington	grdn	11067
	Henry	1822	Duxbury	grdn	11110
	Henry A	1864	Abington	admn	11068
	Henry A	1868	Duxbury	admn	11069
	Hiram	1824	Duxbury	grdn	11070
	James	1740	Weymouth	grdn	11105
	Joanna	1740	Weymouth	grdn	11105
	John	1804	Bridgewater	admn	11071
	John	1854	Abington	admn	11072
	Joseph	1865	Abington	admn	11074
	Joseph S	1805	Middleboro	admn	11073
	Joseph W	1878	Rockland	will	11075
	Josiah	1776	Abington	will	11076
	Josiah	1817	Abington	admn	11077
	Josiah	1880	Scituate	admn	11078
	Josiah P	1827	Abington	grdn	11079
	Lot	1822	Duxbury	will	11080

SURNAME	FIRST NAME	YEAR	PLACE	CASE	DOCKET
HUNT	Lucy	1872	Duxbury	admn	11081
	Lydia	1854	Abington	will	11082
	Mary	1711/2	Duxbury	admn	11083
	Mary	1740	Weymouth	grdn	11105
	Mary	1822	Duxbury	grdn	11110
	Mary	1825	Abington	grdn	11067
	Mary A	1875	Hingham	will	11084
	Mehitable	1849	Abington	will	11085
	Mehitable	1872	Abington	admn	11086
	Micah	1795	Abington	will	11087
	Nancy	1825	Abington	grdn	11067
	Nathaniel T	1871	Abington	admn	11088
	Noah	1842	Abington	admn	11089
	Owen	1869	Bridgewater	will	11090
	Reuben	1825	Abington	grdn	11067
	Reuben	1825	Abington	admn	11091
	Samuel	1707	Duxbury	will	11092
	Samuel	1824	Duxbury	admn	11093
	Sarah	1756	Plymouth/Duxb'y	grdn	11109
	Sarah K	1827	Abington	grdn	11079
	Sarah P	1877	Abington	grdn	11094 a
	Sarah P	1878	Abington	admn	11095
	Seth	1832	Abington	will	11096
	Seth	1880	Abington	will	11097
	Silas Jr	1834	Abington	admn	11098
	Thomas	1740	Weymouth	grdn	11105
	Thomas	1755	Duxbury	will	11099
	Thomas	1807	Duxbury	will	11100
	Thomas	1825	Abington	admn	11101
	Thomas	1827	Abington	divi	11102
	Thomas	1847	Abington	admn	11103
	Thomas J	1873	Abington	will	11104
	Warren	1867	Abington	admn	11106
	Winifred	1842	Hull	will	11107
	Winifred	1853	Hull	admn	11108
	Ziba	1756	Plymouth/Duxb'y	grdn	11109
	Ziba	1822	Duxbury	grdn	11110
HUNTER	Samuel	1757	Middleboro	admn	11111 i
	William	1719	Scituate	will	11112
HURLEHY	Mary	1871	N. Bridgewater	will	11113
HURLEY	Dennis	1862	N. Bridgewater	grdn	11114
	Mary	1862	N. Bridgewater	grdn	11114
	Richard	1862	N. Bridgewater	grdn	11114
HUSE	Mary T	1870	N. Bridgewater	will	11115
HUSSEY	Alfred	1872	Lakeville	grdn	11116
	Alice	1872	Lakeville	grdn	11116
	Charles	1872	Lakeville	grdn	11116
	Emily	1872	Lakeville	grdn	11116
	George Jr	1872	Lakeville	admn	11117
	Harriet	1864	Rochester	grdn	11119
	Helen	1864	Rochester	grdn	11119
	Robert	1667	Bridgewater	admn	11118
	William	1864	Rochester	grdn	11119
HUTCHINSON	Anthony O N	1877	Rockland	grdn	11120
	Bethiah	1865	Abington	grdn	11123
	Charles W	1873	Abington	admn	11121
	Elizabeth	1865	Abington	grdn	11123
	Henry B	1877	Rockland	admn	11122
	Herbert	1865	Abington	grdn	11123
	John	1795	Middleboro	grdn	11124
	Joseph	1875	Middleboro	admn	11125
	Polly	1872	Middleboro	admn	11126
	Robert	1869	Plymouth	admn	11127
	Robina	1865	Abington	grdn	11123
HYATT	Joseph	1829	Pembroke	grdn	11128 a
HYDE	Anna	1858	Bridgewater	peti	11129
	Ezra	1789	Rehoboth	grdn	11130
	Francis	1858	Bridgewater	peti	11129
	John	1789	Rehoboth	grdn	11130
	Joseph A	1877	Bridgewater	admn	11131
	Martha	1862	Bridgewater	admn	11132

SURNAME	FIRST NAME	YEAR	PLACE	CASE	DOCKET
HYDE	Mary	1789	Rehoboth	grdn	11130
	Samuel	1789	Rehoboth	grdn	11130
HYLAND	Amasa	1878	Hingham	will	11133
	Barden	1816	Scituate	admn	11134
	Chloe S	1874	Hingham	will	11135
	Elizabeth	1865	Scituate	admn	11136
	Isaiah	1823	Scituate	grdn	11137
	James	1776	Scituate	will	11138
	John	1754	Scituate	will	11139
	Samuel	1824	Scituate	grdn	11141 a
	Samuel	1828	Scituate	admn	11142
	Samuel	1876	Scituate	will	11140
	Thomas	1706/7	Scituate	will	11144
	Thomas Jr	1690	Scituate	admn	11143
	William	1765	Scituate	admn	11145
	William	1840	Scituate	admn	11146
	William	1842	Scituate	will	11147
INGHAM	Mary	1708	Scituate	will	11148
INGLEE	Caroline	1854	Selma MO	grdn	11152
	Lemuel	1804	Kingston	admn	11149
	Louisa	1871	N. Bridgewater	grdn	11153
	Lucius	1871	Halifax	admn	11150
	Lucy	1872	Halifax	will	11151
	Maria	1854	Selma MO	grdn	11152
	Marion	1871	N. Bridgewater	grdn	11153
	Mercy	1870	Marshfield	grdn	11154
	Moses	1809	Halifax	will	11155
	Robert	1852	Halifax	admn	11156
	Robert	1870	Marshfield	admn	11157
	Sophronia F	1873	N. Bridgewater	admn	11158
IRIS	Benjamin R	1869	Abington	grdn	11159
	Henry W	1867	Abington	grdn	11160
	Mary E	1869	Abington	grdn	11159
IRISH	William	1777	Rochester	admn	11161
IVES	William	1875	Middleboro	admn	11162
JACKSON	Abraham	1714	Plymouth	will	11163
	Abraham	1734	Plymouth	admn	11164
	Abraham	1760	Plymouth	will	11165
	Abraham	1859	Plymouth	admn	11166
	Adnah	1880	Middleboro	will	11167
	Alfred	1879	Middleboro	will	11169
	Alfred P L	1878	Middleboro	grdn	11168
	Alpheus E	1859	N. Bridgewater	grdn	11171
	Alpheus G	1848	W. Bridgewater	admn	11170
	Ansil A	1859	N. Bridgewater	grdn	11171
	Bathsheba	1863	N. Bridgewater	will	11172
	Benjamin	1757	Halifax	admn	11173
	Benjamin F	1875	Brockton	admn	11174
	Bethiah	1849	Plymouth	admn	11175
	Betsey	1817	Plymouth	grdn	11176
	Caroline	1841	Plymouth	will	11177
	Charles	1818	Plymouth	will	11178
	Charles T	1820	Plymouth	grdn	11221
	Cornelius	1730	Middleboro	grdn	11209
	Cornelius	1741	Middleboro	admn	11179
	Daniel	1829	Plymouth	will	11180
	Daniel	1852	Plymouth	will	11181
	David B	1806	Plymouth	grdn	11215
	Deborah	1765	Halifax	grdn	11196
	Ebenezer	1734	Plymouth	grdn	11182
	Edmund	1724	Abington	will	11183
	Eleanor	1859	Scituate	will	11184
	Eleanor E	1871	Scituate	grdn	11185
	Eleazer	1736	Plympton	will	11186
	Eleazer	1750	Stoughton	grdn	11191
	Eliezer Jr	1719/0	Plymouth	admn	11187
	Elisha T	1844	Middleboro	grdn	11188
	Eliza E	1861	Abington	grdn	11189
	Elizabeth	1775	Plymouth	grdn	11190
	Ephraim	1750	Stoughton	grdn	11191
	Estella	1873	Scituate	grdn	11192

SURNAME	FIRST NAME	YEAR	PLACE	CASE	DOCKET
JACKSON	Francis L	1806	Plymouth	grdn	11215
	Franklin M	1878	Brockton	grdn	11216
	Frederick	1857	Plymouth	will	11193
	George	1873	Scituate	grdn	11192
	Gustavus R	1878	Plymouth	admn	11194
	Hannah	1763	Plymouth	will	11195
	Hannah	1765	Halifax	grdn	11196
	Harriet O	1874	Plymouth	will	11197
	Harry	1823	Middleboro	admn	11198
	Henry	1835	Plymouth	admn	11199
	Henry	1878	Brockton	admn	11202
	Henry F	1868	Plymouth	admn	11200
	Henry H	1877	Plymouth	admn	11201
	Hezekiah	1768	Plymouth	admn	11203
	Hosea	1861	Abington	grdn	11189
	Idella	1873	Scituate	grdn	11192
	Isaac	1763	Plymouth	grdn	11222
	Isaac	1792	Middleboro	grdn	11239
	Isaac C	1875	Plymouth	will	11205
	Isaac R	1861	Abington	admn	11204
	Israel	1727	Plymouth	admn	11206
	Jacob	1857	Plymouth	will	11207
	James	1840	Middleboro	admn	11208
	John	1730	Middleboro	grdn	11209
	John	1792	Middleboro	grdn	11239
	John	1817	Plymouth	grdn	11176
	Jonathan	1725/6	Scituate	will	11210
	Jonathan	1764	Scituate	will	11211
	Joseph	1728	Plymouth	admn	11212
	Joseph	1788	Middleboro	admn	11213
	Joseph	1792	Middleboro	grdn	11239
	Joseph	1875	Middleboro	admn	11214
	Leavitt T	1806	Plymouth	grdn	11215
	Linda M	1878	Brockton	grdn	11216
	Lothrop	1847	Plymouth	grdn	11217
	Lydia	1750	Stoughton	grdn	11191
	Lydia	1820	Plymouth	grdn	11221
	Lydia	1849	Plymouth	will	11220
	Lydia	1873	Scituate	grdn	11192
	Lydia K	1850	N. Bridgewater	will	11218
	Lydia K	1880	Middleboro	will	11219
	Margaret	1763	Plymouth	grdn	11222
	Maria	1817	Plymouth	grdn	11176
	Melzar C	1871	Scituate	admn	11223
	Melzar H	1871	Scituate	grdn	11185
	Nathaniel	1743	Plymouth	will	11224
	Nathaniel	1746	Plymouth	will	11225
	Nathaniel	1768	Middleboro	will	11226
	Oliver	1845	N. Bridgewater	will	11227
	Ransom	1809	Plymouth	admn	11228
	Rebecca	1765	Halifax	grdn	11196
	Rebecca	1792	Middleboro	grdn	11239
	Rebekah S	1876	Plymouth	admn	11229
	Salisbury	1852	Plymouth	will	11231
	Salisbury Jr	1847	Plymouth	admn	11230
	Sally	1848	Plymouth	admn	11232
	Samuel	1745	Plympton	will	11233
	Samuel	1773	Abington	will	11234
	Samuel	1805	Plymouth	will	11235
	Samuel	1836	Wareham	admn	11236
	Sarah	1739	Scituate	grdn	11237
	Sarah	1792	Middleboro	grdn	11239
	Sarah M	1837	Plymouth	will	11238
	Solomon	1792	Middleboro	grdn	11239
	Southworth	1815	Middleboro	grdn	11240 a
	Thomas	1775	Plymouth	admn	11241
	Thomas	1794	Plymouth	will	11242
	Thomas	1879	Plymouth	will	11246
	Thomas Jr	1837	Plymouth	will	11243
	Thomas T	1875	Plymouth	grdn	11244 a
	Thomas T	1876	Plymouth	will	11245

SURNAME	FIRST NAME	YEAR	PLACE	CASE	DOCKET
JACKSON	Varlina	1880	Plymouth	grdn	11247 a
	William	1836	Plymouth	will	11248
	William D	1855	Halifax	admn	11250
	William H	1869	Plymouth	admn	11249
	Woodworth	1816	Plymouth	grdn	11251 a
JACOBS	Amanda	1808	Hanover	grdn	11278
	Andrew	1861	S. Scituate	admn	11252
	Andrew	1861	S. Scituate	grdn	11253
	Anna L	1867	Hingham	grdn	11254
	Arthur L	1866	Hingham	adop	11255
	Bela	1782	Scituate	grdn	11256
	Benjamin	1782	Scituate	grdn	11256
	Benjamin	1792	Scituate	will	11257
	Benjamin R	1880	S. Scituate	will	11258
	Bethiah	1880	S. Scituate	admn	11259
	Betsey T	1861	Scituate	will	11260
	Braddock	1782	Scituate	grdn	11256
	Catherine	1807	Hingham	grdn	11322
	Daniel	1806	Hingham	will	11261
	David	1748	Scituate	will	11262
	David	1808	Hanover	grdn	11278
	David	1809	Hanover	will	11264
	David	1845	Scituate	grdn	11307
	David F	1879	Hingham	admn	11266
	David Jr	1799	Hanover	admn	11263
	David O	1860	Hingham	will	11265
	Deborah	1802	Scituate	will	11267
	Edward	1782	Scituate	grdn	11256
	Edward	1878	S. Scituate	will	11269
	Edward F	1853	S. Scituate	will	11268
	Elisha	1781	Scituate	admn	11270
	Elisha	1879	S. Scituate	will	11271
	Emeline	1861	S. Scituate	grdn	11253
	Eunice	1829	Scituate	grdn	11272 a
	Eunice	1850	S. Scituate	will	11273
	Franklin	1833	Scituate	admn	11274
	George	1838	Scituate	admn	11275
	George	1845	Scituate	admn	11276
	George	1845	Scituate	grdn	11307
	Hannah	1808	Hanover	grdn	11278
	Hannah W	1874	S. Scituate	will	11277
	Hawkes	1818	Hingham	grdn	11280
	Hawkes	1855	Hingham	admn	11279
	Henry	1854	S. Scituate	admn	11281
	Hiram	1808	Hanover	grdn	11278
	Hosea S	1872	Hingham	admn	11282
	Jacob	1734	Plymouth	admn	11283
	James H	1825	Scituate	admn	11284
	John	1807	Hingham	will	11285
	John	1847	Hingham	will	11286
	John	1860	Hingham	will	11287
	Joseph	1781	Scituate	admn	11288
	Joseph	1811	Scituate	admn	11289
	Joshua	1784	Scituate	will	11290
	Joshua	1808	Scituate	will	11291
	Joshua	1840	Scituate	will	11292
	Joshua	1879	Hingham	will	11293
	Jotham	1852	Hingham	admn	11294
	Lemuel	1844	Scituate	will	11296
	Lemuel	1851	S. Scituate	will	11297
	Lemuel Jr	1824	Scituate	grdn	11295 a
	Lincoln	1818	Hingham	grdn	11280
	Loring	1847	Scituate	admn	11298
	Loring	1879	S. Scituate	will	11299
	Lucy	1782	Scituate	grdn	11256
	Lucy	1861	S. Scituate	grdn	11253
	Lusanna	1823	Scituate	will	11300
	Lydia	1782	Scituate	grdn	11256
	Lydia	1794	Scituate	admn	11303
	Lydia	1833	Hingham	will	11301
	Lydia	1833	Hingham	admn	11302

SURNAME	FIRST NAME	YEAR	PLACE	CASE	DOCKET
JACOBS	Lydia M P	1847	Scituate	admn	11304
	Maria	1808	Hanover	grdn	11278
	Mary	1793	Scituate	grdn	11305 a
	Mary	1803	Scituate	will	11306
	Mary J	1807	Hingham	grdn	11322
	Matilda	1845	Scituate	grdn	11307
	Merial	1861	S. Scituate	admn	11308
	Michael	1861	S. Scituate	will	11309
	Nancy	1872	S. Scituate	will	11310
	Nancy	1879	Hingham	will	11311
	Nathaniel	1823	Hanover	admn	11312
	Nellie L	1867	Hingham	grdn	11254
	Olney	1873	Abington	grdn	11313
	Perez	1828	Hanover	admn	11314
	Peter	1810	Hingham	admn	11315
	Peter	1834	Hingham	admn	11316
	Piam	1880	S. Scituate	admn	11317
	Policarpus	1782	Scituate	grdn	11256
	Rachel H	1870	Hanover	will	11318
	Relief	1805	Hanover	will	11319
	Relief	1808	Hanover	grdn	11278
	Samuel	1784	Pembroke	will	11320
	Sarah	1807	Hingham	grdn	11322
	Sarah	1847	Scituate	will	11321
	Stephen	1860	Hanover	admn	11323
	Submit	1844	Hingham	will	11324
	Susanna	1794	Pembroke	will	11325
	Temperance	1880	S. Scituate	grdn	11326 a
	Theodosius	1829	Hanover	grdn	11327
	Thomas M	1845	Scituate	admn	11328
	Walter	1827	Scituate	admn	11329
	William	1867	Hingham	admn	11330
	William A	1867	Hingham	grdn	11254
JAEGER	Conrad P	1862	Hingham	admn	11331
JAMES	Abigail	1862	Scituate	admn	11332
	Benjamin	1796	Scituate	grdn	11333 a
	Benjamin	1797	Scituate	admn	11334
	Charles	1783	Scituate	grdn	11348
	Edward	1877	Scituate	will	11335
	Elisha	1744	Scituate	admn	11336
	Elisha	1797	Scituate	grdn	11351
	Elisha	1827	Scituate	grdn	11337 a
	Elisha	1834	Scituate	admn	11338
	Elisha	1854	Scituate	will	11339
	Emily	1868	S. Scituate	will	11340
	Eunice	1767	Scituate	grdn	11350
	Evan W	1877	Brockton	will	11341
	Hannah	1818	Scituate	admn	11342
	Hannah P	1854	S. Scituate	grdn	11343
	John	1761	Scituate	will	11345
	John	1764	Scituate	admn	11346
	John	1776	Scituate	admn	11347
	John	1783	Scituate	grdn	11348
	John	1862	Scituate	will	11344
	Joseph	1783	Scituate	grdn	11348
	Joshua	1859	S. Scituate	will	11349
	Lydia	1767	Scituate	grdn	11350
	Polly	1797	Scituate	grdn	11351
	Prudence	1783	Scituate	will	11352
	Ruth	1837	Marshfield	will	11353
	Samuel	1814	Bridgewater	grdn	11354 i
	Sarah	1783	Scituate	grdn	11348
	Sarah	1847	Scituate	will	11355
	Thomas	1767	Scituate	grdn	11350
	William	1767	Scituate	grdn	11350
	William	1854	S. Scituate	admn	11356
JAMESON	Adaline	1858	Duxbury	admn	11357
	Joel P	1859	N. Bridgewater	admn	11358
	William	1869	N. Bridgewater	will	11360
	William N	1855	Plymouth	admn	11359
JAQUITH	Henrietta J	1871	Abington	grdn	11361

SURNAME	FIRST NAME	YEAR	PLACE	CASE	DOCKET
JAQUITH	Mary F	1871	Abington	grdn	11361
JEFFERS	John	1869	Middleboro	admn	11362
JEFFERSON	Robert W	1874	Brockton	admn	11363
JEFFERY	John	1772	Pembroke	grdn	11364
	Micah	1756	Pembroke	admn	11365 i
	Sarah	1772	Pembroke	admn	11366
JENCKS	Joseph F	1866	Middleboro	grdn	11367
JENKINS	Abby E	1849	Bridgewater	grdn	11414
	Alden S	1863	Abington	admn	11368
	Ambrose	1858	Scituate	will	11369
	Andrew N	1862	Scituate	grdn	11409
	Benjamin S	1877	Plymouth	admn	11370
	Betsey	1856	Scituate	admn	11371
	Caleb	1820	Scituate	admn	11372
	Calvin	1846	Scituate	admn	11373
	Coleman	1857	Scituate	admn	11375
	Coleman Jr	1839	Scituate	admn	11374
	Content	1730	Scituate	grdn	11380
	Cummings	1834	Scituate	admn	11376
	Daniel	1812	Scituate	will	11377
	David	1730	Scituate	grdn	11380
	David	1792	Abington	will	11378
	David	1832	Abington	will	11379
	David	1838	Abington	grdn	11429
	Davis	1820	Scituate	admn	11381
	Ebenezer	1783	Scituate	admn	11382
	Edward	1699	Scituate	will	11383
	Edward H	1828	Scituate	admn	11384
	Elijah	1863	Scituate	admn	11385
	Elijah	1869	Scituate	admn	11386
	Elisha J	1844	Scituate	grdn	11387
	Eliza	1866	Abington	will	11388
	Eliza	1876	Scituate	will	11389
	Elizabeth	1849	Scituate	admn	11390
	Emily	1874	Scituate	will	11391
	Ephraim S	1865	Abington	will	11392
	Florence	1861	E. Bridgewater	grdn	11393
	Frances M	1876	Scituate	admn	11394
	Frank	1861	E. Bridgewater	grdn	11393
	George O	1865	Abington	grdn	11395
	Gideon	1830	Scituate	admn	11396
	Hannah	1794	Scituate	admn	11397
	Hannah	1849	Scituate	admn	11398
	Harlan W	1877	Plymouth	grdn	11399
	Huldah	1836	Abington	grdn	11400
	Isaiah	1836	Abington	grdn	11400
	James	1730	Scituate	grdn	11380
	James	1789	Scituate	will	11401
	James	1832	Scituate	will	11402
	John	1747	Rochester	agre	11403
	John	1863	Scituate	admn	11405
	John W	1878	Newton	peti	11404
	Joshua	1799	Scituate	admn	11406
	Joshua	1800	Scituate	grdn	11407
	Lemuel	1823	Abington	admn	11408
	Lemuel	1836	Abington	grdn	11400
	Lizzie T	1862	Scituate	grdn	11409
	Lucy O	1838	Abington	grdn	11429
	Luther	1853	Scituate	admn	11410
	Lydia E	1855	Abington	grdn	11411
	Marcy	1755	Rochester	admn	11412
	Martha	1730	Scituate	grdn	11380
	Mary	1704/5	Scituate	will	11413
	Mary	1730	Scituate	grdn	11380
	Mary J	1849	Bridgewater	grdn	11414
	Mary R	1865	Abington	grdn	11395
	Mercy L	1860	Scituate	admn	11415
	Merritt	1861	E. Bridgewater	bond	11416
	Myron A	1864	Abington	grdn	11417
	Nancy	1800	Scituate	grdn	11407
	Nathan	1836	Abington	grdn	11400

SURNAME	FIRST NAME	YEAR	PLACE	CASE	DOCKET
JENKINS	Nathaniel	1868	Abington	admn	11418
	Noah	1842	Scituate	admn	11419
	Peleg	1844	Scituate	will	11420
	Peleg F	1850	Scituate	admn	11422
	Peleg T	1849	Scituate	admn	11421
	Polly	1865	Scituate	admn	11423
	Rebecca	1836	Abington	grdn	11400
	Robert O	1848	Bridgewater	admn	11424
	Samuel	1730	Scituate	grdn	11380
	Samuel	1794	Scituate	admn	11425
	Samuel	1805	Scituate	will	11426
	Sarah	1838	Abington	will	11427
	Sarah	1856	Abington	admn	11428
	Spooner	1838	Abington	grdn	11429
	Thankful	1730	Scituate	grdn	11380
	Thomas	1739	Scituate	will	11430
	Thomas	1791	Scituate	will	11432
	Thomas	1809	Scituate	admn	11431
	Walter	1861	E. Bridgewater	grdn	11393
	William C	1835	Scituate	grdn	11433
	William F	1854	Carver	admn	11434
	Zenas	1834	Abington	admn	11435
	Zenas A	1866	E. Bridgewater	grdn	11436
JENNEY	Charles H W	1863	Mattapoisett	admn	11437
	David	1855	Marion	admn	11438
	Elisha C	1870	Mattapoisett	admn	11439
	Ignatius	1778	Rochester	grdn	11440
	Job	1834	Rochester	will	11441
	Job	1873	Marion	will	11442
	Joseph	1866	Mattapoisett	will	11443
	Lettice	1778	Rochester	grdn	11440
	Nathan	1829	Rochester	admn	11444
	Priscilla	1878	Marion	admn	11445
	Rebecca S	1858	Middleboro	admn	11446
	Samuel	1692	Dartmouth	will	11447
	Samuel	1778	Rochester	will	11448
	Samuel	1855	Rochester	admn	11449
JENNINGS	Abigail	1821	Pembroke	grdn	11450
	Charity	1821	Pembroke	grdn	11450
	Elizabeth	1821	Pembroke	grdn	11450
	Isaac	1762	Pembroke	will	11451
	Isaac	1785	Pembroke	grdn	11453 a
	Isaac	1797	Pembroke	warr	11452
	Isaac	1811	Pembroke	admn	11454
	Isaac	1821	Pembroke	grdn	11450
	Isaac	1873	Pembroke	admn	11455
	Mary	1821	Pembroke	grdn	11450
	Nathaniel	1807	Pembroke	will	11456
	Nathaniel	1808	Pembroke	grdn	11457
	Nathaniel	1871	Marshfield	will	11458
	Richard	1750	Bridgewater	will	11459
	Samuel	1776	Bridgewater	grdn	11460
	Samuel	1785	Bridgewater	admn	11461
JESS	Amy	1814	Bridgewater	admn	11462
JEWETT	Edwin C	1838	Carver	grdn	11463
	Eleanor P	1838	Carver	grdn	11463
	Henry P	1838	Carver	grdn	11463
	William H	1841	Plymouth	admn	11464
JOCOY	Isaac H	1869	N. Bridgewater	admn	11465
	Walter E	1869	N. Bridgewater	grdn	11466
JOEL	Richard	1818	Pembroke	grdn	11467 a
	Richard	1830	Pembroke	admn	11468
JOHNSON	Albert E	1867	Bridgewater	grdn	11475
	Andrew	1829	Rochester	will	11469
	Andrias	1807	Plymouth	grdn	11470
	Benjamin	1768	Bridgewater	will	11471
	Bethiah	1834	Plymouth	will	11472
	Branch	1837	Plymouth	admn	11473
	Caroline M	1873	Kingston	admn	11474
	Charles E	1867	Bridgewater	grdn	11475
	Deborah A	1873	Mattapoisett	admn	11476

SURNAME	FIRST NAME	YEAR	PLACE	CASE	DOCKET
JOHNSON	Edwin	1870	N. Bridgewater	admn	11477
	Eliza	1877	Bridgewater	admn	11479
	Eliza E	1876	Bridgewater	grdn	11478 a
	Emeline O	1879	W. Bridgewater	grdn	11480
	Emery A	1879	Middleboro	will	11481
	Francis	1828	E. Bridgewater	grdn	11513
	Francis	1850	Kingston	admn	11482
	Frederick	1807	Hanover	admn	11483
	Frederick A	1875	Bridgewater	grdn	11485
	Frederick H	1862	N. Bridgewater	grdn	11484
	George P	1869	N. Bridgewater	grdn	11486
	George W	1881	W. Bridgewater	will	11487
	Hannah W	1870	Kingston	admn	11488
	Harriet	1828	E. Bridgewater	grdn	11513
	Henry A	1857	N. Bridgewater	grdn	11489
	Henry A	1864	Plymouth	grdn	11490
	Henry A et al	1877	Hanover	peti	11491
	Horace A	1859	E. Bridgewater	admn	11492
	Isaac Jr	1790	Bridgewater	grdn	11493 a
	Jacob	1798	Plymouth	admn	11494
	James	1800	Bridgewater	will	11495
	John	1770	Bridgewater	admn	11496
	John	1820	Kingston	admn	11497
	John	1873	Kingston	admn	11498
	Joseph	1792	Bridgewater	will	11499
	Josiah	1724	Marshfield	admn	11500
	Josiah	1812	Bridgewater	will	11502
	Josiah	1824	Plymouth	grdn	11501
	Josiah	1835	E. Bridgewater	admn	11503
	Julia	1828	E. Bridgewater	grdn	11513
	Lucy	1860	E. Bridgewater	admn	11504
	Mary	1857	N. Bridgewater	adop	11507
	Mary A	1854	N. Bridgewater	grdn	11508
	Mary A	1874	N. Bridgewater	admn	11506
	Mary T	1852	Kingston	grdn	11505
	Merton C	1867	Bridgewater	grdn	11475
	Nahum	1872	Bridgewater	admn	11509
	Richard	1858	Kingston	admn	11511
	Richard F	1837	Kingston	will	11510
	Seth	1826	E. Bridgewater	will	11512
	Seth	1828	E. Bridgewater	grdn	11513
	Susan	1868	Marion	will	11514
	Thomas	1862	Mattapoisett	admn	11516
	Thomas J	1865	Kingston	admn	11515
	Thomas W	1867	Mattapoisett	will	11517
	Willard	1879	E. Bridgewater	will	11518
	William	1725	Rochester	admn	11519
	William	1768	Bridgewater	grdn	11522
	William	1854	N. Bridgewater	admn	11523
	William B	1878	Plymouth	adop	11520
	William H	1879	Hanover	admn	11521
	William T	1854	N. Bridgewater	grdn	11508
	William T	1864	N. Bridgewater	will	11524
	Winslow	1855	Kingston	admn	11525
	Winslow P	1856	Kingston	grdn	11526
JONES	Abigail	1850	Marshfield	admn	11527
	Abigail A	1842	N. Bridgewater	grdn	11528
	Almira	1843	Bridgewater	grdn	11565
	Alonzo	1864	Scituate	will	11529
	Amos	1749	Marshfield	admn	11530
	Amos	1808	Marshfield	admn	11531
	Andrew	1849	Hanover	grdn	11532
	Ann	1749	Scituate	will	11533
	Ann M	1857	Turner ME	peti	11534
	Asa	1841	N. Bridgewater	will	11535
	Asa B	1865	N. Bridgewater	will	11536
	Baker	1847	Hanover	will	11537
	Benjamin	1752	Marshfield	will	11538
	Benjamin	1853	Hingham	will	11539
	Benjamin	1869	Hingham	will	11540
	Benjamin B	1856	Pembroke	admn	11541

SURNAME	FIRST NAME	YEAR	PLACE	CASE	DOCKET
JONES	Betsey	1815	Pembroke	grdn	11542
	Betsey	1849	Hanover	grdn	11532
	Betsey	1852	Marshfield	will	11543
	Bradford E	1842	N. Bridgewater	grdn	11528
	Caroline	1881	Pembroke	admn	11544
	Catherine	1858	Fairhaven	grdn	11607
	Charles	1813	Pembroke	grdn	11546 a
	Charles	1849	Hanover	grdn	11532
	Charles	1852	Abington	will	11545
	Charles F	1866	Middleboro	grdn	11547
	Christopher B	1849	S. Scituate	will	11548
	Consider	1757	Pembroke	grdn	11557
	Consider	1820	Middleboro	will	11549
	David	1783	Abington	will	11550
	David	1871	Plymouth	admn	11551
	Dearing	1753	Scituate	grdn	11592
	Deborah	1863	Marshfield	will	11554
	Deborah H	1848	Hanover	grdn	11552 a
	Deborah H	1849	Hanover	admn	11553
	Ebenezer	1756	Pembroke	admn	11556
	Ebenezer	1757	Pembroke	grdn	11557
	Ebenezer	1809	Middleboro	admn	11555
	Edwin B	1873	Pembroke	grdn	11558
	Eleanor	1782	Marshfield	will	11559
	Elizabeth	1768	Middleboro	grdn	11583
	Elizabeth	1813	Scituate	admn	11560
	Elizabeth	1856	Hingham	admn	11561
	Ellen	1858	Fairhaven	grdn	11607
	Ellen M	1863	Abington	grdn	11562
	Experience	1753	Scituate	grdn	11592
	Ezekiel	1877	Scituate	will	11563
	Frank S	1859	Halifax	adop	11564
	Franklin	1843	Bridgewater	grdn	11565
	Freeman	1843	Bridgewater	grdn	11565
	Grace	1786	Marshfield	admn	11566
	Hannah	1849	Hanover	grdn	11532
	Hannah A	1854	N. Bridgewater	admn	11567
	Helen E	1875	Brockton	admn	11568
	Hope S	1881	Middleboro	will	11569
	Isabella F	1867	Hingham	admn	11570
	Jeremiah	1792	Middleboro	admn	11571
	John	1740	Marshfield	will	11573
	John	1758	Plympton	admn	11576
	John	1758	Plympton	grdn	11577
	John	1765	Scituate	admn	11579
	John	1767	Middleboro	admn	11578
	John	1768	Middleboro	grdn	11583
	John	1775	Marshfield	will	11574
	John	1830	Marshfield	admn	11575
	John	1849	Hanover	grdn	11532
	John	1871	S. Scituate	will	11581
	John C	1847	Scituate	will	11580
	John E	1873	Pembroke	grdn	11558
	John Sr	1720	Marshfield	will	11572
	Joseph	1727	Marshfield	admn	11582
	Josiah	1768	Middleboro	grdn	11583
	Julia	1858	Fairhaven	grdn	11607
	Laura L B	1874	Bridgewater	admn	11584
	Levi	1768	Middleboro	grdn	11583
	Lot N	1874	Mattapoisett	admn	11585
	Lovisa	1768	Middleboro	grdn	11583
	Lucia	1871	N. Bridgewater	grdn	11586 a
	Lucia	1872	N. Bridgewater	will	11587
	Lydia	1796	Abington	will	11588
	Lysander	1880	Bridgewater	admn	11589
	Margaret	1858	Fairhaven	grdn	11607
	Mary	1849	Hanover	grdn	11532
	Mary	1858	Fairhaven	grdn	11607
	Mary	1862	Hingham	will	11591
	Mary B	1753	Scituate	grdn	11592
	Mary V	1851	Scituate	grdn	11590

SURNAME	FIRST NAME	YEAR	PLACE	CASE	DOCKET
JONES	Moses	1878	Hingham	admn	11593
	Nathan	1867	N. Bridgewater	admn	11594
	Nathaniel	1772	Marshfield	will	11595
	Parker	1861	Duxbury	will	11596
	Persis	1850	Marshfield	admn	11597
	Rosseter	1842	N. Bridgewater	admn	11598
	Samuel	1801	Marshfield	admn	11599
	Samuel	1842	Bridgewater	will	11601
	Samuel	1863	Abington	grdn	11562
	Samuel	1863	Middleboro	admn	11602
	Samuel P	1819	Scituate	admn	11600
	Sarah	----	Carver	grdn	11603 a
	Sarah	1858	Fairhaven	grdn	11607
	Sarah	1859	Plymouth	admn	11604
	Sarah	1873	Pembroke	admn	11606
	Sarah A	1863	Abington	grdn	11562
	Sarah T	1863	S. Scituate	will	11605
	Seth	1757	Pembroke	grdn	11557
	Seth	1879	Pembroke	admn	11608
	Shubael	1760	Rochester	will	11609
	Simeon	1801	Pembroke	admn	11610
	Simeon	1818	Pembroke	will	11611
	Solomon	1831	Hingham	admn	11612
	Thomas	1816	Hingham	will	11613
	Thomas	1844	Hull	admn	11614
	William	1728	Marshfield	grdn	11615
	William	1789	Scituate	will	11616
	William	1840	Scituate	admn	11617
	William H Jr	1865	Hingham	will	11618
JORDAN	Baruch	1699	Plymouth	will	11619
	Charles P	1877	E. Bridgewater	will	11620
	David	1822	Scituate	admn	11621
	Ellen	1877	Plymouth	admn	11622
	Gadlin	1865	Abington	will	11623
	John	1863	Plympton	admn	11624
	John	1877	Plymouth	admn	11625
	Joseph P	1849	Hanson	admn	11626
	Lucy J	1879	Plymouth	admn	11627
	Simeon	1858	Marshfield	admn	11628
JOSSELYN	Abbot	1862	Hanson	grdn	11693
	Abraham	1735	Abington	grdn	11629
	Abraham	1778	Pembroke	admn	11630
	Abraham	1860	Hanover	will	11631
	Albert L	1842	Hanson	grdn	11632
	Algernon	1862	Hanson	will	11633
	Alice A	1864	E. Bridgewater	grdn	11634
	Ambrose	1849	Hanson	admn	11635
	Ann M	1873	Marshfield	will	11636
	Anna	1801	Pembroke	will	11637
	Benjamin	1870	Hanson	will	11638
	Charles	1794	Pembroke	grdn	11639 a
	Charles	1812	Pembroke	admn	11640
	Charles	1861	Hanson	grdn	11683
	Charles S	1861	Duxbury	admn	11641
	Chloe	1852	Hanson	will	11642
	David	1875	Hanson	will	11644
	David A	1870	Pembroke	admn	11643
	Deborah	1824	Pembroke	will	11645
	Deborah	1861	Hanson	will	11646
	Ebenezer	1747	Abington	admn	11647
	Edgar A	1863	Hanson	grdn	11648
	Edward	1860	Hanson	admn	11649
	Eleazer	1778	Pembroke	grdn	11652
	Eleazer	1838	Hanson	will	11651
	Eleazer	1868	Hanover	will	11650
	Eli E	1860	Hanover	grdn	11653
	Elisha	1879	Pembroke	will	11656
	Elisha K	1850	Pembroke	grdn	11654
	Elisha K	1857	Pembroke	admn	11655
	Francis	1827	Hanson	admn	11657
	George R	1863	Hanover	admn	11658

SURNAME	FIRST NAME	YEAR	PLACE	CASE	DOCKET
JOSSELYN	Helen M	1856	Hanover	grdn	11659
	Henry	1787	Pembroke	will	11660
	Henry	1829	Pembroke	grdn	11661 a
	Henry	1829	Pembroke	admn	11662
	Henry	1880	Pembroke	admn	11663
	Ida W	1864	E. Bridgewater	grdn	11634
	Isaac	1778	Pembroke	grdn	11652
	Isaac	1846	Hanson	will	11664
	Isaac	1863	Pembroke	admn	11665
	Isaiah	1788	Hanover	grdn	11666 a
	Isaiah	1804	Pembroke	admn	11667
	Jabez	1734	Hanover	admn	11669
	Jabez	1743	Hanover	grdn	11670
	Jabez	1854	Hanover	admn	11668
	Jacob	1827	Hanson	grdn	11671 a
	James E	1861	Abington	grdn	11672
	Jane	1845	Pembroke	admn	11673
	Jane	1861	Hanson	grdn	11683
	Jarvis	1857	Hanson	admn	11674
	John	1771	Hanover	admn	11675
	Jonathan W	1842	Pembroke	admn	11676
	Joseph	1726	Abington	will	11677
	Joseph	1787	Hanover	will	11678
	Joseph	1842	E. Bridgewater	will	11679
	Joseph	1862	Hanson	grdn	11693
	Joseph B	1848	Hanson	grdn	11680 a
	Leavitt R	1878	Hanson	will	11681
	Luther	1859	Hanson	admn	11682
	Luther	1861	Hanson	grdn	11683
	Lydia	1863	Bridgewater	admn	11684
	Marquis F	1847	Abington	admn	11685
	Martha L	1876	Charlestown NH	grdn	11686
	Mary	1827	Hanover	admn	11687
	Mary	1850	Hanson	admn	11690
	Mary	1852	Hanson	admn	11691
	Mary	1859	Hanson	will	11692
	Mary	1862	Hanson	grdn	11693
	Mary C	1854	Hanover	will	11688
	Mary J	1869	Duxbury	will	11689
	Nathaniel	1726	Scituate	admn	11694
	Nathaniel	1792	Hanover	admn	11695
	Oren	1880	Hanover	will	11696
	Otis P	1864	Pembroke	will	11697
	Patience	1821	Hanson	will	11698
	Phillips	1787	Hanover	admn	11699
	Polly	1875	Hanover	admn	11700
	Priscilla L	1873	Hanover	admn	11701
	Rebecca	1828	Pembroke	admn	11702
	Sage	1775	Hanover	will	11703
	Samuel W	1879	Hanson	admn	11704
	Sarah	1743	Hanover	grdn	11670
	Sophronia	1861	Hanson	grdn	11683
	Stockbridge	1847	Abington	will	11705
	Sylvester	1797	Pembroke	warr	11706
	Sylvester	1801	Pembroke	will	11707
	Tamar	1778	Pembroke	grdn	11652
	Thomas	1782	Pembroke	will	11708
	Thomas	1825	Hanson	admn	11709
	Waldo	1861	Abington	grdn	11672
	William	1852	Hanover	admn	11710
	William W	1854	Pembroke	will	11711
	William W	1864	E. Bridgewater	admn	11712
JOY	Jedediah	1833	Hingham	grdn	11713 a
	Mary	1726	Scituate	will	11714
JOYCE	Abia	1779	Marshfield	grdn	11730
	Allathea	1779	Marshfield	grdn	11730
	Asa	1779	Marshfield	grdn	11730
	Augusta J	1841	Marshfield	grdn	11715
	Daniel T	1842	Marshfield	admn	11716
	David T	1841	Marshfield	admn	11717
	David T	1874	Marshfield	admn	11718

SURNAME	FIRST NAME	YEAR	PLACE	CASE	DOCKET
JOYCE	Ebenezer	1776	Marshfield	admn	11719
	Elizabeth	1754	Marshfield	grdn	11722
	Elizabeth	1842	Marshfield	grdn	11720
	Elizabeth H	1850	Marshfield	will	11721
	Isaac	1754	Marshfield	grdn	11722
	John	1762	Marshfield	will	11723
	John	1822	Marshfield	will	11724
	Jonathan	1809	Marshfield	will	11725
	Joseph	1862	Marshfield	admn	11726
	Leander R	1880	Pembroke	admn	11727
	Samuel	1841	Marshfield	will	11728
	Seth	1750	Marshfield	admn	11729
	Stephen	1779	Marshfield	grdn	11730
	Thomas	1755	Marshfield	will	11731
	Warren	1841	Marshfield	admn	11732
JUDD	Celia	1860	Hanover	will	11733
	Dryden	1852	Hanover	will	11734
JUDSON	Abigail	1842	Plymouth	will	11735
	Adoniram	1827	Plymouth	will	11736
KAY	Joseph	1879	Scituate	admn	11737
	Samuel H	1880	Abington	grdn	11738
KEATING	Peter	1860	E. Bridgewater	admn	11739
KEAY	Anne C	1879	Bridgewater	will	11740
KEEFE	William	1877	Brockton	will	11741
KEELEY	Ellen	1869	E. Bridgewater	grdn	11742
	James	1869	E. Bridgewater	grdn	11742
	Julia	1869	E. Bridgewater	grdn	11742
KEEN	Abel	1880	Pembroke	will	11743
	Abigail	1736	Pembroke	grdn	11756
	Abigail	1798	Pembroke	will	11744
	Abigail	1843	Pembroke	will	11745
	Alethea C	1843	Pembroke	will	11746
	Almira	1877	Hanson	will	11747
	Almira B	1880	Hanson	adop	11748
	Asa	1818	Pembroke	grdn	11749 a
	Asa	1828	Pembroke	admn	11750
	Asa	1871	N.Providence RI	will	11751
	Asher	1755	Pembroke	grdn	11796
	Asher	1790	Pembroke	will	11752
	Benjamin	1732	Pembroke	admn	11755
	Benjamin	1736	Pembroke	grdn	11756
	Benjamin	1738	Hanover	grdn	11790
	Benjamin	1828	Marshfield	will	11753
	Benjamin	1859	Marshfield	will	11754
	Betsey	1858	Abington	admn	11757
	Calvin W	1824	E. Bridgewater	admn	11758
	Celia	1856	E. Bridgewater	admn	11759
	Celia J	1866	N. Bridgewater	adop	11760
	Charles	1813	Pembroke	grdn	11813
	Charles	1816	Bridgewater	admn	11761
	Charles	1879	Pembroke	admn	11762
	Charles E	1874	Abington	grdn	11763
	Daniel	1851	Pembroke	will	11764
	Deborah	1736	Pembroke	grdn	11756
	Deborah	1801	Scituate	will	11765
	Ebenezer	1738	Hanover	grdn	11790
	Elbridge W	1866	E. Bridgewater	grdn	11800
	Elizabeth	1738	Hanover	grdn	11790
	Emma A	1860	Abington	adop	11767
	Frederick	1832	Middleboro	admn	11768
	George	1820	Plymouth	admn	11769
	George H	1874	Middleboro	will	11771
	George M	1865	Marion	admn	11770
	Gilbert	1875	E. Bridgewater	grdn	11774
	Hannah	1710	Duxbury	admn	11775
	Hannah	1837	Pembroke	will	11776
	Ichabod	1852	Pembroke	will	11777
	Isaac	1787	Pembroke	will	11778
	Isaac	1830	Duxbury	will	11779
	Isaac	1845	Duxbury	admn	11780
	Isaac	1873	Hanover	admn	11781

SURNAME	FIRST NAME	YEAR	PLACE	CASE	DOCKET
KEEN	Jairus	1845	Duxbury	grdn	11782
	Jairus	1878	New Orleans	will	11783
	James	1864	Pembroke	will	11784
	John	1738	Hanover	grdn	11790
	John	1744	Pembroke	admn	11788
	John	1776	Pembroke	admn	11789
	John	1812	Rochester	admn	11786
	John	1814	Rochester	grdn	11787
	John Jr	1805	Rochester	admn	11785
	Joseph	1738	Hanover	grdn	11790
	Josiah	1710	Duxbury	will	11791
	Josiah	1732	Pembroke	will	11792
	Josiah	1778	Pembroke	admn	11793
	Josiah	1799	Rochester	admn	11794
	Judah	1765	Pembroke	will	11795
	Judath	1755	Pembroke	grdn	11796
	Lawrence	1738	Hanover	admn	11798
	Lemuel	1810	Pembroke	admn	11799
	Lois M	1866	E. Bridgewater	grdn	11800
	Lot	1826	Pembroke	will	11801
	Lucy	1877	Duxbury	admn	11802
	Lusannah	1736	Pembroke	grdn	11756
	Lydia	1797	Marshfield	admn	11803
	Mahala	1875	Middleboro	admn	11804
	Margaret	1781	Plymouth	will	11805
	Martin	1860	Marshfield	bond	11806
	Martin	1864	Marshfield	will	11807
	Mary	1738	Hanover	grdn	11790
	Mary	1813	Pembroke	grdn	11813
	Mary R	1874	Abington	grdn	11763
	Moses	1755	Pembroke	grdn	11796
	Nathaniel	1811	Pembroke	will	11810
	Nathaniel	1842	Pembroke	admn	11811
	Noah	1738	Hanover	grdn	11790
	Rebecca	1813	Pembroke	grdn	11813
	Rebecca	1836	Pembroke	will	11812
	Ruth	1755	Pembroke	grdn	11796
	Ruth	1863	Pembroke	admn	11814
	Samuel	1754	Pembroke	admn	11815
	Seth	1870	Lakeville	will	11816
	Simeon	1743	Pembroke	grdn	11817
	Simeon	1790	Marshfield	will	11818
	Susanna	1853	Marshfield	will	11819
	Wilbar	1863	Pembroke	grdn	11820
	William	1758	Plymouth	admn	11822
	William	1793	Marshfield	admn	11821
	William	1828	Plymouth	admn	11823
KEENE	Ada S	1864	Marshfield	grdn	11773
	Charles W	1864	Marshfield	grdn	11773
	Ebenezer B	1867	Hanson	admn	11766
	George H	1878	Pembroke	admn	11772
	George M	1864	Marshfield	grdn	11773
	Laura M	1877	Marion	grdn	11797
	Mary	1822	Rochester	admn	11808
	Mehitable	1872	Hanson	will	11809
KEITH	Abby	1871	N. Bridgewater	admn	11824
	Aberdeen	1825	Middleboro	grdn	11831
	Abia	1781	Bridgewater	will	11825
	Abigail	1843	N. Bridgewater	will	11826
	Agnes	1834	E. Bridgewater	grdn	11986
	Albert	1825	Bridgewater	grdn	11864
	Albert	1873	Bridgewater	will	11827
	Albert F	1866	Bridgewater	grdn	11901
	Alexander	1778	Bridgewater	grdn	11828
	Amos	1782	Bridgewater	will	11829
	Ann	1823	N. Bridgewater	will	11830
	Ann	1825	Middleboro	grdn	11831
	Anna	1814	Bridgewater	admn	11832
	Arza	1864	N. Bridgewater	will	11833
	Asa	1793	Bridgewater	admn	11834
	Asa	1860	E. Bridgewater	will	11836

SURNAME	FIRST NAME	YEAR	PLACE	CASE	DOCKET
KEITH	Asa P	1865	Bridgewater	admn	11835
	Asaba	1878	E. Bridgewater	admn	11837
	Azel	1748	Bridgewater	grdn	11919
	Bela	1867	N. Bridgewater	admn	11838
	Benjamin	1801	Bridgewater	will	11839
	Benjamin	1814	Bridgewater	admn	11840
	Benjamin	1844	Bridgewater	will	11842
	Benjamin	1854	N. Bridgewater	admn	11843
	Benjamin	1879	Bridgewater	admn	11845
	Benjamin H	1829	Bridgewater	admn	11841
	Benjamin Jr	1857	Bridgewater	grdn	11844
	Bethiah W	1864	Bridgewater	admn	11846
	Bethuel	1785	Bridgewater	grdn	11968
	Bethuel	1851	E. Bridgewater	admn	11847
	Caleb	1835	Bridgewater	admn	11848
	Calvin	1858	E. Bridgewater	admn	11850
	Calvin F	1842	E. Bridgewater	grdn	11849
	Catherine	1865	Bridgewater	grdn	11851
	Charles	1859	N. Bridgewater	will	11852
	Charles H	1853	W. Bridgewater	grdn	11853
	Charlotte L	1861	Bridgewater	will	11854
	Chester	1858	N. Bridgewater	grdn	11936
	Clara	1858	N. Bridgewater	grdn	11936
	Cordelia	1874	N. Bridgewater	admn	11855
	Cynthia B	1876	Brockton	admn	11856
	David	1748	Bridgewater	grdn	11919
	David N	1844	W. Bridgewater	grdn	11857 a
	Debby	1793	Marshfield	grdn	11934
	Deborah	1750	Bridgewater	grdn	11858
	Dennis	1872	Bridgewater	admn	11859
	Dulcina	1881	E. Bridgewater	admn	11860
	Ebenezer	1778	Bridgewater	will	11861
	Edward H	1880	W. Bridgewater	grdn	11862
	Edwin	1825	Bridgewater	grdn	11864
	Edwin	1861	Bridgewater	admn	11863
	Elbridge	1834	E. Bridgewater	admn	11865
	Elbridge	1865	Bridgewater	admn	11866
	Eleazer	1809	Bridgewater	will	11867
	Eleazer	1820	Bridgewater	will	11868
	Eleazer	1830	E. Bridgewater	grdn	11869 a
	Eliza C	1878	W. Bridgewater	will	11870
	Elizabeth	1758	Bridgewater	will	11871
	Elizabeth M	1847	E. Bridgewater	will	11872
	Ellen K	1879	Bridgewater	grdn	11873
	Elma L	1854	N. Bridgewater	grdn	11874
	Ephraim	1781	Bridgewater	will	11875
	Fred L	1880	E. Bridgewater	grdn	11876
	George	1873	E. Bridgewater	will	11877
	George L	1868	Bridgewater	grdn	11878
	Hannah	1857	Bridgewater	admn	11879
	Hariot	1825	Bridgewater	grdn	11864
	Harriet	1876	Marion	admn	11880
	Harry B	1880	E. Bridgewater	grdn	11881
	Hartwell	1801	Bridgewater	admn	11882
	Heman	1880	E. Bridgewater	will	11883
	Henry	1829	Bridgewater	grdn	11884
	Henry T	1853	Bridgewater	will	11885
	Holman	1835	E. Bridgewater	will	11886
	Holman	1849	E. Bridgewater	will	11887
	Horatio	1846	E. Bridgewater	will	11888
	Howard	1825	Middleboro	grdn	11831
	Howe	1856	Bridgewater	admn	11890
	Howe Jr	1854	Bridgewater	admn	11889
	Ichabod	1754	Bridgewater	admn	11891
	Ichabod	1785	Bridgewater	grdn	11968
	Isaac	1777	Bridgewater	admn	11892
	Isaac	1823	E. Bridgewater	admn	11894
	Isaac	1825	Middleboro	grdn	11831
	Isaac	1844	Bridgewater	admn	11893
	Isaac	1853	N. Bridgewater	will	11895
	Isaiah	1775	Middleboro	admn	11896

SURNAME	FIRST NAME	YEAR	PLACE	CASE	DOCKET
KEITH	Israel	1748	Bridgewater	admn	11897
	James	1719	Bridgewater	will	11899
	James	1780	Middleboro	admn	11898
	James	1793	Marshfield	grdn	11934
	James	1870	N. Bridgewater	admn	11900
	James L	1866	Bridgewater	grdn	11901
	Jane	1874	Bridgewater	admn	11902
	Jason	1815	Bridgewater	grdn	11950
	Jemima	1814	Bridgewater	admn	11903
	Jeremiah	1823	Bridgewater	admn	11904
	John	1761	Bridgewater	will	11908
	John	1809	Middleboro	admn	11905
	John	1827	E. Bridgewater	grdn	11909 a
	John	1872	Bridgewater	grdn	11911
	John H	1852	Duxbury	grdn	11906
	John Jr	1747	Bridgewater	admn	11907
	John et al	1872	Bridgewater	peti	11910
	Jonas	1810	Bridgewater	grdn	11912
	Jonas	1864	N. Bridgewater	will	11914
	Jonas H	1822	W. Bridgewater	admn	11913
	Jonathan	1748	Bridgewater	grdn	11919
	Jonathan	1759	Bridgewater	admn	11918
	Jonathan	1810	Bridgewater	will	11916
	Jonathan	1824	Bridgewater	admn	11917
	Jonathan C	1868	W. Bridgewater	admn	11915
	Jonathan W	1868	W. Bridgewater	grdn	11990
	Joseph	1730/1	Bridgewater	will	11920
	Joseph	1789	Bridgewater	admn	11921
	Joseph	1792	Bridgewater	will	11922
	Juliet	1824	N. Bridgewater	grdn	11923
	Keziah	1826	N. Bridgewater	admn	11924
	Keziah P	1857	Bridgewater	admn	11925
	Levi	1813	Bridgewater	will	11926
	Levi	1873	E. Bridgewater	admn	11927
	Lewis	1859	N. Bridgewater	admn	11928
	Lewis	1878	E. Bridgewater	admn	11929
	Lizzie A	1871	N. Bridgewater	grdn	11930
	Louis	1847	Bridgewater	will	11931
	Lucia	1834	E. Bridgewater	grdn	11986
	Lucia M	1847	Bridgewater	grdn	11976
	Lucian B	1864	N. Bridgewater	admn	11932
	Lucius A	1858	N. Bridgewater	will	11933
	Lusanna	1793	Marshfield	grdn	11934
	Lydia	1844	E. Bridgewater	admn	11935
	Lyman	1858	N. Bridgewater	grdn	11936
	Margaret	1872	Bridgewater	grdn	11911
	Marshal	1874	Mattapoisett	admn	11937
	Martha W	1865	Bridgewater	grdn	11851
	Martin	1810	Bridgewater	admn	11938
	Mary	1804	Bridgewater	will	11939
	Mary	1831	E. Bridgewater	grdn	11941
	Mary	1833	W. Bridgewater	will	11940
	Mary	1872	Bridgewater	grdn	11911
	Mary E	1880	E. Bridgewater	grdn	11991
	Mary J	1866	Bridgewater	grdn	11951
	Mehitable	1873	W. Bridgewater	will	11942
	Mitchell	1861	Bridgewater	will	11943
	Morton L	1868	Bridgewater	grdn	11878
	Morton S	1854	N. Bridgewater	grdn	11874
	Nathan	1786	Bridgewater	will	11944
	Nathaniel	1810	Hingham	grdn	11945
	Pardon	1880	W. Bridgewater	will	11946
	Phidelma	1877	E. Bridgewater	will	11947
	Philander	1866	Wareham	admn	11948
	Philo	1876	Bridgewater	will	11949
	Polly	1815	Bridgewater	grdn	11950
	Rhoda F	1866	Bridgewater	grdn	11951
	Robert	1796	Bridgewater	will	11952
	Robert	1818	Bridgewater	will	11953
	Royal	1847	Bridgewater	grdn	11976
	Ruth	1841	Bridgewater	will	11954

SURNAME	FIRST NAME	YEAR	PLACE	CASE	DOCKET
KEITH	S Elliot	1880	W. Bridgewater	grdn	11862
	S Lorin	1866	Bridgewater	grdn	11973
	Saba	1881	Bridgewater	admn	11955
	Salmon	1815	Bridgewater	will	11956
	Salmon	1880	Bridgewater	will	11957
	Salome	1792	Bridgewater	grdn	11958
	Sam A	1880	E. Bridgewater	grdn	11876
	Samuel	1826	Bridgewater	will	11959
	Samuel	1865	Bridgewater	admn	11960
	Samuel S	1866	Bridgewater	grdn	11951
	Sarah	1800	Bridgewater	will	11961
	Sarah	1864	Bridgewater	will	11962
	Sarah J	1853	W. Bridgewater	grdn	11853
	Sarah M	1859	W. Bridgewater	admn	11964
	Sarah S	1877	Bridgewater	will	11963
	Seth	1785	Bridgewater	will	11967
	Seth	1785	Bridgewater	grdn	11968
	Seth	1830	Middleboro	admn	11965
	Seth Jr	1805	Bridgewater	admn	11966
	Shepard	1826	N. Bridgewater	grdn	11969 a
	Silvester	1866	E. Bridgewater	will	11970
	Simeon	1828	W. Bridgewater	will	11971
	Simeon C	1876	W. Bridgewater	admn	11972
	Solomon	1823	Bridgewater	will	11974
	Solomon	1832	Bridgewater	admn	11975
	Stillman O	1847	Bridgewater	grdn	11976
	Sumner	1828	Bridgewater	admn	11977
	Susan R	1874	Mattapoisett	grdn	11978
	Susanna	1861	N. Bridgewater	will	11979
	Sylvanus	1825	E. Bridgewater	admn	11980
	Sylvanus	1831	E. Bridgewater	grdn	11941
	Sylvanus	1838	Bridgewater	admn	11981
	Sylvanus	1877	Bridgewater	admn	11982
	Thaxter	1866	E. Bridgewater	will	11983
	Thomas	1834	E. Bridgewater	grdn	11986
	Thomas	1878	Bridgewater	admn	11985
	Thomas M	1870	Bridgewater	will	11984
	Timothy	1786	Bridgewater	grdn	11988
	Timothy	1792	Middleboro	admn	11989
	Timothy Jr	1747	Bridgewater	admn	11987
	Wallace C	1868	W. Bridgewater	grdn	11990
	Walter	1880	E. Bridgewater	grdn	11991
	William	1827	E. Bridgewater	will	11992
	William	1863	Bridgewater	will	11993
	William	1865	N. Bridgewater	grdn	11994
	Zebina	1880	E. Bridgewater	will	11995
	Zepheniah	1858	Bridgewater	will	11996
	Ziba	1862	N. Bridgewater	will	11997
	Ziba C	1863	N. Bridgewater	grdn	11998
	Zilpha	1857	E. Bridgewater	will	11999
KELLEHER	Denis	1880	W. Bridgewater	will	12000
KELLEY	Amos	1848	Rochester	admn	12001
	Catherine	1875	Hingham	will	12002
	George	1847	Rochester	will	12003
	John	1880	Middleboro	admn	12004
	Lemuel C	1861	Marion	will	12005
	Rebecca	1807	Rochester	will	12006
	Sands	1848	Rochester	admn	12007
	William H	1875	Hingham	grdn	12008
KELSEY	James R	1842	Hingham	admn	12009
KELTON	Herbert L	1871	Scituate	grdn	12010
	Isadore A	1871	Scituate	grdn	12010
	Mary E	1871	Scituate	grdn	12010
	William H	1871	Scituate	admn	12011
KEMPTON	Deborah	1838	Plymouth	will	12012
	Joanna	1823	Plymouth	will	12013
	John	1815	Plymouth	grdn	12014
	Oliver	1822	Plymouth	admn	12015
	Samuel	1774	Plymouth	admn	12017
	Samuel Jr	1750	Plymouth	admn	12016
	Thomas	1760	Plymouth	admn	12018

SURNAME	FIRST NAME	YEAR	PLACE	CASE	DOCKET
KEMPTON	Zacheus	1825	Plymouth	admn	12019
KENDALL	James	1859	Plymouth	will	12020
	Julia P	1874	Plymouth	will	12021
KENDRICK	Benjamin F	1845	Bridgewater	grdn	12022 a
	James	1834	Plymouth	admn	12023
	James	1872	Plymouth	admn	12024
	John	1799	Wareham	admn	12025
	Lillie B	1874	Plymouth	grdn	12026
	Mary E	1874	Plymouth	grdn	12026
	Reuben F	1874	Plymouth	grdn	12026
	Solomon	1796	Wareham	admn	12027
KENERSON	Eli H	1879	Hingham	will	12028
	Ella Francis	1878	Hingham	adop	12029
	Ella Francis	1879	Hingham	grdn	12030
KENNEDY	Charles F	1865	Abington	grdn	12032
	John	1826	Kingston	will	12031
	Julia E	1865	Abington	grdn	12032
	Robert B	1872	Duxbury	admn	12033
	Walter H	1865	Abington	grdn	12032
KENT	Abigail	1827	Duxbury	admn	12034
	Abigail	1828	Waldboro ME	grdn	12038
	Clarissa	1828	Waldboro ME	grdn	12038
	Desire	1745	Marshfield	grdn	12037
	Elisha	1841	Marshfield	bond	12035
	Elizabeth	1880	Marshfield	admn	12036
	Frederick	1828	Waldboro ME	grdn	12038
	Hannah	1745	Marshfield	grdn	12037
	Huldah	1745	Marshfield	grdn	12037
	Ichabod	1745	Marshfield	grdn	12037
	Ichabod	1828	Waldboro ME	grdn	12038
	Jane	1828	Waldboro ME	grdn	12038
	John	1745	Marshfield	grdn	12037
	John	1753	Marshfield	will	12039
	John	1755	Boston	grdn	12040
	Joseph	1755	Boston	grdn	12040
	Lucy	1828	Waldboro ME	grdn	12038
	Martin	1880	Marshfield	admn	12041
	Mary	1755	Boston	grdn	12040
	Nathaniel	1745	Marshfield	grdn	12037
	Otis	1828	Waldboro ME	grdn	12038
	Peleg	1819	Marshfield	will	12042
	Peleg	1871	Marshfield	admn	12043
	Phebe	1805	Kingston	admn	12044
	Phebe	1843	Marshfield	admn	12045
	Samuel	1745	Marshfield	grdn	12037
	Samuel Jr	1756	Kingston	admn	12046
	Sarah	1745	Marshfield	grdn	12037
	Sarah T	1865	Marshfield	admn	12047
	Thomas	1776	Marshfield	admn	12048
	William	1877	Marshfield	will	12049
KEOUGH	Francis	1875	Brockton	adop	12050
KIDDER	Albert H	1879	Brockton	grdn	12051
	Ruie E	1879	Brockton	grdn	12051
	Wallace W	1879	Brockton	admn	12052
KIERSTEAD	Charlotte	1878	Plymouth	adop	12053
KILBRITH	Asa	1874	Pembroke	admn	12054
KILEY	Alvin A	1867	Hanson	name	12055
	Cornelius J	1868	Hanson	grdn	12056
KILLAM	Phebe S	1859	Hanover	will	12057
	Robert L	1866	Hanover	grdn	12058 a
	Robert L	1867	Hanover	will	12059
KILLAMORE	Benjamin	(see	COLLAMORE)		12060
KIMBALL	Estis	1868	S. Scituate	will	12061
	Hira H	1859	Middleboro	admn	12062
	Putnam	1857	Plymouth	admn	12063
KING	Adelaide	1857	Plymouth	grdn	12084
	Albert M	1852	Bridgewater	grdn	12070
	Alice	1776	Pembroke	admn	12064
	Anna	1732	Marshfield	grdn	12076
	Asa	1842	Rochester	admn	12065
	Benjamin	1777	Plymouth	will	12066

SURNAME	FIRST NAME	YEAR	PLACE	CASE	DOCKET
KING	Benjamin	1858	Abington	will	12067
	Betsey D	1804	Duxbury	grdn	12068
	Caleb	1854	Marion	will	12069
	Calvin B	1852	Bridgewater	grdn	12070
	Charles A	1852	Abington	admn	12071
	Deborah	1711	Scituate	will	12072
	Deborah	1758	Scituate	will	12073
	Edward P	1858	Abington	grdn	12074
	Eleazer	1762	Plympton	admn	12075
	Elisha	1732	Marshfield	grdn	12076
	Elizabeth	1732	Marshfield	grdn	12076
	Florence	1857	Plymouth	grdn	12084
	George	1754	Scituate	will	12077
	George	1852	Rochester	admn	12078
	Hannah	1843	Abington	will	12079
	Hannah	1862	Abington	admn	12080
	Ichabod	1753	Rochester	will	12081
	Isaac	1728	Plympton	will	12083
	Isaac	1767	Halifax	will	12082
	Isaac	1857	Plymouth	grdn	12084
	James	1867	Mattapoisett	will	12085
	Jane	1874	Middleboro	will	12086
	John	1721	Marshfield	will	12087
	John	1752	Plympton	admn	12088
	John	1819	Abington	admn	12089
	John	1823	Middleboro	grdn	12090 a
	John	1829	Middleboro	admn	12091
	John	1860	Plymouth	admn	12092
	Jonathan	1769	Middleboro	admn	12093
	Jonathan	1788	Plymouth	will	12094
	Jonathan	1822	Rochester	will	12095
	Joseph	1736	Plympton	will	12096
	Joshua	1850	Abington	admn	12097
	Joshua H	1864	Abington	admn	12098
	Lucy A	1871	Middleboro	grdn	12099 a
	Mary	1769	Halifax	will	12100
	Mary	1844	Rochester	will	12101
	Mary	1857	Plymouth	grdn	12084
	Mary S	1835	Bridgewater	grdn	12116
	Mercie H	1881	Plymouth	admn	12102
	Nathaniel	1824	Rochester	will	12103
	Nathaniel	1868	Rochester	admn	12104
	Obidiah	1874	Plymouth	will	12105
	Phillip C	1852	Bridgewater	admn	12106
	Rufus	1834	Rochester	admn	12107
	Sarah A	1878	Abington	grdn	12109
	Sarah F	1870	Carver	will	12108
	Susan A	1853	Rochester	grdn	12110
	Sylvia	1863	Marion	admn	12111
	Thomas	1692	Scituate	will	12112
	Thomas	1711/2	Scituate	will	12113
	Thomas	1732	Marshfield	grdn	12076
	Thomas	1805	Hingham	admn	12114
	Uriah S	1835	Bridgewater	grdn	12116
	Uriah S	1841	Bridgewater	admn	12115
	William	1797	Plymouth	admn	12117
	William	1880	Plymouth	will	12118
	William A	1875	Middleboro	will	12119
KINGMAN	Abel	1850	N. Bridgewater	will	12120
	Abiel	1854	N. Bridgewater	will	12121
	Abigail	1811	Bridgewater	admn	12122
	Alexander	1794	Bridgewater	will	12123
	Anna H	1870	Bridgewater	grdn	12124
	Arnold	1865	N. Bridgewater	admn	12125
	Barton E	1862	N. Bridgewater	grdn	12188
	Barza	1829	E. Bridgewater	grdn	12126 a
	Bela	1854	Middleboro	will	12127
	Benjamin	1775	Bridgewater	grdn	12129
	Benjamin	1870	N. Bridgewater	will	12128
	Betsey	1834	N. Bridgewater	grdn	12190
	Caleb	1807	Bridgewater	will	12130

SURNAME	FIRST NAME	YEAR	PLACE	CASE	DOCKET
KINGMAN	Charles	1831	E. Bridgewater	grdn	12131
	Charles E	1878	Brockton	admn	12132
	Crissa	1842	Hingham	grdn	12133 a
	Damon	1846	W. Bridgewater	admn	12135
	Damon 2nd	1841	Bridgewater	grdn	12134
	Daniel	1792	Bridgewater	will	12136
	David	1805	Bridgewater	will	12137
	David	1812	Bridgewater	admn	12138
	Edward	1857	N. Bridgewater	grdn	12140
	Edward A	1867	Rochester	grdn	12171
	Edward S	1866	N. Bridgewater	admn	12139
	Edwin H	1874	Brockton	admn	12141
	Eliphalet	1856	N. Bridgewater	will	12142
	Ezra	1852	E. Bridgewater	admn	12143
	Francis	1815	Bridgewater	grdn	12167
	Franklin	1868	E. Bridgewater	grdn	12175
	Freelove	1815	Bridgewater	will	12144
	George	1815	Bridgewater	grdn	12167
	George H	1865	N. Bridgewater	grdn	12145
	Hannah	1796	Bridgewater	grdn	12146
	Hannah	1844	N. Bridgewater	will	12147
	Hannah	1863	Hingham	will	12148
	Henry	1775	Bridgewater	will	12149
	Henry	1830	N. Bridgewater	will	12150
	Henry C	1878	Middleboro	grdn	12180
	Henry G	1867	Rochester	grdn	12171
	Hosea	1853	Middleboro	will	12151
	Hosea	1854	Bridgewater	grdn	12152
	Huldah	1868	E. Bridgewater	grdn	12175
	Jabez	1864	N. Bridgewater	will	12153
	Jane	1821	Hingham	will	12154
	John	1690/1	Bridgewater	admn	12156
	John	1755	Bridgewater	will	12157
	John	1842	Hingham	admn	12155
	John W	1876	Brockton	will	12158
	Jonathan	1813	Bridgewater	will	12159
	Jonathan Jr	1832	W. Bridgewater	admn	12160
	Joseph	1813	Plymouth	grdn	12161
	Joseph	1876	W. Bridgewater	will	12164
	Joseph W	1853	Hingham	grdn	12162
	Joseph W	1855	Hingham	admn	12163
	Loring	1835	E. Bridgewater	admn	12165
	Lucas	1852	N. Bridgewater	admn	12166
	Lucy	1815	Bridgewater	grdn	12167
	Lucy	1834	N. Bridgewater	grdn	12190
	Lucy	1868	E. Bridgewater	grdn	12175
	Luther	1834	N. Bridgewater	grdn	12190
	Lydia R	1867	Middleboro	will	12168
	Martha	1881	New York	grdn	12169 a
	Mary	1868	E. Bridgewater	grdn	12175
	Mary E	1857	N. Bridgewater	grdn	12140
	Mary W	1876	Plymouth	admn	12170
	Matilda S	1867	Rochester	grdn	12171
	Matthew	1809	Bridgewater	will	12172
	Nathan	1796	Bridgewater	admn	12173
	Nathan	1868	E. Bridgewater	grdn	12175
	Nathan	1877	Brockton	admn	12174
	Nellie F	1870	Bridgewater	grdn	12176
	Olive	1869	N. Bridgewater	will	12177
	Otis	1872	E. Bridgewater	admn	12178
	Phebe	1857	Middleboro	admn	12179
	Phillip E	1878	Middleboro	grdn	12180
	Polly	1871	W. Bridgewater	will	12181
	Sally R	1878	Bridgewater	will	12182
	Samuel	1742	Bridgewater	will	12183
	Seth	1775	Bridgewater	grdn	12129
	Seth	1843	N. Bridgewater	admn	12184
	Submit	1775	Bridgewater	grdn	12129
	Susan	1815	Bridgewater	grdn	12167
	Susanna	1822	Middleboro	admn	12185
	Tempie	1874	Brockton	grdn	12186 a

SURNAME	FIRST NAME	YEAR	PLACE	CASE	DOCKET
KINGMAN	Thomas B	1872	N. Bridgewater	admn	12187
	Thomas S	1862	N. Bridgewater	grdn	12188
	Warren	1852	Hingham	admn	12189
	Willard	1834	N. Bridgewater	grdn	12190
	William B	1873	N. Bridgewater	grdn	12192
	William H	1849	N. Bridgewater	admn	12191
KINGSBURY	Caroline B	1873	Marion	admn	12193
KINGSLEY	Azuba A	1880	Plymouth	will	12194
	Edward	1866	S. Abington	admn	12195
KINLOCK	John Jr	1862	Kingston	will	12196
KINNEY	Elizabeth N	1863	Wareham	admn	12197
	Hannah C	1869	Wareham	will	12198
	Jonathan	1845	Rochester	admn	12199
	Judson	1846	Wareham	admn	12200
	Lewis	1872	Wareham	admn	12201
	Martha J	1846	Wareham	grdn	12202
	Nahum	1846	Wareham	grdn	12202
	William H	1863	Mattapoisett	admn	12203
KINSLEY	Alvan	1834	Middleboro	grdn	12209
	Apollos	1774	Bridgewater	grdn	12205
	Betsey	1834	Middleboro	grdn	12209
	Cephas	1774	Bridgewater	grdn	12205
	Cephas	1800	Middleboro	admn	12204
	Eunice	1774	Bridgewater	grdn	12205
	George H	1842	N. Bridgewater	admn	12206
	Hannah	1774	Bridgewater	grdn	12205
	John	1834	Middleboro	grdn	12209
	Luther	1774	Bridgewater	grdn	12205
	Lydia	1801	Middleboro	grdn	12211
	Lydia	1834	Middleboro	grdn	12209
	Mary	1834	Middleboro	grdn	12209
	Samuel	1773	Bridgewater	admn	12207
	Sophia	1800	Bridgewater	admn	12208
	Susan	1834	Middleboro	grdn	12209
	Unite	1801	Middleboro	grdn	12211
	Unite	1833	Middleboro	admn	12210
KIRBY	John	1779	Rochester	admn	12212
KNAPP	Aaron	1674	Plymouth	admn	12213
	George O	1863	S. Scituate	admn	12214
	Joseph	1690/1	Plymouth	will	12215
	Philip Jr	1836	Middleboro	admn	12216
KNIGHT	John G	1859	Hull	grdn	12217
KNOBB	Alvin P	1858	Rochester	will	12218
	Mary	1867	Mattapoisett	admn	12219
KNOWLES	Harry W	1876	Marshfield	grdn	12220
	Helena R	1878	Marshfield	admn	12221
	John	1790	Middleboro	admn	12222
	Mary D	1840	Plymouth	grdn	12223
	Paul F	1876	Marshfield	admn	12224
	Susan F	1876	Marshfield	grdn	12220
	Susan F	1878	Marshfield	adop	12225
KNOWLTON	Daniel	1786	Ipswich	grdn	12226
	Joshua	1777	Middleboro	grdn	12227
KNOX	Eli	1878	Rockland	will	12228
KONKEAL	Christian	1881	Mattapoisett	will	12229
LAMBERT	James	1783	Scituate	will	12230
	Mercy	1841	Scituate	grdn	12231 a
	Patience E	1865	Bridgewater	will	12232
	Samuel	1795	Scituate	admn	12233
LANCASTER	William K	1864	Pembroke	admn	12234
LANDERS	Mary A	1851	Rochester	grdn	12235
	Nathan	1765	Wareham	will	12236
	Warren P	1877	Brockton	adop	12237
LANE	Abbie M	1880	Kingston	admn	12238
	Abigail	1816	Hingham	will	12239
	Abigail	1846	Hingham	will	12240
	Alma C T	1860	Abington	name	12240 +
	Andrews	1814	Abington	grdn	12241 a
	Annie J	1856	Abington	adop	12242
	Caleb	1833	Abington	grdn	12243
	Caleb	1840	Abington	admn	12244

SURNAME	FIRST NAME	YEAR	PLACE	CASE	DOCKET
LANE	Charles	1849	Abington	will	12245
	Charles	1854	Hingham	will	12246
	Christiana	1840	Abington	grdn	12249
	David	1822	Hingham	will	12247
	David	1831	Abington	admn	12248
	David	1840	Abington	grdn	12249
	Elias	1805	Hingham	grdn	12256
	Elias N	1847	Hingham	admn	12250
	Elisha	1850	Hingham	admn	12251
	Ellen	1875	Hingham	admn	12252
	Emeline	1840	Abington	grdn	12249
	Emma S	1863	Abington	adop	12253
	Enoch	1833	Hingham	will	12254
	Hannah	1805	Hingham	grdn	12256
	Hannah	1839	Hingham	will	12255
	Henry	1840	Abington	grdn	12249
	Henry M	1847	Abington	admn	12257
	Isaac	1818	Hingham	grdn	12258 a
	Isaac	1866	Middleboro	admn	12260
	Isaac	1873	Hingham	admn	12259
	James	1878	New York	admn	12261
	Jared	1839	Hingham	will	12262
	Jenkins	1870	Abington	admn	12263
	John	1835	Hingham	will	12264
	John F	1871	Abington	will	12265
	Josiah	1813	Hingham	will	12266
	Josiah	1848	Hingham	admn	12267
	Leavitt	1813	Hingham	admn	12268
	Leavitt	1836	Hingham	admn	12269
	Marshall	1825	Plymouth	admn	12270
	Mary	1879	Hingham	grdn	12279
	Peter	1805	Hingham	grdn	12256
	Priscilla	1879	Hingham	will	12271
	Quincy	1866	Hingham	will	12272
	Rachel	1840	Abington	admn	12273
	Rachel	1849	Abington	admn	12274
	Rufus	1863	Hingham	will	12275
	Sally	1824	Hingham	admn	12276
	Sally	1873	Hingham	admn	12277
	Sarah	1831	Hingham	will	12278
	Sarah	1879	Hingham	grdn	12279
	Virginia	1879	Hingham	grdn	12279
LANGFORD	Betsey	1870	Plymouth	admn	12280
	William	1860	Plymouth	admn	12281
LANGLEY	Thomas	1880	W. Bridgewater	admn	12282
LANGMAID	Charles H	1871	N. Bridgewater	admn	12283
LANMAN	Deborah	1869	Kingston	will	12284
	Isaac	1871	Plymouth	will	12285
	Jane	1857	Plymouth	admn	12286
	Lucy	1799	Plymouth	grdn	12293
	Mary	1799	Plymouth	grdn	12293
	Nancy	1877	Kingston	admn	12287
	Nathaniel C	1799	Plymouth	grdn	12293
	Nathaniel C	1867	Plymouth	admn	12288
	Peter	1825	Kingston	will	12289
	Peter	1853	Kingston	will	12290
	Rebecca	1799	Plymouth	grdn	12293
	Samuel	1797	Plymouth	admn	12292
	Samuel	1799	Plymouth	grdn	12293
	Samuel	1877	Plymouth	admn	12291
LAPHAM	Abiel	1774	Scituate	grdn	12297
	Adam	1833	Marshfield	grdn	12294 a
	Adam	1845	Marshfield	will	12295
	Amos	1763	Scituate	will	12296
	Amos	1774	Scituate	grdn	12297
	Andrew W	1857	Pembroke	grdn	12298
	Avis W	1877	S. Scituate	admn	12299
	Bethiah	1860	Marshfield	will	12300
	Charles	1796	Marshfield	admn	12301
	Charles	1827	Scituate	will	12302
	Charles H	1849	S. Scituate	admn	12303

SURNAME	FIRST NAME	YEAR	PLACE	CASE	DOCKET
LAPHAM	Chloe	1837	Scituate	will	12304
	David	1773	Marshfield	will	12305
	David	1792	Marshfield	admn	12306
	Ebenezer R	1838	Pembroke	admn	12307
	Elisha	1785	Scituate	admn	12308
	Eliza W	1846	Marshfield	grdn	12309
	George E	1865	Duxbury	grdn	12310
	Hannah A	1866	Pembroke	grdn	12317
	Hannah E	1879	Pembroke	admn	12311
	Harriet	1876	Rockland	will	12312
	Israel	1805	Scituate	admn	12313
	Jabez	1844	Marshfield	admn	12315
	Jabez S	1842	Marshfield	admn	12314
	James	1784	Scituate	will	12316
	James F	1866	Pembroke	grdn	12317
	Jesse	1814	Marshfield	will	12318
	Joseph	1758	Scituate	admn	12319
	Joseph	1815	Marshfield	will	12320
	Lemuel	1844	Pembroke	will	12321
	Lorenzo	1857	Pembroke	grdn	12298
	Lucy	1774	Scituate	grdn	12297
	Luther	1806	Marshfield	admn	12322
	Lydia	1738	Scituate	will	12323
	Lydia	1810	Scituate	grdn	12340
	Lydia	1847	Pembroke	grdn	12325 a
	Lydia L	1846	Marshfield	will	12324
	Mary	1810	Scituate	grdn	12340
	Mary	1876	Marshfield	admn	12326
	Melzar	1856	Pembroke	admn	12327
	Michael	1809	Scituate	will	12328
	Molly	1774	Scituate	grdn	12297
	Nathaniel	1777	Scituate	admn	12329
	Nathaniel	1842	Marshfield	admn	12330
	Nellie M	1865	Duxbury	grdn	12310
	Oliver	1783	Scituate	will	12331
	Oliver	1865	Pembroke	admn	12332
	Prince	1817	Marshfield	grdn	12333 a
	Prince	1838	Marshfield	admn	12334
	Ruth	1847	Duxbury	admn	12335
	Samuel	1757	Scituate	will	12336
	Samuel	1792	Pembroke	admn	12337
	Samuel	1806	Marshfield	admn	12338
	Sarah	1810	Scituate	grdn	12340
	Sarah	1853	S. Scituate	admn	12339
	Sereno	1857	Pembroke	grdn	12298
	Sereno H	1876	Rockland	will	12341
	Temperance	1834	Scituate	will	12342
	Thomas	1720	Scituate	will	12343
	Thomas	1811	Scituate	will	12344
	Thomas	1827	Scituate	will	12345
	William	1843	Marshfield	admn	12346
LARKIN	Ephraim	1848	E. Bridgewater	admn	12347
LARKUM	Albert W	1864	Hanover	grdn	12348
	George H	1864	Hanover	grdn	12348
	Noah	1864	Hanover	grdn	12348
LARTHLY	Phillip	1718	Plymouth	admn	12369
LATHAM	Charles	1817	Bridgewater	grdn	12350
	Charles	1864	Duxbury	will	12349
	Chilton	1751	Bridgewater	admn	12351
	Chilton	1752	Bridgewater	will	12352
	Chilton	1793	Bridgewater	will	12353
	Chilton	1812	Bridgewater	admn	12354
	Dean	1835	E. Bridgewater	will	12355
	Deliverance	1749	Bridgewater	admn	12356
	Galen	1844	E. Bridgewater	admn	12357
	James	1738	Bridgewater	admn	12358
	Jane	1751	Bridgewater	grdn	12359
	Joseph	1758	Bridgewater	will	12360
	Juliet	1873	Duxbury	will	12361
	Mary	1825	Bridgewater	will	12362
	Nathaniel	1758	Bridgewater	admn	12363

SURNAME	FIRST NAME	YEAR	PLACE	CASE	DOCKET
LATHAM	Nathaniel	1817	Bridgewater	grdn	12350
	Nathaniel	1833	E. Bridgewater	grdn	12364 a
	Nehemiah	1751	Bridgewater	grdn	12359
	Robert	1789	Bridgewater	admn	12365
	Susanna	1817	Bridgewater	grdn	12350
	Thomas	1778	Bridgewater	admn	12366
	Woodward	1803	Bridgewater	admn	12367
LATHLY	John	1733	Plymouth	admn	12368
LAWLESS	James	1878	Rockland	will	12370
LAWRENCE	Aaron L	1867	Bridgewater	admn	12371
	Abbie F	1867	Bridgewater	grdn	12373
	Grace	1855	Marshfield	adop	12372
	Herbert	1867	Bridgewater	grdn	12373
	Imogene A	1867	Bridgewater	grdn	12373
	Joseph	1768	Plymouth	admn	12374
	Sarah	1867	Bridgewater	grdn	12373
	Shubael	1841	Falmouth	will	12375
	Thomas	1759	Bridgewater	will	12376
	Thomas	1760	Bridgewater	grdn	12377
LAWSON	Peter	1874	N. Bridgewater	will	12378
	William A	1879	Brockton	will	12379
LAWTON	Benjamin F	1851	N. Bridgewater	admn	12380
LAZELL	Abner	1746	Middleboro	grdn	12381
	Amanda	1863	Abington	grdn	12382 a
	Bethiah	1799	Bridgewater	grdn	12383
	Bethiah	1805	CharlestonSC	grdn	12384
	Charlotte	1810	Bridgewater	grdn	12399
	Daniel	1863	Abington	admn	12385
	Deborah	1864	Bridgewater	will	12386
	Hannah	1832	Hingham	will	12387
	Henrietta	1810	Bridgewater	grdn	12399
	Irene	1810	Bridgewater	grdn	12399
	Isaac	1810	Bridgewater	will	12388
	Jacob	1746	Middleboro	grdn	12381
	Jacob	1751	Middleboro	will	12389
	Jennett	1851	Middleboro	admn	12390
	Joanna	1747	Middleboro	admn	12391
	Jonathan	1820	Hingham	admn	12392
	Joseph	1799	Bridgewater	admn	12393
	Joshua	1749	Middleboro	will	12394
	Nathan	1832	Bridgewater	admn	12395
	Nathan	1839	Bridgewater	grdn	12397
	Nathan Jr	1835	Bridgewater	will	12396
	Rachel	1810	Bridgewater	grdn	12399
	Rachel	1812	Hingham	will	12398
	Samuel	1804	Hingham	admn	12400
	Sarah	1746	Middleboro	grdn	12381
	Sarah H	1874	Bridgewater	will	12401
	Silvanus	1827	E. Bridgewater	will	12402
	Simon	1745	Middleboro	will	12403
	Thomas	1857	Middleboro	will	12404
	William	1746	Middleboro	grdn	12381
LEACH	Abial Jr	1836	Scituate	will	12405
	Abiel Jr	1780	Middleboro	admn	12406
	Abigail T	1871	Bridgewater	will	12407
	Abishai	1747	Middleboro	grdn	12408
	Abraham	1788	Bridgewater	grdn	12481
	Alden	1860	Halifax	admn	12409
	Alpheus	1875	Bridgewater	will	12410
	Ambrose	1865	W. Bridgewater	will	12411
	Anna	1739	Bridgewater	grdn	12412
	Apollos	1832	Bridgewater	admn	12413
	Arnold	1879	Middleboro	will	12414
	Benjamin Jr	1756	Bridgewater	admn	12415
	Caleb	1774	Halifax	grdn	12417
	Caleb	1800	Bridgewater	grdn	12443
	Caleb	1853	Bridgewater	admn	12416
	Catherine	1874	Bridgewater	admn	12418
	Charles W	1872	Lakeville	grdn	12419 a
	Charlotte	1849	N. Bridgewater	grdn	12464
	Chloe	1800	Bridgewater	grdn	12443

SURNAME	FIRST NAME	YEAR	PLACE	CASE	DOCKET
LEACH	Conrad H	1863	Abington	grdn	12420
	Daniel	1800	Bridgewater	will	12421
	David	1726	Bridgewater	will	12421 +
	David	1756	Bridgewater	admn	12422
	Dexter	1828	N. Bridgewater	grdn	12423
	Ebenezer	1750	Bridgewater	will	12424
	Ebenezer	1753	Bridgewater	will	12425
	Ebenezer	1774	Halifax	grdn	12417
	Ebenezer	1803	Bridgewater	admn	12426
	Ebenezer	1835	Bridgewater	will	12427
	Ebenezer	1838	Mt Vernon OH	admn	12428
	Eliphalet	1816	Bridgewater	grdn	12429 a
	Elisha G	1871	Bridgewater	admn	12430
	Ellen F	1851	W. Bridgewater	grdn	12431
	Ephraim	1771	Bridgewater	will	12432
	Eunice	1842	Bridgewater	will	12433
	Ezekiel	1788	Bridgewater	grdn	12481
	Ezra	1877	Plymouth	admn	12434
	Finney	1839	Plymouth	admn	12435
	Franklin S	1845	Plymouth	grdn	12467
	George M	1877	Middleboro	admn	12436
	Giles	1749	Halifax	admn	12437
	Giles	1799	Bridgewater	will	12438
	Hannah	1866	N. Bridgewater	admn	12439
	Hezediah	1826	Bridgewater	admn	12440
	Isaiah	1778	Bridgewater	admn	12441
	James	1800	Bridgewater	admn	12442
	James	1800	Bridgewater	grdn	12443
	James F	1855	Bridgewater	grdn	12444
	Jedediah	1760	Bridgewater	grdn	12445
	Jephthah	1784	Bridgewater	admn	12446
	Jesse	1773	Bridgewater	admn	12447
	John	1743	Bridgewater	admn	12448
	John	1807	Halifax	will	12449
	Joseph	1760	Bridgewater	will	12450
	Josiah	1866	Plymouth	admn	12451
	Lemuel	1820	Plymouth	admn	12452
	Lemuel	1860	Plymouth	admn	12453
	Levi	1849	N. Bridgewater	grdn	12464
	Levi	1861	Bridgewater	will	12454
	Lizzie M	1868	Hingham	grdn	12455
	Lucia H	1872	Bridgewater	will	12456
	Luthera H	1851	W. Bridgewater	grdn	12431
	Maria	1849	N. Bridgewater	grdn	12464
	Mary	1851	Rochester	admn	12457
	Mary A	1855	Bridgewater	grdn	12444
	Mercy	1865	Plymouth	admn	12458
	Nehemiah	1769	Bridgewater	admn	12459
	Olive	1853	Bridgewater	grdn	12460 a
	Olive	1854	Bridgewater	admn	12461
	Oliver	1848	N. Bridgewater	will	12462
	Pamelee	1788	Bridgewater	grdn	12481
	Peleg	1849	N. Bridgewater	grdn	12464
	Peleg	1877	Bridgewater	will	12463
	Philander	1832	Bridgewater	grdn	12465
	Philo	1853	Bridgewater	will	12466
	Phineas A	1845	Plymouth	grdn	12467
	Rebecca	1845	Charleston SC	grdn	12468
	Reuben	1864	Plymouth	will	12469
	Rufus	1788	Bridgewater	grdn	12481
	Samuel	1757	Bridgewater	will	12471
	Samuel	1761	Bridgewater	admn	12470
	Sarah	1739	Bridgewater	grdn	12412
	Seth	1851	W. Bridgewater	admn	12472
	Sheperd H	1875	Bridgewater	grdn	12473 a
	Solomon	1836	Rochester	admn	12474
	Stephen	1729	Bridgewater	admn	12475
	Stephen	1739	Bridgewater	grdn	12412
	Susanna	1862	Plymouth	admn	12476
	Unite K	1871	Bridgewater	admn	12477
	Zadock	1788	Bridgewater	admn	12480

SURNAME	FIRST NAME	YEAR	PLACE	CASE	DOCKET
LEACH	Zadock	1788	Bridgewater	grdn	12481
	Zadock	1805	Bridgewater	admn	12479
	Zadock	1866	Bridgewater	admn	12478
	Zebedee	1788	Bridgewater	grdn	12481
	Zeptha	1784	Bridgewater	admn	12482
LEAHY	Cornelius	1875	Rochester	admn	12483
	Hannah	1876	Brockton	admn	12484
LEAVITT	Celia W	1856	Pembroke	will	12485
	Cushing	1837	Hingham	will	12486
	Cushman	1870	S. Scituate	will	12487
	Cushman	1872	S. Scituate	grdn	12488 a
	David	1876	Hingham	admn	12489
	Elijah	1814	Hingham	admn	12491
	Elijah	1814	Hingham	grdn	12492
	Elijah	1876	Hingham	admn	12490
	Elisha	1806	Hingham	warr	12493
	Elizabeth	1814	Hingham	grdn	12492
	Elizabeth	1869	Hingham	admn	12494
	Elmira	1868	Hingham	peti	12495
	Esther	1865	S. Scituate	will	12496
	Evelina	1879	Hingham	admn	12497
	Ezra	1853	Hingham	admn	12499
	Ezra Jr	1850	Hingham	will	12498
	Franklin	1875	Bridgewater	admn	12500
	Gad	1870	S. Scituate	will	12501
	George	1825	Hingham	grdn	12528
	Hannah	1814	Hingham	grdn	12492
	Hannah	1821	Hingham	admn	12502
	Harvey	1853	S. Scituate	admn	12503
	Isaac	1874	Rockland	will	12504
	Israel	1798	Abington	will	12505
	Jacob	1814	Hingham	grdn	12492
	Jacob	1826	Hingham	will	12506
	Jacob	1879	Hingham	will	12507
	Jairus	1821	Hingham	will	12508
	Jerom	1855	Hingham	will	12509
	John	1838	Hingham	admn	12511
	John	1877	Hingham	will	12512
	John	1879	Hingham	grdn	12513 a
	John C	1824	Hingham	admn	12510
	Joseph	1719	Rochester	will	12514
	Joseph	1803	Rochester	admn	12515
	Joshua	1825	Hingham	will	12516
	Joshua	1872	Hingham	admn	12517
	Josiah	1737	Scituate	admn	12518
	Laban	1820	Pembroke	admn	12519
	Leah	1828	Hingham	admn	12520
	Lydia	1855	Hingham	will	12521
	Martin	1868	Hingham	admn	12522
	Mary J	1856	Hingham	grdn	12523 a
	Moses	1851	Scituate	admn	12524
	Nahum	1859	Pembroke	admn	12525
	Oscar W	1875	Bridgewater	grdn	12526
	Rachel	1861	Hingham	will	12527
	Rachel C	1825	Hingham	grdn	12528
	Sally	1845	Hingham	admn	12529
	Samuel	1857	Hingham	will	12530
	Susannah	1842	Hingham	admn	12531
	Thomas	1846	Hingham	admn	12532
LEBARON	Charles H	1837	Rochester	grdn	12533
	David	1745	Middleboro	grdn	12544
	Eliza	1797	Plymouth	grdn	12557
	Elizabeth	1833	Rochester	grdn	12534
	Elizabeth	1845	Rochester	grdn	12552
	Emeline L	1877	Mattapoisett	will	12535
	Emily	1877	Middleboro	grdn	12536
	Francis	1704	Plymouth	will	12537
	Francis	1731	Plymouth	admn	12538
	Francis	1732	Plymouth	grdn	12556
	Francis	1745	Middleboro	grdn	12541
	Francis	1761	Middleboro	admn	12540

SURNAME	FIRST NAME	YEAR	PLACE	CASE	DOCKET
LEBARON	Francis	1774	Plymouth	admn	12539
	Harry	1877	Middleboro	grdn	12536
	Henry	1833	Rochester	grdn	12534
	Ida	1877	Middleboro	grdn	12536
	Isaac	1732	Plymouth	grdn	12556
	James	1744	Middleboro	admn	12543
	James	1745	Middleboro	grdn	12544
	James	1780	Middleboro	will	12542
	Japheth	1816	Middleboro	will	12545
	John A	1854	Rochester	admn	12546
	Joseph	1784	Plymouth	admn	12547
	Joshua	1745	Middleboro	grdn	12541
	Joshua	1793	Middleboro	admn	12548
	Lazarus	1773	Plymouth	will	12549
	Lemuel	1837	Rochester	will	12550
	Levi	1820	Middleboro	admn	12551
	Lewis	1877	Middleboro	grdn	12536
	Lucy	1797	Plymouth	grdn	12557
	Lucy	1845	Rochester	grdn	12552
	Lydia	1745	Middleboro	grdn	12544
	Marcus B	1877	Mattapoisett	will	12553
	Martha	1745	Middleboro	grdn	12544
	Mary	1732	Plymouth	grdn	12556
	Mary	1745	Middleboro	grdn	12544
	Mary	1792	Plymouth	will	12554
	Mary	1797	Plymouth	grdn	12557
	Priscilla	1797	Plymouth	grdn	12557
	Samuel	1793	Middleboro	grdn	12555
	Sarah	1732	Plymouth	grdn	12556
	Sarah	1797	Plymouth	grdn	12557
	Theophilus P	1877	Middleboro	admn	12558
	William	1831	Rochester	admn	12559
	William	1833	Rochester	grdn	12534
	Ziba	1820	Middleboro	admn	12560
LEDDY	Peter J	1880	Hingham	will	12561
LEE	Henry	1852	Duxbury	will	12562
	Isaac	1762	Bridgewater	admn	12563
	John Adams	1869	Bridgewater	adop	12564
	Sarah H	1867	Duxbury	will	12565
LEEDS	Daniel D	1835	N. Bridgewater	grdn	12566
	Polly	1873	Abington	will	12567
LEMOTE	Matthew	1767	Plymouth	admn	12568
LENDALL	John W	1836	Scituate	admn	12569
LEONARD	Abby L	1874	Marion	grdn	12570
	Abiah	1726	Middleboro	grdn	12571
	Abial	1731	Norton	grdn	12572
	Abial	1739	Plymouth	will	12573
	Abigail	1832	Bridgewater	admn	12574
	Almira B	1838	Pembroke	admn	12575
	Almira B	1838	Mansfield	grdn	12669
	Anna	1830	W. Bridgewater	grdn	12629
	Ansel	1823	Bridgewater	admn	12576
	Ansel	1824	Bridgewater	grdn	12666
	Arza	1812	Middleboro	grdn	12577
	Arza	1857	N. Bridgewater	admn	12578
	Bathsheba	1830	Middleboro	grdn	12651
	Baylies G	1863	Lakeville	grdn	12579
	Benajah	1815	Wareham	admn	12580
	Benjamin	1801	Middleboro	will	12581
	Benjamin	1801	Middleboro	grdn	12582
	Betsey	1819	Middleboro	grdn	12583
	Betty	1781	Bridgewater	grdn	12614
	Caleb F	1840	Bridgewater	admn	12584
	Calvin	1781	Bridgewater	grdn	12614
	Caty D	1880	Plymouth	grdn	12585
	Charles	1869	Lakeville	grdn	12652
	Clara	1866	Bridgewater	grdn	12586
	Clarence H	1877	Marshfield	grdn	12685
	Clarinda	1835	-----	grdn	12587
	Content et al	1793	Middleboro	grdn	12588
	Crocker W	1863	Lakeville	grdn	12579

SURNAME	FIRST NAME	YEAR	PLACE	CASE	DOCKET
LEONARD	Cynthia W	1879	Rochester	admn	12589
	Cyrus	1830	W. Bridgewater	grdn	12629
	Dan	1771	Bridgewater	admn	12590
	Daniel	1801	Middleboro	admn	12592
	Daniel	1802	Middleboro	grdn	12593
	Daniel	1803	Bridgewater	grdn	12591
	David	1814	Bridgewater	will	12594
	Deborah	1824	Bridgewater	grdn	12666
	Deborah	1830	Middleboro	grdn	12651
	Deborah	1847	Wareham	admn	12595
	Diadama	1763	Middleboro	grdn	12647
	Elijah	1834	Marshfield	will	12596
	Elijah H	1860	Bridgewater	will	12597
	Eliza	1830	Middleboro	grdn	12598
	Elkanah	1714/5	Middleboro	admn	12599
	Elkanah	1749	Middleboro	grdn	12600 a
	Elkanah	1802	Middleboro	will	12601
	Elmer	1866	Bridgewater	grdn	12586
	Ephraim	1819	Middleboro	admn	12602
	Eva F	1880	Plymouth	grdn	12585
	Eveline	1869	Lakeville	grdn	12652
	Fanny	1869	Lakeville	grdn	12652
	Flora	1866	Bridgewater	grdn	12586
	Frank	1869	Lakeville	grdn	12652
	Frederick	1867	Lakeville	admn	12603
	George	1801	Middleboro	will	12606
	George	1815	Marshfield	grdn	12604
	George	1824	Bridgewater	grdn	12666
	George	1830	Middleboro	grdn	12651
	George	1832	Middleboro	admn	12607
	George	1849	Rochester	admn	12608
	George A	1849	Rochester	will	12609
	George E	1871	Marshfield	admn	12605
	Gideon	1872	N. Bridgewater	will	12610
	Hannah	1829	Middleboro	will	12611
	Hannah	1830	Middleboro	grdn	12598
	Hannah	1830	Middleboro	grdn	12651
	Hannah K	1881	W. Bridgewater	admn	12612
	Horatio	1880	Middleboro	admn	12613
	Ichabod	1781	Bridgewater	grdn	12614
	Isam	1870	Bridgewater	admn	12615
	Jacob	1717	Bridgewater	will	12616
	Jacob	1728	Bridgewater	admn	12617
	Jacob	1874	W. Bridgewater	will	12618
	James	1875	Lakeville	admn	12622
	James A	1862	Middleboro	admn	12621
	James E	1842	Plymouth	admn	12619
	James E	1876	Plymouth	admn	12620
	James M	1874	Ottawa IL	admn	12623
	James M	1880	Bridgewater	will	12624
	Jane	1819	Middleboro	grdn	12583
	Jemima	1726	Middleboro	grdn	12571
	Jemima	1784	Bridgewater	will	12625
	Jesse W	1874	Marion	grdn	12570
	John	1699	Bridgewater	admn	12627
	John	1792	Middleboro	admn	12626
	John	1825	N. Bridgewater	grdn	12628
	Jonas	1830	W. Bridgewater	grdn	12629
	Jonathan	1814	Bridgewater	admn	12630
	Jonathan	1840	Middleboro	admn	12631
	Jonathan	1848	Middleboro	admn	12632
	Joseph	1784	Middleboro	admn	12633
	Joseph	1793	Middleboro	will	12634
	Joseph	1844	Middleboro	admn	12635
	Joseph	1877	Hanson	will	12637
	Joseph J C	1872	Lakeville	admn	12636
	Josiah	1745	Bridgewater	will	12638
	Josiah	1761	Bridgewater	will	12639
	Josiah	1865	Hanson	will	12640
	Keziah	1763	Middleboro	grdn	12647
	Lewis	1880	Middleboro	admn	12643

SURNAME	FIRST NAME	YEAR	PLACE	CASE	DOCKET
LEONARD	Lewis N	1864	Middleboro	grdn	12641
	Lewis N	1873	Middleboro	admn	12642
	Lizzie	1869	Lakeville	grdn	12652
	Lois	1869	Middleboro	will	12644
	Louisa C H	1875	Bridgewater	will	12645
	Lucy	1763	Middleboro	grdn	12647
	Lucy	1824	Bridgewater	grdn	12666
	Lucy B	1880	Middleboro	admn	12646
	Martin	1845	Bridgewater	admn	12648
	Mary	1761	Bridgewater	grdn	12653
	Mary	1830	Middleboro	grdn	12651
	Mary	1833	Middleboro	admn	12650
	Mary	1835	Marshfield	admn	12649
	Mary	1869	Lakeville	grdn	12652
	Mary A	1877	Brockton	grdn	12654
	Micah	1855	Middleboro	will	12655
	Minot	1824	Bridgewater	grdn	12666
	Mira L	1868	Bridgewater	grdn	12656
	Moses	1761	Bridgewater	grdn	12653
	Nahum	1794	Bridgewater	grdn	12681
	Nahum	1879	W. Bridgewater	will	12657
	Nathan	1765	Bridgewater	will	12658
	Nathaniel K	1877	Brockton	grdn	12654
	Nathaniel W	1880	Plymouth	admn	12659
	Oaks	1869	Lakeville	grdn	12652
	Oliver	1794	Bridgewater	grdn	12681
	Oliver	1866	Duxbury	will	12660
	Otis B	1853	Middleboro	admn	12661
	Perez	1801	Middleboro	admn	12662
	Phillip	1708	Duxbury	admn	12663
	Phillip	1785	Middleboro	admn	12664
	Phillip	1803	Plymouth	admn	12665
	Polly	1794	Bridgewater	grdn	12681
	Rebecca	1761	Bridgewater	grdn	12653
	Rebecca	1763	Middleboro	grdn	12647
	Rebecca	1824	Bridgewater	grdn	12666
	Rhoda	1830	W. Bridgewater	grdn	12629
	Rosamond	1781	Bridgewater	grdn	12614
	Rufus L	1832	Rochester	admn	12667
	Ruth	1830	Middleboro	grdn	12598
	Ruth E	1838	Pembroke	admn	12668
	Ruth E	1838	Mansfield	grdn	12669
	Sally	1862	Middleboro	admn	12670
	Samuel	1841	Bridgewater	will	12671
	Samuel	1867	Bridgewater	will	12672
	Sarah	1781	Bridgewater	grdn	12614
	Sarah	1819	Middleboro	grdn	12583
	Seth	1760	Bridgewater	admn	12673
	Seth	1761	Bridgewater	grdn	12653
	Seth	1778	Bridgewater	will	12674
	Seth C	1872	Marion	admn	12675
	Simeon	1726	Middleboro	grdn	12571
	Simeon	1762	Middleboro	admn	12676
	Simeon	1793	Bridgewater	admn	12680
	Simeon	1794	Bridgewater	grdn	12681
	Simeon	1823	Middleboro	admn	12677
	Simeon	1857	Bridgewater	will	12678
	Simeon W	1863	Bridgewater	admn	12679
	Solomon	1761	Bridgewater	admn	12682
	Solomon	1853	Bridgewater	will	12683
	Spencer	1866	Bridgewater	will	12684
	Susanna	1761	Bridgewater	grdn	12653
	Susie E	1877	Marshfield	grdn	12685
	Theodore W	1881	Rochester	admn	12688
	Thomas F	1847	Middleboro	will	12687
	Thomas N	1839	Middleboro	trus	12686
	Timothy	1855	Lakeville	admn	12689
	Tisdale	1863	Lakeville	will	12690
	William	1722	Bridgewater	inve	12693
	William	1824	Bridgewater	grdn	12666
	William	1835	-----	grdn	12587

SURNAME	FIRST NAME	YEAR	PLACE	CASE	DOCKET
LEONARD	William C	1853	Brooklyn NY	admn	12692
	William C	1866	Middleboro	grdn	12691
	Zadock	1796	Middleboro	admn	12694
	Zebedee	1801	Middleboro	grdn	12582
	Zebedee	1868	Middleboro	will	12695
	Zebedee Jr	1835	-----	grdn	12587
	Zebulon	1795	Middleboro	admn	12696
LEONARDSON	Solomon	1675	Bridgewater	admn	12697
	Solomon	1686	Bridgewater	inve	12698
LESLIE	Edward	1869	N. Bridgewater	grdn	12699
	Patrick	1880	S. Scituate	admn	12700
LEWIS	Abel T	1863	Duxbury	admn	12701
	Abigail	1782	Middleboro	grdn	12702
	Annie	1865	Duxbury	grdn	12724
	Benjamin	1825	Plymouth	grdn	12751
	Betsey	1850	Marshfield	admn	12703
	Catherine	1850	Marshfield	will	12704
	Charles	1871	Marshfield	admn	12705
	Cora M	1870	Plymouth	grdn	12743
	Daniel	1753	Pembroke	admn	12706
	Daniel	1759	Pembroke	admn	12707
	Daniel	1868	Marshfield	admn	12708
	Daniel W	1793	Marshfield	grdn	12730
	David	1782	Middleboro	admn	12709
	David	1846	Hingham	will	12710
	David	1868	Rochester	admn	12711
	Deborah	1782	Middleboro	grdn	12702
	Ebenezer	1758	Rochester	admn	12712
	Ebenezer	1782	Middleboro	grdn	12702
	Ebenezer	1803	Hingham	will	12713
	Ebenezer P	1825	Middleboro	admn	12714
	Edith G	1881	Pembroke	admn	12715
	Edwin	1857	Plymouth	will	12716
	Eleazer	1727	Middleboro	admn	12717
	Elijah	1823	Hingham	will	12719
	Elijah	1846	Middleboro/Roch	admn	12721
	Elijah Jr	1819	Hingham	will	12718
	Elijah W	1869	Hingham	admn	12720
	Elizabeth	1782	Middleboro	grdn	12702
	Elizabeth	1874	Marshfield	will	12722
	Frederick	1771	Marshfield	admn	12723
	Georgiana	1865	Duxbury	grdn	12724
	Hannah	1824	Middleboro	grdn	12744
	Hosea	1822	Hingham	grdn	12725
	Jacob	1879	Hingham	admn	12726
	James	1727	Middleboro	admn	12727
	James	1762	Rochester	grdn	12731
	James	1793	Marshfield	will	12729
	James	1793	Marshfield	grdn	12730
	James	1799	Marshfield	admn	12728
	Jesse J	1848	W. Bridgewater	grdn	12732 a
	Jesse J H	1834	Plymouth	grdn	12733
	John H	1878	Brockton	grdn	12735
	John R	1863	Marion	admn	12734
	Keziah	1730	Middleboro	grdn	12736
	Lothrop	1762	Rochester	grdn	12731
	Lothrop	1782	Middleboro	grdn	12702
	Lothrop	1824	Middleboro	admn	12737
	Lucy	1824	Middleboro	grdn	12744
	Lucy	1833	Middleboro	grdn	12738
	Lucy	1848	Hingham	grdn	12739
	Lucy B	1862	Duxbury	adop	12740
	Marah	1730	Middleboro	grdn	12736
	Marsh	1819	Hingham	grdn	12741
	Mary	1822	Hingham	grdn	12725
	Mary	1824	Middleboro	grdn	12744
	Mary F	1879	Hingham	admn	12742
	Mary L	1870	Plymouth	grdn	12743
	Mercy	1782	Middleboro	grdn	12702
	Mercy D	1834	Plymouth	grdn	12733
	Nancy	1822	Hingham	grdn	12725

SURNAME	FIRST NAME	YEAR	PLACE	CASE	DOCKET
LEWIS	Nathaniel	1824	Middleboro	grdn	12744
	Remember	1782	Middleboro	grdn	12702
	Rosalinda	1824	Middleboro	grdn	12744
	Ruth	1825	Plymouth	grdn	12751
	Samuel	1730	Middleboro	grdn	12736
	Samuel W	1793	Marshfield	grdn	12730
	Sarah	1831	Scituate	admn	12745
	Sarah	1831	Scituate	grdn	12746 a
	Sarah	1831	Scituate	grdn	12747
	Stephen	1782	Middleboro	grdn	12702
	Stephen	1814	Rochester	grdn	12748 a
	Stephen	1822	Rochester	admn	12749
	Thomas	1845	Duxbury	admn	12750
	Welthea	1825	Plymouth	grdn	12751
	William	1821	Marshfield	admn	12753
	William Jr	1806	Plymouth	admn	12752
LIBBY	Mary J	1871	Abington	will	12754
LILE	Arthur	1719	Scituate	admn	12755
LINCOLN	Abigail	1846	Hingham	will	12756
	Abner	1825	Hingham	grdn	12757 a
	Abner	1826	Hingham	will	12758
	Adeline	1870	Hingham	admn	12759
	Alexander	1879	Hingham	admn	12760
	Alexander R	1880	Hingham	grdn	12857
	Alfred	1866	Hingham	admn	12761
	Alfred	1871	Hingham	grdn	12799
	Alonzo F	1871	Hingham	grdn	12762
	Ann	1822	Hingham	grdn	12763
	Asa	1840	Hingham	will	12764
	Barnabas	1822	Hingham	admn	12765
	Barnabas	1850	Hingham	admn	12766
	Barzillia	1858	Hingham	grdn	12767
	Bela	1878	Hingham	will	12768
	Benjamin	1810	Hingham	will	12769
	Benjamin	1842	Wareham	admn	12772
	Benjamin	1866	Hingham	admn	12770
	Benjamin C	1875	Hingham	grdn	12771
	Betsey	1861	Hingham	admn	12773
	Beza	1835	Hingham	will	12774
	Bradford	1865	Wareham	admn	12775
	Caleb	1819	Hingham	grdn	12776 a
	Caleb	1827	Scituate	will	12777
	Calvin A	1877	Hingham	admn	12778
	Charles	1880	Brockton	admn	12779
	Christiana	1849	Hingham	will	12780
	Cyrus	1870	Hanson	admn	12781
	David	1825	Hingham	will	12782
	David	1873	Hingham	will	12783
	Deborah	1822	Hingham	grdn	12763
	Deborah	1865	Hingham	will	12784
	Delight	1813	Hingham	grdn	12785
	Ebenezer	1841	Hingham	admn	12786
	Elijah	1813	Hingham	grdn	12785
	Elijah	1862	Hingham	admn	12787
	Elisha	1816	Abington	will	12788
	Elizabeth	1818	Hingham	will	12789
	Elizabeth S	1819	Hingham	grdn	12790
	Enos	1841	Hingham	admn	12791
	Ezekiel	1828	Hingham	admn	12792
	Ezra	1829	Hingham	admn	12793
	Francis	1828	Hingham	admn	12794
	Gorham	1869	Hingham	will	12795
	Hannah	1805	Hingham	grdn	12797
	Hannah	1811	Scituate	will	12796
	Hannah	1822	Hingham	will	12798
	Helen	1871	Hingham	grdn	12799
	Herman	1871	Hingham	grdn	12799
	Hezekiah	1853	Hingham	admn	12800
	Huldah	1820	Hingham	will	12801
	I Augustus	1871	N. Bridgewater	grdn	12802 a
	Isaac	1792	Scituate	will	12803

SURNAME	FIRST NAME	YEAR	PLACE	CASE	DOCKET
LINCOLN	Isaac S	1854	Wareham	admn	12804
	Israel	1810	Hingham	admn	12805
	Jacob	1780	Scituate	will	12806
	Jairus	1827	Hingham	admn	12807
	Jairus B	1870	Hingham	will	12808
	James	1837	Hingham	will	12810
	James O	1818	Hingham	admn	12809
	Jane	1851	Hingham	will	12811
	Jane	1857	Hingham	will	12812
	Jedediah	1856	Hingham	will	12813
	Job	1818	Hingham	will	12814
	John	1748	Pembroke	admn	12815
	John B	1832	Hingham	will	12816
	John M	1849	Hingham	will	12817
	Jonathan	1800	Abington	admn	12818
	Jonathan	1822	Hingham	will	12819
	Joseph	1762	Abington	will	12820
	Josephine W	1871	Abington	grdn	12821
	Jotham	1825	Hingham	will	12822
	Keziah	1843	Michigan	grdn	12834
	Laurinda	1879	Hingham	will	12823
	Leah	1856	Hingham	will	12824
	Leavitt	1841	Hingham	admn	12825
	Leila M	1870	Middleboro	adop	12849
	Levi	1819	Hingham	admn	12826
	Levi	1829	Hingham	will	12827
	Levi	1846	Hanson	admn	12828
	Levi P	1870	Hanson	grdn	12829
	Lucinda	1840	Hingham	admn	12830
	Lucy	1872	Hingham	will	12831
	Lucy	1877	Hingham	will	12832
	Luke P	1817	Bridgewater	grdn	12833
	Luther W	1843	Michigan	grdn	12834
	Lydia	1764	Scituate	grdn	12842
	Lydia	1863	Hingham	will	12835
	Maria S	1870	Hingham	will	12836
	Marshal	1857	Hingham	will	12837
	Marshal	1866	Hingham	will	12838
	Martha	1854	Hingham	will	12839
	Martha	1879	Hingham	will	12840
	Martin	1837	Hingham	will	12841
	Mary	1764	Scituate	grdn	12842
	Mary	1816	Hingham	admn	12844
	Mary	1822	Hingham	grdn	12763
	Mary	1847	Hingham	will	12843
	Mary	1853	Hingham	will	12845
	Mary	1874	Hingham	admn	12846
	Mary C	1877	Hingham	will	12847
	Mary Louise	1872	N. Bridgewater	adop	12848
	Mary O	1819	Hingham	grdn	12790
	Mary R	1870	Middleboro	adop	12849
	Matthew	1822	Hingham	will	12850
	Mehitable	1873	Hingham	will	12851
	Mercy S	1857	Hingham	admn	12852
	Mordecai	1728	Scituate	will	12853
	Nathan	1810	Hingham	will	12854
	Nathaniel	1804	Hingham	will	12855
	Nehemiah	1818	Bridgewater	will	12856
	Nichols	1822	Hingham	grdn	12763
	Nin Eva	1880	Hingham	grdn	12857
	Noah	1810	Hingham	will	12858
	Obadiah	1797	Scituate	admn	12859
	Perez	1856	Hingham	will	12860
	Rachel	1842	Hingham	will	12861
	Rachel	1864	Hingham	admn	12862
	Rachel	1870	Hingham	will	12863
	Rachel T	1878	Abington	admn	12864
	Rufus	1851	Wareham	admn	12865
	Rufus	1862	Hanson	admn	12866
	Ruth	1798	Pembroke	will	12867
	Ruth	1861	Hingham	admn	12868

SURNAME	FIRST NAME	YEAR	PLACE	CASE	DOCKET
LINCOLN	Samuel	1840	Hingham	grdn	12874
	Samuel B	1825	Hingham	admn	12872
	Samuel B	1827	Hingham	grdn	12873
	Samuel B	1875	Abington	will	12869
	Samuel J	1855	Hingham	admn	12870
	Samuel M	1864	Hingham	admn	12871
	Sarah	1871	Hingham	grdn	12799
	Seth	1839	Hingham	admn	12875
	Solomon	1763	Scituate	will	12876
	Solomon	1832	Hingham	will	12877
	Solomon	1853	Hingham	appt	12878
	Sophronia H	1858	Hingham	grdn	12767
	Stephen	1816	Hingham	will	12879
	Susan	1852	Hingham	will	12880
	Susan B	1869	Hingham	will	12881
	Susanna	1822	Hingham	admn	12882
	Susanna	1841	Hingham	admn	12883
	Tempe F	1833	Hingham	will	12884
	Thomas	1730	Rochester	admn	12885
	Thomas	1764	Scituate	grdn	12842
	Thomas W	1851	Hingham	grdn	12886
	Welcome	1860	Hingham	will	12887
	William	1840	Hingham	grdn	12874
	William	1879	Hingham	admn	12890
	William V	1802	Scituate	grdn	12888
	William V	1876	Brockton	admn	12889
	William W	1827	Hingham	grdn	12873
LINDSEY	Ephraim	1778	Pembroke	admn	12891
	Ernest W	1871	W. Bridgewater	grdn	12892
	James	1814	Pembroke	admn	12893
	Leila A	1871	W. Bridgewater	grdn	12892
	Martin	1843	Hanover	admn	12894
	Martin A	1871	Abington	admn	12895
	Rebecca	1857	Hanover	will	12896
LING	Samuel C	1832	Middleboro	admn	12897
	Thomas	1776	Middleboro	admn	12898
LITCHFIELD	Abial	1835	Scituate	admn	12899
	Abial G	1836	Scituate	grdn	12900
	Abigail	1793	Scituate	grdn	12901
	Abner	1843	Scituate	admn	12903
	Abner H	1801	Scituate	grdn	12902 a
	Albert	1863	Hingham	grdn	12907
	Albert S	1873	S. Scituate	will	12904
	Alfred	1857	S. Scituate	will	12905
	Alice M	1875	Hanover	grdn	12906
	Almena	1863	Hingham	grdn	12907
	Amos	1830	Scituate	will	12908
	Asa	1853	Scituate	admn	12909
	Barnabas	1788	Scituate	admn	12910
	Barnabas	1829	Scituate	will	12911
	Benjamin	1846	Scituate	admn	12912
	Benjamin	1863	Hingham	grdn	12907
	Benjamin	1864	Scituate	will	12913
	Billings	1873	S. Scituate	admn	12914
	Caroline	1844	Scituate	grdn	13019
	Charles	1831	Scituate	will	12915
	Clara	1874	Hingham	grdn	13006
	Cummings	1793	Scituate	grdn	12901
	Daniel	1820	Scituate	will	12916
	Daniel	1850	Scituate	will	12917
	Deborah	1814	Scituate	grdn	12983
	Deborah	1837	Scituate	admn	12918
	Edwin P	1875	Hanover	grdn	12906
	Eleazer	1780	Scituate	will	12920
	Eleazer	1832	Scituate	admn	12921
	Eleazer et al	1757	-----	decr	12919
	Electa W	1875	Scituate	admn	12922
	Elijah	1821	Scituate	will	12923
	Elijah	1870	S. Scituate	will	12924
	Elisha	1751	Scituate	grdn	13004
	Elisha	1751	Scituate	grdn	12925

SURNAME	FIRST NAME	YEAR	PLACE	CASE	DOCKET
LITCHFIELD	Elisha	1812	Scituate	will	12926
	Elisha	1827	Scituate	grdn	12927
	Eliza	1831	Scituate	grdn	13016
	Elizabeth	1836	Scituate	admn	12928
	Enoch	1873	Scituate	admn	12930
	Enoch 2nd	1843	Scituate	grdn	12929 a
	Ephraim	1792	Scituate	will	12931
	Fanny	1846	Abington	admn	12932
	Foster	1821	Scituate	admn	12933
	Frank W	1879	Scituate	grdn	12934
	Freelove	1854	Hingham	admn	12935
	George	1874	Hingham	grdn	13006
	George	1881	Scituate	admn	12936
	George R	1855	Scituate	grdn	13017
	Grace	1874	Hingham	grdn	13006
	Hannah	1793	Scituate	grdn	12901
	Hannah	1832	Scituate	will	12937
	Hannah	1872	Scituate	will	12938
	Harriet T	1839	Scituate	grdn	12939
	Hartwell	1875	Hingham	admn	12940
	Harvey	1877	Scituate	admn	12941
	Hattie	1874	Hingham	grdn	13006
	Helen M	1878	Hull	admn	12942
	Henrietta E	1874	S. Scituate	admn	12943
	Hersey	1806	Scituate	grdn	12944
	Hersey	1862	Scituate	admn	12945
	Howard	1881	Scituate	will	12946
	Hubbard	1875	Scituate	will	12947
	Isaac	1800	Scituate	will	12948
	Isaac	1881	Scituate	admn	12949
	James	1735	Scituate	admn	12950
	James	1787	Scituate	admn	12951
	James	1803	Scituate	admn	12952
	James	1812	Scituate	will	12953
	James	1863	Hingham	grdn	12907
	Jane	1844	Scituate	grdn	13019
	Joab	1842	Scituate	admn	12954
	Joab B	1862	Hingham	admn	12955
	Job	1822	Scituate	admn	12956
	Joseph	1827	Scituate	grdn	12927
	Joseph H	1878	Hingham	admn	12957
	Josiah	1707	Scituate	admn	12958
	Josiah	1718	Scituate	will	12959
	Josiah	1787	Scituate	will	12960
	Josiah	1818	Scituate	grdn	12961 a
	Josiah	1823	Scituate	admn	12962
	Justin	1875	Scituate	admn	12963
	Keziah	1852	Scituate	admn	12964
	Lawrence	1814	Scituate	admn	12965
	Lawrence	1857	Scituate	will	12966
	Lewis	1871	Hanover	grdn	12967 a
	Liba	1819	Scituate	admn	12968
	Lillis	1844	Scituate	will	12969
	Lincoln	1877	Scituate	admn	12970
	Lot	1869	S. Scituate	will	12971
	Lucinda W	1875	Hanover	grdn	12906
	Lydia	1814	Scituate	will	12972
	Lydia	1814	Scituate	will	12973
	Maria	1863	Hingham	grdn	12907
	Maria	1874	Scituate	will	12974
	Martha	1834	Scituate	grdn	12975
	Martha	1877	Scituate	admn	12976
	Mary	1874	Hanover	will	12977
	Mary G	1881	Scituate	admn	12979
	Mary J	1841	Scituate	grdn	12981
	Mary Jane	1859	Scituate	admn	12980
	Mary W	1877	Scituate	will	12978
	Melzar	1831	Scituate	admn	12982
	Merrill	1814	Scituate	grdn	12983
	Meshach	1846	Scituate	admn	12984
	Milton	1875	Scituate	admn	12985

SURNAME	FIRST NAME	YEAR	PLACE	CASE	DOCKET
LITCHFIELD	Nathan	1826	Scituate	admn	12986
	Nellie	1874	Hingham	grdn	13006
	Nicholas	1750	Scituate	will	12987
	Nicholas	1780	Scituate	will	12988
	Nymphus	1875	Scituate	will	12989
	Orange	1855	Scituate	will	12990
	Paul	1876	Scituate	will	12991
	Perez	1860	Scituate	admn	12992
	Persis	1835	Scituate	will	12993
	Peter	1880	Scituate	admn	12994
	Polly	1852	Scituate	will	12997
	Polly D	1829	Scituate	grdn	12995
	Polly D	1835	Scituate	admn	12996
	Priscilla	1793	Scituate	grdn	12901
	Rebecca	1855	Scituate	grdn	13017
	Rebecca L	1841	Scituate	grdn	12981
	Rebecca L	1863	Scituate	grdn	12998 a
	Roland	1829	Scituate	will	12999
	Roswell L	1878	Hingham	grdn	13000
	Rufus	1861	S. Scituate	admn	13001
	Rufus	1878	Scituate	will	13002
	Ruth	1751	Scituate	grdn	13004
	Ruth	1776	Scituate	will	13003
	Samuel	1767	Scituate	admn	13005
	Samuel H	1874	Hingham	grdn	13006
	Sarah F	1821	Scituate	grdn	13007
	Sarah T	1876	Scituate	admn	13008
	Seabury	1793	Scituate	grdn	12901
	Siba	1814	Scituate	grdn	12983
	Simeon	1841	Scituate	will	13009
	Stephen	1844	Scituate	admn	13010
	Stockbridge	1808	Hingham	admn	13011
	Sumner	1833	Scituate	grdn	13013
	Sumner O	1878	Scituate	admn	13012
	Thomas	1803	Scituate	will	13014
	Thomas	1844	Scituate	grdn	13019
	Thomas	1863	Scituate	will	13015
	Turner	1831	Scituate	grdn	13016
	Warren	1831	Scituate	grdn	13016
	Webster	1855	Scituate	grdn	13017
	Wilbur T	1878	Hingham	grdn	13000
	William	1833	Scituate	admn	13018
	William H	1844	Scituate	grdn	13019
	Winnet A	1833	Scituate	grdn	13013
LITTLE	Abigail	1779	Pembroke	grdn	13020
	Almira	1809	Marshfield	grdn	13068
	Almira	1836	Marshfield	grdn	13031
	Amos	1809	Marshfield	grdn	13068
	Amos	1836	Marshfield	grdn	13031
	Amos R	1815	Marshfield	admn	13021
	Anna	1779	Pembroke	grdn	13020
	Anna	1826	Marshfield	grdn	13022 a
	Anna	1881	Marshfield	will	13023
	Barnabas	1789	Scituate	will	13024
	Bethiah	1727	Kingston	grdn	13055
	Charles	1724	Plymouth/King'n	admn	13025
	Charles	1779	Pembroke	grdn	13020
	Charles	1793	Marshfield	grdn	13064
	Charles	1821	Pembroke	will	13026
	Constant	1772	Marshfield	will	13027
	Constant	1821	Marshfield	admn	13028
	Daniel P	1878	Marshfield	grdn	13048
	David	1779	Scituate	will	13029
	Edward	1809	Marshfield	grdn	13068
	Eliza J	1876	Marshfield	admn	13030
	Elizabeth R	1836	Marshfield	grdn	13031
	Ephraim	1719	Marshfield	will	13033
	Ephraim	1724	Plymouth	will	13032
	Ephraim	1808	Marshfield	admn	13034
	Ephraim	1809	Marshfield	grdn	13035 a
	George	1712	Plymouth	grdn	13079

SURNAME	FIRST NAME	YEAR	PLACE	CASE	DOCKET
LITTLE	George	1763	Plympton	admn	13036
	George	1809	Marshfield	will	13037
	George	1811	Scituate	admn	13038
	Isaac	1699	Marshfield	admn	13039
	Isaac	1712	Plymouth	grdn	13079
	Isaac	1755	Plympton	will	13040
	Isaac	1758	Pembroke	will	13041
	Isaac	1774	Pembroke	admn	13042
	Isaac	1779	Pembroke	grdn	13020
	Isaac	1846	Pembroke	will	13043
	Isaac	1864	Hingham	admn	13044
	James	1803	Scituate	admn	13045
	James	1804	Scituate	grdn	13047
	James	1810	Scituate	admn	13046
	James	1826	Marshfield	grdn	13069
	Joanna W	1878	Marshfield	grdn	13048
	John	1767	Marshfield	will	13049
	John	1835	Marshfield	will	13050
	John S	1859	N. Bridgewater	grdn	13051
	Judah	1779	Pembroke	grdn	13020
	Lemuel	1712	Plymouth	grdn	13079
	Lemuel	1725	Edgartown	inve	13052
	Lemuel	1758	Pembroke	grdn	13054
	Lemuel	1799	Marshfield	will	13053
	Lucie	1727	Kingston	grdn	13055
	Lucy	1756	Kingston	will	13056
	Luther	1793	Marshfield	grdn	13058
	Luther	1842	Marshfield	will	13057
	Lydia	1804	Scituate	grdn	13047
	Lydia	1826	Marshfield	grdn	13069
	Marcy	1758	Pembroke	grdn	13054
	Mary	1712	Plymouth	grdn	13079
	Mary	1748	Chilmark	grdn	13060
	Mary	1755	Plymouth	will	13059
	Mary	1835	Pembroke	admn	13061
	Mary J	1836	Marshfield	grdn	13031
	Mayhew	1736	Plymouth	admn	13062
	Mayhue	1712	Plymouth	grdn	13079
	Mercy	1779	Pembroke	will	13063
	Nancy	1793	Marshfield	grdn	13064
	Nathaniel	1715	Marshfield	admn	13065
	Olive	1826	Marshfield	grdn	13069
	Otis	1779	Pembroke	grdn	13020
	Peabody	1793	Marshfield	admn	13066
	Penelope	1803	Marshfield	will	13067
	Polly	1809	Marshfield	grdn	13068
	Priscilla	1826	Marshfield	grdn	13069
	Rachel	1838	Marshfield	will	13071
	Rachel W	1810	Marshfield	admn	13070
	Rebecca W	1870	Marshfield	will	13072
	Sarah	1760	Plymouth	admn	13073
	Sarah	1800	Marshfield	admn	13074
	Sarah	1836	Marshfield	grdn	13031
	Solomon	1877	Marshfield	admn	13075
	Statira	1809	Marshfield	grdn	13068
	Susanna	1793	Marshfield	grdn	13058
	Thomas	1712	Plymouth	admn	13078
	Thomas	1712	Plymouth	grdn	13079
	Thomas	1815	Marshfield	will	13076
	Thomas	1842	Marshfield	admn	13077
	William F	1879	Marshfield	admn	13081
	William H	1844	Marshfield	grdn	13080 a
LITTLEFIELD	Fidelia R	1846	N. Bridgewater	grdn	13082
	Frederick H	1876	Brockton	admn	13083
LITTLEJOHN	William	1826	Wareham	admn	13084
LIVINGSTON	Barzillai	1782	Rochester	will	13085
LOBDELL	Ebenezer	1748	Plympton	will	13086
	Ebenezer	1805	Plympton	admn	13087
	Eliza F	1877	Mattapoisett	will	13088
	Emma F	1877	Brockton	grdn	13093
	George	1811	Plympton	grdn	13091

SURNAME	FIRST NAME	YEAR	PLACE	CASE	DOCKET
LOBDELL	George B	1870	Plympton	admn	13090
	George W	1874	Mattapoisett	will	13089
	Hannah	1811	Plympton	grdn	13091
	Hannah	1820	Plympton	admn	13092
	Ida E	1877	Brockton	grdn	13093
	Isaac F	1876	Plympton	grdn	13094 a
	Isaac F	1876	Plympton	admn	13095
	Jeremiah	1819	Kingston	admn	13096
	Judith	1818	Plympton	will	13097
	Lydia	1748	Plympton	grdn	13098
	Maria	1832	Kingston	admn	13099
	Sally	1818	Plympton	grdn	13100 a
	Thomas	1811	Plympton	grdn	13091
	Thomas J Jr	1820	Plymouth	grdn	13101
LOCKE	Frances C	1880	Plymouth	admn	13102
	Mary A	1873	Plymouth	will	13103
	Sally S	1878	Hingham	will	13104
	Thomas	1727	Plymouth	admn	13105
	William	1861	Hingham	will	13106
LOCKWOOD	Charles	1868	Middleboro	grdn	13108
	Charles M	1868	Middleboro	admn	13107
	Elton	1868	Middleboro	grdn	13108
	Emily	1868	Middleboro	grdn	13108
	J Frank	1868	Middleboro	grdn	13108
	Julia M	1868	Middleboro	grdn	13108
	Samuel	1868	Middleboro	grdn	13108
LOMBARD	Charles	1795	Rochester	grdn	13111
	James L	1876	Middleboro	grdn	13109
	John	1795	Rochester	grdn	13111
	Joseph	1795	Rochester	grdn	13111
	Mary	1795	Rochester	grdn	13111
	Phebe	1795	Rochester	grdn	13111
	Samuel	1795	Rochester	admn	13110
	Samuel	1795	Rochester	grdn	13111
	Thomas	1807	Sandwich	grdn	13112
LONG	Frederick	1880	Hingham	admn	13113
LOOK	Adam	1795	Rochester	admn	13114
	Jane	1844	Rochester	admn	13115
	John	1824	Rochester	admn	13117
	John Jr	1803	Rochester	admn	13116
	Joseph	1857	Rochester	will	13118
LORDAN	Elizabeth A	1872	Hingham	grdn	13120
	Hannah	1872	Hingham	grdn	13120
	John	1872	Hingham	grdn	13120
	Julia	1872	Hingham	grdn	13120
	Michael	1872	Hingham	grdn	13120
	Timothy	1872	Hingham	admn	13119
	Timothy	1872	Hingham	grdn	13120
LORING	Abbott	1848	Duxbury	grdn	13121
	Albert B	1880	S. Scituate	admn	13122
	Alden	1861	Pembroke	will	13123
	Alfred H	1860	Hingham	admn	13124
	Amelia B	1875	Hingham	will	13125
	Anna	1804	Duxbury	will	13126
	Anna	1852	Hingham	will	13127
	Anna B	1822	Rochester	grdn	13183
	Bailey	1830	Duxbury	grdn	13128
	Barnabas	1825	Duxbury	grdn	13136
	Benjamin	1724	Duxbury	grdn	13130
	Benjamin	1833	Plympton	admn	13129
	Caleb	1732	Plympton	will	13131
	Caleb	1742	Plympton	grdn	13153
	Caleb	1746	Plympton	admn	13132
	Caleb	1833	Plympton	will	13133
	Caroline T	1860	Hingham	grdn	13161
	Christiana	1827	Hingham	will	13134
	Daniel	1825	Duxbury	grdn	13136
	Daniel B	1822	Rochester	admn	13135
	David H	1863	Middleboro	will	13137
	Deborah	1724	Duxbury	grdn	13130
	Deborah	1741	Duxbury	grdn	13214

SURNAME	FIRST NAME	YEAR	PLACE	CASE	DOCKET
LORING	Dinah	1837	Bridgewater	will	13138
	Elizabeth	1808	Hingham	will	13139
	Elpalet	1853	Hingham	will	13140
	Enos	1837	Hingham	admn	13141
	Ezekiel	1825	Plympton	will	13142
	Fearing	1857	Hingham	will	13143
	Frederick W	1830	Duxbury	grdn	13128
	Freeman	1820	Duxbury	admn	13144
	George	1847	Duxbury	admn	13145
	George	1868	N. Bridgewater	admn	13146
	Hannah	1724	Duxbury	grdn	13130
	Hannah	1811	Plympton	will	13147
	Hannah	1840	Plympton	will	13148
	Hannah	1874	Marshfield	admn	13149
	Hawkes	1850	Hingham	admn	13150
	Huldah B	1860	Hull	will	13151
	Ignatius	1742	Plympton	admn	13152
	Ignatius	1742	Plympton	grdn	13153
	Isaac T	1879	Duxbury	admn	13154
	Jabez	1818	Plympton	will	13155
	James Jr	1825	Duxbury	grdn	13136
	Joanna	1836	Hingham	will	13156
	Job	1825	Hingham	will	13157
	Job	1839	Hingham	grdn	13158
	Job	1843	Hingham	admn	13159
	Job	1860	Hingham	admn	13160
	Job O	1860	Hingham	grdn	13161
	John	1770	Bridgewater	admn	13162
	John	1820	Plympton	admn	13163
	John	1828	Hull	will	13164
	John	1876	Hingham	will	13165
	Jonathan	1815	Hingham	admn	13166
	Joseph	1742	Plympton	grdn	13153
	Joshua	1741	Duxbury	grdn	13214
	Joshua	1752	Duxbury	admn	13167
	Joshua	1781	Duxbury	will	13168
	Joshua	1799	Plympton	admn	13170
	Joshua	1810	Hingham	will	13169
	Joshua	1858	Marshfield	admn	13172
	Joshua	1864	Plympton	admn	13171
	Joshua	1879	Marshfield	admn	13173
	Judah	1825	Duxbury	grdn	13136
	Judah	1832	Duxbury	will	13174
	Levi	1741	Duxbury	grdn	13214
	Levi	1821	Duxbury	will	13175
	Levi	1864	Duxbury	will	13177
	Levi E	1834	Duxbury	admn	13176
	Lucy	1871	Hull	admn	13178
	Lydia	1742	Plympton	grdn	13153
	Lydia	1771	Plympton	admn	13179
	Lydia	1835	Hingham	will	13180
	Lydia	1837	Hingham	admn	13181
	Mary	1742	Plympton	grdn	13153
	Mary	1822	Rochester	grdn	13183
	Mary A	1840	Hingham	grdn	13207
	Mary R C	1839	Duxbury	will	13182
	Mehitable	1834	Hull	will	13184
	Melzar	1832	Plympton	admn	13185
	Nabby	1840	Hingham	will	13186
	Nancy	1848	Duxbury	admn	13187
	Nat	1837	Hingham	will	13188
	Nathaniel	1774	Pembroke	will	13189
	Nathaniel	1820	Pembroke	admn	13190
	Nathaniel	1851	Pembroke	admn	13191
	Perez	1741	Duxbury	grdn	13214
	Perez	1827	Duxbury	admn	13192
	Peter	1830	Hingham	will	13193
	Policarpus	1770	Plympton	will	13194
	Pyam	1873	Hingham	admn	13195
	Rachel	1813	Hingham	will	13196
	Richardson F	1868	Hingham	will	13197

SURNAME	FIRST NAME	YEAR	PLACE	CASE	DOCKET
LORING	Sally C	1873	Hingham	will	13198
	Samuel	1814	Hull	admn	13199
	Samuel	1816	Duxbury	will	13202
	Samuel	1840	Hull	will	13200
	Samuel	1874	Hull	admn	13201
	Samuel Jr	1847	Duxbury	admn	13203
	Sarah	1746	Plympton	admn	13204
	Sarah	1834	Plympton	admn	13205
	Sarah	1840	Hingham	grdn	13207
	Sarah A	1860	Hingham	grdn	13161
	Sarah J	1881	Hingham	admn	13206
	Simeon	1741	Duxbury	grdn	13214
	Simeon	1842	Plympton	admn	13208
	Southworth	1808	Plympton	admn	13209
	Thomas	1718	Duxbury	admn	13212
	Thomas	1739	Duxbury	admn	13213
	Thomas	1741	Duxbury	grdn	13214
	Thomas	1828	Hingham	will	13210
	Thomas	1863	Hingham	will	13211
	William	1742	Plympton	grdn	13153
	William	1815	Duxbury	admn	13215
	Winslow	1876	Marshfield	will	13216
	Zenas	1836	Hingham	will	13217
LOTHROP	Alice	1868	W. Bridgewater	grdn	13232
	Ambrose	1828	Hingham	admn	13218
	Ancil	1750	Plymouth	admn	13219
	Ancil	1756	Plymouth	grdn	13220
	Anna E	1832	W. Bridgewater	grdn	13223
	Annie M	1859	N. Bridgewater	grdn	13221
	Azel	1832	W. Bridgewater	will	13222
	Azel	1832	W. Bridgewater	grdn	13223
	Barnabas	1838	W. Bridgewater	will	13224
	Benjamin	1787	Kingston	admn	13226
	Benjamin Jr	1757	Plymouth	admn	13225
	Betty	1756	Plymouth	grdn	13220
	Clarissa	1820	Bridgewater	admn	13227
	Daniel I	1824	Bridgewater	admn	13228
	David	1808	Bridgewater	will	13229
	Edward	1796	Bridgewater	admn	13230
	Edward H	1828	Hingham	grdn	13231
	Fanny	1868	W. Bridgewater	grdn	13232
	Hannah R	1847	W. Bridgewater	grdn	13233
	Isaac	1743	Plymouth	will	13234
	Isaac	1750	Plymouth	admn	13235
	Isaac	1808	Plymouth	will	13236
	John	1743	Bridgewater	admn	13240
	John	1761	Plymouth	will	13237
	John	1782	Wareham	admn	13238
	John	1794	Wareham	grdn	13239
	John E	1832	W. Bridgewater	grdn	13223
	John E	1861	W. Bridgewater	will	13241
	John M	1868	W. Bridgewater	will	13242
	Jonathan	1819	Bridgewater	will	13243
	Lizzie	1868	W. Bridgewater	grdn	13232
	Lydia	1756	Plymouth	grdn	13220
	Mark	1690	Bridgewater	will	13244
	Mark	1868	W. Bridgewater	grdn	13232
	Mary	1756	Plymouth	grdn	13220
	Mary	1792	Plymouth	admn	13245
	Melatiah	1771	Plymouth	admn	13246
	Nahum P	1859	N. Bridgewater	grdn	13221
	Nathaniel	1828	Plymouth	will	13247
	Olive J	1873	W. Bridgewater	admn	13248
	Philena C	1852	W. Bridgewater	admn	13249
	Samuel	1724	Bridgewater	will	13250
	Samuel	1777	Bridgewater	will	13251
	Sarah	1743	Bridgewater	grdn	13255
	Seth	1773	Bridgewater	grdn	13252
	Seth	1804	Bridgewater	will	13253
	Simeon	1808	Bridgewater	will	13254
	Spencer	1868	W. Bridgewater	grdn	13232

SURNAME	FIRST NAME	YEAR	PLACE	CASE	DOCKET
LOTHROP	Susanna	1743	Bridgewater	grdn	13255
	Thomas C	1839	Wareham	admn	13256
	Vesta C	1832	W. Bridgewater	grdn	13223
	William	1756	Plymouth	grdn	13220
	Zephaniah	1850	W. Bridgewater	admn	13257
LOUD	Annie C	1874	Plymouth	grdn	13258
	Arthur J	1864	Plymouth	grdn	13259
	Arthur J	1872	Plymouth	admn	13260
	Bezaleel	1839	Abington	admn	13261
	Charles H	1859	Abington	grdn	13262
	Ebenezer	1863	Hingham	admn	13263
	Elizabeth J	1859	Abington	grdn	13262
	Elizabeth L	1861	Plymouth	admn	13264
	Elsebere C	1873	Plymouth	will	13265
	George C	1873	Abington	grdn	13266
	Hugh	1873	Plymouth	admn	13267
	Jacob H	1880	Plymouth	will	13268
	James	1834	Hull	will	13269
	Jason	1874	Duxbury	admn	13270
	Joshua B	1873	Abington	admn	13271
	Thomas	1863	Hingham	admn	13272
	Walter H	1874	Plymouth	grdn	13258
	William D	1874	Plymouth	grdn	13258
LOVELL	Abigail C	1881	Middleboro	admn	13273
	Anna	1719	Middleboro	will	13274
	Jacob	1798	Abington	will	13275
	Jacob	1871	Abington	admn	13276
	James	1720	Weymouth	admn	13277
	John	1759	Wareham	admn	13278
	Joseph	1817	Middleboro	admn	13279
	Leander	1879	Plymouth	will	13280
	Noah	1830	Abington	admn	13281
	Obadiah	1810	Abington	will	13282
	Olive	1844	Hull	admn	13283
	Polly	1806	Abington	grdn	13285
	Samuel	1807	Hull	will	13284
	Sarah	1806	Abington	grdn	13285
	Shubael S	1866	Bridgewater	admn	13286
	Sylvanus	1800	Middleboro	admn	13287
	Thomas	1746	Bridgewater	admn	13288
	Thomas	1870	Middleboro	will	13289
LOVERING	John P	1848	Kingston	grdn	13298
	Joseph F	1848	Kingston	grdn	13290
	Mary A	1848	Kingston	grdn	13298
	Sarah	1848	Kingston	grdn	13298
	Susan	1848	Kingston	grdn	13298
LOVETT	Horace F	1855	Hingham	grdn	13291
LOVEWELL	Joseph	1724	Weymouth	admn	13292
LOW	Arthur	1690/1	Marshfield	admn	13293
	Samuel	1805	Marshfield	admn	13294
	Thomas	1804	Marshfield	admn	13295
	Thomas	1857	Duxbury	admn	13296
LOWDEN	Abner	1776	Duxbury	admn	13297
	Betsey	1840	Duxbury	admn	13298
	Deborah	1862	Duxbury	admn	13299
	Elizabeth	1851	Duxbury	will	13300
	Eunice	1866	Duxbury	will	13301
	Huldah	1817	Duxbury	grdn	13303
	Joanna	1817	Duxbury	grdn	13303
	Joanna P	1866	Duxbury	admn	13302
	John	1805	Pembroke	will	13304
	Josiah	1778	Duxbury	grdn	13305
	Lydia	1817	Duxbury	grdn	13303
	Mary	1817	Duxbury	grdn	13303
	Mercy	1778	Duxbury	grdn	13305
	Michael	1803	Duxbury	will	13306
	Richard	1777	Duxbury	admn	13307
	Richard	1823	Hanson	will	13308
	Ruth	1813	Pembroke	admn	13309
	Silvanus	1817	Duxbury	will	13310
LOWELL	Mabel Warren	1862	Abington	adop	13311

SURNAME	FIRST NAME	YEAR	PLACE	CASE	DOCKET
LUCAS	Abial	1738	Plympton	grdn	13376
	Abigail	1801	Carver	will	13312
	Abigail	1849	Carver	admn	13313
	Abijah	1838	Carver	will	13314
	Abijah	1849	Carver	admn	13315
	Allen	1815	Plymouth	grdn	13358
	Alvin	1865	Kingston	admn	13316
	Anna T	1842	Carver	grdn	13317
	Ansel	1853	Carver	admn	13318
	Augustus H	1880	Plymouth	will	13319
	Barnabas	1746	Plympton	grdn	13320
	Barnabas	1778	Plympton	admn	13321
	Barnabas	1807	Plymouth	admn	13322
	Barnabas	1824	Plymouth	admn	13323
	Bela	1821	Plymouth	admn	13324
	Benjamin	1821	Carver	admn	13325
	Benjamin	1826	Carver	grdn	13338
	Benoni	1730	Plympton	will	13326
	Betty	1839	Plymouth	grdn	13327 a
	Caleb	1818	Carver	grdn	13329 a
	Caleb	1872	Middleboro	admn	13328
	Cynthia	1829	Plymouth	grdn	13330
	Cynthia	1848	Plymouth	grdn	13330 +
	Daniel	1864	Carver	admn	13331
	David	1796	Kingston	admn	13332
	David	1855	Kingston	admn	13333
	Eldora C	1864	Carver	grdn	13334
	Elisha	1756	Plympton	will	13335
	Elisha	1796	Carver	will	13336
	Elizabeth	1738	Plympton	grdn	13376
	Elizabeth	1798	Carver	admn	13337
	Erastus	1826	Carver	grdn	13338
	Ezra	1853	Plympton	will	13339
	Hannah	1768	Plympton	grdn	13362
	Harriet A	1848	Middleboro	grdn	13340
	Harvey	1867	Carver	admn	13341
	Hosea	1861	Kingston	will	13342
	Isaac	1815	Plymouth	grdn	13358
	Isaac	1826	Carver	grdn	13338
	Isaac J	1878	Plymouth	admn	13343
	James	1750	Plympton	admn	13348
	James	1756	Plympton	grdn	13349
	James	1773	Plympton	grdn	13347 a
	James	1825	Plymouth	admn	13344
	James F	1850	Kingston	admn	13345
	James F	1861	Kingston	grdn	13346
	Jennie H	1869	Plymouth	grdn	13350
	Joanna	1845	Middleboro	admn	13351
	John	1768	Plympton	admn	13352
	John	1803	Carver	admn	13353
	John	1826	Carver	grdn	13338
	Joseph	1742	Plympton	will	13354
	Joseph	1774	Plymouth	grdn	13355 a
	Joseph	1807	Carver	admn	13356
	Levi	1814	Plymouth	will	13357
	Levi	1815	Plymouth	grdn	13358
	Lois	1857	Carver	admn	13359
	Lot S	1850	Carver	grdn	13360
	Luther	1867	Plymouth	admn	13361
	Lydia	1768	Plympton	grdn	13362
	Martin L	1864	Carver	admn	13363
	Molly	1738	Plympton	grdn	13376
	Nathan	1796	Carver	grdn	13364
	Nathan	1854	Kingston	admn	13365
	Nathaniel	1805	Carver	grdn	13366
	Persis	1826	Carver	grdn	13338
	Persis	1850	Carver	admn	13367
	Repentance	1738	Plympton	grdn	13376
	Rhoda	1850	Plympton	admn	13368
	Ruth	1855	Carver	will	13369
	Samuel	1715/6	Plymouth	will	13370

SURNAME	FIRST NAME	YEAR	PLACE	CASE	DOCKET	
LUCAS	Samuel	1736	Plympton	admn	13375	
	Samuel	1738	Plympton	grdn	13376	
	Samuel	1749	Plympton	admn	13374	
	Samuel	1756	Plympton	grdn	13349	
	Samuel	1792	Carver	will	13373	
	Samuel	1813	Carver	admn	13372	
	Samuel	1838	Carver	will	13371	
	Seth	1865	Wareham	grdn	13377	
	Susanna	1768	Plympton	grdn	13362	
	Thomas	1760	Marshfield	admn	13378	
	Warren	1860	Middleboro	admn	13379	
	William	1768	Plympton	grdn	13362	
	William	1770	Plymouth	will	13380	
	Zellah	1826	Carver	grdn	13338	
LUCE	Alfred	1877	Mattapoisett	grdn	13381	
	Barnabas	1808	Rochester	will	13382	
	Betsey	1854	Plymouth	will	13384	
	Betsey	1874	Marion	will	13383	
	Crosbe	1808	Plymouth	admn	13385	
	Crosbe	1829	Plymouth	will	13386	
	David	1835	Rochester	admn	13387	
	Edwin	1856	Marion	admn	13388	
	Edwin	1856	Marion	grdn	13389	
	Elisha	1850	Rochester	admn	13390	
	Eunice W	1872	Marion	admn	13391	
	Franklin N	1837	Rochester	grdn	13392	a
	George	1877	Mattapoisett	grdn	13381	
	George A	1875	Marion	admn	13393	
	Hannah	1802	Rochester	grdn	13399	
	Henry C	1873	Marion	admn	13394	
	James	1798	Rochester	admn	13398	
	James	1802	Rochester	grdn	13399	
	James	1837	Rochester	admn	13396	
	James	1837	Rochester	grdn	13397	
	James	1850	Rochester	admn	13395	
	Jonathan	1856	Marion	grdn	13389	
	Lydia	1837	Rochester	grdn	13397	
	Lydia	1860	Mattapoisett	will	13400	
	Mary	1856	Marion	grdn	13401	a
	Mary	1858	Marion	admn	13402	
	Mary A	1877	Mattapoisett	will	13403	
	Roland L	1856	Marion	grdn	13389	
	Rowland	1852	Rochester	admn	13404	
	Seth	1802	Plymouth	admn	13405	
	Sprowell	1802	Rochester	grdn	13399	
	Stephen	1807	Rochester	will	13406	
	Stephen	1808	Rochester	grdn	13407	
	Stephen C	1874	Marion	will	13408	
	Susie	1877	Mattapoisett	grdn	13381	
	Thomas	1837	Rochester	grdn	13397	
	Timothy	1856	Marion	grdn	13389	
	William	1802	Rochester	grdn	13399	
	William	1847	Rochester	admn	13409	
	William	1876	Mattapoisett	admn	13410	
LUCIHE	John	1878	Hull	will	13411	
LUDDEN	Eliza L	1866	E. Bridgewater	grdn	13412	
	George E	1866	E. Bridgewater	grdn	13412	
	Herbert R	1866	E. Bridgewater	grdn	13412	
LUDDY	Eddy	1871	Abington	grdn	13413	
	James	1871	Abington	grdn	13413	
	John	1871	Abington	grdn	13413	
	Mary E	1871	Abington	grdn	13413	
	Mary Jane	1881	S. Abington	adop	13414	
LUDINGTON	Almaria K	1876	Brockton	admn	13415	
	Elliot K	1876	Brockton	grdn	13416	
LUMBARD	Amelia	1832	Rochester	grdn	13417	
	Charles	1829	Rochester	admn	13418	
	Joseph	1818	Rochester	admn	13419	
	Lucy	1832	Rochester	grdn	13417	
	Mary	1832	Rochester	grdn	13417	
LUMBER	Caleb	1749	Rochester	will	13420	

SURNAME	FIRST NAME	YEAR	PLACE	CASE	DOCKET
LUMBER	Caleb	1750	Rochester	admn	13421
LUMBERT	Thomas	1664	-----	admn	13422
LUNT	William	1764	Middleboro	admn	13423
LUTHER	Ada J	1875	Hanson	grdn	13426
	Annie E	1865	Plymouth	grdn	13424
	Austin E	1865	Plymouth	grdn	13424
	Edward Y	1875	Hanson	admn	13425
	Grace G	1875	Hanson	grdn	13426
	Job	1865	Hanson	will	13427
	Lucy A	1875	Hanson	grdn	13426
	Nathaniel C L	1865	Plymouth	grdn	13424
LUZARDER	George E Jr	1873	E. Bridgewater	admn	13428
	Samuel B	1878	S. Abington	will	13429
LYNCH	Catherine	1881	Wareham	grdn	13431
	Dennis	1879	Brockton	admn	13430
	Edward	1881	Wareham	grdn	13431
	James	1871	Plymouth	admn	13433
	James B	1867	Plymouth	admn	13432
	Samuel B	1873	Plymouth	grdn	13434
LYNES	John	1867	E. Bridgewater	will	13435
LYON	Abby J	1866	N. Bridgewater	grdn	13449
	Abner W	1844	Bridgewater	grdn	13436
	Alice B	1881	Bridgewater	adop	13437
	Chloe R	1820	Middleboro	grdn	13457
	Edward	1865	Hanson	grdn	13441
	Eunice J	1858	Middleboro	grdn	13447
	Frederick	1859	Plympton	admn	13438
	Granville W	1866	N. Bridgewater	grdn	13449
	Henry	1821	Halifax	admn	13439
	Isaac	1848	Middleboro	admn	13440
	James	1865	Hanson	grdn	13441
	Jane W	1820	Middleboro	grdn	13457
	Jedediah	1807	Middleboro	will	13442
	Joanna	1822	Halifax	grdn	13443
	Joanna	1830	Halifax	admn	13444
	Lemuel	1789	Middleboro	admn	13445
	Lemuel	1848	Middleboro	admn	13446
	Lemuel M	1858	Middleboro	grdn	13447
	Mary	1865	Hanson	grdn	13441
	Mary W	1866	N. Bridgewater	grdn	13449
	Mary W	1875	E. Bridgewater	admn	13448
	Obadiah	1786	Plympton	admn	13450
	Obadiah	1846	Halifax	will	13451
	Phebe	1820	Middleboro	grdn	13457
	Phebe	1839	Middleboro	will	13452
	Priam	1855	Halifax	admn	13453
	Samuel	1756	Middleboro	admn	13454
	Sarah	1865	Hanson	grdn	13441
	Vinal	1820	Middleboro	admn	13456
	Vinal	1820	Middleboro	grdn	13457
	Vinal	1866	N. Bridgewater	admn	13455
MCALPINE	Olive C	1867	Wareham	will	13756
MCCABE	Patrick	1850	N. Bridgewater	admn	13757
MACCALL	Anna	1709	Marshfield	admn	13458
	James	1693	Marshfield	admn	13459
MCCAMMON	David	1856	Plymouth	admn	13758
	Mary	1856	Plymouth	grdn	13759
MCCARTER	Charles	1864	E. Bridgewater	admn	13760
	Priscilla	1839	Plymouth	grdn	13761
MCCARTY	Daniel	1869	N. Bridgewater	grdn	13763
	Dennis	1869	N. Bridgewater	admn	13762
	Ellen	1868	N. Bridgewater	grdn	13765
	Hannah	1868	N. Bridgewater	grdn	13765
	Hannah	1869	N. Bridgewater	grdn	13763
	James	1755	Abington	admn	13764
	John	1868	N. Bridgewater	grdn	13765
	Katie	1869	N. Bridgewater	grdn	13763
	Michael	1869	Plymouth	will	13766
	Patrick	1869	N. Bridgewater	grdn	13763
	Timothy	1868	N. Bridgewater	admn	13767
	William Henry	1853	Hingham	name	13768

SURNAME	FIRST NAME	YEAR	PLACE	CASE	DOCKET
MCCLINTOCK	James	1872	Abington	will	13769
MCCLOUSKY	Margaret	1866	Hanover	admn	13770
	Margaret	1868	Hanover	grdn	13771
	Mary	1868	Hanover	grdn	13771
	Nancy	1880	Wareham	admn	13772
MCCOURT	Elizabeth	1873	Bridgewater	grdn	13773
	John	1873	Bridgewater	admn	13774
	Margaret	1873	Bridgewater	grdn	13773
	Mary A	1873	Bridgewater	grdn	13773
MCCOURT	William	1873	Bridgewater	grdn	13773
MCCRAITH	Catherine	1881	S. Abington	grdn	13775
MCCUE	Francis	1875	Brockton	grdn	13776
	Hannah/Johanna	1874	Brockton	will	13777
	Katie	1875	Brockton	grdn	13776
	Margaret	1875	Brockton	grdn	13776
	Mary	1875	Brockton	grdn	13776
	Patrick	1875	Brockton	grdn	13776
MCCULLY	Andrew	1790	Middleboro	admn	13779
	Andrew	1790	Middleboro	grdn	13780
	Andrew	1843	Middleboro	admn	13778
	Betsey	1855	Lakeville	admn	13781
	Chloe	1790	Middleboro	grdn	13780
	Elizabeth	1790	Middleboro	grdn	13780
	Ezra	1870	Lakeville	admn	13782
	George	1790	Middleboro	grdn	13780
	Isaac W	1829	Middleboro	grdn	13783
	John	1829	Middleboro	admn	13784
	Joshua	1829	Middleboro	grdn	13783
	Judith	1835	Middleboro	will	13785
	Lois	1790	Middleboro	grdn	13780
	Martha	1790	Middleboro	grdn	13780
	Mary	1790	Middleboro	grdn	13780
	Obed	1838	Middleboro	admn	13786
MCDANIELS	James	1814	Middleboro	admn	13787
MCDEVITT	William	1875	Abington	will	13788
MCDONALD	Edward	1878	Brockton	grdn	13789
	Isabella A	1873	N. Bridgewater	grdn	13790
	Patrick	1878	Brockton	grdn	13789
	William H	1873	N. Bridgewater	grdn	13790
MCDONOGH	Caroline	1871	Hingham	will	13791
	Harriet	1839	Hingham	will	13792
MCFARLIN	Deborah	1823	Pembroke	will	13793
	Delia	1833	Pembroke	grdn	13804
	George O	1859	Pembroke	admn	13794
	Hannah	1726	Pembroke	grdn	13802
	Hannah	1833	Pembroke	grdn	13804
	Henry L	1864	Middleboro	admn	13795
	Hewett	1842	Carver	admn	13796
	Huldah	1879	Middleboro	will	13797
	Isaac	1726	Pembroke	grdn	13802
	Isaac	1803	Pembroke	admn	13798
	James	1866	Pembroke	will	13799
	John	1726	Pembroke	admn	13801
	John	1726	Pembroke	grdn	13802
	John	1781	Middleboro	admn	13800
	John	1831	Pembroke	admn	13803
	John	1833	Pembroke	grdn	13804
	John	1844	Carver	admn	13805
	John	1852	Carver	grdn	13806
	Joseph	1852	Carver	grdn	13806
	Lucretia	1852	Carver	grdn	13806
	Marcena	1833	Pembroke	grdn	13804
	Martha	1726	Pembroke	grdn	13802
	Martha	1749	Pembroke	admn	13807
	Mary	1815	Pembroke	will	13808
	Mercy	1852	Carver	grdn	13806
	Polly S	1880	Carver	grdn	13809
	Rebecca	1726	Pembroke	grdn	13802
	Rebecca	1852	Carver	grdn	13806
	Sampson	1880	Carver	grdn	13809
	Samuel	1854	Pembroke	admn	13810

SURNAME	FIRST NAME	YEAR	PLACE	CASE	DOCKET
MCFARLIN	Seth	1803	Pembroke	admn	13811
	Simeon	1819	Pembroke	grdn	13812
	Thomas H	1880	Carver	admn	13813
	William	1726	Pembroke	grdn	13802
MCGANN	Owen	1867	Plymouth	admn	13814
MCGILL	Charles	1878	Plymouth	admn	13815
MCGRATH	Dennis	1876	Brockton	will	13816
MCHENRY	Emmanuel F	1881	Plymouth	name	13817
MCINTEE	Mary A	1878	Brockton	admn	13818
	William	1879	Brockton	admn	13819
MCINTOSH	Georgia D	1877	Plymouth	grdn	13820
MACK	John	1809	Scituate	admn	13460
	William T	1860	Duxbury	grdn	13461
MCKEEN	John S	1869	Middleboro	admn	13821
MACKIE	Andrew	1817	Wareham	will	13462
	Charity	1844	Wareham	grdn	13463
	Fanny	1864	Wareham	admn	13464
	John	1844	Wareham	grdn	13463
	Mary Rebecca	1845	Providence RI	grdn	13465
	Peter	1858	Wareham	will	13466
	Sarah	1844	Wareham	grdn	13463
	William	1840	Wareham	admn	13467
	William	1844	Wareham	grdn	13463
MCKINSEY	Alexander	1788	Bridgewater	admn	13822
MCLAUTHLIN	Almira	1830	Kingston	grdn	13823
	Angelina	1830	Kingston	grdn	13823
	Ann	1851	Kingston	grdn	13831
	Augusta	1830	Kingston	grdn	13823
	Augusta	1851	Kingston	grdn	13831
	Bartlett	1850	Duxbury	admn	13824
	Deborah	1867	Plympton	admn	13825
	Dominick	1871	Wareham	grdn	13826
	Elisha	1836	Kingston	admn	13827
	Elisha	1869	Kingston	admn	13829
	Elisha Jr	1859	Kingston	admn	13828
	Francis B	1879	Kingston	grdn	13830
	Harvey	1851	Kingston	grdn	13831
	Isabel S	1850	Duxbury	grdn	13846
	James	1880	Plymouth	admn	13832
	John	1772	Duxbury	will	13833
	John	1777	Kingston	admn	13836
	John	1777	Kingston	grdn	13837
	John	1831	Kingston	admn	13834
	John	1836	Kingston	grdn	13835
	Joseph	1819	Pembroke	will	13838
	Judith	1853	Kingston	admn	13839
	Lewis	1830	Pembroke	grdn	13840 a
	Lewis	1875	Pembroke	will	13841
	Lovica T	1865	Plymouth	will	13842
	Lusanna	1874	E. Bridgewater	admn	13843
	Lydia S	1879	Kingston	grdn	13830
	Martin	1860	E. Bridgewater	will	13844
	Mary	1880	Plymouth	admn	13845
	Mary D	1850	Duxbury	grdn	13846
	Miller	1819	Kingston	admn	13847
	Nancy H	1879	Pembroke	admn	13848
	Pamela A	1836	Kingston	grdn	13835
	Robert	1837	Kingston	will	13849
	Robert B	1875	Kingston	admn	13850
	Ruth	1828	Kingston	will	13851
	Sally	1830	Kingston	grdn	13823
	Samuel W	1848	Kingston	admn	13852
	Sarah	1777	Kingston	grdn	13837
	Simeon W	1878	Kingston	admn	13853
MCLEAN	Andrew D	1851	Plympton	grdn	13854 a
	Daniel	1846	Plympton	admn	13855
	Daniel S	1865	Bristol	admn	13856
MCLEOD	Edith	1859	Middleboro	grdn	13857
	Helen	1859	Middleboro	grdn	13857
MCMENAMEN	Bernard	1879	Bridgewater	admn	13858
MCMINAMY	Mary	1876	Brockton	adop	13859

SURNAME	FIRST NAME	YEAR	PLACE	CASE	DOCKET
MCNAUGHT	John	1876	Duxbury	admn	13860
MCNEIL	Peter	1880	Hingham	admn	13861
MCNIFF	Mary A	1874	W. Bridgewater	grdn	13862
MACOMBER	Alethea	1837	Middleboro	will	13468
	Charles	1835	Marshfield	will	13469
	Cyrus	1775	Middleboro	grdn	13476
	Daniel	1861	Lakeville	will	13470
	Elijah	1843	Plymouth	admn	13471
	Elizabeth	1775	Middleboro	grdn	13476
	Elizabeth	1804	Middleboro	grdn	13479
	Enoch	1775	Middleboro	grdn	13476
	Gideon R	1843	Rochester	admn	13472
	Joanna	1791	Marshfield	will	13473
	Job G	1857	Middleboro	grdn	13474 a
MACOMBER	John	1775	Middleboro	admn	13475
	John	1775	Middleboro	grdn	13476
	Joseph	1800	Middleboro	admn	13478
	Joseph	1804	Middleboro	grdn	13479
	Joseph	1862	Middleboro	admn	13477
	Joshua	1829	Middleboro	admn	13480
	Josiah	1804	Middleboro	grdn	13479
	Josiah R	1822	Middleboro	admn	13481
	Luther	1850	Middleboro	admn	13482
	Mary	1775	Middleboro	grdn	13476
	Nathaniel	1814	Middleboro	will	13483
	Nathaniel	1856	Lakeville	admn	13484
	Onesimus	1749	Marshfield	admn	13485
	Onesimus	1791	Marshfield	will	13486
	Roanna	1852	Middleboro	admn	13487
	Samuel	1775	Middleboro	grdn	13476
	Simeon	1827	Middleboro	will	13488
	Thomas	1711	Marshfield	will	13489
	Thomas	1748	Marshfield	grdn	13495
	Thomas	1771	Marshfield	will	13491
	Thomas Jr	1748	Marshfield	admn	13490
	Warren S	1876	Plymouth	admn	13492
	William	1670	Marshfield	admn	13494
	William	1748	Marshfield	grdn	13495
	William	1815	Marshfield	will	13493
MACPHATRES	Daniel	1731	Scituate	grdn	13496
	Martha	1731	Scituate	grdn	13496
	Mary	1731	Scituate	grdn	13496
MCRAITH	John	1873	Abington	will	13863
MACREADING	Charles S	1875	Middleboro	admn	13497
MCSHANE	Patrick	1839	Scituate	admn	13864
MCSWEENEY	Bridget	1878	Brockton	grdn	13865 a
	Bridget	1881	Brockton	will	13866
MAGOUN	Aaron	1828	Pembroke	admn	13499
	Aaron S	1820	Pembroke	admn	13498
	Abigail	1746	Pembroke	admn	13500
	Abigail	1794	Pembroke	admn	13501
	Abner	1868	Hanover	will	13502
	Asaph	1848	Pembroke	admn	13503
	Betsey	1858	Pembroke	admn	13504
	Betsey L	1840	Pembroke	grdn	13505
	Calvin S	1864	Pembroke	admn	13506
	Calvin S	1869	Marshfield	admn	13507
	Charles	1835	Pembroke	grdn	13539
	Cornelius	1861	Pembroke	admn	13508
	Daniel	1876	Pembroke	will	13509
	David	1787	Plympton	will	13510
	David	1803	Bath ME	bond	13511
	David F	1853	Pembroke	grdn	13512
	Edmund	1835	Pembroke	grdn	13539
	Elias	1727	Pembroke	will	13513
	Elias	1823	Pembroke	will	13514
	Eliza H	1840	Pembroke	grdn	13515
	Enoch	1840	Pembroke	admn	13516
	Franklin W	1881	Hanover	admn	13517
	George	1835	Pembroke	grdn	13539
	Hannah	1818	Pembroke	will	13518

SURNAME	FIRST NAME	YEAR	PLACE	CASE	DOCKET
MAGOUN	Henry	1835	Pembroke	grdn	13539
	Henry	1841	Pembroke	grdn	13553
	Huldah S	1840	Pembroke	grdn	13505
	Isaac	1705	Duxbury	grdn	13524
	Isaac	1821	Pembroke	will	13519
	Isaac	1834	Pembroke	admn	13520
	Isaac	1835	Pembroke	grdn	13539
	Jairus	1816	Pembroke	grdn	13551
	James	1705	Duxbury	admn	13523
	James	1705	Duxbury	grdn	13524
	James	1719/2	Pembroke	admn	13522
	James H	1881	Pembroke	will	13521
	Jason	1840	Pembroke	admn	13525
	John	1709	Scituate	will	13526
	John	1739	Pembroke	admn	13527
	John	1743	Pembroke	will	13528
	John	1807	Pembroke	admn	13529
	John Jr	1806	Hanover	admn	13530
	Joseph	1829	Pembroke	grdn	13531 a
	Joseph	1832	Pembroke	admn	13533
	Joseph W	1831	Pembroke	admn	13532
	Joshua	1841	Pembroke	admn	13534
	Lusannah	1798	Pembroke	admn	13535
	Lydia	1826	Pembroke	admn	13536
	Mary	1838	Pembroke	admn	13537
	Mary	1876	Pembroke	admn	13538
	Mary J	1853	Pembroke	grdn	13512
	Matthew	1835	Pembroke	grdn	13539
	Nabby	1803	Bath ME	bond	13511
	Nancy	1852	Pembroke	will	13540
	Nathaniel	1786	Pembroke	admn	13541
	Nathaniel	1853	Pembroke	admn	13542
	Neal	1803	Bath ME	bond	13511
	Paul	1852	Pembroke	admn	13543
	Penelope L	1881	Pembroke	will	13544
	Recompence	1802	Pembroke	will	13545
	Robert	1840	Pembroke	admn	13546
	Ruth	1832	Pembroke	grdn	13556
	Sarah	1705	Duxbury	grdn	13524
	Sarah	1868	Pembroke	admn	13547
	Sarah N	1827	Pembroke	grdn	13548
	Seth	1810	Pembroke	admn	13550
	Seth	1816	Pembroke	grdn	13551
	Seth	1856	Duxbury	admn	13549
	Silvina	1837	Plymouth	will	13552
	Simeon N	1841	Pembroke	grdn	13553
	Snow	1827	Duxbury	admn	13554
	Thomas	1705	Duxbury	grdn	13524
	Thomas	1819	Pembroke	admn	13555
	Waterman	1832	Pembroke	grdn	13556
MAGRANE	Anna	1864	N. Bridgewater	grdn	13557
	Jane	1864	N. Bridgewater	grdn	13557
MAGUIRE	Abbie	1869	N. Bridgewater	grdn	13559
	George	1872	Hingham	admn	13558
	Hugh	1869	N. Bridgewater	grdn	13559
	John	1869	N. Bridgewater	grdn	13559
	Margaret	1869	N. Bridgewater	grdn	13559
	Mary	1878	Brockton	admn	13560
	Mary	1878	Plymouth	admn	13561
	Susan	1869	N. Bridgewater	grdn	13559
	William	1873	Abington	admn	13562
MAHLER	Elizabeth	1878	Plymouth	will	13563
MAHONE	Mary	1748	Scituate	admn	13564
MAHONEY	James	1871	E. Bridgewater	admn	13565
MAKEPEACE	Abel	1833	Middleboro	grdn	13568
	Allen	1833	Middleboro	grdn	13568
	Alvan	1833	Middleboro	admn	13566
	Alvin S	1876	Middleboro	admn	13567
	Francis	1833	Middleboro	grdn	13568
	Isaac	1813	Hanover	admn	13569
MAKER	James	1879	Brockton	will	13570

SURNAME	FIRST NAME	YEAR	PLACE	CASE	DOCKET
MALLARD	Grace	1715	Rochester	will	13571
MALLOY	James	1869	N. Bridgewater	admn	13572
MANCHESTER	Eli	1852	Rochester	admn	13573
MANGAN	Matilda A	1879	Rockland	grdn	13575
	Michael	1873	Abington	admn	13574
	Sarah J	1879	Rockland	grdn	13575
MANLEY	Charles	1853	N. Bridgewater	grdn	13576
	Daniel	1804	Bridgewater	will	13577
	Daniel	1828	N. Bridgewater	will	13578
	Eliza	1848	N. Bridgewater	grdn	13584
	Galen	1876	Brockton	will	13579
	Harriet	1853	N. Bridgewater	grdn	13576
	Harriet	1869	N. Bridgewater	will	13580
	Henry	1853	N. Bridgewater	grdn	13576
	Herbert	1848	N. Bridgewater	grdn	13584
	Herbert	1866	N. Bridgewater	will	13581
	Howard	1848	N. Bridgewater	will	13582
	Julius	1848	N. Bridgewater	grdn	13584
	Julius	1853	N. Bridgewater	admn	13583
	Milo	1853	N. Bridgewater	grdn	13576
	Nathaniel	1834	N. Bridgewater	admn	13585
	Sabine	1857	N. Bridgewater	grdn	13586 a
	Sabine	1857	N. Bridgewater	admn	13587
	Salmon	1853	N. Bridgewater	will	13588
	Sarah	1804	Bridgewater	grdn	13589
	William	1848	N. Bridgewater	grdn	13584
	William H	1859	N. Bridgewater	admn	13590
MANN	Abby	1862	Hanover	grdn	13593
	Abby J	1869	Hanover	admn	13591
	Albert	1862	Hanover	grdn	13593
	Albert G	1865	Hanover	admn	13592
	Ama	1819	Hanover	grdn	13623
	Benjamin	1770	Hanover	will	13594
	Benjamin	1820	Hanover	admn	13595
	Benjamin	1861	Hanover	will	13596
	Betsey	1874	Hanover	will	13597
	Charles	1814	Hanover	grdn	13598 a
	Charles	1878	Rockland	grdn	13600
	Charles F	1862	Hanover	grdn	13599 a
	Comfort	1857	Pembroke	grdn	13601 a
	Comfort	1859	Pembroke	admn	13602
	David	1839	Pembroke	will	13603
	David O	1874	Pembroke	admn	13604
	Deborah	1847	Scituate	will	13605
	Ebenezer	1812	Pembroke	will	13606
	Everett	1862	Hanover	grdn	13593
	Gustavus N	1857	Abington	grdn	13607
	Helen I	1879	Boston MI	grdn	13608
	Horace	1875	Hanover	grdn	13609 a
	Horace E	1857	Abington	grdn	13607
	John	1841	Scituate	admn	13610
	John	1878	Rockland	admn	13612
	John C	1867	Pembroke	will	13611
	Joseph	1806	Hanover	grdn	13613 a
	Joshua	1828	Hanover	admn	13614
	Joshua	1875	Hanover	admn	13615
	Josiah	1708	Scituate	admn	13616
	Josiah	1819	Scituate	grdn	13617 a
	Josiah	1821	Scituate	admn	13618
	Lester	1878	Rockland	grdn	13600
	Levi	1817	Hanover	admn	13619
	Louis	1878	Rockland	grdn	13600
	Mary	1819	Hanover	grdn	13623
	Nathaniel	1688	Scituate	admn	13620
	Patience S	1846	Hanover	will	13621
	Priscilla	1831	Scituate	will	13622
	Sarah	1819	Hanover	grdn	13623
	Sylvia L	1875	Pembroke	admn	13624
	Thomas	1732	Scituate	will	13625
	Thomas	1795	Scituate	will	13626
	Ursula	1822	Pembroke	will	13627

SURNAME	FIRST NAME	YEAR	PLACE	CASE	DOCKET
MANNING	Adelaide E	1880	Abington	admn	13628
	Venus	1860	S. Scituate	will	13629
MANSFIELD	Hannah E	1847	Wareham	will	13630
MANSON	Benjamin	1845	Scituate	grdn	13631
	Charles	1851	Scituate	grdn	13636
	Edward	1845	Scituate	grdn	13631
	George	1825	Scituate	grdn	13638
	George	1839	Scituate	admn	13632
	George	1845	Scituate	grdn	13631
	Hannah L	1840	Scituate	grdn	13641
	Horace	1851	Scituate	grdn	13636
	Joel	1825	Scituate	grdn	13638
	Joel L	1851	Scituate	admn	13633
	John	1762	Scituate	admn	13634
	John	1762	Scituate	grdn	13635
	John	1825	Scituate	grdn	13638
	Mary	1851	Scituate	grdn	13636
	Miriam	1762	Scituate	grdn	13635
	Nehemiah	1762	Scituate	grdn	13635
	Nehemiah	1833	Scituate	admn	13637
	Nehemiah Jr	1825	Scituate	grdn	13638
	Phebe	1821	Hanover	will	13639
	Samuel	1845	Scituate	grdn	13631
	Thomas L	1844	Scituate	admn	13640
	William C	1840	Scituate	grdn	13641
MANTER	Arabella	1834	Plymouth	grdn	13647
	Augusta	1851	Plymouth	grdn	13649
	Belcher	1825	Plymouth	will	13642
	Belcher	1848	Plymouth	admn	13643
	Charles	1834	Plymouth	grdn	13647
	Everett	1834	Plymouth	grdn	13647
	Everett M	1877	Carver	grdn	13645
	Everett T	1877	Carver	will	13644
	George	1876	Plymouth	will	13646
	Harriet	1834	Plymouth	grdn	13647
	Leonice	1834	Plymouth	grdn	13647
	Lucy	1834	Plymouth	grdn	13647
	Mary	1834	Plymouth	grdn	13647
	Naomi	1834	Plymouth	grdn	13647
	Prince	1851	Plymouth	grdn	13649
	Prince Jr	1849	Plymouth	admn	13648
	Susan et al	1880	Plymouth	peti	13650
	Thomas	1843	Plymouth	admn	13651
	Timothy	1879	Plymouth	will	13652
MARBLE	Demerick	1823	Hingham	admn	13653
	Demerick	1824	Hingham	grdn	13654
	Elizabeth	1836	Hingham	grdn	13656
	Isabella	1836	Hingham	grdn	13656
	James	1835	Hingham	admn	13655
	James	1836	Hingham	grdn	13656
	Lucy A	1831	Hingham	grdn	13657
	Olive A	1867	Hingham	grdn	13658 a
	Olive A	1869	Hingham	admn	13659
	William	1836	Hingham	grdn	13656
MARCHANT	Sarah	1881	Abington	admn	13660
MARCY	Charles	1805	Plymouth	grdn	13665
	Charlotte A	1818	Plymouth	grdn	13661
	Edward	1805	Plymouth	grdn	13665
	Hannah	1805	Plymouth	grdn	13665
	Joseph	1805	Plymouth	grdn	13665
	Joseph	1817	Plymouth	admn	13662
	Lucy	1805	Plymouth	grdn	13665
	Lucy	1842	Plymouth	will	13663
	Mary	1805	Plymouth	grdn	13665
	Stephen	1804	Plymouth	admn	13664
	Stephen	1805	Plymouth	grdn	13665
	William	1805	Plymouth	grdn	13665
MARKS	Isaac	1874	Abington	name	13666
MARSH	Benjamin	1823	Hingham	grdn	13674
	Caleb	1849	Hingham	admn	13667
	Caleb	1849	Hingham	grdn	13682

SURNAME	FIRST NAME	YEAR	PLACE	CASE	DOCKET
MARSH	Caleb	1871	Hingham	admn	13668
	Celia	1843	Hingham	grdn	13669 a
	Celia	1843	Hingham	admn	13670
	David	1838	Hingham	will	13671
	Elizabeth	1871	Hingham	grdn	13672
	Fred	1871	Hingham	grdn	13672
	George	1871	Hingham	grdn	13672
	Helen M	1881	Hingham	will	13673
	Jacob	1823	Hingham	grdn	13674
	John	1803	Hingham	will	13675
	John	1823	Hingham	admn	13676
	Josiah	1831	Hingham	admn	13677
	Lot	1843	Hingham	admn	13678
	Louisa	1849	Hingham	grdn	13682
	Louisa	1876	Hingham	admn	13679
	Lucinda	1823	Hingham	grdn	13674
	Lydia	1849	Hingham	grdn	13682
	Mary	1849	Hingham	grdn	13682
	Olive	1833	Hingham	admn	13680
	Robert	1871	Hingham	grdn	13672
	Samuel's ch	1833	Hingham	grdn	13681
	Stephen	1849	Hingham	grdn	13682
	Thomas	1833	Hingham	will	13683
MARSHALL	Albert	1860	N. Bridgewater	grdn	13692
	Alice	1860	N. Bridgewater	grdn	13692
	Allen	1843	Rochester	will	13684
	Benjamin	1878	W. Bridgewater	will	13686
	Benjamin F	1870	W. Bridgewater	will	13685
	Charles	1859	Plymouth	admn	13687
	Charles	1860	N. Bridgewater	grdn	13692
	Emma	1860	N. Bridgewater	grdn	13692
	Hayward	1839	N. Bridgewater	will	13688
	Hazadiah M	1865	Middleboro	admn	13689
	John	1792	Rochester	will	13690
	Louisa	1860	N. Bridgewater	grdn	13692
	Ponsonby	1871	Middleboro	will	13691
	Susan	1860	N. Bridgewater	grdn	13692
	Susanna	1806	Plymouth	grdn	13693
	William H	1867	Middleboro	admn	13694
MARSTON	Frank A	1861	E. Bridgewater	grdn	13695
	Mary J	1861	E. Bridgewater	will	13696
	Theodore	1861	E. Bridgewater	will	13697
MARTIN	Anthony P	1874	Scituate	will	13698
	Frederick D	1870	Middleboro	grdn	13699
	Isabella R	1866	Plymouth	admn	13700
	Jesse	1837	Rochester	admn	13701
	Margaret A	1871	Plymouth	grdn	13702
	Stephen	1783	Rochester	admn	13703
MASON	Albert T	1868	Lakeville	will	13704
	Arlina	1879	Lakeville	admn	13705
	Charles H	1864	N. Bridgewater	admn	13706
	George A	1865	N. Bridgewater	grdn	13707
	Hattie T	1865	N. Bridgewater	grdn	13707
	John D	1877	E. Bridgewater	will	13708
	Louisa	1872	New Hampshire	affi	13709
	Lyman W	1838	E. Bridgewater	admn	13710
	William E F	1865	N. Bridgewater	admn	13711
MATTERN	Barbara	1877	Plymouth	will	13712
MATTHEWS	Alphonso C	1875	Abington	grdn	13714
	Desire	1807	Plymouth	will	13713
	Maria A	1875	Abington	grdn	13714
	Thomas	1807	Plymouth	will	13715
MAXIM	Betsey	1850	Middleboro	grdn	13724
	Caleb	1762	Rochester	grdn	13729
	Caleb	1833	Middleboro	will	13716
	Edna	1844	Wareham	admn	13717
	Elbridge A	1864	Middleboro	admn	13718
	Elizabeth	1762	Rochester	grdn	13729
	Ezra	1762	Rochester	grdn	13729
	Ezra	1788	Middleboro	admn	13719
	Ezra	1879	Middleboro	will	13720

SURNAME	FIRST NAME	YEAR	PLACE	CASE	DOCKET
MAXIM	Jacob	1789	Rochester	will	13721
	John	1827	Carver	will	13722
	Nathan	1833	Rochester	admn	13723
	Nathan	1850	Middleboro	grdn	13724
	Noah	1850	Middleboro	grdn	13724
	Prince W	1849	Middleboro	admn	13725
	Reuben	1825	Middleboro	admn	13726
	Samuel	1762	Rochester	grdn	13729
	Samuel	1763	Rochester	will	13728
	Samuel Jr	1755	Rochester	admn	13727
	Thadeus	1773	Middleboro	admn	13730
	Thomas	1862	Carver	will	13731
	Thomas	1872	Carver	will	13732
MAXWELL	Charles W	1876	Abington	admn	13733
	Georgiana W	1876	Abington	grdn	13734
	Matilda R	1876	Abington	grdn	13734
MAY	Edward	1691/2	Plymouth	admn	13735
	John	1748	Plymouth	grdn	13736 a
	John	1770	Plymouth	admn	13737
	John	1770	Plymouth	grdn	13738
	Nicholas	1713	Plymouth	will	13739
	Sarah	1770	Plymouth	grdn	13738
MAYBURY	Joseph	1878	Plymouth	will	13740
MAYHEW	Lemuel	1796	Scituate	admn	13741
	Matthew	1866	Mattapoisett	admn	13742
	Noah	1745	-----	grdn	13743
	Thomas	1745	-----	grdn	13743
	Thomas	1784	Plymouth	admn	13744
MAYN	William	1841	Bridgewater	grdn	13745
MAYNARD	Elizabeth	1858	Plymouth	admn	13746
	George L	1873	Plymouth	admn	13747
	Henry N	1876	Middleboro	admn	13748
	Solomon	1812	Plymouth	admn	13749
MAYO	Elizabeth	1862	Plymouth	will	13750
	Emily	1862	Scituate	admn	13751
	George	1867	Plymouth	grdn	13754
	Hannah A	1870	Plymouth	admn	13752
	Henrietta	1867	Plymouth	grdn	13754
	John	1867	Plymouth	grdn	13754
	Nathaniel C	1817	Plymouth	admn	13753
	Seth	1867	Plymouth	grdn	13754
	Thomas A	1862	Plymouth	admn	13755
MEARA	Sherman T	1853	N. Bridgewater	name	13867
MEARS	Angela	1851	Hingham	grdn	13868
	Frank	1851	Hingham	grdn	13868
	Hannah	1866	Hingham	name	13869
	Hannah	1876	Hingham	will	13870
	John	1851	Hingham	grdn	13868
	Micajah D	1850	Hingham	admn	13871
	Samuel	1851	Hingham	grdn	13868
MEHURIN	Benjamin	1761	Bridgewater	admn	13872
	Jonathan	1757	Bridgewater	admn	13873
	Josiah	1812	Bridgewater	will	13874
	Martha	1839	Bridgewater	admn	13875
	Patience	1847	Plymouth	admn	13876
	Ruth	1782	Easton	grdn	13877
	Silvia	1842	Bridgewater	will	13878
MEIGS	Abigail	1832	Rochester	will	13879
	Alice	1821	Rochester	will	13880
	Alice	1821	Rochester	will	13880
	Alice	1862	Mattapoisett	will	13881
	Caleb	1814	Rochester	admn	13882
	Caleb	1826	Rochester	grdn	13883
	Ephraim	1812	Rochester	will	13884
	Ephraim	1828	Rochester	admn	13885
	John	1796	Rochester	will	13886
	Joseph	1847	Rochester	admn	13887
	Joseph L	1847	Rochester	grdn	13888
MEIN	Thomas	1871	Bridgewater	admn	13889
MELLBAR	Augustus	1873	N. Bridgewater	will	13890
MEMUNTAGUE	Abigail	1717	Pembroke	admn	13891 i

SURNAME	FIRST NAME	YEAR	PLACE	CASE	DOCKET
MENDALL	Amos	1770	Rochester	admn	13892
	Barnabas	1820	Rochester	admn	13893
	Benjamin W	1877	Mattapoisett	admn	13894
	Caleb	1804	Rochester	will	13895
	Caleb	1843	Rochester	grdn	13896 a
	Charles A	1855	Rochester	admn	13898
	Charles F	1842	Rochester	grdn	13897
	David	1823	Rochester	admn	13899
	David	1829	Rochester	admn	13900
	David	1833	Rochester	grdn	13901
	Ellis	1849	Rochester	grdn	13904
	George W	1850	Rochester	will	13902
	Hannah	1844	Rochester	will	13903
	Henry	1849	Rochester	grdn	13904
	Jabez	1748	Plymouth	admn	13905
	John	1720	Marshfield	will	13906 +
	John	1743	Rochester	will	13906
	John	1853	Rochester	will	13907
	John	1865	Mattapoisett	admn	13909
	John C	1872	Rochester	admn	13908
	Jonathan	1870	Marion	admn	13910
	Lydia	1852	Rochester	will	13911
	Mary A	1854	E. Bridgewater	grdn	13912
	Moses	1843	Rochester	will	13913
	Noah	1831	Rochester	admn	13914
	Samuel	1841	Rochester	admn	13915
	Seth	1796	Plymouth	will	13916
	Seth	1812	Rochester	will	13917
	Seth	1822	Rochester	will	13918
	Seth	1837	Rochester	will	13919
	Sylvanus	1795	Rochester	will	13920
	Walter	1836	Rochester	admn	13921
	William	1858	Marion	will	13922
	William H	1872	Rochester	admn	13924
	William P	1858	Rochester	will	13923
	Zacheus	1777	Plymouth	will	13925
MERCHANT	Sylvia	1869	N. Bridgewater	admn	13926
MERRIAM	Edwin E	1867	Plymouth	admn	13927
	Elisha J	1874	Plymouth	will	13928
MERRIHEW	Charity	1855	Rochester	will	13929
MERRITT	Allen	1869	Scituate	admn	13930
	Ambrose	1813	Scituate	admn	13931
	Amos	1829	Scituate	admn	13932
	Arthur	1872	Scituate	grdn	13933
	Asa	1815	Scituate	will	13934
	Asa	1866	Scituate	admn	13935
	Aurah H	1856	Scituate	grdn	13941
	Bailey	1845	Scituate	admn	13936
	Benjamin	1869	S. Scituate	admn	13937
	Betsey	1832	Scituate	will	13938
	Billings	1825	Scituate	admn	13939
	Billings	1866	Scituate	admn	13940
	Billings	1872	Scituate	grdn	13933
	Charles	1856	Scituate	grdn	13941
	Charles	1864	Abington	grdn	13948
	Consider	1831	Scituate	will	13942
	Daniel	1833	Scituate	grdn	13943 a
	David	1772	Scituate	will	13944
	Deborah	1879	Scituate	admn	13945
	Dexter	1868	Scituate	will	13946
	Diana	1878	Scituate	will	13947
	Edward	1864	Abington	grdn	13948
	Edwin	1880	S. Scituate	admn	13949
	Elizabeth	1734	Scituate	will	13950
	Elizabeth	1832	Scituate	admn	13951
	Elizabeth	1872	Scituate	grdn	13933
	Emily	1879	Scituate	admn	13952
	Ensign	1840	Scituate	admn	13953
	Ezekiel	1846	N. Bridgewater	admn	13954
	Francis	1854	S. Scituate	admn	13955
	Franklin	1864	Abington	grdn	13948

SURNAME	FIRST NAME	YEAR	PLACE	CASE	DOCKET
MERRITT	George	1851	N. Bridgewater	grdn	13956 a
	Henrietta	1872	Scituate	grdn	13933
	Henry	1732	Scituate	admn	13957
	Henry	1771	Scituate	admn	13958
	Henry	1874	S. Scituate	will	13959
	Herbert M	1879	Scituate	grdn	13960
	James	1769	Scituate	will	13961
	James	1795	Scituate	will	13962
	James	1822	Scituate	will	13963
	James	1864	Abington	grdn	13948
	James H	1868	Scituate	will	13965
	James L	1859	Scituate	will	13964
	James L	1877	Scituate	admn	13966
	John	1677	Scituate	admn	13967
	John	1740	Scituate	admn	13968
	John	1748	Scituate	admn	13969
	John	1760	Scituate	admn	13970
	John	1814	Scituate	admn	13971
	Jonathan	1754	Scituate	will	13972
	Jonathan	1773	Scituate	will	13973
	Joseph	1876	S. Scituate	will	13974
	Lydia	1859	Scituate	admn	13975
	Martha	1872	Scituate	grdn	13933
	Martha	1876	Scituate	will	13976
	Martin D	1872	Scituate	will	13977
	Mary B	1877	Scituate	admn	13978
	Melzar	1845	Scituate	will	13979
	Melzar	1858	Abington	admn	13980
	Nehemiah	1818	Scituate	will	13981
	Obadiah	1794	Scituate	will	13982
	Paul	1821	Plympton	bond	13983
	Paul	1851	Scituate	admn	13984
	Peter	1827	Scituate	admn	13985
	Robert C	1870	Scituate	will	13986
	Ruth	1829	Scituate	grdn	13987
	Sally	1856	Scituate	admn	13988
	Sarah	1825	Scituate	grdn	13989 a
	Sarah	1838	Scituate	admn	13990
	Seth	1828	Scituate	will	13991
	Seth	1869	Scituate	will	13992
	Shadrach B	1871	Scituate	will	13993
	Thomas	1724	Pembroke	admn	13994
MERROW	William	1870	Abington	will	13995
MERRY	Helen R	1869	Pembroke	grdn	13996
MERRYFIELD	Francis	1760	Plymouth	admn	13997
MESERVE	George H	1876	Abington	adop	13998
	William F	1874	Abington	adop	13999
MEW	Richard	1741	Newport	grdn	14000
MIDGETT	William	1842	Plymouth	admn	14002
MIGHELL	Thomas	1689/0	Scituate	will	14001
MILES	Lydia	1846	Wareham	admn	14003
MILITARY	4thReg Roster	1778	-----	rost	14004
MILLARD	John	1824	Rochester	admn	14005
MILLER	Abishai	1827	Middleboro	grdn	14006
	Abraham	1817	Middleboro	will	14007
	Adino	1835	Middleboro	admn	14008
	Alden	1828	Middleboro	admn	14009
	Clarinda	1880	Wareham	admn	14010
	Darius	1874	Wareham	admn	14011
	David	1727	Middleboro	grdn	14012
	Elias	1727	Middleboro	grdn	14012
	Elias	1807	Middleboro	will	14013
	Elizabeth	1869	Middleboro	grdn	14014 a
	Francis	1747	Middleboro	will	14015
	Hannah A	1876	Middleboro	grdn	14016 a
	Isaac	1827	Middleboro	will	14017
	Jedediah	1838	Middleboro	will	14018
	John	1720	Middleboro	admn	14019
	John	1727	Middleboro	admn	14020
	John	1759	Middleboro	grdn	14022
	John	1795	Middleboro	admn	14023

SURNAME	FIRST NAME	YEAR	PLACE	CASE	DOCKET
MILLER	John	1808	Middleboro	will	14024
	John	1818	Middleboro	admn	14025
	John 2nd	1759	Middleboro	will	14021
	Joseph	1826	Middleboro	admn	14026
	Lorenzo T	1839	Middleboro	peti	14027
	Lucy	1833	Middleboro	will	14028
	Mary	1817	Middleboro	admn	14029
	Peter	1835	Middleboro	admn	14030
	Samuel	1831	Middleboro	admn	14031
	Seth	1823	Middleboro	will	14032
	Seth	1866	Middleboro	will	14033
	Seth	1876	Wareham	will	14034
	Thankful	1853	Middleboro	will	14035
	William J	1830	Hingham	admn	14036
MILLIKEN	Hurd	1872	E. Bridgewater	will	14037
MILLS	Caroline F	1852	Plymouth	grdn	14039
	Henry	1873	Plymouth	will	14038
	Mary H	1852	Plymouth	grdn	14039
MILN	Isabella A	1868	E. Bridgewater	admn	14040
MINTER	Eli H	1857	Plymouth	admn	14041
MINZY	George W	1880	Brockton	will	14042
MITCHELL	Abiel	1744	Bridgewater	grdn	14114
	Abigail	1839	Bridgewater	will	14043
	Archibald	1875	Scituate	admn	14044
	Asa	1796	Bridgewater	grdn	14045
	Asa	1869	E. Bridgewater	grdn	14046 a
	Betsey	1843	Plymouth	admn	14047
	Betsey	1853	Rochester	will	14048
	Betsey	1869	Bridgewater	admn	14049
	Caleb	1873	Bridgewater	will	14050
	Calvin	1783	Bridgewater	grdn	14111
	Calvin	1825	Rochester	will	14051
	Cary	1821	Bridgewater	admn	14052
	Charles	1857	E. Bridgewater	will	14053
	Charles P	1875	Rockland	admn	14054
	Cushing	1820	Bridgewater	will	14055
	Cushing	1872	E. Bridgewater	will	14056
	Daniel	1847	Bridgewater	admn	14057
	Daniel F	1856	Bridgewater	grdn	14118
	Deborah	1744	Bridgewater	admn	14058
	Edward	1717	Bridgewater	will	14059
	Edward	1802	Bridgewater	will	14060
	Edward	1829	Bridgewater	will	14062
	Edward	1863	Bridgewater	admn	14063
	Edward Jr	1825	Bridgewater	will	14061
	Elisha	1790	Bridgewater	admn	14064
	Elisha	1861	Hanson	will	14065
	Elphaz	1821	Bridgewater	admn	14066
	Eva J	1879	W. Bridgewater	grdn	14067
	Experience	1689	Bridgewater	will	14068
	Ezra	1812	Kingston	admn	14070
	Ezra	1823	Kingston	grdn	14071
	Ezra	1873	Kingston	will	14069
	George	1869	E. Bridgewater	will	14072
	George W	1879	Halifax	admn	14073
	Harriet L	1873	E. Bridgewater	will	14074
	Harvey	1823	Kingston	grdn	14071
	Henry	1862	Bridgewater	admn	14075
	Jacob	1690/1	Dartmouth	admn	14076
	James H	1872	E. Bridgewater	will	14077
	Japheth	1859	Marshfield	will	14078
	John	1711	Bridgewater	admn	14080
	John	1742	Milton	grdn	14079
	John	1779	Scituate	admn	14083
	John	1823	Kingston	admn	14086
	John	1829	Bridgewater	will	14081
	John	1876	Hull	will	14084
	John	1878	Kingston	admn	14087
	John Jr	1770	Marshfield	admn	14082
	John W	1877	Abington	admn	14085
	Joseph	1755	Kingston	will	14088

SURNAME	FIRST NAME	YEAR	PLACE	CASE	DOCKET
MITCHELL	Joseph	1793	Plymouth	admn	14089
	Lavinia H	1873	E. Bridgewater	grdn	14090
	Leonard	1856	W. Bridgewater	will	14091
	Mary	1744	Bridgewater	grdn	14114
	Molly	1846	Kingston	will	14092
	Morton D	1865	E. Bridgewater	admn	14093
	Nahum	1853	E. Bridgewater	will	14094
	Nathan	1744	Bridgewater	grdn	14114
	Nathan	1789	Bridgewater	will	14095
	Nathan	1845	Bridgewater	will	14096
	Philo	1868	Bridgewater	admn	14097
	Ransom	1823	Kingston	grdn	14098
	Ruth	1863	Bridgewater	will	14099
	Sarah	1854	Kingston	will	14100
	Sarah	1875	Marshfield	will	14101
	Seth	1729	Bridgewater	grdn	14102
	Seth	1778	Bridgewater	grdn	14103 a
	Seth	1808	Bridgewater	will	14104
	Sewall	1879	W. Bridgewater	grdn	14105
	Sewall	1879	Standish ME	will	14106
	Simeon W	1879	Bridgewater	admn	14107
	Thomas	1727	Bridgewater	admn	14109
	Thomas	1744	Bridgewater	grdn	14114
	Thomas	1777	Bridgewater	will	14110
	Thomas	1783	Bridgewater	grdn	14111
	Thomas C	1859	Abington	admn	14108
	Timothy	1733	Bridgewater	admn	14112
	Timothy	1744	Bridgewater	grdn	14114
	Timothy	1750	Bridgewater	admn	14113
	William	1851	E. Bridgewater	admn	14115
	William	1852	Bridgewater	will	14117
	William	1866	W. Bridgewater	admn	14116
	William D	1856	Bridgewater	grdn	14118
	William L	1879	W. Bridgewater	grdn	14067
MOAN	Fred Ernest	1870	N. Bridgewater	grdn	14119
MONAHAN	Dennis	1875	Wareham	grdn	14120 a
	Dennis	1876	Wareham	grdn	14121 a
	Patrick	1875	S. Scituate	grdn	14122 a
MONING	August	1879	Plymouth	grdn	14123
	Casper	1878	Plymouth	admn	14124
	Charles	1879	Plymouth	grdn	14123
	Mary	1879	Plymouth	grdn	14123
MONTGOMERY	Ann E	1876	Marion	grdn	14126
	Hugh	1834	Middleboro	will	14125
	James O	1876	Marion	grdn	14126
	John	1787	Middleboro	will	14127
	Katherine	1785	Middleboro	grdn	14129
	Samuel	1785	Middleboro	grdn	14129
	Samuel	1792	Middleboro	admn	14128
	Seth C	1876	Marion	admn	14130
	William	1804	Middleboro	will	14131
MOORE	Caroline	1878	Kingston	will	14132
	Charles G	1868	Pembroke	grdn	14133
	David	1872	Bridgewater	grdn	14142
	David	1880	Hingham	grdn	14134
	Edwin A H	1850	Plymouth	grdn	14135
	Esther B	1875	Brockton	grdn	14136
	Henry R	1854	Peoria IL	peti	14137
	John	1738	Bridgewater	grdn	14148
	John	1819	-----	admn	14138
	Jonathan	1814	Rochester	will	14139
	Margaret	1878	Brockton	will	14140
	Mary A	1872	Bridgewater	grdn	14142
	Mary A	1875	Bridgewater	admn	14141
	Michael	1875	Brockton	will	14143
	Morris	1880	Hingham	grdn	14134
	Patrick	1880	Hingham	grdn	14134
	Patrick	1880	Hingham	admn	14144
	Robert	1872	Bridgewater	grdn	14142
	Samuel D	1865	Abington	admn	14145
	Sarah	1875	Bridgewater	admn	14146

SURNAME	FIRST NAME	YEAR	PLACE	CASE	DOCKET
MOORE	Sarah J	1872	Bridgewater	grdn	14142
	Theodosius	1737	Bridgewater	will	14147
	Thomas	1738	Bridgewater	grdn	14148
	Thomas	1872	Bridgewater	grdn	14142
	William	1872	Bridgewater	grdn	14142
	William	1880	Hingham	grdn	14134
MOORFIELD	James	1835	Hingham	admn	14149
MORAN	Julia	1875	Brockton	admn	14150
MOREY	Benjamin	1744	Plymouth	admn	14151
	Caleb	1845	Halifax	will	14152
	Cornelius	1746	Plymouth	grdn	14161
	Cornelius	1803	Plymouth	will	14153
	Cornelius	1813	Plymouth	admn	14154
	Cynthia A	1880	E. Bridgewater	admn	14155
	Elijah	1746	Plymouth	grdn	14161
	Eunice M	1875	Brockton	grdn	14156
	Hannah	1842	Middleboro	grdn	14157 a
	Hannah	1852	Middleboro	will	14158
	Isaiah S	1875	Brockton	will	14159
	John	1746	Plymouth	grdn	14161
	John	1800	Middleboro	admn	14160
	Jonathan	1708	Plymouth	will	14162
	Jonathan	1733	Plymouth	will	14163
	Josiah	1807	Plymouth	grdn	14170
	Josiah	1841	Plympton	admn	14164
	Josiah	1841	Plympton	grdn	14165
	Mary	1821	Middleboro	admn	14166
	Patrick	1871	E. Bridgewater	admn	14167
	Sarah	1727	Boston	grdn	14168
	Stephen	1872	W. Bridgewater	will	14169
	William	1807	Plymouth	grdn	14170
MORGAN	John L	1873	N. Bridgewater	admn	14171
	Joseph	1827	Bridgewater	admn	14172
MORRILL	Mary S	1876	Bridgewater	grdn	14173
MORRISON	John	1878	Plymouth	admn	14174
	Robert	1764	Bridgewater	will	14175
MORSE	Ann	1858	Middleboro	grdn	14203
	Ansel	1810	Rochester	admn	14176
	Anthony	1858	Plymouth	admn	14177
	Asa	1860	Bridgewater	admn	14178
	Barzilla	1857	Middleboro	admn	14179
	Betsey	1858	Middleboro	grdn	14203
	Betsey	1865	Carver	admn	14180
	Charles T P	1858	Plymouth	grdn	14181
	Clarence	1876	Hanover	grdn	14182
	Cynthia E	1862	Rochester	admn	14183
	Daniel	1875	Hingham	will	14184
	David	1763	Plympton	admn	14185
	Desire	1852	Middleboro	will	14186
	Edward	1784	Rochester	will	14187
	Edward Jr	1806	Rochester	admn	14188
	Edwin	1855	Bridgewater	grdn	14189 a
	Elizabeth E	1878	Mattapoisett	grdn	14190
	Emily A	1879	Arkwright NY	grdn	14191
	Ephraim	1765	Plympton	warr	14220
	Fanny	1857	Halifax	admn	14192
	Franklin M	1863	Halifax	grdn	14193
	George M	1863	Halifax	grdn	14193
	Hannah	1765	Plympton	grdn	14194
	Hannah	1852	Middleboro	grdn	14195 a
	Hattie A	1879	Arkwright NY	grdn	14191
	Hosea	1862	Carver	will	14196
	Isaac	1850	Middleboro	admn	14198
	Isaac 3rd	1826	Middleboro	admn	14197
	Jabez	1843	Pembroke	admn	14199
	Joanna	1839	Middleboro	will	14200
	John	1836	Middleboro	admn	14202
	John	1858	Middleboro	grdn	14203
	John N	1868	Rochester	will	14201
	Jonathan	1709	Middleboro	admn	14204
	Jonathan	1725	Middleboro	will	14205

SURNAME	FIRST NAME	YEAR	PLACE	CASE	DOCKET
MORSE	Jonathan	1740	Middleboro	grdn	14206
	Joseph B	1850	Middleboro	admn	14207
	Joshua	1760	Rochester	admn	14208
	Joshua	1843	Hingham	grdn	14210
	Joshua Jr	1842	Hingham	admn	14209
	Josiah	1868	Rochester	admn	14211
	Julia E	1877	Mattapoisett	admn	14212
	Levi	1857	Middleboro	admn	14213
	Lucy	1763	Plympton	grdn	14214
	Lucy	1858	Middleboro	grdn	14203
	Lucy	1860	Mattapoisett	admn	14215
	Lydia B	1875	S. Scituate	admn	14216
	Marcus	1876	Hanover	admn	14217
	Maria M	1859	Lakeville	will	14218
	Mary	1843	Hingham	grdn	14210
	Nancy C	1880	Plymouth	will	14219
	Noah	1765	Plympton	warr	14220
	Obadiah	1877	Bridgewater	admn	14221
	Ruth	1864	Middleboro	will	14222
	Samuel	1836	Middleboro	admn	14223
	Simeon	1837	Wareham	admn	14224
	Simeon	1863	Wareham	admn	14225
	Sophronia	1843	Hingham	grdn	14210
	Thomas S	1838	Middleboro	admn	14226
	Tilson	1863	Wareham	will	14227
MORTON	Abby Ann	1857	Plymouth	admn	14228
	Abby Ann	1857	Plymouth	grdn	14271
	Abiel	1740	Plymouth	grdn	14361
	Abiel	1778	Plymouth	admn	14229
	Abigail	1740	Plymouth	grdn	14361
	Abigail	1810	Plymouth	grdn	14344
	Abigail	1842	Plymouth	grdn	14230
	Abigail	1850	Middleboro	will	14231
	Abigail	1877	Plymouth	will	14232
	Abner	1828	Abington	admn	14233
	Albert	1828	Halifax	grdn	14234 a
	Alma	1871	Plymouth	grdn	14235
	Amasa	1796	Plymouth	admn	14236
	Amasa	1861	Plymouth	admn	14237
	Amasa	1872	Plymouth	admn	14238
	Barnabee	1745	Plymouth	grdn	14239
	Bartlett	1843	Middleboro	grdn	14261
	Benjamin	1724	Plymouth	grdn	14242
	Benjamin	1745	Plymouth	grdn	14239
	Benjamin	1796	Rochester	admn	14240
	Benjamin	1816	Plymouth	admn	14241
	Betsey	1781	Plymouth	grdn	14243
	Betsey	1791	Plymouth	warr	14244
	Caleb	1798	Plymouth	admn	14245
	Caleb	1878	Plymouth	admn	14246
	Catherine	1850	Middleboro	will	14248
	Catherine 2nd	1847	Middleboro	grdn	14247 a
	Charles	1829	Halifax	grdn	14249
	Charles F	1871	N. Bridgewater	grdn	14251
	Charles G	1842	Plymouth	admn	14250
	Cornelius	1724	Plymouth	grdn	14242
	Cyrus	1873	Halifax	will	14252
	Deborah E	1878	Plympton	admn	14253
	Ebenezer	1724	Plymouth	grdn	14242
	Ebenezer	1750	Middleboro	admn	14254
	Ebenezer	1776	Middleboro	admn	14255
	Edward	1804	Plymouth	admn	14256
	Edward	1854	Plymouth	admn	14257
	Edwin	1871	N. Bridgewater	grdn	14251
	Elbridge G	1876	Halifax	admn	14258
	Eleanor	1805	Plymouth	grdn	14259
	Eleanor	1835	Plymouth	will	14260
	Eleazer	1764	Plymouth	grdn	14369
	Elisha	1724	Plymouth	grdn	14242
	Eliza	1843	Middleboro	grdn	14261
	Elizabeth F	1867	Plymouth	grdn	14262

SURNAME	FIRST NAME	YEAR	PLACE	CASE	DOCKET
MORTON	Ellis	1874	Plymouth	admn	14263
	Ephraim	1692	Plymouth	will	14264
	Ephraim	1717/8	Plymouth	admn	14265
	Ephraim	1729/0	Plymouth	admn	14266
	Ephraim	1731	Plymouth	will	14267
	Ephraim	1758	Plymouth	admn	14268
	Ephraim	1815	Plymouth	admn	14269
	Ephraim	1857	Plymouth	grdn	14271
	Ephraim 2nd	1833	Plymouth	admn	14270
	Eunice	1798	Plymouth	admn	14272
	Experience	1800	Plymouth	grdn	14273
	Experience	1851	Plymouth	grdn	14348
	Ezekiel	1797	Plymouth	admn	14274
	Ezekiel	1811	Plymouth	will	14275
	Ezekiel	1873	Plymouth	admn	14276
	Flora A	1872	Plymouth	grdn	14277
	Freeman	1861	Plymouth	will	14279
	Freeman Jr	1849	Plymouth	admn	14278
	George	1727	Plymouth	will	14280
	George	1731	Plymouth	admn	14281
	George	1764	Plymouth	grdn	14369
	George	1782	Scituate	admn	14283
	George	1819	Plymouth	admn	14282
	George	1843	Middleboro	grdn	14261
	Hannah	1740	Plymouth	grdn	14361
	Hannah	1784	Plymouth	grdn	14285
	Hannah H	1859	Middleboro	name	14284
	Henry	1696/7	Plymouth	grdn	14317
	Henry	1878	Plymouth	admn	14287
	Henry M	1872	Plymouth	admn	14286
	Herbert L	1872	Plymouth	grdn	14277
	Horace	1843	Middleboro	grdn	14261
	Ichabod	1862	Plymouth	admn	14288
	Isaac	1740	Plymouth	grdn	14361
	Isaac	1793	Plymouth	admn	14289
	Jacob T	1871	Plymouth	will	14290
	James	1755	Plympton	grdn	14291
	James	1833	Plymouth	admn	14293
	James	1838	Plymouth	admn	14294
	James 2nd	1832	Plymouth	admn	14292
	Jane B	1863	Plymouth	grdn	14322
	Joanna	1728	Plymouth	will	14295
	Joanna	1740	Plymouth	grdn	14361
	Joanna	1750	Plymouth	admn	14296
	Joanna	1818	Plymouth	admn	14297
	Joanna	1845	Halifax	admn	14298
	Job	1762	Plymouth	admn	14299
	Job	1797	Plymouth	admn	14300
	John	1718	Middleboro	will	14303
	John	1738	Plymouth	will	14301
	John	1785	Plymouth	admn	14302
	John	1786	Middleboro	will	14304
	John	1826	Scituate	admn	14307
	John	1836	Middleboro	will	14306
	John 2nd	1803	Middleboro	grdn	14305 a
	Jonathan	1740	Plymouth	grdn	14361
	Joseph	1754	Plymouth	will	14308
	Joseph	1810	Plymouth	grdn	14344
	Joseph	1843	Middleboro	grdn	14261
	Joshua	1790	Middleboro	admn	14309
	Joshua	1802	Middleboro	grdn	14310
	Josiah	1694	Plymouth	admn	14316
	Josiah	1696/7	Plymouth	grdn	14317
	Josiah	1761	Plymouth	admn	14315
	Josiah	1800	Plymouth	admn	14314
	Josiah	1838	Plymouth	will	14313
	Josiah	1842	Duxbury	admn	14311
	Josiah	1850	Plymouth	will	14312
	Lemuel	1779	Plymouth	will	14318
	Lemuel	1784	Plymouth	grdn	14285
	Lemuel	1827	Plymouth	admn	14319

SURNAME	FIRST NAME	YEAR	PLACE	CASE	DOCKET
MORTON	Lemuel	1867	Plymouth	admn	14320
	Lendall P	1843	Middleboro	admn	14321
	Leonice	1863	Plymouth	grdn	14322
	Livy 2nd	1837	Middleboro	grdn	14323 a
	Lizzie F	1871	N. Bridgewater	grdn	14251
	Lucia W	1859	Plymouth	admn	14324
	Lucy	1751	Middleboro	grdn	14325
	Lucy	1857	Plymouth	grdn	14271
	Lucy L	1851	Plymouth	grdn	14348
	Marcy	1751	Plymouth	will	14326
	Martha	1784	Plymouth	admn	14327
	Martha	1832	Plymouth	admn	14328
	Mary	1817	Plymouth	admn	14329
	Mary	1871	Plymouth	grdn	14235
	Natalie	1871	Plymouth	grdn	14235
	Nathaniel	1709	Plymouth	will	14332
	Nathaniel	1711	Plymouth	grdn	14330
	Nathaniel	1727	Plymouth	admn	14333
	Nathaniel	1731	Plymouth	admn	14334
	Nathaniel	1733/4	Plymouth	grdn	14331
	Nathaniel	1751	Middleboro	grdn	14325
	Nathaniel	1823	Plymouth	admn	14336
	Nathaniel	1829	Halifax	admn	14338
	Nathaniel	1843	Halifax	admn	14339
	Nathaniel H	1871	Plymouth	admn	14337
	Nathaniel Jr	1781	Plymouth	will	14335
	Polly	1858	Plymouth	admn	14340
	Polly	1874	Plymouth	will	14341
	Rebecca	1759	Plymouth	admn	14343
	Rebecca	1764	Plymouth	grdn	14369
	Rebecca	1810	Plymouth	grdn	14344
	Rebecca	1863	Plymouth	grdn	14322
	Rebecca F	1834	Plymouth	grdn	14342
	Ruth	1740	Plymouth	grdn	14361
	Samuel	1745	Plymouth	admn	14345
	Samuel	1843	Middleboro	admn	14346
	Sarah	1751	Middleboro	grdn	14325
	Sarah	1764	Plymouth	grdn	14369
	Sarah	1851	Plymouth	grdn	14348
	Sarah	1871	Plymouth	grdn	14235
	Sarah E	1870	Plymouth	will	14347
	Seth	1751	Middleboro	grdn	14325
	Seth	1847	Middleboro	will	14350
	Seth Jr	1806	Middleboro	will	14349
	Silas	1783	Plymouth	admn	14351
	Silas	1840	Pembroke	will	14352
	Silas	1841	Pembroke	grdn	14353 a
	Silvanus	1740	Plymouth	grdn	14361
	Susanna	1696/7	Plymouth	grdn	14317
	Susannah	1802	Middleboro	grdn	14310
	Thomas	1731	Plymouth	admn	14359
	Thomas	1740	Plymouth	grdn	14361
	Thomas	1748	Plymouth	will	14358
	Thomas	1817	Plymouth	admn	14357
	Thomas	1825	Plymouth	admn	14356
	Thomas	1834	Plymouth	admn	14355
	Thomas	1850	Plymouth	admn	14354
	Thomas Jr	1738	Plymouth	admn	14360
	Timothy	1747	Plymouth	will	14362
	William	1750	Plymouth	admn	14363
	William	1752	Plymouth	grdn	14364
	William	1764	Plymouth	grdn	14369
	William	1851	Plymouth	will	14365
	William H	1879	Plympton	grdn	14366
	Zacheus	1791	Scituate	admn	14367
	Zephaniah	1760	Middleboro	admn	14368
	Zephaniah	1764	Plymouth	grdn	14369
	Zilpha	1843	Middleboro	grdn	14261
MOTT	Atwood	1809	Scituate	will	14370
	Deborah	1826	Scituate	will	14371
	Ebenezer	1777	Scituate	admn	14372

SURNAME	FIRST NAME	YEAR	PLACE	CASE	DOCKET
MOTT	Elenora	1864	Scituate	grdn	14373
	Hannah	1864	Scituate	grdn	14373
	Leurena	1864	Scituate	grdn	14373
	Mercy	1862	Scituate	admn	14374
	Otis	1864	Scituate	grdn	14373
	Ruth	1801	Scituate	will	14375
	Stephen	1862	Scituate	admn	14376
MOUNTFORD	Rebekah	1727	Scituate	bond	14377
MULLANEY	James H	1873	N. Bridgewater	grdn	14378
MULLEN	Patrick	1863	Plymouth	admn	14379
	Thomas P	1863	Kingston	admn	14380
MUNGO	Elias R	1880	Scituate	will	14381
MUNROE	Abigail	1836	Halifax	admn	14382
	Benjamin	1824	Halifax	admn	14383
	Charles J	1842	Hanson	admn	14384
	Cyrus	1872	Hanson	will	14385
	Daniel	1837	Halifax	will	14386
	Deborah	1879	Hanson	admn	14387
	Francis M	1851	Hanover	grdn	14388
	George W	1826	Hanson	will	14389
	Grenville	1880	Bridgewater	will	14390
	Henry	1837	Hanson	admn	14391
	Henry	1848	Hanson	admn	14392
	Hiram	1873	Hanson	admn	14393
	Lucy	1860	W. Bridgewater	admn	14394
	Mary F	1865	Hanson	grdn	14395
	Matthias	1836	Bridgewater	will	14396
	Nathan	1876	Bridgewater	will	14397
MURDOCK	Abigail	1798	Carver	grdn	14403
	Albert	1858	N. Bridgewater	grdn	14398
	Alfred	1838	Carver	admn	14399
	Andrew	1854	N. Bridgewater	admn	14400
	Bartlett	1795	Carver	admn	14401
	Bartlett	1798	Carver	grdn	14403
	Bartlett	1880	Carver	grdn	14409
	Bartlett Jr	1796	Carver	admn	14402
	Calvin	1857	Middleboro	will	14404
	Deborah	1798	Carver	grdn	14403
	Elijah	1827	Carver	grdn	14405
	Elisha	1813	Carver	grdn	14427
	Elisha	1826	Carver	admn	14406
	Eliza Ann	1854	Carver	grdn	14407
	Fanny	1865	Bridgewater	grdn	14408
	George	1880	Carver	grdn	14409
	Henry C	1879	Carver	admn	14410
	Hiram N	1844	W. Bridgewater	will	14411
	Ira	1828	Carver	admn	14412
	Ira	1865	Bridgewater	admn	14413
	Ira	1879	Carver	grdn	14414
	Jennie	1880	Carver	grdn	14409
	Jesse	1798	Carver	grdn	14403
	Jesse	1875	Carver	will	14415
	Jesse	1880	Carver	grdn	14409
	John	1756	Plymouth	grdn	14416
	John	1756	Plymouth	will	14417
	John	1756	Plymouth	will	14418
	John	1817	Middleboro	admn	14419
	John	1880	Carver	admn	14420
	Levi	1850	Middleboro	admn	14421
	Lucy	1820	Carver	will	14422
	Luther	1860	Middleboro	will	14423
	Luther Jr	1854	Middleboro	admn	14424
	Maud	1880	Carver	grdn	14409
	Myrtle	1880	Carver	grdn	14409
	Polly L	1859	Middleboro	admn	14425
	Rebecca	1827	Carver	grdn	14405
	Sally	1798	Carver	grdn	14403
	Seabury	1813	Carver	grdn	14427
	Seabury	1833	Carver	admn	14426
	Thomas	1751	Plymouth	will	14428
	Thomas	1798	Carver	grdn	14403

SURNAME	FIRST NAME	YEAR	PLACE	CASE	DOCKET
MURDOCK	William	1812	Carver	admn	14429
	William B	1879	Carver	grdn	14414
MURPHY	Dennis	1862	Plymouth	admn	14430
	James	1873	N. Bridgewater	will	14431
	James C	1879	Plymouth	will	14432
	John	1855	W. Bridgewater	admn	14433
	Mary	1880	S. Abington	admn	14434
	Michael	1863	W. Bridgewater	admn	14435
	Sarah J	1848	N. Bridgewater	grdn	14436
	William	1856	Abington	admn	14437
	William T	1866	Bridgewater	admn	14438
MURRAY	Cornelius	1875	Bridgewater	will	14439
	Ellen	1879	Abington	will	14440
	James	1852	E. Bridgewater	name	14441
MURRAY	Michael	1866	Abington	will	14443
	Michael	1867	Abington	grdn	14444
	Michael	1873	Abington	will	14442
MUZZEY	Julia A	1880	Hingham	will	14445
MYE	Eliza J	1877	Plymouth	will	14446
MYRICK	Barnabas	1789	Sheph'sfield ME	grdn	14447
	Elizabeth	1789	Sheph'sfield ME	grdn	14447
	William	1870	Duxbury	will	14448
NASH	Abigail	1728	Abington	grdn	14521
	Alexander	1847	Abington	admn	14449
	Arthur D	1869	Abington	grdn	14469
	Asa	1815	Bridgewater	admn	14450
	Benjamin	1730	Weymouth	grdn	14451
	Benjamin L	1850	Abington	grdn	14452
	Betsey	1870	Abington	will	14453
	Betty	1852	Pembroke	will	14454
	Catherine B	1872	Abington	will	14455
	Cornelius	1864	E. Bridgewater	admn	14456
	Cyrus	1850	Abington	will	14457
	Daniel	1785	Abington	grdn	14458
	Daniel	1804	Abington	admn	14459
	David	1848	Hanover	admn	14460
	Edmund	1863	Plymouth	grdn	14472
	Edward E	1861	Abington	grdn	14462
	Edward E	1863	Abington	admn	14461
	Edwin	1852	Abington	admn	14463
	Elias	1857	Abington	will	14464
	Elisha	1769	Scituate	admn	14465
	Eliza J	1874	Abington	admn	14466
	Elizabeth	1768	Scituate	grdn	14489
	Elizabeth	1800	Scituate	will	14467
	Experience	1730	Abington	admn	14468
	George W	1869	Abington	grdn	14469
	Hannah	1768	Scituate	will	14470
	Hannah	1793	Abington	admn	14471
	Henrietta C	1863	Plymouth	grdn	14472
	Ida E W	1874	Abington	grdn	14473
	Ira	1859	Abington	admn	14474
	Irving C	1869	Abington	grdn	14469
	Jacob	1729	Weymouth	admn	14475
	Jacob	1730	Abington	admn	14476
	Jacob	1774	Abington	grdn	14477
	Jacob	1798	Abington	admn	14478
	Jacob	1839	Abington	admn	14479
	Jacob	1851	Abington	admn	14480
	Jacob B	1850	Abington	grdn	14482
	Jacob B	1868	Abington	admn	14481
	James	1725	Abington	admn	14483
	James	1759	Abington	admn	14484
	James	1771	Abington	admn	14485
	James	1773	Scituate	admn	14488
	James	1858	Abington	admn	14486
	James E	1850	Abington	grdn	14452
	James Jr	1768	Scituate	grdn	14489
	James O	1881	Abington	admn	14487
	John	1745	Scituate	admn	14490
	John	1768	Scituate	grdn	14489

SURNAME	FIRST NAME	YEAR	PLACE	CASE	DOCKET
NASH	John	1826	Abington	admn	14493
	John	1851	Abington	admn	14494
	John	1857	S. Scituate	will	14491
	John K	1880	S. Scituate	will	14492
	Jonathan	1827	Abington	will	14495
	Joseph	1732	Scituate	will	14496
	Joseph	1764	Scituate	will	14497
	Joseph	1802	Scituate	grdn	14526
	Joseph	1815	Scituate	will	14498
	Joseph	1818	Scituate	admn	14499
	Leonard	1867	Abington	will	14500
	Loring	1868	E. Bridgewater	admn	14501
	Lucy	1802	Scituate	grdn	14526
	Lydia	1816	Scituate	admn	14502
	Lysander B	1827	Scituate	grdn	14503
	Lysander W	1863	Plymouth	grdn	14472
	Mary	1728	Abington	grdn	14521
	Mary	1761	Abington	will	14504
	Mary	1860	E. Bridgewater	admn	14507
	Mary	1872	Abington	admn	14506
	Mary L	1850	Abington	grdn	14482
	Mary O	1864	Abington	admn	14505
	Mercy	1769	Scituate	admn	14508
	Micah	1849	Abington	admn	14509
	Minot	1873	Abington	will	14510
	Nabby S	1855	Abington	will	14511
	Nancy M	1850	Abington	grdn	14482
	Nathaniel	1836	Abington	will	14512
	Nathaniel	1861	Abington	will	14513
	Nathaniel W	1861	Abington	grdn	14462
	Olive	1860	Abington	will	14514
	Peter	1728	Abington	grdn	14521
	Peter	1773	Abington	admn	14515
	Polly	1869	Abington	will	14516
	Rachel	1851	Abington	grdn	14527
	Rebecca	1730	Weymouth	grdn	14451
	Reuben T	1843	Hingham	admn	14517
	Richmond	1852	E. Bridgewater	admn	14518
	Ruth	1768	Scituate	grdn	14489
	Ruth	1848	Hanover	grdn	14519 a
	Sally	1870	Abington	will	14520
	Samuel	1728	Abington	grdn	14521
	Sarah	1728	Abington	grdn	14521
	Sarah	1843	Abington	admn	14522
	Sarah	1880	Abington	will	14523
	Silence	1728	Abington	grdn	14521
	Simeon	1764	Scituate	admn	14524
	Solon	1802	Scituate	admn	14525
	Solon	1802	Scituate	grdn	14526
	Sylvia A	1851	Abington	grdn	14527
	William	1760	Scituate	admn	14528
	Zadock	1865	Abington	will	14529
NASON	Mary	1879	Brockton	admn	14530
NATHAN	Catherine	1872	N. Bridgewater	will	14531
NEAL	Abigail	1836	Scituate	will	14532
	John	1735	Scituate	admn	14533
	Joseph	1744	Scituate	will	14534
	Joseph	1748	Scituate/Hanovr	admn	14535
	Willie Russell	1862	Plymouth	adop	14536
NEGRO	Francis	1714	Scituate	admn	14537
NELSON	Abiah	1735	Middleboro	grdn	14538
	Abiel	1829	Middleboro	will	14539
	Abigail	1810	Plymouth	grdn	14569
	Abigail	1844	Middleboro	admn	14540
	Amos	1796	Middleboro	will	14541
	Amos	1796	Middleboro	grdn	14542
	Bathsheba	1803	Middleboro	grdn	14543
	Caroline B	1863	Lakeville	grdn	14580
	Charity	1735	Middleboro	grdn	14538
	Cyrus	1849	Plymouth	grdn	14544
	Ebenezer	1809	Plymouth	will	14545

SURNAME	FIRST NAME	YEAR	PLACE	CASE	DOCKET
NELSON	Ebenezer	1829	Plymouth	will	14546
	Ebenezer	1830	Plymouth	admn	14547
	Ebenezer L	1859	Middleboro	admn	14548
	Elisha	1878	Plymouth	admn	14549
	Ezra	1803	Middleboro	admn	14550
	Fatima B	1871	Lakeville	admn	14551
	George	1829	Plymouth	admn	14552
	George	1829	Plymouth	grdn	14553
	Hannah	1827	Middleboro	will	14554
	Hezekiah	1806	Plymouth	admn	14555
	Hope	1735	Middleboro	grdn	14538
	Hope	1821	Middleboro	will	14556
	Horatio	1803	Middleboro	grdn	14543
	Horatio	1869	Lakeville	admn	14557
	Isabella F	1864	N. Bridgewater	grdn	14566
	James	1867	Hingham	will	14558
	Joannah	1697	Plymouth	grdn	14578
	Job P	1862	Lakeville	admn	14559
	John	1697	Plymouth	will	14560
	John	1732	Middleboro	admn	14561
	John	1803	Middleboro	will	14562
	Judith	1859	Lakeville	will	14563
	Lemuel	1810	Plymouth	grdn	14564
	Lydia C	1874	Plymouth	grdn	14586
	Martha	1839	Plymouth	admn	14565
	Martha B	1874	Plymouth	grdn	14586
	Mary C	1864	N. Bridgewater	grdn	14566
	Morgan	1806	Middleboro	grdn	14567
	Phebe	1844	Middleboro	admn	14568
	Polly	1810	Plymouth	grdn	14569
	Polly	1835	Middleboro	grdn	14579
	Ruth	1810	Plymouth	warr	14570
	Ruth	1823	Plymouth	admn	14571
	Ruth J	1829	Plymouth	grdn	14553
	Samuel	1697	Plymouth	grdn	14578
	Samuel	1758	Plymouth	will	14575
	Samuel	1810	Plymouth	grdn	14569
	Samuel	1822	Middleboro	will	14572
	Samuel	1826	New Orleans	admn	14574
	Samuel	1831	Middleboro	admn	14573
	Samuel	1835	Plymouth	admn	14577
	Samuel N	1798	Plymouth	admn	14576
	Sarah	1835	Middleboro	grdn	14579
	Sarah K	1845	Middleboro	grdn	14581
	Sidney T	1863	Lakeville	grdn	14580
	Susan F	1845	Middleboro	grdn	14581
	Susannah	1868	Middleboro	will	14582
	Thomas	1755	Middleboro	admn	14584
	Thomas	1819	Middleboro	admn	14585
	Thomas	1832	Plymouth	admn	14583
	Walter H	1874	Plymouth	grdn	14586
	William	1718	Middleboro	will	14589
	William	1806	Middleboro	will	14590
	William	1820	Plymouth	will	14587
	William	1851	Middleboro	admn	14592
	William	1863	Plymouth	admn	14588
	William W	1845	Middleboro	admn	14591
NETCHER	Star	1848	Rochester	will	14593
NEUFFER	George S J	1849	Plymouth	will	14594
NEVINS	Bridget	1880	S. Abington	grdn	14595 a
	Patrick	1874	Abington	admn	14596
NEWBURY	James	1791	Plymouth	grdn	14597
	Lemuel	1791	Plymouth	grdn	14597
NEWCOMB	Joshua	1749	Plymouth	admn	14598
	Rachel	1880	Hingham	will	14599
	Samuel	1877	Hingham	admn	14600
	Silas	1874	Hingham	admn	14601
NEWELL	Caleb	1781	Scituate	grdn	14605
	Hezekiah	1777	Scituate	admn	14602
	Jacob	1781	Scituate	grdn	14605
	James	1720	Scituate	will	14603

SURNAME	FIRST NAME	YEAR	PLACE	CASE	DOCKET
NEWELL	James	1780	Scituate	will	14604
	James	1781	Scituate	grdn	14605
	John	1805	Scituate	admn	14606
	Joshua	1770	Scituate	admn	14607
	Joshua	1781	Scituate	grdn	14605
	Levi	1806	Scituate	admn	14608
	Mary	1745	Scituate	will	14609
NEWHALL	Horace	1830	E. Bridgewater	grdn	14611
	Martha	1878	Hingham	will	14610
	Nabby	1830	E. Bridgewater	grdn	14611
	Samuel	1830	E. Bridgewater	grdn	14611
	William	1818	Bridgewater	admn	14612
NEWLAND	Jabez	1787	Plympton	will	14613
	Jeremiah	1723	Pembroke	admn	14614
	Sarah	1792	Plympton	will	14615
NEWMAN	Maria P	1874	N. Bridgewater	peti	14616
NEWTON	Ruhamah	1792	Brookfield	grdn	14617
	Sarah M	1863	Bridgewater	will	14618
NICHOLS	Abigail	1850	Scituate	admn	14620
	Adam	1869	Wareham	admn	14619
	Albert O	1874	Plymouth	adop	14621
	Alfred	1868	Hingham	will	14622
	Allen	1871	Hingham	will	14623
	Amos	1721	Scituate	grdn	14654
	Amos	1760	Scituate	grdn	14624 a
	Caleb	1777	Scituate	admn	14625
	Caleb	1830	Scituate	admn	14626
	Charles A	1869	Wareham	grdn	14627
	Cynthia	1850	S. Scituate	admn	14628
	Darius M	1873	Middleboro	admn	14629
	David	1715/6	Pembroke	will	14630
	Eben B	1858	Hingham	admn	14631
	Edward	1816	Plymouth	admn	14632
	Eleazer	1824	Freetown	grdn	14633
	Elizabeth	1777	Scituate	inve	14634
	Ephraim	1749	Pembroke	admn	14635
	Flora	1874	Plymouth	adop	14636
	Harriet L	1870	Kingston	will	14637
	Harriet L	1871	Kingston	will	14638
	Israel	1721	Scituate	grdn	14654
	Israel	1779	Scituate	will	14639
	Israel	1838	Scituate	grdn	14640 a
	Israel	1874	Scituate	will	14641
	Job	1721	Scituate	grdn	14654
	John	1858	Hingham	admn	14643
	John M	1825	Plymouth	admn	14642
	Joseph	1718	Scituate	admn	14644
	Leah	1721	Scituate	grdn	14654
	Leah	1851	Hingham	admn	14645
	Lincoln	1863	Marshfield	admn	14646
	Mary	1762	Scituate	grdn	14647
	Micah	1769	-----	grdn	14648
	Moses	1846	Plymouth	admn	14649
	Nathaniel	1731	Pembroke	will	14650
	Noah	1824	Scituate	will	14651
	Paul L	1868	Kingston	will	14652
	Priscilla	1880	Hingham	will	14653
	Rachel	1721	Scituate	grdn	14654
	Rebecca	1871	Hingham	admn	14656
	Rebecca C	1859	Middleboro	admn	14655
	Robert C	1840	Hingham	grdn	14657
	Ruth	1769	-----	grdn	14648
	Susanna	1750	Pembroke	will	14658
	Thomas	1721	Scituate	grdn	14654
	Thomas	1754	Scituate	will	14659
	Warren	1866	Marshfield	grdn	14660
NICHOLSON	Benoni	1781	Rochester	admn	14661
	Daniel	1816	Plymouth	admn	14662
	Thomas	1798	Plymouth	will	14663
NICKERSON	Ann S	1880	Hingham	admn	14664
	Anson	1877	Hingham	will	14665

SURNAME	FIRST NAME	YEAR	PLACE	CASE	DOCKET
NICKERSON	Carrie J	1870	Rochester	adop	14666
	Edward	1873	Plymouth	grdn	14669
	Emeline R	1854	Plymouth	grdn	14667
	Frederick	1823	Boston	grdn	14668
	Frederick	1873	Plymouth	grdn	14669
	Israel	1853	Plymouth	will	14670
	John	1774	Scituate	admn	14671
	John	1852	Hingham	will	14672
	Lucy Ann	1823	Boston	grdn	14668
	Mary	1816	Provincetown	grdn	14673
	Nicholas	1683	Yarmouth	admn	14674
	Rebecca	1879	Plymouth	admn	14675
	Roland	1873	Plymouth	grdn	14669
	Seth	1774	Plymouth	admn	14676
	Seth	1807	Plymouth	admn	14677
	Sparrow	1810	Hingham	admn	14678
	Uriah	1835	Plymouth	will	14679
	William T	1844	Plymouth	grdn	14680
NIGHTINGALE	Phineas S	1880	Wareham	will	14681
NILES	Asa	1849	Middleboro	will	14682
	Clarissa	1864	Abington	will	14683
	Elizabeth	1863	Abington	will	14684
	Laura	1876	Abington	admn	14685
	Mary	1840	Abington	admn	14686
	Samuel	1805	Abington	admn	14687
	Samuel	1814	Abington	admn	14688
NOBLE	Jesse	1872	Wareham	will	14689
NORCROSS	Joseph W	1863	Abington	admn	14690
	Mary L	1864	Abington	admn	14691
	Sarah	1845	Scituate	admn	14692
NORCUTT	Ephraim	1833	Middleboro	grdn	14694 a
	Ephraim Jr	1756	Middleboro	admn	14693
	Ralph	1716	Marshfield	admn	14695
	Sarah	1721	Marshfield	grdn	14696
	William	1693	Marshfield	will	14697
	Zenas	1833	Middleboro	grdn	14698 a
NORRINGTON	Thomas	1764	Plymouth	admn	14699
NORRIS	Lewis A	1867	N. Bridgewater	admn	14700
	Olive	1860	Plymouth	admn	14701
	Oliver	1715	Plymouth	will	14702
	Samuel	1726	Plymouth	admn	14703
	William	1707	Scituate	will	14704
NORTHEY	Betty	1798	Scituate	grdn	14712
	Eliphalet	1787	Scituate	will	14705
	James	1752	Scituate	will	14706
	John	1720	Scituate	admn	14707
	John	1769	Scituate	grdn	14708
	Joseph	1786	Scituate	will	14710
	Joseph	1796	Scituate	admn	14711
	Joseph	1798	Scituate	grdn	14712
	Joseph	1801	Pembroke	admn	14709
	Mary	1805	Scituate	will	14713
	Mercy	1877	Scituate	will	14714
	Polly	1798	Scituate	grdn	14712
	Sally	1798	Scituate	grdn	14712
NORTON	Anna	1807	Hingham	will	14715
	Elizabeth	1759	Abington	grdn	14731
	Hannah	1831	Abington	admn	14716
	Jabez	1785	Rochester	will	14717
	Jane	1840	Hingham	admn	14718
	John	1843	Hingham	admn	14719
	Mary	1759	Abington	grdn	14731
	Matilda C	1870	Bridgewater	will	14720
	Mehitable R	1873	Abington	will	14721
	Noah	1791	Abington	grdn	14722
	Noah	1814	Abington	admn	14723
	Samuel	1789	Abington	will	14724
	Samuel	1826	Abington	will	14725
	Samuel	1832	Hingham	will	14727
	Samuel	1837	Hingham	admn	14728
	Samuel	1871	Abington	will	14726

SURNAME	FIRST NAME	YEAR	PLACE	CASE	DOCKET
NORTON	Sarah	1759	Abington	grdn	14731
	Sarah	1862	N. Bridgewater	admn	14729
	Sarah E	1870	Bridgewater	grdn	14730
	Shubael	1820	Rochester	admn	14732
	Silence	1840	Abington	admn	14733
	William H	1855	Marion	admn	14734
NORVEILL	Etta	1874	Middleboro	adop	14735
	Levi	1883	Middleboro	will	14736
NORWOOD	Bathsheba	1856	Hull	will	14737
NOURSE	Charles A	1881	Brockton	admn	14738
	George D	1881	Brockton	grdn	14739
NOYES	Benjamin	1833	Abington	admn	14740
	Benjamin	1877	Abington	will	14741
	Daniel	1780	Abington	will	14743
	Daniel	1780	Abington	grdn	14744
	Daniel	1829	Abington	will	14742
	Ebenezer	1832	E. Bridgewater	admn	14745
	Eliab	1826	Abington	admn	14746
	Eliab	1826	Abington	admn	14747
	Eliab M	1873	Abington	will	14748
	Elizabeth	1725	Abington	grdn	14756
	Elizabeth	1879	Abington	admn	14749
	Ephraim	1822	N. Bridgewater	will	14750
	Hannah	1725	Abington	grdn	14756
	Ichabod	1787	Abington	grdn	14763
	Jacob	1743	Abington	grdn	14751
	Jacob	1814	Abington	will	14752
	Jacob	1879	Brockton	admn	14753
	James	1879	Abington	will	14754
	John	1793	Abington	will	14755
	John N	1830	Abington	grdn	14764
	Martha	1725	Abington	grdn	14756
	Mary	1725	Abington	grdn	14756
	Matthew	1837	Abington	grdn	14757
	Mercy	1780	Abington	grdn	14744
	Moses	1795	Abington	grdn	14758
	Nicholas	1719	Abington	admn	14759
	Samuel	1729	Abington	will	14760
	Samuel	1773	Abington	will	14761
	Samuel	1787	Abington	grdn	14763
	Samuel Jr	1776	Abington	admn	14762
	Spencer W	1830	Abington	grdn	14764
	Susan G	1858	Abington	admn	14765
NUDD	Joseph W	1850	Hingham	admn	14766
NUTTER	Frederick	1866	E. Bridgewater	grdn	14767
	Ichabod	1864	E. Bridgewater	admn	14768
	Isaac	1866	E. Bridgewater	admn	14769
	Samuel J	1876	Kingston	will	14770
	Samuel W	1863	Kingston	grdn	14771
	Samuel W	1880	Kingston	admn	14772
NYE	Abigail	1817	Hingham	grdn	14786
	Ann E	1855	Rochester	grdn	14798
	Atkinson	1838	Hingham	grdn	14806
	Barnabas	1816	Rochester	admn	14773
	Barnabas B	1863	Marion	will	14775
	Barnabas Jr	1856	Marion	admn	14774
	Benjamin	1818	Wareham	admn	14776
	Bonum	1762	Plympton	admn	14777
	Charles	1816	Rochester	grdn	14800
	Cornelius	1817	Hingham	grdn	14786
	Cornelius	1833	Hingham	admn	14778
	David	1863	Wareham	will	14779
	Deborah	1817	Hingham	grdn	14786
	Dinah	1833	Rochester	grdn	14780 a
	Elisha	1816	Rochester	grdn	14800
	Ezekiel	1816	Rochester	grdn	14800
	Ezekiel	1828	Rochester	admn	14781
	Francis	1872	Mattapoisett	will	14782
	George	1872	Marion	grdn	14799
	George B	1833	Rochester	will	14783
	Hannah	1872	Marion	grdn	14799

SURNAME	FIRST NAME	YEAR	PLACE	CASE	DOCKET
NYE	Henry	1817	Hingham	admn	14785
	Henry	1817	Hingham	grdn	14786
	Henry	1838	Hingham	grdn	14806
	Henry	1840	Hingham	admn	14784
	Ichabod	1735	Rochester	admn	14787
	Ichabod	1771	Rochester	will	14788
	Icy	1816	Rochester	grdn	14800
	Isaac	1779	Plympton	will	14789
	Isabella L	1859	S. Scituate	grdn	14790
	Jabez	1745	Plympton	will	14791
	James	1816	Rochester	grdn	14800
	James M	1840	Rochester	admn	14792
	John	1737	Plymouth	admn	14793
	John	1809	Rochester	will	14795
	John	1817	Hingham	grdn	14786
	John	1867	Hingham	will	14794
	John B B	1872	Marion	admn	14796
	Joseph	1840	Plympton	admn	14797
	Joseph J	1855	Rochester	grdn	14798
	Lillian	1872	Marion	grdn	14799
	Lois	1817	Hingham	grdn	14786
	Lorenzo	1816	Rochester	grdn	14800
	Lucy	1875	Marion	will	14801
	Lydia R	1871	Plymouth	peti	14802
	Mary et al	1878	Marion	peti	14803
	Nathan	1808	Rochester	will	14804
	Nathan	1872	Marion	grdn	14799
	Phebe	1816	Rochester	grdn	14800
	Richard	1816	Rochester	grdn	14800
	Ruth	1855	Rochester	admn	14805
	Sarah	1838	Hingham	grdn	14806
	Stephen	1810	Rochester	grdn	14807 a
	Stephen	1818	Scituate	grdn	14808 a
	Stephen	1829	Pembroke	admn	14809
	Susan	1816	Rochester	grdn	14800
	Susan	1869	Mattapoisett	admn	14810
	Tabitha	1817	Hingham	grdn	14786
	William	1817	Hingham	grdn	14786
	William	1841	Rochester	admn	14813
	William	1849	Plymouth	admn	14811
	William	1856	Rochester	admn	14814
	William Jr	1831	Rochester	admn	14812
OAKES	George L	1851	Middleboro	will	14815
OAKLEY	Arthur	1868	N. Bridgewater	will	14816
OAKMAN	Alice	1823	Pembroke	will	14817
	Betsey	1796	Marshfield	grdn	14835
	Betsey	1866	Marshfield	will	14818
	Christopher	1875	Marshfield	will	14819
	Constant	1877	Marshfield	admn	14821
	Constant F	1834	Marshfield	admn	14820
	Deborah	1795	Marshfield	admn	14822
	Edward	1757	Marshfield	grdn	14823 a
	Edward	1761	Marshfield	grdn	14824
	Edward	1791	Marshfield	admn	14825
	Ellen B	1876	Marshfield	admn	14826
	Hatch	1843	Marshfield	will	14827
	Hope	1827	Marshfield	admn	14828
	John	1798	Marshfield	grdn	14829 a
	Louisa	1800	Marshfield	admn	14830
	Louisa R	1868	Marshfield	grdn	14831
	Melzar T	1796	Marshfield	will	14832
	Nathan O	1869	Hanover	grdn	14834
	Nathan S	1869	Hanover	will	14833
	Nellie S	1869	Hanover	grdn	14834
	Persis	1796	Marshfield	grdn	14835
	Polly	1796	Marshfield	grdn	14835
	Rachel	1796	Marshfield	grdn	14835
	Rachel	1855	Marshfield	will	14836
	Samuel	1739	Marshfield	admn	14837
	Samuel	1791	Marshfield	will	14838
	Thomas R	1868	Marshfield	admn	14839

SURNAME	FIRST NAME	YEAR	PLACE	CASE	DOCKET
OAKMAN	Tobias	1748	Marshfield	grdn	14840
	Tobias	1750	Marshfield	will	14841
	Wealthy C	1877	Marshfield	admn	14842
	Xoa	1796	Marshfield	grdn	14835
OBER	Elijah	1868	Middleboro	grdn	14843
	Eveline	1868	Middleboro	grdn	14843
	Lucinda	1868	Middleboro	grdn	14843
	Nelson	1868	Middleboro	grdn	14843
OBRIEN	Catherine	1873	Kingston	grdn	14844
	Charles	1879	Abington	grdn	14852
	Daniel	1878	Wareham	admn	14845
	Daniel	1879	Rockland	will	14846
	Denis	1879	Brockton	admn	14847
	Helen	1879	Abington	grdn	14852
	John	1866	Kingston	admn	14848
	Mansfield	1879	Abington	grdn	14852
	Mary A	1865	Plymouth	grdn	14849
	Miles	1850	Scituate	admn	14850
	Patrick	1879	Abington	admn	14851
	Robert	1879	Abington	grdn	14852
OCALLAHAN	Michael	1870	Abington	admn	14853
	Michael J	1870	Abington	grdn	14854
OCONNELL	John	1852	Carver	admn	14855
ODONNELL	William	1875	Middleboro	will	14856
OKEEFE	Ellen	1866	Middleboro	admn	14857
OLDHAM	Annie F	1865	Wareham	grdn	14858
	David	1858	Pembroke	admn	14859
	Deborah	1861	Pembroke	will	14860
	Gracey L	1826	Pembroke	grdn	14861
	Isaac	1736	Pembroke	admn	14862
	Isaac	1796	Pembroke	will	14863
	Job B	1879	Plymouth	will	14864
	Joel	1869	Abington	admn	14865
	John	1822	Pembroke	will	14866
	John	1871	Pembroke	will	14867
	Jonathan	1812	Scituate	admn	14868
	Jonathan	1825	Pembroke	grdn	14869
	Joseph	1825	Pembroke	grdn	14869
	Joseph	1825	Pembroke	will	14870
	Joseph	1841	Duxbury	admn	14871
	Lydia	1831	Hanover	will	14872
	Oliver	1760	Duxbury	admn	14873
	Patience	1735	Scituate	grdn	14878
	Thomas	1713	Scituate	admn	14875
	Thomas	1734	Scituate	will	14876
	Thomas	1735	Scituate	will	14877
	Thomas	1735	Scituate	grdn	14878
	Thomas	1840	Duxbury	admn	14874
	Walter S	1868	Abington	admn	14879
OLIVER	Andrew	1772	Middleboro	admn	14880
	Clarissa	1879	Hingham	admn	14881
	Jonathan	1773	Plymouth	admn	14882
	Peter	1718	Rochester	admn	14883
	Peter (absent)	1777	Middleboro	bond	14884
	Peter Jr (abs)	1777	Middleboro	bond	14885
	Phebe	1831	Middleboro	will	14886
OLNEY	Zaben	1870	Plymouth	will	14887
OLSON	Andrew P	1863	N. Bridgewater	admn	14888
OMANS	Job	1824	Rochester	admn	14889
	Polly	1872	Rochester	admn	14890
	Sally	1851	Rochester	will	14891
OMARRA	Patrick et al	----	(Coogan ch)	----	14892
OMEY	Phillip	1782	Middleboro	admn	14893
ONEIL	Lemuel	1820	Duxbury	grdn	14896
	Patrick	1875	Brockton	will	14894
	Thomas	1820	Duxbury	grdn	14896
	Thomas	1877	W. Bridgewater	admn	14895
	William	1820	Duxbury	grdn	14896
ORCHARD	Robert	1712	Boston	admn	14897
ORCUTT	Anna	1872	Abington	will	14898
	Benjamin	1694	Bridgewater	grdn	14908

SURNAME	FIRST NAME	YEAR	PLACE	CASE	DOCKET
ORCUTT	Benjamin	1777	Bridgewater	admn	14899
	Esther R	1846	Hanover	grdn	14900
	Joseph	1784	Bridgewater	admn	14901
	Mary	1818	Bridgewater	will	14902
	Mercy	1760	Bridgewater	grdn	14903
	Moses	1748	Bridgewater	admn	14904
	Moses	1781	Bridgewater	will	14905
	Nathaniel	1760	Bridgewater	grdn	14903
	Nathaniel	1811	Bridgewater	will	14906
	Rhoda	1836	Scituate	will	14907
	Thomas	1694	Bridgewater	grdn	14908
	William	1693	Bridgewater	admn	14909
	William	1739	Bridgewater	admn	14910
	William	1814	Scituate	admn	14911
	William E	1846	Hanover	grdn	14900
OROHO	Owen	1877	Bridgewater	will	14912
OROURKE	Patrick	1866	Kingston	admn	14913
ORR	Elizabeth C	1871	E. Bridgewater	will	14914
	Hector	1855	E. Bridgewater	will	14915
	Hugh	1798	Bridgewater	admn	14916
	Margaret	1837	E. Bridgewater	admn	14917
	Mary	1859	E. Bridgewater	admn	14918
	Samuel A	1878	E. Bridgewater	admn	14919
OSBORNE	Barak	1868	Hanson	will	14920
	Ebenezer	1838	Scituate	will	14921
	Ebenezer	1874	E. Bridgewater	admn	14922
	Edwin F	1878	Scituate	admn	14923
	Eleanor B	1876	Pembroke	will	14924
	George	1878	Lakeville	will	14927
	George Jr	1809	Pembroke	admn	14925
	George T	1872	Marshfield	admn	14926
	Hannah	1839	E. Bridgewater	admn	14928
	Isabel	1872	Marshfield	grdn	14929
	Jerusha	1826	Pembroke	admn	14930
	Martin	1861	Pembroke	admn	14931
OSGOOD	Esther	1862	Kingston	admn	14932
OSMENT	Mary	1729	Plymouth	will	14933
OSYER	Joseph	1749	Pembroke	admn	14934
OTHEMAN	Bartholomew	1879	Duxbury	will	14935
OTIS	Abigail	1823	Scituate	grdn	14966
	Abigail T	1841	Scituate	will	14936
	Abijah	1818	Scituate	grdn	14937 a
	Abijah Jr	1841	Scituate	grdn	14938
	Almeda L	1833	Scituate	grdn	14939
	Amos S	1840	Scituate	will	14940
	Amy	1846	Scituate	grdn	14941 a
	Amy	1869	Pembroke	grdn	14942 a
	Amy	1870	Pembroke	will	14943
	Barnabas	1847	Plymouth	will	14944
	Benjamin	1813	Scituate	admn	14945
	Charles	1794	Boston	grdn	14946
	Cushing	1838	Scituate	admn	14947
	Cushing	1869	E. Bridgewater	admn	14948
	Daniel	1872	S. Scituate	will	14949
	Ensign	1782	Scituate	will	14950
	Ensign	1787	Scituate	grdn	14951 a
	Ensign Jr	1823	Scituate	will	14952
	Ephraim	1816	Scituate	will	14953
	Fanny	1841	Scituate	will	14954
	Gertrude B	1878	S. Scituate	adop	14955
	Gracie L	1875	Scituate	adop	14956
	Hannah	1688	Scituate	will	14957
	Hannah	1823	Scituate	grdn	14966
	Henry	1823	Scituate	grdn	14966
	Henry T	1841	Scituate	admn	14958
	Ignatius	1781	Scituate	grdn	14959
	Ignatius	1802	Scituate	will	14960
	Isaac	1778	Scituate	will	14961
	Isaac	1786	Bridgewater	will	14962
	James	1807	Scituate	will	14963
	James	1823	Scituate	grdn	14966

SURNAME	FIRST NAME	YEAR	PLACE	CASE	DOCKET
OTIS	James E	1864	Scituate	grdn	14965
	James L	1832	Scituate	will	14964
	Jane	1823	Scituate	grdn	14966
	Job	1760	Scituate	will	14967
	Job	1791	Scituate	will	14968
	Job	1825	Scituate	grdn	14969 a
	Job P	1838	Scituate	admn	14970
	Job P	1838	Scituate	grdn	14971
	John	1823	Scituate	grdn	14966
	John	1832	Scituate	admn	14973
	John C	1851	Scituate	will	14976
	John E	1835	Scituate	will	14975
	John T	1830	Scituate	admn	14972
	John T	1832	Scituate	grdn	14974
	Joseph	1788	Scituate	will	14977
	Joshua	1822	Scituate	will	14979
	Joshua 3rd	1801	Scituate	admn	14978
	Josiah	1808	Bridgewater	will	14980
	Laura	1841	Scituate	grdn	14938
	Lemuel	1762	Scituate	admn	14981
	Lemuel	1845	Key West FL	admn	14982
	Lucy	1823	Scituate	grdn	14966
	Lucy	1841	Scituate	admn	14983
	Lydia	1823	Scituate	grdn	14966
	Lydia	1841	Scituate	grdn	14938
	Lydia C	1838	Scituate	grdn	14971
	Mabel	1816	Scituate	admn	14984
	Martha	1841	Scituate	grdn	14938
	Mary	1841	Scituate	grdn	14938
	Mary	1841	Scituate	will	14985
	Mary	1842	Scituate	will	14986
	Mary	1858	S. Scituate	will	14987
	Mary T	1873	Scituate	admn	14988
	Melville	1853	E. Bridgewater	admn	14989
	Mercy	1815	Scituate	admn	14990
	Noah	1799	Scituate	admn	14991
	Primus	1854	S. Scituate	will	14992
	Prince	1801	Scituate	admn	14993
	Prince	1802	Scituate	will	14994
	Priscilla	1750	Scituate	will	14995
	Ruth	1828	Scituate	will	14996
	Sally B	1844	Scituate	admn	14997
	Samuel	1823	Scituate	grdn	14998 a
	Samuel	1826	Scituate	will	14999
	Sarah	1813	Scituate	will	15000
	Sarah	1827	Scituate	will	15001
	Sarah	1841	Scituate	grdn	14938
	Silas	1864	Scituate	will	15002
	Stephen	1733	Scituate	will	15003
	Stephen	1757	Scituate	will	15004
	Stephen	1775	Hanover	admn	15005
	Susanna	1838	E. Bridgewater	admn	15006
	Thankful	1826	Scituate	will	15007
	William	1765	Scituate	admn	15008
	William	1785	Scituate	grdn	15009
	William	1841	Scituate	grdn	14938
OUR	William	1860	Hingham	grdn	15010 a
	William	1860	Hingham	admn	15011
OURISH	Agnes	1865	Hingham	will	15012
	Agnes F	1865	Hingham	grdn	15013
	Annie L	1865	Hingham	grdn	15013
	Harriet E	1865	Hingham	grdn	15013
	John	1865	Hingham	grdn	15013
	Simeon	1856	Hingham	will	15014
OVERTON	Alfred	1848	Hingham	will	15015
	Charlotte	1848	Hingham	grdn	15016
	Eliza	1848	Hingham	grdn	15016
	Ellen	1848	Hingham	grdn	15016
	Francis	1848	Hingham	grdn	15016
	Sarah	1848	Hingham	grdn	15016
OWENS	Ann	1869	N. Bridgewater	grdn	15019

SURNAME	FIRST NAME	YEAR	PLACE	CASE	DOCKET
OWENS	Ellen	1869	N. Bridgewater	grdn	15019
	Ellen	1879	Brockton	grdn	15020
	John	1879	Brockton	will	15017
	Michael	1869	N. Bridgewater	admn	15018
	Michael	1869	N. Bridgewater	grdn	15019
	Michael J	1879	Brockton	grdn	15020
	Robert	1879	Brockton	grdn	15020
PACKARD	Abbie L	1877	Brockton	will	15021
	Abel	1796	Bridgewater	grdn	15022
	Abiah	1755	Bridgewater	grdn	15023
	Abiah	1809	Bridgewater	admn	15024
	Abiah	1818	Bridgewater	grdn	15025 a
	Abiel	1774	Bridgewater	will	15026
	Abiel	1801	Bridgewater	grdn	15136
	Abiel	1879	W. Bridgewater	admn	15027
	Abigail	1751	Bridgewater	grdn	15120
	Abigail	1768	Bridgewater	grdn	15073
	Abigail	1774	Bridgewater	grdn	15028 a
	Abigail W	1830	Abington	grdn	15160
	Abijah	1775	Bridgewater	admn	15029
	Abijah	1783	Bridgewater	grdn	15030
	Addie L	1881	Brockton	grdn	15031
	Albert	1856	N. Bridgewater	admn	15032
	Almira	1821	N. Bridgewater	grdn	15127
	Alpheus	1812	Bridgewater	admn	15033
	Alvah	1861	W. Bridgewater	admn	15034
	Ambrose	1869	N. Bridgewater	will	15035
	Ames	1815	Bridgewater	will	15036
	Ann	1817	Bridgewater	grdn	15179
	Annie F	1879	Brockton	grdn	15048
	Arza	1853	N. Bridgewater	will	15037
	Arza	1863	N. Bridgewater	will	15038
	Austin	1819	Bridgewater	grdn	15039
	Barnabas	1798	Bridgewater	admn	15040
	Bathsheba	1815	Bridgewater	grdn	15049
	Beniah	1773	Bridgewater	grdn	15157
	Benjamin	1768	Bridgewater	grdn	15073
	Benjamin	1808	Bridgewater	will	15041
	Betsey	1815	Bridgewater	grdn	15049
	Betsey D	1873	N. Bridgewater	will	15042
	Caroline F	1857	N. Bridgewater	grdn	15182
	Charles	1783	Bridgewater	grdn	15030
	Charles	1851	N. Bridgewater	will	15044
	Charles	1876	W. Bridgewater	admn	15045
	Charles A	1815	Bridgewater	grdn	15049
	Charles A	1836	N. Bridgewater	admn	15043
	Charles F	1857	N. Bridgewater	grdn	15182
	Charles J F	1872	N. Bridgewater	grdn	15046 a
	Charles J F	1877	Brockton	will	15047
	Charles W	1879	Brockton	grdn	15048
	Charlotte	1872	W. Bridgewater	will	15050
	Chloe	1778	Bridgewater	grdn	15051
	Clara S	1870	N. Bridgewater	adop	15052
	Clarence M	1872	N. Bridgewater	grdn	15053
	Clifford A	1879	Brockton	grdn	15048
	Content	1804	Bridgewater	grdn	15054
	Cyrus	1854	N. Bridgewater	will	15055
	Dan	1840	Abington	admn	15056
	Daniel	1697	Bridgewater	grdn	15123
	Daniel	1732	Bridgewater	will	15058
	Daniel	1732	Bridgewater	grdn	15059
	Daniel	1745	Bridgewater	admn	15057
	David	1755	Bridgewater	will	15060
	David	1785	Bridgewater	will	15061
	David	1786	Bridgewater	admn	15062
	David	1856	N. Bridgewater	will	15063
	David A	1857	N. Bridgewater	grdn	15182
	Deliverance	1791	Bridgewater	will	15064
	Denison	1861	W. Bridgewater	admn	15065
	Dorothy	1801	Bridgewater	will	15066
	Ebenezer	1803	Bridgewater	will	15068

SURNAME	FIRST NAME	YEAR	PLACE	CASE	DOCKET
PACKARD	Ebenezer Jr	1798	Bridgewater	will	15067
	Edward A	1868	N. Bridgewater	admn	15069
	Edward B	1879	Brockton	will	15070
	Elijah	1766	Bridgewater	admn	15072
	Elijah	1768	Bridgewater	grdn	15073
	Elijah	1832	W. Bridgewater	admn	15071
	Eliphalet	1795	Bridgewater	grdn	15143
	Eliza C	1827	N. Bridgewater	grdn	15074
	Elizabeth	1853	S. Scituate	grdn	15075
	Emma L	1871	N. Bridgewater	grdn	15077
	Emma S	1880	Brockton	will	15076
	Fearnot	1722	Bridgewater	grdn	15078
	Frederick	1871	N. Bridgewater	grdn	15077
	Galen	1869	N. Bridgewater	will	15079
	Gamaliel	1783	Bridgewater	grdn	15030
	George	1736	Bridgewater	admn	15080
	George A	1837	N. Bridgewater	grdn	15102
	George F	1871	N. Bridgewater	admn	15081
	Georgianna F	1872	N. Bridgewater	adop	15083
	Georgianna R	1845	N. Bridgewater	admn	15082
	Hannah	1796	Bridgewater	grdn	15084
	Hannah	1799	Bridgewater	grdn	15085
	Harriet	1827	N. Bridgewater	grdn	15074
	Harriet A	1871	N. Bridgewater	grdn	15077
	Henry R	1834	Duxbury	admn	15086
	Herbert	1879	Brockton	grdn	15048
	Herbert S	1866	N. Bridgewater	grdn	15088
	Herbert T	1868	E. Bridgewater	grdn	15087
	Herbert W	1857	N. Bridgewater	grdn	15182
	Herman	1866	N. Bridgewater	grdn	15089
	Hezekiah	1779	Bridgewater	grdn	15090
	Hezekiah	1857	N. Bridgewater	will	15091
	Horace	1869	W. Bridgewater	grdn	15092
	Horace E	1866	N. Bridgewater	grdn	15088
	Hosea	1838	N. Bridgewater	grdn	15093
	Howard	1837	N. Bridgewater	will	15094
	Ichabod	1754	Bridgewater	grdn	15095
	Isaac	1732	Bridgewater	grdn	15059
	Isaac	1743	Bridgewater	admn	15096
	Isaac	1793	Bridgewater	will	15097
	Isaac	1793	Bridgewater	grdn	15098
	Isaac	1837	N. Bridgewater	admn	15101
	Isaac	1837	N. Bridgewater	grdn	15102
	Isaac	1860	Bridgewater	admn	15100
	Isaac A	1848	N. Bridgewater	admn	15099
	Isaiah	1816	Bridgewater	will	15103
	Israel	1856	N. Bridgewater	will	15105
	Israel Jr	1752	Bridgewater	will	15104
	Jacob	1777	Bridgewater	admn	15106
	James	1765	Bridgewater	will	15107
	Japhet	1832	W. Bridgewater	grdn	15163
	Jennie A	1872	N. Bridgewater	grdn	15108
	Jesse	1773	Bridgewater	grdn	15157
	Jesse	1860	N. Bridgewater	will	15109
	Joanna	1838	N. Bridgewater	will	15110
	Job	1735	Bridgewater	grdn	15111
	Joel	1872	N. Bridgewater	will	15112
	John	1738	Bridgewater	admn	15113
	John	1741	Bridgewater	admn	15114
	John	1862	N. Bridgewater	peti	15115
	Jonas	1819	Bridgewater	admn	15116
	Jonas	1835	N. Bridgewater	will	15117
	Jonathan	1746	Bridgewater	admn	15119
	Jonathan	1751	Bridgewater	grdn	15120
	Jonathan	1805	Bridgewater	will	15118
	Joseph	1697	Bridgewater	grdn	15123
	Joseph	1760	Bridgewater	will	15121
	Joseph	1778	Bridgewater	grdn	15051
	Joseph 2nd	1760	Bridgewater	will	15122
	Josiah	1783	Bridgewater	grdn	15186
	Josiah	1793	Bridgewater	will	15124

SURNAME	FIRST NAME	YEAR	PLACE	CASE	DOCKET
PACKARD	Josiah	1801	Bridgewater	admn	15125
	Josiah	1821	N. Bridgewater	grdn	15127
	Josiah	1864	N. Bridgewater	will	15126
	Julia E	1837	N. Bridgewater	grdn	15102
	Keziah	1795	Bridgewater	grdn	15143
	Leah	1778	Bridgewater	grdn	15051
	Lebbeus	1855	W. Bridgewater	will	15128
	Lemuel	1822	N. Bridgewater	admn	15129
	Lemuel	1875	Marshfield	admn	15130
	Liberty	1877	Brockton	admn	15131
	Loami	1773	Bridgewater	grdn	15157
	Louisa	1827	N. Bridgewater	grdn	15074
	Lucia W	1854	Marshfield	admn	15132
	Lucinda	1872	N. Bridgewater	will	15133
	Lucius	1833	N. Bridgewater	admn	15134
	Luke	1801	Bridgewater	grdn	15136
	Luke	1858	N. Bridgewater	will	15135
	Luther	1783	Bridgewater	grdn	15186
	Marcus	1871	N. Bridgewater	will	15137
	Marcus	1872	N. Bridgewater	admn	15138
	Marlborough	1773	Bridgewater	grdn	15157
	Martha	1732	Bridgewater	grdn	15059
	Martha	1832	N. Bridgewater	will	15139
	Mary	1768	Bridgewater	grdn	15073
	Mary	1821	N. Bridgewater	grdn	15127
	Mary H	1876	W. Bridgewater	grdn	15140
	Matilda G	1859	N. Bridgewater	will	15141
	Matthew	1795	Bridgewater	admn	15142
	Matthew	1795	Bridgewater	grdn	15143
	Mehitable	1821	N. Bridgewater	grdn	15127
	Mercy	1841	Duxbury	admn	15144
	Micah	1850	Bridgewater	admn	15145
	Micha	1854	N. Bridgewater	will	15146
	Minerva	1869	N. Bridgewater	will	15147
	Minnie L	1872	N. Bridgewater	grdn	15108
	Moses	1875	Brockton	grdn	15148 a
	Myra	1876	W. Bridgewater	admn	15149
	Nahum	1821	N. Bridgewater	grdn	15127
	Nahum	1856	Marshfield	will	15150
	Nathan	1773	Bridgewater	admn	15156
	Nathan	1773	Bridgewater	grdn	15157
	Nathan	1791	Bridgewater	admn	15155
	Nathan	1798	Bridgewater	will	15154
	Nathan	1823	N. Bridgewater	will	15153
	Nathan	1840	W. Bridgewater	admn	15152
	Nathan F	1873	N. Bridgewater	will	15151
	Nathaniel	1721	Bridgewater	will	15158
	Nehemiah	1732	Bridgewater	grdn	15059
	Nehemiah	1751	Bridgewater	admn	15159
	Nehemiah	1795	Bridgewater	grdn	15143
	Noah F	1830	Abington	grdn	15160
	Olive	1865	N. Bridgewater	will	15161
	Oliver	1820	Bridgewater	grdn	15162 a
	Orlando	1832	W. Bridgewater	grdn	15163
	Perez	1783	Bridgewater	grdn	15186
	Perez	1832	W. Bridgewater	grdn	15163
	Philo	1821	N. Bridgewater	grdn	15127
	Rebecca	1801	Bridgewater	grdn	15136
	Relief	1843	N. Bridgewater	will	15164
	Robert	1844	N. Bridgewater	will	15165
	Robert	1880	Brockton	admn	15166
	Ruth	1778	Bridgewater	grdn	15051
	Ruth	1789	Halifax	will	15167
	Sally	1873	N. Bridgewater	will	15168
	Samuel	1697	Bridgewater	admn	15169
	Samuel	1749	Bridgewater	will	15170
	Samuel	1775	Bridgewater	admn	15171
	Samuel N	1826	N. Bridgewater	grdn	15191
	Samuel T	1866	N. Bridgewater	admn	15172
	Sarah	1732	Bridgewater	grdn	15059
	Sarah	1783	Bridgewater	grdn	15186

SURNAME	FIRST NAME	YEAR	PLACE	CASE	DOCKET
PACKARD	Sarah	1793	Bridgewater	will	15173
	Sarah	1801	Bridgewater	grdn	15136
	Shepard	1837	N. Bridgewater	will	15174
	Sidney	1821	N. Bridgewater	grdn	15127
	Sidney	1878	E. Bridgewater	admn	15175
	Silas	1851	N. Bridgewater	will	15176
	Silas	1859	N. Bridgewater	admn	15177
	Simeon	1783	Bridgewater	grdn	15030
	Simeon	1815	Bridgewater	will	15178
	Simeon	1817	Bridgewater	grdn	15179
	Sumner E	1866	N. Bridgewater	grdn	15088
	Susan	1815	Bridgewater	grdn	15049
	Susan P	1857	N. Bridgewater	grdn	15182
	Susanna	1732	Bridgewater	grdn	15059
	Susanna	1773	Bridgewater	grdn	15157
	Susannah	1869	N. Bridgewater	will	15180
	Sylvanus	1857	N. Bridgewater	grdn	15181 a
	Sylvanus C	1857	N. Bridgewater	grdn	15182
	Thomas	1819	Bridgewater	admn	15183
	Tiley	1880	Brockton	will	15184
	Timothy	1782	Bridgewater	admn	15185
	Timothy	1783	Bridgewater	grdn	15186
	Vasti	1856	N. Bridgewater	will	15187
	Washburn	1881	Brockton	will	15188
	Weston	1826	N. Bridgewater	grdn	15191
	William	1815	Bridgewater	grdn	15049
	William	1824	N. Bridgewater	admn	15190
	William	1866	N. Bridgewater	admn	15189
	William A	1826	N. Bridgewater	grdn	15191
	Zachariah	1772	Bridgewater	will	15192
	Zacheus	1725	Bridgewater	admn	15193
PACUCHES	David	1733	Assawamsett	will	15194 i
PADDOCK	Angenette F	1873	Plymouth	grdn	15195
	Nathaniel	1758	Rochester	admn	15196
	Septa	1855	Abington	admn	15197
	Thomas	1786	Middleboro	admn	15198
	Thomas Jr	1778	Middleboro	admn	15199
	Zechariah	1795	Middleboro	will	15200
PAGE	Abigail	1858	Plymouth	will	15201
	Aurelia	1877	Middleboro	admn	15202
PAINE	Content	1800	Abington	admn	15203
	Gardner	1877	Rochester	admn	15204
	Hannah	1740	Sandwich	grdn	15208
	Harriet N	1868	Abington	grdn	15205
	Horace E	1868	Abington	grdn	15205
	Isaac	1869	Marshfield	will	15206
	John S	1878	Plymouth	will	15207
	Joseph Jr	1740	Sandwich	grdn	15208
	Lydia R	1876	E. Bridgewater	admn	15209
	Peleg	1786	Rochester	grdn	15210
	Reuben C	1879	Kingston	will	15211
	Stephen	1781	Abington	will	15213
	Stephen	1853	Abington	admn	15214
	Stephen Jr	1778	Abington	admn	15212
	Vesta C	1868	S. Scituate	grdn	15215
	Zebulon	1821	Abington	will	15216
PALMER	Amasa	1870	S. Scituate	will	15217
	Ann	1744	Plymouth	admn	15218
	Ann	1755	Scituate	will	15219
	Anna	1749	Scituate	grdn	15225
	Anna	1847	E. Bridgewater	will	15220
	Benjamin	1749	Scituate	grdn	15225
	Benjamin	1820	Scituate	will	15221
	Bezaliel	1706	Scituate	will	15222
	Bezaliel	1748	Scituate	admn	15224
	Bezaliel	1749	Scituate	grdn	15225
	Bezaliel	1757	Scituate	will	15223
	Eliza	1809	Bridgewater	grdn	15226
	Ephraim	1797	Hanover	will	15227
	Ezekiel	1788	Hanover	will	15228
	George W	1880	Rochester	admn	15229

SURNAME	FIRST NAME	YEAR	PLACE	CASE	DOCKET
PALMER	Huldah	1749	Scituate	grdn	15225
	Huldah	1769	Scituate	grdn	15243
	James	1780	Middleboro	admn	15230
	James	1780	Middleboro	grdn	15231
	Jane	1808	Scituate	will	15232
	Job	1747	Middleboro	admn	15233
	John	1708	Scituate	admn	15234
	John	1785	Middleboro	will	15236
	John	1794	Scituate	will	15235
	Joseph	1789	Scituate	admn	15237
	Joshua	1710	Scituate	admn	15238
	Josiah	1728	Hanover	admn	15239
	Josiah	1736	Hanover	admn	15240
	Josiah	1775	Hanover	will	15241
PALMER	Lydia	1812	Scituate	will	15242
	Nathaniel	1749	Scituate	grdn	15225
	Priscilla	1749	Scituate	grdn	15225
	Sarah	1769	Scituate	grdn	15243
	Sarah	1780	Middleboro	grdn	15231
	Thomas	1689	Scituate	admn	15244
	Thomas	1743	Middleboro	will	15245
	Thomas	1779	Halifax	admn	15246
	Zilpha	1809	Bridgewater	grdn	15226
PARISH	Elizabeth O	1839	N. Bridgewater	grdn	15247
PARKER	Benjamin	1865	Hingham	admn	15248
	Betsey	1873	W. Bridgewater	admn	15249
	Betty	1810	Plympton	will	15250
	Caroline	1877	Plympton	will	15251
	Ebenezer	1783	Rochester	will	15252
	Ebenezer G	1840	Plymouth	admn	15253
	Fanny B	1880	E. Bridgewater	admn	15254
	Hannah	1798	Rochester	grdn	15264
	Henry G	1841	Plymouth	grdn	15255
	Isaac	1851	Rochester	admn	15256
	Jerusha	1837	Plympton	will	15257
	Jesse	1761	Rochester	admn	15258
	John	1798	Rochester	grdn	15264
	Jonathan	1776	Plympton	will	15259
	Jonathan	1825	Plympton	will	15260
	Jonathan	1851	Plympton	will	15261
	Jonathan	1864	Plympton	admn	15262
	Joseph	1798	Rochester	admn	15263
	Joseph	1798	Rochester	grdn	15264
	Joseph	1823	Plympton	grdn	15268
	Lydia	1799	Plympton	will	15265
	Mary	1852	Hanover	admn	15267
	Mary E	1866	Bridgewater	grdn	15266
	Mercy M	1823	Plympton	grdn	15268
	Nathaniel	1690/1	Scituate	admn	15269
	Oliver	1836	Plympton	will	15270
	Oliver	1879	Middleboro	will	15271
	Perry L	1833	Scituate	admn	15272
	Perry L	1860	Scituate	bond	15273
	Polly G	1823	Plympton	grdn	15268
	Polycarpus	1820	Plympton	will	15274
	Susanna	1823	Plympton	grdn	15268
	William	1764	Middleboro	admn	15275
	William	1823	Plympton	grdn	15268
PARKHURST	Mary A	1874	Lakeville	will	15276
PARKINSON	Mary C	1852	Scituate	grdn	15277
PARLOW	Almira	1877	Marion	admn	15278
	Annie F	1876	Marion	grdn	15282
	Charles F	1851	Providence RI	grdn	15279
	Charles H	1876	Marion	admn	15280
	Hannah	1739	Rochester	grdn	15288
	Joseph	1857	Rochester	admn	15281
	Mary	1739	Rochester	grdn	15288
	Mary A	1876	Marion	grdn	15282
	Nathan D	1880	Marion	will	15283
	Nathaniel	1879	Rochester	will	15284
	Thomas	1705	Middleboro	admn	15285

SURNAME	FIRST NAME	YEAR	PLACE	CASE	DOCKET
PARLOW	Thomas	1726	Middleboro	admn	15286
	Thomas	1739	Rochester	grdn	15288
	Thomas	1831	Rochester	admn	15287
PARRIS	Alexander	1852	Pembroke	will	15289
	Ambrose	1877	Pembroke	will	15290
	Benjamin	1816	Pembroke	will	15291
	Benjamin	1817	Bridgewater	admn	15292
	Benjamin	1835	Middleboro	admn	15293
	Cynthia A	1865	Lakeville	grdn	15294
	Elias	1836	Middleboro	admn	15295
	Elias	1836	Middleboro	grdn	15296
	Grace	1754	Pembroke	admn	15297
	Henry	1837	E. Bridgewater	admn	15298
	John	1744	Middleboro	admn	15299
	John	1800	Middleboro	will	15300
	Jonathan	1877	Halifax	will	15301
	Julia D	1854	Kingston	will	15302
	Martin	1840	Kingston	will	15303
	Moses	1833	Middleboro	admn	15304
	Parna	1871	Halifax	admn	15305
	Rebecca	1805	Bridgewater	grdn	15306 a
	Samuel	1730	Pembroke	admn	15307
	Sarah	1879	E. Bridgewater	admn	15308
	Thomas	1786	Pembroke	will	15309
	Thomas	1861	E. Bridgewater	will	15311
	Thomas Jr	1860	E. Bridgewater	admn	15310
PARROT	Ruth	1777	Halifax	admn	15312
PARRY	Annie	1877	Lakeville	grdn	15313 a
PARSONS	Annie M	1880	Plymouth	grdn	15314
	Edith	1865	Plympton	grdn	15315
	Frederick A	1874	Plymouth	grdn	15316
	Grant C	1872	Plymouth	will	15317
	Joseph	1845	Marshfield	admn	15318
	Luella	1874	Plymouth	grdn	15316
	Lydia	1824	Scituate	will	15319
	William	1874	Plymouth	admn	15320
PARTIN	John	1732	Pembroke	grdn	15322
	Thomas	1732	Pembroke	will	15321
	Thomas	1732	Pembroke	grdn	15322
PARTRIDGE	Adoniram J	1865	Abington	will	15323
	Calvin	1815	Duxbury	admn	15324
	George	1695	Duxbury	will	15325
	George	1705	Duxbury	grdn	15332
	George	1768	Duxbury	will	15326
	George	1828	Duxbury	will	15327
	Hannah	1872	Duxbury	will	15328
	Ichabod A	1864	Abington	will	15329
	James	1743	Duxbury	admn	15330
	John	1705	Duxbury	grdn	15332
	John	1731	Duxbury	will	15331
	Mary	1705	Duxbury	grdn	15332
	Mary	1742	Duxbury	will	15333
	Mary	1838	Duxbury	will	15334
	Moses	1824	Plymouth	admn	15335
	Samuel	1705	Duxbury	grdn	15332
	Sarah	1708	Duxbury	will	15336
PATRICK	Edmund	1789	Marshfield	admn	15337
PATTEN	Huldah	1878	Abington	admn	15338
PATTERSON	George A	1848	Wareham	grdn	15339
PATY	Asenath	1861	Plymouth	will	15340
	Carrie H	1867	Plymouth	adop	15341
	Charles W	1850	Plymouth	grdn	15342
	Ellen D	1850	Plymouth	grdn	15342
	Emma T	1880	Plymouth	adop	15343
	Ephraim	1855	Plymouth	will	15344
	Frances W	1850	Plymouth	grdn	15342
	Frank W	1865	Plymouth	grdn	15345
	John	1821	Plymouth	will	15346
	Thomas	1846	Plymouth	admn	15347
	William	1851	Honolulu	admn	15348
PAULDING	Catherine	1872	Plymouth	admn	15349

SURNAME	FIRST NAME	YEAR	PLACE	CASE	DOCKET
PAULDING	Henry B	1863	Duxbury	admn	15350
PAULL	Billings P	1866	Pembroke	will	15351
PAUN	John	1872	Lakeville	will	15352
PEAKES	Daniel	1757	Plymouth	admn	15353
	Eleazer	1705	Scituate	admn	15354
	Eleazer	1784	Scituate	will	15355
	Eleazer	1846	Scituate	will	15356
	Eliza P	1827	Hingham	grdn	15359
	Israel	1706	Scituate	will	15357
	Joseph	1825	Hingham	admn	15358
	Joseph	1827	Hingham	grdn	15359
	Priscilla M	1865	Hingham	admn	15360
	William	1721	Scituate	will	15361
PEARE	Mercy A	1866	Abington	grdn	15362
	Oscar H	1866	Abington	grdn	15362
PEARSON	Annis	1879	S. Abington	admn	15363
	Ezra F	1864	Carver	grdn	15364
	Henry	1866	N. Bridgewater	grdn	15365
	Joannah E	1864	Carver	grdn	15364
	William B	1760	Plymouth	admn	15366
PEASE	Abner	1864	Fairhaven	peti	15367
	Asa	1834	Rochester	will	15368
	Martha	1835	Rochester	will	15369
	Theophilus	1821	Rochester	will	15370
PEASLEY	Melinda	1866	Halifax	admn	15371
	William A	1875	Hanson	admn	15372
PECKHAM	Bertha M	1865	W. Bridgewater	grdn	15373
	David	1761	Newport	grdn	15374
	David	1826	Rochester	will	15375
	David	1851	Rochester	will	15376
	Dorothy	1837	Rochester	will	15377
	Elizabeth	1823	Westport	bond	15378
	Henry Jr	1865	W. Bridgewater	admn	15379
	Isabella F	1865	W. Bridgewater	grdn	15380
	Jacob	1823	Westport	bond	15378
	Judith	1871	Wareham	will	15381
	Percival H	1881	Brockton	admn	15382
	Stephen	1823	Westport	bond	15378
	Zaccheus	1847	Rochester	will	15383
PEGNAM	John S	1873	Abington	grdn	15384
	Thomas	1863	Abington	admn	15385
PEIRCE	Abial	1812	Middleboro	will	15386
	Abial	1853	Middleboro	will	15387
	Abigail	1780	Middleboro	grdn	15508
	Abraham	1785	Pembroke	will	15388
	Abraham	1824	Middleboro	will	15390
	Abraham	1831	Pembroke	admn	15389
	Amy	1794	Middleboro	grdn	15462
	Ann J	1856	Pembroke	grdn	15391
	Anthony	1755	Bridgewater	admn	15392
	Anthony	1756	Bridgewater	grdn	15393
	Atkins	1868	E. Bridgewater	will	15394
	Bathsheba	1794	Middleboro	grdn	15496
	Benjamin	1730	Scituate	will	15396
	Benjamin	1763	Scituate	grdn	15399
	Benjamin	1768	Scituate	admn	15397
	Benjamin	1772	Scituate	will	15398
	Benjamin	1816	Plymouth	grdn	15395
	Caleb	1768	Scituate	grdn	15469
	Caleb	1773	Rochester	will	15400
	Caleb	1783	Scituate	admn	15401
	Caleb	1786	Scituate	grdn	15402
	Calvin	1813	Duxbury	admn	15404
	Calvin	1813	Duxbury	grdn	15405
	Calvin	1818	Scituate	will	15403
	Catherine	1814	Duxbury	grdn	15482
	Charles S	1869	N. Bridgewater	will	15406
	Chloe	1837	E. Bridgewater	admn	15407
	Christopher Jr	1847	Pembroke	admn	15408
	Daniel	1785	Pembroke	grdn	15411
	Daniel	1799	Pembroke	admn	15410

SURNAME	FIRST NAME	YEAR	PLACE	CASE	DOCKET
PEIRCE	Daniel	1807	Pembroke	grdn	15412
	Daniel	1819	Bridgewater	admn	15409
	Deborah	1814	Duxbury	grdn	15482
	Deborah	1881	Rochester	will	15413
	Deliverance	1801	Middleboro	admn	15414
	Dennis	1868	Rochester	will	15415
	Ebenezer	1795	Middleboro	grdn	15448
	Ebenezer	1797	Middleboro	will	15416
	Ebenezer	1863	Plymouth	admn	15417
	Ebenezer N	1864	Plymouth	grdn	15418
	Elijah	1848	Scituate	admn	15419
	Eliphalet	1827	Middleboro	admn	15420
	Elisha	1770	Scituate	will	15421
	Elisha	1776	Middleboro	admn	15423
	Elisha	1776	Middleboro	admn	15424
	Elisha	1853	Scituate	admn	15422
	Elisha	1863	Middleboro	admn	15425
	Eliza	1876	Duxbury	admn	15426
	Eliza W	1865	Bridgewater	admn	15427
	Elizabeth	1807	Pembroke	grdn	15412
	Elizabeth	1846	Middleboro	will	15428
	Elizabeth B	1848	Scituate	grdn	15430
	Elizabeth B	1876	Scituate	admn	15429
	Elkanah	1797	Middleboro	will	15431
	Enos	1790	Middleboro	will	15432
	Enos	1794	Middleboro	grdn	15462
	Enos	1868	Marshfield	will	15433
	Ethan	1794	Middleboro	grdn	15462
	Ethan	1864	Lakeville	admn	15434
	Experience	1845	Middleboro	admn	15435
	Fanny	1873	Lakeville	will	15436
	George	1779	Middleboro	admn	15437
	George	1875	Rochester	admn	15440
	George R	1876	Middleboro	admn	15438
	George W K	1860	Marion	will	15439
	Gilbert	1864	Middleboro	admn	15441
	Hayward	1827	Scituate	admn	15442
	Hayward	1834	Scituate	grdn	15443 a
	Henry	1791	Middleboro	will	15447
	Henry	1795	Middleboro	grdn	15448
	Henry	1826	Rochester	will	15444
	Henry	1826	Rochester	grdn	15445
	Henry G	1879	Abington	admn	15446
	Henry T	1822	Scituate	grdn	15467
	Hermon	1780	Middleboro	grdn	15508
	Hermon	1809	Middleboro	will	15449
	Howard	1768	Scituate	grdn	15469
	Huldah L	1853	Middleboro	bond	15450
	Ignatius	1862	Plymouth	admn	15451
	Isaac	1732	Middleboro	will	15453
	Isaac	1757	Middleboro	will	15454
	Isaac	1782	Middleboro	will	15455
	Isaac	1830	Middleboro	grdn	15452 a
	Jacob	1807	Bridgewater	admn	15456
	James A	1870	Lakeville	grdn	15457
	Job	1790	Middleboro	admn	15461
	Job	1794	Middleboro	grdn	15462
	Job	1819	Middleboro	will	15460
	Job	1868	Middleboro	will	15459
	Job C	1881	Middleboro	admn	15458
	John	1725	Pembroke	admn	15464
	John	1816	Scituate	admn	15465
	John	1879	Rochester	will	15463
	John B	1840	Scituate	grdn	15466
	John W	1822	Scituate	grdn	15467
	Jonathan	1763	Scituate	grdn	15399
	Jonathan	1768	Scituate	grdn	15469
	Jonathan	1851	Rochester	admn	15468
	Joseph	1794	Middleboro	grdn	15462
	Joseph	1797	Rochester	will	15473
	Joseph	1814	Duxbury	admn	15471

SURNAME	FIRST NAME	YEAR	PLACE	CASE	DOCKET
PEIRCE	Joseph	1860	Duxbury	admn	15472
	Joseph D	1822	Scituate	grdn	15467
	Joseph W	1880	Plymouth	will	15470
	Joshua	1848	Rochester	admn	15474
	Judith	1881	Middleboro	will	15475
	Judith S	1881	Middleboro	admn	15476
	Junietta B	1879	Mattapoisett	adop	15477
	Levi	1780	Middleboro	grdn	15508
	Levi	1847	Middleboro	will	15478
	Levi L	1826	Middleboro	grdn	15479
	Lorenzo F	1826	Middleboro	grdn	15479
	Lucinda	1826	Rochester	grdn	15488
	Lucy	1879	Scituate	admn	15480
	Luther	1814	Duxbury	grdn	15482
PEIRCE	Luther	1831	Duxbury	admn	15481
	Lydia	1814	Duxbury	grdn	15482
	Lysander	1839	Middleboro	grdn	15483
	Lysander	1856	Lakeville	will	15484
	Martin B	1877	Abington	admn	15485
	Mary	1786	Scituate	will	15487
	Mary E	1870	Lakeville	grdn	15457
	Mary L	1826	Rochester	grdn	15488
	Mary L	1870	S. Scituate	admn	15486
	Matthew	1802	Scituate	admn	15489
	Mercy	1857	Lakeville	will	15490
	Nathan	1823	Middleboro	admn	15491
	Nathaniel	1838	Scituate	will	15492
	Nathaniel	1845	Scituate	will	15493
	Nehemiah	1726	Pembroke	grdn	15494
	Oliver	1794	Middleboro	grdn	15496
	Oliver	1861	Lakeville	admn	15495
	Otis	1813	Duxbury	grdn	15405
	Otis	1861	Scituate	admn	15497
	Parker	1813	Duxbury	grdn	15405
	Peter H	1861	Middleboro	admn	15498
	Phebe	1866	Middleboro	will	15499
	Phillip R W	1877	Wareham	admn	15500
	Phineas	1841	Plymouth	admn	15501
	Phineas A	1845	Plymouth	grdn	15502
	Priscilla	1849	Duxbury	will	15503
	Rebecca	1826	Rochester	grdn	15445
	Rowland	1844	Middleboro	will	15504
	Rufus	1814	Duxbury	grdn	15482
	Ruth	1811	Middleboro	admn	15505
	Samuel	1826	Rochester	grdn	15488
	Sarah	1780	Middleboro	grdn	15508
	Sarah	1824	Scituate	admn	15506
	Sarah	1849	Middleboro	grdn	15507
	Sarah B	1848	Scituate	grdn	15430
	Sarah E	1864	Plymouth	grdn	15418
	Seth	1810	Scituate	will	15509
	Silas	1816	Middleboro	will	15510
	Susannah	1840	Plymouth	will	15511
	Theodora	1831	Middleboro	admn	15512
	Thomas	1775	Scituate	will	15513
	Walter	1878	Hanover	name	15514
	Willard	1860	Abington	admn	15515
	William	1806	Wareham	admn	15516
	William	1826	Rochester	grdn	15445
	William G	1844	Middleboro	admn	15518
	William R	1794	Middleboro	admn	15517
	William S	1858	Middleboro	admn	15519
PEMBER	Charles	1874	Plymouth	grdn	15520
	Florence	1874	Plymouth	grdn	15520
	Henry S	1874	Plymouth	grdn	15520
	Howard	1874	Plymouth	grdn	15520
	John	1874	Plymouth	grdn	15520
	Mabel	1874	Plymouth	grdn	15520
	Mira	1874	Plymouth	grdn	15520
	Nathaniel	1874	Plymouth	grdn	15520
	Walter	1874	Plymouth	grdn	15520

SURNAME	FIRST NAME	YEAR	PLACE	CASE	DOCKET
PENEY	George	1840	Scituate	admn	15521
PENNIMAN	Betsey	1854	S. Scituate	admn	15522
	Samuel	1852	Hingham	admn	15523
	William	1761	Braintree	grdn	15524
PERKINS	Abbie	1872	Middleboro	grdn	15525
	Abiah N	1855	Middleboro	admn	15526
	Abraham	1872	Middleboro	will	15527
	Alvin	1875	Carver	will	15528
	Andrew J	1863	Lakeville	admn	15529
	Andrew M	1879	Middleboro	admn	15530
	Annie I	1877	Plymouth	grdn	15531
	Ansel	1850	N. Bridgewater	admn	15532
	Anselm	1806	Bridgewater	grdn	15533
	Azel	1818	Bridgewater	grdn	15535
	Azel	1836	Middleboro	grdn	15574
	Azel	1853	Middleboro	will	15534
	Barnabas	1851	Middleboro	will	15536
	Benjamin	1843	N. Bridgewater	grdn	15537
	Betsey	1821	Middleboro	admn	15538
	Betsey	1843	N. Bridgewater	grdn	15537
	Betsey A	1838	E. Bridgewater	grdn	15540
	Betsey M	1827	Plympton	grdn	15539
	Beza	1827	Plympton	grdn	15541
	Calvin	1815	Duxbury	admn	15542
	Charles A S	1866	Plymouth	admn	15544
	Charles H	1852	Plymouth	grdn	15543
	Charles T	1827	Plympton	grdn	15539
	Charlotte B	1878	Hanover	grdn	15545 a
	Clara M	1853	Middleboro	peti	15546
	Cyrus	1775	Bridgewater	grdn	15661
	Daniel	1783	Bridgewater	will	15547
	Daniel	1801	Kingston	admn	15551
	Daniel	1815	Bridgewater	grdn	15548 a
	Daniel	1817	Bridgewater	admn	15549
	Daniel	1836	Middleboro	will	15552
	Daniel H	1852	Bridgewater	admn	15550
	David	1736	Bridgewater	will	15553
	David	1737	Bridgewater	admn	15554
	David	1859	Bridgewater	grdn	15555 a
	Deborah	1775	Bridgewater	grdn	15661
	Ebenezer	1770	Bridgewater	will	15557
	Ebenezer	1771	Bridgewater	grdn	15558
	Ebenezer	1824	Bridgewater	admn	15556
	Edward G	1869	Middleboro	admn	15559
	Edward S	1869	Plympton	admn	15560
	Eleazer	1738	Plympton	grdn	15594
	Eliza	1827	E. Bridgewater	admn	15561
	Elizabeth	1738	Plympton	grdn	15594
	Elizabeth C	1870	N. Bridgewater	admn	15562
	Experience	1817	Middleboro	admn	15563
	Florence L	1856	Scituate	adop	15564
	Foster	1793	Bridgewater	grdn	15665
	Foster	1802	Bridgewater	admn	15565
	Foster	1812	Bridgewater	grdn	15624
	Foster	1857	Plymouth	will	15566
	Francis	1783	Bridgewater	will	15567
	Francis	1783	Bridgewater	grdn	15568
	Frederick	1862	N. Bridgewater	will	15569
	George	1834	Plymouth	admn	15570
	George W	1793	Bridgewater	grdn	15665
	Gideon	1828	Middleboro	admn	15571
	Grace M	1881	W. Bridgewater	grdn	15595
	Hannah	1831	Carver	grdn	15656
	Hannah	1836	Middleboro	grdn	15574
	Hannah H	1878	Hanover	admn	15572
	Harriet	1850	Hingham	admn	15573
	Harriet J	1836	Middleboro	grdn	15574
	Hepsibah	1771	Bridgewater	grdn	15558
	Holmes	1771	Bridgewater	grdn	15558
	Hosea	1837	E. Bridgewater	admn	15575
	Huldah C	1847	Halifax	grdn	15576

SURNAME	FIRST NAME	YEAR	PLACE	CASE	DOCKET
PERKINS	Isaac	1812	Middleboro	will	15577
	Isaac	1836	Middleboro	grdn	15574
	Isaac	1840	N. Bridgewater	grdn	15587
	Isaac N	1859	Middleboro	will	15578
	Jacob	1783	Bridgewater	grdn	15568
	Jacob	1846	Middleboro	admn	15579
	Jacob	1853	Bridgewater	will	15581
	Jacob Jr	1841	Bridgewater	admn	15580
	Jacob L	1878	PlacevilleCA	will	15582
	James	1728	Bridgewater	grdn	15635
	James	1795	Bridgewater	will	15583
	James	1827	Plympton	grdn	15539
	James S	1870	E. Bridgewater	admn	15584
	Jane A	1858	N. Bridgewater	admn	15585
	Jason	1840	N. Bridgewater	grdn	15587
	Jason	1877	Halifax	admn	15586
	Jesse	1826	N. Bridgewater	will	15588
	Jesse	1857	N. Bridgewater	admn	15589
	John	1728	Plympton	admn	15593
	John	1738	Plympton	grdn	15594
	John	1750	Middleboro	admn	15596
	John	1763	Middleboro	grdn	15597
	John	1826	Plympton	will	15592
	John	1849	Middleboro	grdn	15600
	John	1866	Middleboro	admn	15598
	John	1870	Marion	admn	15590
	John	1876	Plymouth	admn	15591
	John C	1872	Middleboro	will	15599
	John R	1881	W. Bridgewater	grdn	15595
	Jonas R	1875	Brockton	bond	15601
	Jonathan	1796	Bridgewater	will	15602
	Jonathan	1802	Bridgewater	will	15603
	Jonathan	1837	N. Bridgewater	will	15604
	Jonathan B	1870	Plympton	admn	15605
	Joseph	1771	Bridgewater	admn	15606
	Joshua	1797	Carver	admn	15607
	Joshua	1833	Plymouth	admn	15608
	Josiah	1798	Bridgewater	will	15610
	Josiah	1818	Bridgewater	grdn	15535
	Josiah	1828	Plympton	admn	15609
	Josiah	1848	N. Bridgewater	will	15611
	Levi	1881	Brockton	will	15612
	Lloyd	1849	Middleboro	grdn	15600
	Lothrop	1867	Middleboro	will	15613
	Louisa	1881	Rochester	will	15614
	Lucia	1849	Middleboro	grdn	15600
	Lucy	1793	Bridgewater	grdn	15665
	Lucy	1829	Wareham	admn	15616
	Lucy W	1808	Kingston	grdn	15615
	Luke	1776	Bridgewater	admn	15617
	Luke	1789	Bridgewater	grdn	15618
	Luke	1831	Carver	grdn	15656
	Marcia	1827	Plympton	grdn	15539
	Mark	1757	Bridgewater	admn	15619
	Mark	1856	N. Bridgewater	will	15620
	Martha	1728	Bridgewater	grdn	15635
	Martin	1879	Plympton	admn	15621
	Mary	1812	Bridgewater	grdn	15624
	Mary	1843	Kingston	will	15622
	Mary	1850	Bridgewater	admn	15623
	Mary G	1852	N. Bridgewater	grdn	15647
	Mercy	1738	Plympton	grdn	15594
	Mercy	1874	Halifax	admn	15625
	Minerva	1849	Bridgewater	grdn	15626
	Morrill	1849	Middleboro	grdn	15600
	Nahum	1873	N. Bridgewater	will	15627
	Nancy	1771	Bridgewater	grdn	15558
	Nancy	1868	Lakeville	admn	15629
	Nancy S	1819	Bridgewater	grdn	15628
	Nathan	1723	Bridgewater	admn	15634
	Nathan	1728	Bridgewater	grdn	15635

SURNAME	FIRST NAME	YEAR	PLACE	CASE	DOCKET
PERKINS	Nathan	1790	Plympton	admn	15633
	Nathan	1846	Halifax	admn	15632
	Nathan	1852	Middleboro	admn	15631
	Nathan	1860	Middleboro	will	15630
	Noah C	1880	Middleboro	admn	15636
	Olive R et al	1880	Bridgewater	peti	15637
	Orman	1847	Bridgewater	will	15638
	Ozias	1873	Hanover	will	15639
	Rachel	1823	N. Bridgewater	will	15640
	Rebecca	1834	Plymouth	grdn	15657
	Rest	1876	Middleboro	will	15641
	Robert	1783	Bridgewater	grdn	15568
	Robert	1794	Bridgewater	admn	15642
	Robert	1865	Bridgewater	will	15643
	Sampson	1829	Carver	admn	15644
	Sarah	1836	Middleboro	grdn	15574
	Sarah B	1852	N. Bridgewater	will	15646
	Sarah E	1858	Middleboro	admn	15645
	Sarah O	1852	N. Bridgewater	grdn	15647
	Sarah W	1849	Middleboro	grdn	15600
	Seabury	1819	Middleboro	admn	15648
	Seth	1819	Kingston	admn	15649
	Seth	1854	Rochester	admn	15650
	Shepard	1817	Bridgewater	admn	15651
	Sidney	1806	Bridgewater	grdn	15533
	Sidney	1838	E. Bridgewater	grdn	15540
	Sidney	1879	Brockton	will	15652
	Silence	1728	Bridgewater	grdn	15635
	Simeon	1877	Bridgewater	will	15653
	Solomon	1728	Bridgewater	grdn	15635
	Solomon	1743	Bridgewater	admn	15654
	Sophia	1874	Kingston	admn	15655
	Stillman	1831	Carver	grdn	15656
	Susanna	1818	Bridgewater	grdn	15535
	Susannah	1771	Bridgewater	grdn	15558
	Theodore	1775/8	Bridgewater	grdn	15661
	Thomas	1761	Bridgewater	will	15659
	Thomas	1773	Bridgewater	will	15660
	Thomas	1775	Bridgewater	grdn	15661
	Thomas	1843	Halifax	will	15658
	Thomas S	1834	Plymouth	grdn	15657
	Thompson	1849	Middleboro	grdn	15600
	Timothy	1728	Bridgewater	grdn	15635
	Timothy	1792	Barrington NH	grdn	15662
	Timothy	1796	Plymouth	admn	15663
	William	1778	Bridgewater	admn	15664
	William	1793	Bridgewater	grdn	15665
	William	1831	Carver	grdn	15656
	Zadock	1804	Bridgewater	admn	15666
	Zadock	1818	Bridgewater	grdn	15535
	Zadock	1843	N. Bridgewater	grdn	15537
	Zephaniah	1808	Plympton	will	15667
PERRY	Adam	1830	Hanover	will	15668
	Alvah	1837	Hanover	will	15669
	Amos	1756	Scituate	admn	15670
	Amos	1782	Scituate	admn	15671
	Andrew	1838	Middleboro	admn	15672
	Anne	1841	Hanover	will	15673
	Barnabas	1753	Pembroke	admn	15674
	Barnabas	1759	Hanover	admn	15675
	Bethiah	1820	Hanson	grdn	15676 a
	Betsey	1834	Middleboro	admn	15677
	Calvin	1854	Scituate	will	15678
	Charles	1847	Pembroke	admn	15679
	Daniel	1875	S. Abington	will	15680
	Edward Y	1821	Hanson	grdn	15694
	Eleazer	1821	Middleboro	admn	15681
	Elijah	1812	Middleboro	will	15682
	Elijah	1814	Pembroke	admn	15683
	Elizabeth	1743	Scituate	will	15684
	Ethan	1880	Hanover	will	15685

SURNAME	FIRST NAME	YEAR	PLACE	CASE	DOCKET
PERRY	George W	1864	Scituate	grdn	15686
	George W	1865	Scituate	admn	15687
	Hannah	1852	Pembroke	admn	15688
	Henry	1734	Pembroke	will	15689
	Henry	1815	Pembroke	will	15690
	Henry	1837	Hanson	admn	15691
	Horatio	1879	Pembroke	will	15692
	Isaac	1724	Scituate	will	15693
	Isaiah S	1821	Hanson	grdn	15694
	Israel	1817	Hanover	admn	15695
	James	1794	Rochester	grdn	15696 a
	John	1847	Plymouth	admn	15697
	John B	1847	Plymouth	grdn	15698
	Jonathan	1714	Pembroke	admn	15699
	Joseph	1761	Scituate	admn	15700
	Joshua	1762	Middleboro	grdn	15701 a
	Joshua	1875	Hanson	will	15702
	Kimball	1852	Rochester	admn	15703
	Lewis	1876	Plymouth	will	15704
	Lucinda C	1847	Plymouth	grdn	15698
	Maria L	1878	S. Abington	grdn	15705 a
	Mary	1762	Sheepscut Rv	grdn	15728
	Mary	1859	Hanson	admn	15707
	Mary	1877	Hanson	will	15708
	Mary C	1880	Hanover	grdn	15710 a
	Mary E	1876	Hanover	admn	15709
	Mary J	1855	Pembroke	adop	15706
	Nabby B	1835	Marshfield	will	15711
	Nabby B	1855	Hanson	admn	15712
	Nathaniel M	1877	Plymouth	admn	15713
	Otis	1858	Middleboro	admn	15714
	Perez E	1838	Hanover	grdn	15715
	Perly L	1876	Hanover	adop	15716
	Rachel	1762	Sheepscut Rv	grdn	15728
	Relief	1824	Hanover	admn	15717
	Rhoda	1855	Plymouth	will	15718
	Robert	1881	Hanson	will	15719
	Salathiel Jr	1848	Wareham	admn	15720
	Samuel	1742	Hanover	admn	15721
	Samuel	1781	Pembroke	will	15722
	Samuel	1869	Pembroke	admn	15723
	Sarah	1792	Rochester	will	15724
	Sarah	1876	Pembroke	admn	15725
	Seth	1846	Hanson	admn	15726
	Seth	1874	Hanover	admn	15727
	Simeon	1762	Sheepscut Rv	grdn	15728
	Sophia A	1879	Wareham	admn	15729
	Stephen	1779	Rochester	will	15730
	Susanna	1762	Sheepscut Rv	grdn	15728
	Susannah B	1881	Plymouth	will	15731
	Thankful	1856	Abington	grdn	15732 a
	Thankful	1873	Abington	peti	15733
	Thomas	1817	Hanover	grdn	15734 a
	William	1693	Marshfield	admn	15735
	William	1716	Scituate	will	15736
	William	1868	Plymouth	admn	15737
PETERSON	Abigail	1845	Duxbury	will	15738
	Andrew E	1878	Duxbury	grdn	15827
	Ann E	1843	Duxbury	grdn	15819
	Asaph T	1863	Abington	admn	15739
	Benjamin Jr	1769	Duxbury	admn	15740
	Betsey	1846	Plymouth	admn	15741
	Betty	1860	Abington	will	15742
	Briggs	1879	Duxbury	admn	15743
	Caleb	1843	Duxbury	admn	15744
	Charles	1846	Plymouth	admn	15745
	Clark	1867	Duxbury	will	15746
	Cora	1875	Duxbury	grdn	15808
	Daniel B	1876	Duxbury	admn	15747
	David	1761	Duxbury	will	15748
	David	1765	Duxbury	grdn	15786

SURNAME	FIRST NAME	YEAR	PLACE	CASE	DOCKET
PETERSON	Delia S	1878	Duxbury	grdn	15827
	Edwin	1835	Duxbury	peti	15749
	Elijah	1820	Duxbury	admn	15750
	Elijah	1871	Duxbury	admn	15751
	Elisha	1875	Duxbury	admn	15752
	Elisha	1875	Duxbury	grdn	15753
	Elizabeth	1806	Duxbury	admn	15754
	Ellen W	1860	Duxbury	grdn	15755
	Emeline T	1843	Duxbury	grdn	15819
	Frank	1864	Hanover	grdn	15757
	Frank I	1879	Brockton	grdn	15756
	Frederick	1847	Duxbury	will	15758
	Frederick W	1874	E. Bridgewater	admn	15759
	George	1820	Duxbury	admn	15761
	George	1827	Duxbury	admn	15762
	George	1860	Duxbury	grdn	15755
	George	1863	Duxbury	will	15764
	George P	1836	Duxbury	grdn	15765
	George S	1877	Plymouth	admn	15760
	George W	1856	Duxbury	admn	15763
	George W	1864	Pembroke	grdn	15766
	Gilbert M	1877	Duxbury	admn	15767
	Harriet	1853	Plymouth	grdn	15769
	Harriet	1870	Marshfield	admn	15770
	Hattie W	1867	Duxbury	adop	15768
	Helen M	1865	Kingston	grdn	15771
	Hiram	1875	Duxbury	admn	15772
	Ichabod	1805	Duxbury	admn	15773
	Isaac	1741	Duxbury	admn	15774
	Isaac	1785	Scituate	admn	15775
	Isaac	1843	Duxbury	grdn	15819
	Jabez	1855	Duxbury	will	15776
	Jacob	1784	Duxbury	will	15777
	Jane	1846	Duxbury	admn	15778
	Joanna	1875	Halifax	admn	15779
	Joel	1856	Duxbury	will	15780
	John	1690	Duxbury	admn	15781
	John	1720	Duxbury	will	15782
	John	1765	Duxbury	grdn	15786
	John J	1836	Duxbury	grdn	15765
	Jonathan	1745	Pembroke	will	15783
	Jonathan	1765	Duxbury	will	15785
	Jonathan	1765	Duxbury	grdn	15786
	Jonathan	1814	Duxbury	admn	15784
	Joseph	1751	Duxbury	admn	15787
	Joshua	1836	Duxbury	will	15788
	Judah	1846	Duxbury	will	15789
	Judah	1859	Duxbury	admn	15790
	Lewis	1803	Duxbury	admn	15792
	Lewis	1863	Duxbury	admn	15793
	Lewis	1863	Duxbury	grdn	15794
	Lewis	1878	Plymouth	admn	15791
	Lucy	1835	Duxbury	peti	15749
	Lurania	1765	Duxbury	grdn	15786
	Luther	1823	Duxbury	admn	15795
	Lydia	1818	Duxbury	grdn	15796 a
	Lydia	1830	Duxbury	will	15797
	Lydia	1860	Duxbury	admn	15798
	Marshall	1838	Duxbury	admn	15799
	Marshall A	1843	Duxbury	grdn	15800
	Mary	1747	Duxbury	grdn	15804
	Mary D	1877	Duxbury	admn	15803
	Mary E	1869	Duxbury	admn	15802
	Mary H	1863	Duxbury	grdn	15794
	Mary J	1847	Duxbury	grdn	15801
	Mary P	1864	Pembroke	grdn	15766
	Mattie P	1880	Plymouth	grdn	15805
	Nancy C	1877	Duxbury	grdn	15806
	Nehemiah	1811	Duxbury	admn	15807
	Nellie	1875	Duxbury	grdn	15808
	Orphan	1747	Duxbury	grdn	15804

SURNAME	FIRST NAME	YEAR	PLACE	CASE	DOCKET
PETERSON	Packard	1843	Duxbury	admn	15809
	Perez	1953	Plymouth	admn	15810
	Priscilla	1843	Duxbury	admn	15811
	Rebecca	1836	Duxbury	grdn	15812 a
	Reuben	1795	Duxbury	admn	15813
	Reuben	1845	Duxbury	will	15814
	Reuben	1856	Plymouth	will	15815
	S Stillman	1881	Duxbury	will	15820
	Sally	1857	Plymouth	admn	15816
	Samuel S	1873	Duxbury	will	15817
	Sarah A	1873	Duxbury	grdn	15818
	Sarah G	1835	Duxbury	peti	15749
	Sarah J	1843	Duxbury	grdn	15819
	Silas T	1864	Hanover	grdn	15757
	Susie T	1881	Marion	grdn	15821
	Thaddeus	1825	Duxbury	admn	15822
	Thankful	1863	Plymouth	will	15823
	Thomas W	1839	Duxbury	admn	15824
	Turner	1765	Duxbury	grdn	15786
	Walter	1863	Duxbury	admn	15825
	Whittemore	1862	Duxbury	admn	15826
	Wilbur F	1878	Duxbury	grdn	15827
	William	1841	Duxbury	admn	15828
	William P	1863	Duxbury	grdn	15794
	Zephaniah S C	1860	Marshfield	will	15829
PETTEE	Alice	1791	Rochester	admn	15830
	Clara A	1872	Middleboro	adop	15831
PETTER	Albert Watfri	1882	Wareham	adop	15832
PETTINGALE	Akerman	1834	N. Bridgewater	admn	15833
	Araminta	1789	Bridgewater	grdn	15837
	Daniel	1726	Abington	will	15834
	John	1747	Abington	admn	15835
	John	1789	Bridgewater	admn	15836
	John	1789	Bridgewater	grdn	15837
	Obadiah	1743	Abington	admn	15838
	William	1789	Bridgewater	grdn	15837
PHELIX	-----	1715	Assawampset	admn	15839 i
PHELPS	Edward	1826	Rochester	will	15840
	Moses	1788	Albany NY	admn	15841
PHILLIPS	Abigail	1812	Marshfield	grdn	15854
	Asa F	1832	N. Bridgewater	grdn	15850
	Benjamin	1750	Marshfield	admn	15842
	Benjamin	1771	Pembroke	admn	15843
	Betty	1851	Hanson	will	15844
	Blaney	1801	Pembroke	will	15846
	Blaney	1812	Pembroke	grdn	15847
	Blaney	1829	Hanson	admn	15845
	Calvin S	1872	N. Bridgewater	will	15848
	Charles H	1832	N. Bridgewater	grdn	15850
	Charles N	1872	N. Bridgewater	grdn	15849
	Christopher	1806	Pembroke	admn	15851
	Daniel	1812	Marshfield	will	15853
	Daniel	1812	Marshfield	grdn	15854
	Daniel	1863	Marshfield	will	15852
	Daniel L	1828	Bridgewater	grdn	15855
	Edmund	1817	Pembroke	grdn	15856
	Edward T	1865	Carver	admn	15857
	Eli W	1865	Halifax	grdn	15858
	Eliphalet	1774	Bridgewater	admn	15859
	Elisha	1770	Marshfield	admn	15863
	Elisha	1773	Marshfield	grdn	15864
	Elisha	1834	Marshfield	admn	15861
	Elisha	1834	Marshfield	will	15862
	Elisha	1859	E. Bridgewater	admn	15860
	Elisha	1865	Halifax	grdn	15858
	Elizabeth	1736	Plymouth	will	15865
	Elizabeth	1771	Boston	grdn	15884
	Ezra	1856	Hanson	admn	15866
	Frederick	1880	Marshfield	admn	15867
	Hannah	1733	Plymouth	grdn	15868
	Henry L	1873	Marshfield	grdn	15869

SURNAME	FIRST NAME	YEAR	PLACE	CASE	DOCKET
PHILLIPS	Joanna	1798	Marshfield	will	15870
	Joanna W	1812	Marshfield	grdn	15854
	John	1692	Marshfield	will	15871
	John	1738	Marshfield	admn	15872
	John	1791	Duxbury	admn	15873
	John	1855	Newburg NY	admn	15874
	Joseph	1767	Marshfield	will	15875
	Joseph	1773	Marshfield	grdn	15864
	Joseph	1784	Marshfield	admn	15876
	LeRoach	1828	Bridgewater	grdn	15855
	Lewis	1827	Bridgewater	admn	15877
	Lot	1812	Pembroke	will	15878
	Lot	1854	Hanson	grdn	15879
	Luther	1861	Kingston	will	15880
	Lydia	1817	Pembroke	grdn	15856
	Mark	1811	Bridgewater	will	15881
	Mark	1851	E. Bridgewater	will	15882
	Mary	1771	Boston	grdn	15884
	Mary	1773	Marshfield	grdn	15864
	Mary	1807	Marshfield	will	15883
	Mary A	1828	Bridgewater	grdn	15855
	Mercy	1769	Marshfield	will	15885
	Mercy	1773	Marshfield	grdn	15864
	Nathaniel	1795	Marshfield	will	15886
	Nathaniel	1812	Marshfield	grdn	15854
	Oreb	1828	Bridgewater	grdn	15855
	Penelope	1750	Marshfield	grdn	15887
	Priscilla	1817	Pembroke	grdn	15856
	Ruth	1845	Marshfield	will	15888
	Sarah	1789	Pembroke	admn	15889
	Theophilus	1817	Pembroke	grdn	15856
	Thomas	1778	Duxbury	will	15890
	Thompson	1731	Plymouth	will	15891
	Tisdale	1828	Bridgewater	grdn	15855
	William	1776	Pembroke	admn	15892
	William	1869	Hanover	admn	15893
PHINNEY			(see FINNEY)	----	-----
PHIPPS	Charles E	1872	Rochester	grdn	15894
	Elmer E	1872	Rochester	grdn	15894
	Henry G	1872	Rochester	grdn	15894
	Joseph H	1871	Kingston	admn	15895
	Mary E	1872	Rochester	grdn	15894
PICKENS	Abby D	1878	Lakeville	grdn	15897
	Abigail	1876	Middleboro	admn	15896
	Albert G	1824	Freetown	grdn	15910
	Carrie I	1878	Lakeville	grdn	15897
	Catherine	1794	Middleboro	grdn	15901
	Ebenezer	1868	Middleboro	will	15898
	Ezra	1794	Middleboro	grdn	15901
	Ezra	1831	Middleboro	grdn	15903
	George	1872	Middleboro	admn	15899
	Henry	1794	Middleboro	grdn	15901
	James	1794	Middleboro	grdn	15901
	James	1821	Middleboro	admn	15902
	James Jr	1791	Middleboro	admn	15900
	James O	1831	Middleboro	grdn	15903
	Lot	1807	Rochester	will	15904
	Mary B	1866	Middleboro	admn	15905
	Phebe	1834	Middleboro	grdn	15906 a
	Priscilla	1831	Middleboro	grdn	15903
	Samuel	1830	Middleboro	will	15907
	Silas	1871	Lakeville	admn	15908
	Silence	1834	Middleboro	admn	15909
	Stephen B	1824	Freetown	grdn	15910
	Susanna	1834	Middleboro	grdn	15906 a
	Thomas	1793	Middleboro	will	15911
	Thomas	1845	Middleboro	will	15912
	Vodisa H	1872	Lakeville	admn	15913
	Zacheus	1880	Lakeville	will	15914
PICKERNELL	Joseph	1873	Abington	admn	15915
PICKLES	Margaret	1778	Scituate	admn	15916

SURNAME	FIRST NAME	YEAR	PLACE	CASE	DOCKET
PICKLES	Nathan	1742	Scituate	will	15917
	Nathan	1770	Scituate	will	15918
PIGIN	Patience	1825	Bridgewater	grdn	15919 i
	Robert	1814	Bridgewater	grdn	15920 i
PIGSLEY	Benjamin	1796	Plymouth	admn	15921
PILSBURY	Jacob	1789	Abington	will	15922
PINCIN	Benjamin	1848	E. Bridgewater	will	15923
	Elizabeth	1839	E. Bridgewater	will	15924
	Lucy	1859	Scituate	will	15925
	Molly	1850	E. Bridgewater	admn	15926
	Perez	1874	Scituate	will	15927
	Sarah	1851	Scituate	grdn	15928 a
	Sarah	1854	Scituate	admn	15929
	Simeon	1850	Scituate	will	15930
	Simeon	1857	Scituate	will	15931
	Thomas	1694	Scituate	will	15932
	Thomas	1714	Scituate	will	15933
	Thomas	1732	Scituate	grdn	15934 a
	Thomas	1732	Scituate	admn	15935
	Thomas	1793	Scituate	will	15936
	William	1828	E. Bridgewater	admn	15937
PITCHER	Anna C	1873	Marion	admn	15938
	Catherine	1871	Marion	admn	15939
	Ezra	1754	Scituate	grdn	15941
	Ezra	1771	Scituate	will	15940
	James S H	1874	Marion	will	15942
	John	1754	Scituate	grdn	15941
	John	1830	Rochester	grdn	15943
	John	1867	Marion	will	15944
	Nathaniel	1723	Scituate	admn	15945
	Nathaniel	1754	Scituate	grdn	15941
	Peleg S	1830	Rochester	admn	15946
PITTEE	Lizzie E	1865	Plymouth	adop	15947
	Mary Ann	1861	Plymouth	adop	15948
PIVORICK	Nicholas	1859	Hull	admn	15949
PLACE	Darius C	1871	N. Bridgewater	will	15950
PLAISTED	Ichabod	1831	Rochester	will	15951
PLIMPTON	Sarah	1875	Plymouth	will	15952
POCONEY	Joseph	1819	Scituate	grdn	15953
	Joseph	1828	Scituate	grdn	15954
	Lydia	1857	S. Scituate	admn	15955
POKE	James	1749	Middleboro	admn	15956
POLDEN	Briggs	1862	Hanover	will	15957
	James	1804	Plymouth	grdn	15958
	John	1848	Pembroke	admn	15959
POMEROY	Emily M S	1870	Plymouth	admn	15960
POOL	Albert W	1866	Abington	grdn	15961
	Alfred	1858	Abington	admn	15962
	Angelina	1876	Rockland	will	15963
	Benjamin	1813	Bridgewater	admn	15964
	Betsey	1796	Abington	grdn	15983
	Charles A	1862	Abington	grdn	15965
	Charles C	1858	Abington	grdn	15969
	Charles H	1879	S. Abington	grdn	15966
	Clarissa	1796	Abington	grdn	15983
	David	1796	Abington	grdn	15983
	David	1862	Abington	will	15967
	Elias	1796	Abington	grdn	15983
	Elias	1803	Abington	admn	15968
	Ella F	1858	Abington	grdn	15969
	Eurilla A	1881	Rockland	admn	15970
	Ferdinand H	1858	Abington	grdn	15969
	George T	1870	Abington	grdn	15971
	Harriet B	1870	Abington	grdn	15971
	Horace W	1863	Halifax	will	15972
	Isaac	1757	Bridgewater	admn	15973
	Isaac	1759	Bridgewater	will	15974
	Jacob	1875	Abington	will	15975
	James M	1875	S. Abington	will	15976
	Jane	1880	Hingham	grdn	15977 a
	John	1728	Gloucester	admn	15978

SURNAME	FIRST NAME	YEAR	PLACE	CASE	DOCKET
POOL	John	1788	Abington	admn	15982
	John	1796	Abington	grdn	15983
	John	1828	Halifax	admn	15979
	John	1855	W. Bridgewater	admn	15980
	John	1866	Abington	admn	15981
	Joseph	1738	Abington	admn	15984
	Joseph Jr	1801	Abington	will	15985
	Julian	1876	S. Abington	admn	15986
	Ludo	1870	Abington	will	15987
	Maria	1860	Hanover	admn	15988
	Mary A	1807	Abington	grdn	15991
	Mary A	1862	Hanover	grdn	15989
	Mary F	1869	Plymouth	adop	15990
	Mehitable	1810	Abington	will	15992
	Micah	1845	Abington	admn	15993
	Nathaniel	1877	Rockland	admn	15994
	Noah	1847	Abington	will	15995
	Noah A	1879	S. Abington	admn	15996
	Noah A	1879	S. Abington	grdn	15997
	Olive	1768	Bridgewater	grdn	15998
	Rebecca	1853	Halifax	will	15999
	Rosamond S	1879	Rockland	grdn	16000 a
	Ruth	1807	Abington	grdn	15991
	Sally	1866	Abington	will	16001
	Sally	1879	S. Abington	admn	16002
	Samuel C	1858	Abington	will	16003
	Susan E	1876	S. Abington	admn	16004
	Thaxter	1870	Abington	will	16005
	Warren	1801	Abington	grdn	16006
POPE	Benjamin P	1849	Bridgewater	will	16007
	Ellen	1849	Bridgewater	grdn	16008
	Eunice C	1849	Bridgewater	grdn	16008
	Eunice M	1877	Bridgewater	admn	16009
	Ezra P	1866	Halifax	grdn	16010
	George W	1866	Halifax	grdn	16010
	Hannah P	1849	Bridgewater	grdn	16008
	Henry	1866	Halifax	will	16011
	Huldah E	1849	Bridgewater	grdn	16008
	Ichabod	1795	Bridgewater	will	16012
	Lydia W	1879	Plymouth	will	16013
	Nahum	1849	Bridgewater	grdn	16008
	Priscilla	1836	Plymouth	grdn	16014
	Seth	1837	Rochester	admn	16015
	Sylvanus P	1849	Bridgewater	grdn	16008
	Sylvanus P	1879	Bridgewater	admn	16016
	Thomas	1820	Plymouth	admn	16017
	Thomas	1843	Halifax	admn	16018
PORCHERON	Charles E	1866	Bridgewater	admn	16019
	Joseph E	1859	Bridgewater	admn	16020
PORTER	Abigail	1785	Middleboro	grdn	16021
	Amasa	1785	Middleboro	grdn	16021
	Avery	1847	Abington	admn	16022
	Calvin	1785	Middleboro	grdn	16021
	David	1784	Abington	will	16023
	Ebenezer	1860	Abington	admn	16024
	Edward	1818	Marshfield	grdn	16043
	Frank	1875	Middleboro	grdn	16033
	Isaac	1809	Middleboro	admn	16025
	James	1803	Bridgewater	admn	16026
	James	1804	Bridgewater	grdn	16027
	John	1724	Weymouth	admn	16028
	John	1730	Abington	grdn	16029
	John	1824	Abington	will	16030
	John	1866	Duxbury	admn	16031
	Jonathan	1791	Middleboro	admn	16032
	Lucy	1785	Middleboro	grdn	16021
	Lucy B	1875	Middleboro	grdn	16033
	Martin	1816	Middleboro	grdn	16034
	Mary	1804	Bridgewater	grdn	16027
	Mary	1836	E. Bridgewater	admn	16035
	Oliver	1831	Marshfield	admn	16036

SURNAME	FIRST NAME	YEAR	PLACE	CASE	DOCKET
PORTER	Oliver C	1875	Middleboro	admn	16037
	Peggy	1818	Marshfield	grdn	16043
	Sally	1845	Bridgewater	will	16038
	Samuel	1725	Abington	will	16039
	Sarah	1839	Abington	will	16040
	William	1800	Marshfield	warr	16041
	William	1816	Marshfield	admn	16042
	William	1818	Marshfield	grdn	16043
POWERS	Betsey R	1868	Kingston	admn	16044
	Edward S	1855	Abington	grdn	16045
	Mary T	1881	Abington	grdn	16046 a
PRAMBERG	Charles G	1873	N. Bridgewater	will	16047
PRATT	Abigail	1760	Plympton	grdn	16048
	Abigail	1762	Bridgewater	grdn	16049
	Abner	1872	Hingham	admn	16050
	Adaline	1840	Hanover	grdn	16179
	Adeline	1841	Hanover	admn	16051
	Albert D	1864	Kingston	grdn	16052
	Albert G	1869	Middleboro	will	16053
	Alvin F	1878	Hingham	grdn	16102
	Alvina F	1856	E. Bridgewater	grdn	16110
	Amanda F	1866	E. Bridgewater	grdn	16054
	Amittai	1845	N. Bridgewater	will	16055
	Andrew	1820	Middleboro	grdn	16082
	Anna	1749	Bridgewater	grdn	16056
	Annis	1760	Plympton	admn	16057
	Arthur J	1851	Middleboro	grdn	16058
	Asa	1832	Bridgewater	will	16059
	Azell	1791	Bridgewater	grdn	16060
	Barnabas	1787	Bridgewater	admn	16061
	Barnabas Jr	1791	Bridgewater	admn	16062
	Benajah	1771	Middleboro	admn	16063
	Benjamin	1757	Plympton	will	16064
	Benjamin	1759	Hanover	grdn	16182
	Benjamin	1762	Bridgewater	will	16065
	Benjamin	1838	Middleboro	will	16066
	Benjamin C	1875	Hanover	will	16067
	Benoni	1820	Middleboro	grdn	16082
	Betsey	1829	Abington	admn	16068
	Calvin	1821	Middleboro	admn	16071
	Calvin	1821	Bridgewater	grdn	16072
	Calvin B	1862	Bridgewater	will	16069
	Calvin W E	1873	Hanson	grdn	16070
	Charles	1846	Abington	admn	16073
	Charles F	1856	E. Bridgewater	grdn	16110
	Charles K	1825	Middleboro	grdn	16105
	Christiana	1821	Bridgewater	grdn	16072
	Clarissa	1821	Bridgewater	grdn	16072
	Cornelius	1823	Bridgewater	admn	16074
	Cornelius	1836	Halifax	admn	16075
	Cyrus	1846	Hanover	admn	16076
	Daniel	1739	Plympton	will	16080
	Daniel	1779	Bridgewater	admn	16081
	Daniel	1820	Middleboro	grdn	16082
	Daniel	1873	Abington	will	16079
	Daniel L	1782	Abington	grdn	16077
	Daniel S	1870	Abington	grdn	16078
	David	1750	Kingston	admn	16083
	David	1810	Bridgewater	will	16084
	David	1817	Bridgewater	admn	16085
	David	1821	Bridgewater	grdn	16086
	David	1863	E. Bridgewater	admn	16087
	Dexter	1866	E. Bridgewater	will	16088
	Diantha	1840	Hanover	grdn	16179
	Dianthe	1843	Hanover	admn	16089
	E Tillson	1875	Carver	will	16104
	Ebenezer	1768	Middleboro	admn	16092
	Ebenezer	1778	Middleboro	admn	16093
	Ebenezer	1779	Middleboro	grdn	16094
	Ebenezer	1818	Weymouth	grdn	16091
	Ebenezer	1880	Bridgewater	will	16090

SURNAME	FIRST NAME	YEAR	PLACE	CASE	DOCKET
PRATT	Eleazer	1795	Middleboro	will	16095
	Eliab	1796	Middleboro	grdn	16096
	Elias W	1880	S. Scituate	admn	16097
	Elizabeth	1864	Carver	will	16098
	Elizabeth B	1850	Abington	grdn	16189
	Elizabeth W	1873	Hingham	admn	16099
	Elizabeth W	1877	Middleboro	admn	16100
	Elkanah	1734	Plympton	admn	16101
	Ella S	1867	Hanson	grdn	16200
	Ellis W	1878	Hingham	grdn	16102
	Else	1836	Hanover	admn	16103
	Eunice	1760	Plympton	grdn	16048
	Everett T	1856	E. Bridgewater	grdn	16110
	Francis G	1825	Middleboro	grdn	16105
	Frank H	1866	Plymouth	grdn	16106
	George	1867	W. Bridgewater	admn	16107
	Greenleaf	1824	Middleboro	admn	16108
	Hampden K	1821	Bridgewater	grdn	16072
	Hannah	1743	Middleboro	grdn	16134
	Hannah	1764	Bridgewater	will	16109
	Harriet A	1856	E. Bridgewater	grdn	16110
	Harrison O	1875	Middleboro	admn	16111
	Harry S	1875	Middleboro	grdn	16112
	Hattie A	1867	W. Bridgewater	grdn	16113
	Henry C	1821	Bridgewater	grdn	16072
	Henry W	1852	St. Charles IL	admn	16114
	Herbert E	1866	E. Bridgewater	grdn	16054
	Homan	1779	Middleboro	grdn	16094
	Huldah T	1877	W. Bridgewater	admn	16115
	Ida C T	1868	Marion	grdn	16116
	Isaac	1864	Middleboro	will	16117
	Isaac	1875	E. Bridgewater	will	16118
	Isaiah	1866	Carver	admn	16119
	Jabez	1710	Duxbury	admn	16120
	James	1741	Plympton	grdn	16121
	James	1861	Kingston	admn	16123
	James	1861	Abington	will	16124
	James H	1861	Kingston	will	16122
	Jared	1864	Middleboro	admn	16125
	Jedediah	1743	Middleboro	grdn	16134
	Jennette	1835	Scituate	will	16126
	Job	1786	Bridgewater	admn	16127
	Job	1857	Middleboro	admn	16128
	John	1730/1	Plympton	will	16132
	John	1743	Middleboro	will	16133
	John	1743	Middleboro	grdn	16134
	John	1779	Middleboro	grdn	16094
	John	1833	Hanson	will	16131
	John Q	1878	Hanover	admn	16129
	John S	1867	Hanson	admn	16130
	Jonathan	1729	Hanover	will	16136
	Jonathan	1759	Hanover	grdn	16182
	Jonathan	1760	Plympton	grdn	16141
	Jonathan	1775	Bridgewater	will	16135
	Jonathan	1814	Hanover	admn	16137
	Jonathan	1825	Halifax	admn	16138
	Joseph	1758	Plympton	admn	16140
	Joseph	1760	Plympton	grdn	16141
	Joseph	1765	Bridgewater	will	16139
	Joshua	1697	Plymouth	will	16142
	Joshua	1705/6	Plymouth	grdn	16143
	Joshua	1758	Plympton	admn	16146
	Joshua	1772	Bridgewater	will	16149
	Joshua	1773	Pembroke	will	16148
	Joshua	1802	Plympton	will	16147
	Joshua	1813	Bridgewater	will	16150
	Joshua	1824	Hanson	admn	16145
	Joshua	1869	Plymouth	will	16144
	Kezia	1743	Middleboro	grdn	16134
	Kimball	1806	Middleboro	admn	16151
	Kimball	1806	Middleboro	grdn	16152

SURNAME	FIRST NAME	YEAR	PLACE	CASE	DOCKET
PRATT	Leonard	1877	Bridgewater	admn	16153
	Lewis	1779	Middleboro	grdn	16094
	Lewis	1862	Carver	will	16154
	Lewis	1872	Hingham	will	16155
	Louisa	1865	Abington	admn	16156
	Louisa M	1825	Middleboro	grdn	16105
	Lucy	1779	Middleboro	grdn	16094
	Lucy	1828	Middleboro	admn	16157
	Lucy	1844	Middleboro	admn	16158
	Lucy	1857	Pembroke	admn	16159
	Lydia C	1861	Hanson	grdn	16160
	Lydia M	1850	Abington	grdn	16189
	Marcia	1825	Middleboro	grdn	16105
	Marcy	1760	Plympton	grdn	16141
	Maria L	1853	Bridgewater	admn	16161
	Martha	1760	Plympton	grdn	16141
	Martha	1806	Middleboro	grdn	16162 a
	Martin	1868	Middleboro	grdn	16163
	Mary	1759	Hanover	grdn	16182
	Mary	1865	Hingham	will	16164
	Mary	1866	Abington	admn	16165
	Mary T	1875	Bridgewater	admn	16166
	Matilda H	1880	Bridgewater	admn	16167
	Molly	1805	Abington	grdn	16168
	Nathan	1750	Bridgewater	admn	16169
	Nathan F C	1879	Middleboro	will	16170
	Nathaniel	1749	Bridgewater	admn	16174
	Nathaniel	1779	Abington	will	16171
	Nathaniel	1793	Abington	grdn	16172
	Nathaniel	1828	Bridgewater	will	16175
	Nathaniel	1840	Hanover	will	16178
	Nathaniel	1844	Hanover	admn	16177
	Nathaniel Jr	1781	Plympton	admn	16173
	Nathaniel O	1840	Hanover	grdn	16179
	Nathaniel O	1848	Hanover	will	16176
	Noah	1825	Hanover	admn	16180
	Othniel	1759	Hanover	will	16181
	Othniel	1759	Hanover	grdn	16182
	Otis	1840	Halifax	grdn	16183
	Otis	1878	Middleboro	will	16184
	Percis	1701/2	Plymouth	cont	16185
	Phebe	1806	Middleboro	grdn	16152
	Philip	1850	Abington	grdn	16189
	Phillip	1831	Abington	will	16187
	Phillip	1849	Abington	will	16188
	Phillip C	1851	Middleboro	admn	16186
	Phineas	1830	Abington	admn	16190
	Relief	1837	Scituate	admn	16191
	Robert	1791	Abington	admn	16192
	Ruth	1840	Hanover	grdn	16179
	Ruth	1843	Hanover	admn	16195
	Ruth	1855	N. Bridgewater	grdn	16196
	Ruth C	1852	S. Scituate	grdn	16193
	Ruth C	1879	S. Scituate	admn	16194
	Sally	1821	Bridgewater	grdn	16072
	Samuel	1745	Middleboro	will	16197
	Samuel	1745	Middleboro	will	16198
	Sarah	1743	Middleboro	grdn	16134
	Sarah	1762	Bridgewater	grdn	16049
	Sarah	1875	Middleboro	will	16199
	Sarah A	1866	E. Bridgewater	grdn	16054
	Sarah E	1852	Carver	grdn	16213
	Sarah E	1866	Plymouth	grdn	16106
	Sarah E	1867	Hanson	grdn	16200
	Seth	1796	Bridgewater	will	16201
	Seth	1845	Abington	admn	16203
	Seth J	1780	Abington	grdn	16202
	Simeon	1848	Bridgewater	admn	16204
	Solomon	1757	Bridgewater	will	16205
	Stillman	1862	Middleboro	admn	16206
	Susan	1880	Pembroke	admn	16207

SURNAME	FIRST NAME	YEAR	PLACE	CASE	DOCKET
PRATT	Sylvanus	1833	Bridgewater	will	16208
	Thomas	1757	Plympton	admn	16209
	Thomas	1777	Bridgewater	admn	16210
	Thomas	1779	Middleboro	grdn	16094
	Thomas	1813	Middleboro	admn	16211
	Thomas	1865	Scituate	admn	16212
	Thomas S	1852	Carver	grdn	16213
	Tillson	1859	Carver	will	16214
	Wibry	1820	Middleboro	grdn	16082
	William	1808	Middleboro	will	16218
	William	1849	Bridgewater	will	16215
	William	1857	Bridgewater	admn	16216
	William	1861	E. Bridgewater	will	16217
	William	1868	Abington	will	16219
	William B	1873	Hanson	admn	16220
	William H	1821	Bridgewater	grdn	16072
	Winslow	1877	Carver	admn	16221
	Zebulon	1808	Middleboro	grdn	16222
	Zebulon K	1860	Middleboro	admn	16223
PREBLE	John R	1856	Marion	will	16224
PRENTISS	Margaret L	1846	Hingham	grdn	16225
PRESTON	Hervey N	1837	Plymouth	admn	16226
	Isadore E	1854	Rhode Island	grdn	16227
	Mary H	1854	Rhode Island	grdn	16227
PRICE	Almira D	1865	Bridgewater	will	16228
	Asaph	1803	Rochester	admn	16229
	Benjamin	1805	Bridgewater	will	16230
	George	1813	Hingham	will	16231
	John	1711	Plymouth	admn	16232
PRIEST	Franklin	1881	Hanover	admn	16233
PRINCE	Benjamin	1704	Boston	grdn	16251
	Betsey	1825	Kingston	grdn	16241
	Christopher	1744	Kingston	grdn	16234
	Elizabeth	1722	Rochester	grdn	16235
	Isaac	1769	Duxbury	admn	16236
	James	1744	Kingston	grdn	16234
	Job	1704	Boston	grdn	16251
	Job	1731	Kingston	admn	16237
	John	1824	Kingston	will	16238
	Kimball	1744	Kingston	grdn	16234
	Kimball	1814	Kingston	will	16239
	Levi	1825	Kingston	grdn	16241
	Levi S	1862	Kingston	will	16240
	Marcy	1756	Middleboro	admn	16242
	Mercy	1733	Middleboro	grdn	16243 a
	Nathan	1757	-----	admn	16244
	Samuel	1730	Rochester/M'bor	will	16245
	Sylvester	1852	Marshfield	admn	16246
	Thomas	1703	Boston	admn	16250
	Thomas	1704	Boston	grdn	16251
	Thomas	1755	Duxbury	admn	16247
	Thomas	1768	Kingston	admn	16248
	Thomas	1783	Kingston	will	16249
	Thomas	1825	Kingston	grdn	16241
PRIOR	Benjamin	1748	Duxbury	admn	16252
	Benjamin	1767	Duxbury	will	16253
	Betsey B	1831	Duxbury	grdn	16254
	Charles	1828	Duxbury	admn	16255
	Charles	1871	Duxbury	admn	16256
	Charles W	1874	Marshfield	grdn	16260
	Deborah	1810	Duxbury	grdn	16259
	Eliphaz	1806	Duxbury	will	16257
	Ezra	1809	Duxbury	admn	16258
	Ezra	1810	Duxbury	grdn	16259
	George J	1874	Marshfield	grdn	16260
	Helen De W	1831	Duxbury	grdn	16254
	Jane	1810	Duxbury	grdn	16259
	Jennie A	1873	Duxbury	grdn	16266
	John	1742	Bridgewater	will	16261
	Joseph	1690/1	Duxbury	admn	16262
	Joseph	1692/3	Duxbury	admn	16263

SURNAME	FIRST NAME	YEAR	PLACE	CASE	DOCKET
PRIOR	Otis	1810	Duxbury	grdn	16259
	Sylvanus	1836	Duxbury	admn	16264
	Sylvanus	1875	Duxbury	admn	16265
	Sylvanus Jr	1873	Duxbury	grdn	16266
	William	1818	Duxbury	grdn	16267
PROCTOR	Samuel	1846	N. Bridgewater	admn	16268
PROUTY	Caleb	1754	Scituate	admn	16269
	Caleb	1759	Scituate	grdn	16270
	Caleb	1840	Scituate	will	16271
	Caleb W	1872	Scituate	admn	16272
	Caleb W	1876	Scituate	will	16273
	David	1805	Scituate	grdn	16274
	Edward	1726	Scituate	admn	16275
	Edward	1749	Scituate	admn	16276
	Elijah	1849	S. Scituate	admn	16277
	Elisha	1729	Scituate	grdn	16278
	Eunice	1729	Scituate	grdn	16278
	Hannah	1729	Scituate	grdn	16278
	Harris G	1869	Abington	will	16279
	Isaac	1754	Scituate	will	16280
	James L	1877	Scituate	admn	16281
	John	1838	Scituate	admn	16282
	John N	1870	Abington	grdn	16283
	Jonathan	1738	Scituate	will	16284
	Lavinia	1870	Abington	will	16285
	Luther	1852	Scituate	admn	16286
	Margaret	1770	Scituate	will	16287
	Maria H	1870	Abington	grdn	16283
	Mary	1729	Scituate	grdn	16278
	Mary	1863	S. Scituate	admn	16288
	Richard	1708/9	Scituate	admn	16289
	Richard	1729	Scituate	grdn	16290
	Thomas L	1827	Scituate	admn	16291
PUFFER	John	1877	Hingham	admn	16292
	John	1881	Hanover	admn	16293
PUGH	George T	1871	Plymouth	grdn	16294
	William H	1871	Plymouth	grdn	16294
PULCIFER	Abiel	1736	Plymouth	admn	16295
PUMPONOOHOO	Peter	1748	Middleboro	admn	16296
PURRINGTON	Cynthia	1779	Middleboro	grdn	16297
	Eleazer	1765	Middleboro	grdn	16309
	Elias	1795	Rochester	admn	16299
	Elias	1796	Rochester	grdn	16300
	Elias	1810	Middleboro	grdn	16298
	George F	1869	Mattapoisett	grdn	16313
	Harriet	1848	Rochester	grdn	16310
	Henry	1823	Rochester	admn	16301
	Henry	1848	Rochester	grdn	16310
	Hezekiah	1765	Middleboro	will	16302
	Hezekiah	1808	Rochester	admn	16303
	Isaac	1773	Middleboro	grdn	16306
	Isaiah	1876	Mattapoisett	will	16304
	Joseph	1848	Rochester	grdn	16310
	Joshua	1770	Middleboro	admn	16305
	Joshua	1773	Middleboro	grdn	16306
	Mary	1765	Middleboro	grdn	16309
	Mary A	1849	Rochester	grdn	16307
	Mary E	1848	Rochester	grdn	16310
	Minerva B	1849	Rochester	grdn	16307
	Nathaniel	1765	Middleboro	grdn	16309
	Nathaniel	1773	Middleboro	admn	16308
	Noble	1796	Rochester	grdn	16300
	Phebe	1848	Rochester	grdn	16310
	Samuel	1789	Middleboro	admn	16311
	Samuel	1847	Rochester	admn	16312
	Sarah D	1869	Mattapoisett	grdn	16313
	Seth	1765	Middleboro	grdn	16309
	Seth	1779	Middleboro	grdn	16297
	Sylvanus	1765	Middleboro	grdn	16309
PUTNAM	Betsey F	1868	Middleboro	will	16314
	Israel W	1868	Middleboro	will	16315

SURNAME	FIRST NAME	YEAR	PLACE	CASE	DOCKET
QUASH	Quamony	1818	Plymouth	grdn	16316 a
QUIGLEY	Charles E	1868	Abington	grdn	16317
	James H	1868	Abington	grdn	16317
	Mary J	1868	Abington	grdn	16317
	William	1868	Abington	grdn	16317
QUINDLEY	John	1856	Abington	will	16318
QUINLAN	Timothy	1871	Plymouth	will	16319
QUINN	Michael	1857	Abington	admn	16320
	Patrick	1868	N. Bridgewater	admn	16321
RACHFORD	James	1755	Bridgewater	admn	16322
	Thomas	1758	Bridgewater	grdn	16323
RADCLIFF	Joseph J	1849	E. Bridgewater	admn	16324
RADICAN	Thomas	1852	N. Bridgewater	grdn	16325
RAMSDELL	Abigail	1806	Hanover	will	16326
	Ada Francis	1858	Abington	adop	16327
	Alberson	1809	Pembroke	admn	16328
	Anna	1797	Pembroke	will	16329
	Anna	1866	Hanson	admn	16330
	Bartlett	1875	Pembroke	admn	16331
	Bathsheba	1824	Hanson	grdn	16341
	Bethiah	1853	Pembroke	admn	16332
	David	1754	Hanover	admn	16333
	David	1835	Pembroke	admn	16334
	Diana	1833	Hanson	admn	16335
	Edmund	1822	Hanover	admn	16336
	Elijah	1829	Hanson	grdn	16337 a
	Elizabeth	1830	Hanson	grdn	16338 a
	Fanny	1824	Hanson	grdn	16341
	Gideon	1795	Abington	admn	16339
	Isaac	1822	Hanson	admn	16340
	Isaac	1824	Hanson	grdn	16341
	James E	1865	Lakeville	grdn	16342
	Joseph	1788	Hanover	will	16344
	Joseph	1817	Hanover	will	16345
	Joseph	1830	E. Bridgewater	admn	16346
	Joseph Jr	1778	Hanover	admn	16343
	Lot	1818	Pembroke	grdn	16347 a
	Lot	1822	Hanson	admn	16348
	Lydia	1846	E. Bridgewater	will	16349
	Nathaniel	1762	Bridgewater	admn	16350
	Nathaniel	1872	E. Bridgewater	will	16351
	Robert	1861	Hanson	admn	16352
	Sabina	1870	E. Bridgewater	admn	16353
	Sally	1824	Hanson	grdn	16341
	Samuel	1830	Hanson	will	16354
	Samuel L	1871	Hanover	will	16355
	William	1854	Lakeville	admn	16356
RAMSDEN	Samuel	1759	Pembroke	will	16357
	Thomas	1788	Middleboro	will	16358
RAND	Alexander B	1870	Pembroke	admn	16359
	William	1779	Kingston	will	16361
	William	1779	Kingston	grdn	16362
	William	1818	Kingston	grdn	16363 a
	William Jr	1769	Kingston	will	16360
RANDALL	Abraham	1854	Abington	admn	16364
	Alfred	1863	Middleboro	admn	16365
	Amanda S	1881	Bridgewater	grdn	16366 a
	Ann M	1865	Rochester	admn	16367
	Benjamin	1764	Scituate	will	16368
	Benjamin	1786	Scituate	admn	16369
	Benjamin	1842	W. Bridgewater	admn	16370
	Bershua	1760	Rochester	will	16371
	Caleb	1761	Hanover	admn	16372
	Charles	1852	Plymouth	admn	16373
	Clement	1862	Mattapoisett	will	16374
	Clement	1877	Mattapoisett	admn	16375
	Deborah	1770	Pembroke	grdn	16438
	Deborah	1771	Scituate	grdn	16386
	Desire	1842	Scituate	will	16376
	Desire D	1880	Mattapoisett	will	16377
	Diadamia	1835	Rochester	grdn	16378

SURNAME	FIRST NAME	YEAR	PLACE	CASE	DOCKET
RANDALL	Elias	1847	Middleboro	admn	16379
	Elijah	1766	Scituate	grdn	16436
	Elijah	1835	Scituate	admn	16381
	Elijah Jr	1811	Hanover	admn	16380
	Elijah W	1863	Mattapoisett	admn	16382
	Elisha	1760	Scituate	admn	16383
	Elisha	1800	Scituate	admn	16384
	Elisha	1803	Pembroke	grdn	16391
	Elizabeth	1713	Scituate	grdn	16412
	Elizabeth	1770	Scituate	grdn	16385 a
	Elizabeth	1771	Scituate	grdn	16386
	Emeline M	1862	Abington	admn	16387
	Enoch	1799	Plymouth	admn	16388
	Enoch	1830	Plymouth	bond	16447
	Ephraim	1799	Pembroke	will	16390
	Ephraim	1803	Pembroke	grdn	16391
	Ephraim	1871	Pembroke	will	16389
	Faith	1770	Pembroke	grdn	16438
	George W	1855	Rochester	grdn	16392
	Gershom	1756	Scituate	admn	16393
	Hannah	1809	Scituate	will	16394
	Henry M	1881	Bridgewater	admn	16395
	Isaiah	1764	Scituate	grdn	16396 a
	Jane	1830	Plymouth	bond	16447
	Jeremiah	1854	Rochester	will	16397
	Job	1727	Scituate	will	16398
	Job	1760	Duxbury	admn	16399
	Job	1765	Rochester	admn	16400
	John	1728	Rochester	will	16401
	John	1758	Rochester	will	16402
	John	1806	Rochester	grdn	16403 a
	John	1826	Rochester	admn	16404
	John	1832	Duxbury	admn	16407
	John H	1842	Rochester	admn	16405
	John T	1865	Rochester	admn	16406
	Joseph	1720/1	Scituate	will	16409
	Joseph	1752	Scituate	admn	16410
	Joseph Jr	1713	Scituate	admn	16408
	Joshua	1713	Scituate	grdn	16412
	Joshua	1776	Scituate	will	16411
	Josiah	1765	Hanover	grdn	16415
	Josiah	1826	Marshfield	admn	16414
	Josiah D	1870	Duxbury	admn	16413
	Lazarus	1744	Rochester	will	16416
	Lemuel	1810	Rochester	admn	16417
	Lewis	1834	Rochester	will	16418
	Lucy	1878	Duxbury	admn	16419
	Margaret	1830	Plymouth	bond	16447
	Martha	1876	Rochester	will	16420
	Mary	1770	Pembroke	grdn	16438
	Mary F	1855	Abington	grdn	16421
	Mercy	1774	Rochester	admn	16422
	Mercy	1803	Pembroke	grdn	16391
	Mercy	1843	Scituate/Pembro	will	16423
	Nathaniel	1792	Kingston	admn	16424
	Nehemiah	1745	Scituate	will	16425
	Patience C	1881	Plymouth	will	16426
	Perez	1786	Kingston	admn	16427
	Ruth	1771	Scituate	admn	16428
	Sally	1835	Rochester	grdn	16378
	Sally	1873	S. Scituate	admn	16429
	Samuel	1745	Scituate	grdn	16432
	Samuel	1759	Scituate	admn	16435
	Samuel	1766	Scituate	grdn	16436
	Samuel	1767	Rochester	will	16430
	Samuel	1801	Kingston	admn	16431
	Samuel	1829	Scituate	will	16433
	Samuel	1842	Scituate	admn	16434
	Sarah	1766	Scituate	grdn	16436
	Sarah	1770	Pembroke	grdn	16438
	Sarah	1864	S. Scituate	will	16437

SURNAME	FIRST NAME	YEAR	PLACE	CASE	DOCKET
RANDALL	Seth	1798	Rochester	will	16439
	Snow	1765	Hanover	grdn	16415
	Thomas	1748	Rochester	will	16441
	Thomas	1769	Pembroke	admn	16440
	Thomas	1816	Rochester	admn	16442
	Walter B	1868	Marion	grdn	16443
	William	1693	Scituate	will	16444
	William	1760	Rochester	admn	16445
	William	1830	Plymouth	bond	16447
	William R	1878	Mattapoisett	will	16446
	Zeporah	1815	Scituate	admn	16448
RANKIN	Alexander	1869	Rochester	admn	16449
	William	1870	N. Bridgewater	admn	16450
RANSFORD	Joseph A	1838	Marshfield	will	16451
	Josiah C	1832	Abington	will	16452
RANSOM	Anna	1723	Plympton	grdn	16456
	Benjamin	1745	Plympton	grdn	16454
	Benjamin	1864	Carver	will	16453
	David	1801	Carver	will	16455
	Deborah	1723	Plympton	grdn	16456
	Deborah	1745	Plympton	grdn	16454
	Ebenezer	1734	Middleboro	grdn	16478
	Ebenezer	1737	Plympton	admn	16457
	Ebenezer	1758	Halifax	admn	16458
	Ebenezer	1798	Carver	grdn	16460
	Ebenezer Jr	1798	Carver	admn	16459
	Eunice	1798	Carver	grdn	16460
	Fred S	1871	Plympton	admn	16461
	Freeman B	1849	Plympton	grdn	16462
	Hannah S	1849	Plympton	grdn	16462
	Harvey L	1865	Kingston	admn	16463
	Henry A	1866	Abington	admn	16464
	John	1729	Plympton	admn	16466
	John	1749	Hanover	admn	16465
	John	1848	Plympton	admn	16467
	John	1877	Plympton	admn	16468
	Jonathan	1745	Plympton	grdn	16454
	Joseph	1723	Plympton	grdn	16456
	Joseph	1793	Carver	admn	16469
	Lemuel	1734	Middleboro	grdn	16478
	Lemuel	1804	Middleboro	will	16470
	Levi	1876	Carver	will	16471
	Lydia	1820	Carver	will	16472
	Mary	1723	Plympton	grdn	16456
	Mary	1833	Scituate	will	16473
	Rebecca	1832	Carver	admn	16474
	Robert	1697	Plymouth	admn	16475
	Robert	1723	Plympton	admn	16476
	Robert	1734	Middleboro	grdn	16478
	Robert	1745	Middleboro	will	16477
	Samuel	1737	Plympton	will	16479
	Samuel	1762	Middleboro	grdn	16480
	Sarah	1734	Middleboro	grdn	16478
	Sarah	1762	Middleboro	grdn	16480
	Thaddeus	1784	Kingston	admn	16481
	William	1734	Middleboro	grdn	16478
	William	1757	Middleboro	admn	16482
RAUNCE	John	1694/5	Scituate	will	16483
	Mary	1695	Scituate	will	16484
RAYMOND	Aaron	1874	Middleboro	will	16485
	Albert	1848	Plymouth	grdn	16512
	Albert	1875	Plymouth	adop	16486
	Alden	1845	Middleboro	admn	16487
	Allen	1821	Plymouth	admn	16488
	Allen L	1865	Plymouth	grdn	16489
	Annie P	1867	Plymouth	adop	16490
	Ansel E	1859	Plymouth	will	16491
	Caleb	1868	Plymouth	will	16492
	Calvin	1867	Plymouth	admn	16493
	Carrie H	1867	Abington	grdn	16494
	Charles	1880	Plymouth	will	16495

SURNAME	FIRST NAME	YEAR	PLACE	CASE	DOCKET
RAYMOND	Deborah	1850	Plymouth	admn	16496
	Ebenezer	1767	Middleboro	admn	16497
	Ezekiel	1816	Plymouth	admn	16498
	George Jr	1850	Plymouth	admn	16499
	Hannah	1774	Middleboro	grdn	16501
	Hannah S	1871	Middleboro	admn	16500
	Ichabod	1792	Rochester	grdn	16502
	Isaiah	1868	Plymouth	admn	16503
	Jacob	1821	Plymouth	admn	16504
	Jerusha	1880	Abington	admn	16505
	Josephine P	1851	E. Bridgewater	grdn	16506
	Joshua	1787	Middleboro	admn	16507
	Lemuel	1757	Wareham	admn	16508
	Lemuel	1834	Plymouth	admn	16509
	Lewis	1830	Plymouth	grdn	16510
	Lewis	1848	Plymouth	grdn	16512
	Lewis	1879	Plymouth	grdn	16511 a
	Lucy	1774	Middleboro	grdn	16501
	Lucy C	1848	Plymouth	grdn	16512
	Martin	1839	Middleboro	admn	16513
	Nathaniel Jr	1805	Plymouth	admn	16514
	Paul	1811	Plympton	admn	16515
	Perkins	1849	Plymouth	will	16516
	Rebecca	1879	Middleboro	admn	16517
	Samuel	1737	Rochester	admn	16518
	Samuel	1846	Middleboro	admn	16519
	Solomon	1793	Middleboro	admn	16520
	Stephen	1824	Rochester	grdn	16521 a
	Stephen	1867	Middleboro	admn	16522
	Stetson	1864	Bridgewater	will	16523
	Zenas	1829	Middleboro	admn	16524
REACH	Mary E	1873	N. Bridgewater	adop	16525
REARDON	Dennis	1879	Brockton	admn	16526
	Jeremiah	1869	E. Bridgewater	grdn	16528
	Joanna	1869	E. Bridgewater	grdn	16528
	John	1852	N. Bridgewater	admn	16527
	John	1869	E. Bridgewater	grdn	16528
	William	1869	E. Bridgewater	grdn	16528
REDDING	Calvin	1822	Middleboro	admn	16529
	Ebenezer	1751	Middleboro	will	16530
	John	1751	Middleboro	admn	16531
	Moses	1773	Middleboro	will	16532
	William	1792	Middleboro	admn	16533
	William	1833	Wareham	admn	16534
REED	Aaron	1759	Abington	grdn	16667
	Abel	1765	Abington	grdn	16605
	Abel	1855	Wareham	admn	16535
	Abiah	1806	Abington	grdn	16698
	Abiah	1867	Abington	will	16536
	Abigail	1737	Abington	grdn	16539
	Abigail	1801	Abington	grdn	16540
	Abigail	1808	Abington	will	16537
	Abigail F	1853	Abington	grdn	16538
	Adam	1765	Abington	grdn	16605
	Adam	1792	Abington	will	16541
	Albert	1863	Abington	admn	16542
	Albert	1873	Abington	will	16543
	Alfred L	1870	Abington	grdn	16544
	Ann E	1864	E. Bridgewater	grdn	16545
	Ann W	1867	N. Bridgewater	will	16546
	Annis	1848	Abington	grdn	16547
	Apollos	1863	Lakeville	admn	16548
	Barnabas	1791	Abington	grdn	16549 a
	Bela	1874	Abington	admn	16550
	Benjamin F H	1844	Rochester	grdn	16551
	Betsey R	1870	Abington	will	16552
	Caleb K	1813	Bridgewater	grdn	16553
	Charles	1806	Abington	grdn	16698
	Charles	1873	W. Bridgewater	admn	16555
	Charles E	1847	Brattleboro	grdn	16554
	Charles E	1867	New York	grdn	16628

SURNAME	FIRST NAME	YEAR	PLACE	CASE	DOCKET
REED	Cordelia	1846	Abington	grdn	16643
	Cyrus	1850	Abington	admn	16556
	Daniel	1776	Abington	will	16557
	Daniel	1806	Abington	will	16558
	Daniel	1867	W. Bridgewater	will	16559
	Daniel W	1867	New York	grdn	16628
	David	1853	Abington	admn	16560
	David R	1875	W. Bridgewater	grdn	16561
	Deborah	1776	Abington	grdn	16704
	Deborah	1805	Abington	will	16562
	Deborah	1851	E. Bridgewater	will	16563
	Ebenezer	1790	Abington	will	16564
	Ebenezer	1864	Abington	admn	16565
	Ebenezer	1878	S. Abington	will	16566
	Edward C	1881	Middleboro	grdn	16705
	Edward S	1857	Abington	grdn	16567
	Edwin et al	1875	Kingston	peti	16568
	Electe	1876	E. Bridgewater	admn	16569
	Elijah	1777	Middleboro	grdn	16570
	Elijah	1816	Middleboro	will	16571
	Elijah	1827	Middleboro	admn	16572
	Elisha	1820	Hull	grdn	16573
	Elizabeth	1864	Abington	grdn	16574
	Elizabeth	1867	Hanson	admn	16576
	Elizabeth	1879	Rockland	will	16575
	Elizabeth E T	1879	Hanson	will	16577
	Emily B	1845	W. Bridgewater	grdn	16717
	Eunice E	1845	W. Bridgewater	grdn	16717
	Eva A	1874	Lakeville	grdn	16627
	Experience	1811	Abington	will	16578
	Ezekiel	1740	Abington	grdn	16580
	Ezekiel	1862	W. Bridgewater	will	16579
	George H	1857	Kingston	grdn	16581
	Goddard	1811	Abington	grdn	16582
	Goddard	1865	Abington	will	16583
	Hannah	1806	Abington	grdn	16698
	Hannah	1849	W. Bridgewater	will	16584
	Hannah	1855	Lakeville	grdn	16585 a
	Hannah	1856	Lakeville	admn	16586
	Helen E	1864	Lakeville	grdn	16587
	Henry L	1861	Abington	grdn	16646
	Hervey	1879	Abington	admn	16588
	Hezekiah	1789	Bridgewater	admn	16589
	Homan T	1846	Abington	grdn	16662
	Horace F	1879	Hingham	admn	16590
	Horatio G	1880	Scituate	will	16591
	Huldah	1765	Abington	grdn	16605
	Huldah	1791	Abington	will	16592
	Ichabod	1818	Rochester	will	16593
	Ichabod	1839	Middleboro	admn	16594
	Isaac	1771	Wareham	admn	16595
	Isaac	1847	Abington	will	16597
	Isaac	1871	E. Bridgewater	admn	16598
	Isaac 2nd	1830	Abington	admn	16596
	Jacob	1828	Scituate	admn	16599
	Jacob	1839	Abington	will	16600
	James	1727	Middleboro	admn	16602
	James	1753	Abington	admn	16603
	James	1765	Abington	grdn	16605
	James Jr	1762	Abington	will	16604
	James T	1875	E. Bridgewater	will	16601
	Jane	1870	Abington	will	16606
	Jared	1856	E. Bridgewater	admn	16607
	Jason M	1850	N. Bridgewater	admn	16608
	Jennette	1880	E. Bridgewater	admn	16609
	Jeremiah	1765	Abington	grdn	16605
	Jeremiah	1777	Bridgewater	admn	16610
	Jeremiah	1854	Abington	admn	16611
	Jesse	1867	Marshfield	will	16613
	Jesse	1874	Abington	will	16612
	Jesse E	1876	Marshfield	grdn	16614

SURNAME	FIRST NAME	YEAR	PLACE	CASE	DOCKET
REED	Joel	1853	Abington	admn	16615
	John	1694	Marshfield	admn	16616
	John	1716	Bridgewater	admn	16621
	John	1739	Abington	admn	16619
	John	1757	Middleboro	admn	16625
	John	1777	Pembroke	will	16617
	John	1778	Pembroke	grdn	16641
	John	1831	W. Bridgewater	will	16622
	John	1843	Abington	admn	16620
	John	1861	Bridgewater	will	16623
	John E	1873	Lakeville	admn	16626
	John E	1874	Lakeville	grdn	16627
	John Jr	1828	Hull	admn	16618
	John M	1867	New York	grdn	16628
	John P	1879	E. Bridgewater	will	16624
	Jonathan Jr	1783	Middleboro	admn	16629
	Jonathan L	1869	Abington	admn	16630
	Joseph	1765	Bridgewater	grdn	16634
	Joseph	1777	Bridgewater	will	16633
	Joseph	1806	Abington	grdn	16698
	Joseph	1868	E. Bridgewater	admn	16632
	Joseph	1879	Rockland	admn	16631
	Joshua	1853	E. Bridgewater	admn	16635
	Josiah	1873	E. Bridgewater	grdn	16637
	Josiah V	1842	Rochester	will	16636
	Levi	1778	Pembroke	grdn	16641
	Levi	1869	Abington	will	16638
	Levi	1877	Lakeville	will	16639
	Levi	1878	Middleboro	admn	16640
	Lorenzo	1845	Abington	admn	16642
	Lorenzo	1846	Abington	grdn	16643
	Louisa	1876	Marshfield	admn	16644
	Lucia E	1861	Abington	grdn	16646
	Lucia W	1875	Abington	grdn	16645
	Lucy	1832	Hanson	grdn	16647 a
	Lucy	1840	Pembroke	admn	16648
	Lucy	1879	Rockland	admn	16649
	Luke	1810	Middleboro	admn	16650
	Luke Jr	1861	Middleboro	admn	16651
	Luther	1862	Pembroke	will	16652
	Lydia	1779	Rochester	grdn	16688
	Lydia J	1871	Abington	admn	16653
	M Ella	1861	Abington	grdn	16646
	Marcia	1806	Abington	grdn	16698
	Marcus M	1863	Pembroke	will	16654
	Marcy	1859	Abington	will	16655
	Martha K	1876	Brockton	admn	16656
	Mary	1779	Rochester	grdn	16688
	Mary	1802	Middleboro	will	16657
	Mary	1806	Abington	grdn	16698
	Mary	1839	Abington	admn	16658
	Mary	1849	Abington	admn	16659
	Mary C	1873	Bridgewater	adop	16660
	Mary E	1870	Abington	grdn	16544
	Mary L	1864	Pembroke	grdn	16735
	Matthew	1755	Abington	grdn	16680
	Matthew	1861	Abington	admn	16661
	Mehitable A	1846	Abington	grdn	16662
	Micah	1801	Abington	admn	16663
	Miriam	1759	Abington	grdn	16667
	Molle	1776	Abington	grdn	16664
	Molly	1765	Abington	grdn	16605
	Molly	1778	Pembroke	grdn	16641
	Molly	1780	Abington	grdn	16665
	Moses	1757	Abington	admn	16666
	Moses	1759	Abington	grdn	16667
	N Augustus	1861	Abington	grdn	16646
	Nahum	1873	Abington	admn	16668
	Nancy	1864	Abington	grdn	16669 a
	Nancy	1865	Abington	admn	16670
	Naomi	1765	Bridgewater	grdn	16634

SURNAME	FIRST NAME	YEAR	PLACE	CASE	DOCKET
REED	Nathan	1842	Plymouth	admn	16671
	Nathaniel	1864	Abington	admn	16672
	Nathaniel F	1871	Pembroke	admn	16675
	Nathaniel L	1864	Abington	admn	16673
	Nathaniel W	1870	Middleboro	will	16674
	Nettie	1866	Abington	adop	16676
	Nettie	1871	Abington	grdn	16677
	Noah	1801	Abington	grdn	16540
	Oakes	1849	E. Bridgewater	admn	16678
	Obediah	1753	Abington	admn	16679
	Obediah	1755	Abington	grdn	16680
	Patty	1820	Hull	grdn	16573
	Peter	1740	Abington	grdn	16580
	Phebe	1759	Abington	admn	16681
	Philip	1715	Bridgewater/Abi	will	16682
	Philip	1737	Abington	grdn	16539
	Philip	1859	Abington	admn	16683
	Polly	1838	Middleboro	will	16684
	Rebecca	1737	Abington	grdn	16539
	Rebecca	1779	Rochester	grdn	16688
	Rebecca	1817	Middleboro	admn	16685
	Rebecca	1831	Middleboro	admn	16686
	Rebecca	1860	Plymouth	admn	16687
	Robert H	1844	Hingham	grdn	16689
	Ruth	1737	Abington	grdn	16539
	Sally	1869	E. Bridgewater	will	16690
	Samuel	1739	Abington	admn	16693
	Samuel	1740	Abington	grdn	16580
	Samuel	1776	Abington	admn	16694
	Samuel	1805	Abington	will	16697
	Samuel	1806	Abington	grdn	16698
	Samuel	1822	Middleboro	will	16691
	Samuel	1859	Middleboro	admn	16692
	Samuel	1870	Abington	will	16695
	Samuel	1875	W. Bridgewater	grdn	16561
	Samuel Jr	1871	Abington	will	16696
	Sarah	1776	Abington	grdn	16704
	Sarah	1811	Bridgewater	will	16701
	Sarah	1842	Rochester	admn	16699
	Sarah	1844	Abington	will	16703
	Sarah	1853	Rochester	will	16700
	Sarah	1862	Plymouth	admn	16702
	Sarah M	1881	Middleboro	grdn	16705
	Silas	1755	Abington	grdn	16680
	Silas	1800	Abington	will	16706
	Silence	1755	Abington	grdn	16680
	Silence	1810	Abington	will	16707
	Silvia	1770	Middleboro	grdn	16708
	Simeon	1860	Pembroke	admn	16711
	Simeon G	1831	Abington	admn	16709
	Simeon G	1832	Abington	grdn	16710
	Solomon	1776	Abington	admn	16712
	Solomon	1785	Middleboro	will	16713
	Solomon	1820	Bridgewater	admn	16714
	Squire	1740	Abington	grdn	16580
	Stephen	1724	Abington	admn	16715
	Stephen	1765	Abington	grdn	16605
	Stephen	1807	Abington	admn	16716
	Susan T	1845	W. Bridgewater	grdn	16717
	Susannah	1848	Rochester	admn	16718
	Thaxter	1846	Abington	admn	16719
	Thomas	1812	Abington	will	16720
	Thomas	1843	Abington	will	16721
	Thomas	1856	Abington	will	16725
	Thomas D	1880	Middleboro	admn	16726
	Thomas F	1846	Abington	grdn	16723
	Thomas F	1854	Abington	admn	16724
	Thomas Jr	1845	Abington	admn	16722
	Timothy	1813	Bridgewater	admn	16727
	Timothy K	1873	E. Bridgewater	admn	16728
	Watson	1822	Middleboro	grdn	16729

SURNAME	FIRST NAME	YEAR	PLACE	CASE	DOCKET
REED	William	1769	Rochester	will	16732
	William	1776	Middleboro	admn	16730
	William	1778	Abington	admn	16731
	William	1842	Rochester	will	16733
	William	1851	Hanover	admn	16734
	William R	1864	Pembroke	grdn	16735
	Zebulon	1774	Abington	admn	16736
REGAN	Delia M	1876	Brockton	grdn	16737
	George F	1876	Brockton	grdn	16737
	John	1876	Brockton	grdn	16737
	Timothy	1873	N. Bridgewater	will	16738
REMINGTON	Bela	1841	Hingham	will	16739
	Bela	1841	Hingham	grdn	16740
	Bridget	1878	Hingham	admn	16741
	Charles	1841	Hingham	grdn	16740
	Elisha	1822	Hingham	admn	16742
	Elisha	1854	Hingham	admn	16743
	Esther	1841	Hingham	grdn	16740
	Foster	1841	Hingham	grdn	16740
	Hosea S	1864	Hingham	grdn	16746
	Joshua	1841	Hingham	grdn	16740
	Thomas	1813	Abington	will	16744
	Thomas	1848	Abington	admn	16745
	Wendall F	1864	Hingham	grdn	16746
REVERE	Epaphroditus	1803	Plymouth	grdn	16747
	Paul	1857	Bridgewater	will	16748
REYNARD	Lucy A	1854	Rochester	grdn	16750
	Owen	1848	Rochester	admn	16749
	Sarah F	1854	Rochester	grdn	16750
REYNOLDS	Alice C	1855	Ohio	peti	16766
	Baruch	1775	Middleboro	grdn	16753
	Charity	1776	Bridgewater	grdn	16778
	Charles	1765	Middleboro	admn	16751
	Clara M	1875	N. Bridgewater	admn	16752
	Daniel	1775	Middleboro	grdn	16753
	David	1796	Bridgewater	grdn	16770
	David P	1867	E. Bridgewater	will	16754
	Edwin	1867	N. Bridgewater	admn	16755
	Electius	1786	Rochester	admn	16756
	Elizabeth	1816	Bridgewater	will	16757
	Elizabeth	1855	Ohio	peti	16766
	Ellen J	1865	N. Bridgewater	grdn	16758
	Ezra	1821	Middleboro	grdn	16759 a
	Ezra	1822	Middleboro	admn	16760
	Fally	1866	N. Bridgewater	admn	16761
	Gardner W	1876	Brockton	admn	16762
	Griffin C	1881	Abington	will	16763
	Hannah M	1877	Brockton	admn	16764
	Henry F	1866	N. Bridgewater	admn	16765
	James B	1855	Ohio	peti	16766
	Jarvis W	1860	N. Bridgewater	admn	16767
	Job	1856	Middleboro	will	16768
	John	1796	Bridgewater	grdn	16770
	John P	1839	N. Bridgewater	admn	16769
	Jonas	1795	Bridgewater	will	16772
	Jonas	1842	N. Bridgewater	will	16771
	Jonathan	1796	Bridgewater	grdn	16770
	Joseph H	1861	N. Bridgewater	admn	16773
	Martin L	1880	Brockton	will	16774
	Mary	1840	N. Bridgewater	admn	16775
	Mary E	1876	Brockton	grdn	16776
	Phillip	1775	Bridgewater	admn	16777
	Phillip	1776	Bridgewater	grdn	16778
	Polly	1776	Bridgewater	grdn	16778
	Polly	1796	Bridgewater	grdn	16770
	Rebecca	1871	N. Bridgewater	will	16779
	Robert	1775	Middleboro	grdn	16753
	Thomas	1795	Bridgewater	will	16780
	William	1776	Bridgewater	grdn	16778
RICE	Caleb	1817	Hingham	grdn	16781 a
	Caleb	1848	Hingham	will	16782

SURNAME	FIRST NAME	YEAR	PLACE	CASE	DOCKET
RICE	Lydia	1845	Hanover	will	16783
RICH	Catherine S	1831	Scituate	grdn	16784
	Moses	1832	Scituate	admn	16785
	Moses P	1848	Scituate	admn	16786
RICHARDS	Abbie R	1881	Duxbury	adop	16787
	Anna	1828	E. Bridgewater	grdn	16788 i
	Augustus	1874	N. Bridgewater	will	16789
	Benjamin	1741	Bridgewater	will	16790
	Benjamin	1812	Bridgewater	admn	16791
	Betsey	1880	Abington	admn	16792
	Clarkson W	1853	W. Bridgewater	grdn	16793
	Daniel	1759	Abington	admn	16794
	Daniel	1789	Bridgewater	will	16795
	Eli H	1860	W. Bridgewater	admn	16796
	Helen J	1878	Preston CT	grdn	16797
	Isaiah D	1873	S. Scituate	will	16798
	John	1813	Bridgewater	will	16799
	John	1854	W. Bridgewater	will	16800
	Joseph	1774	Abington	will	16801
	Josiah	1815	Bridgewater	will	16802
	Lucy M	1853	W. Bridgewater	grdn	16793
	Luther	1881	W. Bridgewater	admn	16803
	Margaret	1854	Hingham	grdn	16807 a
	Mary	1792	Bridgewater	will	16804
	Nathan	1763	Bridgewater	grdn	16805
	Nathaniel	1864	Hingham	will	16806
	Peggy	1854	Hingham	grdn	16807 a
	Polly	1837	E. Bridgewater	admn	16808
	Polly	1853	E. Bridgewater	will	16809
	Prince	1828	E. Bridgewater	grdn	16810 a
	Randall	1872	Abington	will	16811
	Susie D	1879	S. Scituate	grdn	16812
	Ward	1853	W. Bridgewater	will	16813
RICHARDSON	Andrew S	1850	Scituate	grdn	16820
	Anne B	1872	Hingham	will	16814
	Charles	1777	Bridgewater	admn	16815
	Charles F	1875	Plymouth	grdn	16816
	Charles M	1849	N. Bridgewater	grdn	16826
	Edmond	1761	Duxbury	admn	16817
	Emma F	1875	Plymouth	grdn	16818
	George P	1868	Duxbury	will	16819
	George W	1850	Scituate	grdn	16820
	Hannah A	1868	Duxbury	will	16821
	John C	1820	Hingham	admn	16822
	Joseph	1871	Hingham	will	16823
	Leonard T	1850	Scituate	grdn	16820
	Partridge	1768	Woburn	grdn	16824
	Robert	1866	Plymouth	adop	16825
	Sanford H	1849	N. Bridgewater	grdn	16826
	Sarah	1840	Scituate	will	16827
	Sarah E	1850	Scituate	grdn	16820
	William H	1850	Scituate	grdn	16820
	William H	1867	S. Scituate	grdn	16828
	Zimri C	1850	Scituate	grdn	16820
RICHMOND	Abel	1772	Middleboro	admn	16829
	Abel	1843	Halifax	will	16830
	Abigail	1816	Middleboro	will	16831
	Alanson T	1849	Middleboro	admn	16832
	Anderson	1869	Plymouth	grdn	16858
	Andrew	1845	Halifax	will	16833
	Anna	1841	Plymouth	grdn	16878
	Apollos	1832	Middleboro	admn	16834
	Bathsheba	1845	Middleboro	will	16835
	Benjamin	1830	Middleboro	will	16836
	Benjamin	1833	Middleboro	grdn	16837
	Betsey	1841	Plymouth	grdn	16878
	Betsey D	1826	Rochester	grdn	16868
	Caleb	1790	Middleboro	admn	16838
	Cyrus	1870	Halifax	will	16839
	Ebenezer	1729	Middleboro	will	16840
	Edward	1868	Middleboro	will	16841

SURNAME	FIRST NAME	YEAR	PLACE	CASE	DOCKET
RICHMOND	Eleazer	1817	Middleboro	will	16842
	Eleazer	1876	Lakeville	will	16843
	Elias	1817	Middleboro	admn	16844
	Elijah	1879	Abington	will	16845
	Elisha	1849	Middleboro	admn	16846
	Elizabeth	1833	Middleboro	grdn	16837
	Fear	1879	Halifax	grdn	16847 a
	Gershom	1779	Middleboro	admn	16848
	Gershom	1793	Bridgewater	admn	16849
	Hattie N	1878	Halifax	admn	16851
	Hattie V	1872	Abington	grdn	16850
	Hercules	1868	Middleboro	will	16852
	Hiram L	1877	Middleboro	admn	16853
	James	1820	Middleboro	admn	16854
	James E	1868	Middleboro	admn	16855
	John	1767	Middleboro	will	16856
	John	1822	Middleboro	admn	16857
	John A	1869	Plymouth	grdn	16858
	Joseph	1792	Middleboro	will	16859
	Joseph	1821	Middleboro	will	16860
	Josiah	1763	Middleboro	will	16863
	Josiah	1816	Rochester	admn	16861
	Josiah	1822	Rochester	grdn	16862
	Josiah	1849	Middleboro	will	16864
	Keziah	1866	Middleboro	will	16865
	Lucy	1857	Middleboro	will	16866
	Lydia	1822	Middleboro	grdn	16867
	Lydia B	1826	Rochester	grdn	16868
	Mary	1833	Middleboro	grdn	16837
	Micah	1855	Plymouth	admn	16869
	Sally R	1876	Lakeville	admn	16870
	Salome	1836	Plymouth	will	16871
	Silas M	1825	Middleboro	grdn	16872
	Simon	1809	Plymouth	admn	16873
	Solomon	1840	Plymouth	admn	16874
	Stephen	1803	Middleboro	admn	16875
	Susan W	1823	Plymouth	grdn	16876
	Sylvanus B	1828	Plymouth	grdn	16877
	Thomas H	1841	Plymouth	grdn	16878
	William	1797	Plymouth	admn	16879
	William	1816	Plymouth	admn	16880
	William H	1875	Plymouth	admn	16881
	William Jr	1832	Middleboro	grdn	16882 a
RICKARD	Adeline W	1875	Plymouth	admn	16883
	Anselm	1802	Plymouth	admn	16884
	Anselm	1812	Plymouth	grdn	16885
	Bathsheba	1798	Plymouth	admn	16886
	Benjamin	1788	Plympton	will	16887
	Benjamin	1821	Plymouth	admn	16888
	Betsey	1834	Plympton	grdn	16889 a
	Betty	1782	Pembroke	grdn	16911
	Boadicea	1820	Middleboro	admn	16890
	Cynthia	1782	Pembroke	grdn	16911
	Eldora	1874	Plymouth	grdn	16891
	Eleazer	1784	Plympton	will	16893
	Eleazer Jr	1741	Plympton	grdn	16892 a
	Elisha	1736	Pembroke	will	16894
	Giles	1702	Plymouth	will	16895
	Giles	1709	Plymouth	will	16896
	Giles	1719	Plympton	grdn	16897
	Hannah	1690	Plymouth	admn	16898
	Hannah	1739	Plympton	quit	16899
	Henry	1726	Plympton	admn	16900
	Isaac	1713	Pembroke	grdn	16904
	Isaac	1826	Plympton	admn	16901
	Isaac	1873	Plympton	admn	16902
	Isaac	1873	Plympton	grdn	16903 a
	Jacob	1809	Bridgewater	will	16905
	John	1678	-----	admn	16906
	John	1712	Plymouth	will	16907
	John	1713	Pembroke	will	16910

SURNAME	FIRST NAME	YEAR	PLACE	CASE	DOCKET
RICKARD	John	1726	Plympton	will	16909
	John	1742	Plymouth	admn	16908
	John	1782	Pembroke	grdn	16911
	Jonathan	1785	Plympton	will	16912
	Jonathan	1875	Plympton	admn	16913
	Josiah	1765	Plympton	will	16914
	Lazarus	1840	Plympton	admn	16915
	Lemuel	1854	Rochester	admn	16916
	Lemuel	1876	Plymouth	admn	16917
	Lydia	1837	Plympton	admn	16918
	Mehitable	1739	Plympton	quit	16899
	Mercy	1714	Plymouth/Plympt	admn	16919
	Myra E	1868	Middleboro	grdn	16920
	Rebecca B	1843	Plympton	admn	16921
	Ruth	1782	Plympton	grdn	16931
	Ruth	1826	Plympton	will	16922
	Samuel	1714	Plympton	grdn	16923
	Samuel	1768	Plympton	will	16924
	Samuel	1782	Plympton	grdn	16931
	Samuel	1784	Middleboro	will	16926
	Samuel	1816	Plympton	will	16925
	Sarah	1719	Plympton	grdn	16927
	Sarah	1763	Middleboro	grdn	16928
	Simeon	1782	Plympton	grdn	16931
	Simeon	1840	Plympton	admn	16929
	Theophilus	1782	Plympton	admn	16930
	Theophilus	1782	Plympton	grdn	16931
	Thomas	1771	Pembroke	will	16932
	Thomas	1778	Pembroke	will	16933
	Walter	1770	Middleboro	grdn	16934
	Warren	1839	Rochester	admn	16935
	William	1749	Plymouth	grdn	16936
	William	1766	Plymouth	will	16937
	Zilpah	1880	Plymouth	admn	16938
RICKETSON	James H	1868	Rochester	admn	16939
RIDDLE	Adeline	1833	Hingham	grdn	16941
	Charles L	1833	Hingham	grdn	16941
	Gilman	1833	Hingham	grdn	16941
	Mary	1876	Hingham	admn	16940
	Mary E	1833	Hingham	grdn	16941
RILEY	Abby	1875	Bridgewater	admn	16942
	Ann	1871	Abington	admn	16943
	James E	1871	N. Bridgewater	grdn	16944
	John T	1870	N. Bridgewater	admn	16945
	Patrick H	1857	N. Bridgewater	admn	16946
	Thomas	1871	N. Bridgewater	grdn	16944
RING	Andrew	1692/3	Plymouth	will	16947
	Edith E	1868	Abington	grdn	16951
	Eleazer	1735	Plymouth	will	16948
	Eleazer	1749	Kingston	will	16949
	Francis	1820	Kingston	will	16950
	Joseph B	1868	Abington	grdn	16951
	Osgood	1868	N. Bridgewater	grdn	16952 a
	Samuel	1768	Kingston	will	16953
	Samuel	1874	Kingston	admn	16954
	Susan	1871	Kingston	admn	16955
	William	1730	Plymouth	admn	16956
	William	1731	Plymouth	will	16957
RIPLEY	Abigail	1795	Kingston	admn	16958
	Betsey	1845	Duxbury	will	16960
	Betsey F M	1840	Plymouth	grdn	16959
	Cephas	1831	Plympton	grdn	16961 a
	Chipman	1818	Plympton	grdn	16972
	Christopher	1719/0	Bridgewater	grdn	17021
	Clarissa	1876	Rockland	will	16962
	Daty M	1875	W. Bridgewater	admn	16963
	Deborah	1746	Bridgewater	grdn	16987
	Diana	1871	Plympton	admn	16964
	Ebed	1876	Hingham	will	16965
	Eliza	1841	Franklin MA	admn	16966
	Ephraim C	1813	Halifax/Plympto	grdn	16967

SURNAME	FIRST NAME	YEAR	PLACE	CASE	DOCKET
RIPLEY	Ephraim C	1875	Plympton	admn	16969
	Ephraim C Jr	1867	Plympton	admn	16968
	Eunice	1787	Plympton	will	16970
	Ezekiel	1817	Plympton	admn	16971
	Ezekiel	1818	Plympton	grdn	16972
	George	1861	New York NY	admn	16973
	Hannah T	1860	Kingston	will	16974
	Harvey	1858	California	admn	16975
	Harvey C	1849	Plymouth	grdn	16977
	Harvey W	1846	Plymouth	admn	16976
	Henry	1877	Hingham	admn	16978
	Hezekiah	1750	Kingston	admn	16979
	Hezekiah	1842	Kingston	will	16980
	Isaac	1709	Scituate	admn	16981
	Isaiah	1833	Plympton	admn	16983
	Isaiah S	1834	Plympton	grdn	16984
	Isaiah S	1862	Plympton	admn	16982
	John	1737	Bridgewater	will	16986
	John	1746	Bridgewater	grdn	16987
	John W	1859	Plymouth	admn	16985
	Jonathan	1719/0	Bridgewater	grdn	17021
	Jonathan	1772	Halifax	will	16988
	Joseph	1865	Abington	admn	16990
	Joseph S	1876	Plympton	admn	16991
	Joseph T	1856	Kingston	admn	16989
	Josiah	1823	Plympton	will	16992
	Justin	1870	Hingham	will	16993
	Kenelm	1791	Kingston	will	16994
	Kenelm	1831	Kingston	admn	16995
	Lydia	1868	Plymouth	admn	16996
	Lydia S	1876	Hingham	will	16997
	Mary	1746	Bridgewater	grdn	16987
	Mary	1840	Kingston	admn	16998
	Mary E	1877	Plympton	grdn	16999
	Mary F	1881	Hingham	will	17000
	Molbry	1878	W. Bridgewater	admn	17001
	Naomi T	1849	Plymouth	grdn	16977
	Nehemiah	1829	Hingham	admn	17002
	Nehemiah	1863	Hingham	admn	17003
	Nehemiah Jr	1859	Hull	bond	17004
	Peter	1851	Hingham	will	17005
	Rachel	1841	Hingham	will	17006
	Robert	1752	Bridgewater	grdn	17007
	Rufus	1783	Kingston	admn	17008
	Ruth	1818	Plympton	grdn	16972
	Ruth S	1834	Plympton	grdn	16984
	Sally	1876	Plympton	admn	17009
	Samuel	1719/0	Bridgewater	grdn	17021
	Sarah J	1877	W. Bridgewater	will	17010
	Sarah K	1879	Abington	admn	17011
	Silas	1868	Hingham	will	17012
	Solomon	1810	Bridgewater	admn	17013
	Sylvanus	1847	Plympton	admn	17014
	Tilson	1785	Middleboro	admn	17015
	Timothy	1719/0	Bridgewater	grdn	17021
	Timothy	1777	Plympton	will	17016
	Waitstill	1746	Bridgewater	grdn	16987
	William	1719	Bridgewater	admn	17020
	William	1719/0	Bridgewater	grdn	17021
	William	1873	Abington	will	17019
	William P	1842	Plymouth	will	17017
	William W	1859	Plymouth	grdn	17018
	Zenas	1813	Plymouth	admn	17022
RITCHIE	John	1838	N. Bridgewater	will	17023
ROBBINS	Abigail	1726	Plymouth	grdn	17066
	Adelbert P	1872	Carver	grdn	17024
	Albert R	1868	Plymouth	admn	17025
	Alexander	1877	Plymouth	will	17026
	Amasa	1856	Hanson	admn	17027
	Anson	1867	S. Scituate	will	17028
	Arabella T	1844	Plympton	grdn	17068

SURNAME	FIRST NAME	YEAR	PLACE	CASE	DOCKET
ROBBINS	Benjamin	1743	Plympton	grdn	17085
	Benjamin	1805	Kingston	will	17029
	Benjamin	1847	Middleboro	will	17030
	Chandler	1799	Plymouth	will	17031
	Chandler	1839	Boston	grdn	17032
	Charles	1805	Plymouth	admn	17033
	Charles F	1847	Plymouth	grdn	17055
	Consider	1777	Plympton	grdn	17094
	Consider	1844	Carver	admn	17034
	Ebenezer	1743	Plympton	grdn	17085
	Eleanor	1844	Unavilla NY	grdn	17038
	Eleazer	1743	Plympton	grdn	17085
	Eleazer	1777	Plympton	admn	17035
	Elizabeth	1726	Plymouth	grdn	17066
	Elizabeth	1777	Plympton	grdn	17094
	Elizabeth	1844	Unavilla NY	grdn	17038
	Elizabeth C	1879	Plymouth	admn	17036
	Elizabeth H	1875	Harlem IA	admn	17037
	Elizabeth T	1853	S. Scituate	grdn	17045
	Ellen H	1839	Boston	grdn	17032
	Ephraim	1849	Middleboro	admn	17039
	Esther	1835	Kingston	will	17040
	Frederick	1847	Plymouth	admn	17041
	George A	1853	S. Scituate	admn	17044
	George E	1877	Rixford FL	grdn	17043
	George T	1868	New Berne NC	admn	17042
	George W	1853	S. Scituate	grdn	17045
	Grace J	1877	Carver	adop	17046
	Hannah	1860	Hanover	will	17047
	Hannah T	1872	Plymouth	admn	17048
	Harriet L	1839	Boston	grdn	17032
	Heman C	1881	Plymouth	admn	17049
	Henry H	1827	Plymouth	grdn	17050
	Henry H	1864	Plymouth	admn	17051
	Henry H	1874	Plymouth	admn	17052
	Horace	1869	S. Scituate	admn	17053
	Isaac	1880	Abington	will	17054
	Isabella G	1847	Plymouth	grdn	17055
	James	1743	Plympton	grdn	17085
	Jeduthan	1721	Plympton	admn	17056
	Jeduthan	1740	Plympton	will	17057
	Jesse	1855	Plymouth	admn	17058
	John	1740	Plympton	admn	17059
	John	1838	Hanover	admn	17060
	Joseph	1843	Carver	will	17061
	Josiah	1859	Plymouth	admn	17062
	Josiah P	1872	Carver	admn	17063
	Leavitt T	1871	Plymouth	will	17064
	Lemuel	1726	Plymouth	grdn	17066
	Lemuel	1877	Lakeville	admn	17065
	Lewis	1855	Plympton	admn	17067
	Lewis C	1844	Plympton	grdn	17068
	Manassah	1837	Middleboro	admn	17069
	Margaret	1827	Plymouth	will	17070
	Mary	1777	Plympton	grdn	17094
	Mary	1825	Hanover	admn	17071
	Mary A	1880	Brockton	admn	17073
	Mary J	1847	Plymouth	grdn	17055
	Mary L	1872	Carver	grdn	17024
	Mary W	1868	Marshfield	will	17072
	Matilda S	1875	Abington	admn	17074
	Mehitable	1726	Plymouth	grdn	17066
	Moses	1823	Middleboro	will	17075
	Nahum D	1850	Carver	admn	17076
	Nathan B	1866	Plymouth	admn	17077
	Nathaniel	1724	Charlestown	grdn	17079
	Nathaniel	1775	Hanover	admn	17078
	Peter G	1800	Plymouth	grdn	17080
	Philemon	1800	Plymouth	grdn	17081 a
	Rufus	1743	Plympton	grdn	17085
	Rufus	1797	Plymouth	admn	17084

SURNAME	FIRST NAME	YEAR	PLACE	CASE	DOCKET
ROBBINS	Rufus	1826	Plymouth	admn	17083
	Rufus	1877	S. Abington	will	17082
	Samuel	1776	Middleboro	will	17086
	Samuel	1838	Plymouth	admn	17089
	Samuel	1847	Plymouth	admn	17090
	Samuel	1852	Middleboro	admn	17087
	Samuel	1855	Lakeville	admn	17088
	Samuel V	1816	Williamstown NC	grdn	17091
	Sarah	1825	Hanover	grdn	17092 a
	Seth	1777	Plympton	grdn	17094
	Sibel	1855	Hanover	admn	17093
	Sylvanus	1777	Plympton	grdn	17094
	Sylvester H	1844	Plympton	grdn	17068
	Thaddeus	1844	Plympton	grdn	17068
	Thomas	1724	Charlestown	grdn	17079
	Timothy	1807	Hanover	admn	17095
	Timothy	1856	Hanover	will	17097
	Timothy Jr	1850	Hanover	admn	17096
	William A	1877	Kingston	will	17099
	William H	1839	Plymouth	admn	17098
ROBERTS	Agnes	1869	Marshfield	grdn	17100
	Catherine	1869	Marshfield	grdn	17100
	Coolidge S	1869	Marshfield	grdn	17100
	Elizabeth eta	1886	-----	peti	17101
	Mary A	1869	Marshfield	grdn	17100
	William P	1864	N. Bridgewater	admn	17102
ROBINSON	Abigail	1789	Middleboro	grdn	17106
	Anselm D	1878	Plymouth	admn	17103
	Benjamin R	1878	E. Bridgewater	will	17104
	Charlotte	1864	E. Bridgewater	will	17105
	Clarissa	1789	Middleboro	grdn	17106
	Dyer	1826	Bridgewater	grdn	17107 a
	Dyer	1873	Bridgewater	admn	17108
	Elizabeth H	1872	N. Bridgewater	admn	17109
	Floyd	1880	Bridgewater	admn	17110
	Gad	1880	Plymouth	will	17111
	Gain	1763	Bridgewater	will	17112
	Increase	1756	Bridgewater	admn	17113
	Increase	1768	Pembroke	will	17114
	Isaac	1841	Rochester	grdn	17130
	Jacob	1859	Bridgewater	admn	17115
	Joseph	1766	Bridgewater	admn	17116
	Josiah	1878	Middleboro	will	17117
	Kilborn	1852	E. Bridgewater	admn	17118
	Marcus	1863	E. Bridgewater	will	17119
	Maria D	1819	Bridgewater	grdn	17120
	Mary H	1819	Bridgewater	grdn	17120
	Morrill	1873	Middleboro	will	17121
	Rhoda W	1870	Bridgewater	will	17122
	Robert	1763	Bridgewater	grdn	17123
	Sally	1849	S. Scituate	admn	17124
	Sarah F	1877	Bridgewater	grdn	17125
	Stephen	1788	Middleboro	admn	17126
	Susannah S	1880	Wareham	will	17127
	William	1816	Bridgewater	admn	17128
	William H	1841	Rochester	grdn	17130
	William H	1868	Rochester	admn	17129
ROCHE	Aaron L	1870	Abington	will	17131
	Helen	1876	Hingham	grdn	17133
	James	1872	Hingham	admn	17132
	James S	1876	Hingham	grdn	17133
	Mary	1873	Plymouth	will	17134
	Mary	1876	Hingham	grdn	17133
	Michael J	1876	Hingham	will	17135
	Nicholas	1808	Middleboro	will	17136
	William	1867	N. Bridgewater	adop	17137
ROCKWOOD	John	18--	Abington	will	17138
ROGERS	Abigail	1718	Pembroke	will	17139
	Abigail	1851	Plymouth	admn	17140
	Abisha	1851	Rochester	will	17141
	Amos	1802	Marshfield	will	17142

SURNAME	FIRST NAME	YEAR	PLACE	CASE	DOCKET
ROGERS	Arthur F	1848	Marshfield	grdn	17144
	Arthur F	1879	Marshfield	admn	17143
	Asa	1851	Marshfield	admn	17145
	Asenath	1791	-----	grdn	17146
	Benjamin	1747	Kingston	admn	17147
	Benjamin	1846	Pembroke	will	17148
	Bethiah	1844	Marshfield	admn	17149
	Caleb	1833	Hanover	admn	17150
	Charity	1880	E. Bridgewater	will	17151
	Charles R	1828	Marshfield	admn	17152
	Deborah	1791	-----	grdn	17146
	Ebenezer	1781	Rochester	admn	17153
	Ebenezer	1841	Rochester	will	17154
	Edwin	1867	Hanover	grdn	17155 a
	Edwin	1878	Middleboro	admn	17156
	Elisha	1742	Marshfield	admn	17157
	Elisha	1832	Marshfield	admn	17158
	Elizabeth	1791	-----	grdn	17146
	Elizabeth	1831	Marshfield	will	17159
	Ellis	1874	Plymouth	admn	17160
	George H	1876	Marshfield	admn	17161
	Harry S	1877	Middleboro	grdn	17162
	Henry C	1854	Marshfield	grdn	17176
	Herbert T	1854	Marshfield	grdn	17176
	Howland	1816	Marshfield	admn	17163
	Howland	1875	Marshfield	admn	17164
	Isaac	1853	Marshfield	will	17165
	Isabella T	1859	N. Marshfield	adop	17166
	Israel	1812	Marshfield	admn	17167
	Jacob A	1876	E. Bridgewater	will	17168
	Jane	1862	Plymouth	admn	17169
	Jane F	1867	Plymouth	admn	17170
	John	1692	Duxbury	will	17172
	John	1718	Marshfield	will	17174
	John	1738	Scituate	will	17171
	John	1762	Marshfield	admn	17175
	John Jr	1696	Duxbury	admn	17173
	John L	1854	Marshfield	grdn	17176
	Joseph	1716	Pembroke	will	17177
	Joseph	1760	Marshfield	admn	17178
	Joseph	1816	Marshfield	will	17179
	Judith	1867	Mattapoisett	will	17180
	Libni	1818	Rochester	admn	17181
	Luther	1860	Marshfield	admn	17183
	Luther Jr	1853	Marshfield	admn	17182
	Lydia	1866	Marshfield	admn	17184
	Lydia F	1852	Plymouth	grdn	17203
	Mary L	1854	Marshfield	grdn	17176
	Mehitable J	1852	Plymouth	grdn	17203
	Moses	1707	Marshfield	will	17185
	Nancy	1863	Marshfield	admn	17186
	Nancy B	1876	Plymouth	will	17187
	Naomi	1825	Marshfield	admn	17188
	Nathan	1874	Scituate	admn	17190
	Nathan A	1862	Scituate	admn	17189
	Nathaniel C	1875	Abington	admn	17191
	Nellie	1875	Abington	grdn	17229
	Parker	1875	Abington	grdn	17229
	Patience	1791	-----	grdn	17146
	Peleg Jr	1805	Marshfield	admn	17192
	Polly	1802	Marshfield	grdn	17195
	Polly	1862	Marshfield	will	17194
	Polly	1868	Plymouth	grdn	17193 a
	Prince	1832	Marshfield	will	17196
	Rachel	1857	Marshfield	will	17197
	Rachel	1862	Pembroke	admn	17198
	Rachel W	1802	Marshfield	grdn	17195
	Rebecca	1861	Plymouth	admn	17200
	Rebecca M	1850	Rochester	admn	17199
	Reuben	1867	Hanover	admn	17201
	Richard	1851	Plymouth	admn	17202

SURNAME	FIRST NAME	YEAR	PLACE	CASE	DOCKET
ROGERS	Richard	1852	Plymouth	grdn	17203
	Samuel	1747	Marshfield	will	17207
	Samuel	1760	Plymouth	admn	17204
	Samuel	1761	Marshfield	will	17208
	Samuel	1832	Marshfield	admn	17209
	Samuel	1838	E. Bridgewater	will	17206
	Samuel	1865	Plymouth	will	17205
	Sarah	1837	Hanover	will	17210
	Sarah C	1848	Marshfield	grdn	17144
	Sarah S	1876	Brockton	admn	17211
	Stephen	1835	Marshfield	admn	17212
	Stephen	1835	Marshfield	will	17213
	Stephen	1868	Plymouth	admn	17215
	Stephen R	1836	Marshfield	grdn	17214
	Sylvanus	1859	Plymouth	grdn	17216 a
	Thomas	1718	Pembroke	admn	17219
	Thomas	1745	Marshfield	will	17220
	Thomas	1804	Plymouth	admn	17218
	Thomas	1814	Marshfield	will	17221
	Thomas	1865	Marshfield	admn	17222
	Thomas B	1881	Wareham	will	17223
	Thomas Jr	1756	Plymouth	admn	17217
	Timothy	1728	Marshfield	will	17224
	Timothy	1763	Marshfield	will	17225
	Timothy	1845	Marshfield	admn	17226
	William	1764	Marshfield	will	17227
	William	1844	Plymouth	will	17228
	Willis	1875	Abington	grdn	17229
	Zacheus	1817	Marshfield	will	17230
	Zacheus Jr	1816	Marshfield	admn	17231
ROLFE	Mary A	1831	Plymouth	admn	17232
ROLLINS	Ellen O	1876	E. Bridgewater	grdn	17233
	James H	1876	E. Bridgewater	grdn	17233
ROOT	Charles A	1880	Hanover	grdn	17234
ROSE	Annis	1688	Marshfield	will	17235
	Anthony	1737	Marshfield	admn	17236
	Charles E	1875	Hanover	grdn	17237
	Edwin	1875	Hanover	admn	17238
	Elizabeth	1710	Scituate	grdn	17240
	Gideon	1710	Scituate	grdn	17240
	Gideon	1784	Scituate	will	17239
	Hannah	1852	Scituate	admn	17241
	Jabez	1707	Scituate	admn	17242
	Jeremiah	1709	Scituate	admn	17243
	Laban	1816	Scituate	admn	17244
	Laban	1861	Hanover	will	17246
	Laban T	1854	Hanover	admn	17245
	Lucy D	1876	Hanover	will	17247
	Mary	1709	Scituate	grdn	17248
	Rebecca	1872	Hanover	admn	17249
	Seth	1831	Hanover	will	17250
	Seth	1859	Hanover	admn	17251
	Thomas	1710	Scituate	grdn	17240
ROUND	Juliana	1838	Middleboro	grdn	17252
	William W	1831	N. Bridgewater	will	17253
ROUNSEVILLE	Freelove T	1862	Middleboro	will	17254
	Gamaliel	1853	Middleboro	admn	17255
ROUSE	John	1717	Marshfield	will	17256
ROWE	Eliza J	1867	N. Bridgewater	adop	17257
	Michael	1879	Brockton	will	17258
ROYCE	Ashley A	1855	Wareham	grdn	17259
	Harvey B	1855	Wareham	grdn	17259
RUCH	Manuel	1877	Plymouth	will	17260
	Sarah	1877	Plymouth	admn	17261
RUGGLES	Benjamin	1782	Rochester	grdn	17275
	Elisha	1830	Rochester	admn	17262
	Hannah	1776	Rochester	grdn	17263
	Increase S	1825	Rochester	admn	17264
	Increase S	1825	Rochester	will	17265
	Jacob L	1776	Rochester	grdn	17263
	James	1877	Rochester	will	17266

SURNAME	FIRST NAME	YEAR	PLACE	CASE	DOCKET
RUGGLES	Joanna	1780	Scituate	will	17267
	John	1773	Scituate	will	17268
	John	1812	Scituate	will	17269
	Lucy	1854	S. Scituate	will	17270
	Mary	1780	Rochester	admn	17271
	Nathaniel	1777	Rochester	will	17272
	Polly	1776	Rochester	grdn	17263
	Sarah	1862	Portland ME	admn	17273
	Thomas	1782	Rochester	grdn	17275
	Thomas	1830	Scituate	will	17274
	Timothy	1768	Rochester	will	17276
RUHLE	William A	1879	Plymouth	adop	17277
RUMNEY	Mary	1866	Hanover	will	17278
RUSSELL	Abner	1787	Duxbury	admn	17279
	Adriana M	1865	Wareham	grdn	17302
	Amelia	1868	Kingston	will	17280
	Amelia	1870	Kingston	will	17281
	Andrew H	1864	Plymouth	grdn	17283
	Andrew L	1864	Plymouth	admn	17282
	Ann	1871	N. Bridgewater	will	17284
	Betsey	1817	Kingston	grdn	17298
	Betsey F	1868	Plymouth	admn	17285
	Bridgham	1840	Plymouth	will	17286
	Catherine	1860	Kingston	will	17287
	Catherine D	1850	Kingston	grdn	17293
	Catherine E	1861	Plymouth	admn	17288
	Charity A	1865	Wareham	admn	17289
	Deborah	1871	Plymouth	admn	17290
	Elizabeth B	1841	Plymouth	grdn	17292
	Elizabeth B	1869	Plymouth	admn	17291
	Ellen	1874	Brockton	grdn	17318
	Emma T	1850	Kingston	grdn	17293
	Francis	1857	N. Bridgewater	grdn	17294 a
	Francis	1869	N. Bridgewater	will	17295
	George	1817	Kingston	grdn	17298
	George	1822	Kingston	admn	17297
	George	1857	Kingston	will	17296
	James	1792	Plymouth	admn	17299
	James	1819	Plymouth	admn	17300
	James	1857	Wareham	will	17301
	James A	1865	Wareham	grdn	17302
	John	1723	Pembroke	admn	17303
	John	1777	Plymouth	admn	17304
	John	1857	Plymouth	will	17305
	John	1874	Brockton	grdn	17318
	John B	1841	Plymouth	grdn	17292
	Lothrop	1760	Barnstable	grdn	17306
	Martha L B	1864	Plymouth	grdn	17283
	Mary	1874	Brockton	grdn	17318
	Mary Ann	1872	Plymouth	will	17308
	Mary H	1862	Plymouth	will	17307
	Mercy F	1817	Kingston	grdn	17298
	Nathaniel	1852	Plymouth	will	17309
	Nathaniel	1875	Plymouth	admn	17310
	Rebecca	1877	Plymouth	admn	17311
	Solomon	1761	Pembroke	admn	17312
	Susanna	1807	Duxbury	admn	17313
	Thomas	1800	Bridgewater	will	17317
	Thomas	1854	Plymouth	will	17314
	Thomas	1867	Kingston	grdn	17315 a
	Thomas	1868	Kingston	admn	17316
	Thomas	1874	Brockton	grdn	17318
	William	1874	Brockton	grdn	17318
RYAN	Demmy D	1863	Wareham	admn	17319
	Nathaniel	1802	Bridgewater	grdn	17320
	Nathaniel	1823	W. Bridgewater	admn	17321
RYDER	Abigail	1744	Plymouth	grdn	17372
	Abner	1843	Bridgewater	will	17322
	Amelia C	1853	Rochester	grdn	17323
	Amos	1744	Plymouth	admn	17324
	Amos	1744	Plymouth	grdn	17325

SURNAME	FIRST NAME	YEAR	PLACE	CASE	DOCKET
RYDER	Anna	1880	W. Bridgewater	admn	17326
	Armenia	1873	Middleboro	will	17327
	Benjamin	1744	Plymouth	grdn	17372
	Benjamin	1775	Plymouth	will	17328
	Benjamin	1803	Middleboro	admn	17330
	Benjamin	1804	Plymouth	admn	17329
	Benjamin	1838	Rochester	will	17331
	Caleb	1856	Plymouth	grdn	17333
	Caleb	1865	Plymouth	will	17332
	Chapman	1835	Middleboro	admn	17334
	Charles	1735	Plymouth	grdn	17337
	Charles	1761	Plymouth	admn	17336
	Charles	1785	Duxbury	admn	17335
	Daniel	1861	Plymouth	will	17338
	Daniel	1873	Plymouth	admn	17339
	Deborah	1856	Plymouth	grdn	17333
	Drusilla	1835	Rochester	admn	17340
	Ebenezer	1750	Plymouth	admn	17341
	Edward	1840	Wareham	grdn	17342 a
	Elisha	1828	Middleboro	admn	17343
	Elisha	1828	Middleboro	will	17344
	Elisha	1833	Middleboro	admn	17345
	Elizabeth	1805	Plymouth	will	17346
	Ezekiel	1848	Plymouth	admn	17347
	Ezekiel Jr	1869	Plymouth	admn	17348
	Frederick L	1865	Rochester	grdn	17357
	George	1856	Plymouth	grdn	17333
	George	1880	Plymouth	will	17350
	George S	1878	Plymouth	will	17349
	Hannah	1866	Rochester	admn	17351
	Hattie W	1864	Middleboro	grdn	17409
	Hope D	1867	Middleboro	admn	17352
	Hope W	1853	Rochester	grdn	17323
	Isaac	1776	Middleboro	admn	17353
	Isaac	1776	Middleboro	grdn	17354
	James	1775	Plymouth	grdn	17355
	James	1856	Plymouth	grdn	17333
	James	1859	Rochester	admn	17356
	James N	1865	Rochester	grdn	17357
	Jerusha	1735	Plymouth	grdn	17337
	John	1735	Plymouth	admn	17358
	John	1756	Plymouth	admn	17359
	John	1829	Plymouth	admn	17360
	John	1833	Thomaston ME	grdn	17363
	John	1879	Hingham	will	17362
	John C	1871	Marion	will	17361
	Jonathan	1799	Rochester	admn	17364
	Jonathan	1803	Rochester	grdn	17365
	Joseph	1744	Plymouth	grdn	17372
	Joseph	1767	Plymouth	will	17369
	Joseph	1779	Plymouth	will	17370
	Joseph	1794	Plymouth	admn	17368
	Joseph	1803	Plymouth	admn	17367
	Joseph F	1864	Rochester	admn	17366
	Joseph Jr	1737	Plymouth	admn	17371
	Joshua	1801	Plymouth	bond	17373
	Josiah	1771	Middleboro	will	17374
	Linus	1834	Rochester	admn	17375
	Lucinda	1859	Middleboro	admn	17376
	Madison N	1868	Rochester	admn	17377
	Martin L	1875	Rochester	admn	17378
	Mary	1771	Middleboro	grdn	17404
	Mary	1785	Plymouth	admn	17379
	Mary	1859	Middleboro	will	17380
	Merrick	1862	Plymouth	admn	17381
	Nancy	1824	Hanson	grdn	17382
	Nathan	1843	Middleboro	will	17383
	Nathaniel	1826	Plymouth	admn	17384
	Nathaniel	1857	Middleboro	will	17385
	Patience	1821	Middleboro	admn	17386
	Patience	1854	Middleboro	admn	17387

SURNAME	FIRST NAME	YEAR	PLACE	CASE	DOCKET
RYDER	Peter	1778	Marshfield	will	17388
	Phebe H	1835	Rochester	grdn	17389
	Rebecca	1735	Plymouth	grdn	17337
	Rebecca C	1870	Rochester	will	17390
	Samuel	1715	Plymouth	will	17391
	Samuel	1718	Plymouth	admn	17392
	Samuel	1762	Middleboro	admn	17397
	Samuel	1772	Rochester	will	17396
	Samuel	1803	Rochester	grdn	17365
	Samuel	1804	Plymouth	will	17393
	Samuel	1811	Middleboro	will	17398
	Samuel	1845	W. Bridgewater	will	17394
	Samuel	1851	Middleboro	admn	17399
	Samuel	1880	W. Bridgewater	will	17395
	Samuel W	1873	Middleboro	will	17400
	Servia	1833	Thomaston ME	grdn	17363
	Seth	1755	Middleboro	admn	17401
	Seth	1826	Plymouth	admn	17402
	Standish	1871	Middleboro	admn	17403
	Thankful	1771	Middleboro	grdn	17404
	Whitcomb	1865	Rochester	will	17405
	William	1773	Plymouth	admn	17406
	William E B	1858	Plymouth	grdn	17407
	William H	1864	Middleboro	grdn	17409
	William T	1863	Rochester	admn	17408
	Zachariah W	1853	Rochester	admn	17410
	Zenas	1855	Rochester	will	17411
SACHEMUS	William	1706	Plymouth	admn	17412 i
SACKEE	Phoebe	1767	Bridgewater	will	17413
	Scipio	1748	Bridgewater	admn	17414 b
SALER	James	1751	Plymouth	admn	17415
SALMOND	Abigail	1880	Pembroke	admn	17416
	John	1845	Hanover	admn	17417
	Peter	1880	Pembroke	will	17418
	Robert	1829	Hanover	will	17419
	Samuel	1859	Hanover	will	17420
	Sophia B	1873	Pembroke	admn	17421
	William	1842	Hanover	will	17422
SAMPSON	Aaron	1780	Duxbury	grdn	17423
	Abby M	1851	Plymouth	admn	17424
	Abel	1840	Pembroke	admn	17425
	Abel	1844	Pembroke	admn	17426
	Abiah	1802	Plympton	admn	17427
	Abigail	1795	Plympton	admn	17428
	Abigail	1838	Duxbury	admn	17429
	Abigail E	1869	Bridgewater	grdn	17430
	Abner	1780	Duxbury	will	17431
	Abner	1816	Duxbury	grdn	17610
	Abner	1843	Duxbury	will	17432
	Abraham	1727	Duxbury	will	17433
	Abraham	1777	Duxbury	will	17434
	Ahira	1829	Duxbury	admn	17435
	Ahira	1853	Pembroke	admn	17436
	Alden T	1873	Pembroke	will	17437
	Algernon S	1830	Plymouth	grdn	17687
	Alonzo C	1872	Plymouth	grdn	17481
	Alvan	1821	Plymouth	admn	17438
	Amos	1741	Duxbury	grdn	17447
	Andrew	1786	Duxbury	will	17439
	Andrew	1842	Duxbury	admn	17440
	Andrew	1846	Duxbury	admn	17441
	Andrew C	1874	Mattapoisett	admn	17443
	Andrew W	1874	Hanson	will	17442
	Anna	1835	Duxbury	admn	17444
	Anne	1836	Kingston	will	17445
	Anthony	1741	Duxbury	grdn	17447
	Anthony	1815	Duxbury	admn	17446
	Araunah	1812	Scituate	admn	17448
	Asa	1829	Duxbury	admn	17449
	Azel	1872	Kingston	admn	17450
	Barnabas	1750	Middleboro	will	17451

SURNAME	FIRST NAME	YEAR	PLACE	CASE	DOCKET
SAMPSON	Bartlett	1803	Duxbury	admn	17452
	Benjamin	1754	Middleboro	admn	17453
	Benjamin	1758	Kingston	will	17457
	Benjamin	1762	Plympton	will	17454
	Benjamin	1762	Plympton	grdn	17602
	Benjamin	1779	Kingston	will	17459
	Benjamin	1779	Kingston	grdn	17460
	Benjamin	1794	Kingston	admn	17458
	Benjamin	1832	Kingston	grdn	17456 a
	Benjamin	1880	Kingston	admn	17455
	Betsey	1842	Pembroke	admn	17461
	Bradford	1821	Duxbury	admn	17462
	Bradford	1833	Duxbury	admn	17463
	Bradford	1848	Duxbury	grdn	17464 a
	Bradford	1865	Duxbury	admn	17465
	Briggs	1774	Duxbury	grdn	17472
	Byram	1822	Hanson	admn	17466
	Caleb	1745	Middleboro	grdn	17684
	Caleb	1750	Duxbury	admn	17467
	Calvin	1810	Marshfield	admn	17468
	Calvin	1842	Duxbury	grdn	17469
	Caroline	1824	Plympton	grdn	17583
	Chandler	1850	Marshfield	will	17470
	Chapin	1774	Duxbury	admn	17471
	Chapin	1774	Duxbury	grdn	17472
	Charles	1835	Duxbury	grdn	17474 a
	Charles	1840	Kingston	admn	17475
	Charles	1843	Duxbury	grdn	17477
	Charles	1869	Marshfield	will	17473
	Charles D	1847	Duxbury	grdn	17476
	Chloe	1850	Duxbury	will	17478
	Chloe	1879	Pembroke	grdn	17480 a
	Chloe A	1881	Middleboro	admn	17479
	Christopher D	1872	Plymouth	grdn	17481
	Colson	1839	Duxbury	admn	17482
	Constant	1856	Kingston	admn	17483
	Constant	1874	Kingston	admn	17484
	Cordelia A	1869	Bridgewater	grdn	17430
	Cornelius	1796	Kingston	admn	17485
	Croade	1779	Kingston	grdn	17460
	Crocker	1823	Kingston	will	17486
	Daniel	1791	Middleboro	grdn	17504
	Daniel	1795	Middleboro	grdn	17488 a
	Daniel	1814	Middleboro	will	17489
	Daniel	1834	Duxbury	admn	17487
	David	1772	Duxbury	will	17490
	Deborah	1745	Middleboro	grdn	17684
	Deborah	1789	Kingston	will	17491
	Deborah	1796	Kingston	grdn	17551
	Deborah	1842	Duxbury	admn	17492
	Deborah	1871	Plymouth	admn	17493
	Deborah A	1875	Plymouth	admn	17494
	Delana	1880	Lakeville	will	17495
	Desire	1804	Kingston	will	17496
	Desire	1830	Kingston	will	17497
	Dolly	1853	Duxbury	admn	17498
	Ebenezer	1779	Duxbury	will	17499
	Ebenezer D	1881	Lakeville	admn	17500
	Eden	1874	Duxbury	will	17501
	Eden	1881	Duxbury	grdn	17502 a
	Edith M	1872	Plymouth	grdn	17530
	Eleanor	1855	Marshfield	admn	17503
	Elias	1791	Middleboro	grdn	17504
	Elijah	1805	Duxbury	admn	17505
	Elijah	1834	Duxbury	will	17506
	Elisha	1876	Duxbury	will	17507
	Elizabeth	1774	Duxbury	grdn	17472
	Elizabeth T	1835	Duxbury	grdn	17539
	Elizabeth T	1863	Duxbury	admn	17508
	Esther	1766	Middleboro	grdn	17509
	Esther	1782	Kingston	will	17510

SURNAME	FIRST NAME	YEAR	PLACE	CASE	DOCKET
SAMPSON	Frank	1869	Marshfield	grdn	17511
	Gaius	1858	Duxbury	will	17512
	George	1774	Plympton	will	17518
	George	1796	Kingston	grdn	17551
	George	1816	Duxbury	grdn	17610
	George	1827	Plympton	will	17516
	George	1842	Duxbury	admn	17514
	George	1843	Duxbury	grdn	17477
	George B	1865	Duxbury	admn	17515
	George R	1856	Middleboro	grdn	17513
	George W	1796	Plympton	grdn	17517
	Gershom	1795	Middleboro	grdn	17519 a
	Gideon	1780	Plympton	grdn	17528
	Gideon	1794	Plympton	will	17520
	Gideon	1814	Pembroke	admn	17521
	Hannah	1774	Plympton	will	17525
	Hannah	1780	Plympton	grdn	17528
	Hannah	1808	Plymouth	admn	17523
	Hannah	1825	Duxbury	grdn	17592
	Hannah	1836	Plympton	will	17526
	Hannah	1867	Duxbury	admn	17522
	Hannah B	1849	Plymouth	grdn	17524
	Hannah W	1843	Plympton	grdn	17527
	Harriet M	1879	Kingston	admn	17529
	Harvey C	1872	Plymouth	grdn	17530
	Henry	1787	Duxbury	will	17531
	Henry	1830	Duxbury	grdn	17603
	Henry C	1879	Duxbury	grdn	17532
	Hipsaba	1758	Middleboro	grdn	17587
	Hiram	1875	Plymouth	admn	17533
	Hiram Jr	1865	Plymouth	admn	17534
	Howland	1813	Duxbury	admn	17535
	Ichabod	1830	Duxbury	admn	17537
	Ichabod	1834	Duxbury	admn	17538
	Ichabod	1835	Duxbury	grdn	17539
	Ichabod	1856	Middleboro	admn	17536
	Isaac	1726	Plympton	admn	17540
	Isaac	1750	Middleboro	will	17541
	Isaac	1796	Kingston	grdn	17551
	Isaac	1827	Duxbury	admn	17543
	Isaac	1833	Plymouth	admn	17544
	Isaac	1847	Middleboro	admn	17542
	Isaac	1872	Pembroke	admn	17545
	Isaiah	1842	Pembroke	will	17546
	Israel	1745	Middleboro	grdn	17684
	Issachar	1780	Plympton	grdn	17528
	Jacob	1752	Middleboro	grdn	17547
	James	1796	Kingston	grdn	17551
	James B	1865	N. Bridgewater	will	17548
	James L	1872	Duxbury	grdn	17549 a
	James L	1879	Duxbury	admn	17550
	Jane	1862	Wareham	admn	17552
	Jedediah	1730	Plympton	grdn	17553
	Jeremiah	1762	Plympton	grdn	17602
	Jeremiah	1830	Kingston	will	17554
	Job	1774	Duxbury	grdn	17472
	Job	1822	Duxbury	will	17555
	John	1750	Middleboro	admn	17563
	John	1770	Duxbury	admn	17557
	John	1786	Plymouth	admn	17556
	John	1805	Duxbury	will	17558
	John	1821	Middleboro	will	17564
	John	1823	Wareham	grdn	17565 a
	John	1828	Plympton	admn	17559
	John	1838	Wareham	admn	17566
	John	1845	Brunswick NY	will	17562
	John	1869	Plympton	admn	17560
	John	1869	S. Scituate	will	17561
	John	1881	Wareham	admn	17567
	John H	1869	Bridgewater	grdn	17430
	Jonathan	1758	Plympton	admn	17568

SURNAME	FIRST NAME	YEAR	PLACE	CASE	DOCKET
SAMPSON	Joseph	1726	Plympton	admn	17577
	Joseph	1745	Middleboro	grdn	17684
	Joseph	1748	Plympton	grdn	17676
	Joseph	1752	Plympton	grdn	17578
	Joseph	1757	Middleboro	admn	17574
	Joseph	1795	Plympton	will	17576
	Joseph	1804	Kingston	will	17571
	Joseph	1812	Kingston	grdn	17572
	Joseph	1816	Duxbury	grdn	17610
	Joseph	1833	Plymouth	admn	17570
	Joseph	1843	Plymouth	grdn	17569
	Joseph	1845	Kingston	admn	17573
	Joseph Jr	1828	Middleboro	admn	17575
	Josephus	1857	Middleboro	grdn	17579
	Joshua	1741	Duxbury	admn	17580
	Josiah	1730	Plympton	admn	17581
	Judith	1774	Duxbury	grdn	17472
	Lazarus	1753	Plymouth	admn	17582
	Leonice M	1824	Plympton	grdn	17583
	Leora J	1856	Plymouth	grdn	17639
	Leora W	1853	Kingston	grdn	17584
	Levi	1748	Plympton	grdn	17676
	Lloyd G	1838	Duxbury	admn	17585
	Lucy S	1869	Kingston	will	17586
	Luna	1780	Duxbury	grdn	17423
	Lydia	1762	Plympton	grdn	17602
	Lydia	1816	Duxbury	grdn	17610
	Marcia L	1830	Plymouth	grdn	17687
	Margaret	1758	Middleboro	grdn	17587
	Maria L	1830	Plymouth	grdn	17687
	Marston	1823	Plympton	admn	17588
	Marston	1867	Plymouth	admn	17589
	Martha	1752	Plympton	grdn	17578
	Martha C	1821	Duxbury	grdn	17590
	Martin	1825	Duxbury	grdn	17592
	Martin	1852	Duxbury	admn	17591
	Mary J	1879	Duxbury	grdn	17532
	Melzar	1787	Duxbury	admn	17593
	Melzar	1821	Hanover	grdn	17594
	Mercy	1812	Middleboro	will	17595
	Mercy	1834	Middleboro	grdn	17596 a
	Mercy	1877	Plymouth	admn	17597
	Micah	1740	Kingston	admn	17598
	Micah	1744	Kingston	grdn	17599
	Micah	1750	Duxbury	grdn	17600
	Micah	1779	Kingston	grdn	17460
	Miles	1821	Pembroke	admn	17601
	Moses	1762	Plympton	grdn	17602
	Nancy C	1830	Duxbury	grdn	17603
	Nancy R	1830	Plymouth	grdn	17687
	Nathan	1806	Duxbury	admn	17604
	Nathan	1872	Duxbury	will	17605
	Nathan L	1879	Duxbury	grdn	17532
	Nathaniel	1749	Duxbury	will	17607
	Nathaniel	1780	Duxbury	grdn	17423
	Nathaniel	1788	Duxbury	will	17608
	Nathaniel	1813	Duxbury	will	17609
	Nathaniel	1816	Duxbury	grdn	17610
	Nathaniel	1840	Duxbury	admn	17606
	Newland	1762	Plympton	grdn	17602
	Noah	1742	Plymouth	admn	17611
	Obadiah	1766	Middleboro	admn	17612
	Oliver	1813	Kingston	admn	17613
	Oliver	1817	Kingston	grdn	17614
	P Miller	1867	Middleboro	admn	17628
	Parmenas G	1866	Middleboro	admn	17615
	Patience R	1879	Kingston	will	17616
	Paul	1811	Marshfield	will	17617
	Peleg	1841	Duxbury	admn	17618
	Perez	1733	Duxbury	admn	17621
	Perez	1824	Pembroke	admn	17619

SURNAME	FIRST NAME	YEAR	PLACE	CASE	DOCKET
SAMPSON	Perez H	1864	Duxbury	admn	17620
	Peter	1750	Middleboro	grdn	17622
	Phebe	1752	Middleboro	grdn	17547
	Phebe E	1878	Duxbury	will	17623
	Philander	1854	Middleboro	admn	17624
	Philander M	1854	Middleboro	grdn	17625
	Philemon	1756	Plympton	admn	17626
	Philemon	1780	Plympton	grdn	17528
	Philemon	1805	Plympton	admn	17627
	Polly	1816	Duxbury	grdn	17610
	Priscilla	1779	Kingston	grdn	17460
	Priscilla	1796	Kingston	grdn	17551
	Priscilla	1838	Kingston	will	17629
	Priscilla	1862	Pembroke	admn	17630
	Rebecca	1769	Kingston	will	17631
	Rebecca	1805	Duxbury	will	17633
	Rebecca	1821	Duxbury	grdn	17590
	Rebecca	1833	Duxbury	admn	17634
	Rebecca	1844	Kingston	will	17632
	Rebecca	1855	Duxbury	admn	17636
	Rebecca D	1853	Duxbury	admn	17635
	Richard	1854	Middleboro	admn	17637
	Robert	1775	Duxbury	will	17638
	Roscoe N	1856	Plymouth	grdn	17639
	Rufus	1859	Plymouth	admn	17640
	Rufus	1874	Duxbury	will	17641
	Ruth	1748	Plympton	grdn	17676
	Ruth	1813	Middleboro	admn	17642
	Ruth	1847	Duxbury	will	17643
	Ruth	1878	Pembroke	will	17644
	Ruth L	1830	Plymouth	grdn	17687
	Sally	1817	Kingston	grdn	17614
	Samuel	1744	Middleboro	will	17645
	Samuel	1850	Middleboro	will	17646
	Samuel B	1871	Abington	grdn	17647
	Samuel B	1877	Wareham	will	17648
	Sarah	1762	Plympton	grdn	17602
	Sarah	1792	Plympton	admn	17649
	Sarah	1825	Duxbury	grdn	17592
	Sarah A	1805	Duxbury	grdn	17650
	Sarah T B	1849	Plymouth	grdn	17524
	Schuyler	1856	Plymouth	admn	17651
	Seth	1770	Middleboro	will	17652
	Shadrach A	1854	Middleboro	grdn	17625
	Simeon	1789	Plympton	will	17653
	Solomon	1851	Plymouth	admn	17654
	Sophia B	1833	Duxbury	grdn	17655
	Spencer	1841	Duxbury	admn	17656
	Stephen	1714	Duxbury	admn	17657
	Stephen	1866	Kingston	will	17658
	Studley	1834	Duxbury	grdn	17659 a
	Studley	1835	Duxbury	admn	17660
	Sylvanus	1748	Plympton	grdn	17676
	Sylvanus	1800	Plymouth	admn	17662
	Sylvanus	1832	Plymouth	grdn	17663 a
	Sylvanus	1848	Duxbury	will	17661
	Sylvanus	1872	Plymouth	grdn	17530
	Sylvanus 2nd	1865	Plymouth	admn	17664
	Thirza	1880	Plymouth	admn	17665
	Thomas	1748	Plympton	admn	17675
	Thomas	1748	Plympton	grdn	17676
	Thomas	1793	Middleboro	admn	17668
	Thomas	1813	Middleboro	admn	17669
	Thomas	1824	Plympton	will	17674
	Thomas	1829	Franklin LA	admn	17666
	Thomas	1833	Middleboro	admn	17670
	Thomas	1834	Duxbury	admn	17672
	Thomas	1841	Duxbury	admn	17673
	Thomas	1868	Plymouth	will	17667
	Thomas W	1821	Duxbury	grdn	17590
	Thomas W	1833	Duxbury	admn	17671

SURNAME	FIRST NAME	YEAR	PLACE	CASE	DOCKET
SAMPSON	Thomas W	1857	Middleboro	grdn	17579
	Timothy	1821	Hanover	grdn	17594
	Uriah	1790	Middleboro	will	17677
	Uriah	1880	Lakeville	admn	17678
	Uriah 2nd	1881	Lakeville	admn	17679
	Wealthy	1780	Duxbury	grdn	17423
	William	1745	Middleboro	admn	17683
	William	1745	Middleboro	grdn	17684
	William	1753	Middleboro	admn	17682
	William	1815	Duxbury	admn	17681
	William M	1824	Plympton	grdn	17583
	William M	1829	Plympton	admn	17680
	Zabdiel	1776	Plympton	admn	17685
	Zabdiel	1828	Plymouth	admn	17686
	Zabdiel S	1830	Plymouth	grdn	17687
	Zaviah	1864	Plymouth	admn	17688
	Zilpha	1745	Middleboro	grdn	17684
SANBORN	Samuel A	1862	Abington	admn	17689
	Samuel A	1875	Abington	admn	17690
SANDERS	Abigail	1724	Pembroke	grdn	17693
	Edward	1863	Abington	admn	17691
	John	1724	Pembroke	admn	17692
	Lydia	1724	Pembroke	grdn	17693
SANDRESS	James J	1829	N. Bridgewater	admn	17694
SANFORD	Baalis	1880	E. Bridgewater	will	17695
	Lillian E	1865	N. Bridgewater	grdn	17696
	Robert C	1865	N. Bridgewater	grdn	17696
	Walter E	1865	N. Bridgewater	grdn	17696
SANGER	Samuel F	1878	Bridgewater	will	17697
	Susan	1878	Bridgewater	admn	17698
	Zedekiah	1820	Bridgewater	admn	17699
SARGENT	Abimelech H	1834	Hingham	admn	17700
SASH	-----	1730	Bridgewater	admn	17701 b
	Mary	1757	Bridgewater	admn	17702
SAVAGE	Habijah	1755	Boston	grdn	17704
	John	1755	Boston	grdn	17704
	John	1873	N. Bridgewater	will	17703
SAVERY	Aaron	1798	Wareham	grdn	17705
	Anthony	1789	Rochester	will	17706
	Benjamin	1840	Wareham	admn	17707
	Benjamin	1861	Wareham	admn	17708
	Benjamin H	1856	Carver	grdn	17709
	Betsey S	1876	Wareham	grdn	17714
	Cyrus	1828	Wareham	admn	17710
	Daniel	1778	Middleboro	grdn	17711
	Daniel	1836	Middleboro	admn	17712
	Daniel M	1847	Middleboro	grdn	17713
	Deborah	1827	Wareham	grdn	17738
	Elizabeth	1827	Wareham	grdn	17738
	Eveline A	1876	Wareham	grdn	17714
	George H	1877	E. Bridgewater	grdn	17715 a
	Huldah	1876	Rochester	will	17716
	Isaac	1827	Wareham	grdn	17738
	James	1860	Carver	will	17717
	Jane	1827	Wareham	grdn	17738
	Joanna	1873	Carver	will	17718
	John	1752	Middleboro	admn	17719
	John	1778	Middleboro	will	17720
	John	1853	Carver	will	17721
	Mercy	1771	Plympton	grdn	17722
	Nathan	1859	Marion	will	17723
	Nehemiah	1877	Plymouth	will	17724
	Patience E	1827	Wareham	grdn	17738
	Phebe A	1870	Middleboro	admn	17725
	Phineas	1837	Wareham	will	17726
	Robertson	1827	Wareham	grdn	17738
	Ruth E	1827	Wareham	grdn	17738
	Samuel	1812	Wareham	will	17727
	Samuel M	1862	Plymouth	admn	17729
	Samuel et als	1771	Wareham	warr	17728
	Stillman	1851	Rochester	admn	17730

SURNAME	FIRST NAME	YEAR	PLACE	CASE	DOCKET
SAVERY	Susannah L	1869	Carver	will	17731
	Thomas	1731	Plymouth	admn	17732
	Thomas	1812	Wareham	admn	17734
	Thomas	1822	Carver	admn	17733
	Thomas	1873	Wareham	will	17735
	Timothy	1843	Wareham	admn	17736
	Uriah	1824	Wareham	admn	17737
	Uriah	1827	Wareham	grdn	17738
	William S	1870	Carver	will	17739
	Winsor	1874	Plymouth	will	17740
	Zenas	1874	Plymouth	will	17741
	Zilpha	1771	Plympton	grdn	17722
SAWIN	Daniel	1822	Bridgewater	will	17742
	Daniel C	1829	E. Bridgewater	grdn	17743
	Eliza R	1829	E. Bridgewater	grdn	17743
	Hannah B	1829	E. Bridgewater	grdn	17743
SAWYER	Abel	1818	Abington	admn	17744
	Abel	1867	Abington	admn	17745
	Annette W	1855	Taunton	adop	17746
	Annette W	1867	Duxbury	grdn	17747
	George C	1861	N. Bridgewater	grdn	17748
	Hattie M	1861	N. Bridgewater	grdn	17748
	Joshua	1864	Plymouth	admn	17749
	Martha B	1861	N. Bridgewater	grdn	17748
	Mary A	1861	N. Bridgewater	grdn	17748
	Rebecca	1711	Marshfield	admn	17750
	Susan E	1864	N. Bridgewater	admn	17751
	Thomas	1695	Middleboro	admn	17752
SCALES	Catherine	1877	Scituate	admn	17753
SCANLAN	Charles	1872	Bridgewater	will	17754
SCHIEL	Peter	1876	Plymouth	will	17755
SCHROEDER	John D	1864	Abington	admn	17756
SCOTT	Charles	1852	Rochester	will	17757
	Edward	1791	Providence RI	admn	17758
	Eliza R	1877	Pembroke	admn	17759
	Emanuel A	1877	Plymouth	grdn	17760
	Joseph	1781	Boston	warr	17761
	Lionel	1877	Plymouth	grdn	17760
	Sarah J R	1877	Plymouth	grdn	17760
	Sarah/Susan	1852	Plymouth	admn	17762
SCRIVEN	Edward	1880	Brockton	will	17763
SCUDDER	Abby R	1856	Plymouth	grdn	17764
	Alonzo	1853	Plymouth	admn	17765
SCULLY	William	1873	Middleboro	admn	17766
SEABURY	Samuel	1762	Duxbury	admn	17767
	Wiswall	1768	Duxbury	admn	17768
SEALLEY	Edward	1699	Bridgewater	will	17769
SEARS	Abby M	1842	Rochester	grdn	17770
	Abigail F	1839	Rochester	grdn	17810
	Abner J	1862	Lakeville	grdn	17791
	Albert M	1854	Plymouth	will	17771
	Albert N	1869	Plymouth	adop	17784
	Amanda	1851	Halifax	grdn	17778
	Andrew R	1851	Halifax	grdn	17778
	Bartlett	1821	Plymouth	will	17772
	Bathsheba	1852	Plymouth	admn	17773
	Benjamin M	1849	N. Bridgewater	will	17774
	Caroline	1821	Scituate	grdn	17775
	Charles	1821	Scituate	grdn	17775
	David	1782	Rochester	admn	17776
	Earl	1862	Lakeville	admn	17777
	Ebenezer W	1851	Halifax	grdn	17778
	Edmund L	1879	Carver	admn	17779
	Edward	1777	Halifax	admn	17780
	Eleazer	1855	Plymouth	admn	17781
	Elizabeth A	1839	Rochester	grdn	17810
	Elkanah	1783	Middleboro	grdn	17797
	Emily M	1839	Rochester	grdn	17810
	Francis D	1877	Plymouth	admn	17782
	George	1856	Abington	grdn	17783
	Hannah R	1851	Halifax	grdn	17778

SURNAME	FIRST NAME	YEAR	PLACE	CASE	DOCKET
SEARS	Hattie B	1869	Plymouth	adop	17784
	Holmes	1837	Halifax	will	17785
	Isaac	1821	Scituate	grdn	17775
	Isaac	1863	S. Scituate	will	17786
	Ivory H	1880	Middleboro	will	17787
	Jane F	1850	Middleboro	grdn	17788
	John	1827	Rochester	admn	17789
	John	1855	Abington	admn	17790
	John W	1862	Lakeville	grdn	17791
	Jonathan	1770	Halifax	admn	17792
	Joseph	1818	Rochester	grdn	17805
	Josiah	1769	Halifax	admn	17793
	Josiah	1777	Halifax	grdn	17794
	Josiah E	1851	Halifax	grdn	17778
	Judah	1776	Rochester	will	17795
	Judah Jr	1782	Rochester	admn	17796
	Leonard	1783	Middleboro	grdn	17797
	Louisa B	1869	Rochester	grdn	17798
	Lucinda	1851	Halifax	grdn	17778
	Lyman	1855	Duxbury	admn	17799
	Mary	1783	Middleboro	admn	17800
	Mary	1821	Scituate	grdn	17775
	Mary H	1852	Halifax	will	17801
	Mercy	1851	Halifax	admn	17802
	Nancy	1821	Scituate	grdn	17775
	Nathaniel	1816	Rochester	will	17803
	Nathaniel	1818	Rochester	grdn	17805
	Nathaniel Jr	1816	Rochester	will	17804
	Otis F	1867	Plymouth	grdn	17806
	Peter	1821	Scituate	admn	17807
	Peter Jr	1821	Scituate	admn	17808
	Sarah	1870	S. Scituate	will	17809
	Sarah T	1839	Rochester	grdn	17810
	Stephen	1818	Rochester	grdn	17805
	Stephen	1881	S. Abington	admn	17811
	Stephen Jr	1810	Rochester	admn	17812
	Susan W	1880	Mattapoisett	admn	17813
	Thomas	1755	Plymouth	will	17814
	Thomas	1846	Plymouth	admn	17815
	William	1851	Halifax	admn	17816
	William	1871	Rochester	admn	17817
SEATLE	Henry B	1864	Middleboro	admn	17818
SEEPIT	Lurana	1826	Carver	grdn	17819 i
SEVER	Anna D	1864	Kingston	admn	17820
	Catherine E	1834	Plymouth	grdn	17824
	Celinda	1878	W. Bridgewater	admn	17821
	Charles	1809	Kingston	grdn	17834
	Charles	1834	Plymouth	will	17823
	Charles	1851	W. Bridgewater	grdn	17822
	Charles W	1834	Plymouth	grdn	17824
	Charlotte F	1875	Kingston	admn	17825
	Christopher	1858	E. Bridgewater	admn	17826
	James	1809	Kingston	grdn	17834
	James	1846	Kingston	will	17827
	James N	1869	Kingston	will	17828
	Jane A E	1871	Plymouth	will	17829
	Jane E	1834	Plymouth	grdn	17824
	Jane R	1876	Kingston	will	17830
	John	1761	Kingston	admn	17832
	John	1803	Kingston	admn	17833
	John	1809	Kingston	grdn	17834
	John	1855	Kingston	will	17831
	John E	1834	Plymouth	grdn	17824
	Martha	1864	Kingston	admn	17835
	Mary	1861	Bridgewater	admn	17836
	Mercy	1810	Kingston	will	17837
	Nancy	1848	Kingston	admn	17838
	Nicholas	1764	Kingston	will	17839
	Sarah	1757	Kingston	will	17840
	Sarah A W	1846	Kingston	grdn	17841 a
	Sarah W	1809	Kingston	grdn	17834

SURNAME	FIRST NAME	YEAR	PLACE	CASE	DOCKET
SEVER	William	1809	Kingston	will	17842
	William R	1809	Kingston	grdn	17834
	Winslow W	1809	Kingston	grdn	17834
SEVERANCE	Abijah	1865	E. Bridgewater	admn	17843
	Alonzo C	1879	Brockton	admn	17844
	Sarah H	1880	Brockton	admn	17845
SEWALL	Samuel	1853	N. Bridgewater	admn	17846
SEWARD	Andrew	1712	Marshfield	admn	17847
SEYMORE	Benjamin	1819	Plymouth	admn	17848
	Henry	1862	Plymouth	admn	17849
	Joseph	1863	Plymouth	admn	17850
	Webster	1857	Plymouth	admn	17851
SHANTOM	Joshua	1730	Middleboro	peti	17852 i
SHARPLES	Katharine	1863	Bridgewater	will	17853
SHATTUCK	Ada	1863	N. Bridgewater	adop	17854
	Mary	1732/3	Plymouth	grdn	17855
	Randall	1732/3	Plymouth	grdn	17855
	Robert	1732/3	Plymouth	grdn	17855
SHAW	A James	1870	Mattapoisett	grdn	17892
	Abbie C	1879	E. Bridgewater	grdn	17856
	Abigail	1820	Carver	grdn	17932
	Abigail	1844	Middleboro	will	17857
	Abigail	1871	Carver	admn	17858
	Abraham	1813	Abington	will	17860
	Abraham	1823	Middleboro	admn	17863
	Abraham	1837	Abington	will	17861
	Abraham	1838	Middleboro	grdn	17864
	Abraham	1857	Mattapoisett	admn	17859
	Abraham	1859	Abington	admn	17862
	Adeline	1864	Carver	admn	17865
	Alexander	1818	Bridgewater	will	17866
	Alfred	1870	Middleboro	will	17868
	Alfred M	1861	Middleboro	admn	17867
	Alice L	1865	Plymouth	grdn	18046
	Allen	1848	Middleboro	admn	17869
	Allen M	1857	Abington	grdn	17942
	Allen P	1848	Middleboro	grdn	17870
	Almira A	1879	E. Bridgewater	will	17871
	Alvan	1859	E. Bridgewater	will	17872
	Ambrose	1819	Rochester	will	17873
	Anna	1865	Abington	admn	17874
	Anna W	1839	Carver	grdn	17875
	Annette B	1875	Middleboro	grdn	17876
	Arlotha M	1858	Carver	grdn	17986
	Barnabas	1824	Potsdam NY	admn	17877
	Bartlett	1863	Carver	admn	17878
	Benjamin	1732	Abington	admn	17879
	Benjamin	1837	Carver	admn	17881
	Benjamin	1857	Carver	will	17882
	Benjamin	1861	Middleboro	admn	17880
	Brackley	1849	Abington	will	17883
	Brackley	1863	Abington	admn	17885
	Brackley G	1856	Abington	admn	17884
	Calvin	1834	Abington	will	17886
	Calvin H	1851	Abington	will	17888
	Calvin Jr	1805	Abington	admn	17887
	Calvin R	1858	Carver	grdn	17986
	Cephas	1875	Middleboro	admn	17889
	Charles	1867	Abington	admn	17890
	Charles R	1860	N. Bridgewater	grdn	17891
	Charles R	1870	Mattapoisett	grdn	17892
	Crispus	1819	Carver	grdn	17893 a
	Crispus	1825	Carver	admn	17894
	Cynthia	1859	Carver	admn	17895
	Cyrus	1872	Carver	admn	17896
	Cyrus E	1865	Plymouth	grdn	18046
	Daniel	1812	Abington	will	17897
	Daniel	1812	Middleboro	grdn	18016
	Daniel	1829	Middleboro	grdn	17898 a
	Daniel	1837	Middleboro	admn	17899
	Daniel	1876	Carver	admn	17900

SURNAME	FIRST NAME	YEAR	PLACE	CASE	DOCKET
SHAW	David	1797	Middleboro	will	17901
	David	1812	Middleboro	admn	17902
	David	1847	Abington	admn	17903
	Deborah	1860	Middleboro	admn	17904
	Earl	1839	Carver	admn	17905
	Ebenezer	1719	Bridgewater	grdn	18048
	Ebenezer	1776	Bridgewater	will	17906
	Ebenezer	1794	Middleboro	admn	17909
	Ebenezer	1797	Abington	will	17907
	Ebenezer	1862	Abington	admn	17908
	Ebenezer	1871	Middleboro	admn	17910
	Ebenezer 3rd	1825	Dorchester	admn	17911
	Edmund	1854	Abington	admn	17912
	Elias	1860	Abington	admn	17913
	Elijah	1823	Abington	admn	17914
	Elijah	1841	Middleboro	will	17915
	Elisha	1803	Middleboro	admn	17916
	Elisha C	1848	Carver	admn	17917
	Eliza	1873	Carver	admn	17918
	Eliza L	1878	Middleboro	grdn	17976
	Elizabeth L	1879	Carver	admn	17919
	Elkanah	1822	Middleboro	grdn	17920
	Elkanah	1876	Carver	admn	17921
	Ella	1865	Plymouth	grdn	18046
	Ellen A	1857	Abington	grdn	17942
	Ellis	1857	Plymouth	admn	17922
	Elvira	1848	Middleboro	grdn	17870
	Erastus B	1866	Carver	grdn	17923
	Esther	1847	Plymouth	will	17924
	Eugene E	1864	Carver	grdn	17925
	Ezra	1822	Abington	admn	17926
	Ezra	1853	Abington	will	17927
	Ezra	1854	Rochester	grdn	17928 a
	Faith	1749	Plympton	grdn	17979
	Francis R	1873	Middleboro	grdn	18008
	Frederick W	1862	W. Bridgewater	admn	17929
	Freeman	1820	Carver	grdn	17932
	George	1810	Carver	admn	17931
	George	1820	Carver	grdn	17932
	George	1833	Middleboro	admn	17930
	George P	1867	Abington	grdn	18033
	Gilbert	1820	Carver	grdn	18007
	Goddard	1830	Abington	grdn	17977
	Hannah	1719	Bridgewater	grdn	18048
	Hannah	1868	Carver	admn	17933
	Hannah W	1853	Middleboro	grdn	17934
	Harrison	1861	Carver	admn	17935
	Harvey	1850	Middleboro	admn	17936
	Henriette F	1866	Middleboro	grdn	17937
	Henry	1838	Middleboro	grdn	18001
	Henry	1857	N. Bridgewater	will	17938
	Henry	1879	Middleboro	admn	17940
	Henry H	1833	Middleboro	grdn	17941
	Henry M	1870	Abington	admn	17939
	Howard M	1857	Abington	grdn	17942
	Ichabod	1837	Plymouth	will	17943
	Ichabod	1873	Plymouth	admn	17944
	Ira	1876	Middleboro	admn	17945
	Isaac	1852	Carver	admn	17946
	Jacob	1851	Abington	admn	17947
	Jacob S	1822	Abington	grdn	17948 a
	Jacob S	1823	Abington	admn	17949
	James	1746	Plympton	admn	17951
	James	1803	Middleboro	will	17950
	James	1835	Pembroke	admn	17952
	James R	1848	Middleboro	grdn	17870
	Jared	1822	Abington	admn	17953
	Jennette H	1858	Carver	grdn	17986
	Jennie L	1873	Middleboro	grdn	18008
	Jerome	1878	Hanson	admn	17954
	John	1719	Bridgewater	grdn	18048

SURNAME	FIRST NAME	YEAR	PLACE	CASE	DOCKET
SHAW	John	1780	Plympton	will	17957
	John	1791	Bridgewater	will	17958
	John	1853	Middleboro	admn	17955
	John	1876	Carver	admn	17956
	John A	1869	E. Bridgewater	grdn	17959
	John A	1873	Bridgewater	will	17960
	Jonathan	1701	Plymouth	admn	17961
	Jonathan	1730	Plympton	will	17962
	Jonathan	1745	Plympton	admn	17963
	Jonathan	1746	Plympton	grdn	17964
	Jonathan	1772	Middleboro	admn	17965
	Jonathan	1782	Middleboro	will	17966
	Jonathan	1828	Middleboro	grdn	17967
	Joseph	1719	Bridgewater	admn	17969
	Joseph	1761	Bridgewater	will	17970
	Joseph	1804	Carver	will	17971
	Joseph	1820	Carver	grdn	18007
	Joseph	1829	Abington	admn	17968
	Joseph	1855	Carver	admn	17972
	Joseph	1865	Carver	admn	17973
	Joshua	1845	Middleboro	admn	17974
	Josiah	1868	Abington	will	17975
	Josie B	1878	Middleboro	grdn	17976
	Jotham	1830	Abington	grdn	17977
	Juliette C	1879	Middleboro	admn	17978
	Lemuel	1749	Plympton	grdn	17979
	Levi	1838	Abington	will	17980
	Levi	1849	Carver	admn	17982
	Levi	1851	W. Bridgewater	admn	17981
	Lewis	1868	Rochester	will	17983
	Lillian S	1872	Hanson	adop	17984
	Linus	1857	Carver	admn	17985
	Linus A	1858	Carver	grdn	17986
	Lucy	1861	Lakeville	admn	17987
	Lucy	1879	Middleboro	grdn	17988 a
	Lucy	1880	Middleboro	will	17989
	Luther	1820	Carver	grdn	17932
	Lydia	1820	Carver	grdn	18007
	Lydia	1822	Carver	grdn	18032
	Lydia	1830	Abington	grdn	17977
	Lydia	1880	Carver	will	17990
	Lyman	1858	Carver	admn	17991
	Marcia D	1857	N. Bridgewater	will	17992
	Maria	1851	Plymouth	admn	17993
	Mark	1806	Middleboro	admn	17994
	Martha	1719	Bridgewater	grdn	18048
	Martin	1838	Middleboro	grdn	18001
	Martin	1869	E. Bridgewater	admn	17995
	Mary	1754	Middleboro	admn	17998
	Mary	1808	Carver	will	17996
	Mary	1820	Carver	grdn	17932
	Mary	1840	Bridgewater	admn	17997
	Mary A	1818	Middleboro	grdn	17999
	Mehitable	1749	Plympton	grdn	17979
	Mehitable	1839	Abington	will	18000
	Melancy	1838	Middleboro	grdn	18001
	Micah	1850	N. Bridgewater	will	18002
	Micah P	1867	Abington	admn	18003
	Mira	1880	Bridgewater	will	18004
	Nathaniel	1817	Carver	admn	18006
	Nathaniel	1820	Carver	grdn	18007
	Nathaniel H	1865	Mattapoisett	will	18005
	Nellie H	1873	Middleboro	grdn	18008
	Nellie M	1878	Middleboro	grdn	17976
	Nelson	1876	Carver	grdn	18009
	Newton	1856	N. Bridgewater	will	18010
	Nicholas	1756	Abington	admn	18011
	Nicholas	1780	Abington	will	18012
	Olive	1827	Abington	admn	18013
	Olive	1837	Bridgewater	will	18014
	Oliver	1812	Middleboro	grdn	18016

SURNAME	FIRST NAME	YEAR	PLACE	CASE	DOCKET
SHAW	Oliver	1861	Middleboro	will	18015
	Patience	1872	Carver	admn	18017
	Patty	1843	Middleboro	admn	18018
	Perez	1860	Carver	will	18019
	Polly	1806	Abington	grdn	18020
	Polly	1880	Middleboro	will	18021
	Priscilla	1813	Abington	admn	18022
	Rebecca H	1857	Plymouth	grdn	18023
	Reliance R	1845	Middleboro	will	18024
	Relief	1838	Middleboro	grdn	18001
	Ruth	1878	Rochester	admn	18025
	Ruth G	1865	Plymouth	grdn	18046
	Sally	1834	Plymouth	admn	18026
	Sally A	1838	Middleboro	grdn	18001
	Samuel	1820	Bridgewater	admn	18028
	Samuel	1858	Carver	admn	18027
	Samuel	1874	E. Bridgewater	will	18029
	Sarah	1719	Bridgewater	grdn	18048
	Southworth	1851	Plymouth	admn	18030
	Stillman	1873	Carver	admn	18031
	Sullivan B	1822	Carver	grdn	18032
	Susan M	1867	Abington	grdn	18033
	Sylvanus	1795	Middleboro	admn	18034
	Tamar B	1871	Abington	admn	18035
	Thomas	1779	Middleboro	admn	18036
	Thomas	1863	Mattapoisett	admn	18037
	Truman	1822	Carver	grdn	18032
	Truman	1874	Bridgewater	admn	18038
	Willard	1867	Middleboro	admn	18039
	William	1809	Bridgewater	will	18043
	William	1810	Middleboro	admn	18041
	William	1816	Marshfield	will	18040
	William	1843	Middleboro	admn	18042
	William H	1865	Plymouth	admn	18045
	William H	1865	Plymouth	grdn	18046
	William W	1874	Brockton	admn	18044
	Wilson	1820	Carver	grdn	18007
	Zachariah	1719	Bridgewater	grdn	18048
	Zachariah	1736	Bridgewater	admn	18047
	Zacharias	1790	Bridgewater	will	18049
	Zacharias	1820	Bridgewater	will	18050
	Zebedee	1838	Middleboro	will	18051
	Zenas	1808	Abington	admn	18052
	Zephaniah	1829	Middleboro	will	18053
	Zephaniah	1860	Middleboro	admn	18054
	Zeruah T	1876	Carver	admn	18055
	Zibeon	1854	N. Bridgewater	will	18056
SHEAR	Almira	1873	Abington	grdn	18057 a
	Almira	1874	Abington	will	18058
SHEDD	Annie L	1872	Bridgewater	adop	18059
	Mary H	1865	Abington	will	18060
	William	1831	Abington	admn	18061
SHEEHAN	Daniel	1863	N. Bridgewater	admn	18062
	David	1869	N. Bridgewater	grdn	18063
	James	1866	Abington	admn	18064
	William	1869	N. Bridgewater	admn	18065
SHELDON	Frank A	1878	Rockland	grdn	18066
	Isabella	1870	Duxbury	adop	18067
	Samuel W	1870	Duxbury	adop	18067
SHELLY	Joseph	1818	Bridgewater	will	18068
SHEPHERD	Alice R	1851	Pembroke	grdn	18069
	Arthur	1880	Marshfield	grdn	18076
	Calvin	1876	Pembroke	will	18070
	Joseph R	1836	Pembroke	grdn	18071
	Mary R	1872	Rockland	adop	18072
	Nathaniel	1810	Dartmouth	grdn	18073
	Rebecca	1749	Plymouth	admn	18074
	Samuel	1879	Marshfield	admn	18075
	Samuel E	1880	Marshfield	grdn	18076
	Urana	1810	Dartmouth	grdn	18073
SHEPHERDSON	Nancy	1847	N. Bridgewater	admn	18077

SURNAME	FIRST NAME	YEAR	PLACE	CASE	DOCKET
SHERMAN	Abiel	1822	Marshfield	will	18078
	Albert	1877	Mattapoisett	admn	18079
	Amos	1847	Marshfield	admn	18080
	Amos	1870	Marshfield	will	18081
	Anne M	1832	Middleboro	grdn	18082
	Anthony	1859	Carver	admn	18083
	Asa	1836	Plympton	will	18084
	Asa	1878	Marshfield	admn	18085
	Avery T	1865	Marshfield	admn	18086
	Bartlett	1817	Rochester	grdn	18152
	Benjamin	1817	Marshfield	grdn	18176
	Benjamin	1868	Abington	admn	18087
	Betsey S	1829	Plymouth	grdn	18088
	Betsey W	1833	Plympton	grdn	18143
	Betsey W	1880	Plympton	admn	18089
	Bradford	1863	Rochester	admn	18090
	Calvin F	1857	Marshfield	grdn	18091
	Caroline	1832	Middleboro	grdn	18082
	Charles M	1873	Middleboro	admn	18092
	Charles P	1816	Rochester	grdn	18101
	Christopher M	1845	Marshfield	admn	18093
	Clara F	1868	Mattapoisett	grdn	18094
	Cornelius	1808	Rochester	admn	18095
	Daniel	1878	Brockton	will	18096
	David	1829	Middleboro	admn	18097
	David	1832	Rochester	admn	18098
	Deborah	1875	Middleboro	will	18099
	Dennis	1816	Rochester	grdn	18101
	Dennis	1872	Rochester	will	18100
	Earl	1875	Carver	admn	18102
	Ebenezer	1759	Marshfield	will	18103
	Ebenezer	1835	Marshfield	will	18105
	Ebenezer	1862	Marshfield	will	18106
	Ebenezer	1865	Carver	will	18107
	Ebenezer Jr	1786	Marshfield	admn	18104
	Edward	1805	Middleboro	will	18108
	Edward	1867	Marion	admn	18109
	Edwin A	1863	Rochester	will	18110
	Eleanor	1833	Plympton	grdn	18143
	Eleanor	1876	Plymouth	admn	18111
	Eleazer	1723	Marshfield	admn	18112
	Eli	1875	Marion	will	18113
	Elisha	1797	Marshfield	will	18114
	Elizabeth	1796	Plymouth	grdn	18115
	Elizabeth	1845	Scituate	admn	18116
	Elnathan	1785	Middleboro	will	18117
	Fanny J	1881	Wareham	grdn	18118
	Frank T	1878	Plymouth	grdn	18119
	Freeman	1805	Rochester	admn	18120
	George B	1833	Rochester	grdn	18208
	George B	1855	Rochester	will	18121
	George W	1877	Plympton	admn	18122
	Gershom	1745	Marshfield	admn	18123
	Hannah	1866	Carver	will	18124
	Hannah C	1854	Carver	grdn	18168
	Harriet E	1832	Middleboro	grdn	18082
	Henry W	1867	Rochester	grdn	18125 a
	Ichabod	1814	Marshfield	admn	18126
	Ignatius	1814	Marshfield	will	18127
	Isaac	1806	Plymouth	grdn	18128
	Isaac	1865	Middleboro	will	18129
	Isaac W	1833	Rochester	grdn	18208
	Isabel D	1879	Carver	admn	18130
	Jabez	1835	Middleboro	admn	18131
	Jacob	1778	Middleboro	will	18132
	Jennie T	1875	Wareham	grdn	18151
	Jireh F	1867	Wareham	admn	18133
	Job	1830	Middleboro	admn	18134
	Job	1830	Middleboro	will	18135
	John	1722	Marshfield	will	18137
	John	1780	Marshfield	will	18138

SURNAME	FIRST NAME	YEAR	PLACE	CASE	DOCKET
SHERMAN	John	1789	Rochester	will	18136
	John	1801	Carver	admn	18139
	John	1833	Plympton	grdn	18143
	John	1840	Carver	will	18140
	John	1845	Plympton	admn	18142
	John	1860	Carver	grdn	18141
	John W	1833	Rochester	grdn	18208
	John W	1857	Rochester	grdn	18150
	Joseph	1811	Marshfield	will	18144
	Joseph S	1868	Wareham	admn	18145
	Joshua	1816	Rochester	will	18146
	Josiah	1817	Marshfield	grdn	18176
	Lemuel	1807	Rochester	grdn	18147
	Leonard	1871	Rochester	admn	18148
	Levi	1857	Rochester	grdn	18150
	Levi	1859	Carver	admn	18149
	Lizzie O	1875	Wareham	grdn	18151
	Love	1817	Rochester	grdn	18152
	Lucy	1813	Middleboro	admn	18153
	Lucy	1853	Carver	will	18154
	Lucy	1854	Carver	will	18155
	Luther	1880	Duxbury	admn	18156
	Lydia	1833	Plympton	grdn	18143
	Lydia	1844	Marshfield	will	18157
	Lydia	1873	Mattapoisett	will	18158
	Lydia D	1860	Carver	grdn	18141
	Lysander B	1878	Duxbury	admn	18159
	Margaret	1880	Rochester	will	18160
	Mary J	1857	Marshfield	grdn	18091
	Mary W	1857	Rochester	will	18161
	Mary W	1869	Brooklyn NY	grdn	18162
	Mercy	1816	Rochester	grdn	18101
	Mercy	1817	Marshfield	grdn	18176
	Mercy	1833	Plympton	grdn	18143
	Nancy	1816	Rochester	grdn	18163
	Nancy	1854	Plympton	admn	18164
	Nathan	1862	Marshfield	will	18165
	Nathaniel	1829	Carver	will	18166
	Nehemiah	1783	Middleboro	grdn	18167
	Nelson	1854	Carver	grdn	18168
	Nicholas H	1858	Wareham	grdn	18169 a
	Nicholas H	1877	Wareham	admn	18170
	Nicholas J	1880	Wareham	will	18171
	Noah	1877	Mattapoisett	admn	18172
	Otis	1876	Rochester	admn	18173
	Phebe C	1832	Middleboro	grdn	18082
	Phebe C	1839	Middleboro	grdn	18174 a
	Rachel	1817	Marshfield	grdn	18176
	Rachel O	1843	Marshfield	grdn	18175
	Reuben	1879	Plymouth	admn	18177
	Roxana	1817	Rochester	grdn	18152
	Rufus	1832	Carver	will	18178
	Rufus	1850	Carver	will	18179
	Sada J	1872	Wareham	grdn	18180
	Sally	1833	Plympton	grdn	18143
	Sally	1859	Plympton	will	18181
	Samuel	1718	Marshfield	admn	18183
	Samuel	1725	Rochester	admn	18182
	Samuel	1764	Marshfield	will	18184
	Samuel	1819	Plymouth	admn	18185
	Samuel	1857	Plymouth	will	18186
	Samuel T T	1874	Wareham	admn	18187
	Sarah	1832	Middleboro	grdn	18082
	Sarah E	1859	Plympton	grdn	18188
	Sarah P	1816	Rochester	grdn	18101
	Seth	1795	Middleboro	admn	18189
	Simeon	1812	Middleboro	will	18190
	Sophia	1877	Wareham	admn	18191
	Susan A H	1879	Rockland	will	18192
	Sylvia V	1865	Middleboro	will	18193
	Temperance	1829	Rochester	will	18194

SURNAME	FIRST NAME	YEAR	PLACE	CASE	DOCKET
SHERMAN	Thomas B	1861	Plymouth	admn	18196
	Thomas Jr	1824	Plymouth	admn	18195
	Uriel	1816	Rochester	grdn	18101
	Wealthy	1862	Marshfield	admn	18197
	William	1740	Marshfield	will	18199
	William	1786	Marshfield	will	18198
	William	1796	Plymouth	admn	18202
	William 2nd	1814	Rochester	will	18201
	William D	1876	Plymouth	grdn	18203 a
	William D	1878	Plymouth	admn	18204
	William H	1833	Rochester	grdn	18208
	William Jr	1724	Marshfield	admn	18200
	Willis	1867	Rochester	will	18205
	Zacheus	1859	Plympton	will	18206
	Zephaniah	1830	Rochester	admn	18207
	Zephaniah T	1833	Rochester	grdn	18208
SHIELDS	James	1876	W. Bridgewater	will	18209
	James H	1877	W. Bridgewater	grdn	18210 a
	William	1865	W. Bridgewater	admn	18211
SHIPMAN	Lilla	1876	Bridgewater	grdn	18212
	Lizzie	1876	Bridgewater	grdn	18212
SHIVERICK	Foster	1855	N. Bridgewater	will	18213
	Lucinda D	1855	N. Bridgewater	admn	18214
	Salome	1860	Wareham	will	18215
SHOCKLEY	Almy J	1871	Lakeville	will	18216
	Benjamin	1873	Lakeville	grdn	18217 a
	George P	1868	Bridgewater	grdn	18220
	Joseph	1863	Lakeville	will	18218
	Walter A	1868	Bridgewater	grdn	18220
	William	1868	Bridgewater	admn	18219
	William H	1868	Bridgewater	grdn	18220
SHORT	Catherine M	1877	E. Bridgewater	grdn	18221
	Thankful	1794	Middleboro	will	18222
	William	1773	Middleboro	will	18223
SHUCK	Sarah P	1873	Hingham	admn	18224
SHURTLEFF	Abiel	1732	Plympton	admn	18228
	Abiel	1732	Plympton	grdn	18229
	Abiel	1783	Plymouth	admn	18226
	Abiel	1842	Middleboro	admn	18225
	Abiel Jr	1783	Plymouth	admn	18227
	Abigail	1789	Plympton	grdn	18251
	Abigail	1858	Middleboro	admn	18230
	Alvah	1863	Mattapoisett	admn	18231
	Ann S	1876	Wareham	will	18232
	Barnabas	1730	Plympton	grdn	18272
	Barnabas	1759	Plympton	will	18233
	Barnabas	1759	Plympton	grdn	18234
	Benjamin	1789	Plympton	admn	18235
	Betsey	1821	Carver	grdn	18236
	Clark	1813	Carver	grdn	18268
	Deborah	1818	Carver	grdn	18237 a
	Eliza	1820	Carver	grdn	18238
	Elizabeth	1730	Plympton	grdn	18272
	Elizabeth	1759	Plympton	grdn	18234
	Elizabeth	1837	Carver	grdn	18259
	Flavel	1845	Halifax	admn	18239
	Flavel	1846	Halifax	grdn	18240
	Francis	1794	Carver	will	18241
	Ichabod	1730	Plympton	grdn	18272
	Ichabod	1787	Plympton	will	18242
	Isaac	1821	Plymouth	admn	18243
	Isaiah F	1876	Wareham	grdn	18244
	James	1767	Plymouth	admn	18245
	John	1805	Carver	grdn	18246
	John	1828	Rochester	grdn	18247 a
	John	1836	Rochester	admn	18248
	Jonathan	1730	Plympton	grdn	18272
	Joseph	1732	Plympton	grdn	18229
	Joseph	1755	Plymouth	admn	18249
	Joseph	1789	Plympton	grdn	18251
	Joseph	1797	Plymouth	admn	18250

SURNAME	FIRST NAME	YEAR	PLACE	CASE	DOCKET
SHURTLEFF	Lot	1864	Carver	admn	18252
	Lothrop	1813	Carver	grdn	18268
	Lothrop	1874	Wareham	admn	18253
	Luther	1827	Carver	admn	18254
	Lydia	1809	Plymouth	admn	18255
	Mary	1795	Carver	grdn	18256
	Mehitable	1730	Plympton	grdn	18272
	Minerva	1813	Carver	grdn	18268
	Molly	1759	Plympton	grdn	18234
	Nathan F	1878	Wareham	admn	18257
	Nathaniel	1841	Middleboro	admn	18258
	Perez	1837	Carver	grdn	18259
	Peter	1813	Carver	grdn	18268
	Peter	1818	Carver	admn	18260
	Peter	1818	Carver	admn	18261
	Phebe	1730	Plympton	grdn	18272
	Robert	1795	Carver	admn	18262
	Samuel	1757	Marshfield	will	18263
	Sarah	1762	Plymouth	admn	18264
	Susanna	1868	Middleboro	admn	18266
	Susannah	1834	Carver	grdn	18265 a
	Sylvanus	1810	Carver	admn	18267
	Sylvanus	1813	Carver	grdn	18268
	Thomas	1730	Plympton	admn	18271
	Thomas	1730	Plympton	grdn	18272
	Thomas	1748	Plymouth/Plympt	admn	18270
	Thomas	1851	Carver	admn	18269
	William	1729/0	Plymouth/Plympt	will	18273
	William	1730	Plympton	grdn	18272
	William	1813	Carver	grdn	18268
	William 2nd	1853	Middleboro	admn	18275
	William Jr	1790	Middleboro	admn	18274
	Zilpah	1795	Carver	grdn	18256
SHUTE	Cassandana	1867	Hingham	grdn	18276 a
	Cassandana	1870	Hingham	admn	18277
	Charles	1863	Hingham	will	18278
	Daniel	1829	Hingham	will	18279
	Daniel	1838	Hingham	admn	18280
	Deborah	1823	Hingham	will	18281
	Deborah B	1823	Hingham	grdn	18282
	Edwin	1870	Hingham	admn	18283
	Edwin L	1870	Hingham	grdn	18284
	Harriet G	1870	Hingham	grdn	18284
	John	1876	Hingham	will	18285
	Mary C	1823	Hingham	grdn	18282
SIDERS	George E	1850	Hingham	admn	18286
SILSBY	Carrie F	1870	Middleboro	grdn	18287
	Rebecca C	1876	Brockton	name	18288
	Samuel T	1866	Wareham	admn	18289
	Zeno L	1870	Middleboro	grdn	18287
SILVER	Joseph	1881	Hanson	admn	18290
	Marinda	1855	Marion	admn	18291
SILVIN	Joseph	1813	-----	grdn	18292
SIMMONS	Aaron	1718	Scituate	admn	18293
	Aaron	1756	Middleboro	admn	18294
	Aaron	1790	Duxbury	will	18295
	Aaron	1873	Duxbury	will	18296
	Abiah	1749	Duxbury	grdn	18297
	Abigail	1806	Duxbury	grdn	18397
	Abraham	1727	Duxbury	grdn	18306
	Abraham	1741	Duxbury	will	18298
	Albert L	1880	Plymouth	adop	18299
	Alice M	1867	S. Scituate	grdn	18300
	Allen	1818	Hingham	admn	18301
	Allen	1819	Hingham	grdn	18302 a
	Andrew F	1824	Duxbury	admn	18303
	Benjamin	1727	Duxbury	grdn	18306
	Benjamin	1748	Duxbury	admn	18305
	Benjamin	1748	Duxbury	grdn	18307
	Benjamin	1832	Marshfield	admn	18304
	Bethiah	1860	Hanover	admn	18308

SURNAME	FIRST NAME	YEAR	PLACE	CASE	DOCKET
SIMMONS	Betsey P	1880	Duxbury	admn	18309
	Carrie E	1867	S. Scituate	grdn	18300
	Charles	1785	Scituate	grdn	18395
	Charles	1821	Kingston	grdn	18329
	Charles	1835	Scituate	admn	18310
	Charles W	1871	S. Scituate	will	18311
	Content	1727	Duxbury	grdn	18306
	Cordelia	1823	Duxbury	grdn	18312
	Diana	1821	Kingston	grdn	18329
	Ebenezer	1742	Scituate	admn	18313
	Ebenezer	1784	Scituate	admn	18314
	Ebenezer	1841	Hanover	will	18315
	Edgar E	1868	Duxbury	grdn	18324
	Eleazer	1746	Duxbury	grdn	18408
	Elisha	1825	Hanover	admn	18316
	Elizabeth	1748	Duxbury	grdn	18307
	Elizabeth	1825	Hanover	admn	18317
	Elizabeth	1877	Hanover	admn	18318
	Emma D	1867	S. Scituate	grdn	18300
	Ephraim	1863	Middleboro	admn	18319
	Eunice	1756	Kingston	grdn	18321
	Eunice	1872	Kingston	will	18320
	Faith	1756	Kingston	grdn	18321
	Freeman	1852	S. Scituate	will	18322
	George	1793	Scituate	grdn	18325
	George	1863	Plymouth	will	18323
	George A	1868	Duxbury	grdn	18324
	Grace	1849	Abington	admn	18326
	Hannah	1818	Hingham	grdn	18370
	Harriet H	1857	Plymouth	admn	18327
	Hezekiah	1817	Kingston	admn	18328
	Hezekiah	1821	Kingston	grdn	18329
	Hiram	1806	Duxbury	grdn	18397
	Isaac	1767	Duxbury	will	18330
	Isaac B	1851	Rochester	admn	18331
	James	1811	Rochester	grdn	18332 a
	James	1822	Kingston	admn	18333
	James	1867	Duxbury	will	18334
	James H	1878	Middleboro	admn	18335
	Jane W	1872	Duxbury	admn	18336
	Jerusha A	1853	Pembroke	grdn	18337
	Jesse	1836	Duxbury	admn	18338
	Joanna	1868	Kingston	grdn	18339 a
	Joanna	1870	Kingston	admn	18340
	Joel	1739	Duxbury	grdn	18341
	John	1711	Duxbury	admn	18342
	John	1715	Duxbury	admn	18343
	John	1739	Duxbury	admn	18344
	John	1818	Rochester	will	18345
	John 2nd	1811	Rochester	admn	18346
	John D	1827	Scituate	admn	18347
	Jonathan J	1862	Marshfield	will	18348
	Joseph	1761	Duxbury	will	18350
	Joseph	1827	Hanover	admn	18349
	Joseph E	1863	Duxbury	admn	18351
	Joshua	1807	Hanover	will	18352
	Joshua S	1838	Duxbury	admn	18353
	Keen	1821	Kingston	grdn	18329
	Kent	1819	Hingham	grdn	18354 a
	Keturah	1748	Duxbury	grdn	18307
	Keturah	1840	Marshfield	will	18355
	Lea	1739	Duxbury	grdn	18341
	Lemuel	1863	Plymouth	admn	18356
	Levi	1798	Duxbury	will	18357
	Levi	1821	Kingston	grdn	18329
	Lucy	1748	Duxbury	grdn	18307
	Lucy	1851	Duxbury	will	18360
	Lucy A	1841	Duxbury	grdn	18359
	Lucy D	1840	Marshfield	grdn	18358
	Lydia	1768	Scituate	will	18361
	Lydia	1836	Marshfield	admn	18362

SURNAME	FIRST NAME	YEAR	PLACE	CASE	DOCKET
SIMMONS	Marcy	1751	Duxbury	will	18363
	Maria	1821	Kingston	grdn	18329
	Maria	1879	Brockton	grdn	18399
	Marshall E	1874	Wareham	admn	18364
	Marshall V	1881	Marion	admn	18365
	Martha	1833	Hanover	will	18366
	Martha	1834	Hanover	will	18367
	Martin	1863	Duxbury	admn	18368
	Mary	1818	Hingham	grdn	18370
	Mary A	1879	Brockton	grdn	18399
	Mary L	1850	Duxbury	admn	18369
	Mercy	1728	Duxbury	will	18371
	Mercy B	1859	Plymouth	admn	18372
	Micha	1748	Duxbury	grdn	18307
	Moses	1690/1	Scituate	will	18373
	Moses	1691	Duxbury	will	18375
	Moses	1761	Duxbury	will	18376
	Moses	1768	Scituate	will	18374
	Nancy	1818	Hingham	grdn	18370
	Nathan	1746	Duxbury	grdn	18408
	Nathan	1767	Plymouth	admn	18377
	Nathan B	1820	Plymouth	grdn	18378
	Nathaniel	1835	Duxbury	admn	18379
	Nathaniel	1870	Marshfield	will	18380
	Noah	1756	Kingston	grdn	18321
	Noah	1824	Kingston	will	18381
	Otis	1819	Hingham	admn	18382
	Peleg	1744	Scituate	grdn	18389
	Peleg	1818	Kingston	admn	18383
	Perez	1748	Duxbury	grdn	18307
	Polly	1785	Scituate	grdn	18395
	Priscilla	1879	Hingham	admn	18384
	Reuben	1744	Scituate	grdn	18389
	Ruth	1790	Duxbury	will	18385
	Ruth	1837	Scituate	admn	18386
	Sally	1862	Duxbury	will	18387
	Samuel	1744	Scituate	grdn	18389
	Samuel	1824	Scituate	admn	18388
	Sarah	1785	Scituate	grdn	18395
	Sarah	1793	Scituate	grdn	18325
	Sarah	1807	Scituate	will	18394
	Sarah	1839	Duxbury	will	18390
	Sarah	1846	Duxbury	admn	18391
	Sarah	1866	Duxbury	grdn	18392
	Sarah	1879	Marshfield	admn	18393
	Seth	1805	Duxbury	admn	18396
	Seth	1806	Duxbury	grdn	18397
	Sophia	1854	Duxbury	will	18398
	Susan R	1879	Brockton	grdn	18399
	Tamsin	1861	S. Scituate	will	18400
	Thomas	1823	Middleboro	admn	18401
	Thomas	1853	Hanover	admn	18402
	Walter	1852	S. Scituate	grdn	18403
	Weston	1821	Kingston	grdn	18329
	William	1820	Plymouth	grdn	18378
	William	1833	Kingston	will	18404
	William D	1854	Plymouth	admn	18405
	William H	1879	Duxbury	admn	18406
	Zachariah	1727	Duxbury	grdn	18306
	Zachariah	1746	Duxbury	grdn	18408
	Zachariah	1761	Duxbury	admn	18407
SIMON	Abraham	1718	Abington	admn	18409 i
	William	1730	Middleboro	admn	18410 i
SIMPSON	Abigail E	1869	Bridgewater	grdn	18412
	Cordelia A	1869	Bridgewater	grdn	18412
	Freeman	1862	Bridgewater	will	18411
	John H	1869	Bridgewater	grdn	18412
SINCLAIR	Clara E	1873	Hingham	adop	18413
SINGLETON	Jane	1866	S. Scituate	will	18414
	Mary	1878	Abington	admn	18415
	Samuel	1848	Scituate	will	18416

SURNAME	FIRST NAME	YEAR	PLACE	CASE	DOCKET
SINNOTT	Peter A	1880	Duxbury	will	18417
SIRÓVICH	Grace E	1873	Hull	adop	18418
	Nicholas	1858	Hull	admn	18419
SISSON	Claria	1878	Middleboro	admn	18420
SKIFF	George C	1852	Rochester	admn	18421
	James	1847	Rochester	admn	18422
	William H	1852	Rochester	grdn	18423
SKINNER	Evans	1746	Kingston	powe	18424
SLOAN	Calista	1877	Bridgewater	admn	18425
	Francis	1860	N. Bridgewater	will	18426
SMALL	Nathaniel	1856	Hingham	admn	18427
SMALLEY	Louisa J	1874	Middleboro	admn	18428
SMITH	Abigail	1760	Middleboro	grdn	18452
	Abigail	1788	Middleboro	admn	18429
	Abigal	1788	Middleboro	grdn	18512
	Albert	1823	Hanover	will	18430
	Albert	1865	Middleboro	admn	18431
	Albert H	1866	Middleboro	grdn	18432
	Albert N	1835	Roxbury	grdn	18515
	Anna	1703	Scituate	grdn	18514
	Anna E	1835	Roxbury	grdn	18515
	Anna M	1867	Bridgewater	grdn	18473
	Anne L	1835	Hanover	will	18433
	Anne L E	1835	-----	grdn	18434
	Ansel	1872	Middleboro	will	18435
	Asenath S	1876	Middleboro	admn	18436
	Augustus H	1848	Rochester	grdn	18477
	Benjamin	1703	Scituate	grdn	18514
	Benjamin	1765	Plymouth	grdn	18440
	Benjamin	1767	Middleboro	grdn	18439
	Benjamin	1848	Duxbury	will	18437
	Benjamin Jr	1848	Duxbury	admn	18438
	Betsey D	1840	Middleboro	grdn	18526
	Charles	1876	Brockton	grdn	18444
	Charles H	1865	N. Bridgewater	grdn	18443
	Charles L	1816	Hingham	admn	18445
	Charles T	1855	Abington	admn	18442
	Charles W	1818	Hingham	grdn	18446
	Charles W	1875	Mattapoisett	will	18441
	Chrissa	1837	Hingham	admn	18447
	Christopher	1823	Hanson	admn	18448
	Daniel	1760	Middleboro	grdn	18452
	Daniel	1801	Middleboro	grdn	18554
	Daniel	1829	Middleboro	admn	18451
	Daniel	1881	Rockland	will	18449
	Daniel Jr	1835	Middleboro	will	18450
	Darius	1827	Middleboro	grdn	18484
	David	1853	Abington	will	18453
	Deborah	1863	Abington	will	18454
	Deborah	1872	Marshfield	admn	18456
	Deborah	1878	Rockland	admn	18455
	Earl	1842	Middleboro	admn	18458
	Earl C	1831	Rochester	grdn	18457
	Ebenezer	1788	Middleboro	grdn	18512
	Ebenezer	1871	Middleboro	will	18459
	Edward	1826	Pembroke	will	18460
	Elisha	1875	Plymouth	admn	18461
	Eliza	1846	Abington	grdn	18463
	Eliza	1849	Abington	admn	18462
	Elizabeth	1788	Middleboro	grdn	18512
	Elizabeth	1847	Pembroke	admn	18464
	Emma F	1875	Rockland	grdn	18465
	Emma F	1875	Hanson	grdn	18466
	Flora	1865	Hanson	grdn	18467
	George	1846	Rochester	admn	18468
	George H	1845	Middleboro	grdn	18485
	George H	1864	W. Bridgewater	grdn	18469
	George W	1848	Duxbury	grdn	18564
	Hannah	1801	Middleboro	grdn	18554
	Hannah	1861	Abington	will	18471
	Hannah W	1812	Hingham	grdn	18470

SURNAME	FIRST NAME	YEAR	PLACE	CASE	DOCKET
SMITH	Hannah W	1827	Middleboro	grdn	18484
	Harriet A	1866	Middleboro	grdn	18432
	Harriet Jr	1835	Roxbury	grdn	18515
	Harriet T	1864	Hanson	admn	18472
	Helen L	1848	Duxbury	grdn	18564
	Herbert A	1866	Middleboro	grdn	18432
	Horace M	1867	Bridgewater	grdn	18473
	Ichabod	1785	Rochester	will	18474
	Isaac	1800	Middleboro	admn	18475
	Isaac	1849	Rochester	admn	18476
	Isaac B	1848	Rochester	grdn	18477
	Israel	1760	Middleboro	grdn	18452
	Israel	1836	Middleboro	will	18478
	Jabez	1763	Middleboro	grdn	18480
	Jabez	1769	Middleboro	admn	18481
	Jabez	1769	Middleboro	grdn	18482
	Jabez	1826	Middleboro	admn	18483
	Jabez	1827	Middleboro	grdn	18484
	Jabez	1845	Middleboro	grdn	18485
	Jabez	1880	Middleboro	admn	18479
	Jacob	1779	Middleboro	grdn	18505
	Jacob	1844	Marshfield	will	18486
	James	1763	Middleboro	will	18487
	James	1815	Middleboro	will	18488
	James	1820	Middleboro	admn	18489
	Jane M	1821	Hanover	grdn	18490
	Jarvis B	1859	Bridgewater	admn	18491
	Jarvis D	1837	N. Bridgewater	grdn	18492
	Jemima	1825	Duxbury	admn	18493
	Jeremiah	1823	Wareham	admn	18494
	John	1727	Middleboro	admn	18501
	John	1748	Middleboro	admn	18502
	John	1778	Middleboro	admn	18504
	John	1779	Middleboro	grdn	18505
	John	1797	Rochester	will	18500
	John	1809	Middleboro	admn	18503
	John	1831	N. Bridgewater	will	18495
	John	1866	Abington	admn	18496
	John	1874	Rockland	will	18498
	John H	1873	Scituate	admn	18499
	John H	1874	Abington	admn	18497
	Jonathan	1767	Middleboro	will	18506
	Jonathan	1843	Duxbury	will	18507
	Joseph	1702	Scituate	admn	18513
	Joseph	1703	Scituate	grdn	18514
	Joseph	1778	Middleboro	admn	18511
	Joseph	1788	Middleboro	grdn	18512
	Joseph	1816	Pembroke	admn	18508
	Joseph B	1835	Roxbury	grdn	18515
	Joseph B	1860	Abington	admn	18509
	Joseph E	1855	Randolph VT	admn	18510
	Joshua	1851	Hanson	admn	18516
	Josiah	1803	Pembroke	will	18517
	Julia A	1867	Lakeville	grdn	18518
	Lorenzo F	1873	Middleboro	admn	18519
	Lucia	1856	Hanson	will	18520
	Lucia S	1865	Duxbury	will	18521
	Lucy W	1848	Rochester	grdn	18477
	Lydia	1760	Middleboro	grdn	18452
	Lydia	1876	Middleboro	will	18522
	Marcia G	1880	Abington	will	18523
	Margaret	1852	Duxbury	admn	18524
	Maria	1846	Abington	grdn	18463
	Martha	1801	Middleboro	grdn	18554
	Martin	1833	Middleboro	admn	18525
	Martin	1840	Middleboro	grdn	18526
	Mary	1765	Plymouth	grdn	18440
	Mary	1813	Pembroke	will	18527
	Mary	1818	Hingham	grdn	18446
	Mary	1865	E. Bridgewater	admn	18528
	Mary M	1864	W. Bridgewater	grdn	18469

SURNAME	FIRST NAME	YEAR	PLACE	CASE	DOCKET
SMITH	Miller	1819	Hanover	admn	18529
	Minerva	1840	Middleboro	grdn	18526
	Morris T	1848	Duxbury	grdn	18564
	Moses B	1861	Pembroke	admn	18530
	Nahum	1805	Hingham	admn	18531
	Nathaniel	1777	Middleboro	will	18532
	Nathaniel	1782	Middleboro	will	18533
	Nathaniel	1826	Pembroke	grdn	18534
	Nehemiah	1819	Abington	admn	18535
	Percis	1877	Middleboro	will	18536
	Perez	1788	Middleboro	grdn	18512
	Peter	1854	Wareham	will	18537
	Phebe	1881	Rochester	admn	18538
	Philip	1861	N. Bridgewater	admn	18539
	Reuben	1801	Plymouth	grdn	18540
	Rhoda	1778	Middleboro	admn	18543
	Rhoda	1779	Middleboro	grdn	18542 a
	Rhoda	1787	Middleboro	admn	18541
	Richard H	1867	Bridgewater	grdn	18473
	Richard M	1872	E. Bridgewater	will	18544
	Robert	1878	Brockton	admn	18545
	Rose	1876	Brockton	grdn	18546
	Royal	1872	Rochester	admn	18547
	Ruth	1760	Middleboro	grdn	18452
	Ruth C	1874	Hanover	will	18548
	Sally	1855	Abington	admn	18549
	Sally C	1840	Middleboro	grdn	18526
	Samuel	1750	Scituate	admn	18550
	Samuel	1783	Middleboro	will	18551
	Samuel	1854	Middleboro	will	18552
	Sarah	1779	Middleboro	grdn	18505
	Susanna	1801	Middleboro	grdn	18554
	Susanna W	1849	Hingham	admn	18553
	Sylvanus	1865	Duxbury	admn	18555
	Theodore	1858	Abington	admn	18556
	Thomas	1788	Pembroke	will	18557
	Thomas	1872	Bridgewater	will	18558
	Thomas	1876	Brockton	will	18559
	Whelen	1801	Wareham	admn	18560
	William	1852	E. Bridgewater	admn	18561
	William H	1848	Duxbury	grdn	18564
	William J	1846	Abington	grdn	18463
	William M	1865	Duxbury	admn	18563
	William W	1864	E. Bridgewater	admn	18562
	Zenas	1852	Abington	will	18565
	Zenas	1875	Rockland	will	18566
SNELL	Aaron H	1864	Duxbury	admn	18567
	Abigail	1807	Bridgewater	grdn	18569
	Abigail	1859	N. Bridgewater	admn	18568
	Abigail K	1839	N. Bridgewater	grdn	18586
	Adrianna	1856	N. Bridgewater	grdn	18629
	Anna	1824	Newport NH	admn	18570
	Ansel	1855	N. Bridgewater	admn	18571
	Arethusa	1827	N. Bridgewater	grdn	18642
	Asa F	1833	N. Bridgewater	admn	18572
	Bathsheba	1834	E. Bridgewater	will	18573
	Benjamin	1823	Bridgewater	will	18574
	Benjamin	1861	Bridgewater	will	18575
	Betty	1830	W. Bridgewater	admn	18576
	Bradford	1856	N. Bridgewater	grdn	18629
	Brimsley C	1859	N. Bridgewater	admn	18577
	Catherine L	1872	N. Bridgewater	grdn	18578
	Cephas	1819	Bridgewater	grdn	18652
	Charity	1749	Bridgewater	grdn	18627
	Charles	1771	Bridgewater	will	18579
	Charles	1813	Bridgewater	will	18580
	Charles W	1856	N. Bridgewater	grdn	18646
	Cyrus	1805	Bridgewater	admn	18581
	Cyrus	1806	Bridgewater	grdn	18582
	Daniel	1777	Bridgewater	will	18583
	Daniel	1819	Bridgewater	grdn	18652

SURNAME	FIRST NAME	YEAR	PLACE	CASE	DOCKET
SNELL	Daniel	1822	N. Bridgewater	will	18584
	David	1819	Bridgewater	grdn	18652
	Edward	1858	N. Bridgewater	admn	18585
	Edward S	1839	N. Bridgewater	grdn	18586
	Edwin L	1867	E. Bridgewater	admn	18587
	Elbridge G	1819	Bridgewater	grdn	18652
	Elish J	1866	Wareham	grdn	18588
	Ella L	1874	Bridgewater	grdn	18589
	Emeline W	1839	N. Bridgewater	grdn	18586
	Ephraim	1805	Bridgewater	will	18590
	Ephraim	1805	Bridgewater	grdn	18591
	Ephraim	1847	W. Bridgewater	will	18592
	Frederick	1861	N. Bridgewater	grdn	18593
	Gilbert	1818	Bridgewater	grdn	18594 a
	Gilbert	1837	N. Bridgewater	grdn	18595 a
	Gilbert	1841	Bridgewater	admn	18596
	Hannah	1755	Bridgewater	will	18598
	Hannah	1832	N. Bridgewater	grdn	18653
	Hannah	1876	Brockton	will	18599
	Hannah E	1827	Turner ME	grdn	18597
	Harriet	1838	E. Bridgewater	grdn	18601
	Harriet A	1827	N. Bridgewater	grdn	18642
	Harriet F	1861	E. Bridgewater	admn	18600
	Henry	1865	N. Bridgewater	admn	18602
	Henry C	1875	Bridgewater	will	18603
	Henry M	1856	N. Bridgewater	grdn	18629
	Isaac H	1874	Bridgewater	admn	18604
	Issachar	1820	Bridgewater	admn	18605
	Jeremiah	1830	N. Bridgewater	admn	18606
	Jerusha E	1866	Wareham	grdn	18588
	Joanna	1795	Bridgewater	will	18607
	John	1767	Bridgewater	will	18608
	John E	1878	Hingham	admn	18610
	John W	1856	N. Bridgewater	admn	18609
	Jonathan	1801	Bridgewater	will	18611
	Jonathan	1859	W. Bridgewater	will	18612
	Joseph	1736	Bridgewater	will	18613
	Joseph	1793	Bridgewater	admn	18614
	Joseph D	1868	N. Bridgewater	admn	18615
	Josiah	1785	Bridgewater	will	18616
	Linthea	1826	W. Bridgewater	grdn	18617 a
	Linthea	1859	W. Bridgewater	admn	18618
	Linthia	1807	Bridgewater	grdn	18569
	Louisa J	1856	N. Bridgewater	grdn	18646
	Lucia K	1867	N. Bridgewater	admn	18619
	Lucius	1832	E. Bridgewater	admn	18620
	Luther T	1858	N. Bridgewater	grdn	18621
	Marion J	1875	Brockton	grdn	18638
	Martha	1817	Bridgewater	will	18622
	Martha	1838	E. Bridgewater	grdn	18601
	Martha	1860	E. Bridgewater	grdn	18632
	Mary	1749	Bridgewater	grdn	18627
	Mary T	1872	N. Bridgewater	grdn	18578
	Mary W	1839	N. Bridgewater	grdn	18586
	Matthew	1839	N. Bridgewater	admn	18623
	Mehitable	1819	Bridgewater	grdn	18652
	Mehitable	1826	N. Bridgewater	admn	18624
	Molly	1833	N. Bridgewater	will	18625
	Moses	1749	Bridgewater	admn	18626
	Moses	1749	Bridgewater	grdn	18627
	Nahum	1806	Bridgewater	grdn	18582
	Nahum	1866	W. Bridgewater	admn	18628
	Nancy	1856	N. Bridgewater	grdn	18629
	Nathan	1802	Bridgewater	will	18630
	Nathan F	1860	E. Bridgewater	grdn	18632
	Nathan T	1859	E. Bridgewater	admn	18631
	Nathaniel	1841	N. Bridgewater	will	18633
	Oliver	1831	N. Bridgewater	admn	18634
	Oliver	1863	N. Bridgewater	will	18635
	Otis P	1867	Rochester	admn	18636
	Patty	1819	Bridgewater	grdn	18652

SURNAME	FIRST NAME	YEAR	PLACE	CASE	DOCKET
SNELL	Polycarpus	1806	Bridgewater	will	18637
	Preston W	1875	Brockton	grdn	18638
	Rebecca	1849	N. Bridgewater	admn	18639
	Rhoda	1807	Bridgewater	grdn	18569
	Robert	1749	Bridgewater	grdn	18627
	Royal	1881	Brockton	will	18640
	Ruth G	1827	N. Bridgewater	grdn	18642
	Sally	1878	Bridgewater	admn	18641
	Samuel L	1827	N. Bridgewater	grdn	18642
	Sarah	1832	N. Bridgewater	grdn	18653
	Shepard	1774	Bridgewater	grdn	18643
	Shepard	1840	N. Bridgewater	admn	18644
	Stephen	1847	E. Bridgewater	will	18645
	Stephen L	1872	N. Bridgewater	grdn	18578
	Susanna	1819	Bridgewater	grdn	18652
	Sylvia H	1856	N. Bridgewater	grdn	18646
	Thomas	1724	Bridgewater	will	18647
	Thomas J	1827	N. Bridgewater	grdn	18642
	Warren T	1860	E. Bridgewater	grdn	18632
	William	1836	Bridgewater	admn	18648
	William	1879	Brockton	admn	18649
	Zachariah	1768	Bridgewater	will	18650
	Zachariah	1819	Bridgewater	admn	18651
	Zachariah	1819	Bridgewater	grdn	18652
	Zachary	1832	N. Bridgewater	grdn	18653
SNOW	Aaron	1849	Middleboro	admn	18654
	Abia	1711/2	Marshfield	grdn	18655
	Abner Jr	1855	N. Bridgewater	admn	18656
	Allen W	1843	Rochester	grdn	18657
	Anna	1860	Mattapoisett	admn	18658
	Anna F	1854	Rochester	grdn	18697
	Anthony	1692/3	Marshfield	will	18659
	Austin	1879	Brockton	grdn	18660 a
	Benjamin	1743	Bridgewater	will	18661
	Benjamin	1761	Bridgewater	admn	18662
	Charles	1824	W. Bridgewater	will	18663
	Charles	1842	W. Bridgewater	grdn	18664
	Daniel	1819	Bridgewater	admn	18665
	David	1858	W. Bridgewater	will	18666
	Ebenezer	1823	Rochester	admn	18667
	Eleazer	1797	Bridgewater	will	18668
	Elijah	1792	Bridgewater	will	18669
	Elizabeth	1790	Rochester	grdn	18714
	Elnora E	1870	Mattapoisett	grdn	18670
	George	1867	W. Bridgewater	will	18672
	George D	1865	Mattapoisett	admn	18671
	George F	1843	Rochester	grdn	18657
	George H	1875	Brockton	grdn	18674
	George W	1810	Rochester	grdn	18692
	George W	1867	Middleboro	will	18673
	Hannah	1790	Rochester	grdn	18714
	Hannah	1797	Rochester	grdn	18721
	Hannah	1814	Rochester	admn	18675
	Hannah	1841	W. Bridgewater	admn	18676
	Harriet H	1875	Wareham	admn	18677
	Harvey	1871	Mattapoisett	will	18678
	Herbert E	1875	Brockton	admn	18679
	How	1829	Rochester	admn	18680
	Isaac	1789	Rochester	will	18681
	Isaac N	1810	Rochester	grdn	18692
	Ivory	1874	Mattapoisett	admn	18682
	James	1691	Bridgewater	admn	18683
	James	1760	Bridgewater	will	18684
	James	1860	Mattapoisett	admn	18686
	James 2nd	1849	Rochester	admn	18685
	James M	1878	Mattapoisett	admn	18687
	John	1786	Bridgewater	will	18688
	John	1831	W. Bridgewater	will	18689
	Jonathan	1810	Rochester	admn	18691
	Jonathan	1810	Rochester	grdn	18692
	Jonathan	1814	Rochester	admn	18690

SURNAME	FIRST NAME	YEAR	PLACE	CASE	DOCKET
SNOW	Joseph	1803	Rochester	grdn	18696
	Joseph	1808	Rochester	will	18694
	Joseph	1835	Rochester	admn	18693
	Joseph Jr	1800	Rochester	admn	18695
	Joseph L	1854	Rochester	grdn	18697
	Joshua	1825	Rochester	admn	18698
	Josiah	1692/3	Marshfield	admn	18699
	Lemuel	1848	Rochester	admn	18700
	Levi	1880	Mattapoisett	admn	18701
	Levi M	1858	Mattapoisett	grdn	18702
	Linus	1810	Rochester	grdn	18692
	Linus	1858	Rochester	admn	18703
	Lizzie A	1878	Mattapoisett	grdn	18704
	Lucy	1803	Rochester	grdn	18696
	Luella T	1878	Mattapoisett	grdn	18704
	Mark	1799	Rochester	will	18705
	Mary	1797	Rochester	grdn	18721
	Mary	1825	N. Bridgewater	grdn	18710
	Mary A	1853	Duxbury	admn	18706
	Mary H	1874	Middleboro	admn	18707
	Mercy	1790	Rochester	grdn	18714
	Meriah	1790	Rochester	grdn	18714
	Nathaniel	1790	Rochester	grdn	18714
	Nathaniel	1825	N. Bridgewater	grdn	18710
	Nathaniel	1841	Rochester	admn	18709
	Nathaniel	1868	N. Bridgewater	admn	18708
	Nathaniel S	1797	Rochester	grdn	18721
	Nicholas	1754	Rochester	will	18712
	Nicholas	1790	Rochester	will	18713
	Nicholas	1790	Rochester	grdn	18714
	Nicholas	1854	Rochester	admn	18711
	Prince	1859	Mattapoisett	will	18715
	Rebecca	1797	Rochester	grdn	18721
	Rebecca	1872	Marion	will	18716
	Russell	1881	Middleboro	will	18717
	Sally	1810	Rochester	grdn	18692
	Samuel	1797	Rochester	will	18720
	Samuel	1797	Rochester	grdn	18721
	Samuel	1848	Rochester	admn	18719
	Samuel	1854	Rochester	admn	18718
	Seth	1824	N. Bridgewater	admn	18722
	Solomon	1741	Bridgewater	admn	18723
	Sprague	1839	N. Bridgewater	admn	18724
	Susan A	1819	Taunton/Rochest	grdn	18725
	Susan A	1870	Mattapoisett	grdn	18670
	Sylvanus A	1862	Wareham	admn	18726
	Thankful	1790	Rochester	grdn	18714
	Thomas	1850	Rochester	admn	18727
	Thomas	1859	Marion	admn	18728
	William	1708	Bridgewater	will	18730
	William	1726	Bridgewater	admn	18729
SONET	Samuel	1719	Plympton	admn	18731 i
SOPER	Alexander	1801	Pembroke	admn	18732
	Ann	1746	Scituate	grdn	18733
	Anna	1786	Scituate	admn	18734
	Anna	1793	Scituate	grdn	18735 a
	Betty	1757	-----	admn	18736
	Eunice	1848	Hanson	will	18737
	Gad	1865	Hanson	admn	18738
	Heman	1859	Hanson	will	18739
	Isaac	1846	Hanson	admn	18740
	John	1746	Scituate	admn	18741
	John S	1849	Hanson	grdn	18742
	Joseph	1790	Hanover	will	18743
	Joseph Jr	1804	Hanover	will	18744
	Nathaniel	1830	Hanson	will	18745
	Thomas	1722	Scituate	admn	18746
	Thomas	1791	Scituate	admn	18747
SOULE	Aaron	1783	Pembroke	admn	18748
	Aaron	1842	Plympton	grdn	18749
	Abbot L	1864	E. Bridgewater	grdn	18750

SURNAME	FIRST NAME	YEAR	PLACE	CASE	DOCKET
SOULE	Abigail	1748	Scituate	grdn	18751
	Abigail	1752	Plympton	grdn	18860
	Abigail	1768	Duxbury	grdn	18752
	Abigail	1768	Plympton	grdn	18795
	Abigail	1807	Duxbury	grdn	18827
	Abisha	1778	Duxbury	will	18753
	Abisha	1807	Duxbury	grdn	18827
	Abishai	1873	Hanover	will	18754
	Adoniram	1872	Plympton	admn	18755
	Alathea	1868	Duxbury	admn	18756
	Alfred	1833	Middleboro	admn	18757
	Alice	1768	Duxbury	grdn	18752
	Annie G	1872	Duxbury	grdn	18758
	Anson	1783	Middleboro	grdn	18886
	Asa	1807	Duxbury	grdn	18827
	Aurelius	1864	Duxbury	admn	18759
	Benjamin	1729	Plympton	will	18760
	Benjamin	1751	Plympton	admn	18761
	Bennett	1864	Plympton	admn	18762
	Betsey	1864	Middleboro	admn	18764
	Betsey M	1836	Halifax	grdn	18763
	Charles	1869	Duxbury	will	18765
	Charles E	1874	Duxbury	grdn	18766
	Charles E	1878	Duxbury	adop	18767
	Clenthia	1857	Duxbury	admn	18768
	Daniel	1840	Plympton	will	18769
	Dulcina J	1853	Plympton	grdn	18770
	Ebenezer	1729/0	Plympton	grdn	18771
	Ebenezer T	1862	Middleboro	admn	18772
	Elijah	1827	Hartford ME	admn	18773
	Elijah	1835	Duxbury	admn	18774
	Eliza A	1879	Abington	admn	18775
	Elizabeth	1833	Duxbury	grdn	18864
	Ella J	1864	E. Bridgewater	grdn	18750
	Ephraim	1809	Plympton	grdn	18776 a
	Esther	1793	Middleboro	will	18777
	Ezekiel	1844	Duxbury	will	18778
	Ezra	1852	Middleboro	admn	18779
	Fernando	1861	Duxbury	admn	18780
	Francis	1871	Plympton	admn	18781
	Frederick F	1878	Duxbury	admn	18782
	Freeman	1866	Duxbury	admn	18783
	George	1836	Halifax	will	18784
	George	1874	Middleboro	admn	18785
	Gideon	1750	Duxbury/Pembrok	grdn	18786 a
	Gideon	1792	Halifax	admn	18787
	Hannah	1752	Plympton	grdn	18860
	Hannah	1858	Duxbury	admn	18788
	Hannah W	1876	Middleboro	will	18789
	Harriet A	1864	E. Bridgewater	grdn	18750
	Henry	1872	Duxbury	will	18790
	Herbert L	1865	Duxbury	grdn	18881
	Huldah	1783	Middleboro	grdn	18886
	Isaac	1746	Middleboro	grdn	18800
	Isaac	1776	Pembroke	admn	18791
	Isaac 2nd	1850	Middleboro	admn	18792
	Jabez	1751	Halifax	admn	18794
	Jabez	1768	Plympton	grdn	18795
	Jabez	1827	Halifax	will	18793
	Jabez	1880	Halifax	will	18796
	Jacob	1744	Middleboro	admn	18799
	Jacob	1746	Middleboro	grdn	18800
	Jacob	1750	Middleboro	admn	18798
	Jacob	1761	Halifax	grdn	18802
	Jacob	1823	Middleboro	will	18797
	Jacob	1834	Halifax	admn	18801
	James	1744	Middleboro	will	18805
	James	1759	Plympton	admn	18803
	James	1794	Duxbury	admn	18807
	James	1828	Middleboro	admn	18806
	James	1851	Plympton	will	18804

SURNAME	FIRST NAME	YEAR	PLACE	CASE	DOCKET
SOULE	James	1869	Duxbury	will	18808
	James	1877	S. Abington	will	18809
	John	1707	Duxbury	admn	18810
	John	1734	Duxbury	admn	18811
	John	1743	Middleboro	will	18813
	John	1750	Middleboro	admn	18814
	John	1751	Middleboro	grdn	18815
	John	1792	Pembroke	grdn	18812 a
	John	1816	Middleboro	admn	18816
	John	1852	Bridgewater	admn	18817
	John	1869	E. Bridgewater	admn	18818
	Joseph	1763	Duxbury	will	18819
	Joseph	1800	Duxbury	will	18820
	Joseph	1805	Duxbury	admn	18821
	Joshua	1767	Duxbury	will	18822
	Joshua	1803	Duxbury	admn	18823
	Josiah	1764	Duxbury	will	18825
	Josiah	1806	Duxbury	admn	18826
	Josiah	1807	Duxbury	grdn	18827
	Josiah Jr	1870	Abington	admn	18824
	Lewis	1858	Middleboro	will	18828
	Lois	1758	Plympton	grdn	18829
	Lois	1842	Abington	admn	18830
	Lucy	1852	Middleboro	admn	18831
	Lucy N	1864	Plympton	grdn	18832
	Lucy P	1853	Kingston	grdn	18833
	Lydia	1736	Duxbury	grdn	18868
	Lydia	1746	Middleboro	grdn	18800
	Lydia	1768	Duxbury	grdn	18752
	Lydia	1807	Duxbury	grdn	18827
	Marcia	1834	Kingston	grdn	18834
	Marcia	1848	Halifax	will	18835
	Martha	1758	Middleboro	will	18836
	Mary	1773	Plympton	admn	18837
	Mary	1837	Carver	will	18838
	Mary	1861	Duxbury	admn	18840
	Mary C	1833	Duxbury	grdn	18864
	Mary T	1822	Duxbury	grdn	18839
	May	1873	Abington	grdn	18841
	Mercy	1761	Halifax	grdn	18802
	Micah	1778	Duxbury	will	18842
	Micah	1822	Duxbury	admn	18843
	Micah A	1835	Duxbury	grdn	18844
	Moses	1748	Duxbury	admn	18845
	Nabby	1852	Halifax	will	18846
	Nancy	1881	Rockland	will	18848
	Nancy F	1861	Duxbury	admn	18847
	Nathan	1872	Duxbury	will	18849
	Nathaniel	1811	Duxbury	admn	18850
	Nathaniel	1863	Duxbury	admn	18852
	Nathaniel 2nd	1817	Duxbury	admn	18851
	Orphan	1793	Marshfield	admn	18853
	Otis	1822	Duxbury	admn	18854
	Otis	1871	Middleboro	will	18855
	Polly	1873	Plympton	admn	18856
	Preston	1862	Middleboro	admn	18857
	Priscilla	1752	Plympton	grdn	18860
	Priscilla	1845	Duxbury	admn	18858
	Priscilla	1864	Duxbury	admn	18859
	Prudence	1833	Duxbury	grdn	18864
	Rebecca	1747	Middleboro	will	18861
	Rebecca	1759	Middleboro	will	18862
	Rebecca	1783	Pembroke	admn	18863
	Remember	1783	Middleboro	grdn	18886
	Richard Jr	1833	Duxbury	grdn	18864
	Samuel	1736	Duxbury	grdn	18868
	Samuel	1768	Duxbury	admn	18867
	Samuel	1833	Kingston	admn	18865
	Samuel	1854	Kingston	admn	18866
	Sarah	1740	Plympton	admn	18869
	Sarah	1768	Plympton	grdn	18795

SURNAME	FIRST NAME	YEAR	PLACE	CASE	DOCKET
SOULE	Sarah	1857	Middleboro	will	18870
	Silas T	1878	Wareham	admn	18871
	Simeon	1832	Duxbury	will	18872
	Simeon	1843	Duxbury	admn	18873
	Simeon	1845	Duxbury	grdn	18874
	Sophronia	1878	Rockland	grdn	18875
	Stephen	1868	Duxbury	will	18876
	Susannah C	1844	Plympton	admn	18877
	Sylvia	1768	Duxbury	grdn	18752
	Sylvia	1807	Duxbury	grdn	18827
	Thomas	1835	Duxbury	admn	18878
	Thomas B	1847	Middleboro	grdn	18879
	William	1746	Middleboro	grdn	18800
	William	1778	Middleboro	admn	18885
	William	1783	Middleboro	grdn	18886
	William	1820	Middleboro	admn	18884
	William	1853	Kingston	grdn	18833
	William	1858	Duxbury	admn	18880
	William A	1865	Duxbury	grdn	18881
	William H	1871	Plympton	will	18883
	William N	1864	E. Bridgewater	admn	18882
	Zachariah	1690/1	Duxbury	admn	18890
	Zachariah	1751	Plympton	will	18887
	Zachariah	1760	Plympton	admn	18888
	Zachariah	1804	Plympton	admn	18889
SOUTHER	Caroline	1837	Hingham	grdn	18899
	Charles	1809	Hingham	grdn	18902
	Christiana P	1868	Kingston	grdn	18897
	Daniel	1809	Hingham	admn	18891
	Daniel	1846	Hingham	admn	18892
	Deborah	1836	Hingham	will	18893
	Elijah	1873	Hingham	admn	18894
	Emma M	1837	Hingham	grdn	18899
	Frank	1872	Hingham	adop	18895
	Irene	1852	Hingham	admn	18896
	James T	1868	Kingston	grdn	18897
	John	1807	Hingham	will	18898
	Joseph	1837	Hingham	grdn	18899
	Laban	1841	Scituate	will	18900
	Martin	1878	Hingham	will	18901
	Sally	1809	Hingham	grdn	18902
	Sarah A	1837	Hingham	grdn	18899
SOUTHWORTH	Abiel W	1868	Lakeville	admn	18903
	Abigail	1820	Middleboro	grdn	18909
	Abigail	1861	Lakeville	admn	18904
	Andrew	1779	Rochester	admn	18905
	Andrew	1870	Mattapoisett	admn	18906
	Benjamin	1756	Duxbury	will	18907
	Benjamin	1799	Bridgewater	admn	18908
	Betsey	1820	Middleboro	grdn	18909
	Catherine	1778	Bridgewater	grdn	18942
	Constant	1731	Duxbury	admn	18910
	Constant	1775	Bridgewater	will	18911
	David	1778	Bridgewater	grdn	18942
	Ebenezer	1751	Middleboro	admn	18913
	Ebenezer	1755	Middleboro	grdn	18914
	Ebenezer	1770	Middleboro	grdn	18912 a
	Edward	1727	Duxbury	will	18915
	Edward	1871	N. Bridgewater	admn	18916
	Edward Jr	1877	Brockton	will	18917
	Enoch	1871	Lakeville	will	18918
	George	1809	Duxbury	admn	18919
	Gideon	1772	Rochester	admn	18920
	Gideon	1827	Middleboro	admn	18921
	Gideon	1857	Lakeville	will	18922
	Hannah	1765	Middleboro	grdn	18924
	Hannah	1791	Duxbury	admn	18923
	Hannah	1851	Abington	grdn	18955
	Hannah A	1868	Middleboro	admn	18925
	Ichabod	1757	Middleboro	admn	18926
	Jacob	1867	Duxbury	admn	18927

SURNAME	FIRST NAME	YEAR	PLACE	CASE	DOCKET
SOUTHWORTH	James	1767	Duxbury	grdn	18928 a
	James	1812	Duxbury	admn	18929
	James	1841	Duxbury	admn	18930
	Jedediah	1739	Duxbury	admn	18931
	John	1751	Duxbury	will	18932
	Lewis	1822	Hingham	admn	18933
	Lurania	1755	Middleboro	grdn	18914
	Mary P	1864	Duxbury	grdn	18934 a
	Nathan	1851	Abington	admn	18935
	Nathan	1858	Hingham	admn	18936
	Nathaniel	1710/1	Middleboro	will	18937
	Nathaniel	1757	Middleboro	will	18938
	Nathaniel	1762	Middleboro	admn	18939
	Nathaniel	1778	Bridgewater	admn	18941
	Nathaniel	1778	Bridgewater	grdn	18942
	Nathaniel	1819	Middleboro	admn	18940
	Peleg	1755	Middleboro	grdn	18914
	Perez	1837	N. Bridgewater	will	18943
	Perez	1875	Brockton	will	18944
	Priscilla	1761	Duxbury	will	18945
	Rhoda	1880	Brockton	will	18946
	Sarah	1755	Middleboro	grdn	18914
	Sarah	1861	Duxbury	admn	18948
	Sarah	1865	Rochester	admn	18947
	Sarah C	1865	Lakeville	grdn	18949
	Seth	1862	Lakeville	admn	18950
	Simeon	1778	Bridgewater	grdn	18942
	Thomas	1742	Duxbury	will	18953
	Thomas	1819	Scituate	admn	18954
	Thomas	1851	Abington	grdn	18955
	Thomas	1867	Lakeville	will	18951
	Thomas	1878	Carver	admn	18952
	Wilber	1840	Rochester	grdn	18956 a
	Wilber	1842	Rochester	admn	18957
	William	1752	Duxbury	grdn	18958
	William	1817	Hingham	admn	18959
	William	1861	Lakeville	will	18960
SPARRELL	James N	1774	Scituate	admn	18961
	James N	1859	S. Scituate	will	18962
SPARROW	Anna M	1866	Middleboro	grdn	18967
	Edward	1745	Plymouth	admn	18963
	Edward	1816	Middleboro	grdn	18964 a
	Edward	1817	Middleboro	will	18965
	Edward H	1861	Middleboro	admn	18966
	Elizabeth H	1867	Mattapoisett	grdn	18970
	Frank M	1867	Mattapoisett	grdn	18970
	Helen F	1866	Middleboro	grdn	18967
	Henry P	1866	Middleboro	grdn	18967
	Jacob A	1866	Middleboro	grdn	18967
	Josiah	1851	Rochester	admn	18968
	Rhoda	1826	Middleboro	admn	18969
	Solomon E	1867	Mattapoisett	grdn	18970
	William E Jr	1867	Mattapoisett	grdn	18970
SPAULDING	Alfred A	1875	Brockton	admn	18971
	Edwin	1858	Scituate	admn	18972
SPEAR	Ada F	1870	Hingham	grdn	18973
	Anna B	1874	Scituate	grdn	18974
	Catherine H	1868	Plymouth	will	18975
	Hannah B(Dill)	1870	Hingham	grdn	18973
	Henry E	1870	Hingham	grdn	18973
	James	1879	Plymouth	admn	18976
	Joseph	1788	Pembroke	admn	18977
	Thomas	1856	Plymouth	will	18978
	William F	1858	Plymouth	admn	18979
	William H	1864	Plymouth	grdn	18980 a
	William H 2nd	1858	Plymouth	grdn	18981
SPENCE	James	1858	Abington	will	18982
	Mary	1871	Abington	admn	18983
	Robert	1871	Abington	will	18984
SPINK	Eugene	1855	N. Bridgewater	grdn	18985
	Isaac F	1855	N. Bridgewater	grdn	18985

SURNAME	FIRST NAME	YEAR	PLACE	CASE	DOCKET
SPOONER	Allen C	1826	Plymouth	grdn	18986
	Bourne	1870	Plymouth	will	18987
	Ebenezer	1718	Plymouth	admn	18989
	Ebenezer	1778	Middleboro	admn	18988
	Ebenezer	1845	Plymouth	admn	18990
	Ephraim	1777	Abington	will	18991
	Ephraim	1818	Plymouth	admn	18992
	Ida	1867	Plymouth	grdn	18994
	James	1838	Plymouth	admn	18993
	John B	1867	Plymouth	grdn	18994
	Joshua et al	1781	Middleboro	part	18995
	Leonora	1876	Hingham	admn	18996
	Lucy W	1860	Plymouth	admn	18997
	Maria	1878	S. Scituate	will	18998
	Mary	1777	Abington	grdn	19001
	Mary	1844	Plymouth	admn	18999
	Mary E	1869	Plymouth	will	19000
	Nathaniel	1766	Plymouth	grdn	19004
	Nathaniel	1826	Plymouth	will	19003
	Nathaniel Jr	1817	Plymouth	admn	19002
	Ruth	1777	Abington	grdn	19001
	Ruth K	1876	Lakeville	will	19005
	Sally	1855	Plymouth	admn	19006
	Thomas	1763	Plymouth	will	19007
	Thomas	1766	Plymouth	grdn	19004
	Thomas	1844	Plymouth	grdn	19008 a
	William F	1872	Plymouth	admn	19009
SPRAGUE	Abner	1827	Hingham	grdn	19014
	Adna	1861	Hingham	will	19010
	Albert	1855	Hingham	admn	19011
	Alden	1762	Rochester	admn	19012
	Alden	1773	Rochester	grdn	19013
	Amos Jr	1827	Hingham	grdn	19014
	Amos W	1831	Scituate	grdn	19065
	Asenath	1739	Duxbury	grdn	19015
	Asher	1824	Scituate	will	19016
	Augustus F	1873	Marshfield	grdn	19017 a
	Bela	1847	Hingham	admn	19018
	Bela	1878	Hingham	will	19019
	Bela T	1879	Hingham	will	19020
	Benjamin	1779	Bridgewater	admn	19021
	Benjamin	1831	Scituate	grdn	19065
	Benjamin A	1869	Bridgewater	grdn	19074
	Beulah W	1851	Marshfield	grdn	19022
	Caleb	1825	Hingham	admn	19023
	Chandler	1870	N. Bridgewater	will	19024
	Charles	1844	Hingham	admn	19025
	Charles F	1850	Hingham	grdn	19026
	Chillingsworth	1759	Marshfield	grdn	19054
	Chillingsworth	1875	Marshfield	admn	19027
	Chloe	1867	Bridgewater	will	19028
	Cynthia	1876	Hingham	admn	19029
	Daniel D	1831	Scituate	grdn	19065
	David	1832	Hingham	admn	19030
	David	1849	Hingham	will	19031
	Deborah	1870	Hingham	will	19032
	Edgar M	1878	Hingham	grdn	19033
	Elijah	1868	Hingham	will	19034
	Elizabeth	1759	Marshfield	grdn	19054
	Ellen	1871	Marshfield	grdn	19035 a
	Emma	1847	Hingham	grdn	19036 a
	Emma C	1879	Bridgewater	grdn	19095
	Ephraim	1846	Bridgewater	will	19037
	Eunice	1830	Abington	grdn	19038
	Ezekiel	1759	Marshfield	grdn	19054
	Ezekiel	1874	Duxbury	admn	19039
	Ezra	1860	Hingham	admn	19040
	Fisher A	1868	Bridgewater	admn	19041
	Friend	1808	Bridgewater	grdn	19042
	Grace E W	1880	Hingham	grdn	19043
	Hannah	1766	Duxbury	grdn	19124

SURNAME	FIRST NAME	YEAR	PLACE	CASE	DOCKET
SPRAGUE	Hannah	1773	Rochester	grdn	19013
	Hannah	1809	Hingham	will	19044
	Hannah	1833	Rochester	admn	19045
	Isaac	1826	Hingham	admn	19046
	Isaac G	1838	Hingham	admn	19047
	Israel	1859	Hingham	admn	19048
	Jacob	1809	Hingham	will	19049
	Jacob	1846	Hingham	admn	19050
	James	1759	Marshfield	admn	19053
	James	1759	Marshfield	grdn	19054
	James	1766	Marshfield	will	19052
	James	1881	Marshfield	admn	19051
	Jane F	1876	Marshfield	admn	19055
	Jesse	1812	Hingham	admn	19056
	Jethro	1716	Duxbury	grdn	19110
	Joanna	1759	Marshfield	grdn	19054
	John	1739	Duxbury	will	19058
	John	1765	Duxbury	grdn	19059
	John	1873	Marshfield	will	19057
	Jonathan	1756	Bridgewater	will	19060
	Jonathan	1759	Marshfield	grdn	19054
	Jonathan	1841	Marshfield	will	19061
	Joseph	1759	Marshfield	grdn	19054
	Joshua	1757	Abington	admn	19062
	Joshua	1763	Abington	grdn	19063
	Joshua	1766	Duxbury	grdn	19124
	Joshua	1854	Hingham	will	19064
	Joshua C	1831	Scituate	grdn	19065
	Laban	1831	Scituate	grdn	19065
	Leah	1842	Hingham	will	19066
	Leavitt	1875	Hingham	will	19067
	Leonard	1865	Hingham	will	19068
	Lois H	1863	Bridgewater	will	19069
	Louise K	1875	Hingham	adop	19070
	Louise K	1876	Hingham	admn	19071
	Lucius A	1866	Abington	admn	19072
	Lucy	1744	Rochester	grdn	19073
	Lucy A	1869	Bridgewater	grdn	19074
	Luther	1849	Marshfield	admn	19076
	Luther	1868	Hingham	will	19075
	Luther Jr	1842	Marshfield	admn	19077
	Lydia	1766	Duxbury	grdn	19124
	Lydia	1843	Duxbury	will	19078
	Maria	1878	Hingham	admn	19079
	Marion W	1876	Hingham	adop	19080
	Martin	1867	Hingham	will	19081
	Mary	1759	Marshfield	grdn	19054
	Mary	1766	Duxbury	grdn	19124
	Mary	1865	Hingham	will	19083
	Mary E	1855	Hingham	grdn	19082
	Mehitable	1840	Hingham	admn	19084
	Melzar	1844	Marshfield	will	19085
	Melzar	1880	Hanover	will	19086
	Micah	1744	Rochester	grdn	19094
	Michael	1762	Rochester	admn	19087
	Moses	1828	Hingham	will	19088
	Moses	1850	Hingham	will	19089
	Nathan	1758	Marshfield	will	19090
	Nathaniel	1739	Rochester	admn	19093
	Nathaniel	1744	Rochester	grdn	19094
	Nathaniel	1765	Duxbury	grdn	19059
	Nathaniel	1773	Rochester	grdn	19013
	Nathaniel	1797	Rochester	will	19092
	Nathaniel	1865	Hanson	will	19091
	Nathaniel F	1869	Bridgewater	grdn	19074
	Nellie A	1879	Bridgewater	grdn	19095
	Noah	1773	Rochester	will	19096
	Noah Jr	1773	Rochester	admn	19097
	Paul	1773	Rochester	grdn	19013
	Peleg	1755	Duxbury	admn	19098
	Persis	1847	Hingham	admn	19099

SURNAME	FIRST NAME	YEAR	PLACE	CASE	DOCKET
SPRAGUE	Peter	1777	Bridgewater	admn	19100
	Peter	1868	Hingham	admn	19101
	Peter N	1856	Hingham	name	19102
	Phillis	1793	Rochester	admn	19103 b
	Phineas	1776	Duxbury	admn	19104
	Polly	1858	Hingham	will	19105
	Rachel	1839	Hingham	admn	19106
	Reuben	1852	Hingham	will	19107
	Ruth	1716	Duxbury	grdn	19110
	Ruth	1726	Plymouth	grdn	19117
	Ruth	1830	Hingham	admn	19109
	Ruth	1874	Marshfield	admn	19108
	Sally	1868	Hingham	will	19111
	Samuel	1710	Marshfield	admn	19115
	Samuel	1723	Plymouth	admn	19116
	Samuel	1726	Plymouth	grdn	19117
	Samuel	1740	Rochester	admn	19114
	Samuel	1764	Duxbury	will	19112
	Samuel	1766	Duxbury	admn	19113
	Samuel	1766	Duxbury	grdn	19124
	Sarah E	1873	S. Scituate	admn	19118
	Sarah F	1875	Marshfield	admn	19119
	Seth	1831	Hingham	will	19120
	Seth	1847	Duxbury	will	19121
	Sophia	1862	Duxbury	will	19122
	Terah	1716	Duxbury	grdn	19110
	Thomas	1766	Duxbury	grdn	19124
	Thomas	1864	Hingham	will	19123
	Uriah	1766	Duxbury	grdn	19124
	Uriah	1842	Duxbury	will	19125
	Waterman	1879	Bridgewater	will	19126
	William	1712	Duxbury	admn	19128
	William	1754	Abington	admn	19127
	William	1831	Scituate	grdn	19065
	William T	1853	Duxbury	will	19129
	Zarviah	1716	Duxbury	grdn	19110
	Zenas	1809	Hingham	admn	19130
SPROAT	Bethania	1878	Middleboro	admn	19131
	Earl	1786	Middleboro	grdn	19132
	Earl	1864	Middleboro	will	19133
	Ebenezer	1726	Middleboro	will	19135
	Ebenezer	1732	Middleboro	grdn	19136
	Ebenezer	1786	Middleboro	will	19134
	Elizabeth	1726	Middleboro	admn	19137
	James	1732	Middleboro	grdn	19136
	James	1735	Middleboro	grdn	19138
	James	1837	Middleboro	admn	19139
	James R	1878	Wareham	will	19140
	Leonard	1816	Middleboro	admn	19141
	Mary	1726	Middleboro	admn	19137
	Rachel	1738	Middleboro	admn	19142
	Robert	1712	Middleboro	will	19143
	Robert	1798	Middleboro	will	19145
	Robert Jr	1782	Middleboro	admn	19144
	Thomas	1833	Middleboro	will	19146
	Thomas C	1864	Middleboro	grdn	19147
	Thomas C	1881	Middleboro	admn	19148
SPROWL	James L	1875	Sacramento CA	admn	19149
	Matthew	1871	Abington	admn	19150
STACY	Joseph	1741	Kingston	admn	19151
STANDISH	Alexander	1702	Duxbury	will	19152
	Alice	1863	Plymouth	grdn	19153
	David	1795	Hanover	will	19154
	Desire	1732	Duxbury	will	19155
	Ebenezer	1747	Plympton	admn	19156
	Hannah	1803	Hanover	will	19157
	Ichabod	1772	Halifax	will	19158
	Isaiah	1780	Plympton	grdn	19161
	Isaiah	1816	Rochester	admn	19159
	Isaiah	1816	Rochester	grdn	19160
	J Warren	1879	Duxbury	admn	19168

SURNAME	FIRST NAME	YEAR	PLACE	CASE	DOCKET
STANDISH	Job	1842	Pembroke	admn	19162
	John	1786	Halifax	admn	19163
	John C	1805	Pembroke	grdn	19174
	John C	1826	Middleboro	admn	19164
	Jonathan	1837	Middleboro	will	19165
	Joshua	1876	Plymouth	admn	19166
	Julia M	1881	Middleboro	admn	19167
	Miles	1739	Duxbury	will	19172
	Miles	1805	Pembroke	admn	19173
	Miles	1805	Pembroke	grdn	19174
	Miles B	1838	Middleboro	grdn	19169
	Miles B	1849	Middleboro	admn	19170
	Miles T	1849	Middleboro	grdn	19171
	Moses	1769	Halifax	will	19175
	Nathaniel	1833	Middleboro	admn	19176
	Peleg	1780	Plympton	grdn	19161
	Penelope	1740	Duxbury	admn	19177
	Phebe	1818	Halifax	will	19178
	Rebecca	1780	Plympton	grdn	19161
	Rebecca	1816	Rochester	grdn	19160
	Ruth	1805	Pembroke	grdn	19174
	Sally	1816	Rochester	grdn	19160
	Sarah	1780	Plympton	grdn	19161
	Sarah	1805	Pembroke	grdn	19174
	Shadrach	1856	Halifax	will	19179
	Soranus	1866	Middleboro	admn	19180
	Thomas	1805	Pembroke	grdn	19174
	Thomas C	1860	Plympton	will	19182
	Thomas Jr	1780	Pembroke	admn	19181
	William	1829	Pembroke	will	19183
	William	1852	Pembroke	admn	19184
	William H	1854	Duxbury	will	19187
	William Jr	1841	Duxbury	grdn	19186 a
	William S	1861	Middleboro	admn	19185
	Zachariah	1770	Plympton	admn	19188
	Zachariah	1780	Plympton	will	19189
	Zachariah	1816	Rochester	grdn	19160
	Zachary	1780	Plympton	grdn	19161
STANFORD	Robert	1774	Duxbury	will	19190
STANLAKE	Richard	1691	Scituate	will	19191
STANLEY	Sarah	1848	Scituate	will	19192
STANTON	James R	1880	Hingham	admn	19193
STAPLES	Abraham	1734	Bridgewater	admn	19194
	Elias	1863	Middleboro	will	19195
	Lydia	1867	Middleboro	will	19196
	Samuel	1823	Middleboro	admn	19197
	Simeon	1833	Middleboro	admn	19198
	Thomas	1847	Middleboro	grdn	19199 a
STAPLETON	James	1845	Abington	admn	19200
	Patrick	1845	Abington	admn	19201
STARLING	Ruth	1804	Hanover	admn	19202
STCLAIRE	Clara Maud	1867	Lowell	adop	19203
STEARNS	Elizabeth L B	1875	Kingston	will	19204
	George H	1861	Duxbury	grdn	19205
STEIDLE	John G	1879	Kingston	will	19206
STEINGARDT	John F Jr	1864	E. Bridgewater	admn	19207
STEPHENSON	Carrie B	1881	Hingham	grdn	19208
	Charles H	1877	Hingham	grdn	19209
	Clarence L	1881	Hingham	grdn	19208
	Edward W	1863	Hingham	grdn	19210
	Elizabeth	1772	Plymouth	grdn	19216
	Ellen L	1881	Hingham	grdn	19208
	Ezra	1874	Hingham	admn	19211
	Harriet S	1859	Hingham	will	19212
	James	1857	Hingham	admn	19213
	James	1863	Hingham	admn	19214
	Jasper H	1772	Plymouth	grdn	19216
	John	1767	Plymouth	admn	19215
	John	1772	Plymouth	grdn	19216
	Lydia	1878	Hingham	admn	19217
	William	1772	Plymouth	grdn	19216

SURNAME	FIRST NAME	YEAR	PLACE	CASE	DOCKET
STETSON	Abby C	1849	S. Scituate	grdn	19380
	Abby M	1875	Hanover	grdn	19262
	Abel	1776	Pembroke	will	19219
	Abel	1810	Pembroke	will	19220
	Abel	1811	Pembroke	grdn	19221
	Abel	1874	Pembroke	admn	19218
	Abiel	1747	Scituate	grdn	19222
	Abigail	1727	Scituate	admn	19223
	Abigail	1779	Bridgewater	grdn	19227
	Abisha	1777	Bridgewater	admn	19226
	Abisha	1779	Bridgewater	grdn	19227
	Abisha	1843	E. Bridgewater	will	19225
	Abisha	1864	Pembroke	will	19224
	Abner	1805	Scituate	will	19228
	Abner	1839	Pembroke	admn	19229
	Abner	1847	Duxbury	grdn	19230 a
	Adam	1837	E. Bridgewater	admn	19231
	Albert	1874	Hanover	will	19232
	Alice R	1880	Hanover	admn	19233
	Almira	1811	Pembroke	grdn	19221
	Anthony	1747	Scituate	admn	19234
	Barnabas	1727	Scituate	grdn	19235
	Barnabas	1743	Hanover	admn	19236
	Barnabas	1849	Abington	will	19237
	Bathsheba	1782	-----	bond	19335
	Benjamin	1711	Scituate	admn	19238
	Benjamin	1739	Scituate	admn	19239
	Benjamin	1747	Scituate	grdn	19222
	Benjamin	1757	Hanover	will	19240
	Benjamin	1819	Hanover	admn	19241
	Benjamin	1826	Hanover	will	19242
	Benjamin	1866	Hanover	admn	19243
	Bethiah	1779	Bridgewater	grdn	19227
	Betsey	1852	Hanover	grdn	19387
	Betsey C	1879	Hanover	admn	19244
	Bradbury E	1836	Hanover	admn	19245
	Caleb	1827	Plympton	admn	19246
	Charles	1833	Scituate	admn	19247
	Charles	1867	Abington	grdn	19249
	Charles T	1856	Hanson	grdn	19248
	Chloe	1865	Pembroke	will	19251
	Chloe M	1861	Hanson	admn	19250
	Clarissa	1879	S. Abington	will	19252
	Deborah S	1831	Kingston	admn	19253
	Ebenezer	1779	Scituate	admn	19254
	Ebenezer	1881	S. Scituate	will	19255
	Edith R	1869	Hanson	grdn	19325
	Edward	1846	Hanover	will	19256
	Edward G	1849	S. Scituate	grdn	19380
	Eli	1866	Hanson	will	19257
	Elisha	1747	Scituate	grdn	19222
	Elisha	1755	Kingston	admn	19258
	Elisha	1761	Kingston	admn	19259
	Elizabeth	1840	Hanover	admn	19260
	Elizabeth S	1875	Kingston	will	19261
	Ellen	1849	S. Scituate	grdn	19380
	Emma J	1875	Hanover	grdn	19262
	Ephraim	1841	Abington	will	19264
	Ephraim	1854	S. Scituate	admn	19263
	Ephraim T	1867	Abington	admn	19265
	Ethan A	1832	E. Bridgewater	admn	19266
	Experience	1829	Scituate	admn	19267
	Ezra	1747	Scituate	grdn	19222
	Frederick C	1860	Hanson	grdn	19273
	George	1799	Scituate	admn	19271
	George	1867	Kingston	admn	19269
	George A	1860	Hanson	grdn	19273
	George F	1859	Hanson	admn	19272
	George F	1864	Kingston	admn	19270
	George R	1841	Duxbury	grdn	19268
	Gershom	1754	Scituate	will	19274

SURNAME	FIRST NAME	YEAR	PLACE	CASE	DOCKET
STETSON	Gideon	1761	Scituate	admn	19275
	Hannah	1763	Scituate	grdn	19280
	Hannah	1765	Pembroke	grdn	19299
	Hannah	1779	Scituate	admn	19279
	Hannah	1841	Pembroke	will	19277
	Hannah	1841	Abington	will	19278
	Hannah	1865	Hanover	will	19276
	Horace	1842	Hanover	will	19281
	Huldah M	1853	Pembroke	grdn	19282
	Isaac	1806	Abington	admn	19283
	Isaac	1811	Pembroke	grdn	19221
	Isaac O	1868	Pembroke	admn	19284
	James	1792	Scituate	grdn	19312
	James H	1876	Marshfield	will	19287
	James M	1865	W. Bridgewater	admn	19286
	James O	1860	W. Bridgewater	will	19285
	Jane E	1865	Lakeville	admn	19288
	Jeremiah	1805	Pembroke	will	19289
	Jeremiah	1869	Hanson	admn	19290
	John	1690/1	Scituate	admn	19291
	John	1723	Pembroke	grdn	19297
	John	1730	Scituate	decr	19291 +
	John	1765	Halifax	admn	19294
	John	1765	Pembroke	grdn	19299
	John	1776	Pembroke	admn	19298
	John	1787	Scituate	admn	19292
	John	1789	Scituate	grdn	19293
	John	1811	Hanover	will	19295
	John	1831	Pembroke	admn	19296
	John	1860	Hanson	grdn	19273
	Jonah	1766	Scituate	admn	19300
	Jonah	1783	Scituate	admn	19301
	Jonathan	1779	Bridgewater	grdn	19227
	Jonathan	1858	S. Scituate	will	19302
	Joseph	1724	Scituate	will	19303
	Joseph	1776	Pembroke	will	19304
	Joseph	1797	Hanover	admn	19307
	Joseph	1804	Hanover	grdn	19308
	Joseph	1852	Hanover	will	19306
	Joseph S	1816	Pembroke	admn	19305
	Joshua	1795	Hanover	admn	19309
	Julia	1849	S. Scituate	grdn	19380
	Julius	1860	Kingston	admn	19310
	Lillis	1761	Scituate	grdn	19315
	Lincoln	1785	Scituate	admn	19311
	Lincoln	1792	Scituate	grdn	19312
	Lot	1812	Pembroke	admn	19313
	Lucinda	1761	Scituate	grdn	19315
	Lucinda	1861	Pembroke	admn	19314
	Lucy	1804	Hanover	grdn	19308
	Lucy	1815	Pembroke	grdn	19316 a
	Lucy	1846	Hanover	admn	19317
	Lucy	1875	Hanover	admn	19318
	Luke	1785	Halifax	admn	19319
	Luther	1762	Scituate	grdn	19320
	Lydia	1763	Scituate	grdn	19280
	Lydia	1811	Pembroke	will	19321
	Lydia	1821	Scituate	admn	19322
	Lydia T	1880	Marshfield	will	19323
	Malichy	1762	Scituate	grdn	19320
	Maria	1854	Halifax	will	19324
	Marianna	1853	Pembroke	grdn	19282
	Marshall	1869	Hanson	grdn	19325
	Martha	1747	Scituate	grdn	19222
	Martin T	1857	Hanover	admn	19326
	Martin W	1878	Hanover	will	19327
	Mary	1763	Scituate	grdn	19280
	Mary	1782	-----	bond	19335
	Mary	1833	Scituate	will	19332
	Mary	1839	Pembroke	admn	19328
	Mary	1843	E. Bridgewater	will	19330

SURNAME	FIRST NAME	YEAR	PLACE	CASE	DOCKET
STETSON	Mary	1846	Pembroke	will	19329
	Mary	1854	Scituate	will	19333
	Mary	1870	S. Scituate	will	19334
	Mary E	1839	Hanover	admn	19331
	Matthew	1690/1	Scituate	admn	19336
	Mercy	1773	Scituate	will	19337
	Michael	1851	Hanson	will	19338
	Molly	1779	Bridgewater	grdn	19227
	Nahum	1873	Hanson	will	19339
	Nathaniel	1713	Scituate	admn	19340
	Nathaniel	1753	Hanover	admn	19341
	Nathaniel	1787	Pembroke	will	19343
	Nathaniel	1821	Pembroke	will	19344
	Nathaniel	1824	Hanover	admn	19342
	Nehemiah Jr	1756	Halifax	admn	19345
	Peleg	1798	Bridgewater	admn	19347
	Peleg	1806	Abington	admn	19346
	Peleg	1863	E. Bridgewater	will	19348
	Peleg H	1865	Lakeville	admn	19349
	Priscilla W	1871	Lakeville	admn	19350
	Resolved	1748	Plymouth	admn	19351
	Reuben	1770	Hanover	admn	19352
	Rhoda	1762	Scituate	grdn	19320
	Robert	1702/3	Scituate	will	19353
	Rogers	1805	Scituate	grdn	19355 a
	Rogers	1842	Scituate	admn	19354
	Sally	1811	Pembroke	grdn	19221
	Sally	1861	S. Scituate	grdn	19356 a
	Sally	1861	S. Scituate	will	19357
	Samuel	1769	Scituate	will	19364
	Samuel	1789	Scituate	admn	19365
	Samuel	1791	Hanover	admn	19362
	Samuel	1808	Pembroke	admn	19361
	Samuel	1828	Kingston	will	19358
	Samuel	1848	Scituate	admn	19366
	Samuel	1859	Hanover	admn	19363
	Samuel	1871	Duxbury	admn	19359
	Samuel	1876	Marshfield	will	19360
	Sarah	1779	Bridgewater	grdn	19227
	Sarah	1821	Pembroke	admn	19367
	Sarah	1844	Scituate	admn	19368
	Silas	1772	Scituate	admn	19369
	Silas	1773	Scituate	grdn	19370
	Silas	1829	Scituate	admn	19371
	Sophia	1880	Rochester	will	19372
	Stephen	1801	Scituate	admn	19373
	Stephen	1832	Scituate	will	19374
	Susanna	1713	Scituate	grdn	19375
	Sylva	1765	Pembroke	grdn	19299
	Sylvia C	1868	Duxbury	admn	19376
	Sylvina	1852	Hanover	grdn	19387
	Thomas	1732/3	Scituate	will	19378
	Thomas	1747	Scituate	grdn	19222
	Thomas	1838	Scituate	admn	19379
	Thomas	1877	Hanson	will	19377
	Thomas M	1849	S. Scituate	grdn	19380
	Timothy	1759	Pembroke	admn	19381
	Turner	1844	Hanover	will	19382
	William	1761	Scituate	admn	19384
	William	1792	Scituate	grdn	19312
	William	1855	S. Scituate	will	19385
	William	1873	Rochester	admn	19383
	William S	1852	Hanover	grdn	19387
	William V	1830	Bridgewater	admn	19386
	Zenas	1763	Scituate	grdn	19280
	Zenas	1781	Rochester	admn	19388
	Zenas	1811	Pembroke	grdn	19221
	Zilpha	1873	Hanover	admn	19389
STEVENS	Abigail	1797	Wareham	grdn	19437
	Abigail	1863	Rochester	admn	19390
	Abigail L	1832	Rochester	grdn	19442

SURNAME	FIRST NAME	YEAR	PLACE	CASE	DOCKET
STEVENS	Abraham L	1849	Hanson	will	19391
	Adeline L	1877	Brockton	grdn	19392
	Alvan	1797	Wareham	grdn	19437
	Alwilda Helen	1860	Scituate	grdn	19393
	Andrew	1733	Rochester	will	19394
	Ann	1881	Marshfield	will	19395
	Araminta D	1868	Pembroke	admn	19396
	Augusta C	1873	Abington	admn	19397
	Bela	1797	Wareham	grdn	19437
	Bethia	1822	Marshfield	will	19398
	Catherine	1880	Marshfield	will	19399
	Charles	1863	Marshfield	will	19400
	Clarissa W	1871	Pembroke	will	19401
	Deborah	1833	Hanson	will	19402
	Edward	1689/0	Marshfield	will	19403
	Edward	1756	Plymouth	will	19404
	Edward	1788	Plymouth	admn	19405
	Edward	1803	Pembroke	will	19406
	Edward	1813	Carver	admn	19407
	Edward	1819	Carver	grdn	19408
	Edward	1859	Hanson	admn	19409
	Eleazer	1785	Plymouth	admn	19410
	Elijah	1797	Wareham	admn	19411
	Eliza A	1861	Plymouth	grdn	19412
	Elizabeth	1806	Plymouth	will	19413
	Experience	1850	Hanson	grdn	19414 a
	Experience	1851	Hanson	will	19415
	Fitz Henry R	1880	Hingham	admn	19416
	George	1778	Middleboro	admn	19417
	George L	1873	N. Bridgewater	admn	19418
	Hannah	1785	Plymouth	grdn	19455
	Hannah	1802	Plymouth	admn	19419
	Henry T	1851	Pembroke	grdn	19420
	Herbert E	1877	Brockton	grdn	19392
	Hiram F	1851	Pembroke	grdn	19420
	Isaac	1716	Rochester	admn	19421
	Isaac	1798	Wareham	grdn	19422
	Isaac	1832	Rochester	grdn	19442
	Jane	1875	Plymouth	will	19423
	Jemima	1866	Pembroke	will	19424
	John	1787	Marshfield	admn	19425
	John	1808	Rochester	will	19429
	John	1823	Plymouth	will	19426
	John	1867	Plymouth	admn	19427
	John	1876	Rochester	will	19430
	John 2nd	1799	Rochester	admn	19428
	Joseph	1832	Rochester	grdn	19442
	Josephus	1836	Rochester	will	19431
	Josephus	1861	Middleboro	admn	19432
	Josiah	1793	Wareham	will	19433
	Josiah	1798	Wareham	grdn	19422
	Lemuel	1871	Plymouth	admn	19434
	Lucy	1839	Marshfield	grdn	19438
	Lucy	1850	Marshfield	admn	19435
	Lucy	1855	Marshfield	admn	19436
	Lucy M	1868	Marshfield	grdn	19453
	Luther	1797	Wareham	grdn	19437
	Lydia C	1839	Marshfield	grdn	19438
	Malinda	1832	Rochester	grdn	19442
	Mary	1860	Marshfield	admn	19439
	Merial	1880	S. Scituate	will	19440
	Micah	1831	Rochester	admn	19441
	Micah W	1832	Rochester	grdn	19442
	Nabby	1798	Wareham	grdn	19422
	Nathan	1839	Hanson	will	19443
	Nathan	1861	Hanson	admn	19445
	Nathan Jr	1843	Hanson	admn	19444
	Nathaniel	1754	Marshfield	admn	19446
	Nathaniel	1837	Marshfield	admn	19447
	Nettie A	1873	Abington	grdn	19448
	Oliver	1794	Marshfield	admn	19449

SURNAME	FIRST NAME	YEAR	PLACE	CASE	DOCKET
STEVENS	Paul	1798	Wareham	admn	19450
	Phebe	1860	Rochester	grdn	19451 a
	Ray	1839	Marshfield	grdn	19438
	Ray	1867	Marshfield	admn	19452
	Ray T	1868	Marshfield	grdn	19453
	Sarah	1785	Plymouth	grdn	19455
	Sarah T	1839	Marshfield	grdn	19438
	Silas	1797	Wareham	admn	19454
	Susanna	1785	Plymouth	grdn	19455
	Thomas G	1868	Pembroke	admn	19456
	Timothy	1794	Rochester	admn	19457
	William	1805	Marshfield	will	19458
	William	1830	Marshfield	admn	19459
	William	1860	Rochester	will	19460
	William Jr	1857	Plymouth	admn	19461
	Willie L	1873	Abington	grdn	19448
	Zacheus	1872	Plymouth	admn	19462
STEWARD	Benjamin	1765	Rochester	will	19463
	James	1727	Rochester	will	19464
	Sarah	1754	Rochester	will	19465
STILES	Thomas	1835	Middleboro	admn	19466
STILWELL	Elias C	1857	E. Bridgewater	admn	19467
	Elias H	1858	E. Bridgewater	grdn	19468
	Lizzie L	1858	E. Bridgewater	grdn	19468
STOCKBRIDGE	Alexander	1802	Scituate	grdn	19481
	Anna	1722	Scituate	grdn	19512
	Benjamin	1725	Scituate	will	19469
	Benjamin	1847	Hanover	admn	19470
	Charles	1701	Scituate	divi	19472
	Charles	1731	Hanover	will	19471
	Charles	1806	Scituate	admn	19473
	Charles	1807	Scituate	grdn	19474
	Charles S	1864	S. Scituate	grdn	19475
	Dama	1867	S. Scituate	will	19476
	David	1789	Hanover	will	19477
	David	1829	Scituate	grdn	19500
	David	1879	S. Scituate	will	19478
	Deborah	1722	Scituate	grdn	19512
	Deborah	1727	Scituate	admn	19479
	Eleanor S	1807	Scituate	grdn	19474
	Elizabeth B	1864	S. Scituate	grdn	19475
	Hannah	1788	Hanover	will	19480
	Hector	1802	Scituate	grdn	19481
	Hosea	1832	Scituate	will	19482
	Jacob	1851	S. Scituate	admn	19483
	James	1819	Scituate	will	19484
	James	1863	S. Scituate	admn	19485
	John	1763	Abington	grdn	19488
	John	1768	Pembroke	will	19487
	John	1839	Scituate	will	19486
	Joseph	1763	Abington	grdn	19488
	Joseph	1824	Scituate	admn	19489
	Joseph	1873	S. Scituate	admn	19490
	Joseph C	1860	Hanover	admn	19491
	Lebbeus	1855	Hanover	will	19492
	Lucy	1829	Scituate	grdn	19500
	Lucy	1843	Scituate	will	19493
	Lydia	1767	Scituate	grdn	19494
	Lydia	1768	Scituate	admn	19495
	Lydia L	1869	Hanover	will	19496
	Martha	1829	Scituate	grdn	19500
	Mary A	1864	S. Scituate	grdn	19475
	Mary S	1807	Scituate	grdn	19474
	Mercy	1731	Hanover	grdn	19497
	Mercy	1744	Scituate	will	19498
	Micah	1722	Scituate	grdn	19512
	Micha	1763	Abington	admn	19499
	Nancy	1829	Scituate	grdn	19500
	Sally	1829	Scituate	grdn	19500
	Samuel	1758	Scituate	will	19501
	Samuel	1784	Scituate	will	19502

SURNAME	FIRST NAME	YEAR	PLACE	CASE	DOCKET
STOCKBRIDGE	Samuel	1802	Scituate	will	19503
	Sarah	1722	Scituate	grdn	19512
	Sarah	1758	Hanover	will	19504
	Sarah	1763	Abington	grdn	19488
	Sarah	1786	Scituate	will	19505
	Sarah B	1871	Lakeville	admn	19506
	Stephen	1802	Scituate	admn	19507
	Susannah S	1869	S. Scituate	admn	19508
	Thomas	1718	Scituate	admn	19511
	Thomas	1722	Scituate	grdn	19512
	Thomas	1790	Scituate	will	19509
	Thomas Jr	1786	Scituate	admn	19510
	William	1841	Hanover	will	19513
STOCKS	John	1817	Bridgewater	admn	19514
STOCKWELL	Mary W	1880	Plymouth	admn	19515
	Otis	1877	Hingham	admn	19516
STODDARD	Adeline	1855	Abington	grdn	19517 a
	Albion F	1874	Hingham	grdn	19612
	Ashael	1822	Hingham	will	19518
	B Francis	1855	N. Bridgewater	grdn	19521
	Benjamin	1849	Hingham	admn	19519
	Benjamin G	1855	N. Bridgewater	admn	19520
	Caleb	1872	Hingham	will	19522
	Catherine	1804	Hingham	grdn	19590
	Charles	1838	Scituate	grdn	19523
	Charles A	1855	N. Bridgewater	grdn	19521
	Charles P	1871	N. Bridgewater	will	19524
	Christopher	1881	Plymouth	admn	19525
	Cyrus Jr	1852	S. Scituate	will	19526
	David	1830	Baltimore MD	will	19528
	David	1865	Hingham	will	19527
	Demerick	1828	Hingham	will	19529
	Demerick	1828	Hingham	grdn	19530
	Demerick	1840	Hingham	admn	19531
	Demerick	1841	Hingham	grdn	19532
	Desire	1850	Abington	will	19533
	Ebed	1836	Hingham	admn	19534
	Edwin C	1869	Scituate	grdn	19535
	Elijah	1838	Hingham	grdn	19545
	Elizabeth	1827	Scituate	admn	19536
	Elizabeth	1838	Hingham	grdn	19545
	Elizabeth F	1880	Plymouth	grdn	19579
	Elizabeth W	1855	N. Bridgewater	grdn	19521
	Emeline	1831	Hingham	grdn	19537
	Emma S	1855	N. Bridgewater	grdn	19521
	Emma S	1874	Brockton	admn	19538
	Enoch	1818	Hingham	admn	19539
	Esther S	1877	Hingham	admn	19540
	Frederick A	1868	Abington	grdn	19613
	Gridley	1810	Hingham	grdn	19541 a
	Gridley	1864	Hingham	will	19542
	Hannah	1873	Hanover	admn	19543
	Harriet L	1855	N. Bridgewater	grdn	19521
	Henrietta	1838	Hingham	grdn	19545
	Henry	1838	Hingham	grdn	19545
	Henry D W	1835	Hingham	will	19544
	Henry F	1831	Hingham	grdn	19537
	Henry F	1881	Plymouth	grdn	19546
	Hezekiah	1731	Scituate	will	19547
	Hezekiah	1739	Scituate	grdn	19548
	Hezekiah	1801	Scituate	will	19549
	Hezekiah	1817	Scituate	grdn	19550 a
	Hosea	1860	Hingham	will	19551
	Ichabod	1842	Hingham	admn	19552
	Ichabod	1864	Hull	admn	19553
	Isaiah	1811	Hingham	will	19554
	Jacob	1810	Hingham	admn	19555
	James E	1868	Abington	grdn	19613
	Jesse	1813	Hanover	grdn	19556
	John	1828	Hingham	admn	19557
	John F	1866	Hanover	admn	19560

SURNAME	FIRST NAME	YEAR	PLACE	CASE	DOCKET
STODDARD	John S	1864	N. Bridgewater	admn	19559
	John T	1853	Plymouth	grdn	19558
	Joshua	1815	Scituate	admn	19561
	Laban	1874	Hingham	admn	19562
	Leah	1827	Hingham	will	19563
	Levi	1824	Hingham	warr	19564
	Lizzie T	1874	Hingham	grdn	19612
	Lucy	1846	Hingham	admn	19565
	Lucy	1850	Pembroke	will	19566
	Luther	1856	S. Scituate	will	19567
	Lydia	1836	Hingham	will	19568
	Lydia	1851	Hingham	will	19569
	Lydia	1867	Hingham	admn	19570
	Martin	1878	Hingham	will	19571
	Mary	1838	Hingham	admn	19572
	Mary	1855	Hingham	will	19573
	Mary	1859	Hingham	will	19574
	Mary	1874	Hingham	will	19578
	Mary	1877	Hingham	admn	19577
	Mary C	1874	Hingham	grdn	19612
	Mary C	1880	Plymouth	grdn	19579
	Mary E	1867	Hingham	will	19575
	Mary E	1877	Hingham	grdn	19576 a
	Mary LeB	1881	Plymouth	grdn	19546
	Matilda B	1873	S. Scituate	will	19580
	Matthew	1876	Hingham	admn	19581
	Melzar	1832	Duxbury	admn	19582
	Nancy	1814	Hingham	admn	19583
	Nancy	1862	Hingham	will	19584
	Nathan	1855	Abington	admn	19585
	Obadiah	1799	Scituate	grdn	19586
	Obadiah	1832	Scituate	admn	19587
	Olive L	1876	Hingham	admn	19588
	Peggy	1846	Hingham	admn	19589
	Priscilla	1804	Hingham	grdn	19590
	Quincy	1813	Hanover	grdn	19556
	Rachel B	1841	Marshfield	admn	19591
	Rebecca	1804	Hingham	grdn	19590
	Reuben	1827	Hingham	admn	19592
	Robert T	1859	Hingham	will	19593
	Samuel	1762	Scituate	will	19594
	Samuel	1780	Dartmouth	grdn	19596
	Samuel	1838	Hingham	will	19597
	Samuel Jr	1869	Scituate	admn	19595
	Sarah	1838	Hingham	grdn	19545
	Seth	1809	Hingham	will	19599
	Seth	1831	Scituate	will	19598
	Seth	1845	Hingham	will	19600
	Seth	1861	Hingham	admn	19601
	Stephen	1832	Hingham	grdn	19603 a
	Stephen	1835	Hingham	admn	19602
	Stephen Jr	1833	Hingham	will	19604
	Susan	1838	Hingham	grdn	19545
	Susan	1847	Hingham	admn	19605
	Thomas	1838	Scituate	admn	19606
	Washington	1838	Hingham	grdn	19545
	Washington J	1864	Hingham	admn	19607
	William	1822	Hingham	grdn	19617
	William	1837	Scituate	grdn	19608
	William	1851	Hingham	grdn	19609 a
	William	1858	Hingham	admn	19610
	William A	1868	Abington	grdn	19613
	William M	1874	Hingham	grdn	19612
	William T	1874	Hingham	admn	19611
	Xoa	1846	Marshfield	will	19614
	Zenas	1821	Hingham	admn	19616
	Zenas	1822	Hingham	grdn	19617
	Zenas	1847	Hingham	admn	19615
STONE	Cyrus	1867	Scituate	admn	19618
	Ella Pratt	1877	Carver	adop	19619
	Sally	1833	Easton	peti	19620

SURNAME	FIRST NAME	YEAR	PLACE	CASE	DOCKET
STONE	Sarah P	1879	Carver	admn	19622
	Sarah Palmer	1877	Carver	adop	19621
STOUT	James	1757	Rochester	admn	19623
STOVER	Elizabeth	1722	Scituate	will	19624
STOWELL	Abigail	1865	Hingham	admn	19625
	Adam	1807	Hingham	will	19626
	Alice A	1864	Hingham	grdn	19627
	Hersey	1872	Hingham	will	19628
	Issachar	1813	Hingham	will	19629
	Jared	1880	Hingham	will	19630
	Lydia H	1816	Hingham	bond	19631
	Noah	1826	Hingham	grdn	19632 a
STOWERS	Seth	1811	Hingham	warr	19633
STRAFFIN	David	1843	Plymouth	admn	19634
	William	1806	Plymouth	admn	19635
STRAND	John	1873	N. Bridgewater	admn	19636
STRANGER	Charles H	1841	Kingston	grdn	19639
	Charles H	1853	Abington	admn	19637
	Charles H	1859	Abington	grdn	19638
	Edmund B	1875	Brockton	admn	19640
	Edward	1796	Plympton	admn	19641
	Edward F	1879	Plymouth	peti	19642
	Harriet A	1859	Abington	grdn	19638
	Mary A	1878	Plymouth	admn	19643
	Seth F	1841	Kingston	grdn	19639
STRETER	Joseph	1765	Middleboro	grdn	19644
STROBRIDGE	Anna	1792	Middleboro	grdn	19651
	Ebenezer	1841	Middleboro	admn	19645
	Elizabeth	1848	Middleboro	will	19646
	Harriet	1881	Middleboro	admn	19647
	Henry	1799	Middleboro	admn	19648
	Henry	1842	Middleboro	will	19649
	Robert	1790	Middleboro	admn	19650
	Robert	1792	Middleboro	grdn	19651
	Susan	1878	Lakeville	will	19652
	Susan C	1849	Middleboro	grdn	19653
	Susanna	1854	W. Bridgewater	will	19654
	Thomas H	1855	Lakeville	admn	19655
	William	1775	Middleboro	grdn	19656 a
	William	1778	Middleboro	will	19657
	William	1842	Middleboro	admn	19658
	William	1852	Middleboro	will	19659
STUART	Elisha	1757	Rochester	grdn	19660
	James	1811	Hingham	will	19661
	John	1750	Rochester	grdn	19662
	John	1757	Rochester	admn	19663
	John	1871	Plymouth	will	19664
	Joseph	1746	Rochester	admn	19665
	Parney C	1879	Wareham	admn	19666
	Seth	1757	Rochester	admn	19667
STUBS	James	1732	Kingston	will	19668
STUDLEY	Ammiel	1847	Scituate	admn	19669
	Andrew	1877	Rockland	admn	19670
	Arthur S	1878	S. Scituate	adop	19671
	Benjamin	1743	Scituate	will	19672
	Benjamin	1867	Hingham	admn	19673
	Benjamin F	1874	E. Bridgewater	admn	19674
	Benony	1747	Hanover	admn	19675
	Celia	1871	Scituate	will	19676
	Cordelia	1840	Scituate	grdn	19677
	David	1759	Scituate	will	19678
	David	1799	Scituate	will	19679
	David	1873	Hanover	will	19680
	David F	1873	N. Bridgewater	admn	19681
	Eliab	1785	Hanover	will	19682
	Elizabeth	1879	Bridgewater	will	19683
	Fred B	1880	Rockland	grdn	19694
	George D	1848	Hingham	grdn	19684
	George H	1880	Rockland	grdn	19694
	Gideon	1816	Hanover	admn	19685
	Gideon	1850	Hanover	admn	19686

SURNAME	FIRST NAME	YEAR	PLACE	CASE	DOCKET
STUDLEY	Hannah	1864	Hingham	admn	19687
	Hiram	1855	Hanover	admn	19688
	Howland L	1871	Scituate	will	19689
	James	1786	Scituate	admn	19690
	James B	1863	Hanover/Mobile	admn	19692
	James B	1873	Abington	admn	19693
	James G	1880	Rockland	grdn	19694
	James L	1840	Scituate	will	19691
	Jane	1873	Scituate	grdn	19695
	John	1844	Scituate	will	19696
	Joseph	1766	Hanover	admn	19697
	Joshua	1759	Hanover	admn	19698
	Joshua	1760	Hanover	grdn	19699
	Joshua	1848	Hanover	will	19700
	Lewis	1849	Scituate	will	19701
	Lucy	1766	Hanover	grdn	19702
	Lucy	1869	S. Scituate	will	19704
	Lucy	1873	Hanover	admn	19703
	Mary	1873	Scituate	grdn	19695
	Mary	1873	Scituate	admn	19705
	Nancy	1876	Hingham	will	19706
	Nathan	1850	Abington	admn	19707
	Olive	1813	Hanover	will	19708
	Olivia F	1878	Hingham	admn	19709
	Sarah	1806	Scituate	admn	19710
	Sarah	1847	Hanover	admn	19711
	Sarah E	1859	Hingham	admn	19712
	Solon N	1863	Scituate	will	19713
	Susan W	1846	Hingham	admn	19714
	William	1847	Scituate	admn	19715
	William	1868	S. Scituate	will	19716
STURGIS	Catherine G	1864	Hingham	admn	19717
	Elliot T	1866	Hingham	grdn	19718
	Fanny T	1866	Hingham	grdn	19718
STURTEVANT	Abigail	1842	N. Bridgewater	will	19719
	Amos	1810	Carver	admn	19720
	Anna	1774	Bridgewater	grdn	19721
	Bela	1844	Plympton	will	19722
	Betsey	1812	Middleboro	grdn	19723 a
	Betsey	1855	Plymouth	admn	19724
	Caleb	1793	Halifax	will	19725
	Caleb Jr	1793	Halifax	admn	19726
	Caroline M	1841	Middleboro	grdn	19735
	Charles	1816	Rochester	admn	19727
	Cornelius	1763	Plymouth	admn	19728
	Croade	1846	Middleboro	will	19729
	Daniel	1840	Halifax	admn	19730
	David	1771	Lakeville	admn	19732
	David	1806	Wareham	admn	19731
	David Jr	1765	Kingston	admn	19733
	Dependence	1803	Halifax	will	19734
	Eleanor C	1841	Middleboro	grdn	19735
	Elijah	1828	Kingston	admn	19736
	Eliphalet	1802	Worcester	grdn	19737
	Eliza	1843	Rochester	will	19738
	Fanny D	1846	Middleboro	will	19739
	George	1744	Plympton	grdn	19772
	George	1852	Middleboro	will	19740
	George	1865	Pembroke	admn	19741
	Hannah H	1878	Mattapoisett	admn	19742
	Heman	1819	Wareham	admn	19743
	Henry	1877	Kingston	admn	19744
	Irene L	1857	Halifax	grdn	19745
	Isaac	1750	Halifax	admn	19749
	Isaac	1753	Halifax	grdn	19750
	Isaac	1812	Carver	admn	19747
	Isaac	1875	Bridgewater	will	19746
	Isaac R	1856	Plympton	grdn	19748 a
	Jabez	1797	Halifax	admn	19751
	James	1756	Halifax	will	19752
	Jane	1832	Plymouth	admn	19753

SURNAME	FIRST NAME	YEAR	PLACE	CASE	DOCKET
STURTEVANT	Jesse	1753	Halifax	grdn	19750
	Jesse F	1773	Bridgewater	admn	19754
	John	1749	Plymouth	grdn	19756 a
	John	1759	Halifax	admn	19755
	John	1764	Plymouth	will	19757
	Joseph	1723	Plymouth	admn	19759
	Joseph	1808	Wareham	will	19758
	Joseph	1820	Plymouth	admn	19760
	Josiah	1774	Halifax	will	19761
	Josiah	1776	Halifax	admn	19762
	Josiah	1780	Halifax	abse	19763
	Josiah	1785	Halifax	admn	19764
	Judith et al	1811	Halifax	grdn	19765
	Lemuel	1782	Halifax	grdn	19767 a
	Lemuel	1832	Rochester	admn	19766
	Levi	1858	Pembroke	will	19768
	Lucinda	1843	Middleboro	admn	19769
	Lucy	1744	Plympton	grdn	19772
	Lucy	1840	Plymouth	admn	19770
	Lucy	1858	Plympton	will	19771
	Martha	1753	Halifax	grdn	19750
	Mary B	1863	Mattapoisett	admn	19773
	Mercy	1868	Halifax	will	19774
	Nathaniel	1753	Halifax	grdn	19750
	Nathaniel	1773	Halifax	admn	19775
	Nehemiah	1744	Plymouth	will	19777
	Nehemiah	1802	Plympton	grdn	19776 a
	Otis	1811	Rochester	admn	19778
	Peleg S	1866	Pembroke	grdn	19779
	Priscilla	1839	Halifax	will	19780
	Rebecca	1819	Plymouth	grdn	19812
	Robert	1800	Middleboro	admn	19781
	Rowland	1804	Wareham	will	19782
	Ruth	1831	Halifax	will	19783
	Samuel	1736	Halifax	will	19784
	Samuel	1743	Halifax	will	19785
	Samuel	1753	Halifax	grdn	19750
	Samuel	1777	Halifax	admn	19786
	Samuel	1876	Mattapoisett	admn	19788
	Samuel S	1839	Halifax	will	19787
	Sarah	1819	Plymouth	grdn	19812
	Sarah	1822	Rochester	grdn	19791
	Sarah	1833	Plymouth	admn	19789
	Sarah	1837	Duxbury	grdn	19790 a
	Sarah	1839	Middleboro	will	19792
	Sarah S	1854	Halifax	will	19793
	Seth	1856	Wareham	will	19794
	Seth	1856	Wareham	grdn	19795
	Seth Jr	1863	Wareham	admn	19796
	Simeon	1753	Halifax	grdn	19750
	Simeon	1822	Halifax	admn	19797
	Simeon	1851	Halifax	will	19798
	Simeon	1874	Halifax	admn	19799
	Sophia	1872	Plympton	will	19800
	Stafford	1869	Halifax	will	19801
	Thomas	1837	Middleboro	will	19804
	Thomas	1874	Halifax	admn	19802
	Thomas C	1859	E. Bridgewater	admn	19805
	Thomas Jr	1827	Middleboro	admn	19803
	William	1753	Halifax	will	19806
	William	1783	Halifax	admn	19807
	William	1803	Sumner	grdn	19808
	William	1809	Carver	admn	19809
	William	1816	Rochester	grdn	19810
	William	1819	Plymouth	will	19811
	William	1819	Plymouth	grdn	19812
	Zerviah	1774	Halifax	grdn	19813
SULLIVAN	Ann	1859	Ottawa IL	admn	19814
	James	1866	N. Bridgewater	grdn	19815
	Jerry	1852	Middleboro	grdn	19816
	Johannah	1871	Abington	grdn	19817

SURNAME	FIRST NAME	YEAR	PLACE	CASE	DOCKET
SULLIVAN	John	1859	Abington	admn	19819
	John D	1837	Wareham	admn	19818
	John M	1860	N. Bridgewater	grdn	19820
	Joseph S	1860	N. Bridgewater	grdn	19820
	Joseph S	1878	Brockton	admn	19821
	Mark	1864	Wareham	grdn	19822
	Michael	1879	Rockland	admn	19823
	Owen	1860	N. Bridgewater	will	19824
	Thomas	1865	Abington	admn	19825
SUMMERS	Elizabeth	1732	Rochester	grdn	19827
	John	1721	Rochester	admn	19826
	Sarah	1732	Rochester	grdn	19827
SUMNER	Cloe A	1877	Brockton	admn	19828
SUPPLE	Edward	1872	Scituate	admn	19829
SUTTON	Abigail	1713	Scituate	grdn	19837
	Abner	1814	Hanover	grdn	19838
	Abner	1820	Scituate	grdn	19830
	Anna	1713	Scituate	grdn	19837
	Catherine	1855	N. Bridgewater	will	19831
	Jesse	1799	Scituate	will	19832
	Joan	1873	Scituate	admn	19833
	John	1691/2	Scituate	will	19836
	John	1713	Scituate	admn	19834
	John	1713	Scituate	grdn	19837
	John	1784	Scituate	will	19835
	Loring	1814	Hanover	grdn	19838
	Lydia	1798	Plymouth	admn	19839
	Nathan	1693	Scituate	grdn	19842
	Nathan	1710	Scituate	admn	19840
	Nathan	1713	Scituate	grdn	19837
	Nathan	1745	Scituate	admn	19841
	Nathaniel	1693	Scituate	grdn	19842
	Nathaniel	1743	Scituate	will	19843
	Ray	1737	Scituate	admn	19844
	Reuben	1814	Hanover	grdn	19838
	Seth	1713	Scituate	grdn	19837
	Seth	1837	Scituate	grdn	19845 a
SWAIN	Charles	1806	Hull	will	19846
SWAN	Samuel	1868	N. Bridgewater	will	19847
	William G	1873	Abington	admn	19848
SWANSTROM	Frederick W	1877	Brockton	grdn	19849
SWEENEY	Edward	1869	Bridgewater	will	19850
SWEETLOVE	Eliza	1881	W. Bridgewater	admn	19851
SWEETSER	Susan E	1875	Brockton	admn	19852
SWIFT	Abby A	1851	Plymouth	grdn	19873
	Ann	1744	Sandwich	grdn	19853
	Asa	1833	Wareham	will	19855
	Asa 2nd	1816	Wareham	will	19854
	Asa R	1855	Rochester	admn	19856
	Barnabas E	1851	Plymouth	grdn	19873
	Bartlett D	1832	Plymouth	grdn	19883
	Benjamin	1816	Wareham	admn	19857
	Benjamin	1831	Rochester	admn	19859
	Benjamin 2nd	1825	Wareham	admn	19858
	Betty	1825	Wareham	will	19860
	Calvin D	1851	Plymouth	grdn	19873
	Charles G	1839	Wareham	admn	19861
	Chloe	1877	Wareham	will	19862
	Cynthia	1799	Wareham	grdn	19893
	David	1851	Wareham	will	19863
	Deborah T	1832	Plymouth	grdn	19883
	Drusilla	1850	Plymouth	grdn	19864
	Edward D	1864	Duxbury	admn	19865
	Eldora S	1855	Plymouth	grdn	19877
	Elihu B	1878	Plymouth	will	19866
	Elisha	1804	Wareham	will	19867
	Elisha	1859	Plymouth	admn	19869
	Elisha	1871	Wareham	will	19868
	Ellis F	1851	Plymouth	grdn	19873
	Ephraim	1855	Wareham	admn	19870
	Ezra	1850	Wareham	admn	19871

SURNAME	FIRST NAME	YEAR	PLACE	CASE	DOCKET	
SWIFT	Ezra	1850	Plymouth	will	19872	
	Ezra J	1851	Plymouth	grdn	19873	
	Gerard B	1877	Wareham	grdn	19874	
	Hallett	1835	Wareham	admn	19875	
	Harriet	1855	Plymouth	grdn	19877	
	Harriet N	1835	Wareham	grdn	19876	
	Harrison G	1831	Plymouth	grdn	19881	
	Henry	1868	Plymouth	admn	19878	
	Henry W	1879	Duxbury	admn	19879	
	Isaac	1846	Bridgewater	will	19880	
	Isaac S	1831	Plymouth	grdn	19881	
	Jabez	1825	Plymouth	admn	19882	
	Jabez G	1832	Plymouth	grdn	19883	
	Jacob	1818	Plymouth	will	19884	
	Jacob	1854	Plymouth	admn	19885	
	Jacob	1865	Rochester	admn	19886	
	James	1832	Rochester	grdn	19887	a
	James	1833	Rochester	will	19888	
	James R	1863	Wareham	admn	19889	
	Jeroboam	1837	Plymouth	admn	19890	
	Jesse	1795	Wareham	admn	19892	
	Jesse	1799	Wareham	grdn	19893	
	Jesse	1805	Wareham	will	19891	
	Jirah	1749	Wareham	will	19894	
	Joanna	1851	Plymouth	grdn	19873	
	John	1836	Plymouth	will	19896	
	John	1854	Plymouth	admn	19897	
	John 3rd	1832	Plymouth	admn	19895	
	John Q A	1865	Wareham	grdn	19898	a
	John Q A	1866	Wareham	will	19899	
	Joseph	1830	Middleboro	will	19900	
	Joshua	1777	Plymouth	will	19901	
	Joshua	1860	Plymouth	will	19902	
	Josiah	1803	Wareham	will	19903	
	Josiah M	1865	Plymouth	admn	19904	
	Julian W	1868	Wareham	grdn	19905	
	Keziah	1744	Sandwich	grdn	19853	
	Lemuel	1822	Wareham	admn	19906	
	Lemuel	1849	Rochester	admn	19907	
	Lucy	1861	Middleboro	admn	19908	
	Lucy M	1880	Brockton	grdn	19909	
	Martin	1799	Wareham	grdn	19893	
	Martin	1854	Bridgewater	admn	19910	
	Mary	1861	Wareham	will	19911	
	Mary	1870	Wareham	admn	19912	
	Mary	1878	Brockton	admn	19913	
	Mehitable	1852	Rochester	will	19914	
	Melvin	1874	Bridgewater	admn	19915	
	Mercy	1878	Duxbury	will	19916	
	Micah	1820	Wareham	admn	19917	
	Minnie G	1876	Bridgewater	grdn	19918	
	Nancy	1851	Plymouth	grdn	19873	
	Nathan	1851	Plymouth	grdn	19873	
	Obed	1865	Wareham	will	19919	
	Patty	1799	Wareham	grdn	19893	
	Peleg	1811	Rochester	admn	19920	
	Phineas	1793	Plymouth	admn	19921	
	Phineas	1830	Plymouth	admn	19922	
	Reuben B	1863	Marion	admn	19923	
	Reuel	1864	Bridgewater	will	19924	
	Ruth	1853	Plymouth	admn	19925	
	Sadie M	1876	Plymouth	adop	19926	
	Samuel	1870	Wareham	will	19927	
	Sarah	1817	Sandwich	grdn	19930	
	Sarah	1873	Plymouth	admn	19928	
	Sarah H	1866	Plymouth	grdn	19929	
	Silas	1812	Wareham	admn	19931	
	Stephen	1873	Wareham	will	19932	
	Sylvia	1859	Wareham	will	19933	
	Thomas	1795	Rochester	will	19934	
	Thomas	1842	Plymouth	will	19935	

SURNAME	FIRST NAME	YEAR	PLACE	CASE	DOCKET
SWIFT	Timothy	1876	Wareham	admn	19936
	Walton Jr	1874	Wareham	admn	19937
	Willard	1813	Rochester	admn	19938
	William	1822	Wareham	admn	19939
	William	1839	Bridgewater	will	19940
	William 2nd	1843	Plymouth	admn	19941
	William H	1865	Plymouth	admn	19942
SYLVESTER	Abbie S	1873	Bridgewater	admn	19943
	Abner	1832	Plymouth	admn	19944
	Algernon S	1849	N. Bridgewater	grdn	19945 a
	Algernon S	1868	N. Bridgewater	will	19946
	Amos	1753	Hanover	will	19947
	Belcher	1849	Hanover	will	19948
	Benjamin	1760	Hanover	will	19949
	Bethiah	1787	Scituate	grdn	19950
	Caroline	1863	N. Bridgewater	grdn	19951
	Carrie H	1880	Brockton	grdn	19952
	Charles F	1861	Scituate	grdn	19953
	Chester H	1861	Scituate	grdn	19953
	Deborah	1802	Marshfield	will	19954
	Delilah	1808	Scituate	admn	19955
	Edmund	1784	Hanover	admn	19956
	Edna	1841	Scituate	will	19957
	Elijah	1781	Hanover	grdn	19959
	Elijah	1852	Hanover	admn	19958
	Elisha	1767	Scituate	will	19960
	Elisha	1807	Scituate	will	19961
	Elizabeth	1754	Hanover	grdn	19962 a
	Elizabeth	1762	Hanover	admn	19963
	Emma A	1861	Scituate	grdn	19953
	Eunice	1787	Scituate	admn	19964
	Frederick	1879	Brockton	will	19965
	Fruitfull	1839	Scituate	will	19966
	Grace	1717	Duxbury	grdn	19976
	Hannah	1754	Plymouth	will	19991
	Hannah	1858	S. Scituate	admn	19967
	Henchman	1758	Hanover	admn	19968
	Hitti	1861	S. Scituate	admn	19969
	Israel	1716/7	Duxbury	admn	19975
	Israel	1717	Duxbury	grdn	19976
	Israel	1727	Scituate	will	19970
	Israel	1788	Duxbury	will	19974
	Israel	1812	Scituate	admn	19973
	Israel Jr	1800	Scituate	admn	19971
	Israel Jr	1801	Scituate	will	19972
	Jacob	1806	Hanover	will	19977
	James	1781	Scituate	admn	19978
	John	1706	Marshfield	will	19979
	John	1762	Marshfield	will	19980
	John	1764	Plymouth	grdn	19993
	John	1765	Marshfield	admn	19981
	John H	1845	Hull	admn	19982
	John Jr	1853	Plymouth	admn	19983
	Joseph	1690/1	Scituate	will	19986
	Joseph	1744	Marshfield	admn	19984
	Joseph	1744	Marshfield	grdn	19985
	Joseph	1754	Plymouth	will	19991
	Joseph	1764	Plymouth	admn	19992
	Joseph	1764	Plymouth	grdn	19993
	Joseph	1771	Scituate	will	19987
	Joseph	1800	Halifax	admn	19988
	Joseph	1867	Hanover	admn	19989
	Joseph Jr	1724	Plymouth	admn	19990
	Josiah	1840	Plymouth	admn	19994
	Jotham	1852	S. Scituate	will	19995
	Juletta	1843	Hanover	will	19996
	Julia A	1862	Hanover	adop	19997
	Lillis	1812	Scituate	will	19998
	Loammi B	1862	Hanover	admn	19999
	Louisa C	1879	Scituate	will	20000
	Lucretia	1744	Marshfield	grdn	19985

SURNAME	FIRST NAME	YEAR	PLACE	CASE	DOCKET
SYLVESTER	Lucretia	1746	Marshfield	will	20001
	Lucy	1845	N. Bridgewater	admn	20002
	Lucy B	1809	Hanover	grdn	20018
	Luther	1855	Marshfield	will	20003
	Mary	1715	Scituate	admn	20004
	Mary	1774	Scituate	grdn	20005 a
	Mary	1868	Hanover	admn	20006
	Matthew	1818	Pembroke	admn	20007
	Mercy T	1880	Halifax	admn	20008
	Michael	1798	Hanover	will	20009
	Michael	1802	Hanover	will	20010
	Michael	1809	Hanover	grdn	20018
	Nathaniel	1754	Plymouth	grdn	20011
	Nathaniel	1781	Hanover	will	20012
	Nathaniel	1841	Halifax	admn	20013
	Rebecca	1809	Hanover	grdn	20018
	Reuben	1850	Halifax	will	20014
	Rhoda	1860	S. Scituate	will	20015
	Richard	1768	Scituate	will	20016
	Robert	1807	Hanover	admn	20017
	Robert	1809	Hanover	grdn	20018
	Ruth	1717	Duxbury	grdn	19976
	Ruth	1729	Duxbury	admn	20019
	Saba	1876	Halifax	admn	20020
	Samuel	1734	Marshfield	admn	20021
	Sarah	1764	Plymouth	grdn	19993
	Sarah	1781	Hanover	grdn	19959
	Sarah	1864	Plymouth	will	20022
	Sarah E	1809	Hanover	grdn	20018
	Solomon	1754	Plymouth	admn	20023
	Solon	1815	Scituate	will	20024
	Thomas	1760	Hanover	admn	20025
	Thomas	1827	Scituate	admn	20026
	Thomas	1832	Scituate	admn	20027
	Timothy	1779	Marshfield	admn	20028
	Warren	1828	Scituate	will	20029
	Zebulon	1766	Scituate	will	20030
SYMMES	Elizabeth	1792	Plymouth	grdn	20034
	Isaac	1791	Plymouth	admn	20031
	Lazarus	1792	Plymouth	grdn	20034
	Margaret	1792	Plymouth	grdn	20034
	Mary	1859	Plymouth	admn	20032
	Nancy H	1792	Plymouth	grdn	20034
	Nancy H	1858	Plymouth	will	20033
	Nathaniel	1771	Abington	will	20035
	Sarah	1792	Plymouth	grdn	20034
	Timothy	1767	Scituate	will	20036
	Zachariah P	1792	Plymouth	grdn	20034
TABER	Adeline S	1877	Mattapoisett	grdn	20037
	Admiral	1815	Wareham	admn	20038
	Admiral D	1878	Carver	admn	20039
	Barton	1866	Mattapoisett	will	20040
	Joseph R	1804	New Bedford	grdn	20041
	Joseph R	1852	Rochester	will	20042
	Laura A	1873	Mattapoisett	admn	20043
	Mercy A B	1867	Wareham	admn	20044
	Sarah	1856	Wareham	admn	20045
	William R	1865	Wareham	grdn	20046
TALBOT	Agnes	1877	S. Scituate	admn	20047
	Jacob	1864	W. Bridgewater	grdn	20048
	Willard E	1879	Exeter NH	will	20049
TAMAR	Nancy	1867	Pembroke	admn	20050
TANTACHEE	Moses	1705	Scituate	admn	20051
TAPP	Mary	1865	Hingham	admn	20052
TAPPAN	Aurelia	1846	Rochester	admn	20053
TARROW	Will	1698	Plymouth	admn	20054 i
TAYLOR	Abigail	1842	Pembroke	will	20055
	Abigail W	1838	Rochester	grdn	20069
	Abner S	1806	Plymouth	grdn	20074
	Allen C	1851	Pembroke	admn	20056
	Almira T	1853	Marshfield	will	20057

SURNAME	FIRST NAME	YEAR	PLACE	CASE	DOCKET
TAYLOR	Andrew	1872	Plymouth	admn	20058
	Archippus	1802	Pembroke	admn	20059
	Asa	1841	Pembroke	will	20060
	Asa	1862	Abington	admn	20061
	Benjamin	1867	Rochester	admn	20062
	Benjamin A	1867	Rochester	grdn	20063
	Caleb	1834	Pembroke	will	20064
	Charles S	1867	Rochester	grdn	20063
	Ebenezer	1765	Marshfield	will	20065
	Edward	1806	Plymouth	admn	20066
	Eliza J	1838	Rochester	grdn	20069
	Elizeus	1781	Pembroke	admn	20067
	Henry	1835	Rochester	admn	20068
	Henry	1838	Rochester	grdn	20069
	Horace	1861	Marshfield	admn	20070
	Ichabod	1852	Pembroke	will	20071
	Irene A	1864	Pembroke	grdn	20084
	Isaac	1767	Pembroke	will	20072
	Jacob	1806	Plymouth	grdn	20074
	James	1872	Scituate	admn	20073
	Jane	1806	Plymouth	grdn	20074
	Jennet	1816	Baltimore	grdn	20095
	John	1840	Duxbury	admn	20075
	John S	1835	Scituate	grdn	20076
	Joseph	1727	Marshfield	will	20078
	Joseph	1737	Barnstable	admn	20079
	Joseph	1810	Pembroke	grdn	20077
	Julia A	1864	Pembroke	admn	20080
	Lavinia	1872	Plympton	will	20081
	Lewis	1879	Marshfield	admn	20082
	Lucena H	1859	Pembroke	will	20083
	Lucia J	1864	Pembroke	grdn	20084
	Lucy C	1880	Mattapoisett	admn	20085
	Luella A	1864	Pembroke	grdn	20084
	Lydia B	1838	Rochester	grdn	20069
	Lydia F	1880	Marshfield	will	20086
	Mary E	1806	Plymouth	grdn	20074
	Samuel	1788	Pembroke	will	20087
	Sarah P	1838	Rochester	grdn	20069
	Simeon	1863	W. Bridgewater	admn	20088
	Susan F	1858	Bridgewater	admn	20089
	Sylvia S	1880	Marshfield	admn	20090
	Timothy	1810	Pembroke	grdn	20091 a
	William	1717/8	Scituate	will	20092
	William	1816	Baltimore	grdn	20095
	William	1838	Rochester	grdn	20069
	William	1850	Pembroke	will	20093
	William	1876	Providence RI	admn	20094
	William B	1835	Scituate	grdn	20076
	Willis	1868	Pembroke	will	20096
TEBBETS	John S	1864	Kingston	grdn	20097
THARP	Joseph	1727	Rochester	grdn	20098
THATCHER	Huldah	1836	Rochester	will	20099
	John	1871	Middleboro	will	20100
	Josiah	1799	Kingston	admn	20101
	Lot	1833	Rochester	will	20102
	Mary	1771	Middleboro	will	20103
	Oxenbridge	1756	Middleboro	will	20104
	Peter	1744	Middleboro	will	20105
	Rowland	1775	Wareham	will	20106
	Rufus L	1868	N. Bridgewater	will	20107
	Samuel G	1874	Hanson	grdn	20108 a
	Thomas	1744	Middleboro	admn	20109
THAXTER	Abigail	1774	Bridgewater	grdn	20160
	Abigail	1807	Hingham	will	20110
	Abigail S	1812	Abington	grdn	20154
	Anna Q	1840	Hingham	grdn	20113
	Anna Q	1873	Hingham	grdn	20112 a
	Anna Q	1878	Hingham	will	20111
	Bela	1874	Abington	will	20114
	Benjamin	1805	Hingham	will	20115

SURNAME	FIRST NAME	YEAR	PLACE	CASE	DOCKET
THAXTER	Benjamin L	1812	Abington	grdn	20154
	Benjamin L	1833	Abington	admn	20116
	Caleb	1829	Hingham	will	20117
	Catherine K	1870	Hingham	will	20118
	Celia	1829	Hingham	will	20119
	David	1878	Hingham	admn	20120
	Deborah	1812	Abington	grdn	20154
	Duncan McB	1822	Hingham	will	20121
	Edward	1841	Hingham	will	20122
	Edward T	1840	Hingham	grdn	20113
	Eliza A	1869	Hingham	will	20123
	Elizabeth	1824	Hingham	will	20124
	Elizabeth C	1812	Abington	grdn	20154
	Ellen O	1876	Hingham	will	20125
	Emma E	1879	Abington	admn	20126
	Emma E	1879	Abington	grdn	20127
	Ezekiel	1774	Bridgewater	grdn	20160
	Ezekiel	1856	Abington	will	20128
	Gridley	1774	Bridgewater	grdn	20160
	Gridley	1845	Abington	admn	20129
	Gridley	1869	Abington	will	20130
	Hannah	1808	Hingham	admn	20131
	Harriet	1875	Hingham	grdn	20132 a
	Harriet	1880	Hingham	will	20133
	Henry	1774	Bridgewater	grdn	20160
	Henry	1833	Hingham	will	20134
	Henry	1846	Hingham	will	20135
	Henry	1872	Hingham	will	20136
	Jacob	1816	Hingham	will	20137
	James	1825	Hingham	will	20138
	Jane	1836	Hingham	will	20139
	John	1825	Scituate	admn	20140
	John Q	1864	Hingham	will	20141
	Joseph	1808	Hingham	will	20142
	Joseph B	1863	Hingham	will	20143
	Levi	1880	Hingham	admn	20144
	Lucy B	1873	Hingham	will	20145
	Marshall	1774	Bridgewater	grdn	20160
	Mary	1825	Abington	admn	20146
	N Quincy	1873	Hingham	admn	20147
	Quincy	1837	Hingham	will	20148
	Samuel	1745	Hingham	warr	20149
	Samuel	1771	Hingham	will	20150
	Samuel B	1879	Abington	will	20151
	Sarah	1812	Abington	grdn	20154
	Sarah A	1845	Abington	grdn	20152
	Sarah E	1860	Abington	admn	20153
	Seth	1827	Hingham	admn	20155
	Susan B	1840	Hingham	grdn	20113
	Susanna	1810	Hingham	will	20156
	Thomas	1813	Hingham	will	20157
	Thomas	1839	Hingham	will	20158
	William	1774	Bridgewater	grdn	20160
	William R	1846	Hingham	grdn	20159
THAYER	Abigail	1842	W. Bridgewater	will	20161
	Abijah	1805	Bridgewater	admn	20162
	Adeline N	1879	Brockton	admn	20163
	Alexander	1862	N. Bridgewater	admn	20164
	Ann	1877	W. Bridgewater	admn	20165
	Charles	1806	Bridgewater	grdn	20203
	Charles W	1867	N. Bridgewater	grdn	20166
	Charles W	1870	N. Bridgewater	grdn	20167
	Cyrus	1858	Abington	admn	20168
	David	1795	Bridgewater	will	20169
	E Loring	1876	Brockton	admn	20174
	Earl	1861	W. Bridgewater	admn	20170
	Edwin S	1881	Pembroke	admn	20171
	Elijah	1816	Hingham	grdn	20189
	Eliphalet	1806	Bridgewater	grdn	20203
	Eliphalet	1862	N. Bridgewater	will	20172
	Ellis P	1839	N. Bridgewater	grdn	20173

SURNAME	FIRST NAME	YEAR	PLACE	CASE	DOCKET
THAYER	Enos	1806	Bridgewater	grdn	20203
	Enos	1822	N. Bridgewater	will	20175
	Enos	1865	N. Bridgewater	will	20176
	Experience	1762	Abington	grdn	20211
	Experience	1763	Abington	grdn	20177 a
	Experience	1776	Abington	will	20178
	Francis P	1868	Middleboro	grdn	20179
	Hannah	1806	Bridgewater	grdn	20203
	Hannah	1812	Bridgewater	admn	20180
	Hannah W	1878	Hingham	grdn	20181 a
	Hannah W	1879	Hingham	will	20182
	Harriet	1877	Brockton	grdn	20183 a
	Hiram Jr	1871	N. Bridgewater	grdn	20184
	Huldah E	1851	W. Bridgewater	admn	20185
	Jacob	1762	Abington	grdn	20211
	Jairus	1858	Hingham	will	20186
	Jeremiah	1877	W. Bridgewater	will	20187
	Joshua	1816	Hingham	grdn	20189
	Joshua	1874	Hingham	will	20188
	Leavitt	1839	W. Bridgewater	admn	20190
	Mary J	1876	Hanover	will	20191
	Mehitable	1869	N. Bridgewater	admn	20192
	Micha	1806	Bridgewater	grdn	20203
	Randal	1822	Hingham	will	20193
	Randal	1844	Hingham	will	20194
	Richard	1845	W. Bridgewater	will	20195
	Richard	1877	W. Bridgewater	will	20196
	Richmond	1853	N. Bridgewater	grdn	20197
	Sally	1852	N. Bridgewater	admn	20198
	Samuel	1762	Abington	grdn	20211
	Samuel	1806	Bridgewater	grdn	20203
	Samuel	1837	N. Bridgewater	admn	20199
	Sarah	1840	W. Bridgewater	will	20200
	Seth	1798	Bridgewater	will	20201
	Seth	1806	Bridgewater	admn	20202
	Seth	1806	Bridgewater	grdn	20203
	Solomon	1794	Quincy	admn	20204
	Stephen	1855	Abington	will	20205
	Thankful	1813	Bridgewater	will	20206
	Thankful	1813	Bridgewater	will	20207
	Timothy	1752	Abington	will	20209
	Timothy	1761	Abington	admn	20210
	Timothy	1762	Abington	grdn	20211
	Timothy	1815	Hingham	admn	20208
	Zacheriah	1806	Bridgewater	grdn	20203
	Zeba	1806	Bridgewater	grdn	20203
THOMAS	Abiah	1762	Marshfield	grdn	20318
	Abigail	1731	Pembroke	grdn	20342
	Abigail	1802	Marshfield	will	20212
	Abigail	1840	Marshfield	admn	20213
	Abigail	1848	Rochester	admn	20214
	Abigail C	1867	Hanson	admn	20215
	Abijah	1801	Marshfield	admn	20216
	Abraham	1848	Middleboro	admn	20217
	Adoniram	1864	Middleboro	admn	20218
	Adoniram	1869	Plymouth	admn	20219
	Agnes L	1875	Middleboro	grdn	20468
	Alanson	1878	Plymouth	admn	20220
	Albert W	1873	Middleboro	grdn	20221
	Alden	1852	Marshfield	will	20222
	Alice	1742	Marshfield	grdn	20431
	Amos	1860	Middleboro	will	20223
	Amos R	1854	Middleboro	admn	20224
	Andrew	1772	Middleboro	grdn	20380
	Andrew	1853	Middleboro	admn	20225
	Andrew E	1857	Middleboro	grdn	20227
	Andrew E	1863	Middleboro	admn	20226
	Anna	1733	Plymouth	will	20228
	Anna	1823	Plymouth	admn	20229
	Anne	1821	Pembroke	will	20230
	Annie S	1869	Plymouth	grdn	20231

SURNAME	FIRST NAME	YEAR	PLACE	CASE	DOCKET
THOMAS	Anson H	1851	Middleboro	grdn	20281
	Anthony	1781	Marshfield	admn	20232
	Anthony	1848	Marshfield	will	20233
	Arthur P	1861	Marshfield	grdn	20234
	Asa	1810	Marshfield	will	20235
	Asa	1867	Plymouth	will	20237
	Asa Jr	1855	Plymouth	admn	20236
	Augusta	1878	Kingston	will	20238
	Averick	1842	Pembroke	will	20239
	Azel	1821	Middleboro	admn	20240
	Azel	1844	Middleboro	admn	20241
	Bartlett	1871	Middleboro	admn	20242
	Barzillai	1814	Middleboro	admn	20243
	Benjamin	1733	Middleboro	grdn	20254
	Benjamin	1759	Marshfield	will	20244
	Benjamin	1765	Marshfield	grdn	20245
	Benjamin	1800	Middleboro	will	20251
	Benjamin	1805	Middleboro	admn	20252
	Benjamin	1805	Middleboro	grdn	20253
	Benjamin	1848	Hingham	admn	20246
	Benjamin	1854	Hingham	admn	20247
	Benjamin	1874	Middleboro	will	20249
	Benjamin	1875	Pembroke	admn	20248
	Benjamin F	1865	Middleboro	will	20250
	Benjamin L	1879	Plymouth	grdn	20366
	Benjamin S	1789	Middleboro	grdn	20273
	Betsey F	1856	Marshfield	admn	20255
	Betsey M	1876	Middleboro	admn	20256
	Betty	1734	Middleboro	grdn	20257
	Bourne	1844	Marshfield	will	20258
	Briggs	1814	Duxbury	grdn	20443
	Briggs	1833	Marshfield	will	20259
	Briggs	1878	Duxbury	will	20260
	Caleb	1818	Middleboro	admn	20261
	Caleb	1879	Marshfield	will	20262
	Celia	1868	Hanson	admn	20263
	Cephas	1823	Middleboro	admn	20264
	Charles	1814	Duxbury	grdn	20443
	Charles	1848	Hanover	will	20265
	Charles	1848	Marshfield	will	20266
	Charles B	1865	Plympton	grdn	20451
	Charles H	1875	Middleboro	admn	20267
	Churchill	1810	Middleboro	admn	20268
	Clarissa C	1839	Plympton	grdn	20484
	Clinton	1864	Middleboro/Hali	grdn	20269
	Daniel	1789	Middleboro	admn	20272
	Daniel	1789	Middleboro	grdn	20273
	Daniel	1812	Middleboro	admn	20271
	Daniel	1847	Abington	will	20270
	David	1689	Middleboro	admn	20274
	David	1733	Middleboro	will	20275
	David	1742	Middleboro	will	20276
	David	1825	Middleboro	admn	20277
	David	1869	Hingham	admn	20278
	Deborah	1824	Carver	grdn	20282
	Deborah	1874	Middleboro	admn	20280
	Deborah L	1851	Middleboro	grdn	20281
	Deborah S	1865	Middleboro	will	20279
	Ebenezer	1771	Middleboro	will	20283
	Ebenezer S	1846	Pembroke	grdn	20284 a
	Edward	1726	Middleboro	will	20285
	Edward	1731	Pembroke	grdn	20342
	Edward	1757	Middleboro	will	20286
	Edward	1803	Pembroke	will	20289
	Edward	1844	Middleboro	admn	20287
	Edward	1857	Hanson	admn	20290
	Edward Maloy	1875	Middleboro	adop	20288
	Edwin	1832	Rochester	grdn	20331
	Eleazer	1733	Middleboro	grdn	20254
	Eleazer	1826	Middleboro	will	20291
	Eleazer	1868	Middleboro	grdn	20292 a

SURNAME	FIRST NAME	YEAR	PLACE	CASE	DOCKET
THOMAS	Eleazer	1869	Middleboro	admn	20293
	Eli	1806	Carver	admn	20294
	Eli	1824	Carver	admn	20295
	Elias	1789	Middleboro	grdn	20273
	Elias	1856	Plymouth	will	20297
	Elias Jr	1855	Plymouth	admn	20296
	Elihu	1879	Hanson	admn	20298
	Elijah	1829	Middleboro	admn	20299
	Eliphalet	1788	Middleboro	admn	20300
	Eliphalet	1876	Middleboro	will	20301
	Elisha	1814	Middleboro	admn	20302
	Ella F	1880	Middleboro	admn	20303
	Enoch	1789	Middleboro	grdn	20273
	Ephraim	1734	Middleboro	grdn	20304
	Ephraim	1828	Middleboro	admn	20305
	Eunice	1874	Middleboro	will	20306
	Ezra	1811	Middleboro	will	20307
	Ezra	1825	Middleboro	admn	20308
	Fanny	1862	Plymouth	admn	20309
	Finney	1843	Middleboro	will	20310
	Francis	1860	Plymouth	will	20311
	Francis	1878	Scituate	will	20312
	George	1854	Hingham	grdn	20315
	George E	1880	Hanson	grdn	20314
	George H	1857	Kingston	admn	20313
	Georgianna	1857	Plymouth	grdn	20316
	Gershom	1750	Marshfield	will	20317
	Gershom	1762	Marshfield	grdn	20318
	Gideon	1766	Marshfield	will	20319
	Hannah	1746	Plymouth	grdn	20323
	Hannah	1819	Kingston	will	20322
	Hannah	1846	Middleboro	grdn	20320
	Hannah	1848	Middleboro	admn	20321
	Harriet	1857	Scituate	admn	20324
	Harrison	1881	Middleboro	admn	20325
	Harrison G	1878	Plymouth	grdn	20326
	Harvey C	1877	Middleboro	admn	20327
	Heman	1876	Hanson	will	20328
	Henry	1832	Rochester	grdn	20331
	Henry	1842	Middleboro	will	20330
	Henry L	1865	Plympton	admn	20329
	Hercules	1865	Middleboro	will	20332
	Hervey/Harvey	1853	Plymouth	admn	20333
	Hope	1772	Middleboro	grdn	20380
	Hushai	1818	Middleboro	admn	20334
	Ichabod	1742	Marshfield	grdn	20431
	Ichabod	1758	Marshfield	grdn	20391
	Ichabod	1788	Pembroke	admn	20335
	Ichabod	1804	Middleboro	grdn	20337
	Ichabod	1871	Middleboro	admn	20336
	Isaac	1731	Pembroke	admn	20341
	Isaac	1731	Pembroke	grdn	20342
	Isaac	1765	Marshfield	grdn	20245
	Isaac	1826	Hanson	grdn	20397
	Isaac	1831	Hanson	will	20338
	Isaac	1859	Marshfield	will	20339
	Isaac 2nd	1819	Pembroke	admn	20340
	Isabella	1850	Plymouth	admn	20343
	Isaiah Jr	1843	Middleboro	admn	20344
	Israel	1755	Marshfield	will	20345
	Israel	1809	Middleboro	will	20346
	Israel	1809	Middleboro	grdn	20347
	Israel	1814	Middleboro	admn	20348
	Israel	1863	Carver	will	20349
	Jacob	1796	Middleboro	will	20350
	Jacob	1857	Middleboro	will	20351
	Jacob	1870	Middleboro	admn	20352
	James	1718	Duxbury	admn	20353
	James	1750	Duxbury	admn	20354
	James	1767	Duxbury	grdn	20355
	James	1770	Duxbury	grdn	20356 a

SURNAME	FIRST NAME	YEAR	PLACE	CASE	DOCKET
THOMAS	James	1826	Middleboro	admn	20357
	James	1828	E. Bridgewater	will	20358
	Jane	1851	Plymouth	will	20359
	Jemima	1828	Marshfield	will	20360
	Jeremiah	1736	Middleboro	will	20361
	Jeremiah	1763	Middleboro	admn	20362
	Jeremiah	1776	Middleboro	grdn	20404
	Jeremiah Jr	1821	Middleboro	admn	20363
	Jesse	1764	Pembroke	will	20364
	Jesse	1767	Marshfield	grdn	20365
	Joab Jr	1879	Plymouth	grdn	20366
	Joanna M	1839	Plympton	grdn	20484
	John	1691/2	Marshfield	admn	20367
	John	1699	Marshfield	admn	20368
	John	1737	Plymouth	will	20370
	John	1746	Plymouth	grdn	20323
	John	1770	Marshfield	will	20369
	John	1776	Kingston	will	20374
	John	1851	Middleboro	admn	20376
	John	1853	Kingston	will	20375
	John	1866	Plymouth	admn	20373
	John	1875	Hanson	admn	20378
	John A	1824	Carver	grdn	20282
	John B	1852	Plymouth	will	20372
	John H	1865	Plympton	admn	20377
	John Jr	1760	Plymouth	admn	20371
	Jonathan	1724	Middleboro	admn	20379
	Jonathan	1772	Middleboro	grdn	20380
	Joseph	1728	Middleboro	admn	20381
	Joseph	1733	Middleboro	grdn	20254
	Joseph	1744	Plympton	admn	20384
	Joseph	1758	Marshfield	grdn	20391
	Joseph	1759	Marshfield	admn	20388
	Joseph	1759	Marshfield	will	20389
	Joseph	1771	Middleboro	will	20382
	Joseph	1811	Middleboro	will	20383
	Joseph	1823	Hanson	admn	20385
	Joseph	1838	Plymouth	admn	20387
	Joseph	1857	Middleboro	grdn	20227
	Joseph D	1865	Hanover	admn	20386
	Joseph Jr	1758	Marshfield	admn	20390
	Joshua	1821	Plymouth	will	20392
	Josiah	1750	Middleboro	admn	20393
	Josiah	1750	Duxbury	will	20394
	Josiah	1826	Hanson	grdn	20397
	Josiah	1850	Duxbury	will	20395
	Josiah C	1826	Hanson	admn	20396
	Josiah H	1857	Middleboro	grdn	20227
	Judah	1807	Marshfield	admn	20398
	Judith	1826	Middleboro	grdn	20399 a
	Judith	1845	Middleboro	admn	20400
	Justus	1843	Kingston	will	20401
	Keziah	1788	Kingston	admn	20402
	Lemuel	1776	Middleboro	will	20403
	Lemuel	1776	Middleboro	grdn	20404
	Levi	1824	Middleboro	admn	20405
	Levi	1837	Pembroke	grdn	20407 a
	Levi	1860	Middleboro	will	20406
	Lothrop S	1881	Middleboro	will	20408
	Lucy	1789	Middleboro	grdn	20273
	Lucy	1817	Middleboro	admn	20409
	Lucy	1822	Middleboro	will	20410
	Lucy	1826	Middleboro	grdn	20411
	Lucy	1831	Middleboro	will	20412
	Lucy	1881	Plymouth	admn	20414
	Lucy O	1880	Scituate	will	20413
	Luissania	1824	Carver	grdn	20282
	Luther	1831	Marshfield	will	20415
	Luther H	1875	Middleboro	grdn	20468
	Lydia	1805	Middleboro	grdn	20253
	Lydia	1874	Pembroke	admn	20417

SURNAME	FIRST NAME	YEAR	PLACE	CASE	DOCKET
THOMAS	Lydia C	1864	Hanson	will	20416
	Manuel	1869	Plymouth	admn	20418
	Marcia A	1880	Marshfield	will	20419
	Mary	1724	Pembroke	grdn	20420
	Mary	1731	Pembroke	grdn	20342
	Mary	1772	Middleboro	grdn	20380
	Mary	1838	Pembroke	will	20421
	Mary	1866	Middleboro	admn	20422
	Mary A J	1880	Marshfield	admn	20425
	Mary H	1867	Plymouth	will	20423
	Mary H	1869	Marshfield	admn	20424
	Melintha C	1832	Rochester	grdn	20331
	Mercy	1772	Middleboro	grdn	20380
	Micah	1788	Kingston	admn	20426
	Moses	1828	Middleboro	will	20427
	Moses S	1851	Middleboro	grdn	20281
	Nahum C	1859	Hanover	admn	20428
	Nancy J	1857	Middleboro	grdn	20227
	Nathan	1742	Marshfield	admn	20430
	Nathan	1742	Marshfield	grdn	20431
	Nathan	1803	Marshfield	will	20429
	Nathaniel	1718/9	Marshfield	will	20432
	Nathaniel	1738	Plymouth	will	20434
	Nathaniel	1745	Plymouth	admn	20435
	Nathaniel	1811	Pembroke	will	20437
	Nathaniel	1814	Duxbury	grdn	20443
	Nathaniel	1833	Middleboro	admn	20441
	Nathaniel	1838	Plymouth	will	20436
	Nathaniel	1846	Kingston	admn	20438
	Nathaniel	1848	Hanson	admn	20439
	Nathaniel	1878	Duxbury	will	20442
	Nathaniel B	1871	Hanson	will	20440
	Nathaniel R	1737	Plymouth	grdn	20474
	Nathaniel Ray	1779	Marshfield	abse	20433
	Nehemiah	1782	Marshfield	will	20444
	Nehemiah	1831	Scituate	admn	20445
	Nellie	1881	Plymouth	grdn	20446
	Nelson	1823	Middleboro	admn	20447
	Nelson	1848	Hanson	admn	20448
	Noah	1759	Middleboro	will	20449
	Noah	1842	Plympton	will	20450
	Noah	1865	Plympton	grdn	20451
	Otis	1870	Mattapoisett	admn	20452
	Peleg	1814	Duxbury	admn	20453
	Peleg	1859	Marshfield	will	20454
	Perez	1828	Middleboro	will	20455
	Perez	1862	Middleboro	will	20456
	Polly B	1832	Rochester	grdn	20331
	Priscilla W	1873	Middleboro	grdn	20221
	Prudence	1865	Middleboro	grdn	20457
	Rebecca	1828	Middleboro	will	20458
	Richard	1742	Plymouth	admn	20459 i
	Rufus B	1846	Middleboro	will	20460
	Ruth	1731	Pembroke	grdn	20342
	Ruth	1771	Middleboro	will	20461
	Ruth J	1881	Plymouth	admn	20462
	Samuel	1720	Marshfield	will	20463
	Samuel	1733	Middleboro	grdn	20254
	Samuel	1768	Marshfield	will	20464
	Samuel	1795	Middleboro	admn	20465
	Sarah	1742	Marshfield	grdn	20431
	Sarah	1776	Middleboro	grdn	20404
	Sarah A	1875	Middleboro	grdn	20468
	Sarah D	1867	Hingham	admn	20466
	Sarah W	1871	Plymouth	admn	20467
	Seneca	1876	Middleboro	will	20469
	Seth	1845	Middleboro	will	20470
	Seth	1874	S. Scituate	will	20471
	Shadrach	1839	Hanson	admn	20472
	Silas	1848	Middleboro	admn	20473
	Simon	1737	Plymouth	grdn	20474

SURNAME	FIRST NAME	YEAR	PLACE	CASE	DOCKET
THOMAS	Solomon	1830	Middleboro	will	20475
	Spencer	1842	Plymouth	admn	20476
	Susan C	1879	Plymouth	grdn	20366
	Susanna	1804	Middleboro	grdn	20337
	Susannah	1830	Middleboro	will	20477
	Sylvanus	1814	Middleboro	will	20478
	Sylvia V	1847	Middleboro	grdn	20479
	Sylvina	1875	Marshfield	will	20480
	Thankful	1789	Middleboro	grdn	20273
	Thatcher	1838	Pembroke	admn	20481
	Turner	1859	Marshfield	admn	20482
	Walter	1831	Plympton	admn	20483
	Walter H	1839	Plympton	grdn	20484
	William	1734	Middleboro	will	20486
	William	1742	Marshfield	grdn	20431
	William	1777	Middleboro	admn	20488
	William	1781	Middleboro	grdn	20489
	William	1793	Duxbury	admn	20493
	William	1798	Marshfield	will	20494
	William	1802	Pembroke	admn	20496
	William	1806	Middleboro	admn	20490
	William	1817	Marshfield	admn	20495
	William 2nd	1732	Middleboro	admn	20485
	William F	1865	Plympton	grdn	20451
	William H	1854	Hingham	grdn	20315
	William H	1857	Plymouth	grdn	20316
	William Jr	1764	Middleboro	will	20487
	William N	1832	Rochester	admn	20491
	William O	1848	Hanson	grdn	20492
	Winslow	1814	Duxbury	admn	20497
	Winslow	1828	E. Bridgewater	admn	20498
	Winslow	1844	Middleboro	will	20499
	Winslow	1866	Plymouth	admn	20500
	Zenas	1822	Marshfield	will	20501
	Zeruah	1842	Plymouth	will	20502
THOMPSON	Abby W	1854	Middleboro	grdn	20503
	Abel	1779	Halifax	grdn	20504
	Abiah	1853	Rochester	admn	20505
	Abigail	1744	Halifax	will	20506
	Abigail	1779	Halifax	grdn	20504
	Abigail	1794	Halifax	grdn	20567
	Abigail W	1838	Middleboro	will	20507
	Adam	1822	Halifax	admn	20508
	Adam	1868	Halifax	admn	20509
	Alice J	1873	Bridgewater	admn	20510
	Alice K	1876	Middleboro	grdn	20511
	Amasa	1807	Halifax	admn	20512
	Amasa	1872	Middleboro	admn	20513
	Ammiel	1862	Abington	admn	20514
	Andrew	1773	Halifax	admn	20515
	Andrew L	1881	S. Abington	admn	20516
	Anna G	1854	Middleboro	grdn	20503
	Anna M	1879	California	peti	20517
	Arad	1843	Middleboro	will	20518
	Asa	1830	Hanson	will	20519
	Asa	1862	Halifax	admn	20520
	Asaph	1852	Halifax	grdn	20521
	Asaph B	1836	Halifax	grdn	20555
	Benjamin L	1854	Middleboro	grdn	20503
	Betty	1779	Halifax	admn	20522
	Beza	1771	Halifax	grdn	20658
	Beza	1773	Halifax	admn	20523
	Caleb	1726/7	Middleboro	grdn	20612
	Caleb	1771	Halifax	grdn	20658
	Caleb	1787	Middleboro	will	20524
	Cephas	1856	Middleboro	admn	20525
	Charles	1875	E. Bridgewater	admn	20526
	Clara	1852	Middleboro	admn	20527
	Clarissa C	1852	Plympton	grdn	20528
	Cora C	1877	S. Abington	grdn	20529
	Cyrus	1864	Halifax	admn	20530

SURNAME	FIRST NAME	YEAR	PLACE	CASE	DOCKET
THOMPSON	Daniel	1762	Halifax	grdn	20531
	David	1869	Wareham	admn	20532
	Deborah	1843	Middleboro	will	20533
	Dexter C	1881	Halifax	will	20534
	Domick	1876	Hingham	will	20535
	Ebenezer	1727	Middleboro	admn	20536
	Ebenezer	1743	Halifax	grdn	20540
	Ebenezer	1776	Scituate/Halifa	will	20537
	Ebenezer	1813	Halifax	will	20538
	Ebenezer 2nd	1818	Halifax	grdn	20539 a
	Edward	1705	Marshfield	will	20541
	Edwin	1836	Halifax	grdn	20555
	Edwin	1868	Abington	admn	20542
	Edwin	1877	S. Abington	grdn	20529
	Eliab	1818	Halifax/M'boro	admn	20543
	Eliab	1835	Halifax	admn	20544
	Eliab Jr	1835	Halifax	admn	20545
	Elizabeth	1779	Halifax	grdn	20619
	Ephraim	1744	Halifax	admn	20546
	Ephraim	1762	Halifax	grdn	20531
	Esther	1726/7	Middleboro	grdn	20612
	Ezra	1766	Middleboro	grdn	20640
	Ezra	1835	Rochester	grdn	20584
	Ezra	1850	Rochester	admn	20547
	Ezra Jr	1815	Halifax	admn	20548
	Fear	1766	Middleboro	grdn	20640
	Francis	1734	Halifax	admn	20549
	Francis	1798	Middleboro	will	20550
	Frank S J	1862	Halifax	grdn	20551
	Frederick M	1879	Kingston	will	20552
	George	1865	Middleboro	will	20553
	Hannah	1726/7	Middleboro	grdn	20612
	Hannah	1847	Halifax	admn	20556
	Hannah P	1865	Halifax	admn	20557
	Hannah W	1836	Halifax	grdn	20555
	Hannah W	1841	Bridgewater	admn	20554
	Henry W	1849	N. Bridgewater	grdn	20558
	Ichabod	1821	Halifax	will	20559
	Ichabod W	1847	Brighton IL	admn	20560
	Irena	1800	Plymouth	admn	20561
	Isaac	1733	Middleboro	grdn	20643
	Isaac	1740	Middleboro	admn	20562
	Isaac	1783	Halifax	admn	20566
	Isaac	1794	Halifax	grdn	20567
	Isaac	1820	Middleboro	will	20563
	Isaac	1835	Rochester	admn	20564
	Isaac	1859	Halifax	admn	20565
	Israel W	1869	Middleboro	admn	20568
	Jabez	1845	Plympton	admn	20569
	Jabez P	1852	Halifax	will	20570
	Jacob	1726	Middleboro	admn	20571
	Jacob	1746	Marshfield	admn	20576
	Jacob	1751	Halifax	will	20577
	Jacob	1789	Middleboro	admn	20572
	Jacob	1794	Halifax	grdn	20567
	Jacob	1806	Middleboro	will	20573
	Jacob	1818	Halifax	admn	20578
	Jacob	1848	Middleboro	admn	20574
	Jacob	1849	Middleboro	admn	20575
	Jacob	1859	Halifax	will	20579
	Jacob	1879	Bridgewater	will	20580
	James	1739	Halifax	admn	20581
	James G	1853	Middleboro	will	20583
	James S	1852	Kingston	grdn	20582 a
	Jane	1835	Rochester	grdn	20584
	Joan C	1852	Plympton	grdn	20528
	John	1696	Middleboro	will	20588
	John	1725	Middleboro	will	20589
	John	1733	Middleboro	grdn	20643
	John	1757	Halifax	will	20585
	John	1765	Hanover	admn	20587

SURNAME	FIRST NAME	YEAR	PLACE	CASE	DOCKET
THOMPSON	John	1766	Middleboro	will	20590
	John	1777	Halifax	admn	20586
	John	1876	S. Abington	will	20591
	Joseph	1788	Halifax	admn	20592
	Joseph	1809	Halifax	admn	20593
	Josephus	1877	Abington	grdn	20594 a
	Josiah	1779	Abington	will	20597
	Josiah	1828	Halifax	admn	20595
	Josiah	1838	Halifax	will	20596
	Josiah	1870	Abington	admn	20598
	Lewis	1872	Halifax	admn	20599
	Lois	1771	Halifax	grdn	20658
	Loring	1771	Halifax	grdn	20658
	Lucy	1771	Halifax	grdn	20600
	Lucy	1834	Middleboro	will	20601
	Lydia	1766	Middleboro	grdn	20640
	Lydia C	1870	Middleboro	admn	20602
	Lysander	1860	Halifax	will	20603
	Marcy	1756	Halifax	admn	20604
	Martha	1770	Halifax	will	20605
	Martin	1845	Middleboro	admn	20606
	Mary	1726/7	Middleboro	grdn	20612
	Mary	1733	Middleboro	grdn	20643
	Mary	1734	Middleboro	admn	20644
	Mary	1745	Halifax	admn	20608
	Mary	1761	Halifax	admn	20609
	Mary	1766	Middleboro	grdn	20640
	Mary	1771	Halifax	grdn	20658
	Mary	1781	Halifax	will	20610
	Mary E	1872	Marshfield	adop	20607
	Mary E T	1879	California	peti	20517
	Mary W	1848	Middleboro	admn	20611
	Melinda S	1854	Middleboro	grdn	20503
	Mercy F	1842	Middleboro	will	20613
	Michael	1866	Hingham	admn	20614
	Molly	1869	Halifax	admn	20615
	Moses	1775	Halifax	grdn	20630
	Moses	1859	Middleboro	will	20616
	Nancy R	1862	Middleboro	admn	20617
	Nathan	1779	Halifax	grdn	20619
	Nathan	1831	Halifax	will	20618
	Nathaniel	1761	Halifax	admn	20620
	Nehemiah	1844	Halifax	will	20621
	Olive	1794	Halifax	grdn	20567
	Olive	1852	N. Bridgewater	will	20622
	Olive	1859	Halifax	grdn	20623 a
	Peter	1726	Middleboro	admn	20624
	Peter	1731	Plympton	admn	20625
	Polly	1868	Kingston	will	20626
	Polly S	1874	Abington	will	20627
	Priscilla	1766	Middleboro	grdn	20640
	Priscilla	1809	Halifax	grdn	20628
	Rachel	1775	Halifax	grdn	20630
	Rachel	1851	Halifax	admn	20629
	Reuben	1779	Halifax	grdn	20504
	Reuben	1793	Halifax	will	20631
	Reuben	1813	Halifax	warr	20632
	Reuben	1849	Halifax	admn	20633
	Reuben	1875	Plympton	admn	20634
	Reuel	1851	Middleboro	will	20635
	Reuel	1878	Middleboro	will	20636
	Sally	1877	Plympton	admn	20637
	Samuel	1851	Middleboro	will	20638
	Sarah	1766	Middleboro	grdn	20640
	Sarah	1771	Halifax	will	20639
	Sarah	1771	Halifax	grdn	20658
	Seth	1771	Halifax	grdn	20658
	Shubael	1733	Middleboro	admn	20642
	Shubael	1733	Middleboro	grdn	20643
	Shubael	1734	Middleboro	admn	20644
	Shubael	1770	Middleboro	will	20641

SURNAME	FIRST NAME	YEAR	PLACE	CASE	DOCKET
THOMPSON	Sidney H	1865	Halifax	grdn	20645
	Simeon	1860	Abington	admn	20646
	Solomon	1844	Middleboro	will	20647
	Solomon	1860	Kingston	admn	20648
	Stephen	1779	Halifax	grdn	20619
	Susanna	1770	Middleboro	grdn	20649
	Susannah	1779	Halifax	grdn	20619
	Susannah	1854	Middleboro	grdn	20503
	Thaddeus	1779	Halifax	grdn	20619
	Thomas	1733	Middleboro	grdn	20643
	Thomas	1742	Halifax	admn	20655
	Thomas	1756	Bridgewater	admn	20651
	Thomas	1760	Halifax	will	20656
	Thomas	1769	Halifax	admn	20657
	Thomas	1771	Halifax	grdn	20658
	Thomas	1807	Middleboro	admn	20650
	Thomas	1833	Pomfret CT	grdn	20653
	Thomas	1835	N. Bridgewater	will	20652
	Thomas	1838	Halifax	admn	20654
	Venus	1875	Middleboro	will	20659
	Virgil W	1876	Middleboro	grdn	20511
	William	1816	Middleboro	will	20660
	William A	1843	Middleboro	grdn	20661
	Zacheus	1779	Halifax	grdn	20619
	Zadock	1879	Halifax	will	20662
	Zebadiah	1743	Halifax	grdn	20540
	Zebadiah	1775	Halifax	will	20663
	Zebadiah	1853	Halifax	will	20664
THRASHER	Annie Maria	1866	Plymouth	adop	20665
	Azariah	1800	Plymouth	admn	20666
	Azariah Jr	1783	Plymouth	admn	20667
	Daniel Jr	1826	Middleboro	admn	20668
	David	1865	Plymouth	admn	20670
	David Jr	1842	Plymouth	admn	20669
	Elias C	1868	N. Bridgewater	admn	20671
	Elizabeth H	1854	Lakeville	grdn	20672
	George Jr	1870	Plymouth	admn	20673
	Israel H	1869	Plymouth	grdn	20674
	Jonathan	1880	Plymouth	admn	20675
	Joshua	1879	Plymouth	will	20676
	Mary A	1880	Pembroke	admn	20677
THRESHIE	Charles	1870	Carver	admn	20678
	Charles	1870	Carver	grdn	20679
	John W	1870	Carver	grdn	20679
	Joseph E	1870	Carver	grdn	20679
THURBER	James	1857	Plymouth	admn	20680
THURSTON	Freeman C	1876	Portsmouth NH	admn	20681
	John B	1863	E. Bridgewater	admn	20682
THYNG	Deborah	1857	Rochester	admn	20683
	George H	1847	Rochester	grdn	20685
	John	1847	Rochester	admn	20684
	John H	1847	Rochester	grdn	20685
TIDMARSH	Mary T	1863	Hingham	will	20686
TIERNAN	Patrick	1863	Kingston	will	20687
TIFFANY	Experience	1785	Hanover	admn	20688
	Recompence	1771	Hanover	will	20689
TIGHE	George H	1879	Brockton	adop	20690
TILDEN	Abigail	1749	Marshfield	grdn	20704
	Allen C	1834	Marshfield	grdn	20751
	Amos	1849	Scituate	admn	20691
	Atherton	1844	Marshfield	will	20692
	Benjamin	1693	Scituate	admn	20693
	Benjamin	1761	Marshfield	will	20694
	Betsey	1855	S. Scituate	will	20695
	Caleb	1769	Marshfield	will	20696
	Calvin	1832	Hanson	admn	20697
	Charles L	1835	Hingham	grdn	20699
	Charles L	1866	Marshfield	bond	20698
	Christopher	1712	Marshfield	grdn	20701
	Christopher	1773	Pembroke	admn	20700
	Christopher C	1835	Hanson	grdn	20703

SURNAME	FIRST NAME	YEAR	PLACE	CASE	DOCKET
TILDEN	David	1712	Marshfield	grdn	20701
	Elisha	1852	Marshfield	will	20702
	Eliza A	1835	Hingham	grdn	20699
	Elizabeth	1749	Marshfield	grdn	20704
	Elizabeth	1835	Hanson	grdn	20703
	Elzina Warren	1869	Marshfield	adop	20705
	Fanny H	1835	Hanson	grdn	20703
	Frank H	1865	Marshfield	admn	20707
	Frank W	1869	Boston	grdn	20706
	Frederick	1834	Marshfield	grdn	20751
	Frederick A	1867	Marshfield	grdn	20708
	Frederick A	1880	Marshfield	admn	20709
	George	1869	Marshfield	will	20710
	George W	1850	Marshfield	grdn	20711
	Georgianna	1850	Marshfield	grdn	20711
	Hannah	1746	Pembroke/Marshf	will	20712
	Hannah H	1869	Marshfield	admn	20713
	Hannah H	1869	Marshfield	grdn	20714
	Hatch	1861	Marshfield	admn	20715
	Israel	1763	Marshfield	grdn	20731
	Israel	1779	Marshfield	abse	20716
	Jerusha	1718	Marshfield	grdn	20729
	Job	1830	Hanover	will	20717
	John	1718	Marshfield	grdn	20729
	John	1739	Scituate	will	20721
	John	1762	Marshfield	admn	20727
	John	1763	Marshfield	will	20730
	John	1763	Marshfield	grdn	20731
	John	1774	Scituate	admn	20722
	John	1800	Marshfield	will	20726
	John	1839	N. Bridgewater	will	20718
	John	1860	Scituate	admn	20723
	John	1873	Marshfield	will	20725
	John	1874	Brockton	will	20720
	John Jr	1792	Marshfield	will	20728
	John Jr	1852	Scituate	bond	20724
	John L	1850	N. Bridgewater	grdn	20719
	Jonathan	1712	Marshfield	grdn	20701
	Joseph	1712	Marshfield	admn	20732
	Joseph	1764	Scituate	will	20733
	Joseph	1780	Scituate	admn	20734
	Joshua	1749	Marshfield	will	20735
	Joshua	1803	Marshfield	will	20736
	Jotham	1844	Marshfield	admn	20737
	Jotham Jr	1828	Marshfield	admn	20738
	Leah	1763	Marshfield	grdn	20731
	Lendal	1833	Hingham	admn	20739
	Lucy T	1844	Portland ME	peti	20740
	Lusanna	1763	Marshfield	grdn	20731
	Luther A	1865	S. Scituate	will	20741
	Lydia M	1844	Portland ME	peti	20740
	Mary	1783	Marshfield	will	20742
	Mercy	1873	Marshfield	will	20743
	Nabby	1858	Scituate	will	20744
	Nathaniel	1731	Scituate	will	20747
	Nathaniel	1732	Scituate	admn	20748
	Nathaniel	1735	Scituate	admn	20749
	Nathaniel	1819	Hanover	grdn	20745 a
	Nathaniel	1822	Hanover	will	20746
	Nathaniel C	1834	Marshfield	grdn	20751
	Nathaniel C	1844	Marshfield	admn	20750
	Sagy B	1835	Hanson	grdn	20703
	Samuel	1739	Marshfield	will	20752
	Samuel	1774	Marshfield	will	20753
	Samuel F	1828	Marshfield	grdn	20754
	Sarah	1765	Scituate	will	20755
	Sarah	1808	Hanover	will	20756
	Stephen	1711/2	Scituate	admn	20757
	Stephen	1732	Marshfield	will	20758
	Susanna	1876	Marshfield	admn	20759
	Thatcher	1843	Scituate	will	20760

SURNAME	FIRST NAME	YEAR	PLACE	CASE	DOCKET
TILDEN	Thomas	1705	Marshfield	will	20763
	Thomas	1718	Marshfield	grdn	20729
	Thomas	1718	Marshfield	will	20764
	Thomas	1793	Scituate	will	20762
	Thomas H	1835	Hingham	grdn	20699
	Thomas H	1862	Halifax	grdn	20761
	Waldo H	1875	Marshfield	admn	20765
	Wales	1850	Marshfield	will	20766
	Wales	1863	Marshfield	will	20767
	William H	1834	Marshfield	grdn	20751
	William M	1880	Marshfield	admn	20768
TILESTON	Georgia F	1874	Duxbury	grdn	20769
TILLINGHAST	Nicholas	1856	Bridgewater	will	20770
	William H	1856	Bridgewater	grdn	20771
TILLSON	Benjamin	1730/1	Plympton	grdn	20792
	Betsey P	1866	Pembroke	grdn	20785
	Calvin	1852	Middleboro	will	20772
	Caroline	1877	Halifax	will	20773
	Edmond	1730	Plymouth	admn	20774
	Elisha	1800	Bridgewater	admn	20775
	Elizabeth	1743	Plymouth	admn	20776
	Elizabeth	1745	Plymouth	grdn	20802
	Ephraim	1716	Plympton	admn	20777
	Ephraim	1730/1	Plympton	grdn	20792
	Ephraim	1808	Halifax	will	20778
	Ephraim	1834	Halifax	admn	20779
	Ephraim	1872	Bridgewater	will	20780
	George M	1877	Carver	grdn	20781
	Hamblin	1850	Plymouth	will	20782
	Hannah E	1877	Carver	grdn	20781
	Henry	1835	Plymouth	admn	20783
	Henry W	1853	Plymouth	admn	20784
	Henry W	1866	Pembroke	grdn	20785
	Ichabod W	1877	Carver	grdn	20781
	James	1839	Halifax	admn	20786
	James M	1880	Quincy IL	admn	20787
	Jessie F	1877	Carver	grdn	20781
	Joanna	1730/1	Plympton	grdn	20792
	Joanna	1866	Middleboro	admn	20788
	John	1718	Plympton	admn	20790
	John	1729/0	Plympton	admn	20791
	John	1730/1	Plympton	grdn	20792
	John	1821	Carver	admn	20789
	Jonathan	1783	Plympton	will	20793
	Joseph	1730/1	Plympton	grdn	20792
	Joseph	1830	Halifax	admn	20794
	Lydia F	1857	Pembroke	will	20795
	Maria	1856	Plymouth	admn	20796
	Martha E	1866	Pembroke	grdn	20785
	Mary	1730/1	Plympton	grdn	20792
	Mary	1871	Middleboro	will	20797
	Mary A	1874	Pembroke	admn	20798
	Nabby	1836	Carver	grdn	20799 a
	Perez	1745	Plymouth	grdn	20802
	Perez	1769	Plymouth	admn	20800
	Ruth	1872	Carver	will	20801
	Sarah	1745	Plymouth	grdn	20802
	Sylvanus	1822	Middleboro	admn	20803
	Thomas	1829	Carver	admn	20804
	Walter S	1877	S. Abington	will	20805
	William	1756	Plympton	grdn	20806
	William	1876	Halifax	will	20807
	Zenas	1876	Carver	admn	20808
TINKHAM	Abigail	1773	Middleboro	grdn	20845
	Abishai	1811	Middleboro	will	20809
	Abraham	1848	Rochester	admn	20810
	Abraham	1879	Mattapoisett	admn	20811
	Alanson H	1848	New Orleans	admn	20812
	Alice S	1850	Middleboro	grdn	20848
	Almanda M	1841	Middleboro	grdn	20885
	Alonzo E	1841	Middleboro	grdn	20885

SURNAME	FIRST NAME	YEAR	PLACE	CASE	DOCKET	
TINKHAM	Amos	1776	Middleboro	admn	20813	
	Amos	1776	Middleboro	grdn	20814	
	Anna	1730	Kingston	grdn	20876	
	Asa	1807	Plymouth	grdn	20815	
	Asa	1847	Wareham	admn	20816	
	Asaph	1821	Middleboro	grdn	20817	a
	Betsey	1842	Middleboro	grdn	20818	a
	Betsey	1858	Mattapoisett	grdn	20819	a
	Caleb	1763	Plymouth	admn	20820	
	Caleb	1865	Middleboro	admn	20821	
	Calvin	1877	Middleboro	will	20822	
	Chandler	1838	Middleboro	admn	20823	
	Charles	1822	Rochester	will	20824	
	Charles	1841	Rochester	will	20825	
	Cornelius	1824	Middleboro	admn	20826	
	Cornelius G	1841	Middleboro	grdn	20885	
	Cyrus	1776	Middleboro	grdn	20814	
	Ebenezer	1718	Middleboro	will	20828	
	Ebenezer	1720	Middleboro	grdn	20868	
	Ebenezer	1726	Middleboro	admn	20829	
	Ebenezer	1739	Middleboro	grdn	20835	
	Ebenezer	1747	Plymouth	grdn	20836	
	Ebenezer	1752	Boston	admn	20827	
	Ebenezer	1802	Middleboro	will	20830	
	Ebenezer	1820	Middleboro	admn	20831	
	Ebenezer	1856	Middleboro	admn	20834	
	Ebenezer 2nd	1824	Middleboro	admn	20832	
	Ebenezer 3rd	1825	Middleboro	grdn	20833	
	Edward	1730	Kingston	grdn	20876	
	Elisha	1836	Middleboro	will	20837	
	Elizabeth	1722	Middleboro	grdn	20838	
	Elizabeth	1750	Middleboro	grdn	20910	
	Elizabeth	1763	Plymouth	admn	20839	
	Ephraim	1713	Middleboro	admn	20841	
	Ephraim	1714/5	Middleboro	will	20842	
	Ephraim	1727	Middleboro	grdn	20843	
	Ephraim	1730	Kingston	grdn	20876	
	Ephraim	1770	Middleboro	admn	20844	
	Ephraim	1773	Middleboro	grdn	20845	
	Ephraim	1807	Halifax	grdn	20840	a
	Frank A	1880	Mattapoisett	grdn	20846	
	George F	1877	Middleboro	grdn	20849	
	George H	1850	Middleboro	grdn	20848	
	George W	1838	Middleboro	admn	20847	
	Hannah	1865	Middleboro	admn	20850	
	Harriet A	1867	Middleboro	grdn	20851	a
	Harriet B	1877	Middleboro	grdn	20849	
	Harvey	1865	Middleboro	will	20852	
	Hazael	1839	Middleboro	admn	20853	
	Hazael	1865	Middleboro	admn	20854	
	Hilkiah	1731	Plymouth	will	20855	
	Hilkiah	1746	Plymouth	admn	20856	
	Huldah	1780	Middleboro	grdn	20857	
	Huldah	1835	Middleboro	admn	20858	
	Ira	1856	Middleboro	admn	20859	
	Isaac	1732	Plymouth	will	20863	
	Isaac	1750	Halifax	admn	20864	
	Isaac	1780	Middleboro	will	20861	
	Isaac	1818	Middleboro	will	20862	
	Isaac	1854	Middleboro	admn	20860	
	Jacob	1740	-----	grdn	20865	
	Jeremiah	1718	Middleboro	admn	20867	
	Jeremiah	1720	Middleboro	grdn	20868	
	Jeremiah	1790	Middleboro	will	20866	
	Joanna	1720	Middleboro	grdn	20868	
	Joanna	1747	Middleboro	grdn	20869	
	Joanna	1750	Middleboro	grdn	20910	
	John	1730	Kingston	admn	20875	
	John	1730	Kingston	grdn	20876	
	John	1748	Kingston	admn	20874	
	John	1766	Middleboro	will	20870	

SURNAME	FIRST NAME	YEAR	PLACE	CASE	DOCKET
TINKHAM	John	1793	Middleboro	will	20871
	John	1829	Middleboro	will	20873
	John 2nd	1818	Middleboro	grdn	20872 a
	Joseph	1730	Kingston	grdn	20876
	Joseph	1739	Middleboro	grdn	20835
	Joseph	1759	Kingston	grdn	20878
	Joseph	1767	Middleboro	will	20879
	Joseph	1767	Middleboro	grdn	20880
	Joseph	1842	Halifax	will	20877
	Keziah	1747	Middleboro	grdn	20869
	Keziah	1757	Middleboro	grdn	20881
	Lavinia	1850	Middleboro	admn	20882
	Levi	1857	Middleboro	will	20883
	Levi 2nd	1840	Middleboro	admn	20884
	Levi F	1841	Middleboro	grdn	20885
	Lucretia	1829	Middleboro	will	20886
	Lydia	1747	Plymouth	grdn	20836
	Lydia	1747	Middleboro	grdn	20869
	Marcy	1750	Middleboro	grdn	20910
	Mary	1749	Middleboro	admn	20887
	Mary	1839	Middleboro	admn	20888
	Mary	1842	Middleboro	grdn	20889
	Moses	1727	Middleboro	grdn	20843
	Moses	1767	Middleboro	grdn	20880
	Noah	1765	Halifax	will	20890
	Oliver G	1880	Brockton	admn	20891
	Omar A	1877	Middleboro	grdn	20849
	Patience	1726/7	Middleboro	grdn	20898
	Patience	1745	Middleboro	grdn	20897
	Patience	1814	Middleboro	will	20892
	Perez	1739	Middleboro	grdn	20835
	Perez	1760	Middleboro	will	20893
	Perez	1767	Middleboro	grdn	20880
	Peter	1709/0	Middleboro	admn	20895
	Peter	1726/7	Middleboro	grdn	20898
	Peter	1745	Middleboro	admn	20896
	Peter	1745	Middleboro	grdn	20897
	Peter	1756	Middleboro	admn	20894
	Priscilla	1726/7	Middleboro	grdn	20898
	Priscilla	1739	Middleboro	grdn	20835
	Priscilla A	1847	Middleboro	admn	20899
	Reland	1854	Middleboro	admn	20900
	Ruth	1747	Plymouth	grdn	20836
	Ruth	1805	Middleboro	will	20901
	Samuel	1717	Middleboro	grdn	20902
	Samuel	1747	Middleboro	admn	20903
	Samuel	1773	Middleboro	grdn	20845
	Samuel	1776	Middleboro	will	20904
	Samuel	1796	Middleboro	will	20905
	Sarah	1739	Middleboro	grdn	20835
	Sarah	1745	Middleboro	grdn	20897
	Sarah	1747	Plympton	grdn	20906
	Sarah	1773	Middleboro	grdn	20845
	Sarah	1832	Halifax	will	20907
	Sarah E	1841	Middleboro	grdn	20885
	Seth	1750	Middleboro	admn	20909
	Seth	1750	Middleboro	grdn	20910
	Seth	1765	Middleboro	admn	20908
	Seth	1767	Middleboro	grdn	20880
	Shubael	1739	Middleboro	will	20911
	Shubael	1776	Middleboro	admn	20912
	Silas	1816	Middleboro	will	20913
	Squire	1776	Middleboro	grdn	20814
	Sylvanus	1823	Middleboro	grdn	20914 a
	Thomas P	1853	Middleboro	will	20915
	Warren F	1865	Bridgewater	admn	20916
	William L	1872	Plympton	admn	20918
	William M	1856	Middleboro	grdn	20917 a
	Zebedee	1820	Middleboro	admn	20919
TINSLEY	Mary Ann	1877	Hingham	will	20920
	Thomas	1863	Hingham	admn	20921

SURNAME	FIRST NAME	YEAR	PLACE	CASE	DOCKET
TIPPENREITE	George	1879	Hingham	will	20922
TIRRELL	Adeline	1855	E. Bridgewater	grdn	20937
	Alonzo	1859	Scituate	will	20923
	Bethiah	1876	E. Bridgewater	will	20924
	Betsey	1843	N. Bridgewater	will	20925
	Edwin S	1869	Abington	admn	20926
	Emma C	1875	Brockton	admn	20927
	Ezra	1794	Abington	admn	20928
	Gideon	1823	Hull	admn	20929
	Isaac	1824	Abington	will	20930
	Jacob	1776	Weymouth	grdn	20932
	Job	1759	Abington	admn	20931
	Job	1776	Weymouth	grdn	20932
	John	1816	Abington	admn	20933
	John	1866	Scituate	will	20934
	Lemuel	1802	Abington	will	20935
	Lydia	1764	Abington	grdn	20936
	Mary	1776	Weymouth	grdn	20932
	Nancy J	1855	E. Bridgewater	grdn	20937
	Nathaniel	1811	Abington	admn	20938
	Polly	1873	Scituate	will	20939
	Polly	1876	E. Bridgewater	will	20940
	Sarah	1764	Abington	grdn	20936
	Sarah	1842	Abington	will	20941
	Thomas	1732	Abington	admn	20942
	Thomas	1773	Abington	admn	20943
	William	1728	Abington	will	20944
	William	1777	Abington	will	20945
	William	1863	E. Bridgewater	admn	20947
	William M	1854	Abington	will	20946
TISDALE	Amanda R	1877	W. Bridgewater	admn	20948
	Ann M	1851	Middleboro/Fish	grdn	20949
	Charlotte L	1861	Baltimore MD	grdn	20950
	Clara N	1851	Middleboro	grdn	20949
	Diana	1809	Bridgewater	grdn	20951
	Dora M	1881	W. Bridgewater	grdn	20953
	Joanna	1809	Bridgewater	grdn	20951
	Mary	1728	Taunton	will	20952
	Mary A	1881	W. Bridgewater	grdn	20953
	Mary E	1851	Middleboro	grdn	20949
	Samuel T	1870	New York	will	20954
	Sarah J	1851	Middleboro	grdn	20949
TOAR	Matthew	1763	Abington	grdn	20955
TOBEY	Abigail A P	1825	Wareham	grdn	20970
	Abisha H	1837	Rochester	admn	20956
	Benjamin	1825	Wareham	admn	20957
	Curtis	1827	Wareham	will	20958
	Elisha	1859	Iowa	peti	20959
	Eliza H	1876	Middleboro	admn	20960
	Elizabeth	1866	N. Bridgewater	will	20961
	Hetty	1838	Rochester	will	20962
	Joshua B	1871	Wareham	admn	20963
	Luke	1776	Rochester	admn	20964
	Maria	1876	Lakeville	admn	20965
	Mary A	1859	Iowa	peti	20959
	Moses S	1828	Wareham	grdn	20967
	Moses S F	1879	Wareham	will	20966
	Nathan	1805	Wareham	admn	20968
	Rachel	1871	Lakeville	admn	20969
	Sarah A	1825	Wareham	grdn	20970
	Seth	1828	Wareham	grdn	20967
	Silas	1817	Kingston	admn	20971
	Thomas	1753	Hanover	admn	20972
	Thomas	1832	Rochester	will	20973
	William	1748	Plymouth	admn	20974
TOBIN	Thomas	1875	Brockton	will	20975
TODD	James	1832	Hingham	will	20976
	Rebecca F	1818	Hingham	grdn	20977
TOLMAN	Alfred	1878	S. Scituate	grdn	20978
	Benjamin	1807	Marshfield	admn	20980
	Benjamin	1824	Pembroke	admn	20979

SURNAME	FIRST NAME	YEAR	PLACE	CASE	DOCKET
TOLMAN	Benjamin	1853	Marshfield	will	20981
	Bethiah	1866	S. Scituate	will	20982
	Betty	1808	Marshfield	will	20983
	Charles	1815	Scituate	admn	20986
	Charles	1829	Scituate	will	20987
	Charles	1829	Scituate	grdn	20988
	Charles	1846	Scituate	will	20984
	Charles	1847	S. Scituate	grdn	20985
	Daniel	1829	Bridgewater	will	20989
	Deborah Alden	1854	S. Scituate	adop	20990
	Edward P	1866	S. Scituate	grdn	20991 a
	Elisha	1783	Scituate	will	20992
	Elisha	1826	Scituate	admn	20993
	Elisha	1827	Scituate	grdn	20994
	Elizabeth	1826	Scituate	will	20995
	George P	1827	Scituate	grdn	20994
	James H	1860	E. Bridgewater	admn	20996
	John	1863	Hanson	admn	20997
	Joseph	1793	Scituate	will	20998
	Judith	1827	Scituate	grdn	20994
	Marcus	1835	Scituate	grdn	20999 a
	Mary C	1829	Scituate	grdn	20988
	Mercy	1821	Marshfield	admn	21000
	Michel	1821	Scituate	admn	21001
	Molly	1853	Marshfield	will	21002
	Nathaniel W	1827	Scituate	grdn	20994
	Polly	1827	Scituate	grdn	20994
	Rebecca	1862	Hanover	admn	21003
	Roxana	1843	Scituate	will	21004
	Samuel	1835	Scituate	admn	21005
	Sarah H	1827	Scituate	grdn	20994
	Sarah W	1857	S. Scituate	admn	21006
	Sylvester	1819	Scituate	will	21007
	Thomas J	1874	S. Scituate	will	21008
	William	1749	Scituate	admn	21009
	William C	1829	Scituate	grdn	20988
	William P	1877	Marshfield	will	21010
TOM	Joseph	1746	Pembroke	admn	21011 i
TOMELTY	Margaret	1855	Hingham	admn	21012
TOMKINS	Samuel	1695	Bridgewater	will	21013
TOMLINSON	Russell	1878	Plymouth	admn	21014
TOOHEY	Elizabeth	1870	E. Bridgewater	grdn	21016
	Hannah M	1870	E. Bridgewater	grdn	21016
	James	1870	E. Bridgewater	admn	21015
	James E	1870	E. Bridgewater	grdn	21016
	Margaret	1870	E. Bridgewater	grdn	21016
	Mary C	1870	E. Bridgewater	grdn	21016
	Nellie F	1870	E. Bridgewater	grdn	21016
	Thomas	1870	E. Bridgewater	grdn	21016
TORRANCE	William	1865	Pembroke	admn	21017
TORREY	Almira	1835	Easton	grdn	21018
	Alvin W	1878	Hingham	grdn	21087
	Ann M	1855	Abington	grdn	21019
	Benjamin D	1843	Hanover	admn	21020
	Caleb	1772	Scituate	will	21021
	Caroline	1851	Abington	grdn	21056
	Carrie J	1878	Hingham	grdn	21087
	Charles	1815	Scituate	admn	21022
	Charles T	1819	Scituate	grdn	21023
	Charlotte S	1878	Hingham	grdn	21087
	David	1783	Hanover	will	21027
	David	1830	Abington	admn	21024
	David	1851	Abington	will	21025
	David	1877	S. Scituate	will	21026
	David B	1855	Abington	grdn	21019
	Edward P	1851	Abington	grdn	21056
	Eliab	1793	Hanover	grdn	21028 a
	Elizabeth	1848	Plymouth	grdn	21029 a
	Elizabeth	1852	Abington	will	21030
	Flora W	1878	Hingham	grdn	21087
	Francis B	1835	Easton	grdn	21018

SURNAME	FIRST NAME	YEAR	PLACE	CASE	DOCKET
TORREY	Franklin J	1877	Hingham	admn	21031
	George	1777	Plymouth	grdn	21060
	George	1813	Scituate	admn	21032
	Hannah T	1817	Scituate	will	21033
	Harvey	1855	Abington	admn	21034
	Haviland	1750	Plymouth	will	21035
	Haviland	1865	Hanover	admn	21036
	Huldah	1876	Abington	will	21037
	Isaac	1811	Scituate	will	21038
	Isaac	1879	Duxbury	will	21039
	James	1719	Scituate	will	21040
	James	1820	Scituate	will	21041
	Jennie L	1878	Hingham	grdn	21087
	Jesse	1793	Hanover	admn	21042
	Jesse H	1790	Plymouth	grdn	21046
	John	1777	Plymouth	admn	21045
	John	1790	Plymouth	grdn	21046
	John D	1855	Scituate	will	21043
	John E	1855	Abington	grdn	21019
	John T	1777	Hanover	grdn	21044 a
	Jonathan	1783	Abington	will	21047
	Jonathan C	1878	Hingham	grdn	21087
	Joseph	1714	Scituate	admn	21048
	Joseph	1822	Hanson	will	21049
	Joshua	1839	Plymouth	will	21050
	Josiah	1717	Scituate	will	21051
	Josiah	1762	Plymouth	admn	21052
	Josiah	1783	Abington	will	21053
	Josiah	1822	Abington	will	21054
	Josiah	1880	Rockland	admn	21055
	Levi	1851	Abington	grdn	21056
	Lewis	1811	Middleboro	admn	21057
	Lottie S	1878	Scituate	grdn	21062
	Lucy H	1847	Plymouth	grdn	21058
	Maria	1876	Hanson	admn	21059
	Martha	1777	Plymouth	grdn	21060
	Mary A	1878	Scituate	will	21061
	Mary G	1878	Scituate	grdn	21062
	Mehitable	1847	Abington	will	21063
	Meriah M	1790	Plymouth	grdn	21046
	Meriam	1807	Hanover	will	21064
	Minnie E	1878	Hingham	grdn	21087
	Miranda	1855	Abington	grdn	21019
	Nancy	1837	Scituate	grdn	21065 a
	Nathaniel	1753	Hanover	admn	21066
	Nellie W	1878	Scituate	grdn	21062
	Nettie J	1873	Abington	grdn	21067
	Otis	1814	Scituate	grdn	21068
	Otis	1820	Scituate	admn	21069
	Phillip	1841	E. Bridgewater	admn	21070
	Ruth	1829	E. Bridgewater	admn	21071
	Sarah	1860	N. Bridgewater	admn	21072
	Sarah	1875	Hingham	admn	21073
	Susan	1855	Plymouth	admn	21074
	Thankful	1816	Scituate	grdn	21075 a
	Thomas	1778	Hanover	admn	21076
	Thomas	1806	Bridgewater	admn	21077
	Thomas	1847	Plymouth	admn	21078
	Turner	1858	N. Bridgewater	will	21079
	Walter R	1878	S. Scituate	grdn	21081
	Walter S	1876	Scituate	will	21080
	Warren	1783	Hanover	admn	21082
	William	1768	Hanover	admn	21083
	William	1828	Pembroke	admn	21084
	William	1846	Abington	will	21085
	William	1875	Hingham	admn	21086
	William F	1878	Hingham	grdn	21087
	Ziba	1866	Abington	will	21088
TOTMAN	Adeline	1847	Plymouth	grdn	21089
	Benjamin O	1860	Scituate	admn	21090
	Charles	1825	Scituate	admn	21091

SURNAME	FIRST NAME	YEAR	PLACE	CASE	DOCKET
TOTMAN	Hannah	1863	S. Scituate	will	21092
	Hannah B	1863	Abington	admn	21093
	Harris	1853	S. Scituate	will	21094
	Isaac Jr	1866	S. Scituate	admn	21095
	John	1815	Abington	will	21096
	Joshua	1727	Plymouth	admn	21097
	Joshua	1746	Plymouth	grdn	21100
	Joshua	1761	Plymouth	admn	21098
	Mary	1866	S. Scituate	grdn	21099
	Priscilla	1746	Plymouth	grdn	21100
	Samuel	1749	Plymouth	admn	21101
	Seth	1759	Plymouth	admn	21102
	Sophia	1868	Abington	admn	21103
	Stephen	1830	Scituate	admn	21104
TOUT	Sarah	1880	Kingston	admn	21105
	Thomas	1879	Kingston	will	21106
TOWER	Ada F	1877	Brockton	grdn	21107
	Anna	1876	Hingham	admn	21108
	Bela	1837	Hingham	will	21109
	Benjamin	1757	Scituate	will	21110
	David	1844	Hull	admn	21111
	Emma	1852	Hingham	will	21112
	Frederick	1845	Hingham	admn	21113
	Helen A	1865	Halifax	grdn	21126
	Horace	1823	Scituate	admn	21114
	Isaac	1834	N. Bridgewater	admn	21115
	Isaiah	1811	Hingham	will	21117
	Isaiah	1842	Hingham	admn	21118
	Isaiah G	1842	Hingham	admn	21119
	Isaiah Jr	1807	Hingham	will	21116
	John	1795	Hanover	admn	21120
	John	1809	Scituate	admn	21121
	Jonathan	1759	Scituate	admn	21122
	Joshua	1810	Hingham	will	21123
	Joshua	1845	Hingham	will	21124
	Laban	1824	Hingham	will	21125
	Lorenzo	1834	N. Bridgewater	grdn	21138
	Lorenzo	1865	Halifax	grdn	21126
	Lydia	1749	Abington	grdn	21132
	Lydia C	1848	Hull	grdn	21130
	Malachi	1806	Hingham	will	21127
	Martha C	1875	Hingham	will	21128
	Mary A	1842	Hingham	grdn	21129
	Mary B	1848	Hull	grdn	21130
	Matthew	1749	Abington	admn	21131
	Matthew	1749	Abington	grdn	21132
	Moses	1863	Hingham	admn	21134
	Moses B	1843	Hull	bond	21133
	Olive G	1848	Hull	grdn	21130
	Persis	1787	Hanover	will	21135
	Reuben	1814	Hingham	grdn	21136
	Sarah E	1843	Hingham	grdn	21137
	Silas D	1834	N. Bridgewater	grdn	21138
	Susannah	1830	Abington	admn	21139
	Thomas J	1847	Hingham	will	21140
	William	1879	Hingham	admn	21141
TOWNSEND	Elizabeth W	1870	Abington	grdn	21142
	Ezekiel	1818	Abington	admn	21143
	Ezekiel	1833	Abington	admn	21144
	George A	1870	Abington	grdn	21142
	Jeremiah H	1875	Bridgewater	admn	21145
	Job	1842	Middleboro	will	21146
	John	1835	Middleboro	will	21147
	Paul	1877	W. Bridgewater	will	21148
	Samuel S	1834	Abington	grdn	21150
	William	1834	Abington	grdn	21150
	William	1870	Abington	admn	21149
TRACEY	Asaph Jr	1789	Pembroke	admn	21151
	Lydia C	1794	Pembroke	grdn	21154
	Thomas	1756	Pembroke	admn	21153
	Thomas	1794	Pembroke	grdn	21154

SURNAME	FIRST NAME	YEAR	PLACE	CASE	DOCKET
TRACEY	Thomas	1811	Pembroke	admn	21152
TRASK	Abigail	1814	Bridgewater	grdn	21155 a
	James	1820	Plymouth/Duxbur	grdn	21156
	James	1875	Duxbury	will	21157
	Jerusha	1807	Plymouth	will	21158
	Joseph	1802	Plymouth	admn	21159
TRAVERS	John A	1853	Wareham	admn	21160
TREFRY	Susan B	1878	Middleboro	admn	21161
TRIBBLE	Betsey	1848	Plymouth	admn	21162
	Gideon H	1856	Plymouth	admn	21163
	Isaac	1865	Plymouth	admn	21164
	John	1863	Plymouth	will	21165
	Joseph	1743	Plymouth	grdn	21167
	Joseph	1833	Plymouth	admn	21166
	Joseph Jr	1815	Plymouth	grdn	21168 a
	Lydia	1876	Plymouth	admn	21169
	Thomas	1817	Plymouth	grdn	21170
	Thomas	1864	Plymouth	will	21171
	William	1834	Plymouth	admn	21172
TRIBOU	Asa	1832	N. Bridgewater	grdn	21187
	Asa	1880	Brockton	will	21173
	Charles	1832	N. Bridgewater	grdn	21187
	David O	1874	Middleboro	admn	21174
	Emma F	1832	N. Bridgewater	grdn	21187
	Hannah	1872	Middleboro	admn	21175
	John	1848	Hanover	will	21176
	Levi W	1877	Hanover	will	21177
	Martha	1863	W. Bridgewater	grdn	21178 a
	Martha	1863	W. Bridgewater	will	21179
	Martha	1865	W. Bridgewater	admn	21180
	Mary C	1866	Middleboro	grdn	21183
	Melzar	1852	Middleboro	will	21181
	Nahum M	1866	Middleboro	grdn	21183
	Nahum M	1873	Middleboro	will	21182
	Peter	1849	W. Bridgewater	will	21184
	Samuel	1881	Brockton	will	21186
	Samuel F	1832	N. Bridgewater	grdn	21187
	Samuel F	1874	Brockton	will	21185
	Sarah	1832	N. Bridgewater	grdn	21187
	Sarah H	1865	Middleboro	admn	21188
	Walter S	1839	E. Bridgewater	admn	21189
	William	1855	N. Bridgewater	will	21190
TRIPLETT	John	1752	England	admn	21191
TRIPP	Alice R	1834	Middleboro	will	21192
	Angeline S	1873	Middleboro	grdn	21193
	Elizabeth W	1858	Wareham	grdn	21194
	Emma C	1871	Marion	adop	21195
	James M	1854	Kingston	admn	21196
	Jesse	1806	Rochester	will	21197
	Lucy	1861	Mattapoisett	will	21198
	Sarah	1851	Rochester	admn	21199
	Sarah C	1868	Middleboro	will	21200
	Stillman	1852	Rochester	admn	21201
	Sylvanus	1861	Mattapoisett	will	21202
	Warren	1833	Rochester	admn	21203
TROUANT	Church C	1855	Marshfield	will	21205
	Church C Jr	1821	Marshfield	grdn	21204
	David	1785	Middleboro	admn	21206
	John	1749	Marshfield	will	21208
	John	1749	Marshfield	grdn	21209
	John	1811	Marshfield	will	21207
	Joseph	1761	Middleboro	will	21210
	Joseph	1832	Marshfield	admn	21211
	Lydia	1749	Marshfield	grdn	21209
	Mary	1749	Marshfield	grdn	21209
	Nathan	1837	Middleboro	admn	21212
	Samuel	1749	Marshfield	grdn	21209
	Samuel	1819	Marshfield	will	21213
	Samuel	1853	Marshfield	grdn	21214 a
TROW	Adda F	1865	E. Bridgewater	grdn	21217
	Bartholomew	1863	E. Bridgewater	will	21215

SURNAME	FIRST NAME	YEAR	PLACE	CASE	DOCKET
TROW	George A	1863	E. Bridgewater	admn	21216
	Lucia R	1865	E. Bridgewater	grdn	21217
TROWBRIDGE	Joseph	1853	Hingham	will	21218
	Roswell Jr	1858	Hingham	admn	21219
	Susanna	1859	Hingham	admn	21220
TRUFANT	Ezra	1873	Abington	admn	21221
	Hattie A	1870	Abington	grdn	21223
	Jno	1730	Marshfield	will	21222
	Philip P	1870	Abington	grdn	21223
	Walter E	1870	Abington	grdn	21223
TUBBS	Benjamin	1870	Hanson	admn	21224
	Daniel P	1862	Marshfield	will	21225
	Deborah	1870	Hanson	admn	21226
	Ebenezer	1754	Pembroke	grdn	21227
	Ephraim	1763	Pembroke	admn	21228
	Ephraim	1848	Pembroke	admn	21229
	Eunice W	1879	Hanson	will	21230
	Holbrook	1824	Marshfield	admn	21231
	Isaac	1781	Pembroke	will	21232
	Jacob	1740	Pembroke	grdn	21233
	Joseph	1739	Pembroke	will	21234
	Joseph	1743	Pembroke	will	21235
	Joseph	1816	Pembroke	will	21236
	Joseph	1854	Hanover	admn	21237
	Lucy	1834	Pembroke	will	21238
	Lucy	1866	Hanover	will	21239
	Mary	1764	Abington	admn	21240
	Mary	1840	Pembroke	will	21241
	Morris	1750	Pembroke	admn	21242
	Morris	1831	Pembroke	admn	21243
	Nehemiah	1828	Hanson	admn	21244
	Samuel	1792	Pembroke	admn	21245
	Samuel	1799	Pembroke	grdn	21246
	William	1688	Duxbury	will	21247
TUCK	Silas V	1879	Brockton	will	21248
TUCKER	Amariah	1874	Pembroke	admn	21249
	Andrew	1854	Middleboro	admn	21250
	Andrew	1858	Bridgewater	admn	21251
	Benjamin	1778	Bridgewater	grdn	21262
	Benjamin	1781	Middleboro	will	21252
	Benjamin	1849	Bridgewater	admn	21253
	Daniel	1842	Middleboro	admn	21254
	Elisha	1878	Middleboro	admn	21255
	Elizabeth	1778	Bridgewater	grdn	21262
	Ella A	1867	Bridgewater	grdn	21256
	Eugenia J	1867	Bridgewater	grdn	21256
	George E	1877	Duxbury	admn	21258
	George W	1855	Middleboro	admn	21257
	James H	1862	Abington	admn	21259
	Jeremiah	1876	Bridgewater	admn	21260
	Manassah	1778	Bridgewater	admn	21261
	Manassah	1778	Bridgewater	grdn	21262
	Mary	1851	N. Bridgewater	will	21263
	Mary B	1859	Middleboro	grdn	21267
	Mary E	1862	Abington	grdn	21264
	Mercy	1868	Middleboro	admn	21265
	Nancy S	1859	Middleboro	grdn	21267
	Nathan T	1842	New York	admn	21266
	Nathan T	1859	Middleboro	grdn	21267
	Roscoe G	1866	Bridgewater	admn	21268
	Samuel	1820	Middleboro	will	21269
	Susan H	1859	Middleboro	grdn	21267
	Susanna	1850	Middleboro	will	21270
	Woodward	1761	Middleboro	admn	21271
	Woodward	1858	Middleboro	admn	21272
TUFTS	Jonathan	1821	Plymouth	will	21273
TULLY	Carrie L	1879	Hingham	grdn	21275
	Elizabeth	1878	Almeda CA	admn	21274
	James W	1879	Hingham	grdn	21275
	John H	1879	Hingham	grdn	21275
TUPPER	Hannah	1771	Middleboro	will	21276

SURNAME	FIRST NAME	YEAR	PLACE	CASE	DOCKET
TUPPER	Ichabod	1748	Middleboro	will	21277
	Martin L	1829	Kingston	grdn	21278
	Peleg	1842	Kingston	will	21279
	Peleg Jr	1828	Kingston	admn	21280
	Sarah B	1829	Kingston	grdn	21278
	Seth	1783	Kingston	admn	21281
	Seth	1814	Plymouth	will	21282
TURNER	Abial	1880	S. Scituate	will	21283
	Abiel	1719/0	Scituate	grdn	21285
	Abiel	1798	Scituate	will	21284
	Abiezer	1745	Scituate	grdn	21287
	Abiezer	1752	Scituate	admn	21286
	Abigail	1719	Scituate	admn	21288
	Abigail	1744	Scituate	will	21289
	Abigail	1787	Pembroke	will	21290
	Abner	1721	Scituate	will	21291
	Albion	1853	S. Scituate	admn	21292
	Amasa	1712	Scituate	admn	21293
	Amos	1739	Scituate	will	21294
	Amos	1746	Scituate	grdn	21295
	Amos	1822	Hanover	will	21296
	Anna	1868	S. Scituate	grdn	21348
	Arthur W	1853	Bridgewater	grdn	21297
	Austin	1853	Bridgewater	grdn	21297
	Avis	1857	Hanover	will	21298
	Barker	1873	Pembroke	will	21299
	Benjamin	1734/5	Scituate	will	21301
	Benjamin	1748	Scituate	will	21302
	Benjamin	1764	Scituate	inve	21304
	Benjamin	1768	Scituate	admn	21303
	Benjamin	1771	Pembroke	will	21305
	Benjamin	1861	S. Scituate	will	21300
	Betsey	1854	Scituate	will	21306
	Caleb	1767	Hanover	admn	21307
	Caleb	1844	Bridgewater	admn	21308
	Caroline C	1845	Scituate	grdn	21446
	Charles	1718	Scituate	admn	21309
	Charles	1722	Scituate	grdn	21310
	Charles	1782	Scituate	will	21311
	Charles	1804	Pembroke	admn	21316
	Charles	1810	Pembroke	grdn	21318
	Charles	1812	Pembroke	will	21317
	Charles	1838	Scituate	grdn	21313
	Charles	1839	Scituate	will	21314
	Charles H	1821	Scituate	admn	21312
	Charles N	1875	Scituate	grdn	21315
	Daniel	1761	Pembroke	grdn	21365
	Daniel	1779	Pembroke	will	21319
	David	1698	Scituate	will	21320
	David	1769	Plymouth	will	21322
	David	1775	Plymouth	admn	21323
	David	1821	Scituate	admn	21321
	David	1869	Plymouth	admn	21324
	David W	1845	Scituate	grdn	21446
	Deborah	1719/0	Scituate	grdn	21285
	Deborah L	1857	Plymouth	will	21325
	Desire	1745	Scituate	grdn	21287
	Ebenezer	1799	Pembroke	grdn	21326 a
	Eleazer S	1864	Plymouth	will	21327
	Eliab	1701/2	Scituate	admn	21328
	Eliab	1725	Scituate	grdn	21329
	Elijah	1823	Scituate	will	21330
	Elijah B	1865	S. Scituate	admn	21331
	Elisha	1700	Scituate	will	21334
	Elisha	1710	Scituate	grdn	21335
	Elisha	1761	Pembroke	grdn	21365
	Elisha	1793	Scituate	admn	21333
	Elisha	1848	Hull	admn	21332
	Elizabeth	1703	Scituate	grdn	21421
	Elizabeth	1710	Scituate	grdn	21335
	Elizabeth	1710	Scituate	will	21336

SURNAME	FIRST NAME	YEAR	PLACE	CASE	DOCKET
TURNER	Elizabeth	1712	Duxbury	grdn	21375
	Elizabeth	1744	Scituate	will	21337
	Elizabeth	1760	Scituate	will	21338
	Elizabeth	1823	Scituate	grdn	21426
	Ellen A	1874	Hanover	grdn	21340
	Elnathan	1712	Scituate	will	21339
	Emily C	1874	Hanover	grdn	21340
	Ephraim	1694	Scituate	admn	21341
	Esther	1873	S. Scituate	admn	21342
	Ezekiel	1773	Hanover	will	21343
	Ezekiel	1856	Middleboro	will	21344
	George	1695/6	Bridgewater	admn	21345
	George	1747	Bridgewater	grdn	21346
	George	1805	Pembroke	will	21347
	George	1868	S. Scituate	grdn	21348
	Grace	1745	Scituate	grdn	21287
	Gustavus J	1845	Scituate	grdn	21446
	Hallet	1845	Rochester	dowe	21349
	Hannah	1712	Duxbury	grdn	21375
	Hannah	1712	-----	grdn	21406
	Hannah	1717	Pembroke	will	21354
	Hannah	1745	Scituate	grdn	21287
	Hannah	1746	Scituate	grdn	21350 a
	Hannah	1751	Scituate	admn	21351
	Hannah	1768	Scituate	admn	21352
	Hannah C	1867	S. Scituate	admn	21353
	Hannah L	1869	Hingham	will	21355
	Harriet T	1845	Scituate	grdn	21446
	Harris	1793	Scituate	grdn	21399
	Hawkins	1771	Scituate	admn	21356
	Isaac	1769	Hanover	grdn	21357 a
	Isaac	1772	Hanover	admn	21358
	Israel	1689	Scituate	admn	21359
	Israel	1712	Duxbury	grdn	21375
	Israel	1760	Pembroke	will	21364
	Israel	1761	Pembroke	grdn	21365
	Israel	1769	Scituate	will	21360
	Israel	1799	Scituate	grdn	21361 a
	Israel	1802	Scituate	admn	21362
	Israel	1849	Scituate	admn	21363
	Jael	1710	Scituate	grdn	21335
	James	1776	Scituate	will	21366
	James	1803	Scituate	will	21367
	James	1835	Scituate	will	21368
	James	1863	Plymouth	will	21369
	James H	1867	N. Bridgewater	will	21370
	Japhet	1710	Duxbury	admn	21374
	Japhet	1712	Duxbury	grdn	21375
	Japhet	1748	Middleboro	admn	21372
	Japhet	1802	Pembroke	grdn	21371 a
	Japheth	1690	Duxbury	admn	21373
	Jesse	1799	Scituate	will	21378
	Jesse	1832	Plymouth	admn	21376
	Jesse H	1834	Plymouth	grdn	21377
	Jesse H	1869	S. Scituate	admn	21379
	Job	1823	Pembroke	admn	21380
	John	1697	Scituate	will	21382
	John	1719	Scituate	admn	21383
	John	1728	Bridgewater	admn	21381
	John	1754	Scituate	grdn	21384
	John	1778	Scituate	will	21386
	John	1794	Pembroke	will	21390
	John	1821	Pembroke	will	21389
	John	1838	Scituate	grdn	21313
	John B	1849	Scituate	will	21387
	John B	1875	Scituate	admn	21388
	John Jr	1766	Scituate	grdn	21385 a
	John P	1810	Pembroke	grdn	21318
	Jonathan	1724	Scituate	will	21392
	Jonathan	1796	Hanover/Pembrok	admn	21391
	Jonathan	1823	Scituate	admn	21393

SURNAME	FIRST NAME	YEAR	PLACE	CASE	DOCKET
TURNER	Joseph	1723/4	Scituate	admn	21394
	Joseph	1770	Duxbury	admn	21395
	Joseph G	1813	Pembroke	grdn	21396
	Joshua	1728	Pembroke	will	21400
	Joshua	1730	Pembroke	grdn	21401
	Joshua	1763	Scituate	grdn	21397
	Joshua	1793	Scituate	grdn	21399
	Joshua	1795	Scituate	admn	21398
	Joshua	1816	Pembroke	will	21402
	Joshua D	1836	Hingham	admn	21404
	Joshua D	1837	Hingham	grdn	21403
	Lazarus	1690/1	Scituate	admn	21405
	Lazarus	1712	-----	grdn	21406
	Lemuel	1843	Scituate	admn	21407
	Lothrop	1835	Plymouth	admn	21408
	Lucy B	1878	S. Scituate	admn	21409
	Lusannah	1861	S. Scituate	will	21410
	Lydia	1719/0	Scituate	grdn	21285
	Lydia	1880	S. Scituate	admn	21411
	Maria W	1845	Scituate	grdn	21446
	Mary	1749	Pembroke	will	21412
	Mary	1813	Scituate	grdn	21424
	Mary	1833	Scituate	will	21414
	Mary A	1854	S. Scituate	grdn	21460
	Mary B	1865	S. Scituate	grdn	21416
	Mary C	1865	Scituate	will	21415
	Mary R	1851	Hanson	will	21413
	Melzar S	1866	Scituate	will	21417
	Mercy	1823	Scituate	will	21418
	Meriam	1722	Scituate	grdn	21310
	Miles S	1865	S. Scituate	grdn	21416
	Nancy O	1869	Abington	admn	21419
	Nathan	1694	Scituate	admn	21420
	Nathan	1703	Scituate	grdn	21421
	Nathan	1824	Hanson	grdn	21450
	Nathaniel	1796	Scituate	will	21422
	Nathaniel	1812	Scituate	admn	21423
	Nathaniel	1813	Scituate	grdn	21424
	Noah B	1824	Hanson	grdn	21450
	Perez	1822	Scituate	admn	21425
	Perez	1823	Scituate	grdn	21426
	Perez 2nd	1874	S. Scituate	will	21427
	Philip	1736	Scituate	will	21429
	Philip	1792	Rochester	admn	21428
	Philip	1793	Scituate	will	21430
	Plato	1818	Plymouth	grdn	21431 a
	Plato	1820	Plymouth	admn	21432
	Plato	1857	Bridgewater	will	21433
	Polly	1861	Scituate	will	21434
	Priscilla	1865	Abington	admn	21435
	Rachel	1794	Scituate	grdn	21439
	Rachel	1813	Scituate	grdn	21424
	Richard	1719/0	Scituate	grdn	21285
	Richard	1752	Scituate	will	21436
	Robert V	1823	Scituate	grdn	21426
	Roland et al	1878	Scituate	peti	21437
	Ruth	1753	Scituate	will	21438
	Ruth	1794	Scituate	grdn	21439
	Ruth S	1874	Hanover	grdn	21340
	Sally	1821	Scituate	grdn	21440
	Samuel	1759	Scituate	will	21442
	Samuel	1777	Scituate	admn	21443
	Samuel	1843	Scituate	admn	21445
	Samuel	1845	Scituate	grdn	21446
	Samuel	1847	Plymouth	admn	21441
	Samuel H	1807	Scituate	admn	21444
	Sarah	1712	-----	grdn	21406
	Sarah	1793	Scituate	grdn	21399
	Sarah	1832	Pembroke	grdn	21447 a
	Sarah S	1823	Scituate	grdn	21426
	Seth	1743	Scituate	will	21448

SURNAME	FIRST NAME	YEAR	PLACE	CASE	DOCKET
TURNER	Seth	1823	Hanson	admn	21449
	Seth	1824	Hanson	grdn	21450
	Simeon	1761	Scituate	will	21451
	Theodore	1867	S. Scituate	will	21452
	Thomas	1688	Scituate	will	21453
	Thomas	1721	Scituate	will	21454
	Thomas	1722	Scituate	grdn	21310
	Thomas	1733	Rochester	admn	21455
	Thomas	1794	Pembroke	will	21456
	Thomas	1809	Pembroke	admn	21457
	Thomas	1829	Hanover	admn	21459
	Thomas	1862	Pembroke	will	21458
	Vesta L	1854	S. Scituate	grdn	21460
	Vine	1760	Scituate	admn	21461
	Waitstill	1772	Hanover	grdn	21462 a
	Warren	1852	Bridgewater	admn	21463
	William	1747	Bridgewater	admn	21464
	William	1759	Scituate	will	21466
	William	1808	Marshfield	admn	21465
	William	1823	Scituate	grdn	21426
	William	1866	S. Scituate	admn	21467
	William	1880	Duxbury	will	21468
TUTTLE	George S	1866	Abington	grdn	21469
	Harriet E	1866	Abington	grdn	21469
	James	1847	Hingham	admn	21470
	Mehitable A	1866	Abington	grdn	21469
TWOMEY	Catherine	1876	Brockton	admn	21471
	Ellen	1876	Brockton	grdn	21473
	John	1876	Brockton	grdn	21473
	Michael	1876	Brockton	admn	21472
	Michael	1876	Brockton	grdn	21473
TYSON	Mary A	1879	E. Bridgewater	will	21474
	William H	1872	E. Bridgewater	will	21475
UFFALL	George	1785	Duxbury	will	21476
UNDERHAY	William	1878	Abington	grdn	21477 a
UNDERWOOD	James A R	1871	Abington	grdn	21479
	James M	1871	Abington	admn	21478
	James P	1852	Hingham	grdn	21480
	John H	1852	Hingham	grdn	21480
	Jonas	1850	Hingham	admn	21481
	Rachel S	1875	Rockland	admn	21482
	Walter T	1871	Abington	grdn	21479
VAIL	Ellen	1876	Hanover	admn	21483
	Isaac B	1861	Carver	grdn	21484
	Jacob	1821	Carver	admn	21486
	Jacob	1832	Middleboro	admn	21485
	Jacob	1857	Carver	admn	21487
	John C	1859	Carver	will	21488
	Rebecca D	1861	Carver	will	21489
VALLER	Abby W	1871	Plymouth	admn	21490
	John	1758	Plymouth	admn	21491
	Lydia J	1880	Plymouth	will	21492
	Simeon	1826	Plymouth	grdn	21493 a
	Simeon	1828	Plymouth	admn	21494
	Simeon	1849	Plymouth	admn	21495
	Sylvanus	1760	Plymouth	admn	21496
	Sylvanus	1847	Plymouth	admn	21497
	Sylvester H	1869	Plymouth	will	21498
	Taylor J	1871	Plymouth	admn	21499
VAN SCHAACK	Kate A	1881	Carver	will	21500
VARNEY	Hollis B	1859	Abington	admn	21501
VAUGHN	Abbie J	1867	Middleboro	grdn	21508
	Abby W	1856	Carver	grdn	21567
	Abraham	1813	Middleboro	admn	21502
	Adoniram J	1830	Middleboro	grdn	21549
	Albert C	1842	Middleboro	grdn	21503
	Alvan	1874	Abington	will	21504
	Alvin P	1856	Carver	grdn	21567
	Barzillai	1839	Carver	admn	21505
	Betsey	1855	Middleboro	admn	21506
	Betsey	1865	Middleboro	admn	21507

SURNAME	FIRST NAME	YEAR	PLACE	CASE	DOCKET
VAUGHN	Betty	1809	Middleboro	grdn	21556
	Callie F	1867	Middleboro	grdn	21508
	Charles	1856	Carver	grdn	21567
	Charles H	1867	Middleboro	grdn	21508
	Cornelius P	1868	Halifax	admn	21509
	Cushman	1809	Middleboro	grdn	21556
	Cushman	1856	Middleboro	admn	21510
	Daniel	1730	Middleboro	bond	21514
	Daniel	1786	Plympton	will	21511
	Daniel	1830	Rochester	will	21512
	Daniel	1865	Middleboro	will	21513
	David	1815	Middleboro	will	21516
	David	1818	Carver	admn	21515
	David A	1858	Middleboro	will	21517
	Diana	1879	Plymouth	grdn	21518 a
	Ebenezer	1810	Middleboro	admn	21519
	Ebenezer	1856	Middleboro	admn	21520
	Elias	1792	Middleboro	admn	21521
	Elias	1814	Carver	admn	21522
	Elisha	1724	Middleboro	admn	21523
	George	1694	Middleboro	will	21524
	George	1767	Middleboro	admn	21525
	George	1805	Middleboro	will	21526
	George	1816	Middleboro	will	21527
	George	1818	Middleboro	grdn	21528
	Harrison W	1880	Middleboro	admn	21529
	Huldah	1822	Carver	will	21530
	Isaac	1853	Carver	admn	21531
	Jabez	1773	Middleboro	will	21532
	James	1849	Carver	will	21533
	James S	1856	Carver	grdn	21567
	Jesse	1860	Middleboro	admn	21534
	John	1821	Middleboro	admn	21535
	Jonathan	1849	Rochester	will	21536
	Joseph	1734	Middleboro	will	21538
	Joseph	1747	Middleboro	admn	21539
	Joseph	1809	Middleboro	grdn	21556
	Joseph	1838	Carver	will	21537
	Joseph	1852	Middleboro	admn	21540
	Josiah	1814	Middleboro	will	21541
	Julia	1818	Middleboro	grdn	21528
	Lemuel	1879	Plymouth	grdn	21542 a
	Levi	1823	Middleboro	admn	21543
	Levi	1845	Carver	admn	21544
	Levi C	1856	Carver	grdn	21567
	Lydia	1844	Carver	admn	21545
	Mary	1881	Middleboro	admn	21546
	Mary R	1865	Middleboro	admn	21547
	Nancy L	1869	Kingston	admn	21548
	Nancy T	1830	Middleboro	grdn	21549
	Nathan	1785	Middleboro	admn	21550
	Nathan	1795	Middleboro	grdn	21551
	Nathaniel	1866	E. Bridgewater	will	21552
	Oliver	1856	Plymouth	admn	21553
	Peter	1788	Middleboro	will	21554
	Peter	1806	Middleboro	admn	21555
	Peter	1809	Middleboro	grdn	21556
	Phebe	1823	Middleboro	grdn	21557 a
	Phebe	1849	Carver	will	21558
	Polly	1845	Carver	admn	21559
	Priscilla	1819	Middleboro	will	21560
	Robert	1809	Middleboro	admn	21561
	Robert	1810	Middleboro	grdn	21562
	Samuel	1747	Plympton	admn	21563
	Samuel	1837	Carver	will	21564
	Samuel	1864	Carver	will	21565
	Samuel E	1856	Carver	grdn	21567
	Samuel M	1866	Carver	grdn	21566
	Sarah	1865	Abington	will	21568
	Sarah E	1866	Carver	grdn	21566
	Stillman	1809	Middleboro	grdn	21556

SURNAME	FIRST NAME	YEAR	PLACE	CASE	DOCKET
VAUGHN	Susan	1830	Middleboro	grdn	21549
	Susan E	1867	Middleboro	grdn	21508
	Sylvia	1862	Rochester	will	21569
	William E W	1856	Carver	grdn	21567
	Zebulon	1824	Middleboro	admn	21570
VEAZIE	Abigail S	1813	-----	grdn	21571
	Catherine E	1853	Abington	grdn	21572
	Sally	1813	-----	grdn	21571
	William E	1853	Abington	grdn	21572
VERRY	William	1880	Plymouth	will	21573
VINAL	Abel	1839	Scituate	admn	21574
	Adelia T	1856	Hanson	grdn	21588
	Adeline M	1836	Scituate	grdn	21620
	Alvyn	1866	Scituate	will	21575
	Arthur J	1874	Scituate	grdn	21576
	Beckey	1804	Scituate	admn	21577
	Benjamin	1782	Scituate	admn	21578
	Benjamin	1796	Scituate	grdn	21579
	Betsey C	1836	Scituate	grdn	21620
	Catherine M	1846	Scituate	grdn	21580
	Charles	1813	Scituate	grdn	21581
	Charles	1837	Scituate	bond	21582
	Charles	1871	Scituate	will	21583
	Charles	1875	Scituate	admn	21584
	Cushing	1855	Hanson	admn	21585
	David	1801	Scituate	admn	21586
	David H	1841	Scituate	admn	21587
	Deborah C	1856	Hanson	grdn	21588
	Dexter	1872	Scituate	will	21589
	Eaton	1845	Scituate	admn	21590
	Edwin F	1876	Scituate	grdn	21591
	Elizabeth	1750	Scituate	admn	21592
	Elizabeth	1750	Scituate	grdn	21622
	Ella G	1860	Scituate	grdn	21593
	Ezekiel	1750	Scituate	grdn	21622
	Ezra	1821	Scituate	admn	21594
	Frank T	1860	Scituate	grdn	21593
	George E	1848	Scituate	grdn	21634
	Gideon	1786	Scituate	will	21595
	Gideon	1840	Scituate	admn	21596
	Gideon	1845	Scituate	grdn	21597
	Hannah	1759	Marshfield	grdn	21638
	Hayward	1860	Scituate	will	21598
	Henry A	1848	Scituate	grdn	21634
	Ignatius	1736	Scituate	grdn	21601
	Ignatius	1796	Scituate	will	21600
	Ignatius	1802	Scituate	will	21599
	Israel	1789	Scituate	will	21602
	Israel	1804	Scituate	will	21603
	Issachar	1799	Scituate	will	21604
	Jacob	1736	Scituate	will	21605
	Jacob	1770	Scituate	will	21606
	Jacob	1788	Scituate	will	21608
	Jacob	1873	Scituate	will	21609
	Jacob Jr	1786	Scituate	admn	21607
	James	1839	Scituate	grdn	21610
	James C	1877	Plymouth	admn	21611
	Job	1786	Scituate	will	21612
	Job	1825	Scituate	admn	21613
	Job H	1874	Scituate	admn	21614
	John	1698	Scituate	will	21617
	John	1748	Scituate	admn	21621
	John	1750	Scituate	grdn	21622
	John	1782	Scituate	will	21618
	John	1870	S. Scituate	will	21615
	John S	1836	Scituate	admn	21619
	John T	1836	Scituate	grdn	21620
	John T	1860	Scituate	admn	21616
	Joseph	1768	Scituate	grdn	21623
	Joshua	1759	Marshfield	grdn	21638
	Joshua	1793	Marshfield	admn	21624

SURNAME	FIRST NAME	YEAR	PLACE	CASE	DOCKET	
VINAL	Josie	1860	Scituate	grdn	21593	
	Lemuel	1886	Scituate	admn	21625	
	Lot	1871	Scituate	will	21626	
	Lucy	1805	Marshfield	will	21627	
	Lucy	1829	Scituate	will	21628	
	Lucy	1879	Scituate	will	21629	
	Lydia	1754	Scituate	grdn	21632	
	Lydia	1804	Scituate	admn	21631	
	Lydia	1825	Scituate	admn	21630	
	Maria	1878	Scituate	will	21633	
	Maria E	1848	Scituate	grdn	21634	
	Martha	1768	Scituate	grdn	21623	
	Mary	1750	Scituate	grdn	21622	
	Mary A	1836	Scituate	grdn	21620	
	Mary Ann	1838	Scituate	admn	21635	
	Robert	1754	Scituate	grdn	21632	
	Ruth	1750	Scituate	grdn	21622	
	Sally	1804	Scituate	grdn	21639	
	Sarah	1785	Bridgewater	admn	21636	
	Sarah	1836	Scituate	grdn	21620	
	Sarah E	1839	Scituate	admn	21637	
	Seth	1736	Scituate	grdn	21601	
	Seth	1759	Marshfield	grdn	21638	
	Sophia	1804	Scituate	grdn	21639	
	Stephen	1712	Scituate	will	21640	
	Stephen	1759	Scituate	grdn	21641	
	Stephen	1805	Scituate	grdn	21642	a
	Thankful	1844	Scituate	will	21643	
	Thomas	1880	Scituate	will	21644	
	Walter S	1874	Scituate	grdn	21576	
	William	1813	Scituate	admn	21645	
	William	1849	Scituate	admn	21646	
	William L	1857	Scituate	will	21647	
	Zeruiah	1817	Marshfield	will	21648	
	Zerviah	1759	Marshfield	grdn	21638	
VINCENT	Isaac	1846	Fairhaven	will	21649	
	Stanford W	1872	N. Bridgewater	will	21650	
VINING	Adeline	1819	Scituate	grdn	21652	
	Alexander	1818	Abington	admn	21651	
	Alexander	1819	Scituate/Abingt	grdn	21652	
	Benjamin	1819	Abington	grdn	21653	a
	Benjamin	1835	Abington	admn	21654	
	Benjamin F	1819	Scituate	grdn	21652	
	David	1860	Hanover	will	21655	
	Ebed	1857	Abington	admn	21656	
	Elisha	1822	Abington	admn	21657	
	Hannah	1790	Abington	will	21658	
	Martha	1881	Hanover	admn	21659	
	Mary J	1819	Scituate	grdn	21652	
	Polly I	1819	Scituate	grdn	21652	
	Richard	1845	Abington	will	21660	
	Thomas J	1864	Hanover	will	21661	
VINTON	William	1840	E. Bridgewater	admn	21662	
VIRGIN	Abby D	1823	Plymouth	grdn	21663	
	George W	1869	Plymouth	admn	21664	
	George W	1870	Plymouth	admn	21665	
	John	1815	Plymouth	admn	21666	
	John	1823	Plymouth	admn	21667	
	Mary	1879	Plymouth	admn	21668	
	Samuel	1824	Plympton	admn	21669	
VOSE	Benjamin F	1868	Marion	grdn	21671	
	Frances A I	1827	Boston	grdn	21670	
	Mary E	1868	Marion	grdn	21671	
	Robert L	1868	Marion	grdn	21671	
WADE	Abednago	1797	Scituate	grdn	21673	
	Abednago	1808	Scituate	admn	21672	
	Abiel	1743	Bridgewater	grdn	21687	
	Abigail	1789	Bridgewater	will	21674	
	Amos	1743	Bridgewater	grdn	21687	
	Arnold	1864	Abington	admn	21675	
	Bathsheba	1761	Scituate	admn	21676	

SURNAME	FIRST NAME	YEAR	PLACE	CASE	DOCKET
WADE	Betsey	1797	Scituate	grdn	21673
	Betsey	1797	Scituate	grdn	21724
	Betsey L	1868	Halifax	grdn	21688
	Betty	1828	E. Bridgewater	admn	21677
	Caroline	1874	E. Bridgewater	admn	21678
	Charles H	1832	E. Bridgewater	grdn	21702
	Charles L	1830	Scituate	grdn	21704
	Debby	1823	Scituate	admn	21679
	Deborah	1797	Scituate	grdn	21724
	Delphina L	1871	Carver	adop	21680
	Ebenezer	1743	Bridgewater	grdn	21687
	Ella A	1868	Halifax	grdn	21688
	George	1837	Plymouth	admn	21681
	George F	1855	Halifax	admn	21682
	Hannah	1743	Bridgewater	grdn	21687
	Hannah	1797	Scituate	grdn	21673
	Hannah	1797	Scituate	will	21683
	Hannah	1838	Scituate	will	21684
	Henry S	1831	Hanover	admn	21685
	Ichabod	1741	Bridgewater	admn	21686
	Ichabod	1743	Bridgewater	grdn	21687
	Irene F	1868	Halifax	grdn	21688
	Issachar	1789	Scituate	will	21689
	Jacob	1703	Scituate	admn	21690
	Jacob	1791	Scituate	will	21691
	James	1802	Bridgewater	admn	21692
	James	1860	Halifax	will	21693
	Jetson	1865	Scituate	grdn	21731
	John	1798	Bridgewater	admn	21694
	John	1873	E. Bridgewater	will	21695
	John J	1881	Plymouth	admn	21696
	Joseph	1762	Scituate	will	21697
	Joseph	1829	Scituate	will	21698
	Jotham	1805	Scituate	will	21699
	Levi	1796	Scituate	will	21700
	Lewis	1832	E. Bridgewater	grdn	21702
	Lewis T	1839	E. Bridgewater	grdn	21701
	Mabel	1797	Scituate	grdn	21673
	Maliren	1743	Bridgewater	grdn	21687
	Maria	1830	Scituate	grdn	21704
	Maria	1838	Scituate	will	21703
	Mary	1816	Scituate	will	21705
	Molly	1743	Bridgewater	grdn	21687
	Molly	1842	E. Bridgewater	will	21706
	Nancy	1848	Scituate	admn	21707
	Nathaniel	1781	Scituate	will	21708
	Nathaniel	1808	Scituate	will	21709
	Nathaniel	1815	Scituate	will	21710
	Nicholas	1712	Scituate	will	21715
	Nicholas	1724	Scituate	will	21714
	Nicholas	1767	Bridgewater	will	21711
	Nicholas	1780	Bridgewater	admn	21712
	Nicholas	1852	E. Bridgewater	admn	21713
	Otis	1797	Scituate	grdn	21724
	Polly	1843	Scituate	will	21716
	Robert	1813	Bridgewater	will	21717
	Sabina	1859	Halifax	admn	21718
	Sally	1797	Scituate	grdn	21724
	Samuel	1797	Halifax	will	21719
	Sarah	1759	Scituate	admn	21720
	Shadrach	1797	Scituate	grdn	21673
	Simeon	1783	Scituate	will	21721
	Snell	1795	Scituate	admn	21723
	Snell	1797	Scituate	grdn	21724
	Snell	1859	S. Scituate	admn	21722
	Sophia L	1852	Halifax	admn	21725
	Stephen	1797	Scituate	admn	21726
	Thankful	1789	Scituate	admn	21727
	Thomas	1726/7	Bridgewater	will	21728
	Thomas	1832	E. Bridgewater	will	21729
	William W	1863	Scituate	admn	21730

SURNAME	FIRST NAME	YEAR	PLACE	CASE	DOCKET
WADE	William W	1865	Scituate	grdn	21731
WADSWORTH	Abigail	1723	Duxbury	admn	21732
	Benjamin	1745	Duxbury	grdn	21734
	Benjamin	1782	Duxbury	will	21733
	Briggs C	1861	Duxbury	will	21735
	Cephas	1819	Kingston	admn	21736
	Christopher	1748	Duxbury	will	21737
	Eden	1878	Duxbury	admn	21738
	Elisha	1755	Duxbury	will	21739
	Grace	1688	-----	will	21740
	Hannah	1745	Duxbury	grdn	21734
	Ichabod	1745	Duxbury	will	21741
	Ichabod	1771	Duxbury	will	21742
	Ichabod	1864	Marshfield	admn	21743
	Isaac	1749	Pembroke	admn	21744
	John	1700	Duxbury	will	21745
	John	1750	Duxbury	admn	21746
	John	1799	Duxbury	admn	21747
	John	1862	Middleboro	will	21748
	Joseph	1690	Duxbury	will	21749
	Joseph F	1865	Duxbury	will	21750
	Luke	1830	Marshfield	will	21751
	Lydia	1745	Duxbury	grdn	21734
	Mary	1871	Marshfield	will	21752
	Mehitable	1754	Duxbury	admn	21753
	Mercy	1739	Hanover	will	21754
	Molly	1828	Kingston	admn	21755
	Nathaniel	1840	Marshfield	admn	21756
	Peleg	1799	Duxbury	will	21757
	Prince	1754	Duxbury	grdn	21761
	Priscilla	1858	Duxbury	admn	21758
	Samuel	1809	Duxbury	admn	21759
	Sarah	1738	Duxbury	admn	21760
	Sarah	1754	Duxbury	grdn	21761
	Seneca	1825	Duxbury	admn	21762
	Susanna	1749	Pembroke	grdn	21763
	Unis	1754	Duxbury	grdn	21761
	Uriah	1784	Duxbury	admn	21764
	Uriah	1823	Duxbury	will	21765
	Wait	1840	Duxbury	admn	21766
WAIT	Returne	1751	Plymouth	will	21767
WALDRON	Cynthia	1876	Middleboro	will	21768
	George W	1871	Rochester	admn	21770
	Hiram	1868	Rochester	will	21771
	Isaac	1685/6	Boston	admn	21769
	Roswell W	1872	Middleboro	will	21772
WALES	Austin	1853	Abington	admn	21773
	Catherine B	1871	Abington	admn	21774
	Charles H	1854	Abington	grdn	21776
	Charles H	1869	Abington	will	21775
	Deborah O	1869	W. Bridgewater	admn	21777
	Edward C	1854	Abington	grdn	21776
	Elizabeth F	1841	Hanson	grdn	21778
	James L	1833	Boston	grdn	21779
	John	1823	N. Bridgewater	admn	21780
	Maria J	1856	Abington	grdn	21783
	Mary G	1854	Abington	grdn	21776
	Nathaniel	1826	N. Bridgewater	will	21781
	Samuel R	1873	Cheyenne WY	admn	21782
	Susan J	1856	Abington	grdn	21783
	Thomas	1840	N. Bridgewater	will	21784
	Thomas	1865	N. Bridgewater	admn	21785
	Welcome H	1879	Brockton	will	21786
	William	1776	Abington	admn	21787
	William	1839	Abington	admn	21788
	William	1851	Abington	admn	21789
WALKER	Abigail	1813	Pembroke	will	21802
	Abraham	1786	Marshfield	admn	21790
	Alexander	1793	Middleboro	admn	21791
	Almeda	1853	Marshfield	grdn	21792
	Asa	1820	Marshfield	admn	21793

SURNAME	FIRST NAME	YEAR	PLACE	CASE	DOCKET
WALKER	Bethiah	1763	Marshfield	admn	21794
	Bethiah	1809	Pembroke	grdn	21795
	Betsey T	1823	Hanson	grdn	21796
	Betty	1802	Marshfield	will	21797
	Charles	1852	Marshfield	admn	21798
	Edmund D	1853	Marshfield	grdn	21792
	Gideon	1784	Marshfield	admn	21799
	Isaac	1750	Marshfield	will	21801
	Isaac	1813	Pembroke	will	21802
	Isaac	1822	Hanson	admn	21800
	Isaiah	1793	Marshfield	admn	21803
	Joanna C	1841	Middleboro	grdn	21804
	Joel	1836	Duxbury	will	21805
	John	1747	Marshfield	will	21806
	John	1809	Pembroke	admn	21807
	Laura	186-	-----	dope	21808
	Levi	1879	Marshfield	admn	21809
	Mary Ann	1874	Bridgewater	admn	21810
	Olive H	1866	Abington	grdn	21811
	Olney	1840	Middleboro	admn	21812
	Ruth G	1841	Middleboro	grdn	21804
	Sally	1853	Duxbury	admn	21813
	Solomon D	1854	Duxbury	admn	21814
	Sylvanus W	1867	Bridgewater	admn	21815
WALL	Walter	1872	Scituate	will	21816
WALLING	Alice J	1878	Abington	admn	21817
	Jennie G	1878	Hanover	grdn	21818
WALLIS	James	1777	Plympton	will	21819
	John	1758	Pembroke	will	21820
WALSH	Ardis	1864	E. Bridgewater	admn	21821
	Ella F	1864	Pembroke	grdn	21823
	Ellen M	1856	Philadelphia	peti	21822
	Joseph A	1864	Pembroke/E. B'w	grdn	21823
	Robert F	1856	Philadelphia	peti	21822
	Sophia B	1856	Philadelphia	peti	21822
	Susan	1868	Philadelphia	grdn	21824 a
	Walter H	1856	Philadelphia	peti	21822
WANTON	Edward	1716	Scituate	will	21825
	Lydia	1711	Scituate/Abingt	grdn	21827
	Lydia	1718	Abington	admn	21826
	Mary	1711	Scituate/Abingt	grdn	21827
	Michael	1741	Scituate	will	21828
	Stephen	1709	Scituate	admn	21829
WAPENIT	Robert/Robin	1723	Plymouth	will	21830 i
WARD	Adeline	1836	Carver	grdn	21835
	Alva N	1864	N. Bridgewater	grdn	21831
	Benjamin	1771	Bridgewater	admn	21832
	Benjamin	1812	Carver	will	21833
	Benjamin	1832	Carver	admn	21834
	Benjamin	1836	Carver	grdn	21835
	Betsey	1812	Carver	grdn	21836
	Betsey	1836	Carver	grdn	21835
	Chandler	1812	Carver	grdn	21836
	Edward 2nd	1873	Scituate	admn	21837
	Eliab	1797	Carver	admn	21838
	Eliab	1866	Carver	admn	21839
	Ephraim	1856	Lakeville	will	21840
	Franklin	1863	N. Bridgewater	admn	21841
	George	1856	Lakeville	will	21842
	George F	1864	N. Bridgewater	grdn	21831
	Hannah	1836	Carver	grdn	21835
	James W	1873	Lakeville	admn	21843
	John	1720	Plymouth	will	21844
	Julia	1836	Carver	grdn	21835
	Lothrop	1823	Middleboro	grdn	21845
	Patrick	1875	Abington	will	21846
	Randall	1864	Abington	will	21847
WARLAND	Sarah	1845	Plymouth	will	21848
WARNER	Henry	1878	Rockland	admn	21849
WARR	Charles	1876	Wareham	admn	21850
	Mary E	1872	Wareham	admn	21851

SURNAME	FIRST NAME	YEAR	PLACE	CASE	DOCKET
WARREN	Abigail	1772	Plymouth	grdn	21853
	Abigail	1832	Plymouth	will	21852
	Alva	1873	N. Bridgewater	grdn	21854 a
	Anna	1770	Middleboro	will	21855
	Benjamin	1746	Plymouth	will	21858
	Benjamin	1757	Middleboro	grdn	21860
	Benjamin	1825	Plymouth	admn	21857
	Benjamin	1862	Plympton	will	21856
	Benjamin Jr	1740	Plymouth	admn	21859
	Charles H	1874	Plymouth	will	21861
	Daniel	1838	Middleboro	admn	21862
	Ebenezer	1824	N. Bridgewater	admn	21863
	Elizabeth	1747	Plymouth	admn	21864
	Elizabeth	1799	Plymouth	admn	21865
	Ellen G	1869	N. Bridgewater	grdn	21866
	Eunice	1767	Bridgewater	admn	21867
	Ezra	1791	Bridgewater	admn	21868
	Galen	1853	Middleboro	admn	21869
	Galen	1869	N. Bridgewater	admn	21870
	George O	1869	Abington	grdn	21871
	Hannah	1767	Bridgewater	admn	21867
	Henry	1835	Plymouth	admn	21872
	James	1709/0	Plymouth	admn	21873
	James	1715	Plymouth	will	21874
	James	1757	Plymouth	will	21875
	James	1808	Plymouth	will	21876
	James	1821	Plymouth	will	21877
	John	1768	Middleboro	will	21878
	John	1865	Middleboro	will	21879
	Joseph	1689	Plymouth	will	21880
	Joseph	1696/7	Plymouth	admn	21881
	Joseph	1705	Plymouth	grdn	21886
	Joseph	1756	Plymouth	will	21882
	Joseph	1770	Plymouth	admn	21883
	Joseph	1771	Plymouth	grdn	21884
	Joseph	1779	Plymouth	grdn	21885
	Joshua	1775	Bridgewater	will	21887
	Josiah	1760	Middleboro	admn	21888
	Lois	1803	Plymouth	admn	21889
	Lucia A	1877	Kingston	will	21890
	Mary	1795	Plymouth	admn	21891
	Mary	1858	Plymouth	admn	21892
	Mercy	1747	Plymouth	admn	21893
	Mercy	1872	Middleboro	will	21894
	Nathan	1807	Middleboro	admn	21895
	Nathaniel	1707	Plymouth	will	21896
	Nathaniel	1767	Plymouth	admn	21897
	Phebe	1855	Plymouth	will	21898
	Priscilla	1705	Plymouth	grdn	21886
	Rebecca P	1874	Rockland	admn	21899
	Richard	1696/7	Middleboro	admn	21900
	Ruth	1772	Plymouth	grdn	21853
	Samuel	1750	Middleboro	admn	21901
	Seth	1824	N. Bridgewater	grdn	21902 a
	Seth	1845	N. Bridgewater	admn	21903
	Simeon	1855	Abington	admn	21904
	Sylvanus	1809	Middleboro	admn	21905
	Sylvanus	1872	Middleboro	will	21906
	William	1793	Plymouth	admn	21907
	Winslow	1870	Plymouth	will	21908
WASHBURN	Abbie W	1869	Kingston	grdn	21909
	Abby M	1874	Mattapoisett	grdn	22008
	Abiel	1766	Middleboro	grdn	21915
	Abiel	1780	Kingston	grdn	22004
	Abiel	1837	E. Bridgewater	grdn	21987
	Abiel	1843	Middleboro	will	21910
	Abiel	1868	Middleboro	admn	21911
	Abigail	1766	Middleboro	grdn	21915
	Abigail	1837	E. Bridgewater	grdn	21987
	Abigail	1856	E. Bridgewater	admn	21912
	Abigail	1860	E. Bridgewater	admn	21913

SURNAME	FIRST NAME	YEAR	PLACE	CASE	DOCKET
WASHBURN	Abigail	1860	Middleboro	will	21914
	Abraham	1757	Bridgewater	grdn	22048
	Abraham	1785	Bridgewater	admn	21916
	Abraham	1789	Bridgewater	grdn	21917
	Abram	1854	Bridgewater	will	21918
	Albert	1851	Lynchburg VA	admn	21919
	Alden	1764	Bridgewater	grdn	21956
	Alden	1857	E. Bridgewater	admn	21920
	Amos	1794	Middleboro	admn	21921
	Anna	1764	Bridgewater	grdn	21956
	Anna D	1870	N. Bridgewater	grdn	21962
	Anna E	1816	Bridgewater	grdn	22013
	Asa	1764	Bridgewater	grdn	21956
	Asa	1840	Bridgewater	admn	21922
	Barnabas	1721	Plymouth	grdn	21961
	Barnabas	1770	Kingston	will	21923
	Benjamin	1690/1	Bridgewater	will	21924
	Benjamin	1740	Bridgewater	admn	21925
	Benjamin	1796	Bridgewater	admn	21926
	Benjamin	1812	Bridgewater	will	21927
	Benjamin	1822	Middleboro	admn	21930
	Benjamin	1875	Wareham	admn	21929
	Benjamin F	1865	E. Bridgewater	admn	21928
	Bildad	1780	Kingston	grdn	22004
	Bildad	1833	Kingston	will	21931
	Bradford	1849	Dadeville AL	grdn	22036
	Bradford S	1878	Middleboro	will	21932
	Caleb F	1877	Kingston	grdn	21933 a
	Calvin	1819	Bridgewater	will	21934
	Calvin	1843	Bridgewater	grdn	21935 a
	Caroline	1860	Bridgewater	grdn	21936
	Caroline M	1849	Opheliki AL	grdn	21941
	Carver	1862	Bridgewater	admn	21937
	Cephas	1873	Bridgewater	admn	21938
	Charles	1806	Kingston	grdn	21994
	Charles	1880	Kingston	admn	21939
	Charles C	1849	Opheliki AL	grdn	21941
	Charles E	1870	Lakeville	admn	21940
	Charlotte	1855	Lakeville	admn	21942
	Chloe	1806	Bridgewater	grdn	22072
	Cornelius	1779	Bridgewater	will	21943
	Cyrus	1865	Middleboro	will	21944
	Cyrus	1875	Lakeville	admn	21945
	Daniel	1801	Bridgewater	will	21946
	Deborah	1722	Bridgewater	grdn	22000
	Deborah	1871	Plymouth	admn	21947
	Dorothy	1805	Kingston	grdn	22023
	Ebenezer	1721	Plymouth	grdn	21961
	Ebenezer	1728	Bridgewater	admn	21948
	Ebenezer	1738	Kingston	admn	21949
	Ebenezer	1810	Kingston	admn	21950
	Edward	1793	Middleboro	will	21951
	Edward Jr	1767	Middleboro	admn	21952
	Edward P	1848	Kingston	will	21953
	Elbridge F	1873	E. Bridgewater	grdn	21954
	Eleazer	1762	Bridgewater	admn	21955
	Eleazer	1764	Bridgewater	grdn	21956
	Elford K	1870	N. Bridgewater	grdn	21962
	Eli	1879	Bridgewater	admn	21957
	Eliab F	1806	Bridgewater	grdn	22072
	Elisha	1721	Plymouth	grdn	21961
	Elisha	1734	Kingston	admn	21960
	Elisha	1839	Kingston	will	21959
	Elisha	1870	N. Bridgewater	admn	21958
	Eliza H	1816	Bridgewater	grdn	22013
	Elizabeth J	1870	N. Bridgewater	grdn	21962
	Ellen	1860	Bridgewater	grdn	21963
	Ephraim	1721	Plymouth	grdn	21961
	Ephraim	1755	Plympton	admn	21965
	Ephraim	1775	Kingston	admn	21966
	Ephraim	1870	Plymouth	will	21964

SURNAME	FIRST NAME	YEAR	PLACE	CASE	DOCKET
WASHBURN	Ephraim Jr	1775	Kingston	admn	21967
	Ezekiel	1785	Bridgewater	admn	21968
	Ezra E	1816	Bridgewater	grdn	22013
	Fanny	1875	Middleboro	grdn	21969 a
	Fanny	1878	Middleboro	admn	21970
	Francis	1862	E. Bridgewater	admn	21971
	Frank B	1858	Middleboro	grdn	21977
	Frederick	1860	Bridgewater	grdn	21963
	George	1786	Plymouth	grdn	21972
	George	1829	Plymouth	admn	21973
	George	1829	Plymouth	grdn	21974
	George	1853	New Orleans	admn	21975
	George B	1857	Middleboro	admn	21976
	George H	1858	Middleboro	grdn	21977
	Gideon	1777	Bridgewater	admn	21978
	Hannah	1757	Bridgewater	grdn	22048
	Hannah	1839	Middleboro	will	21979
	Hannah	1856	Bridgewater	will	21980
	Hannah J	1864	Plymouth	admn	21981
	Harriet	1866	Bridgewater	grdn	21982 a
	Henry O	1849	Dadeville AL	grdn	22036
	Herman	1863	E. Bridgewater	admn	21983
	Hervey	1806	Kingston	grdn	21985
	Hervey/Harvey	1847	Kingston	admn	21984
	Hiram	1837	E. Bridgewater	admn	21986
	Hiram	1837	E. Bridgewater	grdn	21987
	Horatio	1858	Kingston	admn	21988
	Horatio N	1877	Marion	admn	21989
	Hugh	1819	Bridgewater	grdn	21990 a
	Hugh	1828	Bridgewater	admn	21991
	Huldah S	1880	Wareham	admn	21992
	Ichabod	1721	Plymouth	grdn	21961
	Ichabod	1798	Kingston	admn	21993
	Ichabod	1806	Kingston	grdn	21994
	Isaac	1764	Bridgewater	grdn	21956
	Isaac	1874	E. Bridgewater	will	21995
	Isaac S	1838	E. Bridgewater	admn	21996
	Israel	1721	Bridgewater	admn	21999
	Israel	1722	Bridgewater	grdn	22000
	Israel	1864	Middleboro	will	21997
	Israel A	1865	Schnectady NY	grdn	21998
	Jabez	1721	Plymouth	grdn	21961
	Jabez	1780	Kingston	grdn	22004
	Jabez	1794	Kingston	will	22001
	Jabez	1799	Kingston	admn	22002
	Jabez Jr	1775	Kingston	admn	22003
	Jacob P	1847	Bridgewater	grdn	22114
	James	1749	Bridgewater	will	22005
	James	1815	Middleboro	admn	22006
	James M	1874	Mattapoisett	admn	22007
	Jane	1805	Kingston	grdn	22023
	Jane D	1874	Mattapoisett	grdn	22008
	Japhet	1763	Plympton	grdn	22009
	Jehiel	1836	Kingston	grdn	22010 a
	Jehiel	1837	Kingston	admn	22011
	Jeremiah	1810	Bridgewater	will	22012
	Jeremiah	1816	Bridgewater	grdn	22013
	Jerome	1847	Kingston	grdn	22056
	Joanna H	1831	Bridgewater	admn	22014
	Job M	1806	Kingston	grdn	21985
	John	1686	Bridgewater	will	22015
	John	1746	Bridgewater	will	22020
	John	1769	Plymouth	admn	22016
	John	1780	Kingston	grdn	22004
	John	1801	Kingston	admn	22022
	John	1805	Kingston	grdn	22023
	John	1861	Plymouth	admn	22017
	John	1868	Bridgewater	will	22021
	John	1871	Plymouth	name	22018
	John H	1860	Bridgewater	grdn	21963
	John L	1880	Halifax	admn	22019

SURNAME	FIRST NAME	YEAR	PLACE	CASE	DOCKET
WASHBURN	Jonathan	1725	Bridgewater	admn	22024
	Jonathan	1824	Middleboro	will	22026
	Jonathan	1859	Bridgewater	will	22025
	Joseph	1767	Bridgewater	will	22027
	Joshua	1832	Bridgewater	admn	22028
	Josiah	1734	Bridgewater	admn	22029
	Josiah	1751	Bridgewater	admn	22030
	Josiah	1789	Bridgewater	admn	22031
	Judah	1824	Kingston	admn	22032
	Judith	1780	Kingston	grdn	22004
	Judith	1862	N. Bridgewater	will	22033
	Julia M	1849	Dadeville AL	grdn	22036
	Keziah	1825	Bridgewater	grdn	22034 a
	Keziah	1826	Bridgewater	will	22035
	Lavonia	1849	Dadeville AL	grdn	22036
	Levi	1764	Bridgewater	grdn	21956
	Levi	1859	E. Bridgewater	admn	22037
	Levi J	1861	E. Bridgewater	grdn	22039
	Levi J	1862	E. Bridgewater	admn	22038
	Lewis	1861	Middleboro	will	22040
	Linus	1857	Lakeville	will	22041
	Linus	1858	Lakeville	grdn	22042
	Lois	1823	Bridgewater	admn	22043
	Lois	1825	Bridgewater	admn	22044
	Louisa	1879	Lakeville	admn	22045
	Lucy	1757	Bridgewater	grdn	22048
	Lucy	1780	Kingston	grdn	22004
	Lucy	1789	Bridgewater	grdn	21917
	Lucy	1850	N. Bridgewater	will	22047
	Lucy	1858	Kingston	admn	22046
	Lydia	1784	Kingston	will	22049
	Lydia	1827	Kingston	grdn	22050 a
	Lydia	1829	Plymouth	grdn	21974
	Lydia	1860	E. Bridgewater	will	22051
	Lydia L	1874	E. Bridgewater	will	22052
	Mahala	1855	Middleboro	admn	22053
	Marcia	1860	Bridgewater	grdn	21963
	Marcia P	1847	Bridgewater	grdn	22114
	Marcia P	1851	Bridgewater	will	22054
	Margaret	1829	Plymouth	grdn	21974
	Mariah L	1860	W. Bridgewater	grdn	22055
	Martha J	1847	Kingston	grdn	22056
	Mary	1860	Bridgewater	grdn	21963
	Mary	1866	Bridgewater	will	22057
	Mary G	1879	Brockton	admn	22058
	Mary R	1874	Mattapoisett	grdn	22008
	Mary R	1878	Bridgewater	will	22059
	Mehitable	1754	Kingston	admn	22060
	Nancy	1838	Bridgewater	admn	22061
	Nathan	1847	Bridgewater	grdn	22114
	Nathan	1848	Middleboro	will	22062
	Nathan	1866	Bridgewater	admn	22063
	Nathaniel	1750	Bridgewater	admn	22066
	Nathaniel	1862	Kingston	admn	22064
	Nathaniel A	1868	Kingston	admn	22065
	Nathaniel Jr	1829	Bridgewater	admn	22067
	Nehemiah	1749	Bridgewater	admn	22068
	Noah	1717	Bridgewater	admn	22069
	Olive M	1864	Kingston	admn	22070
	Oliver	1764	Bridgewater	grdn	21956
	Oliver	1818	Bridgewater	will	22071
	Oliver Jr	1806	Bridgewater	grdn	22072
	Pamelia	1806	Kingston	grdn	21994
	Philip	1854	Kingston	will	22073
	Priscilla D	1864	Plymouth	will	22074
	Rebecca	1831	Bridgewater	admn	22075
	Reuben	1759	Middleboro	grdn	22076
	Rhobe S	1816	Bridgewater	grdn	22013
	Rotheus	1870	Bridgewater	admn	22077
	Rowland	1794	Wareham	admn	22078
	Rowland	1857	Wareham	admn	22079

SURNAME	FIRST NAME	YEAR	PLACE	CASE	DOCKET
WASHBURN	Ruel	1806	Bridgewater	grdn	22072
	Sally	1806	Kingston	grdn	21985
	Sally C	1860	Bridgewater	grdn	21963
	Sally S	1794	Wareham	grdn	22080
	Salmon	1810	Middleboro	admn	22081
	Salmon M	1864	Lakeville	admn	22082
	Sampson	1863	E. Bridgewater	admn	22083
	Samuel	1720	Bridgewater	will	22084
	Samuel	1837	Bridgewater	grdn	22085 a
	Samuel	1838	Bridgewater	admn	22086
	Sarah	1722	Bridgewater	grdn	22000
	Sarah	1826	Kingston	admn	22088
	Sarah	1836	Bridgewater	will	22090
	Sarah	1864	Middleboro	admn	22087
	Sarah	1864	Bridgewater	admn	22091
	Sarah	1867	Bridgewater	will	22089
	Sarah A	1849	Opheliki AL	grdn	21941
	Sarah P	1864	N. Bridgewater	admn	22092
	Sears	1863	Bridgewater	will	22093
	Seldon	1873	E. Bridgewater	admn	22094
	Seth	1722	Bridgewater	grdn	22000
	Seth	1789	Bridgewater	grdn	21917
	Seth	1826	Plymouth	will	22095
	Seth	1858	Bridgewater	admn	22097
	Seth	1860	Kingston	admn	22096
	Seth	1866	Bridgewater	grdn	22098 a
	Simeon	1764	Kingston	will	22099
	Simeon	1806	Kingston	admn	22100
	Solomon	1825	Middleboro	will	22101
	Solomon	1848	Duxbury	admn	22102
	Solomon	1850	Bridgewater	admn	22103
	Sumner F	1881	Middleboro	admn	22104
	Susan L	1880	Halifax	grdn	22105
	Thaddeus R	1864	Kingston	admn	22106
	Thankful	1721	Plymouth	grdn	21961
	Thomas	1732	Bridgewater	will	22111
	Thomas	1806	Bridgewater	grdn	22072
	Thomas	1825	Bridgewater	will	22112
	Thomas	1827	Plymouth	admn	22107
	Thomas	1852	Wareham	admn	22108
	Thomas	1866	-----	will	22108 +
	Thomas	1870	Middleboro	will	22110
	Thomas	1877	Wareham	admn	22109
	Thomas J	1847	Bridgewater	grdn	22114
	Thomas J	1866	Bridgewater	admn	22113
	Willard	1873	Bridgewater	will	22115
	William	1756	Bridgewater	will	22117
	William	1805	Kingston	grdn	22023
	William	1811	Carver	will	22116
	William	1837	E. Bridgewater	grdn	21987
	William S	1866	E. Bridgewater	grdn	22118
	Zenas	1824	E. Bridgewater	admn	22119
WATERMAN	Abia	1715	Marshfield	grdn	22122
	Abigail	1715	Marshfield	grdn	22122
	Abigail	1772	Pembroke	admn	22120
	Abigail	1796	Marshfield	will	22121
	Alice	1868	Middleboro	grdn	22123
	Anthony	1715	Marshfield	admn	22124
	Anthony	1770	Halifax	admn	22125
	Anthony	1770	Halifax	will	22126
	Anthony	1799	Scituate	admn	22127
	Anthony	1859	Scituate	admn	22128
	Arthur G	1879	E. Bridgewater	grdn	22129
	Asa	1807	Marshfield	will	22130
	Asa	1863	Marshfield	will	22131
	Betsey	1876	Middleboro	will	22132
	Blanche H	1858	Marion	grdn	22210
	Calvin	1770	Halifax	grdn	22149
	Debby	1820	Marshfield	grdn	22133
	Deborah	1784	Scituate	grdn	22182
	Eleazer	1841	Rochester	admn	22134

SURNAME	FIRST NAME	YEAR	PLACE	CASE	DOCKET
WATERMAN	Eliphalet	1836	Duxbury	admn	22135
	Elisha Jr	1808	Halifax	admn	22136
	Elizabeth	1837	Hingham	will	22137
	Elizabeth O	1873	Middleboro	will	22138
	Elkanah	1760	Plymouth	admn	22139
	Ephraim	1820	Duxbury	grdn	22140 a
	Freeman	1830	Halifax	admn	22141
	George	1820	Halifax	grdn	22183
	George	1857	Halifax	will	22142
	Hannah	17--	Plympton	grdn	22198
	Hannah	1798	Halifax	will	22143
	Hannah	1855	Carver	admn	22144
	Hannah	1876	Middleboro	will	22145
	Harriet	1858	N. Bridgewater	adop	22146
	Jabez	1836	Halifax	will	22147
	James	1770	Halifax	grdn	22149
	James	1877	S. Scituate	admn	22148
	Jane P	1866	Halifax	will	22150
	Joanna	1833	Halifax	will	22151
	John	17--	Plympton	grdn	22198
	John	1718	Plympton	will	22155
	John	1761	Halifax	will	22152
	John	1781	Plymouth	admn	22156
	John	1788	Plymouth	grdn	22157
	John	1791	Halifax	will	22153
	John	1800	Marshfield	will	22158
	John	1835	Halifax	admn	22154
	John	1850	Carver	will	22159
	John	1879	E. Bridgewater	admn	22160
	Jonathan	1764	Plympton	admn	22161
	Jonathan	1843	Halifax	admn	22162
	Joseph	1710	Marshfield	will	22163
	Joseph	1715	Marshfield	admn	22164
	Joseph	1717	Marshfield	grdn	22186
	Joseph S	1862	Halifax	will	22165
	Joshua	1801	Middleboro	will	22166
	Josiah	1831	Hingham	admn	22167
	Lewis C	1877	Hanover	admn	22168
	Lydia C	1857	Marion	admn	22169
	Lydia M	1858	Marion	grdn	22210
	Martha	1770	Halifax	admn	22170
	Martin	1860	Duxbury	will	22171
	Mary	1732	Plympton	grdn	22194
	Mary	1876	Hingham	will	22172
	Mercy	1784	Scituate	grdn	22182
	Mercy	1834	Scituate	grdn	22173 a
	Mercy	1834	Scituate	will	22174
	Moses	1820	Halifax	grdn	22175 a
	Nathaniel	1784	Scituate	admn	22181
	Nathaniel	1784	Scituate	grdn	22182
	Nathaniel	1813	Marshfield	grdn	22176 a
	Nathaniel	1819	Marshfield	admn	22177
	Nathaniel	1820	Halifax	grdn	22183
	Nathaniel	1868	Duxbury	admn	22180
	Nathaniel	1872	Marshfield	will	22178
	Nathaniel	1878	Kingston	will	22179
	Olive A	1805	Richmond VA	grdn	22185
	Olive A	1863	Halifax	will	22184
	Orphan	1717	Marshfield	grdn	22186
	Otis	1856	Kingston	admn	22187
	Polly	1784	Scituate	grdn	22182
	Priscilla	1827	Plympton	will	22188
	Rebecca	1763	Halifax	grdn	22189
	Robert	1732	Plympton	grdn	22194
	Robert	1749	Halifax	will	22191
	Robert	1761	Halifax	admn	22192
	Robert	1768	Plympton	grdn	22193
	Robert	1813	Hingham	divi	22190
	Ruth L	1843	Marshfield	admn	22195
	Samuel	17--	Plympton	grdn	22198
	Samuel	1718	Plympton	admn	22197

SURNAME	FIRST NAME	YEAR	PLACE	CASE	DOCKET
WATERMAN	Samuel	1732	Plympton	grdn	22194
	Samuel	1847	Scituate	will	22196
	Susan	1867	Hingham	will	22199
	Thomas	1717	Marshfield	grdn	22186
	Thomas	1774	Marshfield	will	22200
	Thomas	1784	Marshfield	admn	22201
	Thomas	1789	Halifax	will	22202
	Thomas	1792	Scituate	admn	22205
	Thomas	1799	Scituate	grdn	22206
	Thomas	1803	Plympton	will	22203
	Thomas	1813	Hingham	divi	22204
	Thomas	1861	S. Scituate	admn	22207
	William	1809	Halifax	admn	22208
	William B	1858	Marion	grdn	22210
	William B	1860	Kingston	will	22209
	Zebulon	1717	Marshfield	grdn	22186
WATERS	Daniel	1821	Hingham	grdn	22211 a
	Daniel	1854	Hingham	admn	22212
	Daniel	1864	Hingham	admn	22213
	Deborah	1865	Hingham	admn	22214
	Ebenezer	1759	Boston	grdn	22215
	Elijah	1809	Hingham	divi	22216
	Isaac	1820	Hingham	admn	22217
	Isaac	1859	Hingham	admn	22218
	Lewis	1858	Wareham	admn	22219
	Mehitable	1808	Hingham	will	22220
	Nancy	1804	Hingham	admn	22221
	William	1759	Boston	grdn	22215
WATSON	Abby	1865	Plymouth	admn	22222
	Albert M	1853	Plymouth	admn	22223
	Albert M	1853	Plymouth	grdn	22224
	Benjamin M	1835	Plymouth	admn	22225
	Benjamin M	1837	Plymouth	grdn	22226
	Charles L	1811	Plymouth	admn	22227
	Daniel H	1839	Duxbury	admn	22228
	Edward W	1853	Plymouth	grdn	22224
	Edward W	1876	Plymouth	will	22229
	Eliza Ann	1848	Plymouth	will	22230
	Elizabeth G	1841	Duxbury	grdn	22242
	Elkanah	1689/0	Plymouth	admn	22231
	Elkanah	1731	Plymouth	grdn	22240
	Elkanah	1804	Plymouth	will	22232
	George	1688	Plymouth	admn	22233
	George	1731	Plymouth	grdn	22240
	George	1800	Plymouth	will	22234
	George	1836	Hingham	will	22235
	George	1881	Duxbury	will	22236
	Horace H	1841	Duxbury	grdn	22242
	James M	1853	Plymouth	grdn	22224
	John	1731	Plymouth	admn	22239
	John	1731	Plymouth	grdn	22240
	John	1753	Plymouth	will	22237
	John	1826	Plymouth	admn	22238
	John	1835	Duxbury	will	22241
	John C	1841	Duxbury	grdn	22242
	Laura	1841	Duxbury	grdn	22242
	Lucia	1807	Plymouth	grdn	22243
	Lucretia B	1864	Plymouth	admn	22244
	Nathan B.	1853	Plymouth	grdn	22224
	Phebe	1825	Plymouth	will	22245
	Susan A	1816	Plymouth	grdn	22246
	William	1731	Plymouth	grdn	22240
	William	1815	Plymouth	admn	22247
	William	1869	Duxbury	admn	22248
WEATHERBEE	Eunice P	1875	Rockland	admn	22249
	George H	1877	Scituate	will	22250
	Joseph	1873	Abington	admn	22251
	Sarah B	1882	Scituate	will	22252
	Thomas P	1880	Middleboro	admn	22253
WEBB	Barnabas	1834	Scituate	admn	22254
	Barnabas	1836	Scituate	admn	22255

SURNAME	FIRST NAME	YEAR	PLACE	CASE	DOCKET
WEBB	Charles D	1852	Scituate	grdn	22259
	Edward	1877	Scituate	grdn	22256
	Eliza	1871	Scituate	admn	22257
	Eliza	1877	Scituate	admn	22258
	Ellen M	1852	Scituate	grdn	22259
	Frederick	1877	Scituate	grdn	22256
	George H	1852	Scituate	grdn	22259
	Henry	1852	Scituate	grdn	22259
	Lydia	1828	Scituate	grdn	22260 a
	Margaret	1852	Scituate	grdn	22259
	Maria E	1878	Scituate	admn	22261
	Marsena	1879	Scituate	admn	22262
	Marsena	1880	Scituate	admn	22263
	Martha	1879	Scituate	will	22264
	Nicholas B	1817	Pembroke	admn	22265
	Paul	1824	Scituate	admn	22266
	Paul	1877	Scituate	admn	22267
	Seth	1870	Scituate	admn	22268
	Seth Jr	1862	Scituate	admn	22269
	Stephen	1877	Scituate	admn	22270
	Thomas	1777	Scituate	admn	22271
WEBQUISH	Alice G	1870	Plymouth	grdn	22272
	Miranda V	1870	Plymouth	grdn	22272
	Rosa L	1870	Plymouth	grdn	22272
WEBSTER	Ashburton	1862	Marshfield	grdn	22273
	Daniel	1852	Marshfield	will	22274
	Eliza Ann	1853	Abington	grdn	22275
	Ervin	1856	Plymouth	admn	22276
	Fletcher	1862	Marshfield	will	22277
WEEKS	Ansel	1876	Mattapoisett	will	22278
	Ansel Jr	1873	Mattapoisett	will	22279
	Charles W	1858	Mattapoisett	grdn	22280
	Charles W	1858	Mattapoisett	admn	22281
	Delia C G	1842	N. Bridgewater	will	22282
	Ethel C L	1873	Mattapoisett	grdn	22283
	Hannah F	1873	Marion	grdn	22284
	Horace D	1873	Marion	grdn	22284
	Lot	1820	Plymouth	admn	22285
	Oceana B L	1873	Mattapoisett	grdn	22283
	Paul M	1871	Marion	admn	22286
WELD	Addison H	1860	Brooklyn NY	grdn	22287
	Carrie A	1860	Brooklyn NY	grdn	22287
	George H	1860	Brooklyn NY	grdn	22287
	Lucy H	1860	Brooklyn NY	grdn	22287
	Quartus	1805	Abington	admn	22288
WELLS	Daniel S	1865	Plymouth	grdn	22289
	Edward A	1874	Hingham	admn	22290
	Elizabeth	1817	Duxbury	will	22291
	Mercy E	1866	Plymouth	admn	22292
	Phineas	1865	Plymouth	admn	22293
WELSH	Bridget A	1881	Brockton	grdn	22294
	Catherine	1874	N. Bridgewater	grdn	22295
	Edward	1874	N. Bridgewater	grdn	22295
	Honora	1874	N. Bridgewater	grdn	22295
	James	1874	N. Bridgewater	grdn	22295
	James	1881	Brockton	will	22296
	John	1873	N. Bridgewater	admn	22297
	John 2nd	1876	Hingham	will	22298
	Margaret	1874	N. Bridgewater	grdn	22295
	Maurice	1874	N. Bridgewater	grdn	22295
	Robert	1857	Marshfield	admn	22299
WENTWORTH	Darius	1841	Bridgewater	admn	22300
	Darius C	1842	Bridgewater	grdn	22301
	Jonathan	1819	Plymouth	admn	22302
	Martin	1880	Brockton	admn	22303
	Mary R	1859	Middleboro	admn	22304
	Olive F	1842	Bridgewater	grdn	22301
	Susan G	1879	Bridgewater	admn	22305
	Theophilus	1861	Bridgewater	will	22306
WEST	Benjamin H	1878	Rochester	will	22307
	Elisha	1738	Kingston	will	22309

SURNAME	FIRST NAME	YEAR	PLACE	CASE	DOCKET
WEST	Elisha	1738	Kingston	grdn	22310
	Elisha	1790	Rochester	will	22308
	Fear	1738	Kingston	grdn	22310
	Francis	1693	Duxbury	admn	22311
	Hannah	1814	Kingston	admn	22312
	Hannah S	1862	Rochester	adop	22313
	Josiah	1803	Kingston	will	22314
	Mary	1738	Kingston	grdn	22310
	Pelatiah	1757	Duxbury	will	22315
	Peleg	1738	Kingston	grdn	22310
	Peter	1721	Plympton	will	22316
	Peter	1738	Kingston	grdn	22310
	Peter	1786	Kingston	will	22317
	Richard	1727	Middleboro	admn	22318
	Samuel	1689/0	Duxbury	admn	22319
	Samuel	1770	Plymouth	admn	22320
	Sarah	1738	Kingston	grdn	22310
	Sophronia P	1880	Hingham	admn	22321
	Thomas	1738	Kingston	grdn	22310
	Thomas	1790	Rochester	will	22322
	Tryphosa	1703	Duxbury	admn	22323
WESTCOTT	Charles J	1837	W. Bridgewater	admn	22324
WESTERMEYER	Matthias	1872	Bridgewater	will	22325
WESTGATE	Benjamin	1824	Rochester	admn	22326
	Bradford F	1871	Wareham	grdn	22327
	Daniel	1863	Wareham	admn	22328
	Ezra T	1864	Middleboro	admn	22329
	Frederick	1822	Rochester	grdn	22330
	James	1822	Rochester	grdn	22330
	Jonathan	1822	Rochester	will	22331
	Joseph	1863	Wareham	grdn	22332
	Leland	1822	Rochester	grdn	22330
	Mary B	1877	Mattapoisett	admn	22333
	Matilda	1822	Rochester	grdn	22330
	Obed	1856	Middleboro	will	22334
	Sarah A	1875	Mattapoisett	will	22335
	Stephen	1862	Kingston	grdn	22336 a
	Susan	1853	Middleboro	will	22337
	Sylvanus	1875	Middleboro	will	22338
	William	1841	Middleboro	admn	22339
WESTON	Abigail A	1821	Middleboro	grdn	22464
	Alden B	1880	Duxbury	admn	22340
	Alonzo	1860	Duxbury	grdn	22452
	Andrew	1871	Middleboro	admn	22341
	Ann W	1866	Duxbury	admn	22342
	Annie S	1853	Duxbury	grdn	22343
	Arabella	1835	Duxbury	grdn	22424
	Arunah	1765	Duxbury	grdn	22344
	Baker	1798	Marshfield	grdn	22397
	Baker	1817	Duxbury	admn	22345
	Barzillai	1802	Middleboro	admn	22346
	Benjamin	1773	Plympton	admn	22347
	Benjamin	1835	Plympton	admn	22348
	Benjamin	1858	Plymouth	will	22349
	Benjamin F	1854	Bridgewater	admn	22350
	Bethania	1837	Middleboro	will	22351
	Betsey	1852	Plymouth	admn	22352
	Caroline E	1873	Middleboro	will	22353
	Charles F A	1874	Wareham	admn	22355
	Charles P	1864	Duxbury	admn	22354
	Church	1848	Duxbury	admn	22356
	Content	1821	Middleboro	will	22357
	Coomer	1796	Plymouth	admn	22359
	Coomer	1800	Plymouth	grdn	22360
	Coomer	1870	Plymouth	admn	22358
	Daniel	1767	Duxbury	admn	22361
	Daniel	1830	Plympton	admn	22365
	Daniel	1837	Halifax	admn	22362
	Daniel	1840	Plympton	grdn	22366
	Daniel	1841	Marshfield	admn	22363
	Daniel	1853	Wareham	will	22364

SURNAME	FIRST NAME	YEAR	PLACE	CASE	DOCKET
WESTON	Darius A	1821	Middleboro	grdn	22464
	David	1836	Middleboro	will	22367
	David	1875	Hamilton NY	will	22368
	Deborah	1878	Marshfield	will	22369
	Eden	1859	Duxbury	will	22370
	Edmond	1686	Duxbury	will	22371
	Edmond	1773	Middleboro	admn	22372
	Edmund	1727	Plympton	admn	22374
	Edmund	1814	Middleboro	will	22373
	Edward B	1868	Duxbury	will	22375
	Elias E	1853	Duxbury	grdn	22376
	Elijah	1803	Plympton	grdn	22377
	Eliphas	1762	Duxbury	admn	22378
	Elkanah	1837	Duxbury	admn	22379
	Ellen C	1848	Duxbury	grdn	22380
	Elnathan	1729	Duxbury	will	22381
	Elnathan	1764	Duxbury	grdn	22382 a
	Enoch	1868	Middleboro	will	22383
	Ezra	1822	Duxbury	admn	22384
	Ezra	1842	Duxbury	admn	22385
	Frances White	1860	Duxbury	grdn	22452
	George	1833	Duxbury	admn	22386
	Gershom B	1838	Duxbury	bond	22387
	Gershom B	1869	Duxbury	admn	22388
	Hannah	1881	Duxbury	will	22389
	Hannah B	1798	Marshfield	grdn	22397
	Harvey	1876	Plymouth	will	22390
	Henry	1836	Middleboro	grdn	22391
	Henry L	1854	Duxbury	admn	22392
	Huldah	1838	Middleboro	will	22393
	Ichabod	1797	Marshfield	admn	22396
	Ichabod	1798	Marshfield	grdn	22397
	Ichabod	1818	Duxbury	admn	22395
	Ichabod	1874	Duxbury	will	22394
	Isaac	1800	Plymouth	grdn	22360
	Jacob	1760	Plympton	admn	22398
	Jacob	1834	Duxbury	admn	22399
	James	1875	Duxbury	admn	22400
	Job	1783	Plympton	admn	22401
	John	1736	Duxbury	admn	22402
	John	1805	Marshfield	grdn	22457
	John	1818	Duxbury	admn	22403
	Joseph	1778	Duxbury	admn	22404
	Joseph	1814	Duxbury	admn	22405
	Joseph	1871	Duxbury	admn	22406
	Joshua	1814	Duxbury	grdn	22438
	Judith	1814	Duxbury	grdn	22438
	Judith T	1868	Duxbury	admn	22407
	Lewis	1825	Plymouth	admn	22408
	Lewis	1864	Duxbury	will	22409
	Lucy	1815	Middleboro	grdn	22410
	Luther F	1853	Duxbury	will	22411
	Lydia	1814	Duxbury	admn	22412
	Marcia	1821	Middleboro	grdn	22413
	Maria E	1840	Plympton	grdn	22366
	Martha G	1836	Duxbury	grdn	22414
	Mary	1778	Duxbury	admn	22415
	Matilda	1854	Duxbury	admn	22416
	Mercy	1776	Duxbury	grdn	22450
	Mercy	1794	Plympton	admn	22417
	Nathan	1754	Plympton	admn	22418
	Nathan	1814	Middleboro	admn	22419
	Nathaniel	1835	Duxbury	grdn	22424
	Nathaniel	1867	Duxbury	will	22420
	Nathaniel B	1848	Duxbury	grdn	22425
	Nathaniel B	1866	Duxbury	admn	22422
	Nathaniel C	1846	Duxbury	admn	22423
	Nathaniel Jr	1834	Duxbury	admn	22421
	Olive D	1838	Duxbury	grdn	22460
	Olive W	1849	Duxbury	admn	22426
	Otis	1798	Marshfield	grdn	22397

SURNAME	FIRST NAME	YEAR	PLACE	CASE	DOCKET
WESTON	Peleg	1776	Duxbury	grdn	22450
	Peleg	1836	Duxbury	will	22427
	Peleg 2nd	1830	Duxbury	admn	22428
	Persis P	1866	Marshfield	admn	22429
	Phebe A	1869	Duxbury	will	22430
	Polly	1844	Middleboro	admn	22431
	Priscilla	1778	Duxbury	admn	22432
	Priscilla	1853	Plymouth	will	22433
	Prudence	1766	Plymouth	will	22434
	Rebecca	1776	Duxbury	grdn	22450
	Roxalana	1817	Duxbury	grdn	22435
	Roxalana	1833	Duxbury	admn	22436
	Rufus	1814	Duxbury	grdn	22438
	Rufus	1853	Duxbury	will	22437
	Sally	1868	Kingston	admn	22439
	Samuel	1752	Duxbury	will	22440
	Samuel	1754	Duxbury	admn	22441
	Samuel	1845	Skowhegan ME	admn	22442
	Sarah	1796	Middleboro	admn	22443
	Sarah L	1839	Duxbury	grdn	22444
	Seth	1876	Marshfield	will	22445
	Sylvanus	1832	Duxbury	admn	22446
	Thomas	1743	Plymouth	admn	22448
	Thomas	1776	Duxbury	will	22449
	Thomas	1776	Duxbury	grdn	22450
	Thomas	1800	Plymouth	grdn	22360
	Thomas	1834	Middleboro	will	22447
	Timothy	1765	Duxbury	grdn	22344
	Waldo E	1865	Marshfield	grdn	22451
	Walter	1860	Duxbury	grdn	22452
	Warren	1799	Duxbury	admn	22453
	William	1805	Marshfield	will	22456
	William	1805	Marshfield	grdn	22457
	William	1820	Plymouth	will	22455
	William	1848	Duxbury	grdn	22425
	William	1861	Duxbury	admn	22454
	Willie H	1872	Duxbury	grdn	22458
	Zabdiel	1805	Duxbury	admn	22459
	Zabdiel	1838	Duxbury	grdn	22460
	Zachariah	1794	Middleboro	admn	22461
	Zechariah	1764	Middleboro	will	22462
	Zechariah	1820	Middleboro	admn	22463
	Zechariah	1821	Middleboro	grdn	22464
WETHERED	John	1748	Plymouth	admn	22466
	John	1778	Plymouth	admn	22465
WHEELDEN	Henry	1730	Scituate	admn	22467
WHEELER	Austin E	1868	Abington	grdn	22475
	Charles E	1868	Abington	grdn	22475
	Clara A	1853	Bridgewater	grdn	22468
	Clara M	1868	Abington	grdn	22475
	Edward A	1871	Abington	admn	22469
	Henry E	1853	Plymouth	grdn	22470
	Jane	1822	Scituate	will	22471
	Joseph W	1868	Abington	grdn	22475
	William	1853	Plymouth	grdn	22470
	William	1853	Plymouth	admn	22473
	William	1868	Abington	admn	22474
	William H	1868	Abington	grdn	22475
	William W	1810	Scituate	admn	22472
WHEELWRIGHT	David	1799	-----	grdn	22476
	John	1824	Scituate	grdn	22477 a
	Martin	1846	Scituate	admn	22478
WHISTONE	John	1693	Scituate	admn	22479
	John	1693	Scituate	grdn	22480
	Joseph	1693	Scituate	grdn	22480
	Susanna	1693	Scituate	grdn	22480
WHITBRIDGE	Peleg	1821	Rochester	will	22481
WHITCOMB	Asa	1870	Marshfield VT	admn	22482
	Asa	1873	Troy NH	admn	22483
	Bertha T	1873	N. Bridgewater	grdn	22484
	Charles	1857	Scituate	will	22485

SURNAME	FIRST NAME	YEAR	PLACE	CASE	DOCKET
WHITCOMB	Elizabeth	1837	N. Bridgewater	admn	22486
	Hervey	1867	Scituate	will	22487
	Israel	1733	Scituate	admn	22488
	James	1730	Rochester	will	22489
	John	1787	Scituate	admn	22490
	Mary	1730	Rochester	will	22491
	Moses	1759	Rochester	grdn	22492
	Noah	1734	Scituate	grdn	22494
	Noah	1851	Scituate	admn	22493
	Olive	1759	Rochester	grdn	22492
	Robert	1696/7	Scituate	admn	22495
	Robert	1705/6	Scituate	admn	22496
	Robert	1745	Rochester	admn	22497
	Samuel	1841	Scituate	admn	22498
WHITE	Abigail	1757	Abington	grdn	22564
	Albert	1861	Hanover	will	22499
	Albert E	1876	Hull	grdn	22500
	Alice	1868	E. Bridgewater	grdn	22501
	Almira B	1844	Duxbury	grdn	22502
	Almira H	1854	Fall River	grdn	22566
	Alvin	1846	Rochester	admn	22503
	Andrew	1746	Marshfield	grdn	22578
	Andrew	1776	Middleboro	grdn	22505
	Andrew	1792	Middleboro	admn	22504
	Ann E	1849	Rochester	grdn	22596
	Anna	1838	Wareham	admn	22506
	Anna	1838	Marshfield	grdn	22508 a
	Anna	1875	S. Scituate	admn	22507
	Asa	1847	W. Bridgewater	will	22509
	Bartlett	1844	Duxbury	grdn	22502
	Benjamin	1724	Marshfield	admn	22511
	Benjamin	1774	Middleboro	admn	22515
	Benjamin	1786	Hanover	will	22512
	Benjamin	1819	Marshfield	admn	22510
	Benjamin	1821	Carver	will	22514
	Benjamin	1835	Middleboro	grdn	22516 a
	Benjamin	1839	Hanover	will	22513
	Benjamin	1849	Middleboro	admn	22517
	Benjamin F	1867	Middleboro	grdn	22518
	Bethuel	1851	Hanson	will	22519
	Briggs	1846	Duxbury	will	22520
	Charles	1867	Middleboro	admn	22522
	Charles	1880	Halifax	admn	22521
	Charles F	1865	Middleboro	will	22523
	Clarissa	1853	Middleboro	will	22524
	Cora A	1867	Bridgewater	grdn	22525
	Cornelius	1756	Marshfield	will	22526
	Cornelius	1841	Hanover	will	22527
	Cornelius	1869	Hanson	will	22528
	Cornelius Jr	1851	Hanson	admn	22529
	Cushing	1880	E. Bridgewater	admn	22530
	Cyrus	1830	Middleboro	will	22531
	Cyrus	1849	Rochester	admn	22532
	Daniel	1724	Marshfield	will	22533
	Daniel	1761	Middleboro	admn	22535
	Daniel	1786	Marshfield	will	22534
	Daniel P	1877	Pembroke	admn	22536
	Darius	1879	Plympton	admn	22537
	David	1757	Easton	grdn	22538
	Ebenezer	1776	Middleboro	grdn	22505
	Edna F	1871	N. Bridgewater	will	22539
	Edwin	1664	-----	admn	22540
	Eliza A R	1880	W. Bridgewater	will	22541
	Elizabeth	1858	Hanson	admn	22542
	Elizabeth C	1843	Plymouth	admn	22543
	Elkanah	1737	Marshfield	grdn	22544
	Elmer	1870	Bridgewater	grdn	22586
	Elmer	1880	Bridgewater	admn	22545
	Ernest W	1867	Bridgewater	grdn	22546
	Ernest W	1876	E. Bridgewater	admn	22547
	Eugenia	1877	Middleboro	admn	22548

SURNAME	FIRST NAME	YEAR	PLACE	CASE	DOCKET
WHITE	Eugenia F	1849	Rochester	grdn	22596
	Ezra S	1841	Plympton	admn	22549
	Frank E	1875	Plympton	grdn	22550
	Friend	1810	Pembroke	admn	22551
	Friend	1810	Pembroke	grdn	22552
	Gideon	1779	Plymouth	will	22553
	Gideon C	1828	Plymouth	admn	22554
	Gideon T	1836	Pembroke	will	22555
	Gilman Jr	1839	Rochester	admn	22556
	Gowan	1664	-----	admn	22555 +
	Hannah	1746	Marshfield	grdn	22578
	Hannah	1768	Marshfield	will	22557
	Hannah	1776	Marshfield	will	22558
	Hannah	1792	Marshfield	will	22559
	Henry	1870	Bridgewater	grdn	22586
	Hiram	1810	Pembroke	grdn	22552
	Hitty	1797	Bridgewater	grdn	22602
	Howard	1855	Scituate	admn	22560
	Irene A	1864	Duxbury	adop	22561
	Jacob	1756	Abington	admn	22563
	Jacob	1757	Abington	grdn	22564
	Jacob	1866	N. Bridgewater	will	22562
	James	1746	Marshfield	grdn	22578
	James	1853	Marshfield	will	22565
	Jane F	1854	Fall River	grdn	22566
	Jeremiah	1794	Abington	will	22567
	Jeremiah	1809	Abington	will	22568
	Joanna	1811	Plymouth	will	22569
	Joel	1822	Halifax	will	22570
	John	1746	Marshfield	grdn	22578
	John	1748	Rochester	will	22571
	John	1753	Marshfield	will	22576
	John	1835	N. Bridgewater	will	22572
	John	1848	Hanson	admn	22573
	John A	1843	Marshfield	grdn	22574 a
	John A	1861	Marshfield	admn	22575
	John Jr	1746	Marshfield	admn	22577
	Joseph	1711	Scituate	will	22582
	Joseph	1722	Scituate	admn	22583
	Joseph	1766	Marshfield	admn	22581
	Joseph	1803	Scituate	admn	22584
	Joseph	1824	Scituate	grdn	22585
	Joseph	1843	Duxbury	admn	22579
	Joseph	1857	Hanson	admn	22580
	Josephine	1870	Bridgewater	grdn	22586
	Judah	1709	Rochester	grdn	22593
	Lemuel	1827	Wareham	admn	22587
	Lucy	1813	Bridgewater	admn	22588
	Lucy M	1876	Hull	grdn	22500
	Luther	1816	Marshfield	will	22589
	Luther M	1867	Middleboro	grdn	22518
	Lydia	1797	Bridgewater	grdn	22602
	Lydia	1837	Marshfield	will	22590
	Malatiah	1799	Rochester	admn	22591
	Maletiah	1709	Rochester	admn	22592
	Maltiah	1709	Rochester	grdn	22593
	Margaret	1709	Rochester	grdn	22593
	Maria A	1849	Rochester	grdn	22596
	Maria A	1875	Marshfield	admn	22594
	Martin	1826	Bridgewater	admn	22595
	Mary	1765	Weymouth	grdn	22600
	Mary B	1849	Rochester	grdn	22596
	Mercy	1709	Rochester	grdn	22593
	Micah	1751	Abington	grdn	22599
	Micah	1765	Weymouth	grdn	22600
	Micah	1795	Bridgewater	admn	22597
	Micah	1805	Bridgewater	admn	22598
	Nabby	1797	Bridgewater	grdn	22602
	Nabby	1864	Abington	will	22601
	Nathan	1746	Marshfield	grdn	22578
	Nathan	1776	Middleboro	grdn	22505

SURNAME	FIRST NAME	YEAR	PLACE	CASE	DOCKET
WHITE	Paul	1776	Marshfield	will	22603
	Paul	1785	Marshfield	will	22604
	Peregrine	1704	Marshfield	will	22605
	Polly	1797	Bridgewater	grdn	22602
	Resolved	1780	Rochester	admn	22606
	Reuben B	1864	Wareham	will	22607
	Richard	1728	Plymouth	will	22608
	Ruth	1776	Middleboro	grdn	22505
	Samuel	1776	Middleboro	grdn	22505
	Samuel	1786	Marshfield	will	22610
	Samuel	1822	Middleboro	admn	22609
	Sarah	1740	Middleboro	grdn	22611
	Sarah	1797	Bridgewater	grdn	22602
	Silas	1835	Middleboro	will	22612
	Solomon	1857	Middleboro	will	22613
	Susanna	1746	Marshfield	grdn	22578
	Sybil	1849	Rochester	will	22614
	Sybil	1875	Marshfield	will	22615
	Sybilline	1781	Marshfield	will	22616
	Sylvanus	1688	Scituate	admn	22617
	Sylvanus	1742	Marshfield	admn	22618
	Sylvanus	1812	Marshfield	will	22619
	Thomas	1797	Bridgewater	grdn	22602
	Thomas	1838	N. Bridgewater	admn	22621
	Thomas F	1819	Marshfield	grdn	22620
	Timothy	1704	Scituate	will	22623
	Timothy	1756	Scituate	admn	22624
	Timothy	1773	Scituate	admn	22625
	Timothy	1824	Scituate	admn	22622
	Timothy Jr	1774	Scituate	admn	22626
	Wadsworth	1844	Duxbury	grdn	22502
	Welcome	1876	Hanson	admn	22627
	Wendall H	1867	Middleboro	grdn	22518
	William	1817	Marshfield	grdn	22628 a
	William	1818	Marshfield	admn	22629
	William B	1875	Middleboro	admn	22630
	William H	1843	N. Bridgewater	admn	22631
	William L	1871	Bridgewater	adop	22632
WHITEHEAD	Enoch	1867	Plymouth	admn	22633
	Harriet	1869	Hingham	admn	22634
	William	1858	Hingham	admn	22635
WHITFIELD	John	1741	Rochester	admn	22636
WHITING	Abel	1822	Hanover	will	22637
	Abigail	1824	Hingham	admn	22638
	Abijah	1808	Halifax	will	22639
	Adoniram	1826	Plymouth	grdn	22641
	Adoniram	1857	Plymouth	grdn	22640
	Alfred B	1872	Hingham	admn	22642
	Amasa	1818	Hingham	admn	22643
	Amasa	1839	Hingham	grdn	22644
	Amos	1793	Hanover	grdn	22682
	Barzillai	1852	Abington	will	22645
	Benjamin	1793	Hanover	grdn	22682
	Benjamin	1858	S. Scituate	admn	22646
	Benjamin 2nd	1867	Plymouth	admn	22647
	Betsey	1829	Hanover	admn	22648
	Betsey	1839	Plymouth	grdn	22707
	Betsey	1856	Plymouth	admn	22649
	Caleb	1867	Hanover	will	22650
	Carrie F	1867	Plymouth	grdn	22662
	Catherine B	1871	Hingham	will	22651
	Charles	1849	Hingham	admn	22652
	Comfort	1869	Plymouth	bond	22653
	Davis	1833	Hingham	admn	22654
	Davis Jr	1828	Hingham	admn	22655
	Dexter	1869	Hingham	admn	22656
	Edwin	1825	Hingham	grdn	22688
	Eleanor	1869	Plymouth	admn	22657
	Eleazer	1868	Abington	will	22658
	Ellis	1880	Plymouth	admn	22659
	Enoch	1838	Hingham	will	22660

SURNAME	FIRST NAME	YEAR	PLACE	CASE	DOCKET
WHITING	Esther	1826	Plymouth	grdn	22641
	Ezra	1831	Hanover	admn	22661
	Florence L	1867	Plymouth	grdn	22662
	Frank	1862	Plymouth	grdn	22719
	George M	1848	Duxbury	will	22663
	Gilman	1825	Hingham	grdn	22688
	Hannah	1826	Plymouth	grdn	22641
	Hannah	1839	Plymouth	grdn	22707
	Henry	1875	Plymouth	admn	22664
	Homer	1794	Hanover	admn	22665
	Homer	1794	Hanover	grdn	22666
	Hosea	1869	Hingham	admn	22667
	Jacob	1880	Rockland	admn	22668
	James	1812	Hanover	admn	22669
	James	1813	Plymouth	admn	22671
	James	1820	Scituate	admn	22670
	James H	1847	Plymouth	grdn	22672 a
	Jared	1876	Hanover	admn	22673
	Joanna	1874	Abington	admn	22674
	John	1851	Plymouth	admn	22675
	John B	1867	Hanover	grdn	22676
	Joseph	1825	N. Bridgewater	admn	22678
	Joseph	1835	Plymouth	admn	22677
	Joseph J	1838	Hingham	admn	22679
	Jotham	1828	Hingham	admn	22680
	Justus	1793	Hanover	grdn	22682
	Justus	1863	Hanover	will	22681
	Leavitt	1857	Plymouth	grdn	22640
	Levi	1821	Plymouth	will	22683
	Levi	1826	Plymouth	grdn	22641
	Lewis	1826	Hanover	admn	22684
	Loisa	1826	Plymouth	grdn	22641
	Lydia	1864	S. Scituate	admn	22685
	Marcia	1859	Marshfield	admn	22686
	Maria	1825	Hingham	grdn	22688
	Maria A	1872	Hingham	grdn	22687
	Martha	1848	Hingham	admn	22689
	Martha	1848	Plymouth	admn	22690
	Martha	1854	Duxbury	will	22691
	Martin	1870	E. Bridgewater	will	22692
	Mary	1818	Plymouth	will	22693
	Mary	1826	Hanover	admn	22694
	Nabby	1854	E. Bridgewater	admn	22695
	Nancy B	1851	Plymouth	grdn	22696
	Nathan	1823	Plymouth	will	22697
	Nathan	1846	Plymouth	admn	22698
	Olive A	1866	Hingham	peti	22699
	Oran	1866	Hanover	admn	22700
	Pelham	1869	Plymouth	admn	22701
	Perez	1860	Hingham	will	22702
	Polly	1857	Plymouth	admn	22703
	Priscilla	1851	Hanover	will	22704
	Pyam C	1825	Hingham	grdn	22688
	Pyam C	1845	Hanover	admn	22705
	Richard	1870	Hingham	will	22706
	Ruth	1793	Hanover	grdn	22682
	Ruth	1839	Plymouth	grdn	22707
	Sarah	1793	Hanover	grdn	22682
	Sarah	1806	Hanover	admn	22708
	Sarah A	1863	Plymouth	admn	22709
	Stephen	1826	Plymouth	grdn	22641
	Sylvanus	1825	Hanover	grdn	22717
	Sylvanus	1859	Hanover	will	22710
	Sylvanus	1872	Hingham	admn	22711
	Thomas	1793	Hanover	admn	22714
	Thomas	1806	Hanover	admn	22713
	Thomas	1826	Abington	will	22712
	Thomas Jr	1805	Hanover	admn	22715
	Tryphena	1794	Hanover	grdn	22666
	Walter	1862	Plymouth	grdn	22719
	William	1825	Hanover	admn	22716

SURNAME	FIRST NAME	YEAR	PLACE	CASE	DOCKET
WHITING	William	1825	Hanover	grdn	22717
	Winslow	1862	Plymouth	admn	22718
	Winslow	1862	Plymouth	grdn	22719
	Zechariah	1814	Hingham	admn	22720
	Zenas L	1825	Hingham	grdn	22688
	Zenas L	1873	Abington	admn	22721
WHITMAN	Abigail	1713	Bridgewater	grdn	22741
	Abigail	1825	Bridgewater	admn	22722
	Abigail	1875	E. Bridgewater	admn	22723
	Alfred	1842	E. Bridgewater	admn	22724
	Alice	1833	E. Bridgewater	grdn	22725
	Amos	1797	Bridgewater	admn	22726
	Anna	1870	E. Bridgewater	admn	22727
	Asa T	1875	E. Bridgewater	admn	22728
	Barzillai A	1853	E. Bridgewater	grdn	22729
	Benjamin	1802	Bridgewater	will	22730
	Betsey	1792	Bridgewater	grdn	22750
	Betsey	1801	Bridgewater	grdn	22731
	Betty	1785	Bridgewater	warr	22732
	Calvin	1808	Bridgewater	grdn	22765
	Celia M	1827	Bridgewater	grdn	22733
	Charles C	1853	E. Bridgewater	grdn	22729
	Chloe	1778	Bridgewater	grdn	22799
	Content	1799	Pembroke	will	22734
	Daniel	1777	Bridgewater	admn	22735
	Daniel	1826	Bridgewater	admn	22736
	Daniel	1879	E. Bridgewater	will	22737
	David A	1858	Scituate	admn	22738
	Ebenezer	1713	Bridgewater	grdn	22741
	Ebenezer	1713/4	Bridgewater	admn	22740
	Ebenezer	1804	Bridgewater	will	22739
	Ebenezer F	1853	E. Bridgewater	grdn	22729
	Eleazer	1728	Bridgewater	grdn	22744
	Eleazer	1747	Bridgewater	grdn	22783
	Eleazer	1847	E. Bridgewater	will	22743
	Eleazer	1857	E. Bridgewater	admn	22742
	Eliab	1862	N. Bridgewater	admn	22745
	Elizabeth	1854	Pembroke	will	22746
	Enos	1790	Bridgewater	admn	22747
	Ephraim	1839	Abington	will	22748
	Ezekiel	1792	Bridgewater	grdn	22750
	Ezekiel	1853	E. Bridgewater	grdn	22729
	Ezekiel	1866	E. Bridgewater	will	22749
	Ezra	1814	Bridgewater	will	22751
	Frank H	1875	E. Bridgewater	grdn	22776
	Freedom	1851	E. Bridgewater	admn	22752
	Freelove	1778	Bridgewater	grdn	22799
	Hannah	1713	Bridgewater	grdn	22741
	Hannah H	1872	E. Bridgewater	will	22753
	Hannah M	1870	E. Bridgewater	grdn	22754
	Harrison	1869	E. Bridgewater	admn	22755
	Henry	1846	Abington	admn	22756
	Independence	1778	Bridgewater	grdn	22796
	Isaac	1828	E. Bridgewater	will	22757
	Joan	1870	E. Bridgewater	admn	22758
	John	1727	Bridgewater	will	22761
	John	1765	Abington	admn	22762
	John	1787	Bridgewater	admn	22760
	John	1842	E. Bridgewater	will	22759
	John F	1870	E. Bridgewater	grdn	22754
	Jonathan	1778	Bridgewater	will	22763
	Joseph	1807	Bridgewater	admn	22764
	Joseph	1808	Bridgewater	grdn	22765
	Joshua	1779	Abington/B'wate	admn	22766
	Joshua	1779	Abington	grdn	22767
	Josiah	1754	Bridgewater	will	22768
	Josiah	1789	Bridgewater	admn	22769
	Josiah	1866	N. Bridgewater	grdn	22771 a
	Josiah	1867	E. Bridgewater	will	22770
	Kilborn	1836	Pembroke	admn	22772
	Levi	1765	Abington	grdn	22773

SURNAME	FIRST NAME	YEAR	PLACE	CASE	DOCKET
WHITMAN	Lucinda	1778	Bridgewater	grdn	22799
	Martin	1829	E. Bridgewater	admn	22774
	Mary	1778	Bridgewater	grdn	22796
	Mary B	1879	Rockland	admn	22775
	Mary J	1875	E. Bridgewater	grdn	22776
	Matilda	1778	Bridgewater	grdn	22796
	Nabby	1873	E. Bridgewater	will	22777
	Nancy	1843	E. Bridgewater	will	22778
	Nathan	1784	Bridgewater	admn	22780
	Nathan	1785	Bridgewater	grdn	22781
	Nathan	1862	E. Bridgewater	admn	22779
	Nicholas	1747	Bridgewater	admn	22782
	Nicholas	1747	Bridgewater	grdn	22783
	Noah	1823	Bridgewater	will	22784
	Peter	1802	Bridgewater	will	22785
	Rachel	1878	E. Bridgewater	will	22786
	Samuel	1774	Bridgewater	admn	22787
	Sarah	1827	Bridgewater	grdn	22733
	Sarah	1864	E. Bridgewater	will	22788
	Sela	1785	Bridgewater	grdn	22781
	Seth	1778	Bridgewater	will	22789
	Seth	1784	Bridgewater	admn	22790
	Seth	1786	Bridgewater	grdn	22791
	Seth A	1842	N. Bridgewater	admn	22792
	Simeon	1811	Bridgewater	admn	22793
	Simeon	1833	E. Bridgewater	grdn	22725
	Snow	1808	Bridgewater	grdn	22765
	Sophronia M	1877	E. Bridgewater	admn	22794
	Stephen	1778	Bridgewater	admn	22795
	Stephen R	1778	Bridgewater	grdn	22796
	Susan F	1847	Abington	grdn	22797
	Susannah	1778	Bridgewater	grdn	22799
	Susannah	1878	Hanson	will	22798
	Sylve	1778	Bridgewater	grdn	22799
	Sylvia	1808	Bridgewater	grdn	22765
	Theron	1842	Weymouth	grdn	22801
	Theron	1876	Rockland	admn	22800
	Thomas	1712	Bridgewater	will	22802
	Thomas	1789	Bridgewater	will	22803
	Thomas	1832	E. Bridgewater	admn	22804
	Willard	1871	E. Bridgewater	will	22805
	William	1797	Pembroke	admn	22806
	Zachariah	1773	Bridgewater	will	22807
	Zachariah	1819	Bridgewater	admn	22808
	Zacheriah	1713	Bridgewater	grdn	22741
WHITMARSH	Asa	1809	Bridgewater	admn	22809
	Asaph	1870	E. Bridgewater	admn	22810
	Charity	1840	E. Bridgewater	admn	22811
	Diana	1875	E. Bridgewater	admn	22812
	Ebenezer	1719	Abington	will	22813
	Ebenezer	1784	Abington	admn	22814
	Henry M	1874	Abington	admn	22815
	Jacob	1803	Bridgewater	will	22816
	John	1739	Abington	admn	22818
	John	1880	S. Abington	will	22817
	Joshua	1870	Abington	will	22819
	Levi	1805	Abington	admn	22821
	Levi	1873	E. Bridgewater	will	22820
	Lot	1836	E. Bridgewater	will	22822
	Oliver G	1864	E. Bridgewater	will	22823
	Sarah T	1874	Abington	grdn	22824
	Susan	1845	E. Bridgewater	will	22825
	Thomas	1781	Abington	admn	22826
	Thomas	1869	E. Bridgewater	admn	22827
WHITNEY	Anna	1864	Hingham	will	22828
	Charles B	1874	Hingham	will	22829
	George R	1847	Duxbury	grdn	22830
	Isaac	1837	Rochester	will	22831
	Julia W	1847	Duxbury	grdn	22830
	Simon	1846	Duxbury	admn	22832
WHITON	Abby	1863	Hingham	grdn	22872

SURNAME	FIRST NAME	YEAR	PLACE	CASE	DOCKET
WHITON	Abraham	1812	Plymouth	admn	22833
	Abraham Jr	1799	Halifax	admn	22834
	Alice L	1860	Hingham	grdn	22862
	Alvan	1881	Hingham	grdn	22835 a
	Amos	1817	Plymouth	admn	22836
	Ann	1851	Hingham	admn	22837
	Anna	1785	Plympton	grdn	22866
	Asenath	1840	Hingham	will	22838
	Azariah	1773	Plympton	will	22839
	Bela	1870	Hingham	will	22840
	Benjamin	1809	Hingham	will	22841
	Benjamin	1815	Hingham	will	22842
	Bethiah	1812	Hingham	grdn	22860
	Betty	1780	Hanover	grdn	22894
	Charity	1848	Hingham	will	22843
	Charles F	1863	Hingham	grdn	22872
	Charles W	1861	Plymouth	grdn	22844
	Christopher	1812	Hingham	grdn	22860
	Columbus	1859	Kingston	will	22845
	Columbus	1863	Duxbury	grdn	22846
	Comfort	1752	Hingham	grdn	22847
	Daniel	1821	Hingham	will	22848
	David	1843	Hingham	will	22849
	Effie A	1875	Hingham	grdn	22850
	Elias	1817	Hingham	warr	22851
	Elijah	1814	Hingham	will	22852
	Elijah	1837	Hingham	admn	22853
	Elijah	1841	Hingham	admn	22854
	Elijah	1871	Hingham	will	22855
	Elijah	1880	Hingham	grdn	22865
	Elisha	1819	Hingham	will	22856
	Elisha C	1864	Plymouth	admn	22857
	Emma S	1865	Hingham	grdn	22858
	Enoch	1812	Hingham	admn	22859
	Enoch	1812	Hingham	grdn	22860
	Ezra	1850	Hingham	will	22861
	Fanny	1863	Hingham	grdn	22872
	Frances H	1860	Hingham	grdn	22862
	George	1863	Hingham	will	22863
	Grace	1780	Hanover	grdn	22894
	Grace	1841	Hingham	will	22864
	Henry E H	1880	Hingham	grdn	22865
	Homer	1780	Hanover	grdn	22894
	Isaac	1785	Plympton	grdn	22866
	Isaiah	1871	Hingham	will	22867
	Israel Jr	1825	Hingham	admn	22868
	James	1760	Plympton	admn	22869
	Joanna	1812	Hingham	grdn	22860
	Job S	1875	Hingham	will	22870
	John	1766	Plympton	will	22871
	Joshua D	1841	Kingston	grdn	22881
	Laura	1863	Hingham	grdn	22872
	Leah S	1812	Hingham	grdn	22860
	Lucy D	1863	Hingham	grdn	22872
	Luther	1842	Hingham	admn	22873
	Lydia	1865	Hingham	will	22874
	Lydia N	1860	Plymouth	will	22875
	Martha	1812	Hingham	grdn	22860
	Martha L	1871	Hingham	will	22876
	Mary A	1861	Plymouth	grdn	22844
	Mary R	1875	Hingham	admn	22877
	Mary W	1812	Hingham	grdn	22860
	Mathew	1776	Plympton	admn	22878
	Melzar	1863	Kingston	will	22879
	Melzar Jr	1836	Kingston	will	22880
	Melzar Jr	1841	Kingston	grdn	22881
	Molly	1785	Plympton	grdn	22866
	Morris F	1873	Hingham	grdn	22882
	Moses	1823	Hingham	will	22883
	Moses	1862	Hingham	admn	22884
	Rachel	1843	Hingham	will	22885

SURNAME	FIRST NAME	YEAR	PLACE	CASE	DOCKET
WHITON	Royal	1877	Hingham	will	22886
	Samuel	1785	Plympton	grdn	22866
	Samuel	1812	Hingham	grdn	22860
	Sarah	1817	Hingham	admn	22887
	Sylvanus	1854	Hingham	admn	22888
	Thomas	1774	Plympton	admn	22889
	Thomas	1785	Plympton	grdn	22866
	Thomas F	1873	Hingham	admn	22890
	Wallace	1860	Hingham	grdn	22862
	Welthea	1837	Kingston	will	22891
	William	1780	Hanover	admn	22893
	William	1780	Hanover	grdn	22894
	William	1876	Hingham	admn	22892
	Wilson	1855	Hingham	will	22895
	Wilson	1873	Hingham	admn	22896
WHITRIDGE	Elizabeth	1731	Rochester	grdn	22897
	Rebecca	1731	Rochester	grdn	22897
	Sarah	1731	Rochester	grdn	22897
	Thomas	1795	Rochester	will	22898
	Thomas	1813	Rochester	will	22899
	William	1726	Rochester	admn	22900
	William	1815	Rochester	will	22901
WHITTAKER	James	1841	Scituate	admn	22902
	John L	1849	Scituate	admn	22903
WHITTEMORE	Benjamin	1857	Plymouth	admn	22904
	Eunice F	1863	Plymouth	will	22905
	Harriet G	1829	Plymouth	grdn	22907
	Henry C	1873	Plymouth	admn	22906
	Isaac	1819	Scituate	admn	22908
	Jabez	1755	Marshfield	admn	22909
	Joseph J L	1821	Scituate	grdn	22910
	Nathaniel	1855	Hingham	will	22911
	Sophia	1853	Hingham	will	22912
WHITTIER	Albert S	1835	Maine	grdn	22913
	David A	1835	Maine	grdn	22913
	Harriet S	1835	Maine	grdn	22913
	Ida May	1875	Brockton	adop	22914
	Joseph E	1835	Maine	grdn	22913
	Mary A	1835	Maine	grdn	22913
	Sarah E	1835	Maine	grdn	22913
WHITWELL	Benjamin	1857	Hanover	will	22915
WILBAR	Aberdeen	1839	Bridgewater	admn	22916
	Austin B	1843	Bridgewater	grdn	22932
	Calvin H	1863	Bridgewater	admn	22917
	Catherine	1843	Bridgewater	grdn	22932
	Charles E	1865	Bridgewater	grdn	22933
	David W	1870	Bridgewater	admn	22918
	Edwin	1864	Bridgewater	admn	22919
	Elnathan W	1863	Middleboro	admn	22920
	George	1803	Bridgewater	will	22921
	George	1868	Bridgewater	will	22922
	Harry S	1866	Bridgewater	grdn	22923
	Howard B	1877	W. Bridgewater	grdn	22924
	Isaac	1834	Bridgewater	will	22925
	Isaac	1854	Bridgewater	will	22926
	Isaac	1862	Bridgewater	will	22927
	Isaiah	1879	Rochester	will	22928
	Jason	1856	Middleboro	admn	22929
	Kilea	1876	Bridgewater	admn	22930
	Lizzie H	1866	Bridgewater	grdn	22923
	Louisa	1867	Bridgewater	admn	22931
	Luther C	1843	Bridgewater	grdn	22932
	Lydia E	1843	Bridgewater	grdn	22932
	Mary W	1865	Bridgewater	grdn	22933
	Olive	1868	Bridgewater	will	22934
	Olive S	1879	Rochester	admn	22935
	Oliver C	1877	Bridgewater	will	22936
	Sanford	1873	N. Bridgewater	admn	22937
	Sebra	1875	Bridgewater	will	22938
	Seth	1806	Bridgewater	will	22939
	William H	1843	Bridgewater	grdn	22932

SURNAME	FIRST NAME	YEAR	PLACE	CASE	DOCKET
WILBAR	Willie S	1865	Bridgewater	grdn	22933
WILCOX	Ellery	1852	Rochester	admn	22940
WILDE	Elijah D	1854	Hingham	admn	22941
	Franklin A	1849	Hingham	admn	22942
	John	1857	Abington	will	22943
	Patrick	1877	Brockton	admn	22944
	Samuel	1828	Middleboro	admn	22945
	William	1822	Middleboro	admn	22946
WILDER	Abiel	1838	Hingham	will	22947
	Abiel	1839	Hingham	grdn	22948
	Albert	1844	Hingham	grdn	22951
	Albert	1864	Hingham	admn	22949
	Albert G	1858	Hingham	admn	22950
	Asa	1866	S. Scituate	adop	22952
	Bela	1828	Hingham	admn	22953
	Bela	1835	Hingham	admn	22954
	Benjamin	1826	Hingham	grdn	22955
	Caleb	1859	Hingham	admn	22956
	Crocker	1847	Hingham	will	22957
	Crocker	1876	Hingham	will	22958
	Daniel	1839	Hingham	will	22960
	Daniel	1839	Hingham	grdn	22961
	Daniel	1879	Hingham	will	22962
	Daniel Jr	1829	Hingham	admn	22959
	David	1818	Hanover	grdn	22976
	Deborah	1844	Hingham	will	22963
	Ebenezer	1848	Middleboro	admn	22964
	Edward	1817	Hingham	will	22965
	Edward	1852	Hingham	admn	22966
	Everett	1869	Scituate	grdn	22967
	Hannah	1811	Hingham	will	22968
	Hannah B	1818	Hanover	grdn	22976
	Hannah H	1818	Hingham	grdn	22993
	Hannah H	1873	Hingham	will	22969
	Harriet et al	1818	Hingham	grdn	22993
	Henry C	1826	Hingham	grdn	22955
	Isaac	1810	Hingham	admn	22970
	Isaac	1818	Hanover	will	22975
	Isaac	1828	Hingham	grdn	22971
	Isaac	1835	Hingham	admn	22972
	Isaac	1878	Hanover	admn	22973
	Isaac M	1818	Hanover	grdn	22976
	Isaac M	1879	Hanover	will	22974
	Isaiah	1843	Hingham	will	22977
	Jairus	1866	Hingham	admn	22979
	James D	1854	Middleboro	admn	22980
	James Jr	1845	Hingham	grdn	22978 a
	Joanna	1823	Scituate	will	22981
	Joanna	1826	Hingham	grdn	22955
	Joanna	1854	Hingham	will	22982
	John	1829	Hanover	admn	22983
	John	1874	Hingham	admn	22985
	John C	1818	Hanover	grdn	22976
	John C	1855	N. Bridgewater	will	22984
	John C	1873	S. Scituate	grdn	22986
	Joseph	1839	Hingham	will	22987
	Joseph	1870	Hingham	will	22988
	Joshua	1860	Hingham	admn	22989
	Louisa C	1844	Hingham	grdn	22951
	Lydia	1873	S. Scituate	grdn	22986
	Martin 2nd	1863	Hingham	will	22990
	Mary	1848	Middleboro	admn	22991
	Mary E	1869	Boston	grdn	22992
	Matilda	1818	Hingham	grdn	22993
	Nathaniel	1823	Hingham	admn	22994
	Nathaniel	1851	Kingston	will	22995
	Olive	1843	Hingham	admn	22996
	Oscar K	1869	Scituate	grdn	22967
	Peter	1821	Hingham	admn	22997
	Ruth	1818	Hanover	grdn	22976
	Samuel	1825	Hingham	will	22998

SURNAME	FIRST NAME	YEAR	PLACE	CASE	DOCKET
WILDER	Samuel	1842	Hingham	will	22999
	Sarah J	1826	Hingham	grdn	22955
	Sarah L	1844	Hingham	grdn	22951
	Seth S	1849	Hingham	admn	23000
	Susannah	1848	Hingham	admn	23001
	Tamah	1867	Hingham	will	23002
	Tamsin	1847	Hingham	will	23003
WILKES	Elizabeth	1854	Abington	admn	23004
	John	1793	Abington	will	23005
	John	1848	Abington	will	23006
	Joseph	1854	Abington	admn	23007
	Lucia	1872	Abington	will	23008
	Ruth E	1878	S. Abington	admn	23009
	Samuel D	1864	Abington	will	23010
	Sarah	1854	Abington	admn	23011
	Thomas	1788	Abington	will	23012
WILKINS	Alice F	1879	N. Rochester	grdn	23013 a
WILL	Indian	1695	Scituate	will	23014
WILLET	Anna	1878	Rockland	will	23015
	John	1861	Hanson	admn	23016
	Thomas	1792	Abington	admn	23017
WILLEY	James B	1862	Abington	admn	23018
	Samuel	1866	Wheelock CA	admn	23019
WILLIAMS	Abner	1792	Middleboro	will	23020
	Amelia	1870	W. Bridgewater	admn	23021
	Calvin	1803	Bridgewater	will	23022
	Charles	1874	Bridgewater	admn	23023
	Edward	1842	E. Bridgewater	grdn	23024
	Elijah	1818	Middleboro	will	23025
	George	1827	W. Bridgewater	will	23027
	George	1843	Middleboro	admn	23028
	George	1870	Lakeville	admn	23029
	George Jr	1809	Bridgewater	will	23026
	Henry	1770	Bridgewater	admn	23030
	Henry	1867	Rochester	admn	23031
	James	1868	Mattapoisett	will	23032
	John	1694	Scituate	will	23033
	John	1852	Plymouth	will	23034
	Joseph	1759	Middleboro	admn	23036
	Joseph	1798	Duxbury	admn	23035
	Joseph	1847	W. Bridgewater	admn	23037
	Josiah	1794	Bridgewater	will	23038
	Josiah	1822	W. Bridgewater	admn	23039
	Josiah P	1842	W. Bridgewater	grdn	23040
	Lavinia	1861	W. Bridgewater	will	23041
	Lydia	1856	E. Bridgewater	will	23042
	Martha S	1829	Hingham	admn	23043
	Mary A	1854	Hingham	will	23045
	Mary Ann N	1834	Brooklyn	will	23044
	Narcissus	1863	Lakeville	admn	23046
	Nathan	1867	Middleboro	will	23047
	Nellie M	1869	Hingham	grdn	23048
	Pamela	1829	Middleboro	grdn	23049 a
	Patience	1875	Lakeville	admn	23050
	Perez	1819	Bridgewater	will	23051
	Rufus	1737	Boston	grdn	23052
	Samuel P	1841	W. Bridgewater	will	23053
	Sarah	1846	Middleboro	admn	23054
	Sylvia K	1880	Brockton	will	23055
	William	1873	Plymouth	admn	23056
WILLIAMSON	Aaron P	1861	Marshfield	admn	23057
	Anthony A	1842	Marshfield	admn	23058
	Anthony W	1844	Marshfield	grdn	23059
	Calvin	1874	Marshfield	will	23060
	Deborah	1735	Marshfield	admn	23068
	Elijah	1879	Marshfield	admn	23061
	Erastus E	1862	Marshfield	grdn	23063
	George	1764	Middleboro	admn	23062
	George H	1862	Marshfield	grdn	23063
	Hannah S	1844	Marshfield	grdn	23059
	Laura J	1844	Marshfield	grdn	23059

SURNAME	FIRST NAME	YEAR	PLACE	CASE	DOCKET
WILLIAMSON	Nathan	1718	Marshfield	admn	23064
	Ruth M	1844	Marshfield	grdn	23059
	Sarah	1846	Marshfield	will	23065
	Susanna	1861	Marshfield	admn	23066
	Timothy	1735	Marshfield	admn	23068
	Timothy	1824	Marshfield	admn	23067
	William	1854	Marshfield	will	23069
WILLIS	Abigail	1764	Bridgewater	grdn	23113
	Arthur H	1875	Bridgewater	grdn	23070
	Benjamin	1696	Bridgewater	will	23071
	Benjamin	1713/4	Bridgewater	grdn	23072
	Benjamin	1779	Bridgewater	admn	23073
	Benjamin	1807	Bridgewater	will	23074
	Benjamin	1809	Bridgewater	admn	23075
	Benjamin	1815	Bridgewater	grdn	23076
	Beriah	1741	Bridgewater	grdn	23082
	Betty	1738	Bridgewater	grdn	23114
	Caroline	1880	Brockton	admn	23077
	Cyrus A	1851	N. Bridgewater	admn	23078
	David	1831	N. Bridgewater	grdn	23079 a
	Ebenezer	1741	Bridgewater	admn	23081
	Ebenezer	1741	Bridgewater	grdn	23082
	Ebenezer	1840	Middleboro	admn	23080
	Elijah	1870	Mattapoisett	will	23083
	Emily C	1868	Kingston	grdn	23084
	Ephraim	1816	Bridgewater	will	23085
	Ezra	1813	Bridgewater	admn	23086
	Hannah	1738	Bridgewater	grdn	23114
	Hannah	1764	Bridgewater	grdn	23113
	Horace W	1880	Brockton	grdn	23087
	Joab	1805	Bridgewater	will	23088
	John	1693	Bridgewater	will	23089
	John	1712	Bridgewater	will	23090
	John	1732	Bridgewater	admn	23091
	John	1835	W. Bridgewater	will	23092
	John	1840	N. Bridgewater	will	23093
	John	1869	N. Bridgewater	will	23094
	Jonathan	1738	Bridgewater	admn	23095
	Jonathan	1741	Bridgewater	grdn	23082
	Jonathan S	1880	Brockton	admn	23096
	Joshua	1758	Bridgewater	will	23097
	Joshua	1856	Middleboro	admn	23098
	Keturah	1738	Bridgewater	grdn	23114
	Keziah	1741	Bridgewater	grdn	23082
	Lucy J	1874	Bridgewater	admn	23099
	Mary J	1846	Middleboro	grdn	23100
	Mehitable	1733	Bridgewater	grdn	23101
	Nathan E	1874	Bridgewater	admn	23102
	Nathaniel	1686	Bridgewater	admn	23103
	Nathaniel	1728	Bridgewater	admn	23104
	Nathaniel T	1872	Kingston	admn	23105
	Philinda	1851	N. Bridgewater	will	23106
	Ruth	1740	Bridgewater	will	23107
	Samuel	1767	Bridgewater	admn	23108
	Samuel	1778	Bridgewater	admn	23109
	Sarah	1738	Bridgewater	grdn	23114
	Sarah M	1852	Middleboro	will	23110
	Seth	1749	Wareham	admn	23111
	Stoughton	1738	Bridgewater	grdn	23114
	Stoughton	1750	Bridgewater	admn	23112
	Stoughton	1764	Bridgewater	grdn	23113
	Susan P	1869	Mattapoisett	will	23115
	Susanna	1784	Bridgewater	will	23116
	Thomas	1784	Bridgewater	will	23117
	William H	1847	Plympton	admn	23118
	William H	1880	Brockton	will	23119
	Zephaniah	1776	Bridgewater	admn	23120
	Zephaniah	1847	Kingston	admn	23121
WILLS	Rowland	1689/0	Scituate	will	23122
	Samuel	1708	Marshfield	admn	23123
	William	1688	Scituate	will	23124

SURNAME	FIRST NAME	YEAR	PLACE	CASE	DOCKET
WILSON	George	1798	Bridgewater	admn	23125
	James	1862	Mattapoisett	will	23126
	Mary	1760	Scituate	admn	23127
	Rebecca	1878	Middleboro	will	23128
	William	1773	Scituate	admn	23129
WING	Alden	1839	Rochester	admn	23130
	Batchelor	1740	Hanover	will	23131
	Benjamin	1756	Rochester	admn	23132
	Benjamin	1846	Wareham	admn	23133
	Bersheba	1777	Wareham	will	23134
	Butler	1765	Wareham	grdn	23136
	Butler	1769	Wareham	admn	23135
	Clifton	1765	Wareham	admn	23137
	David F	1847	Rochester	admn	23138
	Elijah	1840	Hanover	admn	23139
	Elisha	1757	Wareham	will	23140
	Elisha	1762	Wareham	admn	23141
	Elizabeth	1756	Rochester	will	23142
	Eunice	1757	Rochester	admn	23143
	Eunice D	1879	Marion	admn	23144
	Hannah	1765	Wareham	grdn	23136
	Hannah	1840	Hanover	will	23145
	Jedediah	1765	Wareham	grdn	23136
	John	1717	Rochester	will	23146
	John	1750	Rochester	will	23147
	John	1756	Rochester	grdn	23151
	John	1826	Rochester	will	23148
	Joseph	1715	Rochester	admn	23150
	Joseph	1756	Rochester	grdn	23151
	Joseph	1835	Rochester	admn	23149
	Mary	1853	Marion	will	23152
	Moses	1797	Rochester	admn	23153
	Paul	1822	Rochester	admn	23154
	Roger	1800	Rochester	will	23155
	Ruth	1767	Rochester	admn	23156
	Ruth	1840	Hanover	will	23157
	Samuel	1717	Rochester	grdn	23158
	Samuel	1773	Rochester	admn	23159
	Samuel	1810	Rochester	admn	23160
	Shubill	1756	Rochester	grdn	23151
	Stephen	1824	Rochester	admn	23161
	Stephen S	1810	Rochester	admn	23162
	Timothy	1814	Rochester	admn	23163
	Timothy	1850	Wareham	admn	23164
WINSLOW	Abiah	1736	Marshfield	grdn	23165
	Anthony et al	1765	Bridgewater	warr	23166
	Asa T	1878	Lakeville	will	23167
	Benjamin	1731	Marshfield	grdn	23220
	Benjamin	1818	Middleboro	admn	23168
	Bethiah	1759	Scituate	grdn	23216
	David	1770	Rochester	grdn	23178
	David	1804	Rochester	admn	23169
	Deborah	1778	Marshfield	will	23170
	Dorcas	1779	Rochester	grdn	23198
	Dorcas	1800	Rochester	grdn	23171 a
	Ebenezer	1779	Rochester	grdn	23198
	Ebenezer	1793	Rochester	grdn	23172 a
	Edward	1760	Rochester	will	23176
	Edward	1770	Rochester	grdn	23178
	Edward	1780	Rochester	will	23175
	Edward	1851	Duxbury	grdn	23173 a
	Edward	1854	Duxbury	admn	23174
	Edward Jr	1770	Rochester	admn	23177
	Eleanor	1770	Rochester	grdn	23178
	Frances	1846	Hingham	will	23179
	Frances G	1868	Hingham	will	23180
	George	1878	Duxbury	admn	23181
	Gilbert	1731	Marshfield	will	23182
	Hannah	1759	Wareham	grdn	23183
	Isaac	1739	Marshfield	will	23184
	Isaac	1815	Marshfield	bond	23185

SURNAME	FIRST NAME	YEAR	PLACE	CASE	DOCKET
WINSLOW	Isaac	1819	Marshfield	will	23186
	Isaac	1878	Middleboro	will	23187
	James	1733	Rochester	will	23188
	Jirah	1818	Middleboro	grdn	23190
	Jirah	1875	Lakeville	will	23189
	Job	1731	Marshfield	grdn	23220
	John	1755	Rochester	will	23195
	John	1758	Wareham	will	23192
	John	1759	Scituate	grdn	23216
	John	1774	Marshfield	admn	23193
	John	1774	Rochester	will	23197
	John	1776	Rochester	will	23196
	John	1779	Rochester	grdn	23198
	John	1822	Marshfield/Hano	admn	23194
	John B	1870	Bridgewater	will	23191
	Joseph	1759	Scituate	grdn	23216
	Joseph	1780	Marshfield	grdn	23199
	Josiah	1803	Bridgewater	admn	23200
	Josiah	1879	Hanover	admn	23201
	Kenelm	1757	Marshfield	will	23202
	Kenelm	1779	Rochester	grdn	23198
	Kenelm	1780	Marshfield	admn	23203
	Kenelm	1868	Bridgewater	admn	23204
	Lemuel	1839	Rochester	will	23205
	Lucy T	1820	Hanover	grdn	23206
	Mercy	1761	Marshfield	admn	23207
	Micah	1816	Rochester	will	23208
	Nathaniel	1720	Marshfield	will	23209
	Nathaniel	1736	Marshfield	admn	23210
	Nathaniel	1759	Scituate	grdn	23216
	Nathaniel	1786	Marshfield	will	23211
	Nathaniel	1808	Scituate	admn	23213
	Nathaniel	1830	Hanover	admn	23212
	Nathaniel W	1854	S. Scituate	grdn	23231
	Nathaniel W	1863	S. Scituate	admn	23214
	Oliver	1759	Scituate	admn	23215
	Oliver	1759	Scituate	grdn	23216
	Orra	1875	E. Bridgewater	admn	23217
	Paul	1779	Rochester	grdn	23198
	Pelham	1779	Plymouth	abse	23218
	Pelham	1784	Plymouth	admn	23219
	Rebecca	1731	Marshfield	grdn	23220
	Richard	1816	Rochester	admn	23221
	Ruth	1736	Marshfield	grdn	23165
	Ruth	1759	Scituate	grdn	23216
	Ruth G	1820	Hanover	grdn	23206
	Samuel R	1857	Plymouth	admn	23222
	Sarah	1754	Marshfield	will	23223
	Sarah	1826	Scituate	admn	23224
	Snow	1770	Marshfield	will	23225
	Susan	1825	Hingham	admn	23226
	Sylvina	1856	Rochester	admn	23227
	Timothy	1779	Rochester	grdn	23198
	Tisdell	1818	Middleboro	grdn	23190
	William	1759	Wareham	admn	23228
	William	1853	S. Scituate	admn	23229
	William S	1854	S. Scituate	grdn	23231
	William S	1878	S. Scituate	will	23230
WINSOR	Abigail S	1862	Duxbury	admn	23232
	Ada J	1842	Duxbury	grdn	23241
	Albert	1853	Duxbury	will	23233
	Calvin	1836	Duxbury	grdn	23264
	Charles	1836	Duxbury	admn	23234
	Charlotte	1858	Kingston	will	23235
	Eliza	1806	Duxbury	grdn	23262
	Ellis	1845	Marshfield	admn	23236
	Ezra M	1840	Duxbury	admn	23237
	Florence	1842	Duxbury	grdn	23241
	George	1874	Duxbury	will	23238
	George A	1836	Duxbury	grdn	23239
	Gershom	1841	Duxbury	admn	23240

SURNAME	FIRST NAME	YEAR	PLACE	CASE	DOCKET
WINSOR	Gershom C	1842	Duxbury	grdn	23241
	Hannah	1874	Duxbury	admn	23242
	Hannah	1878	Duxbury	will	23243
	Hattie F	1866	Duxbury	grdn	23244
	Henry T	1836	Duxbury	grdn	23239
	Horace E	1842	Duxbury	grdn	23241
	Hosea	1851	Duxbury	admn	23245
	Isaac	1849	Duxbury	will	23246
	John	1843	Duxbury	will	23247
	Joseph	1862	Duxbury	will	23248
	Kezia D	1866	Duxbury	admn	23249
	Lucy	1836	Duxbury	grdn	23264
	Mary A	1836	Duxbury	grdn	23264
	Meria	1806	Duxbury	grdn	23262
	Nathaniel	1839	Duxbury	will	23250
	Nathaniel	1859	Duxbury	admn	23251
	Olive S	1853	Duxbury	grdn	23252
	Otis	1822	Duxbury	admn	23253
	Otis	1865	Duxbury	admn	23254
	Pauline	1842	Duxbury	grdn	23241
	Peter	1845	Kingston	will	23255
	Peter	1845	Kingston	grdn	23256
	Rhoda M	1863	Duxbury	admn	23257
	Samuel	1770	Duxbury	admn	23260
	Samuel	1806	Duxbury	grdn	23262
	Samuel	1835	Duxbury	will	23258
	Samuel G	1874	Bridgewater	will	23259
	Samuel Jr	1805	Duxbury	admn	23261
	Spencer	1835	Duxbury	admn	23263
	Spencer	1836	Duxbury	grdn	23264
	Temperance A	1874	Duxbury	will	23265
	William D	1879	Kingston	admn	23266
	Zenas	1801	Kingston	grdn	23267
WISE	Sally	1880	S. Scituate	admn	23268
	William	1861	S. Scituate	will	23269
WISWALL	Ichabod	1700	Duxbury	will	23270
	John	1843	Plymouth	admn	23271
	John B	1843	Plymouth	grdn	23272
	Priscilla S	1843	Plymouth	grdn	23272
WITHERELL	Addie	1872	Duxbury	grdn	23283
	Amasa C	1859	Duxbury	admn	23273
	Amos	1864	Pembroke	admn	23274
	Arthur C	1866	Pembroke	grdn	23275
	Elizabeth	1814	Plymouth	will	23276
	George M	1863	Pembroke	admn	23277
	Gershom W	1869	Duxbury	admn	23278
	Hannah	1756	Plymouth	grdn	23279
	Hannah	1841	Plymouth	will	23280
	Harriet	1810	Plymouth	grdn	23281
	Harriet	1815	Plymouth	will	23282
	Isabel	1872	Duxbury	grdn	23283
	Jabez	1816	Pembroke	admn	23284
	Jabez	1877	Bridgewater	admn	23285
	John	1690/1	Scituate	will	23286
	John	1764	Plymouth	admn	23287
	Joseph	1779	Pembroke	admn	23288
	Joshua	1700	Scituate	grdn	23301
	Joshua	1727	Plymouth	admn	23289
	Prince	1822	Halifax	admn	23290
	Rebecca	1755	Plymouth	admn	23291
	Ruth	1772	Marshfield	will	23292
	Samuel	1755	Pembroke	grdn	23293 a
	Theophilus	1702/3	Scituate	will	23294
	Theophilus	1758	Pembroke	admn	23295
	Theophilus	1795	Hanover	admn	23296
	Thomas	1700	Scituate	grdn	23301
	Thomas	1743	Plymouth	will	23297
	Thomas	1744	Plymouth	admn	23298
	Thomas	1756	Plymouth	grdn	23299
	Thomas	1809	Plymouth	admn	23300
	William	1748	Plymouth	admn	23304

SURNAME	FIRST NAME	YEAR	PLACE	CASE	DOCKET
WITHERELL	William	1750	Hanover	admn	23302
	William	1757	Plymouth	admn	23303
	William	1803	Plymouth	admn	23305
	Zephaniah	1763	Hanover	admn	23306
WITHINGTON	Newell	1861	Bridgewater	admn	23307
	Susan	1871	N.Y.	grdn	23308
WITTET	James	1872	Marion	will	23309
WOOD	Abiel	1719	Middleboro	admn	23310
	Abigail	1745	Middleboro	grdn	23452
	Abijah	1757	Halifax	grdn	23312
	Abijah/Abia	1746	Halifax	admn	23311
	Abisha	1864	Middleboro	admn	23313
	Abner	1745	Middleboro	grdn	23452
	Abner	1761	Middleboro	grdn	23440
	Abner	1852	Middleboro	admn	23314
	Albert F	1866	Halifax	grdn	23382
	Alexander	1868	Hanover	admn	23315
	Alfred	1876	Middleboro	admn	23316
	Alvinzer	1871	Halifax	admn	23317
	Amasa	1745	Middleboro	grdn	23452
	Amaziah/Amaza	1757	Middleboro	admn	23318
	Anna W	1875	Middleboro	admn	23319
	Asaph S	1871	Halifax	admn	23320
	Azel	1829	N. Bridgewater	will	23321
	Barnabas	1730	Middleboro	admn	23322
	Benjamin	1690	Middleboro	will	23323
	Benjamin F	1879	Middleboro	admn	23324
	Consider	1772	Middleboro	grdn	23426
	Cyrus	1854	Halifax	admn	23325
	Daniel	1787	Middleboro	grdn	23326
	Daniel	1825	Middleboro	admn	23327
	David	1718	Middleboro	admn	23330
	David	1738	Middleboro	will	23331
	David	1739	Middleboro	grdn	23332
	David	1855	Middleboro	will	23329
	David B	1843	Plymouth	grdn	23328
	Deborah E	1880	Middleboro	admn	23333
	Diantha	1843	Middleboro	admn	23334
	Diantha W	1879	Middleboro	admn	23335
	Eben	1863	Middleboro	grdn	23336
	Ebenezer	1769	Middleboro	admn	23337
	Ebenezer	1803	Middleboro	admn	23338
	Ebenezer	1862	Halifax	will	23340
	Ebenezer	1863	Middleboro	admn	23339
	Ebenezer	1866	Halifax	admn	23341
	Edmond	1739	Middleboro	grdn	23332
	Edmond	1806	Middleboro	will	23342
	Eliab	1842	Plymouth	admn	23343
	Eliab	1852	Middleboro	will	23344
	Eliza	1842	N. Bridgewater	will	23345
	Ellen A	1865	Hanover	admn	23346
	Elnathan	1752	Middleboro	will	23347
	Ephraim	1731	Middleboro	grdn	23350
	Ephraim	1744	Middleboro	will	23349
	Ephraim	1783	Middleboro	will	23348
	Experience	1736	Middleboro	grdn	23351
	Ezra	1823	Middleboro	admn	23352
	Foster	1824	Middleboro	grdn	23353
	Francis	1739	Middleboro	grdn	23332
	Francis	1745	Bridgewater	will	23354
	George	1802	Bridgewater	grdn	23446
	George	1843	Middleboro	grdn	23358
	George F	1868	Plymouth	admn	23356
	George H	1855	Plymouth	will	23355
	George W	1881	Rockland	will	23357
	Gorham	1816	Middleboro	grdn	23359 a
	Gorham	1836	Middleboro	admn	23360
	Hannah	1734	Plympton	admn	23361
	Hannah	1745	Middleboro	grdn	23452
	Hannah	1843	Halifax	will	23362
	Harriet C	1863	Bridgewater	grdn	23398

SURNAME	FIRST NAME	YEAR	PLACE	CASE	DOCKET
WOOD	Harriet N	1860	Halifax	grdn	23363
	Henry	1752	Middleboro	will	23364
	Henry	1876	Bridgewater	will	23365
	Henry A	1865	Hanover	admn	23366
	Hervey	1831	Middleboro	will	23367
	Hope	1843	Rochester	admn	23368
	Horatio G	1861	Middleboro	admn	23369
	Horatio G	1863	Middleboro	grdn	23336
	Horatio W	1863	Middleboro	admn	23370
	Ichabod	1787	Middleboro	will	23371
	Ichabod	1826	Middleboro	admn	23372
	Ida Cheney	1868	Plymouth	adop	23373
	Irene	1826	Middleboro	grdn	23374 a
	Isaac	1870	Halifax	will	23375
	Isaiah	1793	Middleboro	bond	23376
	Israel	1829	Middleboro	will	23377
	Jabez	1772	Middleboro	will	23378
	Jacob	1806	Middleboro	grdn	23379 a
	Jacob	1824	Middleboro	will	23380
	James	1728	Middleboro	admn	23381
	James C	1863	Bridgewater	grdn	23398
	Jane	1866	Halifax	grdn	23382
	Jeremiah	1859	Middleboro	admn	23383
	Jerusha	1757	Halifax	grdn	23312
	Joanna	1739	Middleboro	grdn	23332
	Joanna	1755	Middleboro	divi	23385
	Joanna	1757	Middleboro	admn	23384
	John	1701	Plymouth	admn	23387
	John	1842	Middleboro	admn	23386
	Joshua	1879	Middleboro	admn	23388
	Josiah	1768	Middleboro	admn	23389
	Judah	1783	Middleboro	admn	23390
	Judah	1848	Halifax	will	23391
	Keziah	1855	Bridgewater	admn	23392
	Leavitt	1864	Halifax	admn	23393
	Lemuel	1745	Middleboro	grdn	23452
	Levi	1798	Middleboro	grdn	23394 a
	Lewis	1802	Bridgewater	grdn	23446
	Lorenzo	1861	Middleboro	admn	23395
	Lorenzo	1879	Middleboro	admn	23396
	Lorenzo	1881	Middleboro	grdn	23397
	Lucinda	1810	Middleboro	grdn	23450
	Lucius C	1863	Bridgewater	grdn	23398
	Lucy	1856	Middleboro	will	23400
	Lucy C	1848	Middleboro	will	23399
	Lydia	1736	Middleboro	grdn	23351
	Lydia	1793	Middleboro	admn	23401
	Lydia	1802	Bridgewater	grdn	23446
	Lydia	1824	Middleboro	grdn	23353
	Lydia	1832	Bridgewater	will	23403
	Lydia	1849	Middleboro	admn	23402
	Lydia	1852	N. Bridgewater	will	23404
	Lydia J	1860	Middleboro	grdn	23409
	Lysander	1837	Middleboro	admn	23405
	Manassa	1731	Middleboro	grdn	23350
	Manassa	1774	Middleboro	grdn	23408
	Manassah	1764	Middleboro	admn	23407
	Manassah	1800	Middleboro	admn	23406
	Maria A	1860	Middleboro	grdn	23409
	Mary	1868	Middleboro	admn	23410
	Mary S	1838	Middleboro	grdn	23411
	Mehitable	1874	Halifax	will	23412
	Moses	1779	Middleboro	admn	23413
	Nathaniel	1867	Plymouth	admn	23414
	Nichals	1829	Middleboro	will	23415
	Nichols	1774	Middleboro	grdn	23408
	Norman	1881	Middleboro	grdn	23397
	Olive	1858	Middleboro	will	23416
	Orville J	1860	Middleboro	grdn	23409
	Orville J	1873	Middleboro	admn	23417
	Pelham	1774	Middleboro	grdn	23408

SURNAME	FIRST NAME	YEAR	PLACE	CASE	DOCKET
WOOD	Pelham	1793	Middleboro	admn	23418
	Philander	1802	Bridgewater	grdn	23446
	Philander	1866	Bridgewater	will	23420
	Philander Jr	1844	Bridgewater	admn	23419
	Priscilla	1745	Middleboro	grdn	23452
	Priscilla	1826	Middleboro	grdn	23422
	Priscilla C	1868	Middleboro	will	23421
	Ransom T	1863	Middleboro	will	23423
	Rebecca	1731	Middleboro	grdn	23350
	Rebecca	1736	Middleboro	grdn	23351
	Reuben	1790	Middleboro	admn	23424
	Rhoda	1861	Middleboro	admn	23425
	Robert	1772	Middleboro	grdn	23426
	Rufus	1845	Bridgewater	admn	23427
	Rufus W	1862	Bridgewater	admn	23428
	Sally	1811	Middleboro	will	23429
	Samuel	1718	Middleboro	divi	23436
	Samuel	1731	Middleboro	grdn	23350
	Samuel	1747	Middleboro	admn	23437
	Samuel	1750	Middleboro	will	23439
	Samuel	1761	Middleboro	grdn	23440
	Samuel	1777	Middleboro	admn	23438
	Samuel	1798	Middleboro	admn	23435
	Samuel	1827	E. Bridgewater	grdn	23431 i
	Samuel	1835	Wareham	grdn	23430 a
	Samuel	1844	N. Bridgewater	will	23432
	Samuel	1849	Halifax	admn	23433
	Samuel	1860	Halifax	admn	23434
	Sarah	1701	Plymouth	admn	23387
	Sarah	1774	Middleboro	grdn	23408
	Sarah W	1843	Middleboro	grdn	23358
	Serena	1876	Middleboro	will	23441
	Silas	1807	Middleboro	admn	23442
	Simeon	1802	Bridgewater	will	23445
	Simeon	1802	Bridgewater	grdn	23446
	Simeon	1819	Middleboro	admn	23443
	Simeon	1880	E. Bridgewater	will	23444
	Sophronia	1826	Middleboro	grdn	23422
	Susan W	1863	Bridgewater	grdn	23398
	Sylvanus	1841	Middleboro	admn	23447
	Thomas	1744	Middleboro	admn	23451
	Thomas	1745	Middleboro	grdn	23452
	Thomas	1774	Middleboro	grdn	23408
	Thomas	1809	Middleboro	admn	23449
	Thomas	1810	Middleboro	grdn	23450
	Thomas	1860	W. Bridgewater	admn	23448
	Timothy	1756	Halifax	admn	23453
	Timothy	1834	Halifax	admn	23454
	Timothy	1840	Halifax	admn	23455
	Walter F	1865	Scituate	peti	23456
	Warren	1851	Bridgewater	grdn	23457
	Wilkes	1843	Middleboro	will	23458
	William H	1858	Middleboro	oath	23459
	Zephaniah	1745	Middleboro	grdn	23452
WOODBURY	Ruth F	1832	Abington	grdn	23461
	William	1827	Abington	will	23460
	William W	1832	Abington	grdn	23461
WOODING	Bashiah	1722	Rochester	grdn	23462
	Hosea	1722	Rochester	grdn	23462
	Lydia	1722	Rochester	grdn	23462
	Peter	1717	Rochester	admn	23463
WOODMAN	Anna	1875	Hanover	admn	23464
	Barnabas M	1834	Scituate	admn	23465
	Harriet A	1856	Duxbury	adop	23466
WOODWARD	Elizabeth	1774	Bridgewater	will	23467
	Henry H	1852	Duxbury	grdn	23471
	James	1758	Scituate	will	23468
	James	1855	Duxbury	will	23469
	John	1763	Scituate	grdn	23470
	John D	1852	Duxbury	grdn	23471
	Nathaniel	1748	Bridgewater	will	23472

SURNAME	FIRST NAME	YEAR	PLACE	CASE	DOCKET
WOODWARD	Orzo W	1869	Duxbury	admn	23473
	Robert	1744	Scituate	admn	23474
	Rufus	1833	Duxbury	admn	23475
	William B	1852	Duxbury	admn	23476
WOODWORTH	Benjamin	1732	Scituate	will	23477
	Benjamin	1755	Scituate	admn	23478
	Ebenezer	1769	Scituate	will	23479
	James	1743	Abington	will	23480
	Joseph	1718	Scituate	will	23481
	Thomas	1718/9	Scituate	will	23482
WORCESTER	Esther	1872	Mattapoisett	admn	23483
	Samuel	1845	Bridgewater	admn	23484
WORMALL	Benjamin	1739	Halifax	grdn	23492
	Desire	1748	Duxbury	grdn	23489
	Ebenezer	1743	Duxbury	admn	23485
	Ezuba	1748	Duxbury	grdn	23485 +
	Grace	1758	Duxbury	will	23486
	Ichabod	1741	Duxbury	admn	23488
	Ichabod	1748	Duxbury	grdn	23489
	Ichabod	1758	Duxbury	admn	23487
	John	1711	Bridgewater	admn	23490
	John	1739	Halifax	admn	23491
	John	1739	Halifax	grdn	23492
	Joseph	1739	Halifax	grdn	23492
	Josiah	1738	Duxbury	admn	23493
	Josiah	1748	Duxbury	will	23494
	Patience	1748	Duxbury	grdn	23485 +
WORRICK	Paul B	1879	Hingham	will	23495
WRIGHT	Abigail	1774	Marshfield	grdn	23496
	Adam	1724	Plympton	will	23497
	Adam	1776	Plympton	admn	23498
	Anna	1774	Marshfield	grdn	23496
	Ansel	1872	Plymouth	admn	23499
	Barzillai E	1850	Plympton	will	23500
	Benjamin	1776	Plympton	grdn	23526
	Benjamin	1792	Plympton	admn	23501
	Betsey	1857	Marshfield	will	23502
	Billya	1836	Plympton	will	23503
	Caleb	1844	Wareham	admn	23504
	Cora S	1869	Mattapoisett	grdn	23505
	Daniel	1829	Marshfield	will	23506
	Daniel D	1880	Plympton	will	23507
	Ebenezer	1816	Plympton	admn	23508
	Ebenezer	1848	Plympton	will	23509
	Edmond	1773	Plympton	grdn	23510
	Emma	1860	Marshfield	grdn	23541
	Fernando N	1868	Plympton	grdn	23511
	George E	1872	Plympton	will	23512
	Hannah	1797	Plympton	grdn	23551
	Harriet S C	1877	Bridgewater	will	23513
	Henry O	1872	N. Bridgewater	admn	23514
	Isaac	1766	Plympton	will	23515
	Isaac	1797	Plympton	will	23516
	Isaac	1866	Halifax	admn	23517
	Jabez	1774	Marshfield	grdn	23496
	Jabez	1840	Marshfield	will	23518
	James	1774	Marshfield	grdn	23496
	James	1797	Plymouth	admn	23519
	James	1801	Scituate	admn	23520
	James W	1850	S. Scituate	grdn	23521
	John	1712	Scituate	admn	23522
	John	1774	Plympton	will	23525
	John	1776	Plympton	grdn	23526
	John	1821	Plympton	admn	23523
	John G	1863	Plympton	admn	23524
	Jonathan	1855	Scituate	admn	23527
	Joseph	1804	Plymouth	will	23528
	Joseph	1821	Plympton	grdn	23529 a
	Josephine	1860	Marshfield	grdn	23541
	Levi	1776	Plympton	grdn	23526
	Levi	1837	Plympton	grdn	23530 a

SURNAME	FIRST NAME	YEAR	PLACE	CASE	DOCKET
WRIGHT	Lydia	1776	Plympton	grdn	23526
	Lydia	1821	Plympton	grdn	23531
	Marcia	1880	Plymouth	will	23532
	Martin	1760	Plymouth	admn	23533
	Mary	1774	Marshfield	grdn	23496
	Mercy T	1864	S. Scituate	admn	23534
	Nancy	1821	Plympton	grdn	23531
	Nathan	1762	Kingston	admn	23535
	Patience	1842	Plympton	will	23536
	Patience	1852	Carver	admn	23537
	Peleg	1856	Plympton	will	23538
	Richard	1691	Plymouth	will	23539
	Ruth	1859	Marshfield	admn	23540
	Ruth B	1860	Marshfield	grdn	23541
	Sallie A	1860	Marshfield	grdn	23541
	Samuel	1773	Plympton	will	23542
	Samuel	1815	Plympton	admn	23543
	Sarah	1809	Plympton	admn	23544
	Sarah	1850	Plympton	will	23545
	Thomas	1710	Scituate	admn	23547
	Thomas	1712	Marshfield	will	23546
	Thomas	1852	S. Scituate	admn	23548
	Thomas B	1850	S. Scituate	grdn	23521
	Thomas Jr	1851	S. Scituate	admn	23549
	William	1863	Plympton	admn	23550
	Winslow	1797	Plympton	grdn	23551
	Zebedee	1866	Abington	admn	23552
WRIGHTINGTON	Hope	1850	Middleboro	will	23553
	Joseph E	1882	Middleboro	adop	23554
	Thomas	1847	Wareham	will	23555
	William B	1864	Bridgewater	will	23556
WYAT	Samuel	1729	Rochester	admn	23557
YOUNG	Alvin	1857	Marion	will	23558
	Clarissa	1817	Wareham	grdn	23559
	Elisha	1873	Hanson	will	23560
	Eliza	1879	Scituate	will	23561
	Ephraim L	1858	Scituate	admn	23562
	Ezekiel	1814	Scituate	admn	23563
	Gideon	1847	Scituate	will	23564
	Hannah	1778	Scituate	will	23565
	Henry	1826	Wareham	will	23566
	Henry P	1857	Rochester	admn	23567
	James	1760	Scituate	admn	23568
	Job	1781	Hanover	admn	23569
	John	1798	Bridgewater	will	23570
	Joseph	1763	Scituate	admn	23571
	Joseph	1846	Wareham	admn	23572
	Joshua	1757	Scituate	grdn	23573
	Joshua	1811	Scituate	admn	23574
	Joshua Jr	1812	Scituate	admn	23575
	Leah	1801	Bridgewater	admn	23576
	Lusanna	1825	Scituate	admn	23577
	Lydia	1802	Scituate	grdn	23578
	Mary C	1846	Wareham	grdn	23579
	Mary E	1861	Abington	grdn	23580
	Rebecca	1855	Phipsburg ME	admn	23581
	Reuben	1853	Scituate	admn	23583
	Reuben B	1811	Scituate	admn	23582
	Sally	1819	Scituate	grdn	23584 a
	Sarah J	1876	Rockland	will	23585
	Simeon	1861	Abington	admn	23586
	Solomon	1812	Wareham	admn	23587
	Solomon	1816	Wareham	admn	23588
	Thomas	1732	Scituate	admn	23589
	Thomas	1776	Scituate	admn	23590
	Warren	1817	Wareham	grdn	23559
	Welcome	1871	E. Bridgewater	will	23591
	Zacheus	1847	Wareham	admn	23592
	Zeruiah	1841	Wareham	admn	23593

a h2y
G-MA Historical Society
4/25/98